MW01624625

HIDDEN FACES

COVERED PORTRAITS OF THE RENAISSANCE

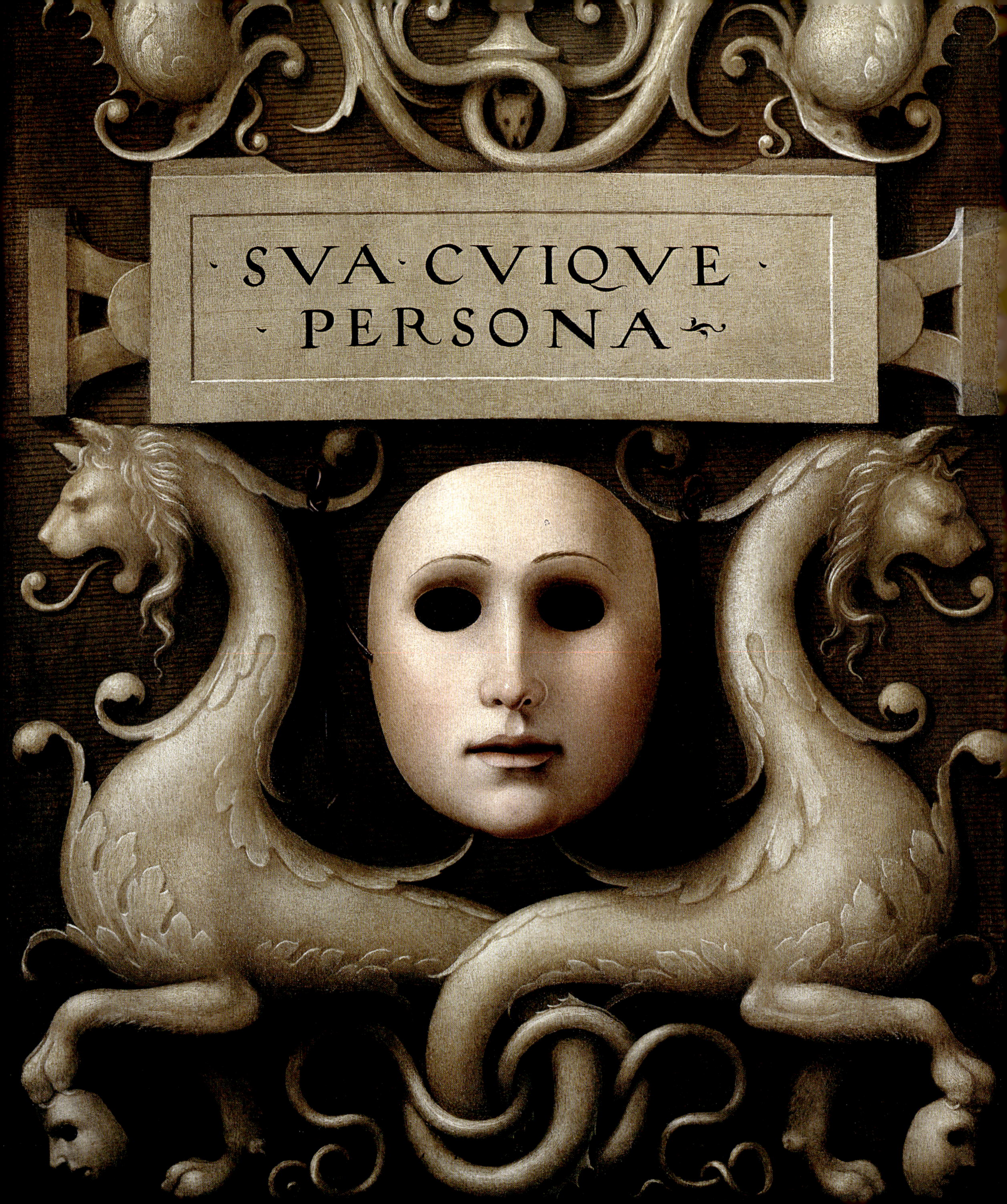
·SVA·CVIQVE·
·PERSONA·

HIDDEN FACES

COVERED PORTRAITS OF THE RENAISSANCE

Edited by Alison Manges Nogueira

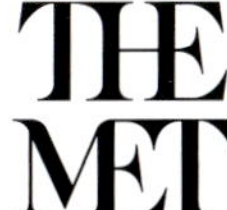

The Metropolitan Museum of Art, New York

Distributed by Yale University Press, New Haven and London

CONTENTS

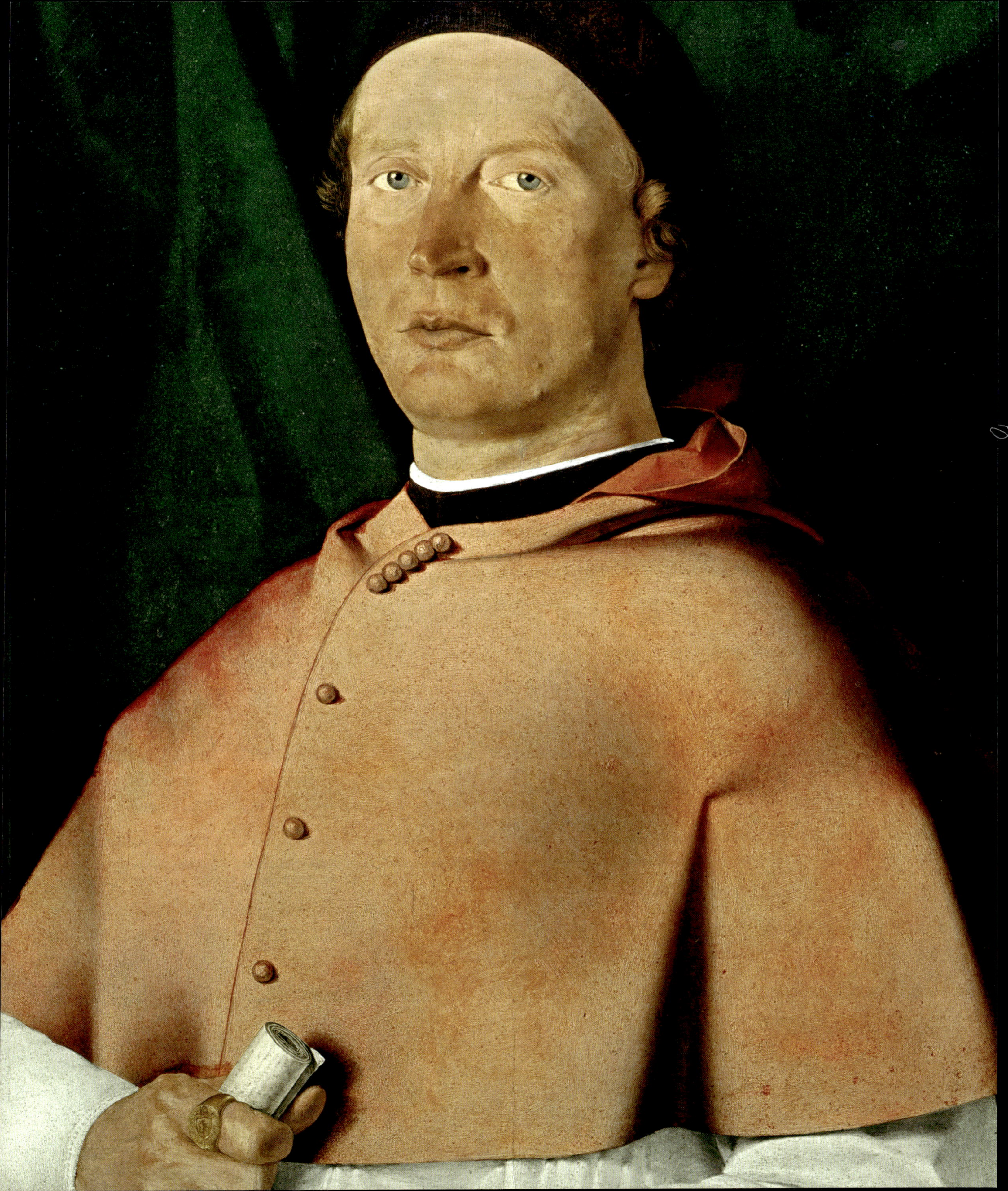

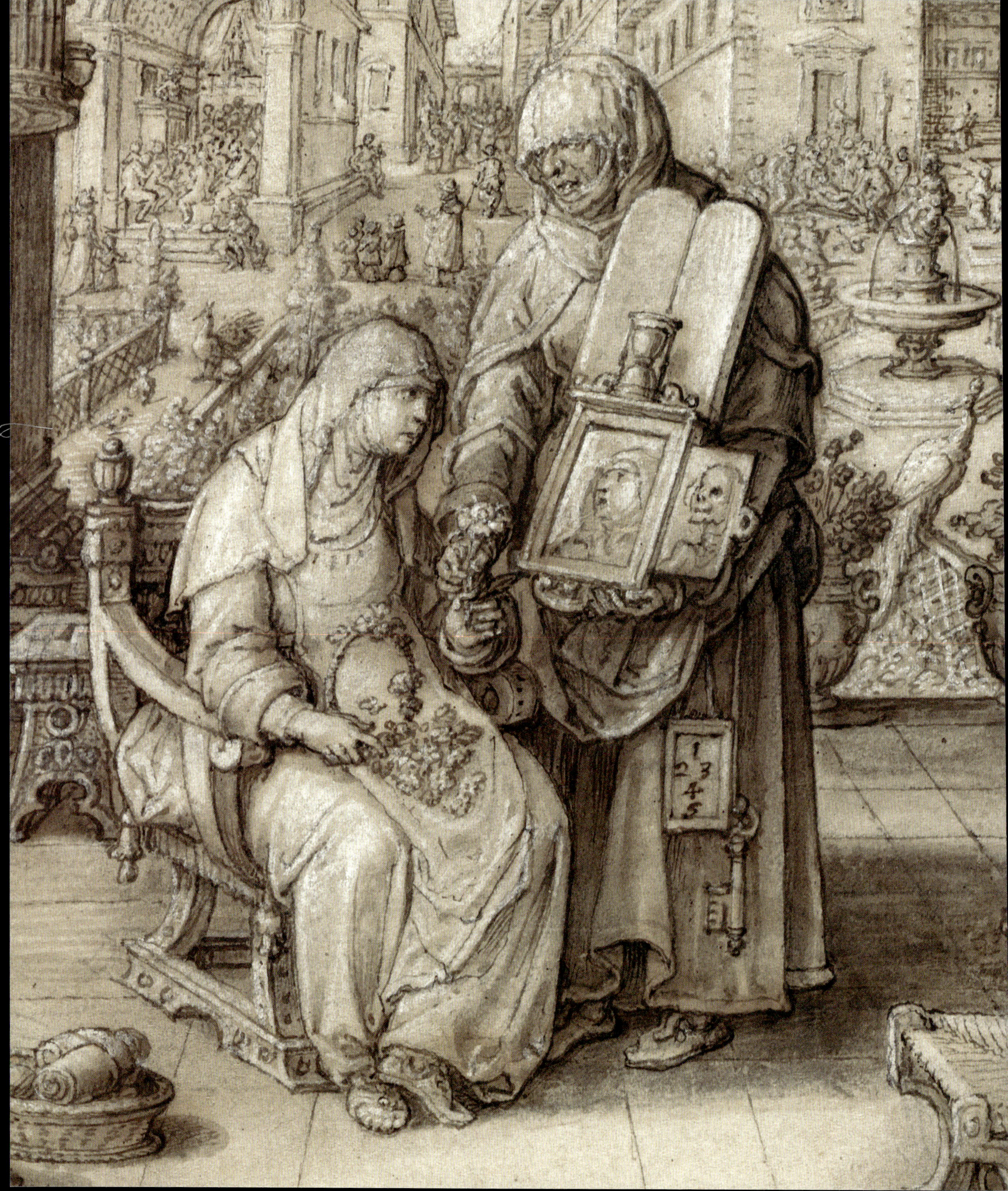
1
2 3
4 5

DIRECTOR'S FOREWORD

Today, we typically envision the painted portrait as an immutable, two-dimensional object, affixed to a wall and permanently visible. However, during the Renaissance, a private portrait often formed part of a three-dimensional, moveable, and interactive ensemble whose layered format and expansive visual program simultaneously concealed the sitter's physical likeness and presented other facets of his or her identity. Such works ranged widely in form and were frequently double-sided or furnished with sliding or hinged covers. Richly adorned with emblems and allegories depicting the sitter's character, the reverse or cover introduced, celebrated, and protected the physical likeness hidden below. The viewer, in fact, was invited to judge the portrait by its cover.

This exhibition, the first to trace the development of multisided portraits in Italy and northern Europe during the fifteenth and sixteenth centuries, challenges many of our fundamental conceptions regarding the definition, forms, and viewership of the genre during the period. By examining a broad range of objects, from portraits with sliding covers to double-sided panels to boxes and lockets, it aims to reconstruct this once-pervasive tradition, reuniting paired works separated over time. From Hans Memling's late fifteenth-century *Portrait of a Man,* whose reverse features one of the earliest independent still lifes, to Titian's large canvas portrait cover depicting an allegory of love, these works represent some of the most innovative and experimental secular images of the Renaissance.

For generously lending works to the exhibition, I thank the Ashmolean Museum of Art and Archaeology, University of Oxford; The Courtauld Gallery, London; Gallerie degli Uffizi, Florence; Germanisches Nationalmuseum, Nuremberg; Historisches Museum, Frankfurt am Main; Institut de France, Musée Jacquemart-André, Paris; Kunsthistorisches Museum, Vienna; The Morgan Library and Museum, New York; Musée des Beaux-Arts, Dijon; Musée du Louvre, Paris; Museo Nacional Thyssen-Bornemisza, Madrid; The National Gallery, London; National Gallery of Art, Washington, D.C.; Niedersächsisches Landesmuseum Hannover, Landesgalerie; Philadelphia Museum of Art; Smith College Museum of Art, Northampton, Massachusetts; Staatliche Museen zu Berlin—Preussischer Kulturbesitz, Gemäldegalerie; Städel Museum, Frankfurt am Main; and Suermondt-Ludwig-Museum, Aachen.

The exhibition was conceived and organized by Alison Manges Nogueira, Curator in the Robert Lehman Collection at The Met, with the support and encouragement of Dita Amory, Robert Lehman Curator in Charge of the Robert Lehman Collection. I extend my gratitude to Alison for assembling this significant material with diligence and dedication. I also wish to thank the colleagues, both inside and outside the Museum, who have contributed their distinguished scholarship to the publication. For lending their works of art and their expertise to the exhibition, I am grateful to many colleagues throughout The Met for their support and collaboration, which helped bring this important project to fruition.

For their generous support of the exhibition, I wish to thank the William Randolph Hearst Foundation, the Robert Lehman Foundation, and the Mellon Foundation, all of whom also have my sincere appreciation for their gifts to scholarly programs at The Met. My gratitude goes to the Drue E. Heinz Fund for bringing the accompanying catalogue to fruition.

Max Hollein
Marina Kellen French Director and CEO
The Metropolitan Museum of Art

ACKNOWLEDGMENTS

This exhibition is the first to examine the tradition of multisided portraits that flourished across Europe in the fifteenth and sixteenth centuries, offering new perspectives on the definition, forms, and viewership of the genre. During the Renaissance, painted portraits were often designed as three-dimensional ensembles in which the sitter's likeness was protected and concealed by a hinged or sliding cover, within a small box, or by its dual-faced format. Portrait covers and reverses were adorned with highly inventive and puzzle-like emblems, epigrams, allegories, and mythologies that celebrated the sitter's character. The exhibition explores the various facets of these portraits as integral parts of the sitter's presentation and the object as a whole.

I owe profound gratitude to many colleagues at The Metropolitan Museum of Art and other institutions who have made the exhibition possible. For their leadership and support at The Met, I am deeply grateful to Max Hollein, Marina Kellen French Director and CEO; Andrea Bayer, Deputy Director for Collections and Administration; Quincy Houghton, Deputy Director for Exhibitions; Inka Drögemüller, Deputy Director for Digital, Education, Publications, Imaging, Libraries, and Live Arts; the members of the Exhibition Advisory Committee; Thomas P. Campbell, former Director; and Daniel H. Weiss, former President and CEO.

For their generous endorsement of the exhibition, I extend my gratitude to the William Randolph Hearst Foundation, the Robert Lehman Foundation—with special thanks to its President, Philip Isles, and its Executive Director, Francesca Valerio, for their steadfast support—and the Mellon Foundation. All these supporters offered significant resources to make the exhibition possible, and I greatly appreciate their dedication to projects like this at the Museum. For its support of this publication, I would like to recognize the Drue E. Heinz Fund and offer my sincere thanks.

I gratefully acknowledge the generosity and collaboration of colleagues at many museums who have lent works of art to the exhibition: Alexander Sturgis and Catherine Whistler, Ashmolean Museum of Art and Archaeology, University of Oxford; Deborah Swallow and Karen Serres, The Courtauld Gallery, London; Eike Schmidt and Anna Bisceglia, Gallerie degli Uffizi, Florence; Daniel Hess, Markus Huber, and Benno Baumbauer, Germanisches Nationalmuseum, Nuremberg; Jan Gerchow and Wolfgang P. Cillessen, Historisches Museum, Frankfurt am Main; Alain Pasquier and Pierre Curie, Institut de France, Musée Jacquemart-André, Paris; Sabine Haag, Katja Schmitz-von Ledebur, and Guido Messling, Kunsthistorisches Museum, Vienna; Colin B. Bailey and John Marciari, The Morgan Library and Museum, New York; Frédérique Goerig-Hergott and Sandrine Champion-Balan, Musée des Beaux-Arts, Dijon; Laurence des Cars, Vincent Delieuvin, and Stéphane Loire, Musée du Louvre, Paris; Guillermo Solana and María del Mar Borobia, Museo Nacional Thyssen-Bornemisza, Madrid; Gabriele Finaldi, Caroline Campbell (former Director of Collections and Research), Susan Foister, Imogen Tedbury, and Laura Llewellyn, The National Gallery, London; Kaywin Feldman, Eve Straussman-Pflanzer, Marjorie Wieseman, David Alan Brown (former Curator of Italian Painting), Gretchen Hirschauer, and Elizabeth Walmsley, National Gallery of Art, Washington, D.C; Katja Lembke, Antje-Fee Köllermann, and Hülya Vidin, Niedersächsisches Landesmuseum Hannover, Landesgalerie; Sasha Suda, Jennifer Thompson, and Mark Tucker, Philadelphia Museum of Art; Jessica Nicoll and Danielle Carrabino, Smith College Museum of Art, Northampton, Massachusetts; Dagmar Hirschfelder and Neville Rowley, Staatliche

Museen zu Berlin–Preussischer Kulturbesitz, Gemäldegalerie; Philipp Demandt and Jochen Sander, Städel Museum, Frankfurt am Main; and Till-Holger Borchert, Michael Rief, Sarvenaz Ayooghi and Ulrike Villwock, Suermondt-Ludwig-Museum, Aachen.

I thank the numerous colleagues in curatorial departments across The Met who have generously lent works in their collections: in European Paintings, Stephan Wolohojian (John Pope-Hennessy Curator in Charge), Keith Christiansen (Curator Emeritus), Maryan Ainsworth (Curator Emerita), Adam Eaker, Anna-Claire Stinebring, Lisa Cain, and John McKenna; in Drawings and Prints, Nadine M. Orenstein (Drue Heinz Curator in Charge), Carmen Bambach (Marica F. and Jan T. Vilcek Curator), Femke Speelberg, Joanna Sheers Seidenstein, Elizabeth Zanis, Clara Goldman, Ricky Luna, and David Del Gaizo; in European Sculpture and Decorative Arts, Sarah E. Lawrence (Iris and B. Gerald Cantor Curator in Charge), Wolfram Koeppe (Marina Kellen French Senior Curator), Denise Maria Allen, Pilar Lia Ferrer, Juan Stacey, Sam Winks, and Denny Stone; in Medieval Art and The Cloisters, C. Griffith Mann (Michel David-Weill Curator in Charge), Shirin Fozi (Paul and Jill Ruddock Associate Curator), Farhan Ali, Christine Brennan, Jeff Elliott, and Andrew Winslow; in Greek and Roman Art, Seán Hemingway (John A. and Carole O. Moran Curator in Charge), Delphine Tonglet, Cecilia Flores, Lenka Maskova, and Katherine Daniels.

I owe a tremendous debt of gratitude to the authors who have contributed to the publication (see page 11): Maryan Ainsworth, Carmen Bambach, Andrea Bayer, Angelica Dülberg (whose scholarship is foundational to the exhibition as a whole), Shirin Fozi, Wolfram Koeppe, Sarah E. Lawrence, Joanna Sheers Seidenstein, Femke Speelberg, Delphine Tonglet, Joshua Waterman, and Catherine Whistler.

Many other colleagues throughout The Met have enriched the exhibition through their invaluable support and dedication, including, in the Exhibitions Office, Christine McDermott, who stewarded the exhibition as project manager, Quinn Corte, Marci King, and Melissa Klein; in the Registrar's Office, Meryl Cohen, Allison Bosch Barone, for her ongoing coordination of myriad logistics, Timothy Shrider, and the Packing Shop; and in Design, Alicia Cheng, Lin Sen Chai, and Tiffany Kim, who masterfully shaped the exhibition's design and presentation, Christopher DiPietro, Dana Citrin, Alexandre Clement Viault, Gretchen Scott, Maanik Singh Chauhan, Kate Truisi, and Jourdan Taylor Ferguson.

I am tremendously grateful to the team in Publications and Editorial, who have diligently overseen the catalogue's editing, design, and production—Mark Polizzotti, Michael Sittenfeld, Peter Antony, Josephine Rodriguez, Paul Booth, Elizabeth Benjamin, and Robyn Fohouo—as well as to designer Jean Wilcox, typesetter Matt Mayerchak, translator Elisabeth Lauffer, and indexer Theresa Duran. I especially wish to thank Margaret Donovan and Margaret Aspinwall for their meticulous editing.

I extend my sincere gratitude to the following colleagues: in Paintings Conservation, Michael Gallagher (Conservator Emeritus), Charlotte Hale, Michael Alan Miller, Sophie Scully, and Kristin Holder; in Paper Conservation, Rachel A. Mustalish (Sherman Fairchild Conservator in Charge), Rebecca Capua, and Yana van Dyke; in Objects Conservation, Lisa Pilosi (Sherman Fairchild Conservator in Charge), Linda Borsch, Dorothy Abramitis, Jack Soultanian, Anne Grady, Mechthild Baumeister, Marina Kastan, Lucretia Kargère, Frederick Sager, Matthew Cumbie, Jacob Goble, Laila Lott, Andrew Estep, and Warren Bennett; in the Counsel's Office, Sharon H. Cott, Emily Balter, Amy Lamberti, Kimberly Nastro, and Edlin Flores; in Development, Whitney W. Donhauser, John L. Wielk, Evie Chabot, and Kate Dobie; in External Affairs, Kenneth Weine, Ann Bailis, and Jennifer Erin Isakowitz; in the Director's Office,

Meghan Kase and Elizabeth Doorly; in Digital, Douglas Hegley, Melissa Bell, Skyla Choi, Isabella Garces, Christopher Alessandrini, Bryan Martin, Paul Caro, Kate Farrell, and Tess Solot-Kehl; in Education, Heidi Holder (Frederick P. and Sandra P. Rose Chair), Elizabeth Perkins, and Marianna Siciliano; in Imaging, Juan Trujillo; in Musical Instruments, Tim Caster; in Scientific Research, Marco Leona (David H. Koch Scientist in Charge); in Buildings, Tom Scally, Taylor Miller, Deepesh Dhingra, Matthew Lytle and the carpenters, Angela Reynolds and the painters, Maria Nicolino and the Plexi Shop, Paul McHale and the Metal Shop, and Gordon Hairston.

I am immensely indebted to my colleagues in the Robert Lehman Collection, who have been integral to the project through their unwavering and invaluable support. I owe profound thanks to Dita Amory, Robert Lehman Curator in Charge, for her steadfast encouragement, wisdom, and guidance on all aspects of the exhibition since its inception. Sarah Nicole Gonzalez provided critical assistance with myriad administrative aspects, diligently overseeing loan agreements, correspondence, provenance research, and many other tasks. Manus Gallagher guided all the complex moving parts of the installation, coordinating with myriad departments, preparing the works, and lending his expertise for their installation.

I also owe thanks to Barriane Franks, Caroline Partamian, Eveline Baseggio-Omiccioli, and Timothy Newberry.

Finally, I wish to thank my wonderful family—my husband, John, and my two daughters, Olivia and Marina—for their endless support, dedication, patience, and love during my work on this project over the past several years.

Alison Manges Nogueira
Curator
Robert Lehman Collection
The Metropolitan Museum of Art, New York

CONTRIBUTORS

MWA Maryan W. Ainsworth, Curator Emerita, Department of European Paintings, The Metropolitan Museum of Art, New York

CCB Carmen C. Bambach, Marica F. and Jan T. Vilcek Curator, Department of Drawings and Prints, The Metropolitan Museum of Art, New York

AB Andrea Bayer, Deputy Director for Collections and Administration, The Metropolitan Museum of Art, New York

AD Angelica Dülberg, independent art historian, Member of the Commission for the History of Art of Central Germany, Saxon Academy of Sciences, Leipzig

SF Shirin Fozi, Paul and Jill Ruddock Associate Curator, Department of Medieval Art and The Cloisters, The Metropolitan Museum of Art, New York

WK Wolfram Koeppe, Marina Kellen French Senior Curator, Department of European Sculpture and Decorative Arts, The Metropolitan Museum of Art, New York

SL Sarah Lawrence, Iris and B. Gerald Cantor Curator in Charge, Department of European Sculpture and Decorative Arts, The Metropolitan Museum of Art, New York

AMN Alison Manges Nogueira, Curator, Robert Lehman Collection, The Metropolitan Museum of Art, New York

JSS Joanna Sheers Seidenstein, Assistant Curator, Department of Drawings and Prints, The Metropolitan Museum of Art, New York

FS Femke Spielberg, Curator, Department of Drawings and Prints, The Metropolitan Museum of Art, New York

DT Delphine Tonglet, Assistant Curator, Department of Greek and Roman Art, The Metropolitan Museum of Art, New York

JPW Joshua P. Waterman, independent art historian

CW Catherine Whistler, Research Keeper, Ashmolean Museum of Art and Archaeology, and Professor of the History of European Art, Fellow of St. John's College, University of Oxford

LENDERS TO THE EXHIBITION

Ashmolean Museum of Art and Archaelogy, University of Oxford

The Courtauld Gallery, London

Gallerie degli Uffizi, Florence

Germanisches Nationalmuseum, Nuremberg

Historisches Museum, Frankfurt am Main

Institut de France, Musée Jacquemart-André, Paris

Kunsthistorisches Museum, Vienna

The Metropolitan Museum of Art, New York

The Morgan Library and Museum, New York

Musée des Beaux-Arts, Dijon

Musée du Louvre, Paris

Museo Nacional Thyssen-Bornemisza, Madrid

The National Gallery, London

National Gallery of Art, Washington, D.C.

Niedersächsisches Landesmuseum Hannover, Landesgalerie

Philadelphia Museum of Art

Smith College Museum of Art, Northampton, Massachusetts

Staatliche Museen zu Berlin–Preussischer Kulturbesitz, Gemäldegalerie

Städel Museum, Frankfurt am Main

Suermondt-Ludwig-Museum, Aachen

UNCOVERING RENAISSANCE PORTRAITS

ALISON MANGES NOGUEIRA

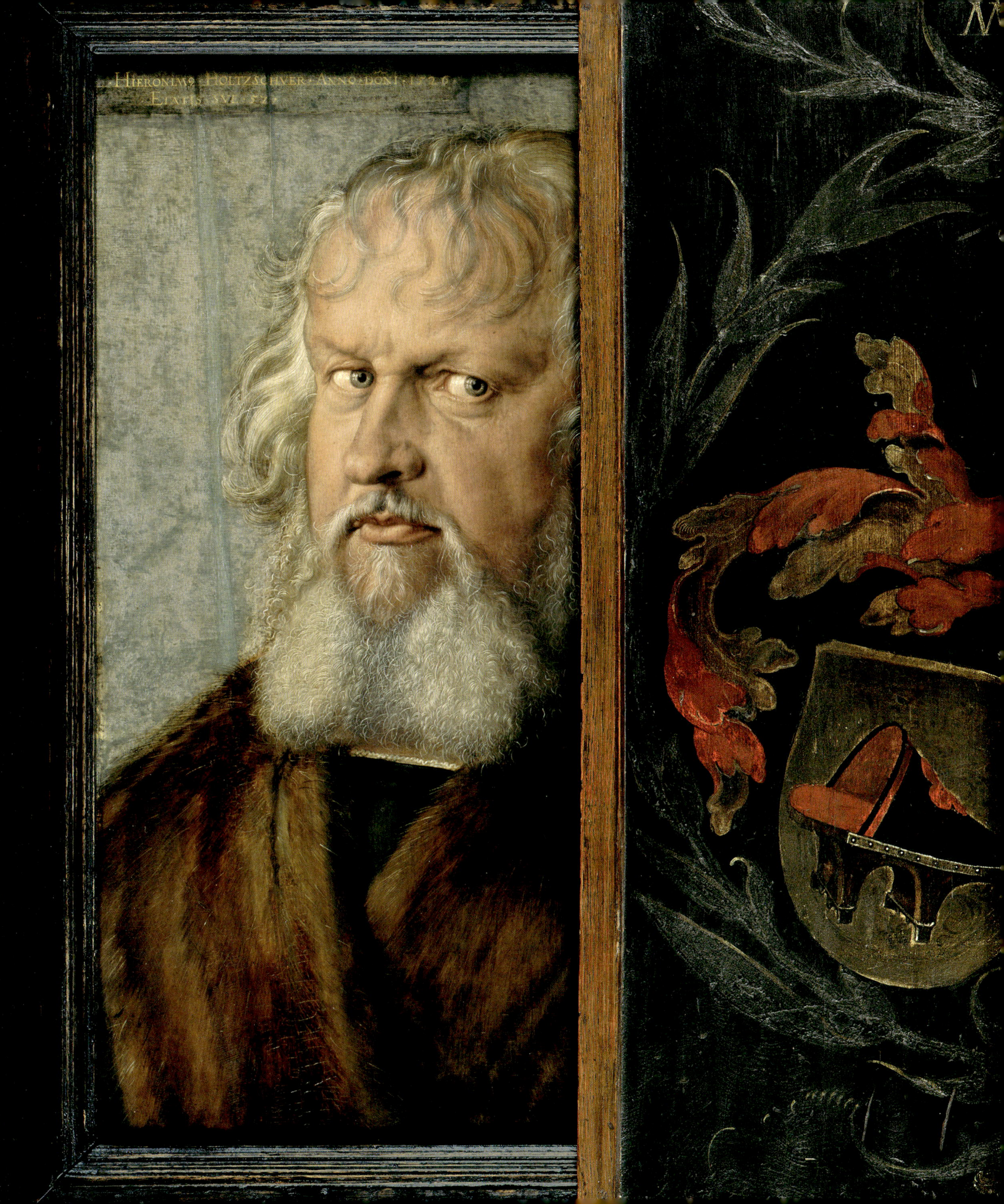
·HIERONIMVS HOLTZSCHVER·ANNO·DOMI·1526·
·ETATIS·SVE·57·

The early sixteenth-century *Portrait of a Woman* (cat. 27B), attributed to the Florentine artist Ridolfo Ghirlandaio, was originally hidden beneath another painting that served as a witty prologue, an enriching counterpart, and a protective cover for the sitter's likeness (cat. 27A). This removable wooden lid fit into into channels carved into the picture frame that allowed it to slide over the portrait. The dramatic effect was heightened by the imagery painted on the cover: a mask whose delicate features echo those of the sitter. The accompanying Latin inscription, translated as "To each his own mask," evokes not only the human condition and the artifice of portraiture but also the ability of such covers to both disguise and unveil the persona beneath.

While the long-standing tradition of shrouding sacred objects is well known, the widespread and varied practice of concealing secular works is less recognized, particularly with regard to painted portraits of the Renaissance that were furnished with embellished covers and reverses expounding upon the identity of the sitters. During the fifteenth and sixteenth centuries in Italy and northern Europe, small-scale paintings produced as private works for the domestic realm often remained veiled by curtains, covers, cases, or cabinets, both in situ and in transit. Evidence of this custom is provided by documents and the objects themselves as well as by images depicting figures in the act of unveiling works of art (fig. 1).[1]

A Medici inventory compiled in 1418 describes a painting of the Madonna that was housed in a cabinet with painted doors and covered by a silk veil.[2] As recorded in 1492, Lorenzo de' Medici owned a painting of Saint Jerome by Jan van Eyck that was kept in a leather case as well as two small cabinets with hinged shutters containing painted female portraits.[3] In 1604 the Dutch painter and historian Karel van Mander recounted in his *Schilder-Boeck* that a small panel by Cornelis Ketel was stored by its owner "inside a chest, hidden from daylight and too many art-loving eyes."[4] Van Mander evokes here both the practical nature of the storage practice—protection against light, dirt, moisture, and other forms of damage—and its ability to mediate access and ensure privacy.

Fig. 1. Unknown artist (Italo-Flemish School). *Portrait of a Man Unveiling a Portrait of a Lady,* 17th century. Oil on canvas, 41 × 35⅞ in. (104 × 91.1 cm). Private collection

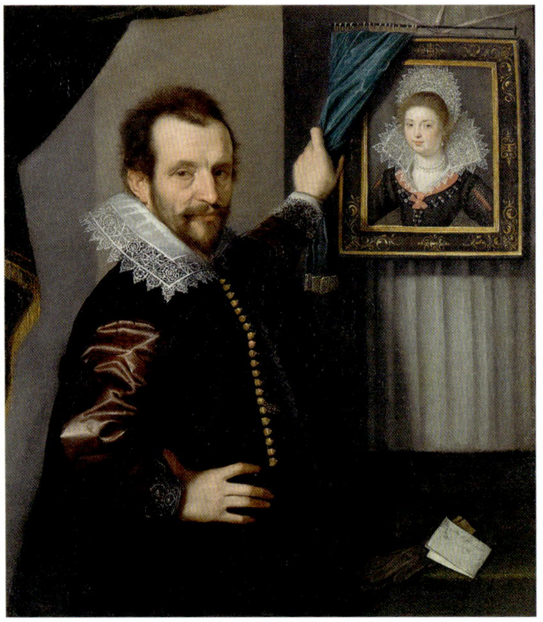

Paradoxically, concealing an object could serve to elucidate deeper levels of meaning through the very act of unveiling and the viewer's haptic participation. Covers were especially revelatory when they were adorned with imagery that functioned as a prelude or gloss, enriching the significance of the work beneath.[5] Equally prohibitive and inviting, these surfaces engaged viewers in a process of revelation, requiring them to uncover the object in a particular narrative sequence. For multisided Renaissance portraits, this process was akin to revealing layers of the sitter's identity through physical and intellectual discovery.

Portraits were designed in a broad range of formats that concealed the sitter's image behind or beneath covers of various sizes and materials. In addition to sliding in and out of picture frames, covers could also be affixed by means of a hinge to individual portraits, as opposed to paired panels that folded close as in a diptych.[6] Although covers of full-scale portraits were most often made of thin wooden panels, they could also be fashioned from copper (cat. 41), mirrors (fig. 2 and cat. 43), or canvas (cats. 32 and 33).[7]

These portraits with embellished covers and reverses are distinguished by their innovative visual programs that incorporated heraldry, emblems, epigrams, allegories, and mythologies to form a symbolic depiction of the sitter, expanding upon his or her character. Modeled on ancient coins, whose reverses celebrated the deeds and virtues of illustrious rulers (see cats. 1 and 2), bilateral portraits fused the sitter's likeness with imagery alluding to his or her moral, intellectual, spiritual, and social ideals. The covers and reverses of painted portraits often bear puzzle-like imagery that required decoding, as do the reverses of Renaissance medals, with their enigmatic pictorial language. The bipartite structures of these ensembles present a range of physical and ideological dualities: interior / exterior, front / back, before / after, earthly / heavenly, public / private, body / soul, ideal / real, transient / eternal.[8]

Multisided portraits, designed as handheld, touchable, interactive objects, frequently had moving parts that required the viewer to turn them over or open the cover. Often stored away, they could be brought out for special viewings, perhaps for a patron's guests in a *studiolo* or *Kunstkammer*, where they served as conversation pieces (see "Covered Portraits in Italy, 1475–1550" by Catherine Whistler in this volume). Although small-scale, private portraits were typically not exhibited on a wall, they could sometimes be suspended by a hook and chain and concealed by pivoting or turning them over to their embellished reverse side.[9] Painting the backs of wooden panels was a long-standing practice, used since antiquity to mitigate the damaging effects of moisture.[10]

Fig. 2. Jan van der Straet (Giovanni Stradano; Flemish, 1523–1605). *Vanitas*, 1594. Pen and brown ink, wash, highlighted in white, 7 9/16 × 11 1/16 in. (19.3 × 28.1 cm). Teylers Museum, Haarlem (1904, n. 7)

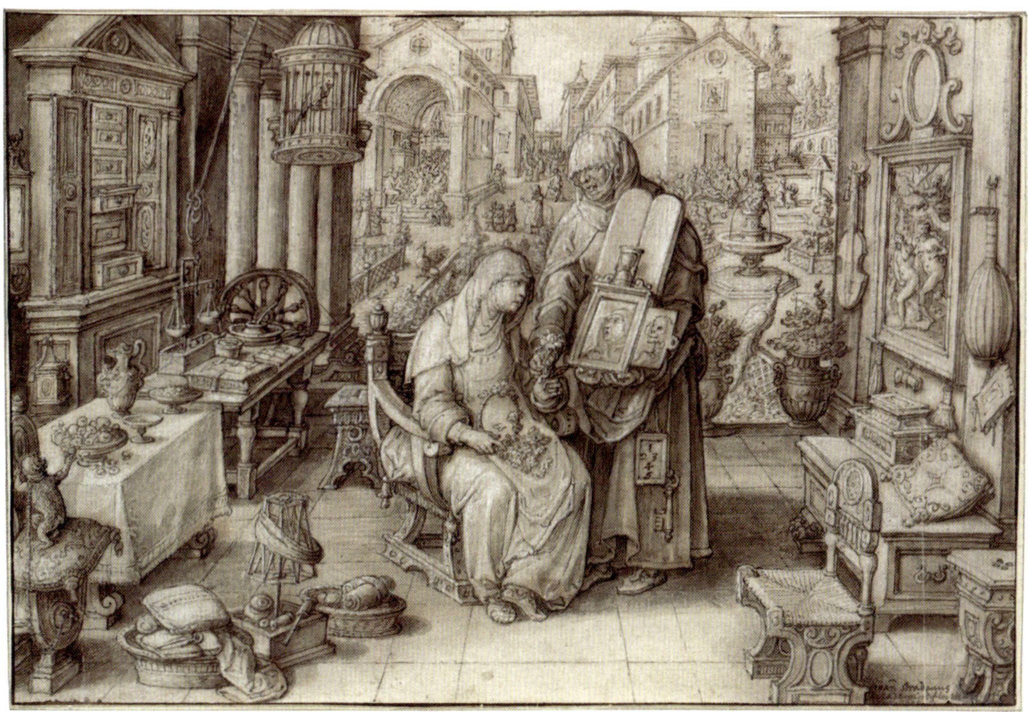

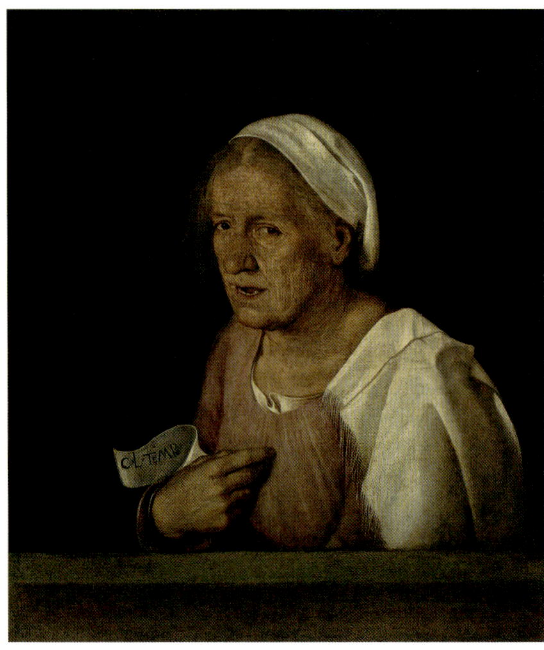

Fig. 3. Giorgione (Italian, 1477/78–1510). *La Vecchia*, ca. 1510. Tempera and oil on canvas, transferred from canvas, 26⅞ × 23¼ in. (68 × 59 cm). Gallerie dell'Accademia, Venice (272)

While very few portrait covers survive today, inventories from England, Spain, Germany, the Netherlands, and Italy attest to their previously widespread use.[11] Dozens of examples are recorded, for instance, in the sixteenth-century inventories of the merchant Octavian Secundus Fugger in Augsburg and in those of Margaret of Austria in Mechelen; the latter, quite significantly, noted paintings that lacked covers ("*sans couverte*"), suggesting that this was an unusual feature.[12] According to a 1516 inventory, Margaret ordered a lock for the now-lost shutters, adorned with fictive stone, that covered Jan van Eyck's *Giovanni(?) Arnolfini and His Wife* (see fig. 32).[13] The shutters may have been original to the painting or added around 1500 by its previous owner, Diego de Guevara.[14] The renowned collection of Gabriele Vendramin in Venice contained more than twenty portrait covers by artists such as Titian and Giorgione, including one for the latter's *La Vecchia* (fig. 3).[15] Seventeenth-century inventories of the Barbarini collection in Rome record shutters for Raphael's *La Fornarina* (1518–19, Galleria Nazionale d'Arte Antica, Rome).[16]

The vast majority of these complex, multilayered structures have been dismembered over time through the loss of their original frames, the cradling or thinning of panels (thereby eradicating the imagery on the reverse), or the separation of portraits from their covers.[17] The result is that many of the extant portraits and covers are fragments of an ensemble. Yet they are often not recognized as such, leading to a distorted and obscured understanding of this aspect of Renaissance portraiture. It is significantly easier to identify cases in which a devotional portrait, depicting a sitter in prayer, has been separated from an adjoining panel of a diptych that originally showed the object of their veneration.

This volume aims to reconstruct the once-pervasive but largely unknown tradition of the multisided portrait and to trace its development from the mid-fifteenth to the mid-sixteenth century in northern Europe and Italy. During this period, the imagery that adorned portrait covers and reverses grew increasingly prominent and innovative, representing some of the most imaginative allegories of the Renaissance, painted by artists such as Hans Memling, Lorenzo Lotto, and Titian. To consider this crucial side (in the literal sense) of Renaissance portraiture, the covers and reverses are examined as integral parts of the object as a whole, symbiotically bound in structure and meaning like the two faces of the coins and medals on which they were modeled. In several instances, portraits and their original covers that have been split into separate collections have been reunited. Exploring these works as paired objects presents the opportunity to investigate significant new questions about the definition, function, meaning, and viewership of portraiture in Italy and northern Europe during the period.

CONCEALING ART THROUGH THE CENTURIES

The flourishing of multisided portraits in the Renaissance constitutes a rich chapter in a long-standing and varied tradition, stretching from antiquity to the modern age, of covering individual likenesses as well as other secular and sacred works of art. An examination of the highly complex, prominent roles that covers played across centuries sheds significant light upon the precedents for the Renaissance formats. It also reveals the deep-rooted associations attached to the concealing and revealing of objects, which were undoubtedly ingrained in those who both produced and viewed covered portraits in this period.

While direct, unmediated visual access to objects is widely available today in museums and sacred spaces, in many historical contexts such viewership was highly restricted.[18] Beyond measures of protection, sacred and secular works were shrouded for a wide range of reasons. The veiling of a holy object enhanced its sanctity, while its revelation activated the image and imparted knowledge of the divine to the beholder. Containing a beloved's portrait within a box or behind a shuttered mirror concealed his or her identity, and veils or covers for painted nudes or erotic scenes—such as the cassoni lids that hid reclining figures or the sliding shutter for Gustave Courbet's *Origin of the World* (1866, Musée d'Orsay, Paris)—served as fig leaves but also enhanced anticipation.[19] Agnolo Bronzino's painting *Pygmalion and Galatea*, forming the cover for Pontormo's *Portrait of a Halberdier* (figs. 4 and 5), enabled its patron to restrict viewership to those with whom he was politically aligned.[20] By mediating and controlling access, the veiling of objects created an intermediary threshold, glorified the hidden object, sparked curiosity and wonder, and invited uncovering and discovering through a performative act of revelation.

From Lenten veils and reliquary covers to shrouded relics and shuttered altarpieces, the covering and revelation of sacred objects has long been an integral aspect of liturgical rituals. According to early fourteenth-century Florentine statutes, the image of a Madonna in the Church of Orsanmichele "should be kept covered with a veil or veils of silk soft and fine" and "should only be uncovered on Sundays and feast days with two torches lit."[21] Bernardo Daddi's *Madonna and Child* (1346–47), at the same site, was concealed by a mechanism of shutters that emerged from the stonework of Orcagna's surrounding tabernacle.[22]

Fifteenth-century accounts of the spiritual and emotional impact of covering and unveiling sacred objects reveal a keen awareness of this powerful dynamic.[23] A Florentine regulation of 1435 restricted the appearances of a miraculous image because "sacred objects . . . are normally respected and held in greater reverence if they are rarely seen."[24] Leonardo da Vinci evocatively described the revelation of divine works: "Do we not see pictures representing divine beings constantly kept under coverlets of the greatest price? And whenever they are unveiled there is first great ecclesiastical solemnity with much hymn singing, and then at the moment of unveiling the great multitude of people who have gathered there immediately throw themselves to the ground, worshipping and praying to the deity."[25]

Veils and Curtains Since antiquity, veils and curtains of various forms have been employed to cover sacred and secular works (fig. 6).[26] While the long-standing use of textile covers is evidenced in documents and in painted and illuminated images of church and domestic interiors, the vast majority of these do not survive, and thus the fundamental relationship of these covers to the works they concealed has been obscured.

A second-century description of the Temple of Zeus at Olympia states that the god's statue was concealed beneath a "woolen curtain adorned with Assyrian weaving and Phoenician purple" that was

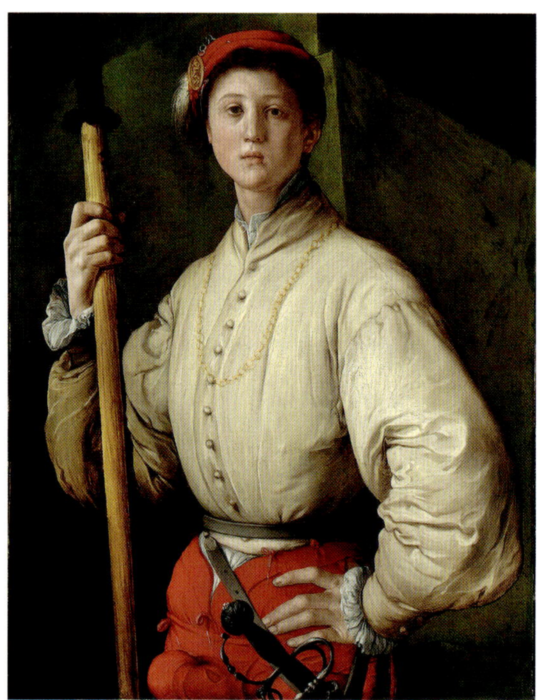

Fig. 4. Jacopo Pontormo (Italian, 1494–1557). *Portrait of a Halberdier (Francesco Guardi?)*, 1529–30. Oil (or oil and tempera) on panel, transferred to canvas, 36¼ × 28¼ in. (92 × 72 cm). J. Paul Getty Museum, Los Angeles (89.PA.49)

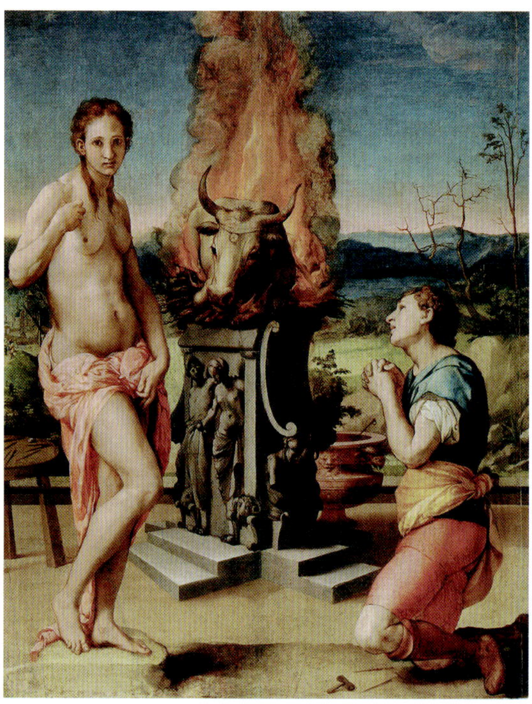

Fig. 5. Agnolo Bronzino (Agnolo di Cosimo di Mariano; Italian, 1503–1572). *Portrait Cover with Pygmalion and Galatea*, 1529–32. Oil on panel, 31⅞ × 25¼ in. (81 × 64 cm). Gallerie degli Uffizi, Florence (1890, 9933)

let down from the ceiling with cords.[27] In the Judeo-Christian tradition, curtains played a central role in liturgical rituals, acting as sanctuary screens, Lenten veils, and altar coverings. They were deeply symbolic as allusions to the veil in the Temple of Jerusalem, which was torn at the moment of Christ's death (fig. 7).[28] Silk veils for icons (*podeia*), often embroidered with images echoing those of the paintings below, were inscribed with dedicatory epigrams that expressed the donor's piety, thereby acting as an intermediary between the patron and the sacred object.[29]

Curtains also served as instruments and symbols of revelation in imperial ceremonies of the Late Antique and Byzantine periods, during which they regulated the ruler's image and propaganda.[30] The tradition of imperial epiphany (*prokypsis*), which emerged in the twelfth century, involved the dramatic opening of a curtain, enhanced by music and light, to reveal the ruling family.[31] The various uses of this device in staging the revelation of sacred objects and imperial figures are reflected in the abundant number of images depicting curtains framing emperors, officials, and holy figures, especially the Virgin and the Evangelists.[32]

By the fifteenth century, curtains frequently appear as framing elements in paintings of sacred subjects as well as in portraits, not solely as theatrical visual devices but also as reflections of the above-mentioned customs. Significant examples include Jean Fouquet's *Charles VII* (1440–60, Musée du Louvre, Paris), in which the ruler emerges from parted curtains, and Vincenzo Foppa's *Madonna and Child* (1479–80, Gallerie degli Uffizi, Florence). Of particular interest is Foppa's illusionistic rendering of the rail and rings from which the curtain is suspended, an early instance of a trompe l'oeil tradition best

Below: **Fig. 6.** Attributed to the Master of the Cité des Dames (Flemish, active ca. 1400–1415). Illumination from Ricoldo de Montecroce, *The Voyages of Jean de Mandeville* and the *Liber peregrinationis*, ca. 1410–12. Bibliothèque Nationale de France, Paris, Département des Manuscrits (Fr. 2810, fol. 171v)

Right: **Fig. 7.** Simon Bening (Flemish, ca. 1483–1561). *The Mass of Saint Gregory*, 1535–40. From the *Munich-Montserrat Hours*. Tempera, gold paint, and ink, sheet: 5⅜ × 3¹⁵⁄₁₆ in. (13.7 × 10 cm). J. Paul Getty Museum, Los Angeles, Ms. 3, leaf 1v (84.ML.83.1.verso)

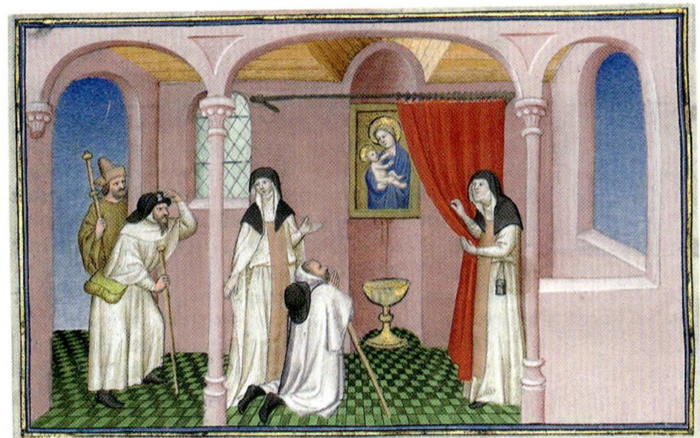

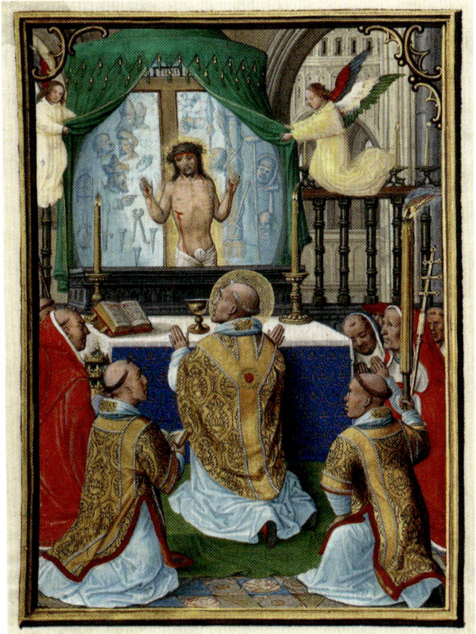

known through Raphael's *Sistine Madonna* (1512–13; Gemäldegalerie Alte Meister, Dresden) and through the works of Dutch masters such as the *Trompe l'Oeil Still Life with Flower Garland and Curtain* by Adriaen van der Spelt and Frans van Mieris the Elder (fig. 8). These virtuosic displays have often been interpreted as allusions to Pliny the Elder's account of the competition between the artists Zeuxis and Parrhasius, the latter of whom painted an illusionistic curtain with such skill that it deceived onlookers.[33]

Numerous household inventories and paintings of domestic interiors, including David Teniers's *Archduke Leopold Wilhelm in His Picture Gallery in Brussels* (1647–51, Kunsthistorisches Museum, Vienna), illustrate the widespread use of curtains as covers for paintings in the private realm. As early as 1413–16, the inventory of Jean de Berry recorded the use of curtains and a protective glass plate to cover works of art.[34] Pietro Aretino vividly evoked the strong association between the veiling of private paintings and sacred objects when he described a portrait of a woman painted by Titian that her lover concealed "like a relic" behind a silk curtain.[35]

Nicolas Poussin explained the advantage of such covers in a letter of 1648 addressed to the collector Paul Fréart de Chantelou: "The intention of covering your paintings is excellent, and to make them visible one by one will mean we do not grow tired, for seeing them all at the same time fills the senses too much at once."[36] In 1655, when Chantelou showed Poussin's *Seven Sacraments* (1645–48, National Galleries of Scotland, Edinburgh) to Bernini, he unveiled them one by one, prompting the sculptor to describe the event as being like a sermon.[37] Chantelou had commissioned Poussin to paint *The Vision of Saint Paul* (1649–50, Louvre) as a pendant to a work in his collection, Raphael's *Vision of Ezekiel* (1517–18, Galleria Palatina, Florence). In July 1643, the artist wrote to Chantelou expressing his anxiety about producing a work that could be compared with the Italian master's and inquiring if his painting could serve merely as a cover to Raphael's work rather than being displayed beside it.[38] While Poussin's suggestion was ostensibly intended to convey his humility, the cover being understood to be an inferior work, this configuration would also, of course, make it possible for his work to eclipse that of Raphael.[39]

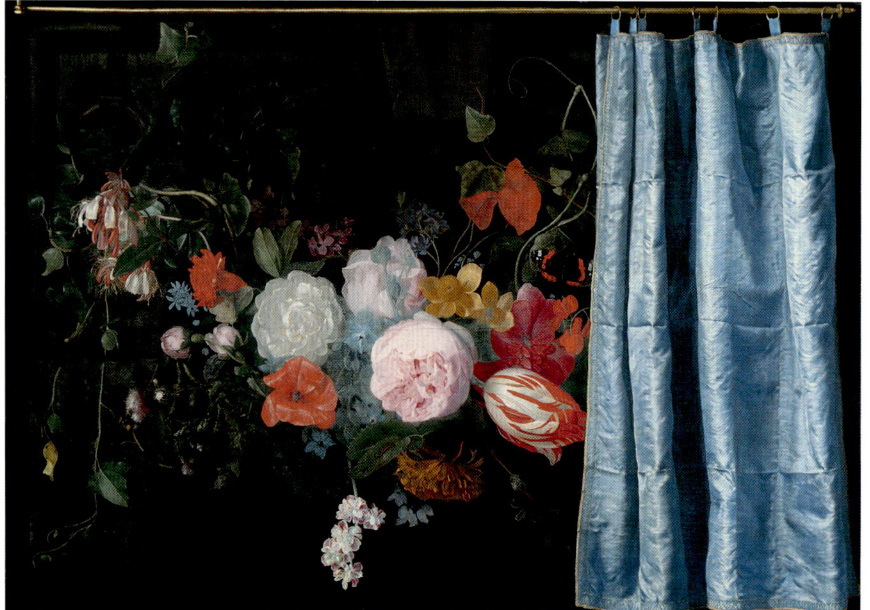

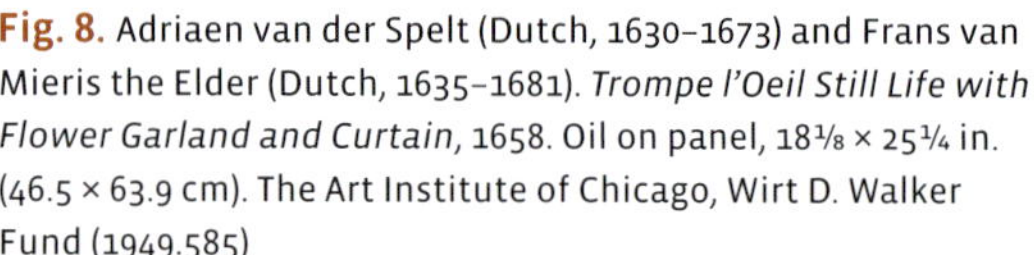

Fig. 8. Adriaen van der Spelt (Dutch, 1630–1673) and Frans van Mieris the Elder (Dutch, 1635–1681). *Trompe l'Oeil Still Life with Flower Garland and Curtain*, 1658. Oil on panel, 18⅛ × 25¼ in. (46.5 × 63.9 cm). The Art Institute of Chicago, Wirt D. Walker Fund (1949.585)

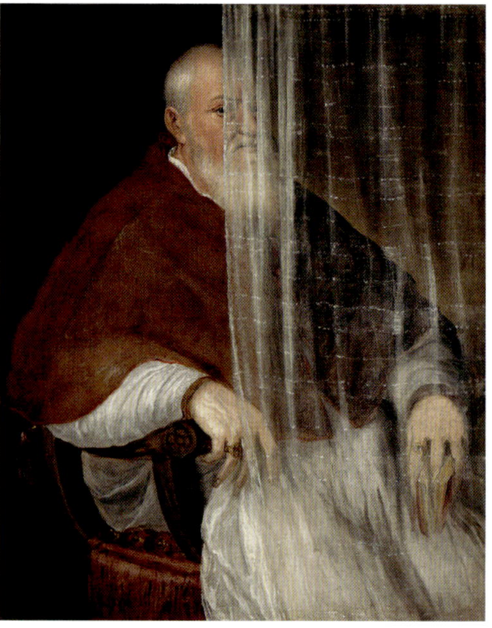

Fig. 9. Titian (Tiziano Vecellio; Italian, 1485/90?–1576). *Archbishop Filippo Archinto*, ca. 1558. Oil on canvas, 45¾ × 35 in. (114.8 × 88.7 cm). Philadelphia Museum of Art, John G. Johnson Collection, 1917 (204)

Curtains were also used to control access to images of nudes and erotic scenes deemed inappropriate for certain guests, women, and children. In the background of Hogarth's *Marriage A-la-Mode* (no. 2, *The Tête à Tête*, ca. 1743, National Gallery, London), the only painting with a curtain is a horizontal image of a reclining nude, identifiable by the bare foot apparently resting on a bed. In the early seventeenth century, Giulio Mancini, a physician, art collector, and critic, recommended keeping erotic works in inner chambers and covered in order to regulate who views them as much as when to view them.[40]

The depiction of paintings with partially drawn curtains, especially with figures in the act of unveiling them, signifies the beholder's active role in accessing them, as in Gabriel Metsu's *Woman Reading a Letter* (1665, National Gallery of Ireland, Dublin). In the *Portrait of a Man Unveiling a Portrait of a Lady* (see fig. 2), the main figure shows a portrait to the viewer, while the fastened curtain at the upper left corner playfully references the revelation of his own image. The transparent curtain that partially obscures the sitter in Titian's *Archbishop Filippo Archinto* (fig. 9) simultaneously alludes to the above-mentioned practices of concealing sacred figures, rulers, and portraits behind textiles and to the bishop's political demise.[41]

Books The book bindings of medieval and Renaissance manuscripts offer significant parallels to multisided painted portraits in their format and in the interrelation between the cover and the folios. Best known through Byzantine examples, so-called treasure bindings were opulently adorned with precious materials and narrative scenes in gold or silver repoussé, enamel, or carved ivory with the aim of glorifying the sacred texts and foreshadowing the events recounted within them. Echoing the format of multisided portraits, the frontispieces of codices frequently bore full-page illuminated portraits of the authors, subjects, or patrons of manuscripts along with portrait-like representations of the Evangelists. A large-scale, bust-length profile portrait of Petrarch that serves as the frontispiece of a fifteenth-century copy of the *Canzoniere* (Musée Atger, Montpellier) mirrors the configuration of panel portraits with their hinged or sliding covers.

Furthermore, various forms of covers could be affixed to individual folios within a manuscript to shield sacred or erotic imagery below.[42] Small textiles, often sewn into the parchment or vellum just above miniatures, served the same protective and theological functions as those for monumental works.[43] In an early sixteenth-century manuscript made for King François I of France, known as *Tutte le dame del re* (*All the Ladies of the King*; Biblioteca Trivulziana, Milan, Ms. 2159), a series of portrait roundels depicting beautiful Milanese women had paper covers opening to the side inscribed with virtues. Donato Bertelli's late sixteenth-century *Le vere imagini et descritioni delle più nobili città del mondo* (*The True Images and Descriptions of the Noblest Cities of the World*) included engravings of Venetian courtesans whose skirts were liftable to expose their undergarments.[44] The presence of hinged textiles and paper flaps in a manuscript would have dramatically heightened the inherently layered, interactive quality of the codex.

Hinged Shutters Relative to textile covers, there is far more surviving evidence of the practice of protecting sacred images behind hinged shutters, as altarpieces and private devotional works in the form of triptychs or diptychs (see cat. 7). Significant precedents from Roman antiquity indicate that these formats were also used for secular images, including portraits.[45] Pliny and other sources report that during the first century CE ancestor portraits in the form of wax masks (*imagines*) were stored in wooden cupboards (*armaria*) in the atrium of a house and displayed on specific occasions.[46] The cupboard doors were opened to exhibit the masks for visitors and on festive days, and they were removed for use during funerary processions.[47] An inscription with the name and a biographical summary of the successes and merits of the deceased (*elogium*) was placed under each image. Ancient Roman grave reliefs depicting portraits inside cabinets with open shutters may refer to this custom, although their bust-like format suggests that the practice of concealing effigies also applied to works in stone or wood.[48]

Just as Lenten veils and altar curtains could be adorned with imagery that foreshadowed and enhanced the significance of the works they concealed, so too could the lateral hinged panels of altarpiece triptychs.[49] Rooted in the tradition of chancery doors in Byzantine churches, the exteriors of triptych wings frequently depicted the Annunciation; during the period of Lent, they also functioned to illustrate this sacred event, which otherwise could not be shown. The unfolding of altarpiece wings also evoked the Virgin's role in opening the doors to paradise.[50] The shutters occupied a liminal space between the beholder and the narratives depicted within—a notion further emphasized through the use of the traditional grisaille technique, often cited as a means of emphasizing the distinction between the physical and the spiritual realms.[51] In this context, it is worth noting that many of the Venetian painted covers in Vendramin's inventory were described as being executed in "chiaroscuro," including Titian's grisaille *Cupid and the Wheel of Fortune*, a rare extant example (cat. 32).

Covered and Bilateral Icons As small-scale devotional images designed in various multisided formats, Byzantine icons—especially those with bust-length, portrait-like depictions of holy figures—appear as significant precedents for later multidimensional portraits.[52] The inextricable connection

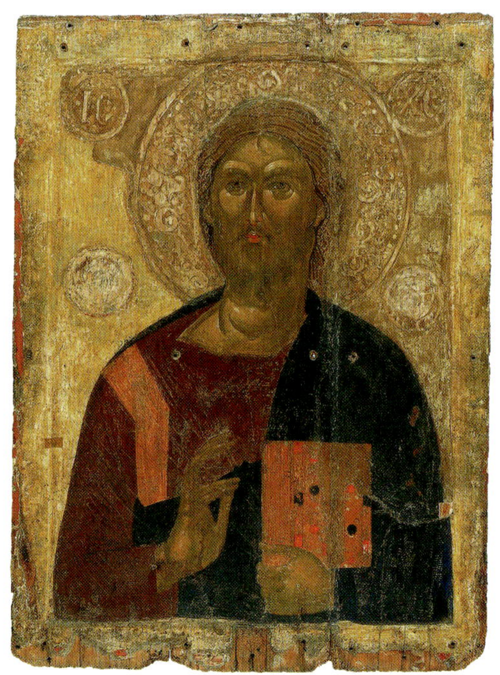

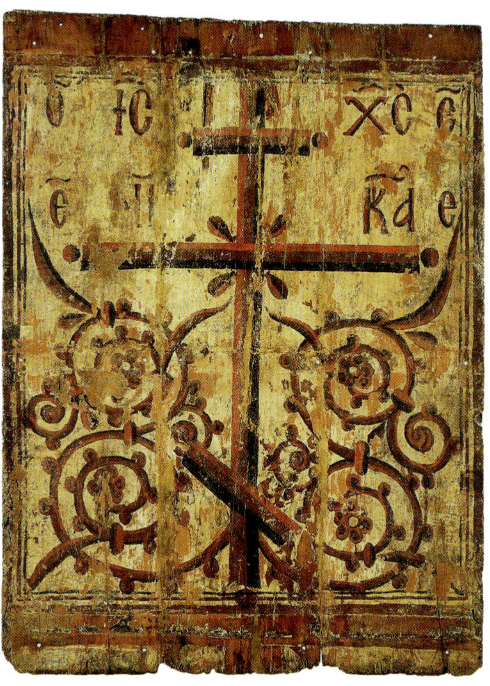

between icons and their covers is revealed by their physical and theological integration as well as by the notion that the cover's removal activated the icon's divine power.

Beginning in the ninth century, metal revetments embellished with sacred figures and narratives were frequently added as partial covers for painted icons. These could include dedicatory offerings or images of the donor in prayer, serving to celebrate his or her piety and wealth.[53] Discussing the revetment of the Icon of Christ in the Sancta Sanctorum (Lateran Palace, Rome), Kirstin Noreen argues that the "cover itself became part of the identification of the icon" and "structured an understanding of the image."[54]

Just as the bust-length depictions of holy figures in Byzantine icons have been considered significant precedents for panel portraits, the frequent double-sided format of the icons was also a source of inspiration. Bilateral icons were used in processions or set within screens (iconostases), with one side facing the sanctuary and the other visible from the nave.[55] The recto of a fourteenth-century icon depicts a bust-length image of Christ, while the reverse bears a cross surrounded by an ornate pattern of acanthus leaves, a motif symbolizing the Resurrection (fig. 10; see also cat. 7) that also appears on the twelfth-century apse mosaic in San Clemente, Rome. The contemporaneous *Head of Christ,* attributed to the Master of the Orcagnesque Misericordia (ca. 1370, The Metropolitan Museum of Art, New York), anticipates the portrait format of the following century. Like many devotional panels, the reverse is adorned with a geometric pattern that echoes the designs found on the interiors of Italian churches of that period, such as Santa Croce in Florence.[56]

The *Christ Crowned with Thorns* on the reverse of the *Portrait of a Lady* (cat. 9), attributed to the workshop of Rogier van der Weyden, vividly illustrates the seminal influence of icons and double-sided devotional images upon the format and visual language of this genre of portraiture. While numerous portraits had sacred narratives painted on their reverses that appeared to reflect the mind's eye of the devout sitter, the paired figures on this panel are particularly expressive of the dynamic interrelationship of its two sides.

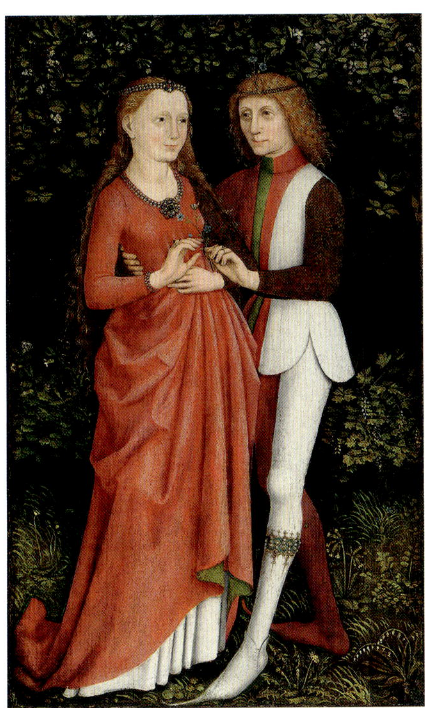
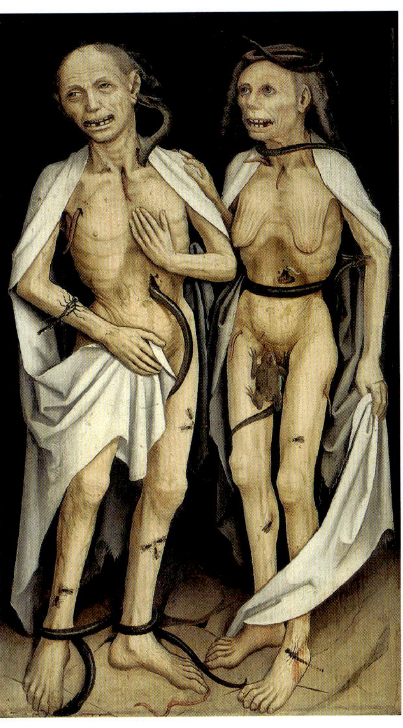

Opposite: **Fig. 10.** Unknown artist (Byzantine). *Christ Pantokrator* (recto); *Crucifix* (verso), 14th century. Tempera on wood panel, 48¾ × 35⅞ in. (124 × 91 cm). Byzantine and Christian Museum, Athens (BXM 00991)

This page: **Fig. 11.** Unknown artist (South German). *A Bridal Couple* (recto), ca. 1470. Oil on panel, 24⅝ × 14⅜ in. (62.3 × 36.5 cm). Cleveland Museum of Art, Delia E. Holden and L. E. Holden Funds (1932.179); *The Dead Lovers* (verso), ca. 1470. Oil on panel, 24⅝ × 15¾ in. (62.5 × 40 cm). Musée de l'Oeuvre Notre-Dame, Strasbourg (MBA 1442)

Since the second century in Roman Egypt, artists have painted double-sided portraits, employing the verso in a variety of ways—to serve as an additional working surface, to present an alternative perspective on the sitter, or to suggest an abstract concept—thereby offering a multiplicity of interrelationships between the painting's two faces.[57] The practical, economical function of the verso as a draft or supplemental surface appealed both to Fayum portraitists and to Ludwig Kirchner, who commented in 1919, "I too have to be a little economical now, and the material has become very expensive. But thank heavens a canvas has two sides."[58] A late fifteenth-century full-length portrait of a betrothed young couple depicts, on its reverse, a very different vision of the same pair, namely, as decrepit corpses (fig. 11). Bronzino cleverly employed the bilateral format to portray Nano Morgante from the front and back (1552, Palazzo Pitti, Florence).

THE DEVELOPMENT OF DOUBLE-SIDED DEVOTIONAL PAINTINGS AND PORTRAITS, 1350–1450

Like devotional works, many early autonomous panel portraits, painted in the early to mid-fifteenth century by the Netherlandish masters Robert Campin, Jan van Eyck, and Rogier van der Weyden, were conceived as handheld, double-sided works and were embellished on their reverses with fictive stone and coats of arms—traditions that would continue through the sixteenth century.[59] While this accompanying imagery did not rival the physiognomic likenesses in virtuosity and innovation, it is noteworthy that these bilateral adornments were integrated into independent painted portraits from the foundational period of the genre's development. A central question regarding these parallel forms of decoration is how their meaning and function varied when used in conjunction with portraits.

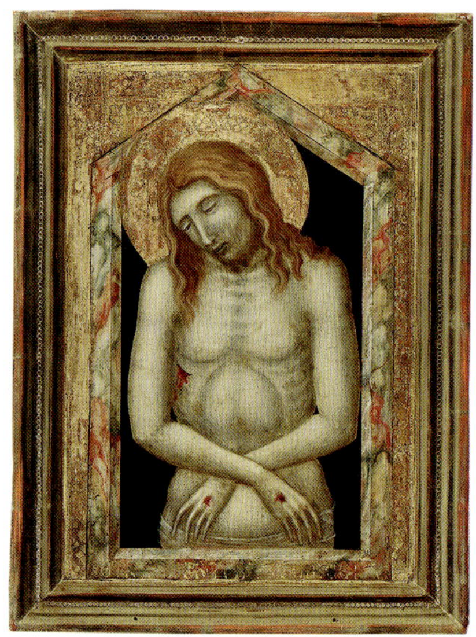
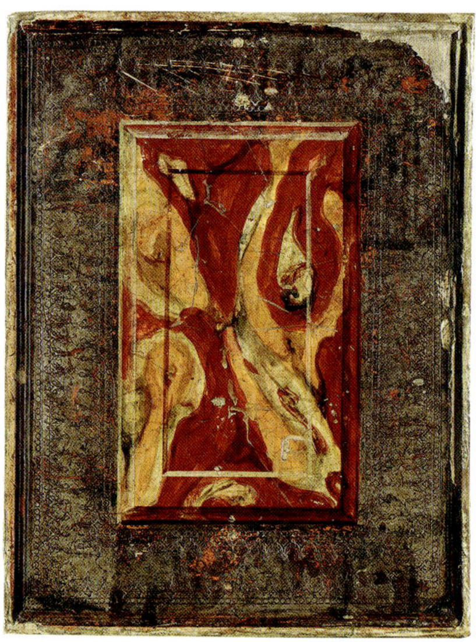

Fictive Stone As Victor Schmidt states, "Almost every small panel originally had a worked verso. . . . This is not only true of panel paintings with religious representations, because such decoration is also found in the earliest private portraits."[60] Since the thirteenth century, the backs of small devotional works were painted in imitation of various types of stone, including marble, jasper, agate, and porphyry, reflecting the design of inlaid liturgical furnishings and wall revetments in sacred interiors.[61] The vast majority depicted stones of reddish tone, symbolizing Christ's Passion, as evidenced by the viscous sanguine pattern of agate painted on the reverse of Pietro Lorenzetti's *Man of Sorrows* (fig. 12), which also alludes to the Stone of Unction (the porphyry slab on which Christ's body was prepared for burial).[62] With its wide frame of pseudo-embossed silver and its central stone panel, the reverse closely recalls contemporary portable altars, such as that made in the eleventh century for Countess Gertrude of Brunswick (Cleveland Museum of Art), further emphasizing the Eucharistic message of the *Man of Sorrows*. More than a decorative element, then, the imitation stone both formed part of and enhanced the devotional narrative on the recto, while also creating the illusion that the panel was a three-dimensional, shrine-like object made of precious and enduring materials.[63]

The remarkably widespread appearance of fictive stone on the reverses of portraits and sacred paintings from the thirteenth to the sixteenth century (see cats. 7, 19, 20A,B, and 24) may also stem from other sources. One is the topos, codified in texts by Pliny, Albertus Magnus, Leon Battista Alberti, and Leonardo, of comparing the anthropomorphic forms perceivable in lithic patterns with painted images; another is the broader (acheiropoietic) notion that art originated in nature and not through human hands. Pliny's account of King Pyrrhus's agate jewel, whose organic shapes formed images of Apollo and the Muses, was discussed by Alberti in his *De pictura* (*Treatise on Painting*, 1435), which subsequently asserts, "Nature itself takes pleasure in painting. We often find it creating hippocentaurs and the bearded faces of kings in marble."[64]

Alberti's reference to the bearded kings recalls a passage from Albertus Magnus's treatise on mineralogy dating around 1260, in which he perceives a portrait in the marble revetment of the Basilica of San Marco: "When I was at Venice as a young man, marble was being cut with saws to decorate the walls of a church. And it happened that when one [piece of] marble had been cut in two and the cut slabs were placed side by side, there appeared a most beautiful picture of a king's head with a crown and a long beard."[65] A century later, this passage was reiterated in Franciscus de Retza's text regarding divine creation, which was illustrated with a depiction of masons sawing apart two marble blocks carved with bust-length portraits of kings that were presented in a format resembling that of a panel painting.[66] The recurring motif of the regal portrait in marble in several highly influential texts from antiquity to the Renaissance may have contributed to the appearance of fictive stone on the very earliest Netherlandish portraits, which date to the beginning of the fifteenth century.

Fictive stone simultaneously alluded to both divine and artistic creation. The coarse-grained material, identified variously as porphyry or jasper, depicted on the reverse of Van Eyck's portrait of his wife (fig. 13), contains spattered drops of white and red paint, poignantly evoking liquid materiality and the artist's working process.[67] In fact, Cennino Cennini's seminal handbook on the practice of painting, written in the late fourteenth century, recommends that artists grind and mix their paints on "a slab of pink porphyry, which is a strong and resistant stone."[68]

Porphyry, known for its rarity and durability as well as for its imperial and funerary associations, was the stone most frequently replicated on the reverses of portraits. It was employed for the tombs of Roman and Byzantine emperors, the Norman kings of Sicily, and the Medici. Its appearance on Renaissance portraits could signal a departed patron's or sitter's wealth, status, and antiquarian tastes, but it was not reserved exclusively for deceased individuals.[69] The presence of fictive porphyry on the reverse of a portrait signified the genre's powerful ability to preserve an individual's image for posterity.[70] The contrast between the sitter's transience and the primordial, immutable nature of stone—and the particularly enduring quality of porphyry—acted as a form of memento mori, a theme often depicted allegorically on portrait reverses.

While most double-sided portraits surviving from the first half of the fifteenth century are Netherlandish or German, numerous Italian examples reveal parallel developments in terms of the use of fictive stone and heraldry. One of the earliest independent Florentine female portraits, Filippo Lippi's *Portrait of a Lady* (fig. 14), depicts the sitter before a window open to a blue sky, signifying eternity. The red marble

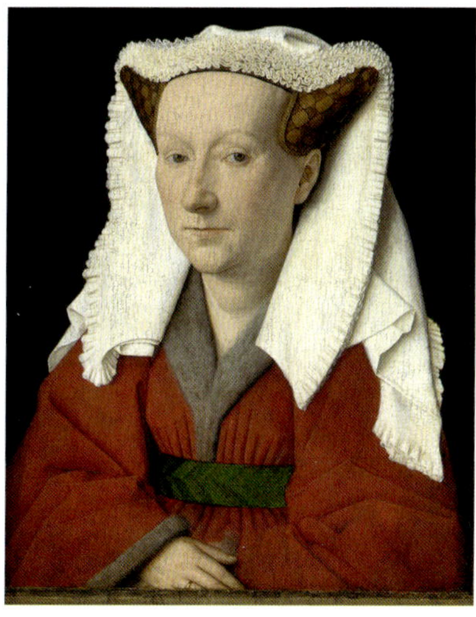

Opposite: **Fig. 12.** Pietro Lorenzetti (Italian, active by 1306, died ca. 1348). *Man of Sorrows* (recto); *Fictive Metalwork and Stone* (verso), ca. 1340–45. Tempera on poplar panel, 13⅞ × 10¼ in. (35 × 26 cm). Lindenau-Museum, Altenburg, Germany (48)

This page: **Fig. 13.** Jan van Eyck (Netherlandish, ca. 1390–1441). *Margareta van Eyck* (recto); *Fictive Stone* (verso), 1439. Oil on wood panel, 12⅞ × 10¼ in. (32.6 × 25.8 cm). Groeningemuseum, Bruges (GRO0162.I)

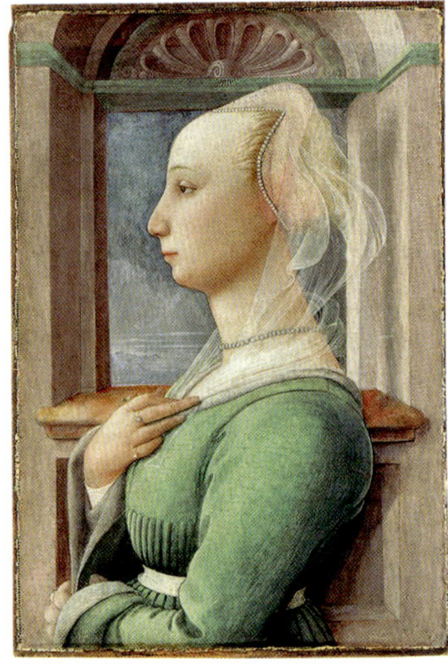
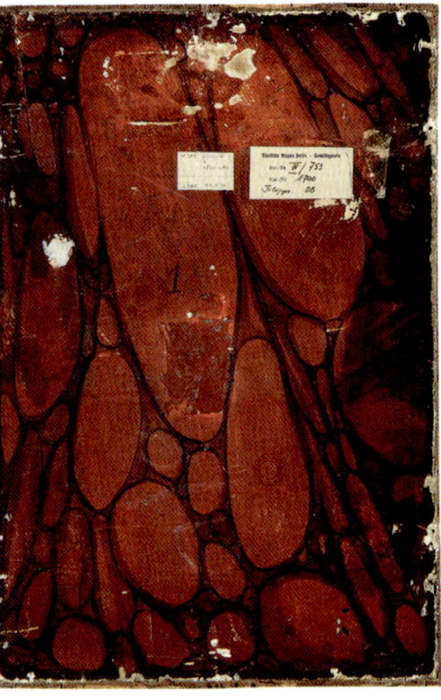

Fig. 14. Fra Filippo Lippi (Italian, ca. 1406–1469). *Portrait of a Lady* (recto); *Fictive Stone* (verso), ca. 1445. Tempera on poplar panel, 19½ × 13 in. (49.5 × 32.9 cm). Staatliche Museen zu Berlin–Preussischer Kulturbesitz, Gemäldegalerie (1700)

Opposite: **Fig. 15.** Unknown artist (English or French). *The Wilton Diptych* (front and back), ca. 1395–99. Tempera on oak panel, each wing: 20⅞ × 14⅝ in. (53 × 37 cm). The National Gallery, London (NG4451)

windowsill echoes the fictive stonework painted on the panel's reverse, which David Alan Brown has described as a "visual metaphor" of "immutability" associated with fidelity and conjugal love, thereby celebrating the sitter's virtue.[71]

Heraldry Like fictive stone, coats of arms frequently adorned the backs of devotional paintings beginning in the 1300s (see cat. 8) and were regularly adopted on the reverses of portraits early in the following century (see cats. 10, 13–16, 25, 35A,B, and 40A,B).[72] The reverse of Simone Martini's panel *The Way to Calvary* (1325–50, Louvre), which originally was part of a double-sided quadriptych, is a significant early example combining the two traditions: it bears the Orsini coat of arms against a fictive stone ground with red striations that evoke the sacrificial narrative on the other side.[73]

Simone Martini is among the earliest artists to whom a small corpus of double-sided paintings can be ascribed, including two works with fictive stone on the back: *Christ Taking Leave of His Mother* (1342, National Museums, Liverpool) and *Saint Luke* (ca. 1326, J. Paul Getty Museum, Los Angeles), the latter being the only panel from a polyptych that retains its original reverse.[74] Alluding to its Angevin patron, the back of Simone's *Saint Louis of Toulouse Crowning Robert of Anjou* (ca. 1317, Museo Nazionale di Capodimonte, Naples) bears a pattern of fleur-de-lis. Like the pseudo-marblework on many panels, the reverse was painted to imitate an armorial textile hanging, possibly the back of the one suggested on the panel's front side.[75] The reverse of Simone's *Virgin and Child with Saints* (ca. 1325, Isabella Stewart Gardner Museum, Boston) is adorned with gold leaf that could be highly polished to form a reflective surface. A mirror was thus formed in which the beholder's likeness could be viewed in relation to the sacred subject on the obverse, a process similar to that of portraits with divine images on their reverse.[76]

Heraldry, a celebration of the patron's status, wealth, and ownership, was frequently included on the reverses of sacred paintings. With some exceptions, such as Simone's *Saint Louis of Toulouse* (ca. 1317, Museo Nazionale di Capodimonte) and *The Wilton Diptych* in the fourteenth century (see fig. 15), coats of arms were often small in scale compared with the painted panel, as for example, those belonging to Philip the Bold, duke of Burgundy on the back of Jean Malouel's *Pietà* (late 14th–early 15th century, Louvre). Unlike other instances in which heraldry was carried out by a workshop member, Malouel may

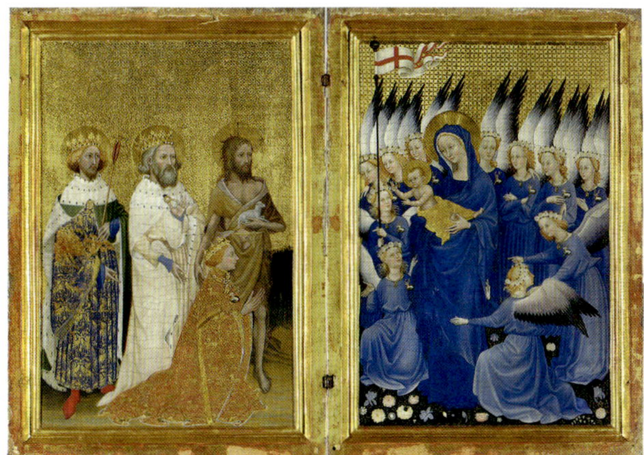
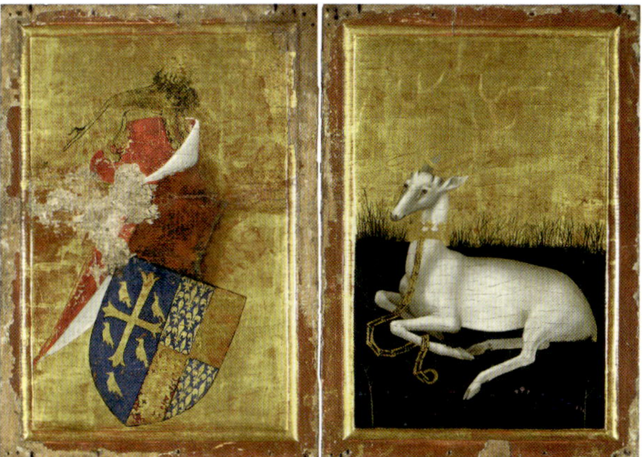

well have painted the reverse himself, given that he served as a heraldic painter at the court of the dukes of Guelders.[77]

The role of heraldry is substantially heightened visually and ideologically in *The Wilton Diptych* (fig. 15), datable to around 1395–99, in which Richard II's coat of arms and emblem of the white hart constitute a vital part of the ensemble: they serve as royal propaganda in parallel with the badges worn by the angels, which signify their loyalty to the king.[78] This prominent display reflects the broader flourishing of heraldry and emblems in the late fourteenth century, as evidenced by the production of numerous heraldic treatises.[79] Scholars such as Stephen Perkinson, Hans Belting, and Michel Pastoureau have emphasized the close connections between fourteenth-century systems of heraldry and emblems and the development of autonomous painted portraits, which represented another form of identity symbol.[80]

Medieval coinage played a significant role in the association of portraiture and heraldry, even in cases where the ruler's numismatic image was not a physiognomic likeness but rather a schematic symbol of authority. The obverse of Richard II's coinage (1377–99, British Museum, London), for example, depicts a boat carrying a crowned, sword-wielding figure identifiable as the English king by his heraldic shield and the armorial reverse.

Beginning in the early fifteenth century, the coats of arms on the reverses of northern European and Italian portraits frequently filled the entire picture plane with their bold colors and designs, forming dramatic decorative paintings in their own right and signaling their essential role in the presentation of the sitter.[81] These heraldic displays closely recall the painted armorials associated with the Order of the Golden Fleece, attributed to the Burgundian court painter Pierre Coustain.[82] Discussing the armorial reverse of Rogier van der Weyden's *Francesco d'Este* (cat. 10), Belting asserts that "only to the modern gaze does the coat of arms mean merely the back of the panel. Likeness and heraldic emblem, which give expression to two different concepts of the body, share the same medial body (the panel)."[83] Francesco d'Este was the illegitimate son of Leonello d'Este, and in order to solidify this dynastic connection, he incorporated his father's emblem of the hooded linx, a symbol of Leonello's astuteness as a ruler, which had appeared on the reverse of Pisanello's medal in the early 1440s.

The inextricable connection between the bodily and heraldic faces, according to Belting, stemmed from the coats of arms emblazoned on knights' shields to identify them in battle, when they were unrecognizable behind the closed visor of their helmets—a thirteenth-century change in armor design

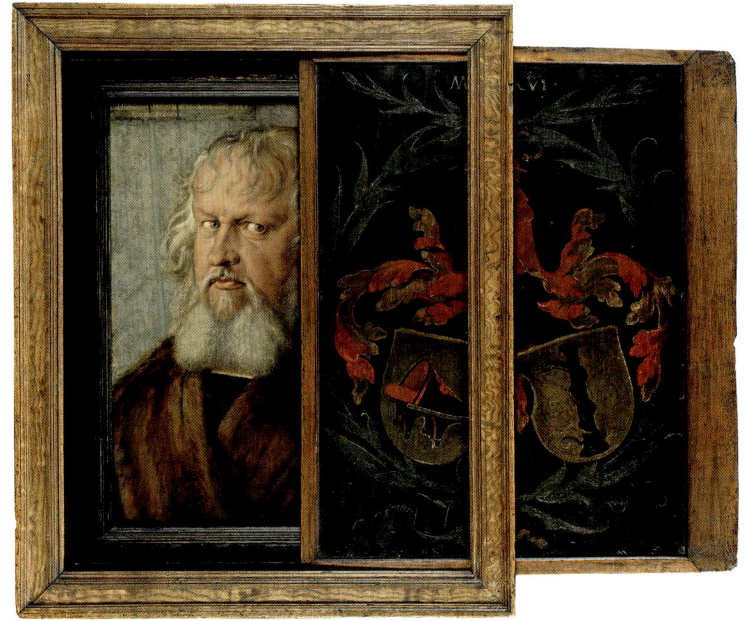

Fig. 16. Albrecht Dürer (German, 1471–1528). *Hieronymus Holzschuher, with Sliding Portrait Cover with Coat of Arms*, 1526. Oil on wood panel, 20⅛ × 14⅝ in. (51 × 37 cm). Staatliche Museen zu Berlin–Preussischer Kulturbesitz, Gemäldegalerie (557E)

Opposite: **Fig. 17.** Unknown artist (Roman). *Portrait of a Woman*, 50–70 CE. Made in Egypt. Tempera on wood panel, H., with frame, 18 in. (45.7 cm). The British Museum, London (1889,1018.1)

Fig. 18. Jean-Etienne Liotard (Swiss, 1702–1789). *Trompe l'Oeil with a Partial Portrait of Maria Theresa of Austria*, 1762–63. Oil on panel, 14¼ × 17⅛ in. (36.2 × 43.4 cm). Private collection

through which "the body's real face is concealed by the official face of the escutcheon."[84] The role of the heraldic shield in simultaneously protecting and identifying the individual behind it has remarkable analogies with sliding portrait covers with armorial designs, such as the panel originally adjoined to Albrecht Dürer's *Hieronymus Holzschuher* (fig. 16).

Portrait Covers Portraits with hinged or sliding covers began to flourish in the second half of the fifteenth century.[85] While examples from earlier in the century have not been identified, it is very likely that this format developed in tandem with bilateral portraits and diptychs. The earliest work with a recognized cover appears to be *Heinrich zum Jungen*, dated 1477 (cat. 15A), ascribed to an anonymous German artist active in Frankfurt. The coat of arms on its cover (cat. 15B) parallels in scale and prominence the heraldry on contemporary portrait reverses and echoes the red, white, and greenish-gray palette of the sitter's garment and the background. A nearly contemporaneous panel, Memling's *Allegory of Chastity* (cat. 18), very likely represents an early cover for a lost portrait, given its small scale and the fact that paintings of the same subject frequently concealed female likenesses.

While earlier European precedents are unknown, the tradition of sliding covers for portraits dates back to the second century in Roman Egypt. The abraded Fayum *Portrait of a Woman* (fig. 17) survives in its original frame, which bears carved channels on its interior that allowed the now-lost cover to slide in and out above the painting's surface.[86] Affixed to the top of the frame is the original palm-fiber cord used to hang the portrait on a wall. David Thompson points out that framed portraits of this period may have been hung in the sitter's home during his or her lifetime before being placed with their mummy.[87] The Fayum portrait was discovered leaning against the legs of the mummy in a tomb in Hawara. The missing cover, like the frame, was probably made of wood, as were the majority of those produced during the Renaissance. Whether it was adorned with imagery relating to the sitter, thus providing a precise model for fifteenth-century examples, remains a significant question.

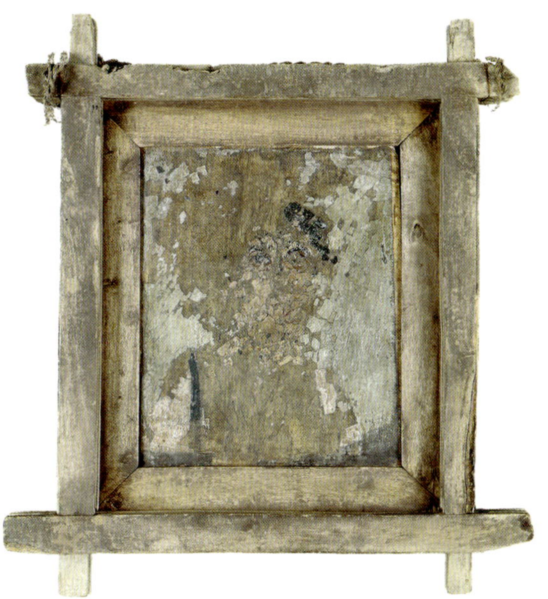

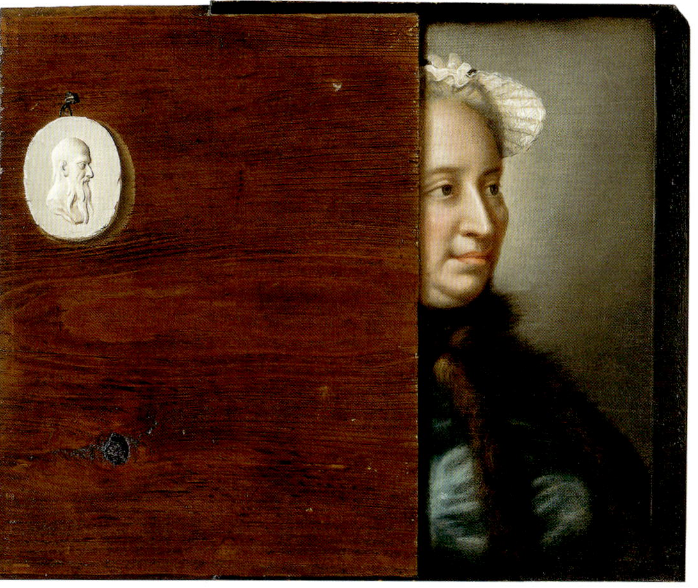

Just as seventeenth-century Dutch paintings with trompe l'oeil curtains and rods reflected the practice of covering images with textiles, Jean-Etienne Liotard's *Trompe l'Oeil with a Partial Portrait of Maria Theresa of Austria* (fig. 18) indicates that the tradition of sliding covers for portraits continued into the eighteenth century. Liotard's portrait depicts the sitter behind a fictive, partially open sliding cover, a wooden panel adorned with a miniature male portrait in relief suspended from a small hook. The disproportionately large number of trompe l'oeil paintings simulating curtains relative to Liotard's unicum suggests that sliding covers were more of a rarity by this time, as echoed in documentary sources.[88]

THE EMERGENCE OF NEW SECULAR GENRES ON PORTRAIT REVERSES, 1450–1500

The second half of the fifteenth century witnessed a major flourishing in the production of portrait covers and a significant expansion in the repertoire of symbolic imagery that adorned the panels' reverses. In the 1450s and 1460s, artists such as Rogier van der Weyden and his circle continued adorning the backs of portraits with fictive stone in the manner of their Netherlandish predecessors, but they also increasingly began to feature personalized references to the sitter through heraldry and emblems. However, it was during the 1470s and 1480s that the most dramatic development occurred. The reverses and covers of portraits became the supports for an experimental secular imagery—still lifes, botanical studies, vanitas scenes, and allegories—that often represented very early examples of those genres, which otherwise would not have been the subjects of independent paintings during the period.

Emblems Personal emblems, known as imprese, were among the expanding types of imagery found on the reverses of painted portraits in the mid-fifteenth century. While emblems had been used by members of the French and Burgundian courts since the previous century, for example, in the margins of manuscript illuminations, their appearance on portrait reverses highlighted their significance as symbols

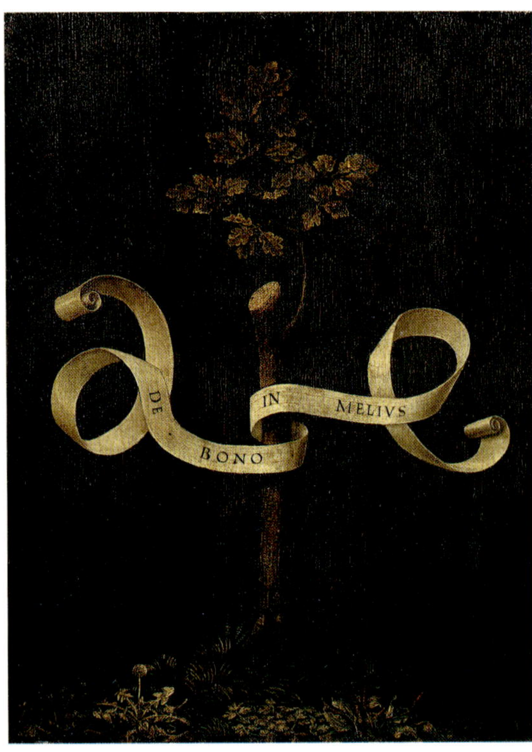

Fig. 19. Hans Memling (Netherlandish, active by 1465–died 1494). *Laurel Stem with Banderole*, verso of right wing of the *Triptych of Benedetto Portinari*, 1487. Oil on oak panel, 17 × 13³⁄₈ in. (43.2 × 34 cm). Gallerie degli Uffizi, Florence (1890, n. 1090)

Opposite: **Fig. 20.** Giovanni Antonio Boltraffio (Italian, 1466/67–1516). *Portrait of a Man (Girolamo Casio?)* (recto); *Memento Mori* (verso), ca. 1500. Oil on panel, 16 × 9¹⁄₈ in. (40.5 × 23 cm). Devonshire Collection, Chatsworth

Fig. 21. Attributed to Ansano Ciampanti (Italian, active 16th century). *Portrait of a Man* (recto); *Landscape with Two Bears and a Tree* (verso), ca. 1500–1510. Tempera on panel, 15⁵⁄₈ × 10⁵⁄₈ in. (39.6 × 27 cm). Museo Poldi Pezzoli, Milan (1549)

of the sitter's identity and character.[89] An important source of inspiration was the frequent appearance of emblems on the reverses of Pisanello's portrait medals, which began to flourish in the late 1430s (see cats. 4 and 5). In their resemblance to ancient numismatic models, both double-sided painted portraits and Renaissance medals enabled the sitter to emulate illustrious figures of antiquity.[90]

A fundamental distinction between coats of arms and emblems was that the former were intended to be clear and legible, while the latter, as described by Paolo Giovio (see cat. 21), were designed to be accessible to a more limited audience owing to chivalric customs that employed allegories to conceal or discreetly express amorous feelings.[91] This tradition is reflected in a letter written in 1490 by the humanist Angelo Poliziano, in which he states that he was asked by a patron to devise an impresa that would be understood only by his lover.[92] The enigmatic nature of imprese meant that the medals and paintings bearing them served as conversation pieces that generated multiple interpretations.

The impresa was rooted in the contract between a knight and his lord, which was understood as an undertaking, or enterprise (*emprise* in French), symbolizing the cavalier's virtues and aspirations.[93] The remarkable proliferation of emblems as personal devices is evidenced by the publication of numerous treatises on the subject, especially those of Paolo Giovio and Andrea Alciato in the 1550s (see cats. 21 and 34).

Images of the Natural World, Still Lifes, and Vanitas Subjects A major milestone in the burgeoning of these new subject matters is marked by the meticulously rendered branch of holly, resembling a botanical study, that fills the entire picture plane on the reverse of the *Portrait of a Man with an Open Book* (cat. 11), attributed to Rogier's workshop and datable to the mid-fifteenth century. The sitter has been plausibly identified as Guillaume Fillastre, counselor to the Burgundian court and bishop of Tournai, although

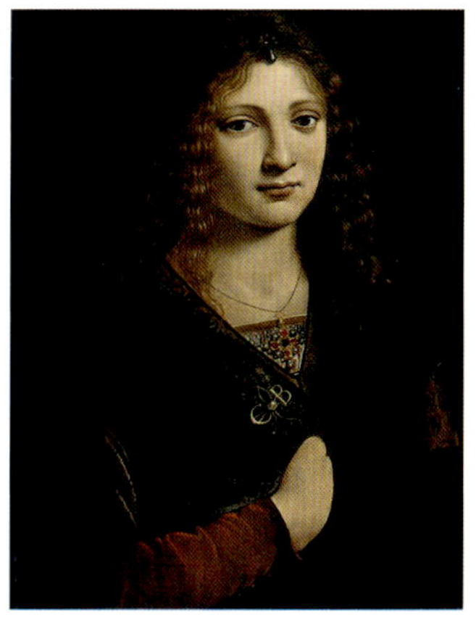

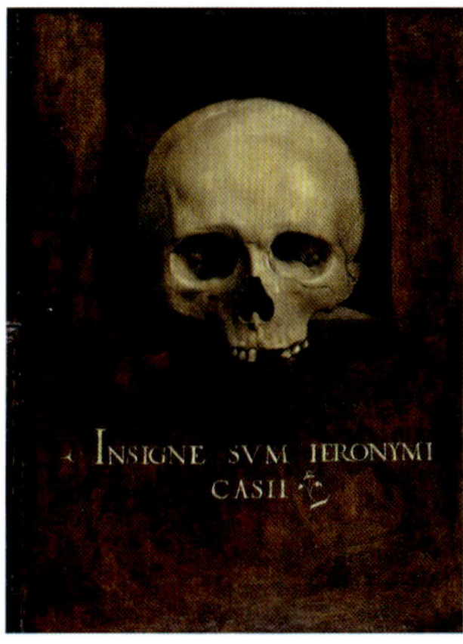

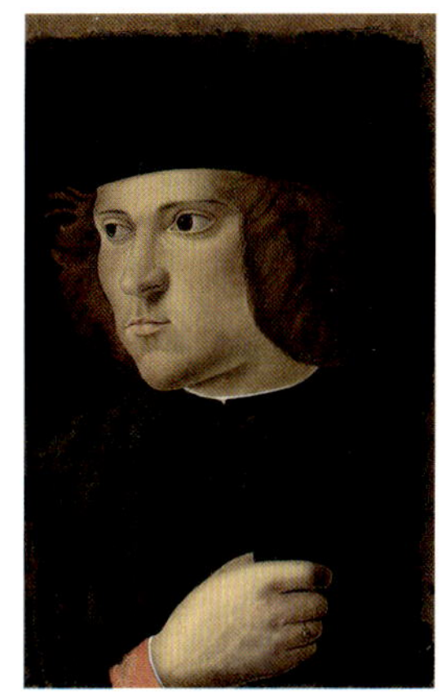

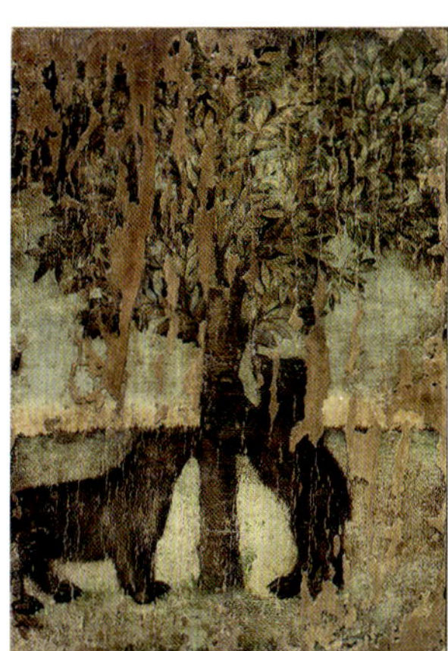

neither the holly nor the inscribed motto has been recognized as his device. The branch's cut stem suggests the brevity of the plant's existence and therefore serves as a memento mori. In the branch's large scale and naturalism, as well as in the absence of other motifs within the composition, the image differs markedly from those on the reverses of contemporary paintings and medals, including the botanical emblem and motto on the reverse of Memling's portrait of Benedetto Portinari (fig. 19; see also fig. 36).

Imprese and other secular imagery also adorned the reverses of devotional portrait diptychs, in which a half-length portrait of the sitter in prayer was portrayed in a panel adjacent to the object of his or her veneration, usually the Madonna and Child (see figs. 33 and 34).[94] Frequently identified as one of the earliest examples of the genre, Memling's *Flowers in a Jug*, on the reverse of the *Portrait of a Man* (cat. 17), parallels other Netherlandish works in which scenes of daily objects were imbued with sacred symbolism. Memling was also crucial to the development of other types of still-life subjects, as seen in the early vanitas images that adorned the reverses of two sacred works from the early 1480s.[95] While Jacques de Gheyn's *Vanitas Still Life* (1603, Metropolitan Museum, New York) is widely considered the earliest independent painting of this genre, memento mori in the form of skulls had been frequently depicted on the reverses of portraits since the late fifteenth century, including Giovanni Antonio Boltraffio's *Portrait of a Man* (*Girolamo Casio?*) (fig. 20) and Andrea Previtali's *Portrait of a Man* (ca. 1502, Museo Poldi Pezzoli, Milan).[96]

Beginning in the second half of the fifteenth century, animals symbolizing sitters' virtues frequently appeared as the primary subjects of portrait reverses and covers, reflecting the tradition of zoological motifs in heraldry and imprese as well as a deepening interest in depictions of the natural world. Examples include the enchained roebuck on the reverse of Jacometto Veneziano's *Alvise Contarini* (cat. 20A) and the pair of bears on the back of the *Portrait of a Man* (fig. 21), attributed to Ansano Ciampanti, the latter having been interpreted as a semiheraldic reference to the sitter's identity as a member of the Orsucci family (*orso* meaning "bear" in Italian).[97] Angelica Dülberg has construed the deer and monkey on the reverse of Sandro Botticelli's *Judith with the Head of Holofernes* (1469–70, Cincinnati Art Museum) as an allegory that may have been joined, perhaps as a cover, to a lost female portrait, with both the sacred and secular images alluding to the sitter's virtues.[98]

The innovative depictions of the natural world painted on the reverses of sacred images during this period further emphasize the role of multisided paintings as supports for experimental subject matters.

The reverse of Dürer's small panel depicting Saint Jerome (ca. 1496, National Gallery, London) bears a remarkable image of a celestial body that probably alludes to the major meteor fall recorded in Ensisheim in the Alsace region in 1492.[99] Dürer incorporated visionary images of the natural world on the backs of two other works, namely, the *Man of Sorrows* (1492–93, Staatliche Kunsthalle, Karlsruhe), with its luminescent lithic form, and the portrait of his mother, Barbara Dürer (1490, Germanisches Nationalmuseum, Nuremberg), with its fantastic nocturnal landscape.

Ancient Numismatics and Renaissance Virtue Whether heraldry, emblem, inscription, or allegory, the imagery that adorned the reverses and covers of Renaissance portraits was intended to celebrate the sitter's social, moral, intellectual, and religious virtues. The multisided format of these portraits enabled the sitter to identify a specific virtue for inclusion as the "symbolic portrait." In doing so, Renaissance patrons aligned themselves with their ancient predecessors, who employed numismatics in the same fashion. Furthermore, the virtues most frequently celebrated on the reverses of ancient coinage and the pictorial language that conveyed them both provided direct inspiration for multisided Renaissance portraits (see cats. 1 and 2).

As Luke Syson and Dora Thornton assert, Renaissance humanists were of pivotal importance in codifying ancient virtues as measures of conduct, which they furthered through their teaching, the treatises they composed on exemplary behavior, and their promotion of texts such as Plutarch's *Vitae Parallelae* (*Parallel Lives*) and *Mulierum virtutes* (*On the Virtues of Women*), written by the Greek philosopher and author in the early second century.[100] Ancient Roman virtues were widely known in the fifteenth century through the circulation of texts like Valerius Maximus's *Facta et dicta memorabilia* (*Memorable Acts and Sayings*), written in the first century CE and dedicated to Emperor Tiberius.[101] Organized by qualities such as moderation, modesty, chastity, and avarice, Valerius's text enumerates positive and negative instances exemplified by the lives of ancient figures. The frontispiece of a manuscript copy of his text, produced in the late fifteenth century for Cardinal Giovanni d'Aragona, son of King Ferdinand I of Naples (New York Public Library, Spencer MS 20), bears profile portraits of four ancient male figures. Their respective virtues—prudence, temperance, fortitude, and justice—are signified both by the female personifications directly above them and by allegories depicted in roundels that simulate the reverses of ancient coins. At the upper right, Augustus is accompanied by the personification of prudence, above whom is the image of a numismatic reverse that portrays the emperor on a chariot drawn by elephants.[102] The frontispiece illustrates how ancient numismatics acted as vehicles for conveying and celebrating antique values and virtues, both in the manuscript itself and in Renaissance culture as a whole.

According to Frank Zöllner, the portrayal of virtue and its survival after death is an essential function of portraiture: "Portraits claim maxims for living and also give evidence of a broader ideal of moral conduct which expresses the hope for the spiritual survival of the individual."[103] He argues that Renaissance portraits convey the sitter's soul through "attributes, signs, symbols, metaphors and references to a number of texts, both antique and . . . Christian. Portraits thus correspond to well-known humanists' attempts to reconcile antique ideas with Christian belief and to describe the immortality of the soul with the help of antique metaphor."[104] When applied to multisided portraits, this reasoning suggests that the portrayal of the sitters' virtues, which forms half of the visual program of the work as a whole, was intended as a profound and powerful expression of his or her soul.

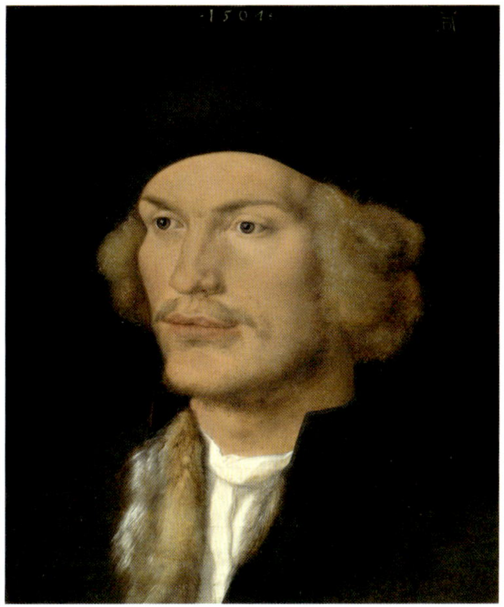

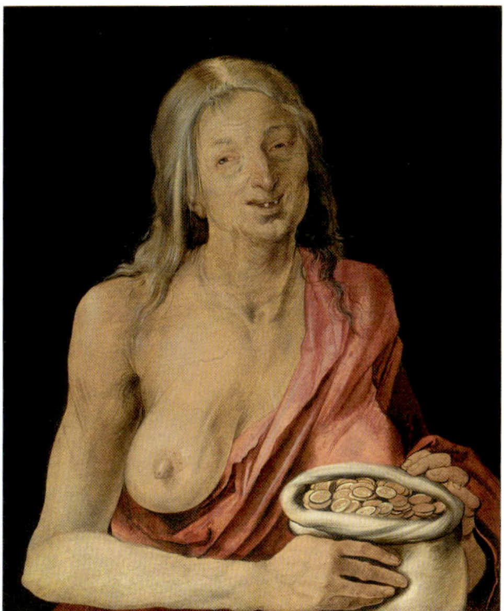

Fig. 22. Albrecht Dürer. *Portrait of a Young Man* (recto); *Avarice* (verso), 1507. Oil on linden panel, 13⅞ × 11½ in. (35 × 29 cm). Gemäldegalerie, Kunsthistorisches Museum, Vienna (849)

Allegories of Virtue

The most pronounced development in the evolution of the imagery on portrait covers and reverses occurred in the late fifteenth to the early sixteenth century in the realm of allegory, resulting in some of the most remarkable examples of the genre, including *Interior with Two Nudes* (cat. 26), attributed to Jacopo de' Barbari, and Dürer's *Avarice* (fig. 22), works that reveal variations on the vanitas theme, which frequently adorned the reverses of male portraits.[105]

Among the most significant early allegorical reverses are those found on Piero della Francesca's portraits of Federico de Montefeltro and Battists Sforza (fig. 23), from the early 1470s. Their *all'antica* triumphal processions, alluding to the sitters' respective virtues, reflected a motif often depicted on ancient coinage and contemporary medals and echoed in Petrarch's celebrated poem dedicated to various triumphs. Federico's chariot, drawn by horses, carries figures personifying the cardinal virtues (prudence, justice, temperance, and fortitude); Battista's bears allegorical figures of the theological virtues (faith, hope, and charity) as well as an additional one (chastity), symbolized by the accompanying unicorns.

A particularly significant corpus of allegories on the reverses and covers of female portraits from the same period articulates the ideals of moral perfection. Reflecting social norms, these female virtues were narrowly circumscribed and related, above all, to chastity and other virtues applying to marriage.[106] However, the artists' treatments of these subjects vary considerably and demonstrate great inventiveness. The reverse of Pisanello's medal of Cecilia Gonzaga of 1447 (cat. 4) alludes to the sitter's chastity through the motif of the Maiden and the Unicorn, while Piero di Cosimo's *Allegory* (ca. 1500, National Gallery of Art, Washington, D.C.), the presumed cover for *Simonetta Vespucci* (ca. 1500, Musée Condé, Chantilly), depicts a winged female figure's facile control over the equine symbol of lust, while a mermaid, evocative of the same vice, swims below. The small size and subject matter of Memling's *Allegory of Chastity* (cat. 18) suggest that it may well have been a cover for a female portrait. A portrait of a woman ascribed to Agnolo

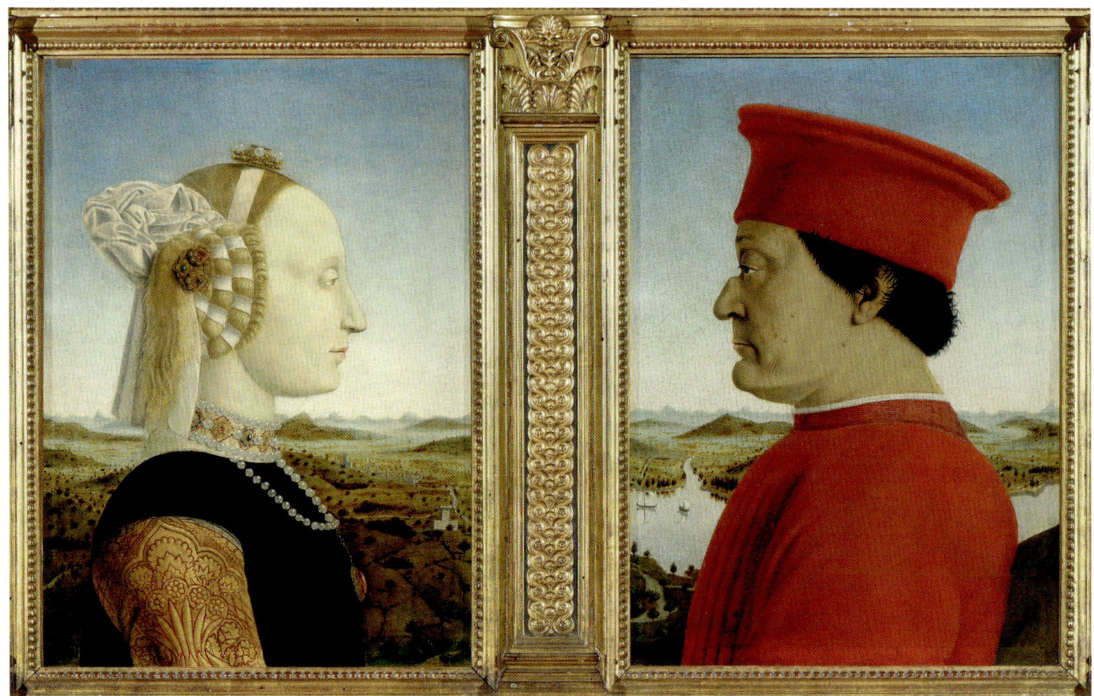

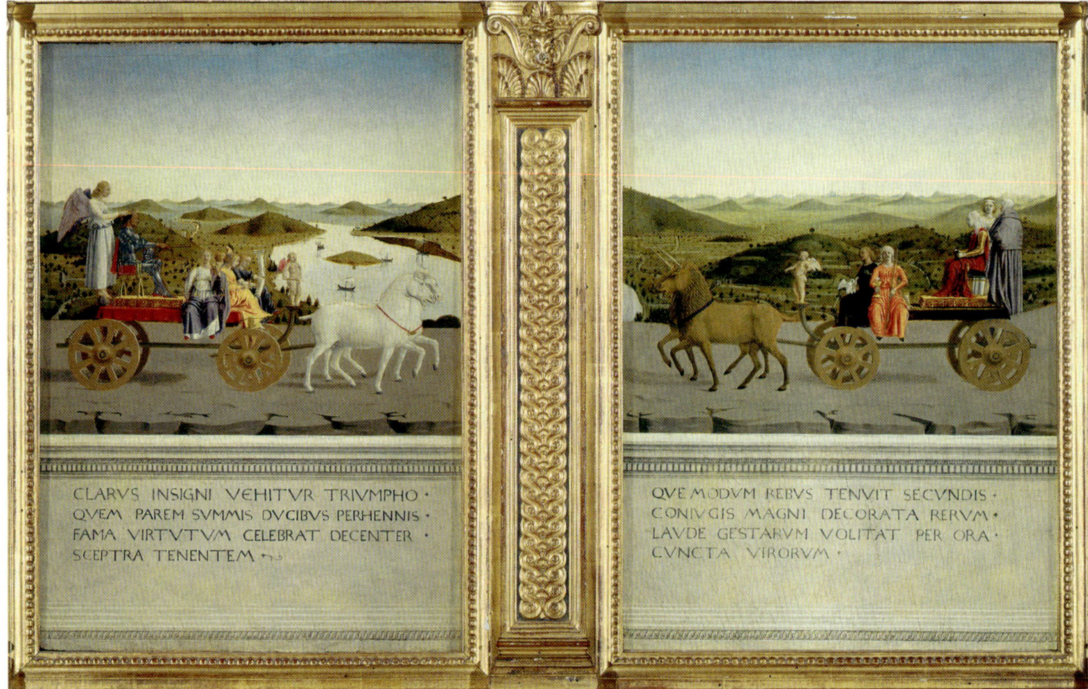

Fig. 23. Piero della Francesca (Italian, ca. 1415–1492). *Federico da Montefeltro* and *Battista Sforza* (recto); *Triumphs of Federico da Montefeltro* and *Battista Sforza* (verso), ca. 1472. Tempera on panel, 18½ × 26 in. (47 × 66 cm). Gallerie degli Uffizi, Florence (1890, 1615, 3342)

Opposite: **Fig. 24.** Leonardo da Vinci (Italian, 1452–1519). *Ginevra de' Benci* (recto); *Wreath of Laurel, Palm, and Juniper* (verso), ca. 1474–78. Oil on panel, 15 × 14⅝ in. (38.1 × 37 cm). National Gallery of Art, Washington, D.C. (1967.6.1a,b)

di Domenico di Donnino Del Mazziere, the Master of Santo Spirito (cat. 28), is adorned on its reverse with inscriptions alluding to the virtues of marriage, including a quote from Petrarch's *Trionfo della castità* (*Triumph of Chastity*, 1340–44). Portraits trumpeting the chaste virtues of female sitters may have been commissioned for potential suitors or on the occasion of the women's marriages.

MULTISIDED PORTRAITS IN ITALY, 1475–1550

The evolution of multisided portraits in Italy between the mid-fifteenth and mid-sixteenth centuries was not always precisely in step with developments in northern Europe. Nevertheless, the broader transalpine crosscurrents that facilitated reciprocal influences in portraiture can also be discerned in covers and reverses. While portraits with painted reverses were produced in Italy in the 1440s and echoed northern European examples in the use of fictive stone and heraldry, there are far fewer surviving examples from the mid-fifteenth century relative to those produced in the Netherlands and Germany.

By the late fifteenth and early sixteenth centuries, however, multisided portraits abounded in Italy and exhibited the same inventive allegorical language as their Northern counterparts. Among the surviving double-sided and covered portraits made in Renaissance Italy, the majority appear to be Venetian (a discrepancy reflected in inventories), which may relate to the city's particularly close ties to northern Europe.[107] The dialogue between the Venetian and northern European traditions of covered portraits is highlighted through two moments of exchange.

The first centers upon Jacometto Veneziano, who appears to have specialized in small, private multisided portraits for humanist patrons in Venice. He was responsible for most of the extant examples (cats. 19, 20A,B, and 23), which marked the initial development of a genre that would flourish in the lagoon during the early sixteenth century under Lotto, Giorgione, and Titian. Jacometto's works, like those of many of his contemporaries, reveal the stylistic and technical influence of Netherlandish portraits, yet he also drew inspiration from their elaborately painted reverses and covers. In fact, during

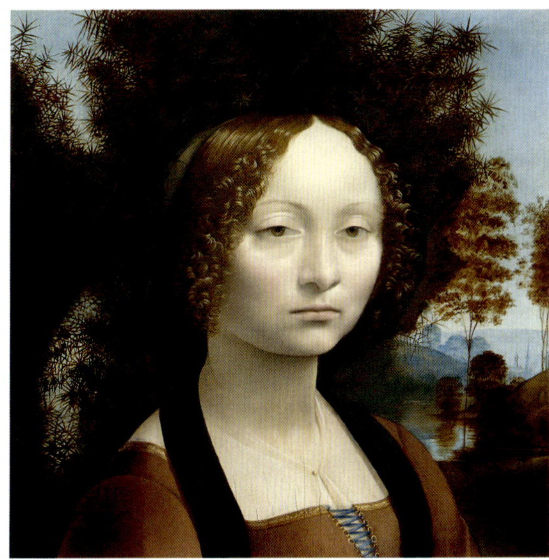

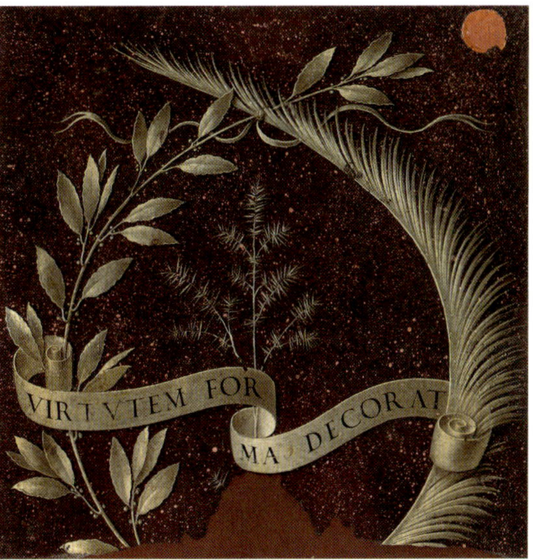

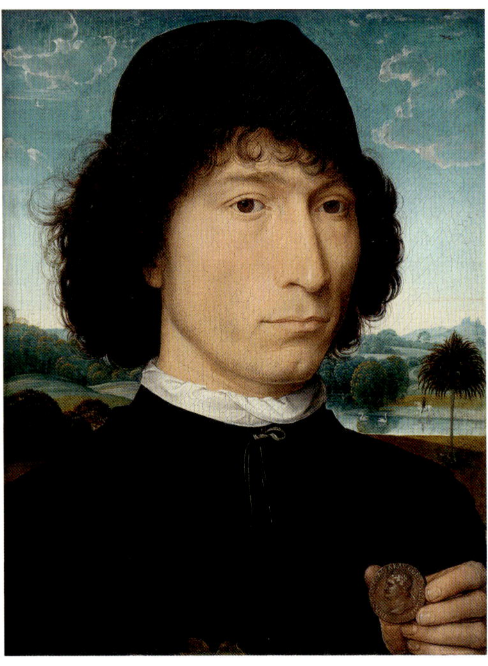

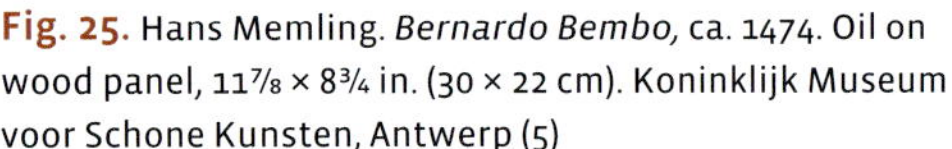

Fig. 25. Hans Memling. *Bernardo Bembo,* ca. 1474. Oil on wood panel, 11⅞ × 8¾ in. (30 × 22 cm). Koninklijk Museum voor Schone Kunsten, Antwerp (5)

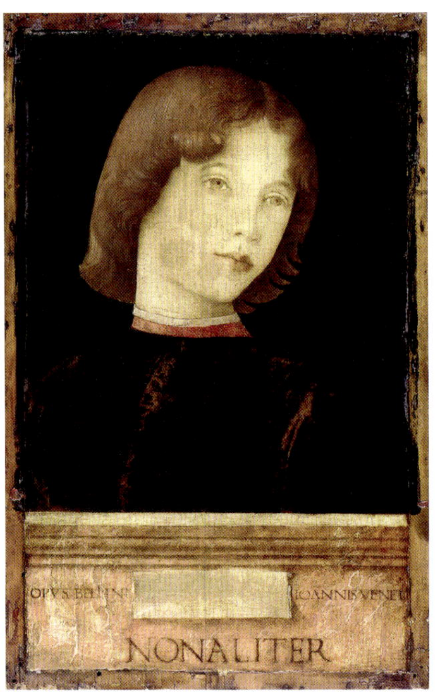

Fig. 26. Giovanni Bellini (Italian, 1431/36–1516). *A Portrait of a Boy,* ca. 1475. Oil on wood panel, 15 × 9⅛ in. (38 × 23 cm). The Barber Institute of Fine Arts, University of Birmingham, United Kingdom (46.11)

the 1470s, Jacometto and Memling had a common patron, the Venetian humanist Bernardo Bembo, who probably commissioned Leonardo's *Ginevra de' Benci* (fig. 24) in the same period (see "Coining Multisided Portraits: Precedents and Parallels" in this volume).

While serving as the Venetian ambassador to the court of Burgundy in 1472, Bembo may have acquired Memling's double-sided diptych depicting Saints John the Baptist and Veronica (ca. 1470/75, Alte Pinakothek, Munich, and National Gallery of Art, Washington, D.C.) and commissioned a portrait from the artist (fig. 25) that could easily have inspired Jacometto's analogous treatment of the landscape backgrounds in *Alvise Contarini* and *Portrait of a Woman (Daria Querini?)* (cat. 20A,B).[108] Among Memling's numerous double-sided likenesses, the motto with intertwined branches painted on the reverse of the portrait of Benedetto Portinari (see fig. 19) has close affinities with the reverses of Jacometto's *Portrait of a Man* (cat. 23) and Leonardo's *Ginevra de' Benci*. Bembo's simultaneous patronage of Memling, Leonardo, and Jacometto in the early 1470s was presumably crucial to the latter's formation as the first Italian artist to "consistently adopt" the Netherlandish practice of adorning the reverses and covers of portraits.[109]

Another significant nexus in the flourishing of multisided portraits in Venice and northern Europe occurred between Giorgione and Dürer during the latter's sojourns to the lagoon in the first decade of the sixteenth century. In the years 1508 to 1510, Giorgione and Dürer both painted multisided portraits of male sitters paired with allegorical figures of aged women depicted with uncompromising realism. According to Vendramin's 1601 inventory, Giorgione's *La Vecchia* (see fig. 3) originally had a cover showing "a man dressed in black fur," while Dürer's *Avarice* (see fig. 22) formed the reverse of a male portrait—both works serving as foils and moralizing figures for their younger male counterparts.[110]

The inventories of the Vendramin collection are among the most significant sources for the proliferation of Venetian portrait covers, recording more than twenty examples by masters such as Bellini, Titian, and Giorgione.[111] Included among these works are two male portraits painted in gouache by Bellini described, respectively, as "a small painting with its box" and "a box with a painting inside."[112] In fact, the two earliest extant portrait boxes, now in fragments, were painted in the late fifteenth century by Bellini and his Venetian contemporary Jacometto (see cat. 20A,B). Both works, which appear to have had funerary functions, differ from the various extant and documented portrait boxes of the fifteenth and sixteenth centuries in their complex structures and extensive visual programs, presumably reflecting a larger tradition that has otherwise been lost.

Bellini's *Portrait of a Boy* (fig. 26), from about 1475, formed the cover of a small wooden cabinet, embellished with arabesques, that contained a marble bust of the youth's deceased father, Angelo Probi, the Venetian ambassador of Ferrante d'Aragona, king of Naples.[113] A panel depicting a memento mori in the form of a skull (private collection, Florence) may originally have formed the portrait's reverse.[114] Upon Probi's death in 1474, the bust was commissioned by the Venetian government and given to his son along with a poem, also kept inside the box, that encouraged the young boy's hope in salvation. As a container for these objects, the box recalls a reliquary casket.

The tradition of multisided portraits in Venice continued in the early sixteenth century under Lotto, a pivotal figure for both the inventiveness of his covered portraits (cats. 29A,B and 30A,B) and his written accounts of their production, which shed invaluable light on the genre.[115] In his account book, the *Libro di spese diverse*, compiled between 1538 and 1556, Lotto records wooden covers and canvas *timpani* as well as mirrors, which traditionally formed a shutter over the image of a beloved (see cat. 43).[116] The same source documents Lotto's commission to copy a now-lost portrait of the humanist Giovanni Aurelio Augurello that had both a painted cover and a reverse.[117] This tripartite configuration provided space for further elaboration of the sitter's virtues or the inclusion of an additional figure.

Moreover, Lotto's correspondence regarding his designs for covers—albeit in the context of a sacred commission—provides invaluable insight into his perception of their complex interrelation with the works they concealed. In 1524 he produced a series of inlaid wood (*intarsia*) panels depicting Old Testament scenes for the choir stalls of Santa Maria Maggiore in Bergamo along with a set of accompanying covers that, according to the contract, should "correspond in meaning to the panels over which they will be respectively placed."[118] However, when the symbolic imagery that Lotto devised for the intarsia covers confounded his patrons, he offered the following wisdom: "Concerning the designs for the covers, please be informed that they are things which are not written; imagination is needed to bring them to light."[119] To Lotto, then, the meaning of the covers' innovative pictorial language could not be readily grasped by means of an explanatory text but was intended to be enigmatic and to engage the viewer in a process of decoding.

While Lotto's account book provides significant information about the production of canvas covers, none by his hand survive. Titian is the artist to whom a significant corpus of such *timpani* can be ascribed.[120] Two allegories painted by him are important examples of covers for lost portraits (cats. 32 and 33). His *Cupid and the Wheel of Fortune* (cat. 32) is one of the few extant covers painted in grisaille, which, according to the Vendramin inventory, was a technique used extensively and, like the exterior of altarpiece wings, served to evoke the cover's role as an intermediary space between the viewer and the painting in color beneath.

MINIATURE PORTRAITS IN BOXES AND LOCKETS

The documented and surviving multisided portraits painted by Jacometto, Bellini, Lotto, and Titian reflect a wide range of formats, scales, and media, from large canvas *timpani* to miniature wooden boxes. Jacometto's portrait box (cat. 20A,B) reflects the practice of incorporating and storing painted, illuminated, or carved likenesses within handheld, portable formats (fig. 27).[121] These highly personal objects provided the owner with continuous access to his or her beloved's image, which could be viewed in a private and intimate manner. As tokens of friendship, love, or political allegiance, small-scale portraits were frequently given as gifts on the occasion of a betrothal, marriage, or journey.[122] In addition to their wooden, metal, or ivory covers, these diminutive portraits, like other small-scale objects, were designed with cases or bags of leather (cat. 51C), velvet (cat. 12C), silk, or other textiles for protection and portability.[123]

As the author and collector Giulio Mancini asserted in the early seventeenth century, miniatures and small paintings were the ideal presents for nobles.[124] A double-sided portrait of the Venetian noblewoman Bianca Cappello (see fig. 53), painted on copper, may have formed the cover of a walnut box commissioned by Francesco de' Medici during their affair.[125] The box could have contained gifts for his beloved, as was customary for brides.

Giorgio Vasari's biography of the celebrated sixteenth-century miniaturist Giulio Clovio evokes the restricted access to such enclosed portraits, recounting that "some private persons have in little cases the most beautiful portraits by his hand, of various lords, their friends, or ladies loved by them. But ... the works of men such as Don Giulio are not public, nor in places where they can be seen by everyone."[126] The format of Clovio's encased images recalls that of the *Kapsel*, or capsule, portrait, which flourished in Germany, France, and England beginning in the early sixteenth century: a painted, illuminated, or carved likeness enclosed within a small, shallow, circular box. In a fictional dialogue written in the 1450s by the humanist Angelo Decembrio, a Ferrarese court member states, "What I keep, framed in this small *pyxis* [round box], is the countenance of a golden-haired maiden.... Not long ago I wrote a tearful elegy on her death, and now I treasure this proof of sweet and everlasting remembrance."[127]

In northern Europe during the early sixteenth century, capsule portraits by German artists such as Lucas Cranach and Hans Holbein (cats. 44A,B and 46A,B) paralleled the development of miniature likenesses painted on vellum at the French and English courts beginning in the 1520s.[128] Holbein's *Anne of Cleves* (1539, Victoria and Albert Museum, London) is encased in an ivory box (which may date to the late sixteenth century), whose lid is carved in the form of a Tudor rose.[129] Holbein painted the miniature when he was in Germany to paint a full-scale portrait of Anne, the prospective bride of Henry VIII, who may also have commissioned this smaller version.[130]

The transmissible format of capsule portraits was exploited by Martin Luther when he commissioned Cranach to paint numerous small roundel images of himself and his wife that fit together in small wooden boxes and were widely distributed as propaganda on the occasion of their controversial marriage in 1525 (cat. 44A,B).[131] Painted and carved capsule portraits flourished in Germany in the early sixteenth century, especially in Luther's circle, which included Philipp Melanchthon (cat. 46A,B) and the electors of Saxony (cat. 47A,B).[132] In Cranach's *Gregor Brück* (1533, Germanisches Nationalmuseum, Nuremberg), the chancellor of the electors of Saxony wears a gold chain from which is suspended a medal of Johann Friedrich I, displaying his allegiance to the ruler.

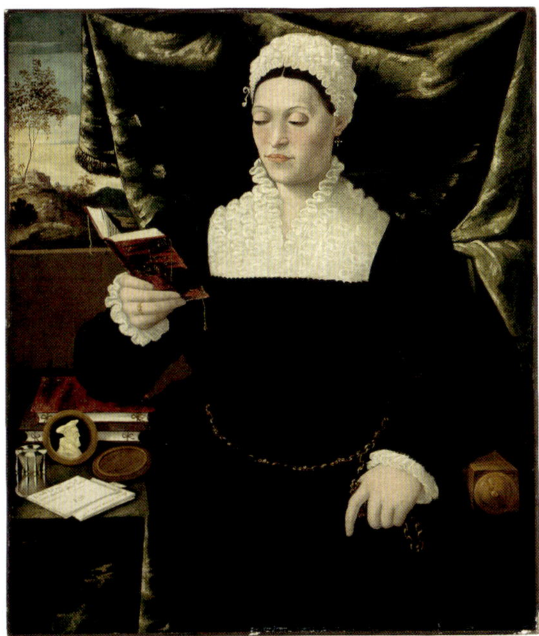

Fig. 27. Unknown artist (Italian, Romagna, active ca. 1540). *Orsina de Grassi*, 1540. Oil on canvas, 40 × 33½ in. (101.5 × 85 cm). Szépművészeti Múzeum, Budapest (69.21)

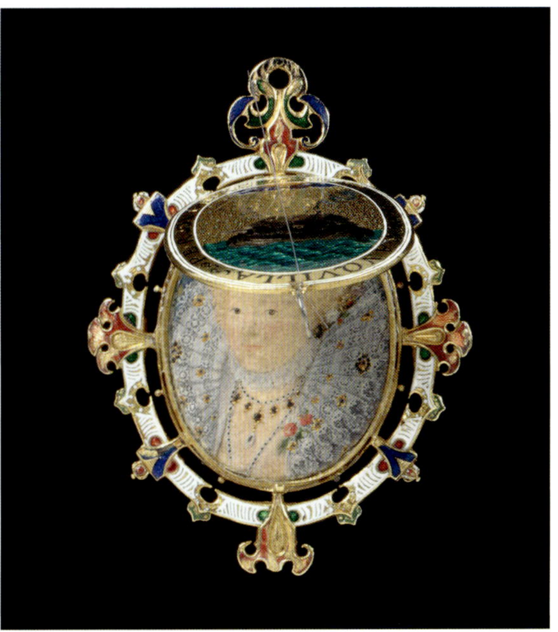

Fig. 28. Nicholas Hilliard (English, 1547–1619). *The Heneage Jewel*, ca. 1600. Watercolor on vellum, gold, enamel on gold, diamonds, rubies, and rock crystal, 2¾ × 2 in. (7 × 5.1 cm). Victoria and Albert Museum, London (M.81-1935)

The incorporation of likenesses into various forms of jewelry, including pendants and brooches, was especially fashionable at the European courts.[133] In the sixteenth century, colored wax carved in relief was frequently employed for miniature portraits encased either in lockets or in wooden boxes.[134] Although the portraits were covered with embellished lids and could remain private, the fact that they could be worn on the body rather than stored away reflects a more public display of small-scale likenesses.

Particularly elaborate in its layered design is the Heneage Jewel (fig. 28), datable around 1600, which may have been among the miniature portraits commissioned by Elizabeth I for her courtiers to demonstrate their loyalty to her.[135] The obverse bears a gold profile bust of the queen set below rock crystal and encircled by gems. The reverse has a hinged cover adorned with Noah's Ark amid stormy seas, signifying her peaceful reign during religious turmoil.[136] The cover, whose reverse is adorned with the Tudor rose, conceals another image of the queen: an illuminated likeness painted by Nicholas Hilliard.

Combining double portraits with allegories and emblems, the Heneage Jewel constitutes a particularly elaborate and complex version of the larger-scale, multisided portrait. Intended to be worn on the body as a sign of political loyalty, such lockets, with their intricate formats, simultaneously existed for the public realm and retained a level of intimacy and privacy. The owner or beholder was required to manipulate and unveil their facets and layers to discover the dynamic interconnections between the subjects' likenesses and the symbolic portraits surrounding them.

The tradition of multisided painted portraits in Italy and northern Europe evolved and expanded during the sixteenth and early seventeenth centuries to encompass works of wide-ranging scales, media, formats, and functions that were gradually integrated into such personal objects as lockets, miniature boxes, and watches.

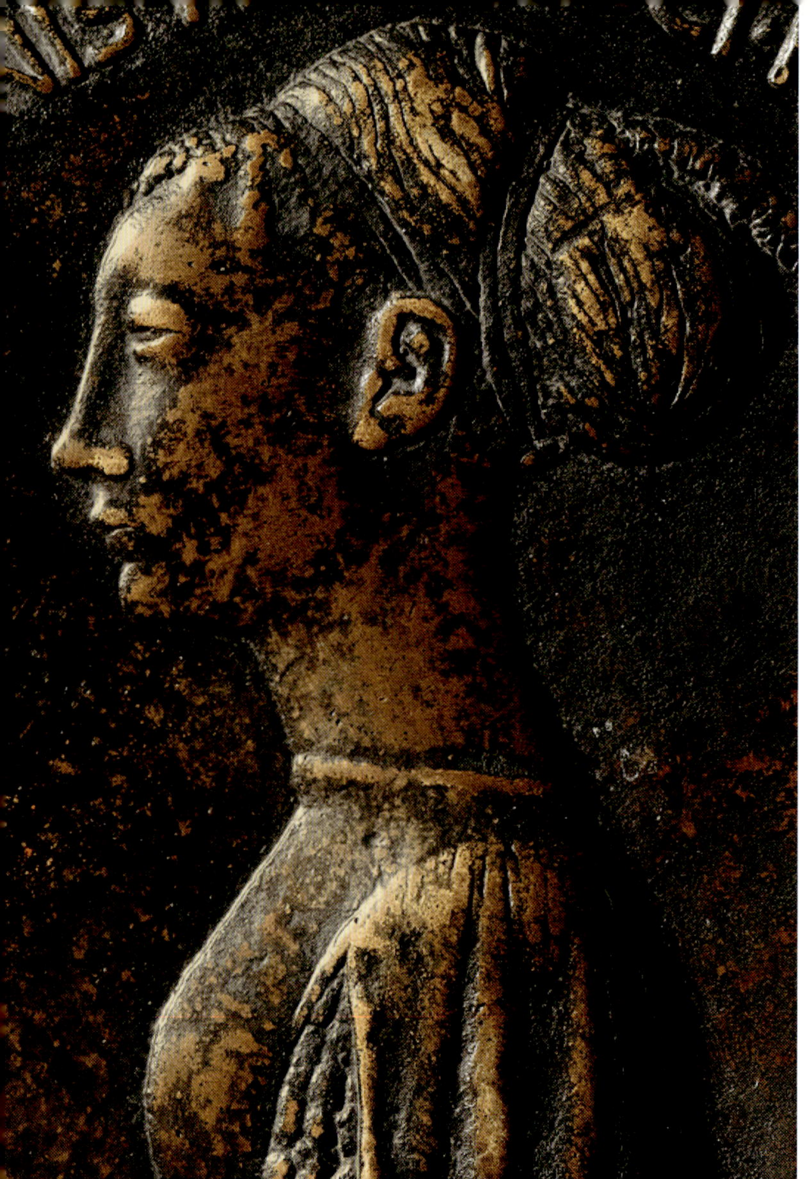

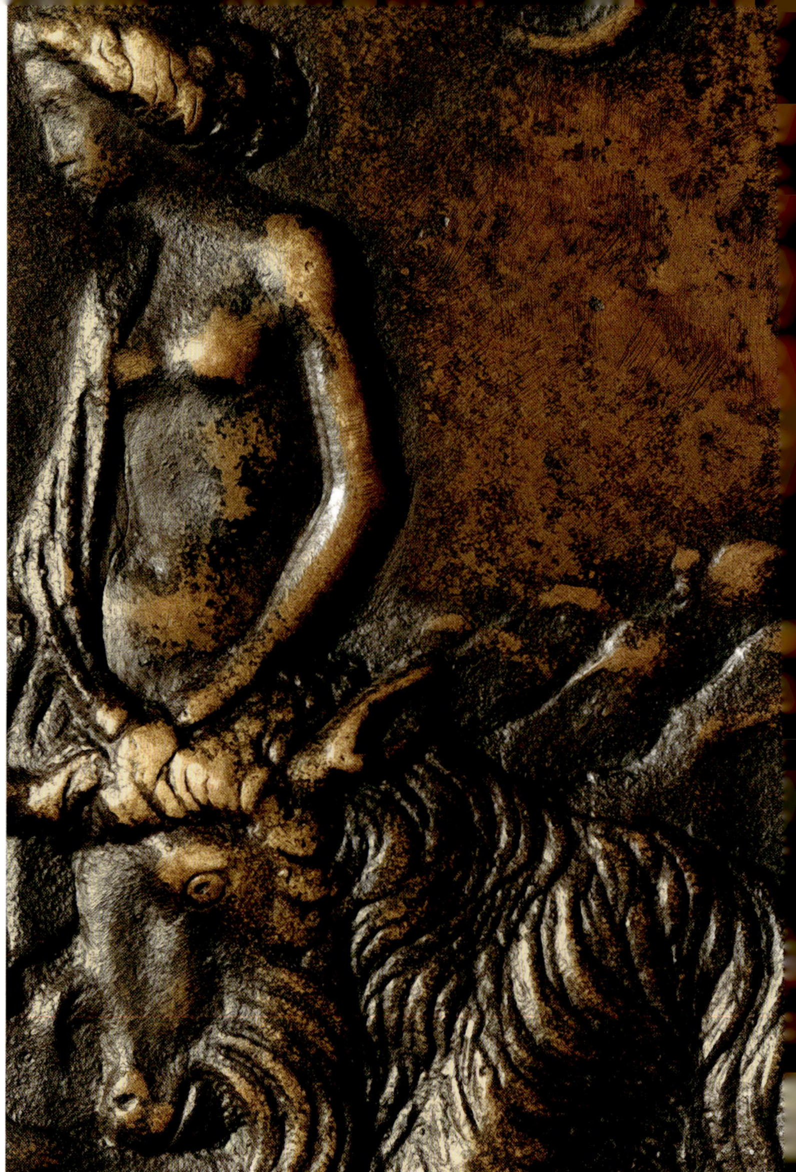

COINING MULTISIDED PORTRAITS: PRECEDENTS AND PARALLELS

ALISON MANGES NOGUEIRA

Traveling from Milan to Mantua in December 1354, the renowned poet and humanist Francesco Petrarch transported several ancient Roman coins to offer King Charles IV on the eve of his coronation as Holy Roman Emperor, with the intention of presenting them as models of virtuous rulership.[1] Petrarch recounted the event the following year: "[The coins] bore the portraits of our rulers, with inscriptions in tiny ancient lettering, among which was the head of Caesar Augustus, almost breathing. 'Here, O Caesar,' I said, 'here are the men whom you have succeeded, here are those whom you must try to imitate and admire, after whose model and image you should compose yourself.'"[2] Although the particular coins presented by Petrarch cannot be identified, one of the many issued by Augustus is a gold aureus whose reverse bears emblems signifying courage, clemency, justice, and piety, granted to a military figure who saved the life of a comrade in battle (cat. 1).[3]

Along with their inscriptions, the reverses of ancient coinage featured a rich visual language of allegories and emblems that bolstered many aspects of rulers' propaganda, from their authority, legitimacy, and ancestry to their victories, patronage, and divine protection.[4] Ancient coinage preserved for posterity, in a portable, durable format, the names, likenesses, and achievements of illustrious figures, thereby upholding the values and historical record of antiquity. Highly esteemed by Renaissance collectors, humanists, and rulers, ancient numismatics served as inspiration for their own multifaced portraiture on coins, medals, and painted panels.[5]

The nature of this relationship is reflected in a manuscript copy of *The Lives of the Twelve Caesars* by the second-century Roman historian Suetonius that was commissioned around 1474 by the Venetian humanist Bernardo Bembo.[6] Its full-page miniatures illustrate events in the emperors' lives as they were portrayed on the reverse sides of their coinage. The folio dedicated to the life of Nero depicts the reverses of five coins issued by the emperor as well as an obverse bearing his likeness (fig. 29). A similar numismatic effigy of Nero is held by the male sitter in Hans Memling's roughly contemporaneous *Bernardo Bembo* (see fig. 25), plausibly identified as the humanist by the presence of laurel and palm trees in the background, the botanical elements of his personal emblem.[7]

The Suetonius manuscript, with its particular emphasis on numismatic reverses as vehicles for conveying imperial deeds, signals Bembo's keen interest in the symbolic language of such images and the interrelation of the coins' dual faces. This fascination paralleled his patronage of several double-sided paintings during the same period, including a devotional diptych he commissioned from Memling in the mid-1470s with memento mori painted on the back (Alte Pinakothek, Munich, and National Gallery of Art, Washington, D.C.).[8]

Between 1474 and 1478, Bembo was probably also the patron of Leonardo's *Ginevra de' Benci* (see fig. 24), whose reverse depicts his laurel-and-palm-wreath emblem as well as a Latin motto, translated as "Virtue adorns Beauty."[9] The presence of the wreath on the reverse of *Ginevra de' Benci* immediately recalls long-standing numismatic models dating back to Hellenistic examples of the second century BCE known as *stephanophori* (wreath-bearers), which combined the bust of a god or goddess on the obverse and a wreath encircling an inscription or image on the reverse.[10] An aureus of Julius Caesar, for instance, depicts a bust-length image of Venus on the obverse and a laurel wreath encircling an inscription on the reverse (44 BCE, British Museum, London).[11] Especially evocative of numismatic models are the female personifications on the reverses of painted portraits, such as the figure of Victory adorning the back of *A Lady in Profile*, attributed to a follower of Sandro Botticelli (fig. 30), which closely recalls the paired images of Empress Faustina II and the standing image of Juno on the aureus of Antoninus Pius (141–161 CE, British Museum).[12]

In addition to numismatics, ancient bronze box mirrors furnished with embellished lids provided inspiration for multisided Renaissance portraits, including those that incorporated mirrored surfaces. Since antiquity, mirrors were closely associated with portraiture (and love), as suggested by a Greek example dating to the fourth century BCE (cat. 3), whose cover, adorned with an idealized female head in bronze relief, served both as a model of beauty and as a memento mori for the beholder's transient likeness reflected beneath (see cat. 43).

Many of the Renaissance humanists and rulers who assembled significant collections of ancient coinage, such as Gianfrancesco Gonzaga of Mantua, were also patrons of a burgeoning, closely related medium: bronze portrait medals, which flourished under the celebrated painter and sculptor Pisanello beginning in the late 1430s (cats. 4 and 5).[13] Adopting the format and iconography of ancient coins enabled Pisanello's subjects to align themselves with imperial predecessors as well as to emphasize similar personal virtues through the allegories, emblems, and inscriptions on the medals' reverses.[14] Multisided painted portraits later enabled a broader section of the populace to emulate the same models.

Medieval coinage was another significant precedent for multisided painted portraits for its use of heraldry, both as an independent symbol of identity and in combination with portraiture. Coinage issued between 1232 and 1250 by the Holy Roman Emperor Frederick II, for instance, follows ancient examples by depicting the ruler in a bust-length, profile portrait with an imperial eagle on the reverse.[15] However, since the eleventh century, numismatic imagery often featured highly schematic depictions of sovereignty in the form of full-length enthroned or crowned figures or, more often, combinations of emblems and heraldry. Between 1266 and 1285, Charles I of Anjou circulated coinage featuring a bust-length (albeit idealized) portrait with his fleur-de-lis coat of arms on the reverse, a formula that would frequently find parallels in later numismatics as well as in painted portraits.[16] Owing to the long-standing tradition of heraldry as a signifier of identity, the two sides of a coin, medal, or painting that combined a sitter's likeness and coat of arms were regarded as inextricably bound.

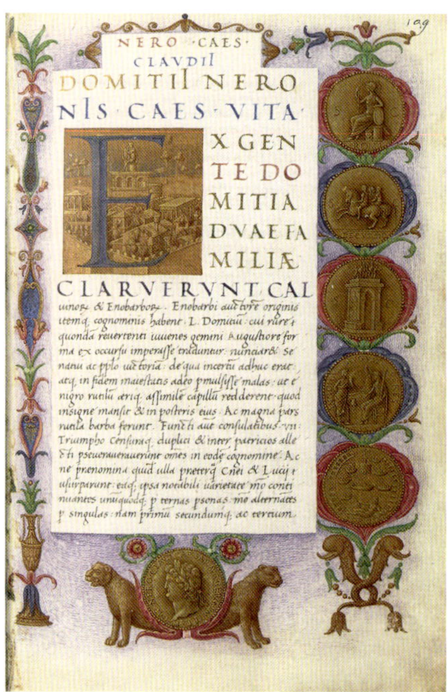

Fig. 29. Attributed to Gaspare da Padova (Italian, active 1466/67–died ca. 1493). Leaf from Caius Suetonius Tranquillus, *The Lives of the Twelve Caesars*, ca. 1474. Tempera and gold on parchment, 10¾ × 7⅛ in. (27.5 × 18 cm). Bibliothèque Nationale de France, Paris, Département des Manuscrits (Latin 5814, fol. 109r)

Since the fourteenth century, heraldry adorned the reverses of many devotional paintings as a mark of patronage, ownership, and piety. On the reverse of Simon Marmion's *Lamentation* (cat. 8), the combined coats of arms of Charles the Bold of Burgundy and Margaret of York fill the picture plane with bold colors and forms along with four love knots uniting their initials. While heraldry painted on the reverses of portraits or devotional works could be small in scale and inconspicuous, there are many such cases in which their prominent display forms part of the decorative program of the composition.[17]

Another long-standing decorative tradition — embellishing the reverses of paintings with fictive stone — had been employed on devotional works since the thirteenth century and was consistently adopted in portraiture from the early fifteenth century. Various stone types, with numerous sacred and secular connotations, were painted on the backs of private devotional panels, diptychs, and triptychs. Not simply ornamental motifs, these lithic patterns evoked the revered and eternal nature of the object itself and the divine subject depicted.[18] As Angelica Dülberg

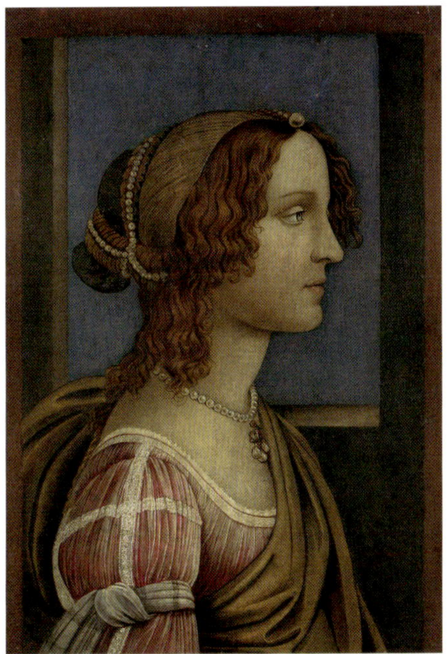
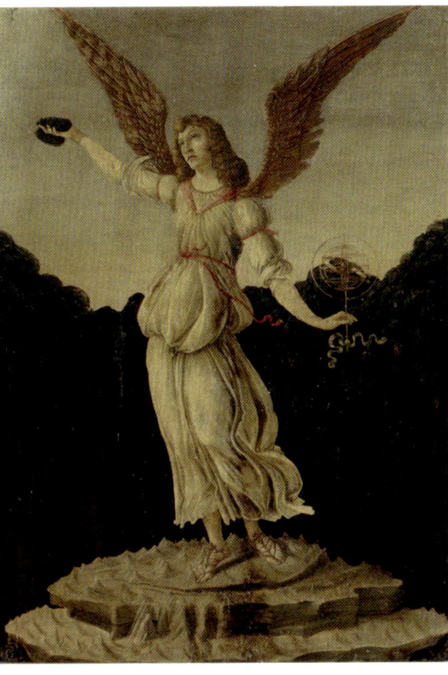

Fig. 30. Follower of Sandro Botticelli (Italian, 1444/45–1510). *A Lady in Profile* (recto); *Allegorical Figure* (verso), ca. 1490. Tempera on wood panel, 23¼ × 15¾ in. (59.1 × 40 cm). The National Gallery, London (NG2082)

asserts, the painted marble reverses and frames of early Netherlandish portraits transform the works from two-dimensional paintings into precious three-dimensional, shrine-like objects.[19]

The colorful pattern of seemingly inlaid marbles on the reverse of Gentile da Fabriano's *Madonna and Child* (ca. 1421, Museo Nazionale di San Matteo, Pisa) reveals the inspiration of the liturgical furnishings and wall revetments of ecclesiastical interiors.[20] Porphyry, the lithic material most imitated, was a costly, highly durable stone used in antiquity for imperial tombs and monuments.[21] The depiction of porphyry and other stones of sanguine color evokes Christ's Passion and the Stone of Unction (upon which his body was prepared for burial), thereby enhancing the devotional message of the subject depicted on the recto.

Acanthus leaves represent another ornamental form with ancient funerary associations that adorned the reverses of both sacred works and portraits (see fig. 10 and cat. 7). Employed in architecture and sepulchral monuments, acanthus was frequently associated with Christ's Crown of Thorns as well as with his Crucifixion and Resurrection.[22]

A late fifteenth-century private devotional shrine (cat. 7) has numerous painted sides, adorned with both ornamental and figurative imagery, that contribute to its sacred narrative. The fictive stone on its reverse emphasizes the universal nature of its divine subjects, while the acanthus leaves on its sides symbolize and foreshadow Christ's Passion, as does the image of Veronica's veil painted on the base. The owner of this small, highly portable, boxlike shrine — perhaps the female donor depicted on the interior — would view its many interior and exterior facets in an interactive, sequential, and revelatory process. She would pay homage to the saints on the exterior before opening the doors to see her own image next to that of Saint Catherine, whose standard attribute, the wheel on which she was martyred, is replaced by a book, emphasizing her scholarly achievements.[23] Like portraits with embellished covers and reverses, the multifaceted structure and visual program of this shrine created a nuanced, layered narrative around the image of the sitter.

CAT. 1
Aureus of Augustus

Roman, Early Imperial, 20–19 BCE
Gold, 11/16 × 3/4 in. (1.8 × 1.9 cm)
Possibly minted in Colonia Patricia (Córdoba, Spain)[1]
Inscribed (on reverse): (at top and bottom) *CAESAR/AUGUSTUS*; (at center, on shield) *CL V* (*Clipeus Virtutis* [Shield of Virtue]); (around shield) *SPQR* (*Senatus Populusque Romanus* [The Senate and the Roman People])
The Metropolitan Museum of Art, New York, Gift of Joseph H. Durkee, 1899 (99.35.6)

SINCE THE SIXTH century BCE, Greek cities had decorated their coins with various types of symbols, such as animals (a turtle in Aegina, an owl in Athens), plants (a grain ear in Metapontum), allegories (Victory flying over a chariot in Messina), mythological figures (Phalanthos riding a dolphin in Tarentum), or a divinity's head presented in profile. The latter motif then served as a model for the first rulers' idealized portraits represented on coins, appearing in the Hellenistic kingdoms after Alexander the Great's death in 323 BCE.[2] Those first portraits were directly inspired by the profile heads of Zeus and Herakles (fig. 31) on coinage struck by Philip II of Macedon and his son Alexander the Great. Roman coinage with the portrait of the ruler in profile derives from that tradition.

Beginning in the second century BCE, a crucial innovation appeared in Roman portraiture—a hyperrealistic style called Verism that depicted a person in a harshly accurate manner, even accentuating ugliness, in order to emphasize virtues such as wisdom and severity. But when Augustus became the first Roman emperor (r. 27 BCE–14 CE), official art, and especially representations of the princeps, took a radical turn from Late Republican Verism. The new style, although still true to nature, was idealized and consciously referred to the classical canons of Greek art.

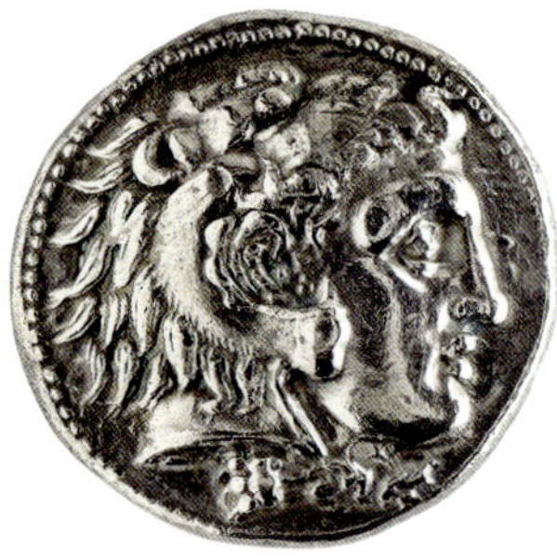
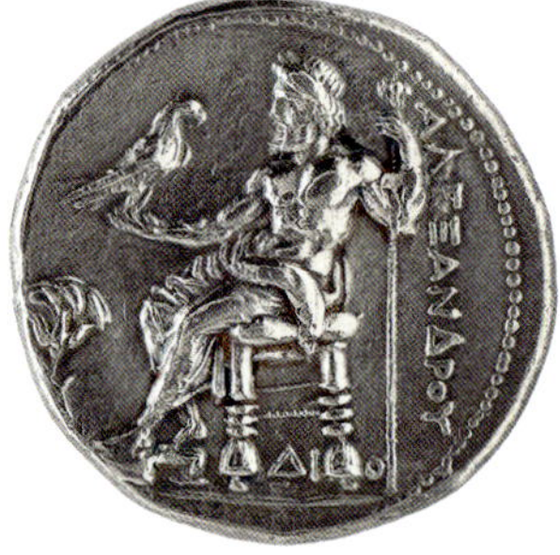

Fig. 31. Tetradrachm of Alexander the Great with profile of Herakles (obverse) and Zeus Enthroned (reverse). Macedonian (minted in Memphis, Egypt), ca. 332–323 BCE. Silver. Museum of Art, Rhode Island School of Design, Providence (40.015.221)

On the obverse of this gold coin, known as an aureus, the emperor appears as an ageless and composed man, depicted with simple and balanced lines.[3] He wears a laurel crown, a symbol of triumph and glory. On the reverse, *CAESAR AUGUSTUS* surrounds a shield and the letters *SPQR*, while laurel trees, symbols of victory, appear at the sides. The letters *CL V* on the shield identify it as the golden "Shield of Virtue" that the Senate presented to Augustus in 27 BCE in thanks for having saved the state and the people in the civil wars.[4]

After a violent and unstable period, this kind of public distinction served as a crucial tool in reshaping the structure and imagery of the new regime. It was communicated across the empire through stone copies of the shield, its frequent reproduction on coins, and its prominent mention in the *Res gestae divi Augusti* (*The Deeds of the Divine Augustus*), Augustus's political testament.[5] The inscription on the shield, invoking virtue, clemency, justice, and piety, expressed the qualities expected from Augustus, and he in turn used the shield in his propaganda to present himself as a savior.[6] Such symbols helped to develop a message of unification, enhancing Augustus's authority and legitimacy.[7] Both sides of the aureus are thus complementary: a dignified portrait of the princeps, savior of the people, is linked to his official core values.

In the Italian states of the fifteenth century, ancient Roman and Greek coins were an important part of the collections amassed by princes, prelates, and humanists. In particular, imperial coins from Augustus to Trajan served as models for the casting of coins and medals meant to glorify Renaissance rulers, their families, and court members (see cats. 4 and 5).[8] By combining the emperors' likenesses with personalized and celebratory allegories, emblems, and inscriptions, ancient numismatics directly inspired the multisided painted portraits of the fifteenth and sixteenth centuries.

DT

SELECTED REFERENCES: Richter 1948, pp. [ii], [11] no. 22; Fowlkes-Childs and Seymour 2019, cat. 6, p. 10.

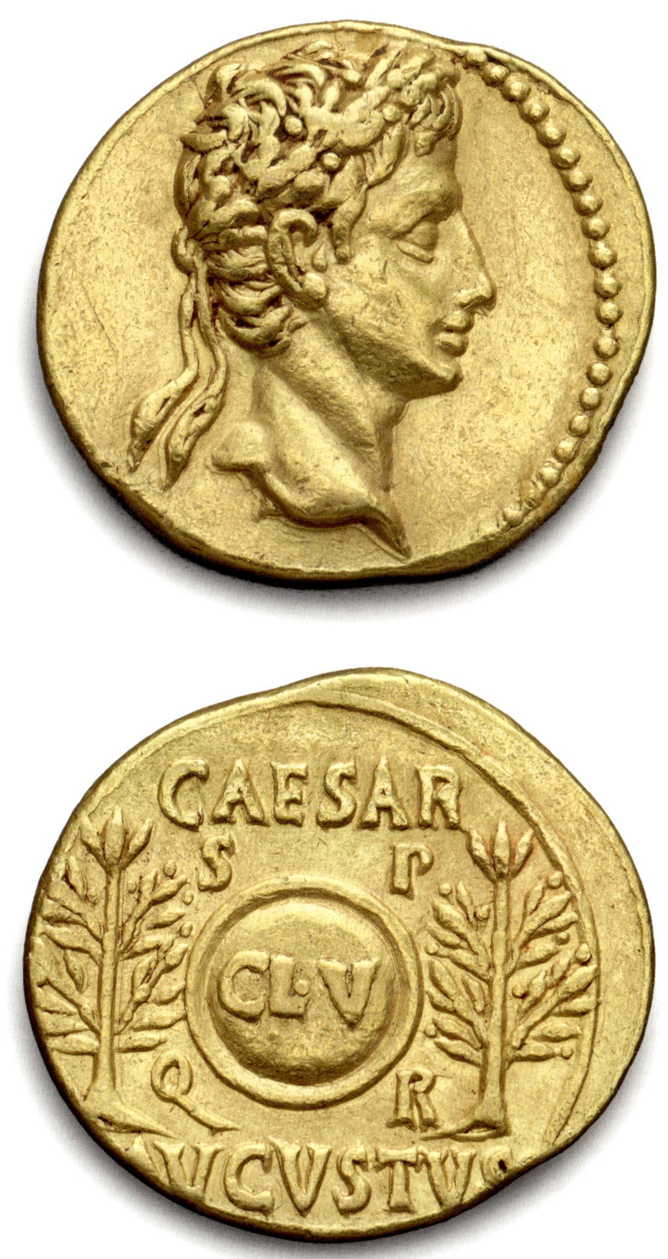
CAESAR
S P
CL·V
Q R
VCVSTVS

CAT. 2

Aureus of Diocletian

Roman, Late Imperial, 293 CE
Gold, ¾ × ⅛ in. (1.8 × 0.2 cm)
Minted in Rome
Inscribed: (on obverse) *DIOCLETIANVS P*[*IUS*] *F*[*ELIX*] *AVG*[*USTUS*] (Diocletian the Pious and Fortunate Emperor); (on reverse) *IOVI CONSERVAT*[*ORI*] *AVGG* (*Duorum Augustorum* [To Jupiter, Protector of the Two Emperors])
Marked: *PROM* (*Percussa Romae* [Struck at Rome])
The Metropolitan Museum of Art, New York, Rogers Fund, 1908 (08.170.444)

THE BEARDED PROFILE of the Roman emperor Diocletian, crowned with a laurel wreath, appears on the obverse of this gold aureus with his title, translated as "Diocletian the Pious and Fortunate Emperor," inscribed around his head.[1] On the reverse, the naked figure of Jupiter stands holding his emblematic thunderbolt in his right hand and a long scepter in his left. The legend surrounding him is dedicated to "Jupiter, Protector of the Two Emperors." The exergual mark, *PROM* (*Percussa Romae*), indicates that the coin was minted in Rome. Legends on the obverse and reverse, as here, are seldom found together on the same coin.[2]

Chief god of the Roman religion, Jupiter often appears on imperial coinage in a wide variety of types. Naked or draped in a mantel, standing or seated, Jupiter alternately holds a scepter, a globe, or the thunderbolt; his symbol, the eagle, is sometimes at his feet. In other instances, he may hold a statuette of Victory (a winged woman), which he may offer to the emperor. On Diocletian's coins, the god represents military victory, stability, and imperial power. Diocletian also minted coins with representations of Mars (god of war) holding trophies or Sol (the Sun), both dragging a bounded captive.

Diocletian became emperor in 284 CE and, two years later, chose to reign as co-emperor with Maximian, whom he had proclaimed Caesar (the designated heir's title) in 285 and Augustus (the full imperial title) in 286. The rulers were not, however, equals, and Diocletian, the elder, was considered the planner. Around 286/87, he formalized his higher status by taking the epithet Iovius, identifying him as the son of Jupiter and explaining the god's depiction on the present coin. Maximian was the younger emperor, charged with the execution of imperial power, including military campaigns. He took the epithet Herculius, meaning son of Hercules, the hero who rid the earth of many monsters and was seen as a protector of emperors. Unsurprisingly, Hercules's image often appears on the reverse of Maximian's coinage.

The exergue *PROM*, instead of the much more frequent abbreviation *PR*, dates this aureus to 293 CE, since this rare form appeared on coins only after a reform established in that year.[3] Diocletian reorganized the imperial power into a tetrarchy (a group of four rulers): two new emperors, both with the title of Caesar, joined the first two Augusti and inherited their epithets, according to their importance. Galerius became Iovius, and Constantius I (the father of Constantine the Great) became Herculius. The association of the tetrarchs with Jupiter and Hercules was not meant as an identification with the divine but rather as a way to share responsibilities and formalize rank among the rulers.[4]

The coinage struck by the four tetrarchs presents highly standardized bearded portraits, barely distinguishable from one another without the legend. This sameness probably expresses a desire for unity and stability in an empire that had suffered from decades of military chaos.[5]

DT

SELECTED REFERENCES: *O'Hagan Coin Collection* 1908, lot 696.

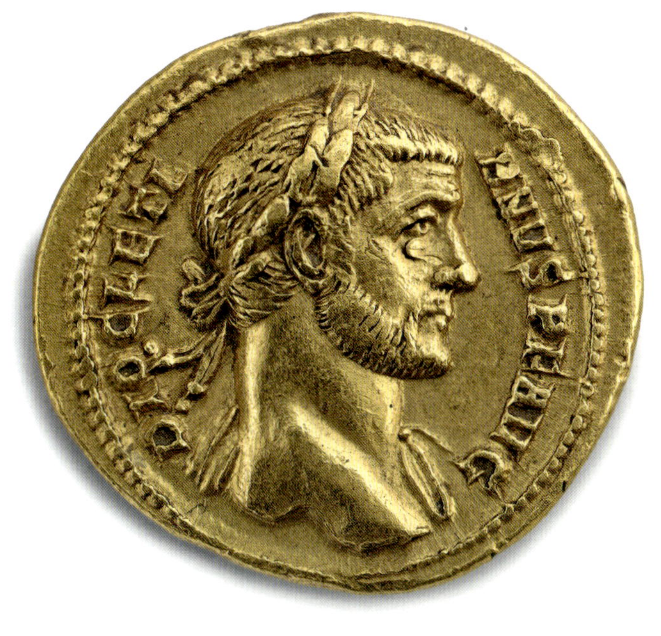

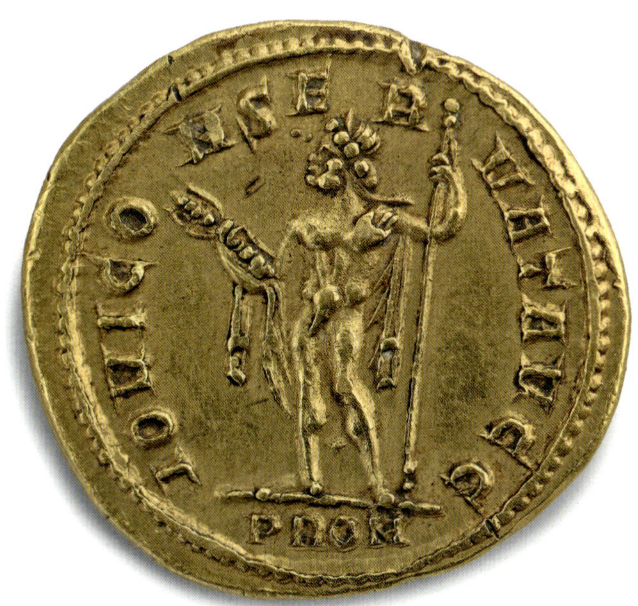

CAT. 3

Box Mirror with the Head of a Woman

Greek, Late Classical, 2nd quarter of the 4th century BCE

Bronze, Diam. 7⅞ in. (20 cm)

The Metropolitan Museum of Art, New York, Rogers Fund, 1907 (07.255)

A SYMBOL OF WEALTH and elite status, this large box mirror is a costly, ostentatious item made of bronze — a metal otherwise used for weapons and coins and thus associated with the masculine world. Lifting the cover by the ring on its lower edge reveals the actual mirror, a cast-bronze disk with a highly polished surface. The protective cover is decorated with a large female head that has been hammered in high relief and applied separately. The woman grasps a lock of wavy hair in her right hand, while her wrist and the curls on the top of her head extend over the lines incised around the edge of the frame. The image radiates erotic beauty, inviting the female user to emulate a feminine ideal by illustrating how her hair can enhance beauty and sexual appeal.[1]

In ancient Greece, the mirror was very much a gendered object, overwhelmingly connected with the female world. Both in literature and in the iconography of vases, terracottas, funerary stelae, gemstones, and other objects, mirrors are almost exclusively depicted in the hands of women, whether respectable matrons, young brides, or courtesans. Archaeology attests that the mirrors offered as dedications in sanctuaries were mostly connected with female divinities, including Artemis, Hera, and Aphrodite. Box mirrors appeared in Greece at the end of the fifth century BCE, supplanting the "caryatid" model, which featured a disk mirror fixed to a handle in the shape of a woman. Although some of the female figures represented on both types of mirrors may have been meant as Aphrodite herself, they were most likely generic, idealized maidens.[2]

The conventional ties between women and mirrors shed further light on the male conception of women in ancient Greece. According to Françoise Frontisi-Ducroux, mirrors in the box configuration belong to the category of pyxides, boxes designed to hold female goods such as jewelry and cosmetics. By extension, the box mirror evokes both the secluded female world within the domestic sphere and the function of women's bodies as "vessels of reproduction."[3]

Mirrors were also tools of magic, used not only for divination in contexts of love and marriage but also as prophecies of death in Greek tragedies. In this regard, following Mireille Lee, mirrors represent feminine agency and knowledge, since only women could employ them to perform these supernatural arts, considered mysterious and obscure by men.[4]

Finally, in the patriarchal ancient Greek world, mirrors and women were also assigned negative qualities as sources of disillusion, deception, and duplicity. The first woman, Pandora, for example, was a puppet fabricated and decorated by the gods to trick men. She was responsible for unleashing all of humanity's pains and evils when she opened the container — a jar or a box — where they had been concealed. Similarly, the mirror was seen as the instrument of alluring beauty but also of cunning seduction.[5] When it was closed, the present mirror showed an ideal image of the woman, hammered in solid, shiny bronze and conveying a sense of eternal beauty; when opened, it reflected her animated likeness, suggesting the fragility and ephemeral nature of life.
DT

SELECTED REFERENCES: Robinson 1908, pp. 68–69, fig. 2; Richter 1915, no. 758, pp. 257–59; Richter 1930, pp. 148–49, fig. 103; Richter 1953, pp. 96, 237, pl. 77c; *Lexicon Iconographicum Mythologiae Classicae* 1981–99, vol. 2, pt. 1, p. 111, no. 1122; Bol 2004, pp. 466, 473, pl. 448.

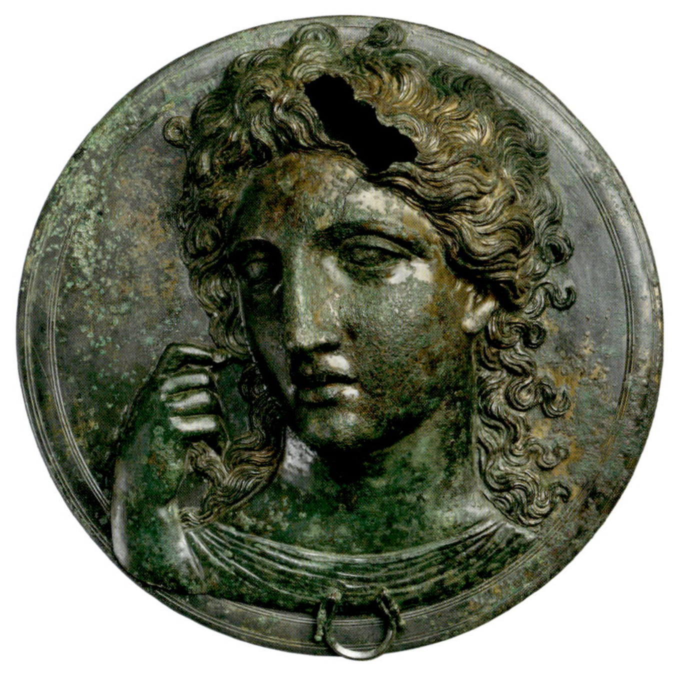

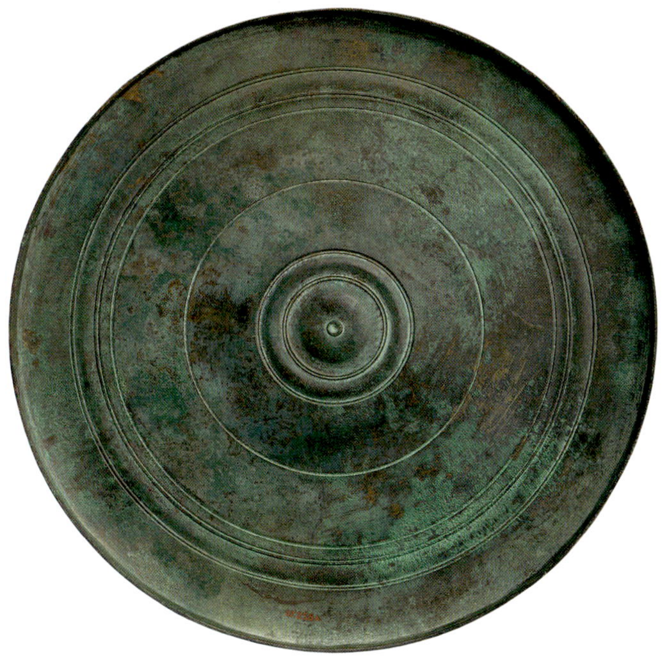

CAT. 4

PISANELLO (ANTONIO PISANO)

Italian, active by 1395–1455

Portrait Medal of Cecilia Gonzaga (obverse); *Innocence and a Unicorn in a Landscape* (reverse), 1447

Bronze, Diam. 3 5/16 in. (8.4 cm)

Inscribed, signed, and dated: (on obverse) *CICILIA VIRGO FILIA IOHANNIS FRANCISCI PRIMI MARCHIONIS MANTVE* (Cecilia, virgin daughter of Gianfrancesco, first marquess of Mantua); (on reverse) *OPVS PISANI PICTORIS MCCCCXLVII* (The work of Pisano the painter, 1447)

The Metropolitan Museum of Art, New York, Robert Lehman Collection, 1975 (1975.1.1307)

THE ARTISTIC LEGACY of Pisanello, one of the most celebrated Italian masters of the mid-fifteenth century, includes fresco and panel paintings as well as a remarkable corpus of drawings that range from sketches of courtly figures to portraits and animal studies. These sheets often served as preparatory designs for Pisanello's narrative paintings and for his most innovative contribution in another medium: the development of bronze portrait medals depicting contemporary rulers, their families, and members of their courts.

Among the medals Pisanello produced for the court of Mantua was that of Cecilia Gonzaga (1426–1451), identified in the inscription as the "virgin daughter of Gianfrancesco, first marquess of Mantua." This likeness is distinguished not only for the poetic quality of its reverse but also as the first Renaissance medal to depict a woman. The young Cecilia, praised by contemporaries for her intellectual achievements, excelled as a pupil at the school founded by the humanist Vittorino da Feltre. Her precocious mastery of Greek was praised by the scholar Ambrogio Traversari: "a ten-year-old girl, daughter of the prince, who writes so well in Greek that I was embarrassed thinking about how many I have taught who can barely write [vernacular] elegantly."[1]

Cecilia again defied expectations by repudiating the strategic marriage that her father had arranged to Oddantonio da Montefeltro of Urbino. In a letter of 1443, she pleaded with her father to release her from the impending wedding so that she could seek sanctuary in a life devoted to God. The following year marked the death of both Oddantonio and Gianfrancesco Gonzaga, who, in his will, granted his daughter permission to become a nun.[2] In 1444 the eighteen-year-old Cecilia entered the convent of Santa Paola in Mantua and was soon joined by her mother, Paola Malatesta.[3]

Cecilia's medal may have been commissioned by her brother, Ludovico, who inherited his father's title as marquess of Mantua. Ludovico was presumably the patron of two other medals by Pisanello in 1447: one with his own image and another honoring their teacher, Vittorino (cat. 5).[4] Given that Cecilia's medal dates to three years after she was cloistered as a Clarissan nun, Pisanello probably based her image, which depicts her in courtly attire, on an earlier portrait.[5]

Cecilia embodies the female ideals of virtue and beauty both through her likeness on the obverse and through the allegory on the reverse, where the unicorn and the crescent moon, the sign of the goddess Diana, symbolize purity and chastity. Only a woman in possession of these virtues could tame a unicorn, according to the Latin *Physiologus,* an early Christian treatise on animals.[6] The long, wavy hair of the present unicorn may have been inspired by this influential text, which describes the mythical beast as resembling a goat, an animal also associated with knowledge and therefore an apt reference to Cecilia's erudition.[7] Moreover, the unicorn, as a symbol of Christ, celebrated Cecilia's piety. The image of a maiden and a unicorn appeared frequently in medieval and Renaissance art, including drawings by Leonardo da Vinci that have been associated with his *Ginevra de' Benci* (see fig. 24) and an emblem of chastity in a late fifteenth-century drawing attributed to Baccio Baldini (1465–80, British Museum, London).[8]

AMN

SELECTED REFERENCES: Hill 1930, p. 11, no. 37, pl. 8; Stephen K. Scher, cats. 7, 7a, in Scher 1994, pp. 52–53; Eleanora Luciano, cat. 7, in Brown 2001, pp 119–20; Pollard 2007, vol. 1, no. 20, pp. 30–31; Eleanora Luciano, cat. 87, in Christiansen and Weppelmann 2011, pp. 231–32; Scholten 2011, no. 50, p. 85; Syson and Gordon 2001, pp. 116–17.

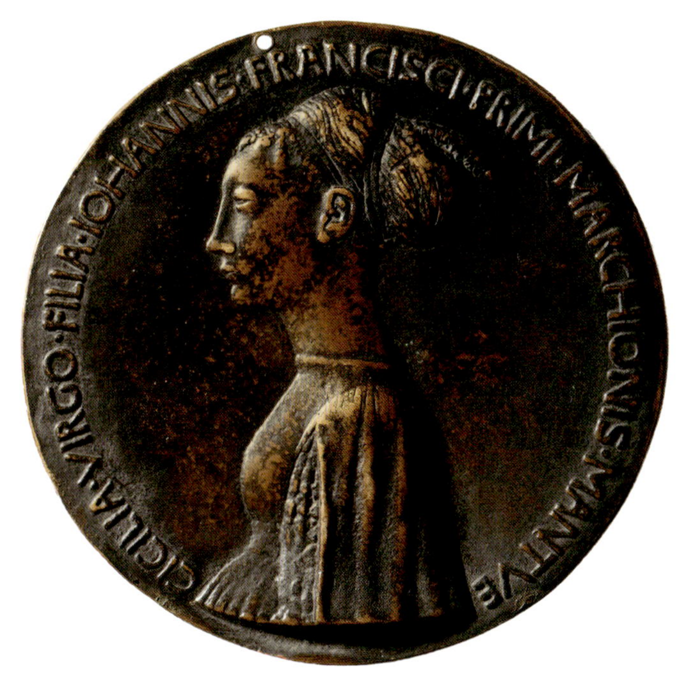
CICILIA·VIRGO·FILIA·IOHANNIS·FRANCISCI·PRIMI·MARCHIONIS·MANTVE

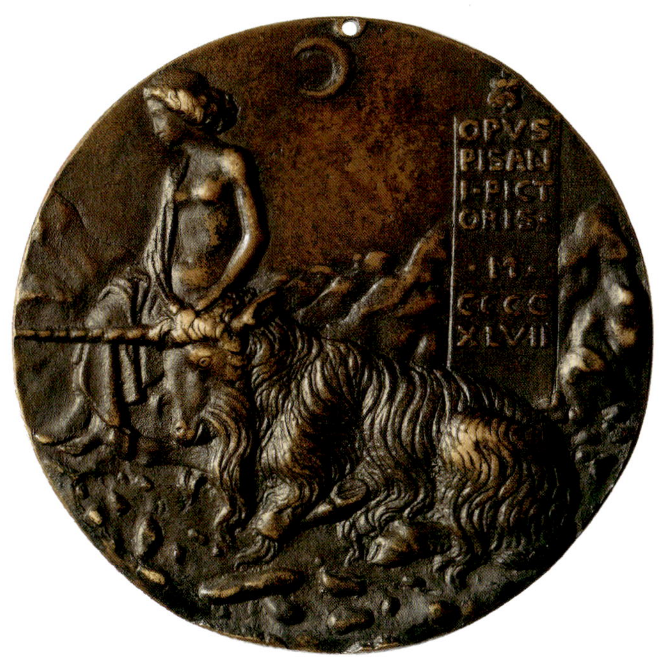
OPVS
PISAN
I·PICT
ORIS·
·M·
CCCC
XLVII

CAT. 5

PISANELLO (ANTONIO PISANO)

Italian, active by 1395–1455
Portrait Medal of Vittorino Rambaldoni da Feltre (obverse); *A Pelican in Her Piety* (reverse), model: 1446–47 (possibly cast 15th or 16th century)

Bronze, Diam. 2 9/16 in. (6.5 cm)

Inscribed and signed: (on obverse) *VITTORINVS FELTRENSIS SVMMVS* (Vittorino da Feltre the most distinguished); (on reverse) *MATHEMATICVS ET OMNIS HVMANITATIS PATER* (Mathematician and father of all the humanities)[;] *OPV PISANI PICTORIS* (The work of Pisano the painter)

The Metropolitan Museum of Art, New York, Robert Lehman Collection, 1975 (1975.1.1302)

THE RENOWNED HUMANIST educator Vittorino da Feltre (1378–1446) studied at the University of Padua, where he later taught grammar, mathematics, and rhetoric before opening his own private school in the city. In 1423 the lord (and future marquess) of Mantua, Gianfrancesco Gonzaga, invited Vittorino to establish a school for his children, including his heir, Ludovico, and his daughter, Cecilia (cat. 4). Several years later, one of Vittorino's teachers, the Greek scholar Guarino da Verona, played a similar pedagogical role in nearby Ferrara, and the two courts became seminal centers of humanist learning for the rising generation of scholars and rulers.[1]

As its reputation grew, Vittorino's school in Mantua, known as the Casa Giocosa (Joyful House), attracted students from patrician families across northern Italy, including, from 1434 to 1437, the young Federico da Montefeltro, the future duke of Urbino. Vittorino also opened the school to students who were unable to attend for financial reasons, using his own salary to support them.[2]

Intensely devoted to his students and his mission, Vittorino created an influential curriculum that combined the liberal arts, religious education, and physical exercise.[3] According to a biography written by the Florentine bookseller Vespasiano da Bisticci, Vittorino strove "to give a good example in his own life; to exhort and stimulate all about him to live worthily.... All teachers should be fashioned after this model, not merely to teach Latin and Greek, but also good conduct, which is the most important thing in life."[4]

Pisanello's posthumous medal of Vittorino was likely commissioned by another former pupil, the newly instated marquess of Mantua, Ludovico Gonzaga, who was also the presumed patron of his sister's medal that same year.[5] The inscriptions on Vittorino's medal praise him as "most distinguished ... mathematician and father of all the humanities"; a small sunflower, emblem of the Gonzaga, is tucked between two letters.

The reverse inscriptions encircle a pelican feeding its young with blood from its pierced breast, a theme known as "a pelican in her piety." According to medieval bestiaries as well as the Latin *Physiologus*, an early Christian text containing moralizing tales featuring animals, the pelican was a symbol of sacrifice and, particularly, of Christ's Passion. In the present context, the bird embodies Vittorino's piety, compassion, and selfless devotion to his young students, whom he nourished intellectually.[6] The pelican may also be an allusion to Vittorino's own teacher in Padua, Biagio Pelacani (meaning "pelican" in Italian), a philosopher, astrologer, and mathematician whose achievements in the latter field were imparted to his student, as highlighted in the inscription on the medal.[7]

With their rich symbolic associations—both sacred and secular—animals were frequently employed in heraldry, emblems, and allegories on the reverses of coins, medals, and multisided portraits, giving zoomorphic form to the virtuous traits possessed by their human counterparts.
AMN

SELECTED REFERENCES: Hill 1930, pp. 6, 11, no. 38, pl. 8; Stephen K. Scher, cats. 8, 8a, in Scher 1994, pp. 53–54; Syson and Gordon 2001, pp. 118–19; Pollard 2007, vol. 1, no. 19, p. 29; Stephen K. Scher, cat. 88, in Christiansen and Weppelmann 2011, pp. 232–34; Scholten 2011, no. 49, p. 84.

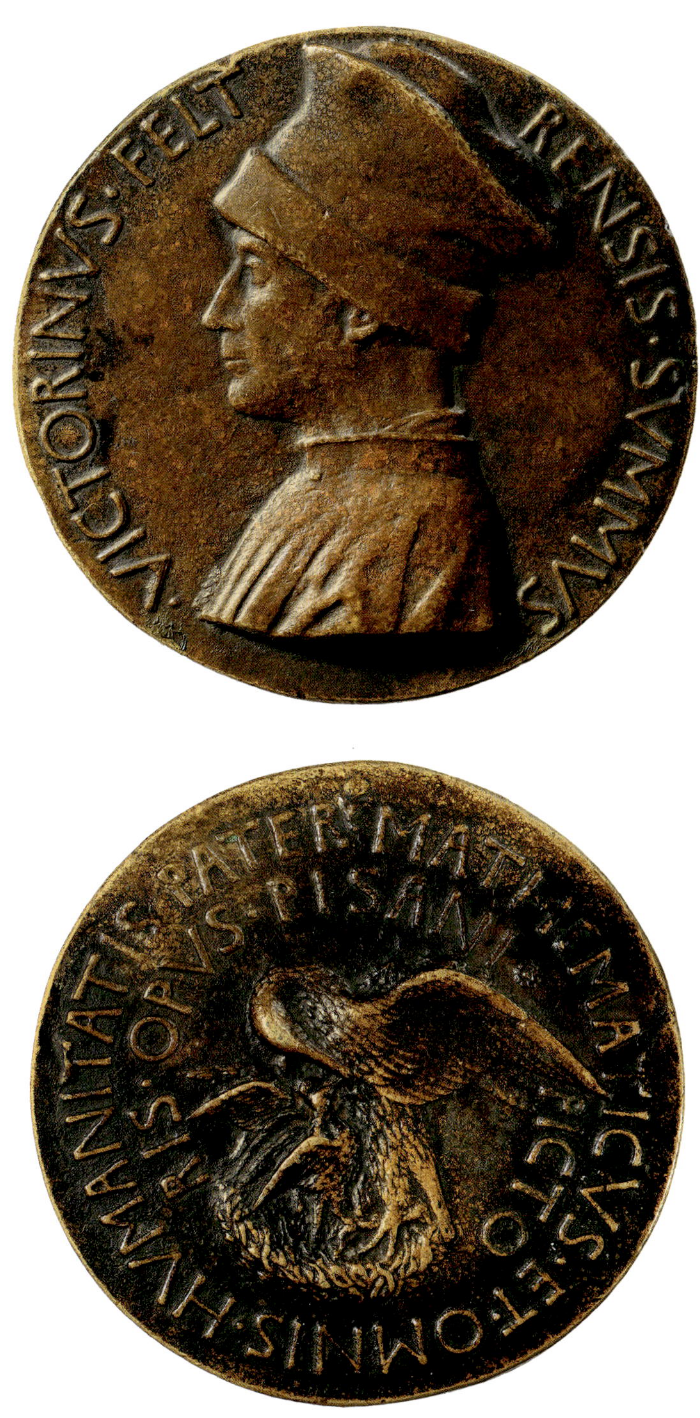
VICTORINVS·FELT
RENSIS·SVMMVS
PATER·MATHEMATICVS·ET·OMNIS·HVMANITATIS
OPVS·PISANI·PICTORIS

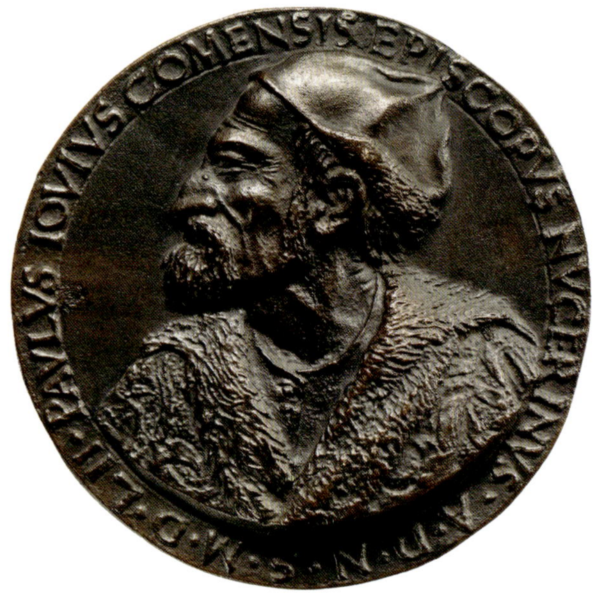

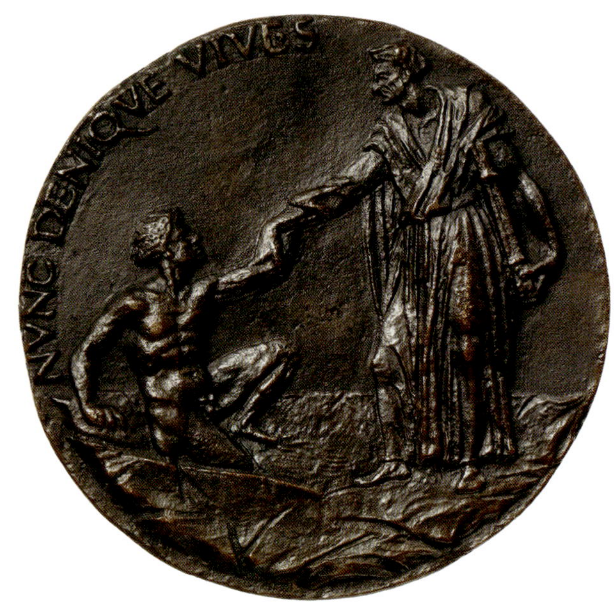

CAT. 6

FRANCESCO DA SANGALLO (FRANCESCO GIAMBERTI)

Italian, 1494–1576

Portrait Medal of Paolo Giovio (obverse); *Allegorical Portrait of Giovio Raising a Man from the Ground* (reverse), 1552[1]

Bronze (copper alloy with brown patina under a layer of dark wax), Diam. 3¾ in. (9.5 cm), weight 308.61g

Inscribed: (on obverse) • *PAVLVS IOVIVS COMENSIS EPISCOPVS NVCERINVS* • *A*[*nno*] • *D*[*omini*] • *N* • *S* • *M* • *D* • *LII* (*Paolo Giovio of Como, Bishop of Nocera, Year of our Lord 1552*); (on reverse) *NVNC DENIQVE VIVES* (Now at last you will live)

The Metropolitan Museum of Art, New York, Robert Lehman Collection, 1975 (1975.1.1314)

ALTHOUGH HIGHLY SUGGESTIVE in the context of the present volume, the fascinating imagery on Giovio's portrait medal by the Florentine sculptor Francesco da Sangallo has gone unexamined in the literature. If my hypothesis is correct, many historical details point to Giovio's own involvement in crafting his identity for posterity in this portrait medal. Artist and subject had likely met in the autumn of 1550, and became friends. Born of minor nobility in Como in Lombardy, in April of either 1483 or 1486, Giovio had been a Renaissance cleric and polymath—a prolific author of books, a student of Greek and a refined Latin philologist, a meticulous historian and art collector, a humanist scholar of anatomy and trained physician, not to mention a famous personality in his day.[2] He became bishop of Nocera de' Pagani in 1528. Giovio's friendship with Giorgio Vasari deepened in 1532, and by 1546 Giovio had become one of the editorial advisers for the first edition of Vasari's influential *Vite de' piú eccellenti pittori, scultori e architettori* (*Lives of the Most Eminent Painters, Sculptors, and Architects*), published by Lorenzo Torrentino in 1550.[3] In 1525–27 Giovio himself wrote (unpublished) biographies of Leonardo da Vinci, Michelangelo, and Raphael from firsthand acquaintance with these artists, planning to incorporate the texts into his larger projects on the biographies of famous figures of ancient and contemporary European history. An ardent admirer and collector of medals, Giovio also owned several specimens by Antonio Pisanello, the great fifteenth-century master of this medium. Vasari's biography of Gentile da Fabriano and Pisanello in the 1568 edition of the *Vite* quotes extensive text directly from Giovio's letter to Duke Cosimo de' Medici, in which Giovio passionately defended Pisanello's portrait medals as evidence of his virtuosic technique and ingenuity of imagery.[4] Giovio died in Florence in December 1552.

As Giovio understood, portrait medals since Pisanello's time had offered one of the most original and complete visual means of glorifying and memorializing the self in the pursuit of earthly immortality. Renaissance portrait medals had functioned as the currency of fame for nearly a century.[5] The imagery and Latin inscriptions on both sides of Giovio's portrait medal by Sangallo pointedly advertise the Lombard author's intellectual ambitions, and with an unusual degree of immediacy. As I suggest here, Sangallo began sculpting the original of Giovio's portrait medal based on direct study of his physiognomy, probably from life, recording his well-known likeness, with an unsparing naturalism—his craggy, gaunt face, visibly sunken cheeks, and a mole on the side of his long nose. The facial expression projects a fierce inner strength that was probably true to his personality. Sangallo later designed Giovio's funerary monument, installed in 1570 in the cloister of the Church of San Lorenzo (Chiostro della Biblioteca Laurenziana), which includes a life-size, more idealized portrait sculpture that had been completed in 1560.

As Giovio also knew, the reverses of portrait medals amplified on the "*virtus*" (the moral character and excellence) of their subjects with allegorical imagery of personal significance. The artistic conceit on the reverse of Sangallo's medal was likely Giovio's invention, as was the inscription, "*Nunc Denique Vives*" (Now at last you will live). Giovio had written his highly popular *Dialogo delle imprese eroiche ed amorose* (*Dialogue on Heroic and Love Devices*), an erudite, much reprinted treatise on the heraldic devices of famous historical figures, during the summer of 1551, one year before his death. It is therefore nearly contemporary with Sangallo's production of the portrait medal. By the end of his life, Giovio was deeply conscious of his literary self, preoccupied with his fame and legacy, as he especially endeavored to right the political record regarding his prolific writings for posterity. The ups and downs in the political power of the patrons to whom Giovio had tied his fortunes too closely in the 1530s and 1540s had eventually contributed to his personal losses of status, especially in Florence. The bishopric of his hometown of Como evaded him in 1548; a much-desired cardinal's hat did not materialize; and heated political and literary controversies accompanied the publication and revisions of his major work, the *Historiarum sui temporis* (*History of His Own Time*), between 1550 and 1552.[6] In a probable act of self-censorship, in my view, Giovio left his biographies of Leonardo, Michelangelo, and Raphael unpublished, as he was acutely aware of the ramifications from his negative portrayal of Michelangelo, who was still alive.[7]

The reverse of Sangallo's portrait medal of Giovio depicts a man in a long tunic, slit to show his bare legs, as he stands in profile at right. He entwines his right arm and hand with those of the nude man at left to raise him from the ground. The muscular, uncovered arm of the standing man, holding a large book, and his hand gesture with bent wrist are both self-conscious quotations of Michelangelesque physical types, but the man's face is clearly a portrait of Giovio himself, resembling his profile on the other side of the medal. Although a source for the scene on the reverse has been said to be the Raising of Lazarus, this is unpersuasive.[8] More compellingly, Sangallo's design borrows from the famous iconography of God the Father creating Adam and Eve, but especially Adam, in medieval and Renaissance art, as in Paolo Uccello's *Creation of Adam* mural (ca. 1436, Chiostro Verde, Florence), and in this line of comparisons, the imagery on the medal's reverse also echoes Michelangelo's famous *Creation of Adam* fresco in the Sistine Ceiling of 1508–12.

In my interpretation of the allegorical imagery on the medal's reverse, therefore, Paolo Giovio stands in the place of God the Father, the Creator, while the "Adam-like" nude man being raised from the ground at left alludes to the spirit of the deceased personages of history whom Giovio resurrects through his writings.

CCB

SELECTED REFERENCES: Armand 1883–87, vol. 1, pp. 156–57; Attwood 2003, vol. 1, no. 795, p. 333; Scholten 2011, no. 102, p. 136 (with further bibliography).

CAT. 7

UNKNOWN ARTIST

German, Swabia

Private Devotional Shrine, ca. 1490

Wood, paint, gold, translucent glazes, and metal fixtures, 13¼ × 11⅞ × 3 in. (33.5 × 30.2 × 7.5 cm) (open)

The Metropolitan Museum of Art, New York, The Cloisters Collection, 1991 (1991.10)

THIS DELICATE TRIPTYCH, a rare intact survival from the end of the fifteenth century, deliberately references the mechanics of the grandest German Gothic altarpieces, but does so on a miniature scale. While its monumental counterparts featured life-size saints on imposing wings that opened and closed to suit the liturgical needs of a church, this tiny version was intended for private devotion. Its painted wings feature four female saints, Catherine and Barbara on the interior, Ursula and Dorothy on the exterior. Inside the boxlike shrine is a statuette of Saint Anne, mother of the Virgin Mary, holding her daughter with one hand and her grandson, Christ, with the other.

The emphasis on saintly women may well indicate that the original owner was female, a possibility underscored by the carved donor figures kneeling at Anne's feet, a veiled woman at the left and a bearded man in a hair shirt at the right. Their hands, once held in gestures of prayer, are lost, but the pair are otherwise remarkably well preserved, with luminous red glazes highlighting their richly polychromed robes. The placement of the woman on the left, the position of honor, offers further indication that she was the probable patron. The small figure itself, however, bears a strong resemblance to contemporaneous images of the Virgin in Passion iconography, in which she usually appears veiled. The corresponding figure at the right—perhaps her husband or another family member—is shown with the clothing and hairstyle associated with John the Baptist.

It is possible, though not certain, that the patrons here were represented in the guise of these popular saints to indicate particular devotion toward them. The woman may have been named for one of the female saints in the ensemble, and it has been suggested that the man could either have been named after John or else have been a member of a lay

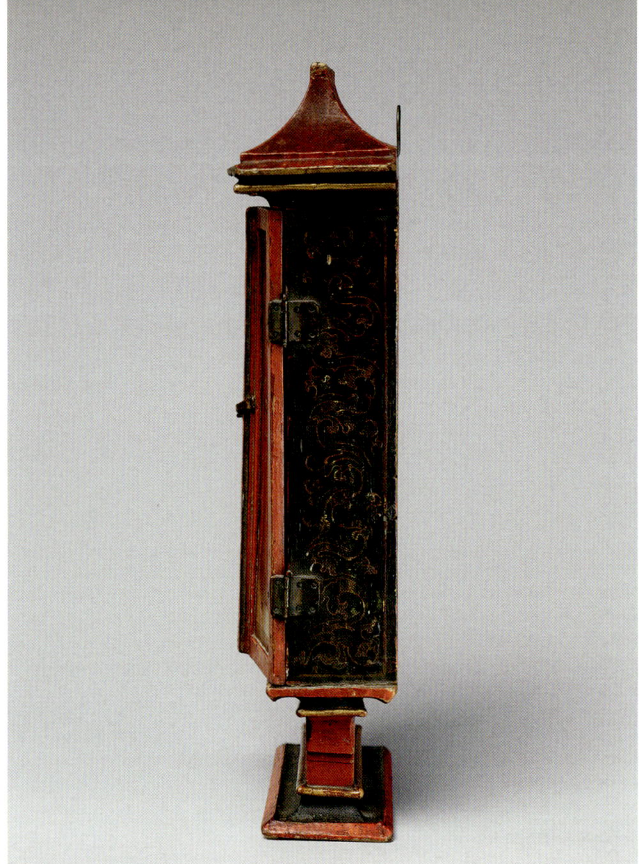

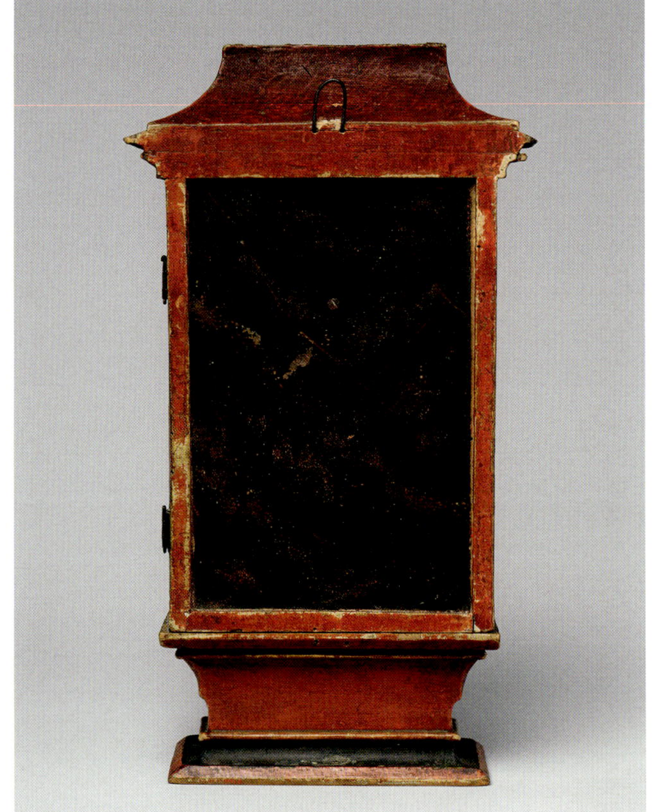

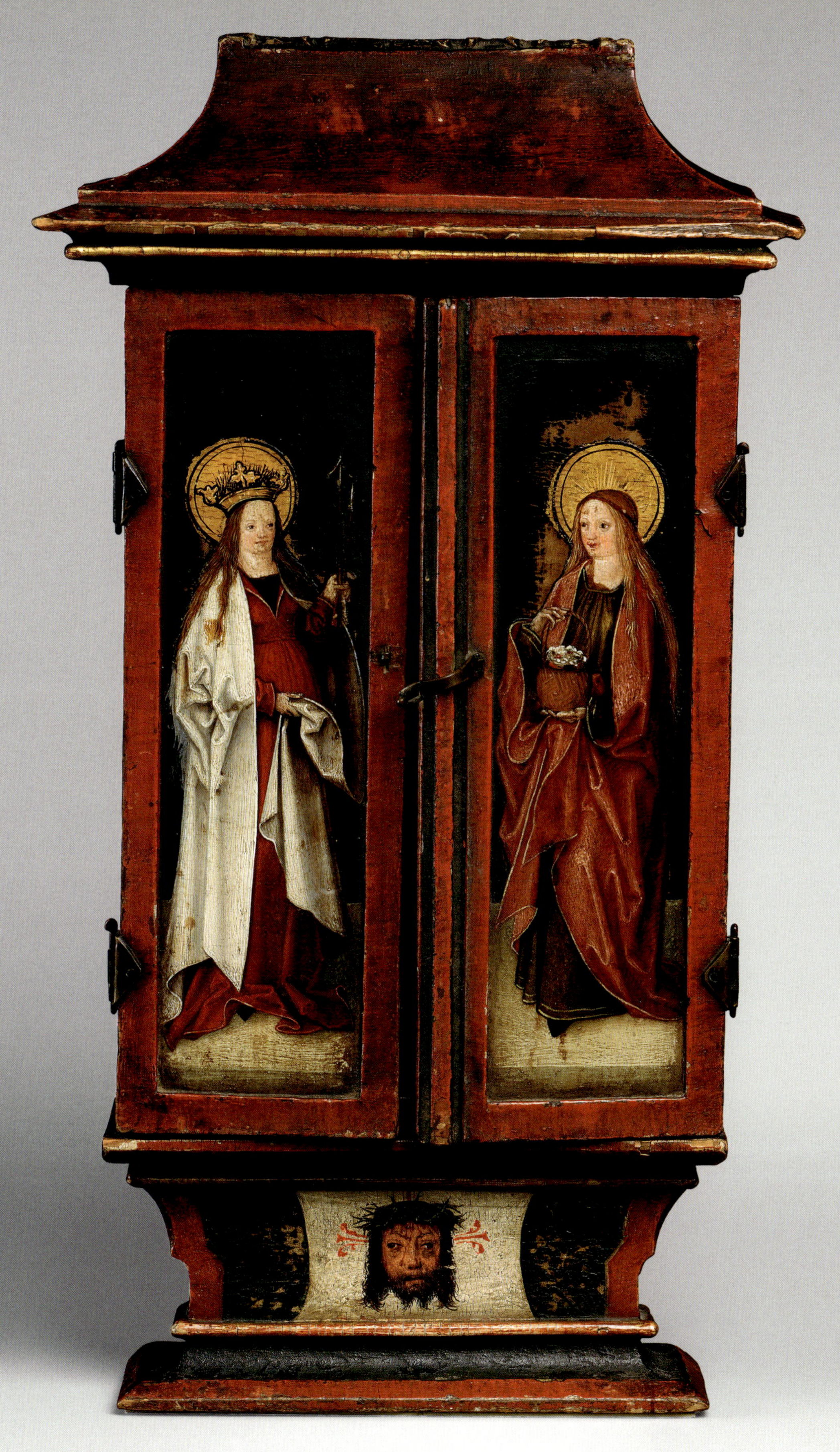

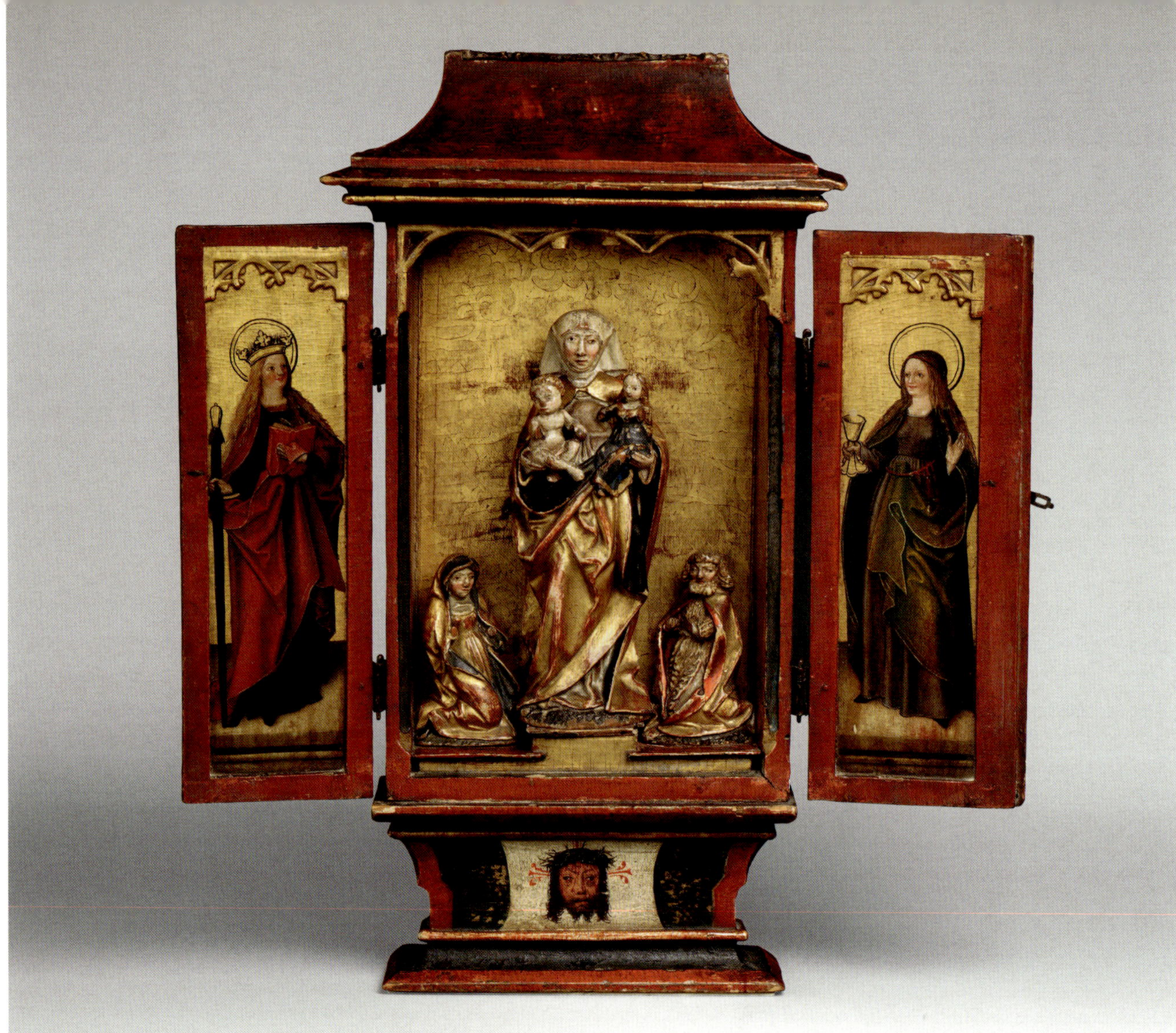

penitent order, or that both donors were members of a lay confraternity devoted to the cult of Saint Anne.[1] In any case, the blurring between portraiture and the conventional depictions of saints reflects a late medieval tendency to privilege communal rather than individualistic notions of identity, at least in the realm of devotional practice.

The sides and back of the shrine are painted with illusionistic details that enhance its precious qualities and underscore its role as a portable object intended to be viewed from multiple sides. The elaborate vine scrolls on the sides serve as more than a generic ornamental motif: they represent acanthus leaves, symbolic of the Resurrection, and thus strengthen the work's devotional message. These vegetal motifs are set within borders that are carefully painted to emulate carved frames. The same trompe l'oeil effect is found on the back, which has been painted to give a marbled effect. The faux stone even bears irregular diagonal lines, as if the panel were assembled from seven blocks of stone rather than from a single piece of wood. These efforts to create fictive materials through the sensitive application of paint follow a tradition established by painters such as Jan van Eyck and Hans Memling.[2] By the end of the fifteenth century, such techniques were highly valued by wealthy patrons who sought redemption through the transformative power of painting.

SF

SELECTED REFERENCES: Nixon 2004, pp. 146–47; Wixom 2007, pp. 4, 5 fig. 2; Timothy B. Husband, no. 59, in Ainsworth and Waterman 2013, pp. 254–57.

CAT. 8

SIMON MARMION

French, ca. 1425–1489

The Lamentation (recto); *Initials and Arms of Charles the Bold and Margaret of York* (verso), ca. 1473

Oil and tempera(?) on oak panel, 20⅜ × 12⅞ in. (51.8 × 32.7 cm)
The Metropolitan Museum of Art, New York, Robert Lehman Collection, 1975 (1975.1.128)

FOLLOWING HER MARRIAGE in 1468 to Charles the Bold, duke of Burgundy, Margaret of York commissioned numerous devotional works that prominently feature her portrait and personal motto as well as emblems and heraldry evoking her ancestral lineage and marital union.[1] The vast majority are illuminated manuscripts adorned in the margins with the couple's initials bound by love knots, her coat of arms impaled by that of her husband, and two principal types of flowers: daisies (*marguerites* in French, alluding to her given name) and white roses (symbolizing the House of York).[2] Three of these volumes were illuminated around 1475 by the French master Simon Marmion, who also produced manuscripts, altarpieces, portraits, and ceremonial decorations for other members of the Burgundian court, including Charles, his father, Philip the Good, and Guillaume Fillastre (see cat. 11).[3]

In 1473 Margaret accompanied Charles to Valenciennes, where he presided over the assembly of the Order of the Golden Fleece.[4] Marmion, who had been active in Valenciennes since 1458, was commissioned to design courtly decorations for the occasion, which presumably included heraldic motifs. Margaret probably commissioned *The Lamentation* from Marmion during this period, and based upon these circumstances, the panel is one of only two works in the artist's oeuvre—along with the *Saint Bertin Altarpiece* of 1459 (Staatliche Museen zu Berlin, Gemäldegalerie; National Gallery, London)—that can be dated with relative certainty.[5]

Possibly intended for Margaret's private devotion, *The Lamentation* is adorned on the back with the couple's conjoined coat of arms surrounded by four pairs of their interlaced initials, paralleling the heraldic and emblematic imagery found on the manuscripts she commissioned.[6] Since the fourteenth century, heraldry ranging from small-scale depictions to highly prominent displays had appeared on the reverses of devotional paintings in both northern Europe and Italy. A mark of piety, patronage, and ownership, it was also a significant aspect of the overall visual program of the object.[7] This tradition was adopted on the reverses and covers of painted portraits throughout Europe beginning in the mid-fifteenth century.

On the reverse of *The Lamentation*, red cords with tasseled ends bind the couple's initials with horizontal loops, forming a "true lovers' knot," known since antiquity as a symbol of love, marriage, and the bride's chastity.[8] Similar knots with irregular shapes appear on several folios of two manuscripts Marmion illuminated for Margaret around the same time: *Les visions du chevalier Tondal* and *La vision de l'âme de Guy de Thurno* (J. Paul Getty Museum, Los Angeles).[9] However, the most of these examples are wider, symmetrical, and cruciform in shape.[10] The interlaced geometric patterns that form the letters on the panel's reverse are also echoed in certain monograms in the two Getty manuscripts.[11] The armorial reverses of paintings, like the marginal decorations of manuscripts, were often painted by assistants, perhaps in this case by the same hand.

Marmion's depiction of the Lamentation, a subject not described in the Gospels, probably derives from popular devotional texts, which fostered intense meditation on the Passion.[12] Christ's lifeless body is lowered by Joseph of Arimathea and Nicodemus onto the lap of his mother, who, like the other mourners, grieves with solemn restraint.[13] In the lower left corner a wilting poppy, symbolic of death, sacrifice, and the Passion, echoes the form of Christ's body.[14] The white flowers with narrow, pointed, raylike petals at the lower right represent daisies, evoking Margaret's piety as a witness to the sacred event depicted.

AMN

SELECTED REFERENCES: Maryan W. Ainsworth, "New Observations on the Working Technique in Simon Marmion's Panel Paintings," in Kren 1992, pp. 246–48, figs. 237–40, 242; Maryan W. Ainsworth, cat. 9, in Ainsworth and Christiansen 1998, pp. 109–12; Charles Sterling and Maryan W. Ainsworth, no. 1, in Sterling et al. 1998, pp. 2–6; Maryan W. Ainsworth, cat. 11, in Kren and McKendrick 2003, pp. 107–8; Nenagh Hathaway, 2019, https://www.metmuseum.org/art/collection/search/459070.

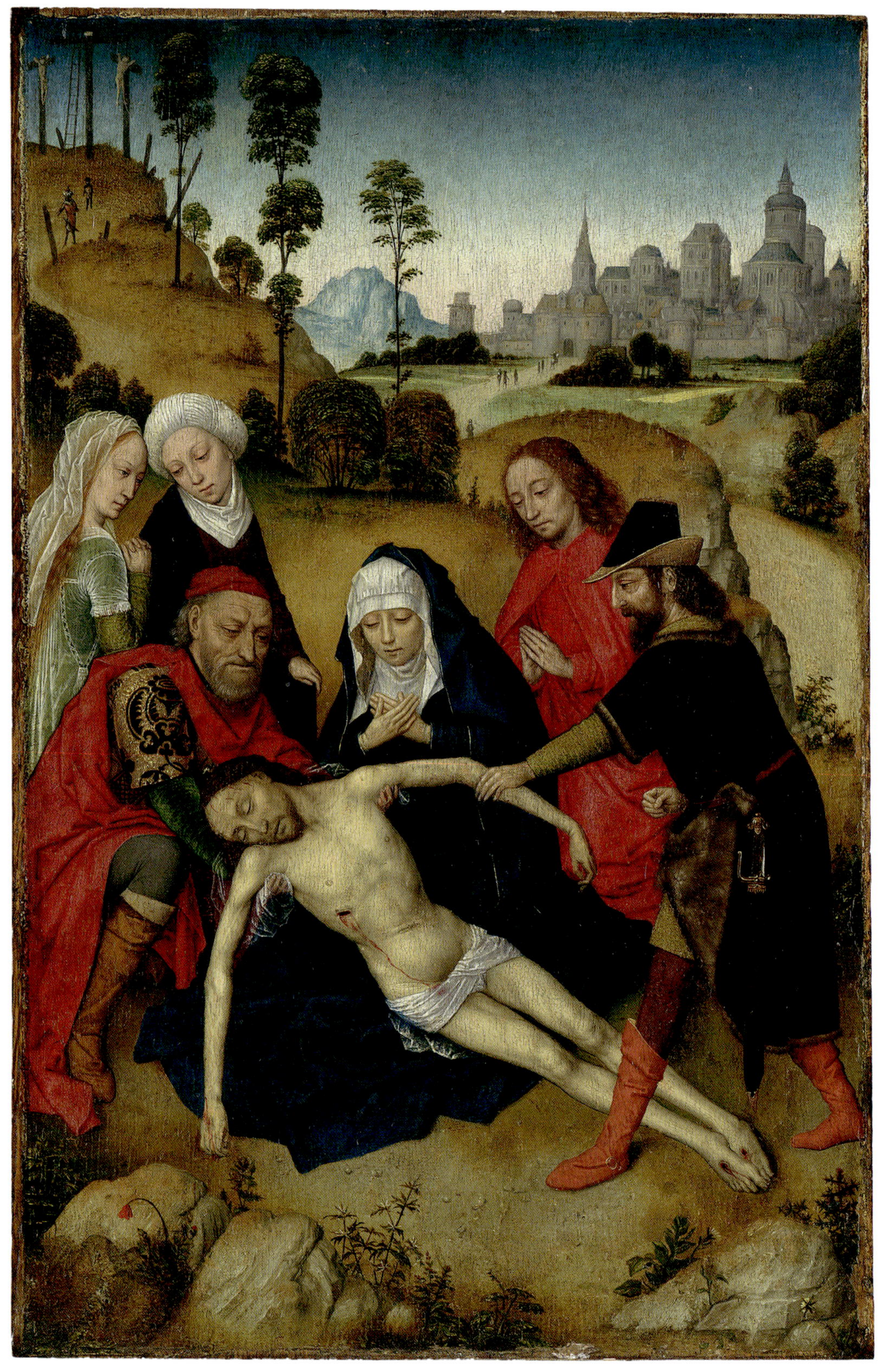

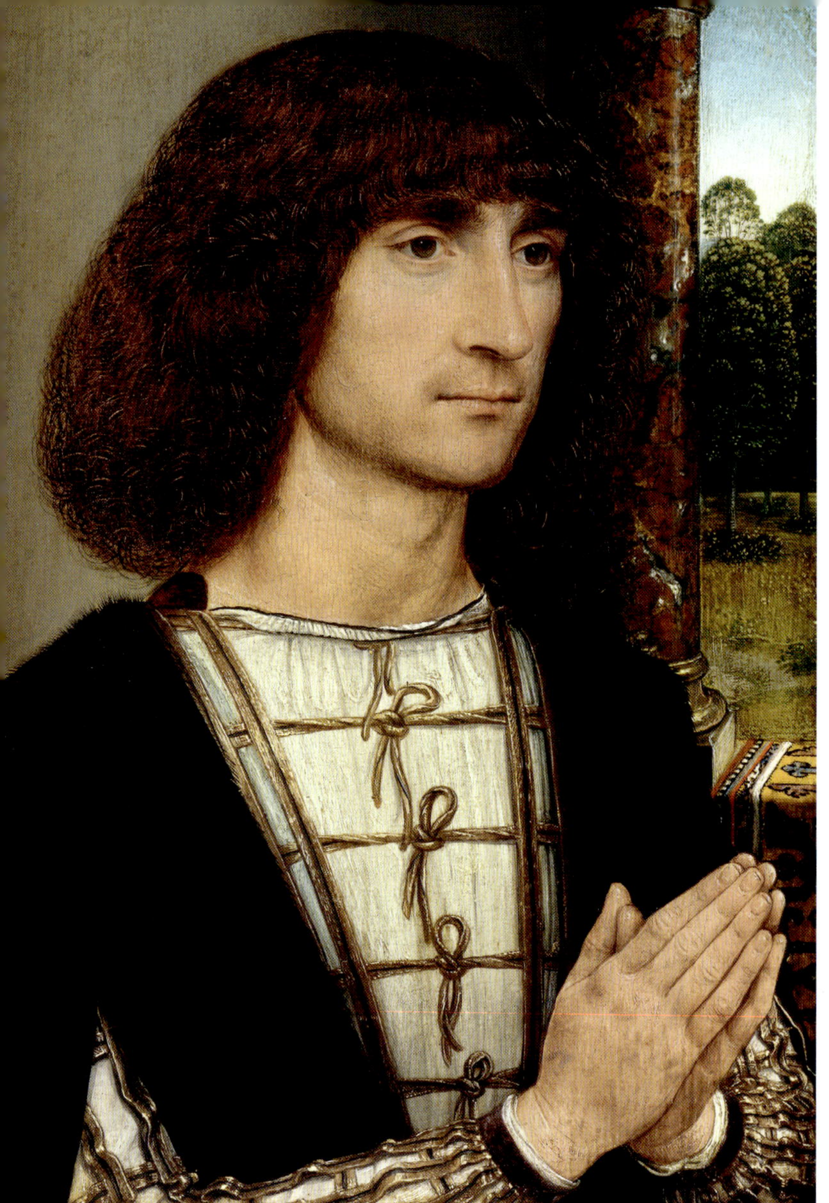

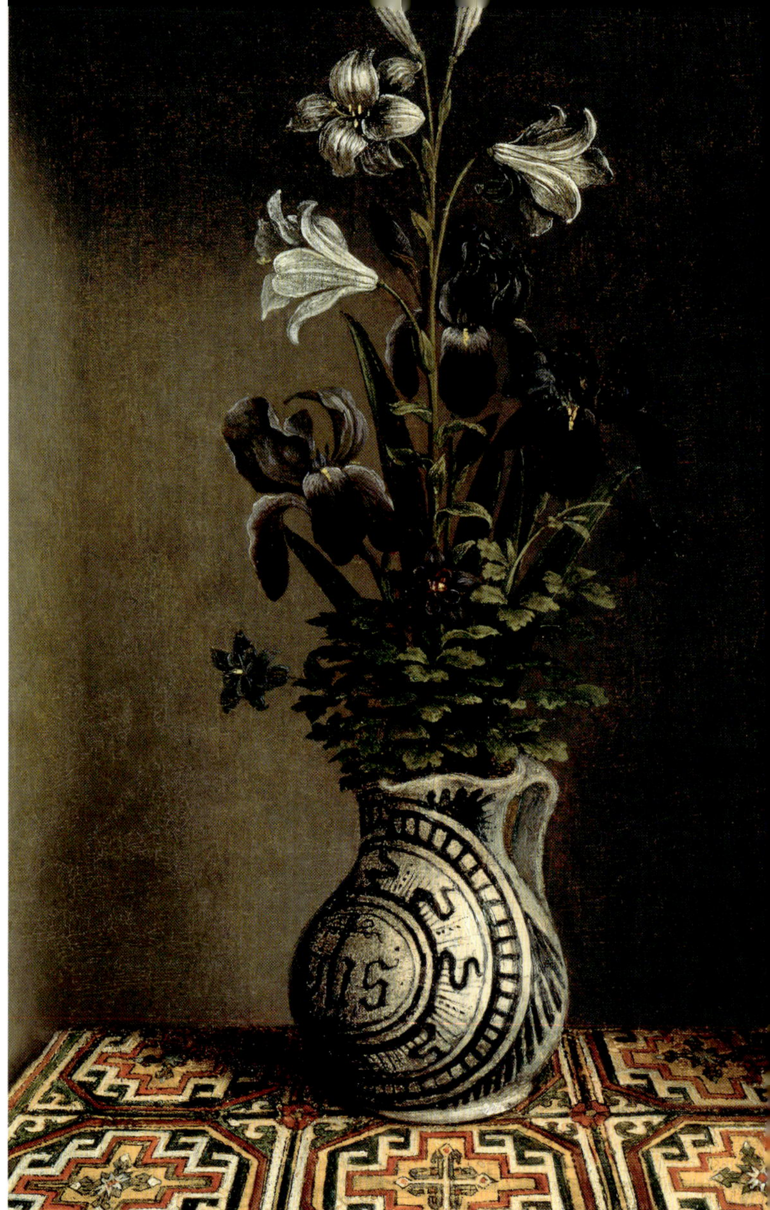

COVERED PORTRAITS IN NORTHERN EUROPE, 1430–1500

MARYAN W. AINSWORTH

What we know about the development of double-sided and covered portraits of the Early Renaissance in northern Europe comes from a variety of sources, especially inventories and the objects themselves.[1] Yet the surviving works often present puzzles to solve. Original frames are frequently lacking or have been altered by later owners (see cats. 9 and 10). Extant portraits can be missing their covers, or vice versa. The images on the rectos or versos may have undergone significant changes, attesting to the ongoing symbiotic relationship between the front and back or the exterior and interior of ensembles.[2] Nonetheless, certain trends can be charted as they developed both at ducal courts and within rising wealthy bourgeois communities.

Along with religious subjects, portraiture dominated the artistic output during the fifteenth century in the Burgundian Netherlands. Certain painters, notably Jan van Eyck, Rogier van der Weyden, and Hans Memling, excelled in the genre and were sought after for their remarkable ability to bring sitters to life through extraordinary technique and execution in paint. Van Eyck's portraits, such as the 1439 portrait of Margareta van Eyck (see fig. 13), were often painted on the verso with imitation stonework. Especially when imitating porphyry, as in that case, the image also conveyed a sense of eternity and an assurance that the person represented on the recto lived on in memory even after death.[3]

Van Eyck's famous *Giovanni(?) Arnolfini and His Wife* of 1434 (fig. 32) was once protected by shutters painted with the coat of arms and device of Don Diego de Guevara, designating ownership by this Spanish nobleman at least by 1516.[4] Julius Held's notion that the *Woman at Her Toilet* (early 16th century copy, Fogg Art Museum, Harvard University, Cambridge) functioned as a sliding door for the Arnolfini painting has not found support.[5] However, the theory that, by showing a nuptial bath preparation, such a painting could have served as an introduction to a marriage portrait is not out of the question.[6] The theme prefigures later examples in Hans Memling's oeuvre, such as an *Allegory of True Love*, which comprises two separated panels, *Young Woman with a Pink* and *Two Horses and a Monkey* (ca. 1485–90, The Metropolitan Museum of Art, New York, and Museum Boijmans Van Beuningen, Rotterdam, respectively),[7] and the *Allegory of Chastity* (cat. 18). The former aimed to introduce the betrothed couple on the interior of a triptych, the latter to praise the virtues of the maiden portrayed on the reverse.

The most common form of the covered, or "hidden," portrait was the devotional diptych, which blossomed during the middle of the fifteenth century in the circles of Duke Philip the Good and the aristocracy.[8] The popularization of this type can be credited to Rogier van der Weyden and his workshop in Brussels.[9] The reverses of the portraits, with their coats of arms and devices, essentially advertise the lineage of the sitters and sometimes provide hints concerning the function of the portrait.[10] The versos of the *Diptych of Jean de Gros* (figs. 33 and 34) carry the motto, emblem, coat of arms, and initials of the nobleman de Gros.[11] The inscribed motto—*Graces/A DIEV* (Thanks to God)—is an appropriate accompaniment to the devotional aspect of the diptych, in which Jean joins his hands in prayer in adoration of the Virgin and Child.

In an unusual instance, the coat of arms and devices on the reverses of Nicolas Froment's portraits of René I d'Anjou and his wife, Jeanne de Laval (cat. 12A–C), are not those of the king but of Jean de Matheron, a counselor and confidant to whom René presented this token of his appreciation. The reverse of the portrait of Francesco d'Este (cat. 10) reveals the well-known coat of arms of the d'Este family and thereby Francesco's identity. However, inscriptions have been added that convey what transpired while

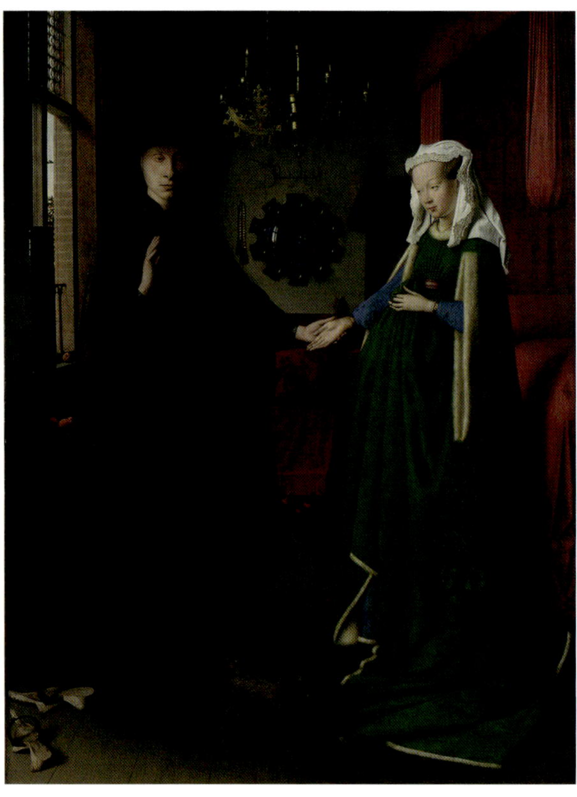

Fig. 32. Jan van Eyck (Netherlandish, ca. 1390–1441). *Giovanni(?) Arnolfini and His Wife*, 1434. Oil on oak panel, 32³/₈ × 23⁵/₈ in. (82.2 × 60 cm). The National Gallery, London (NG186)

Francesco was being trained in military skills at the court of Philip the Good. In French at the top is "*v[ost]re tout*" (Entirely yours), a dedication to the recipient of the portrait, probably a court companion. Squeezed in at the upper left is an enigmatic inscription, *non plus/courcelles* (No longer Courcelles), which possibly refers to the village of Corcelles, in Burgundy, where Francesco served in battle. Occasionally, as with the *Portrait of a Man with an Open Book* (cat. 11), the reverse is purely emblematic, there showing a holly branch and motto that reveal the essence of the man's professional life. His motto, *Je he [hais] ce que mord* (I hate what bites), refers not only to the spiky holly but also to the way the man protected himself against unwanted scholarly attacks.

Painted imagery related to a portrait could also serve for daily devotions, as in *Christ Crowned with Thorns* on the reverse of the *Portrait of a Lady* from the workshop of Rogier van der Weyden (cat. 9). The lamentable condition of the verso may be due to the fact that the painting was habitually displayed with Christ's image facing outward to encourage supplications to and empathy with the Savior. If the woman was half of a devotional diptych that included her husband, then the ensemble, when opened, would present the couple united in their piety.

In the later fifteenth century, the approach was even more deliberately oriented toward the viewer, as in Hans Memling's exquisite *Portrait of a Man* (recto) and *Flowers in a Jug* (verso) (cat. 17).[12] When the triptych including the portrait was closed, the trompe l'oeil image of the flowers in the jug appeared to be in an actual niche in the wall, blurring the border between reality and fiction. For the viewer, this enhanced the sensual experience of the flowers—their scent and vibrant color—and encouraged

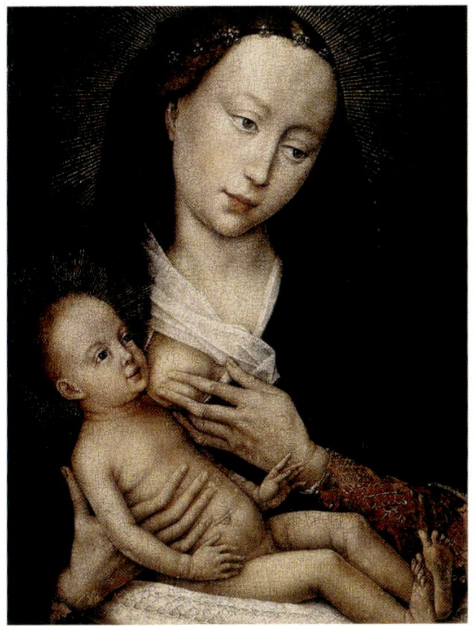

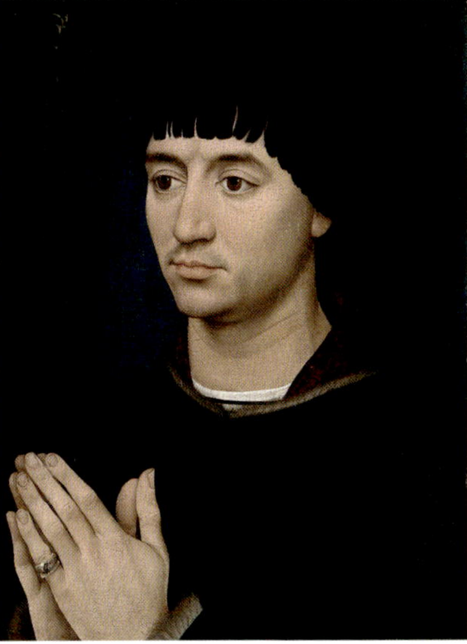

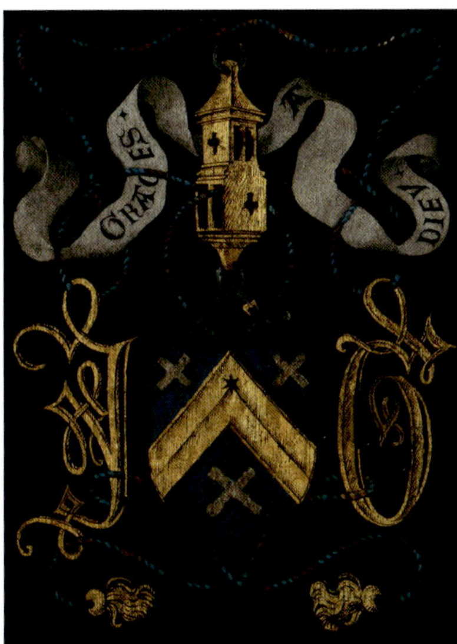

Fig. 33. Rogier van der Weyden and workshop (Netherlandish, ca. 1399–1464). *Diptych of Jean de Gros,* 1460–64. Oil on panel, left wing: $15\frac{1}{4} \times 11\frac{1}{8}$ in. (38.7 × 28.5 cm); right wing: $13\frac{7}{8} \times 11\frac{3}{8}$ in. (35.5 × 28.8 cm). Left wing: Musées des Beaux-Arts, Tournai; right wing: Art Institute of Chicago, Mr. and Mrs. Martin A. Ryerson Collection (1933.1051a–b)

Fig. 34. Reverse of right wing of fig. 33

devotional meditation, which would be deepened by the religious image on the interior of the triptych when opened.[13] Thus, the viewer would assume the devotional demeanor of the man portrayed on the interior left wing of the triptych.

The previous examples represent, in their incipient stages, the images and themes that adorned the reverses or covers of portraits in the fifteenth century. Over the next hundred years, they were richly developed in northern Europe and increasingly appreciated not only by the clients who commissioned them but also by other viewers.

CAT. 9

WORKSHOP OF ROGIER VAN DER WEYDEN

Rogier: Netherlandish, ca. 1399–1464

Portrait of a Lady (recto); *Christ Crowned with Thorns* (verso), ca. 1460

Oil with egg tempera on oak panel, 14⅝ × 10¾ in. (37 × 27.1 cm)
The National Gallery, London (NG1433)
Not exhibited

EXTANT EXAMPLES of a religious image on the reverse of an independent portrait are quite rare.[1] Such is the case with the *Portrait of a Lady*, the verso of which is *Christ Crowned with Thorns*. The original frame of this double-sided panel has not survived, so there are no helpful clues about how the work was initially displayed. Other observations may, however, suggest a likely hypothesis. *Christ Crowned with Thorns* is in poor condition, badly worn and considerably overpainted, while *Portrait of a Lady* is in good condition. This indicates that it was probably the image of Christ that was normally on view, the portrait having been "hidden" and protected from ongoing wear. One possibility is that the original frame had a metal fixture at its top that allowed for a chain to hang the painting, and the portrait side routinely faced the wall.

Another scenario is perhaps more likely. No pendant painting of the woman's spouse has convincingly been identified,[2] but presuming one existed, the two portraits would have been hinged together as a diptych, the man positioned to the left of the woman.[3] In a hypothetical reconstruction, when the diptych was closed, the image of *Christ Crowned with Thorns* would have been available for daily devotional practice. When it was opened toward the right, the man and his wife would come into view.[4] Such a configuration not only would present the couple for posterity but also would have associated them closely with their spiritual dedication to the Savior. The diptych form is portable, and thus it could accompany the couple to various locations.

The *Portrait of a Lady* is most closely associated with those paintings by Rogier van der Weyden that portray fashionably dressed aristocratic women with ring-adorned hands folded in the lower left corner of the composition and with a highly stylized treatment of their bodies.[5] However, when the present work is compared with Rogier's *Portrait of a Lady* in the National Gallery of Art, Washington, D.C. (fig. 35), the difference in quality is so striking that the London portrait can only be attributed to a workshop assistant.[6] The Washington portrait is a late work by Rogier, painted around 1460, which is also probably the date of the London portrait.

The poor condition of *Christ Crowned with Thorns* excludes any possibility of a definitive attribution. Yet, very general stylistic similarities to the images of Christ in Rogier's *Last Judgment Triptych* (ca. 1445–50, Hôtel-Dieu Museum, Beaune) and the *Braque Triptych* (1452, Musée du Louvre, Paris) tend to support a connection with Rogierian types.[7]
MWA

SELECTED REFERENCES: Friedländer 1967–76, vol. 2, no. 34, p. 67, pl. 56; Davies 1968, pp. 170–71; Davies 1972, pp. 221–22; L. Campbell 1998, pp. 428–32; De Vos 1999, no. C7, p. 406.

Fig. 35. Rogier van der Weyden. *Portrait of a Lady*, ca. 1460. Oil on oak panel, 14⅝ × 10⅝ in. (37 × 27 cm). National Gallery of Art, Washington, D.C., Andrew W. Mellon Collection (1937.1.44)

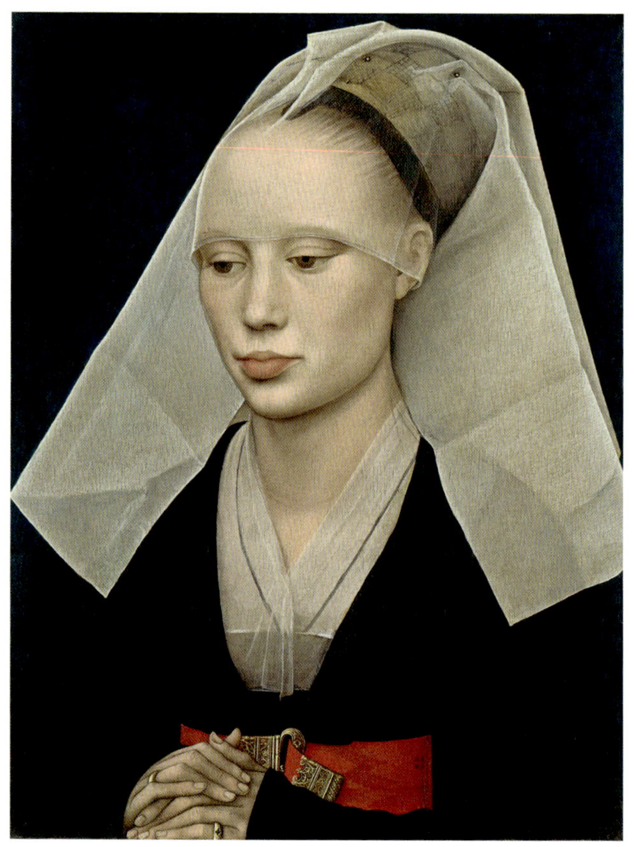

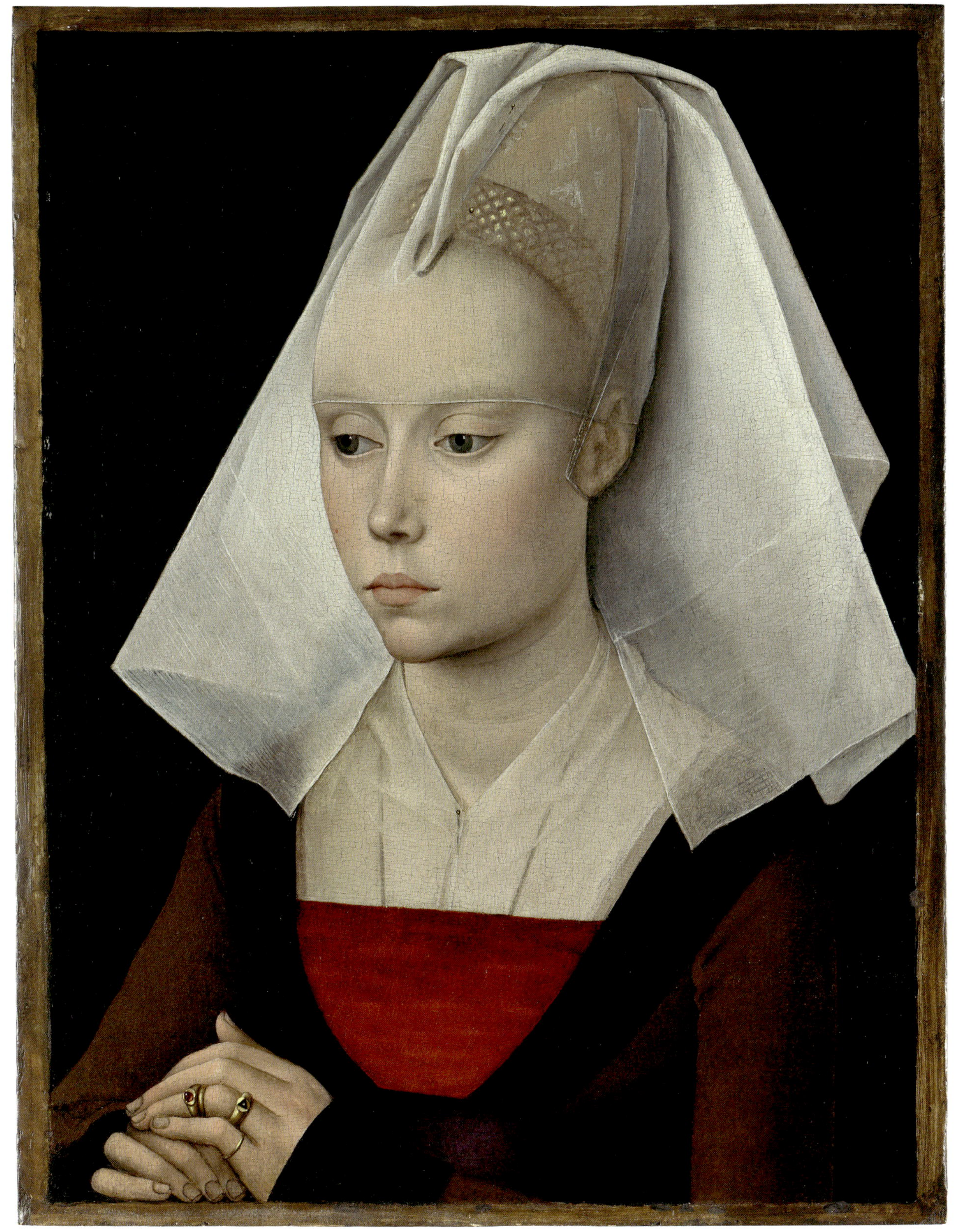

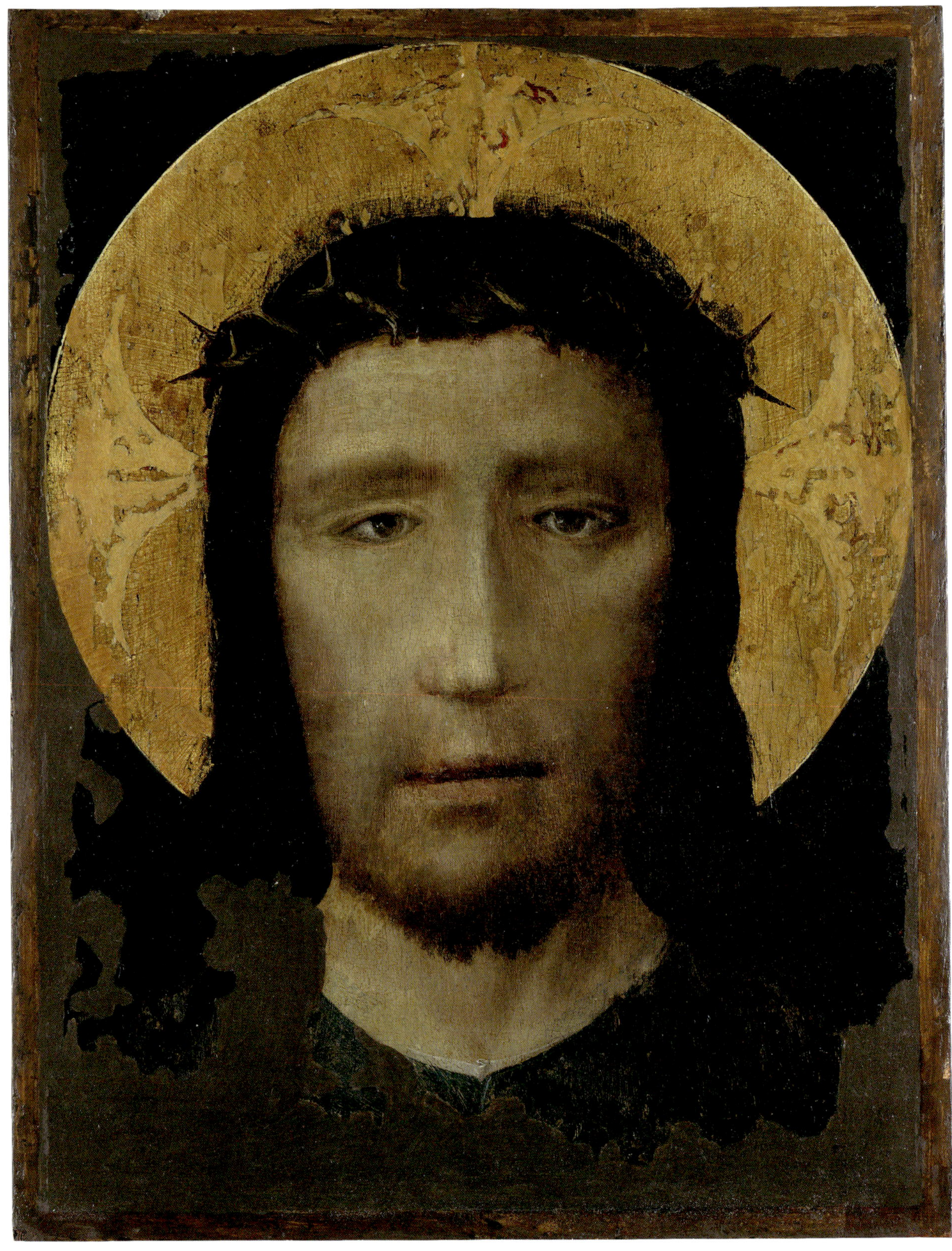

CAT. 10

ROGIER VAN DER WEYDEN AND WORKSHOP

Rogier: Netherlandish, ca. 1399–1464
Francesco d'Este (recto); *Coat of Arms* (verso), ca. 1460

Oil on oak panel, overall: 12½ × 8¾ in. (31.8 × 22.2 cm); painted surface, each side: 11¾ × 8 in. (29.8 × 20.3 cm)

Inscribed (on reverse): *v*[*ost*]*re tout* (Entirely yours) / *m*[*archio*] *e*[*stensis*] (marquess of Este) [twice] / *francisque* (Francesco); incised (on reverse, upper left, at slightly later date) *non plus / courcelles* (No longer Courcelles)

The Metropolitan Museum of Art, New York, The Friedsam Collection, Bequest of Michael Friedsam, 1931 (32.100.43)

THE SITTER IN THIS refined portrait is among those by Rogier van der Weyden that can be identified by the coat of arms on the reverse. The arms and crest are those of Lionello d'Este (1407–1450), marquess of Ferrara, Modena, and Reggio Emilia from 1441 to 1450. But, as proposed by Roger Fry, the likely dating of this portrait of a young man excludes Lionello.[1] Instead, the work represents Lionello's illegitimate but favored son, Francesco (ca. 1429–1476), his designated successor.[2] The twice intertwined letters inscribed on the reverse designate Francesco's title as marquess of Este. The French words at the top are a dedication to the recipient of the portrait, while those in the upper left corner possibly refer to the village where Francesco may have met his death.

Francesco d'Este was sent by his father to the court of Philip the Good to be trained in military skills. He arrived in Liège in 1444 and stayed on to serve both Philip and his successor, Charles the Bold. Francesco participated in jousts and in battles waged by the dukes of Burgundy in their efforts to maintain and expand their territories. In 1475 he served as captain of the Westerloo Division at the battle of Courcelles; he was appointed governor of Montpellier by Louis X in July 1477 and served again in 1484. He is last documented in 1486.[3]

Given his noble birth and privileged position at the ducal court, it is not surprising that Francesco sat for his portrait with Rogier, the favored painter of the dukes of Burgundy. The composition accords well with Rogier's portraits in the 1450s and 1460s of Philip and Charles (ca. 1450–64, Musée des Beaux-Arts, Dijon, and ca. 1460–65, Staatliche Museen zu Berlin, Gemäldegalerie, respectively).[4] The difference is the white background here instead of the standard deep blue for the ducal portraits.[5] Dressed appropriately in aristocratic finery, Francesco wears a fur-trimmed doublet, the high red collar of his undergarment showing at his neck, along with a heavy gold chain. Prominently placed at the lower left corner, Francesco's elegantly posed hands with elongated fingers hold a steel-headed hammer and a gold ring with a ruby. The meaning of these accoutrements is not entirely clear, but C. A. J. Armstrong noted that hammers were employed for inspecting the shields, crested helmets, and pennons of tournament contestants as well as "to knock out disqualified shields before the combats and to referee the contest once the fighting had begun."[6] The hammer was thus a princely attribute of power, while gold rings were sometimes given as prizes to the victor.

Rogier's portraits of other members of high rank associated with the Burgundian ducal court, including those of Jean de Gros (see fig. 33) and Philippe de Croÿ (Huntington Museum of Art, San Marino, and Koninklijk Museum voor Schone Kunsten, Antwerp), display the family coats of arms in a similar manner on the versos.[7] Each of these cases is, however, a devotional portrait linked to an image of the Virgin and Child at the left as a diptych. Thus, the diptychs most often would have been viewed in the closed position, showing the coats of arms. This may explain why more attention has been given to the painting of these reverses than to that of Francesco d'Este, which is weaker in execution and certainly not by Rogier himself, but by a workshop assistant. Since the frame of The Met painting is not original, we cannot know how the portrait was ordinarily shown. Most likely, it was suspended by a chain into a hook on a wall and thus could be turned to the portrait or coat of arms side as desired.

MWA

SELECTED REFERENCES: Fry 1911, pp. 200–202; Kantorowicz 1940; Armstrong 1977; De Vos 1999, no. 26, pp. 302–4; Keith Christiansen, cat. 71, in Christiansen and Weppelmann 2011, pp. 208–10; Keith Christiansen, https://www.metmuseum.org/art/collection/search/437487.

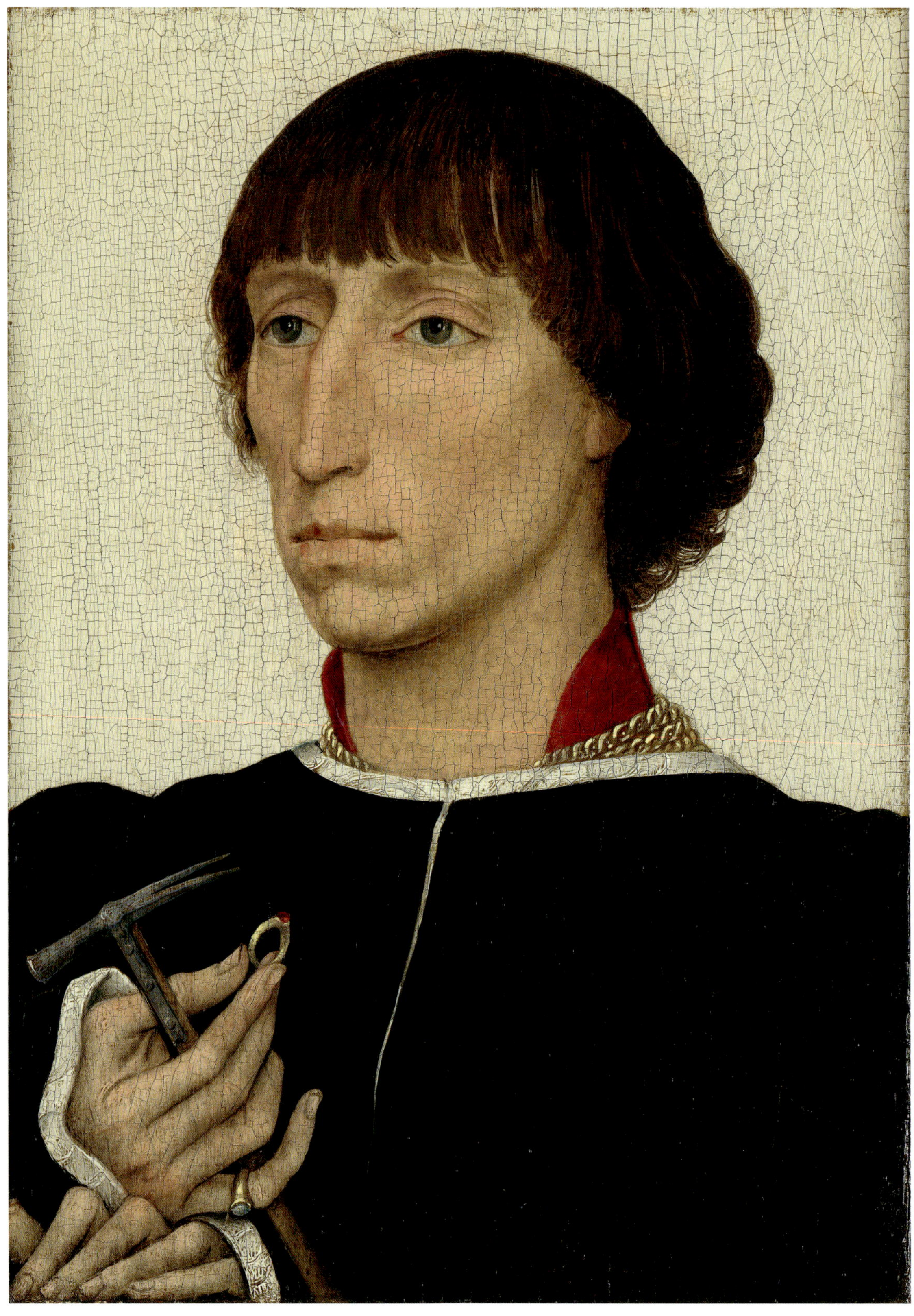

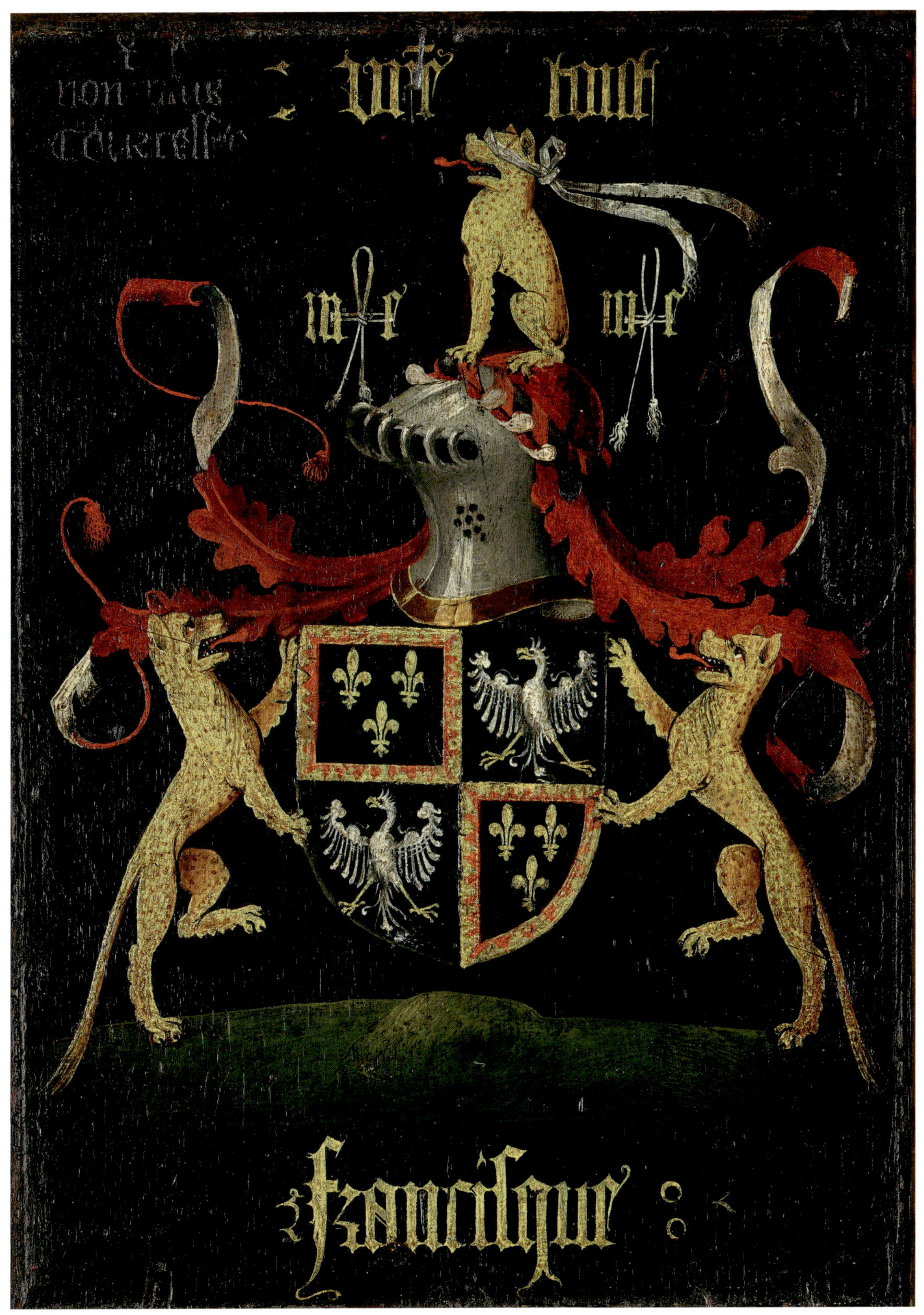

CAT. 11

WORKSHOP OF ROGIER VAN DER WEYDEN

Rogier: Netherlandish, ca. 1399–1464
Portrait of a Man with an Open Book (Guillaume Fillastre?) (recto); *Branch of Holly and Inscription* (verso), 1430s

Oil on oak panel, 13¼ × 9¼ in. (33.7 × 23.5 cm)

Inscribed (on recto, at bottom, and on reverse, at top, on frame): *Je he [hais] ce que mord* (I hate what bites)

The Courtauld Gallery, London, Samuel Courtauld Trust (P.1987.XX.486)

DESPITE THE VICISSITUDES of time, this portrait has survived for more than five centuries with its reverse image and original frame, albeit with a deeper outer molding added in the early seventeenth century.[1] Although the iron hardware at the top of the frame is from the later intervention, there would likely have been something similar on the original frame top by which to hang the portrait so that it could be viewed from either side.

Against a dark blue background, the recto shows a tightly cropped portrait of a man with an open book cradled between his hands, both of which display large gold rings. The text of the book is illegible, but its single-column layout and the man's prominently displayed gold pinkie ring featuring an antique cameo suggest it may be a classical tome. The sitter, quite likely a scholar and a humanist, wears a chaperon and a purple fur-trimmed robe over which there is a transparent sleeveless *heuque*. He gazes off to his right as if pausing to contemplate what he has read.

Alfred Scharf, followed by Erwin Panofsky, identified the man as Guillaume Fillastre, a French cardinal, canon, humanist, and geographer.[2] However, his appearance does not correspond to that seen in other portraits of him, namely, in Jacques Le Boucq's *Recueil d'Arras* (mid-16th century, Médiathèque Municipal, Arras, MS 266, fol. 265) and on an altarpiece wing of Simon Marmion's *Saint-Bertin Altarpiece* for Saint-Omer Cathedral (ca. 1459, now in the Staatliche Museen zu Berlin, Gemäldegalerie).[3] Fillastre is not known to have used the motto or the emblem on the recto of the Courtauld portrait. Moreover, as he was already a prior of a Benedictine abbey by 1426, it would not have been appropriate for him to be dressed in secular attire.[4]

The verso of the panel shows a meticulously rendered branch on a black background; ubiquitous in northern Europe, it is the common holly (*Ilex aquifolium*). The depiction probably was based on a botanical drawing, since it is rendered as a specimen cut from a larger plant. Above on the frame, appearing more conspicuously than it did on the bottom of the recto, and likely part of the later intervention, is the man's motto, which translates as "I hate what bites." Thomas Lüttenberg solved the long-standing riddle of the motto and emblem by arguing that, just as the thorny leaves of the holly protect it against animals who want to eat it, so, too, the man defends himself against those who would attack him.[5]

The portrait has been attributed to Rogier van der Weyden,[6] although the overly large hands of the sitter lack the elegance of the artist's signature style (see cat. 10). Nonetheless, as Stephan Kemperdick has pointed out, the man's large, stylized eyes and the blue background of the painting point to a possible assistant in Rogier's workshop.[7] Dirk De Vos, noting the disproportionate hands in relationship to the small, "clumsily defined upper body," has suggested the Rogier follower who produced the portrait of Anthony of Burgundy in the J. Paul Getty Museum, Los Angeles.[8] Lorne Campbell instead proposed an artist in the circle of the Master of Flémalle in the 1430s.[9] Although a definitive attribution is lacking, this portrait and its intact recto, providing revelations about the man's character, occupy a prominent place as an early representation of a humanist scholar.

MWA

SELECTED REFERENCES: Scharf 1950, no. XXI, pp. 74–77; Winkler 1950; Panofsky 1953, vol. 1, pp. 292, 477–78n5, vol. 2, pl. 221, no. 362; Friedländer 1967–76, vol. 2, suppl. 134, p. 89, pl. 139; Davies 1972, p. 227; Schabacker 1972; L. Campbell 1990b, pp. 65–66, 96, 98 pl. 113; Dülberg 1990, pp. 127–28, 233 no. 153, pl. 40 figs. 89, 90; L. Campbell 1996; De Vos 1999, no. C9, p. 409; Lüttenberg 2000; Lorne Campbell, cat. 22, in Campbell and Stock 2009, pp. 329–31; Stephan Kemperdick, cat. 41, in Kemperdick and Sander 2009, pp. 368–70.

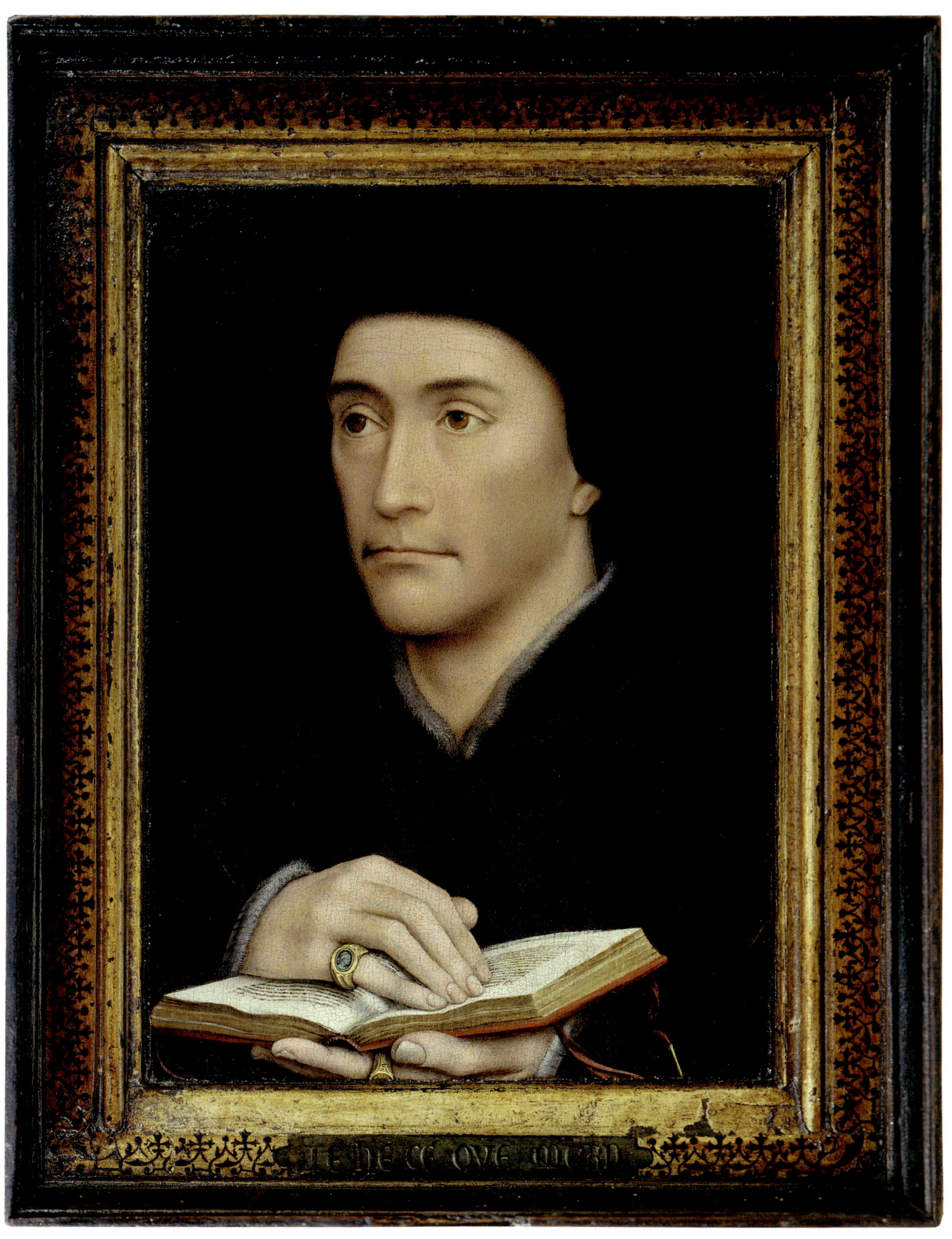

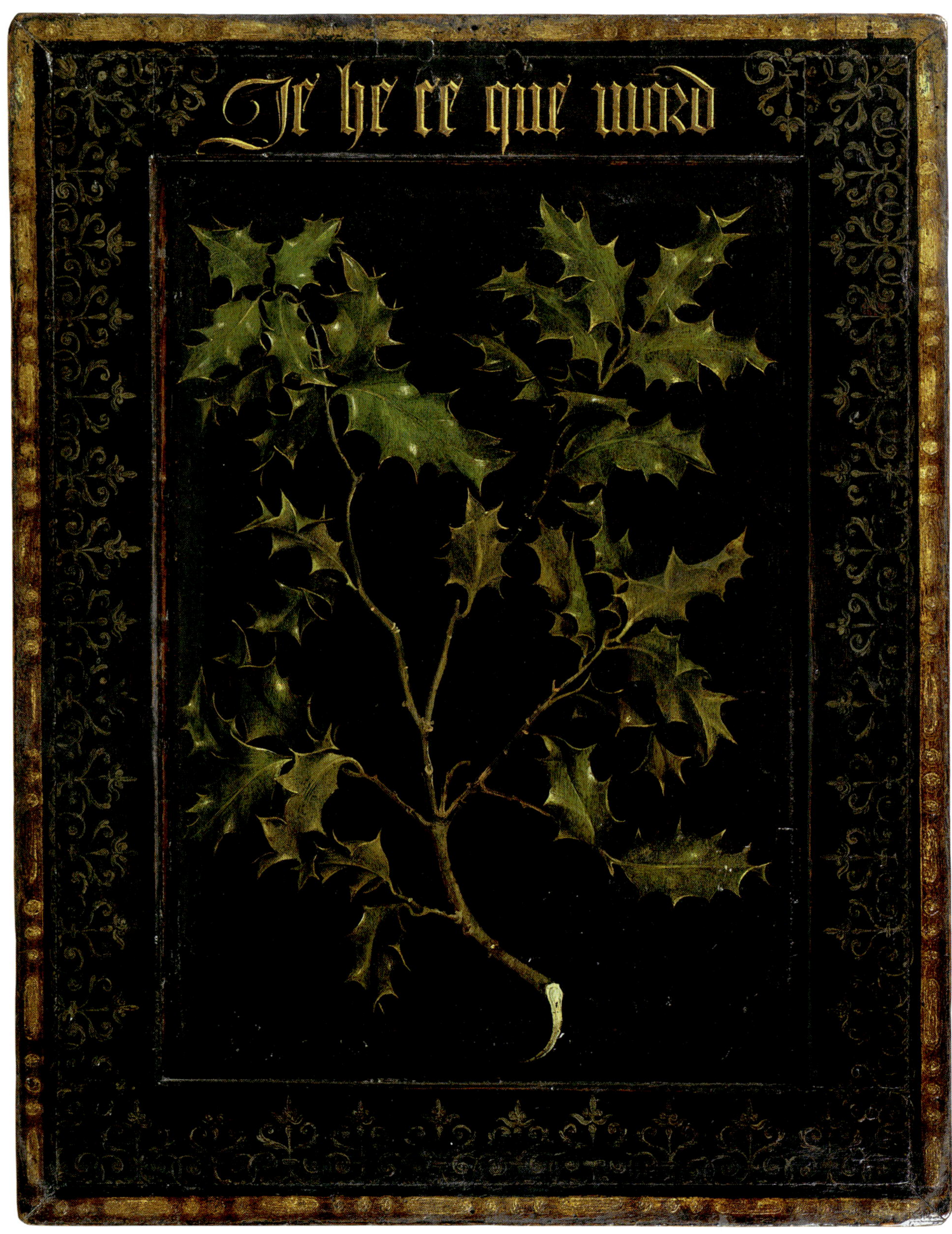
Je he ce que mord

CAT. 12A–C

WORKSHOP OF NICOLAS FROMENT

Froment: French, active by ca. 1460–1484
René d'Anjou and *Jeanne de Laval* (rectos); *Emblems of Jean de Matheron* (versos); *Carrying Case*, ca. 1475

Oil on poplar panel, each wing: 7 × 5⅜ in. (17.7 × 13.4 cm.); velvet, linen, and silk carrying case: 8⅞ × 6⅜ in. (22.5 × 16 cm)

Inscribed (on reverse of each panel): [device of Jean de Matheron, against a field of fleurs-de-lis]; (on banderole) *DIDAT SERVATA FIDES* (Loyalty enriches)

Musée du Louvre, Paris, Départment des Peintures (RF 665 [diptych], OD 125 [case])

Not exhibited

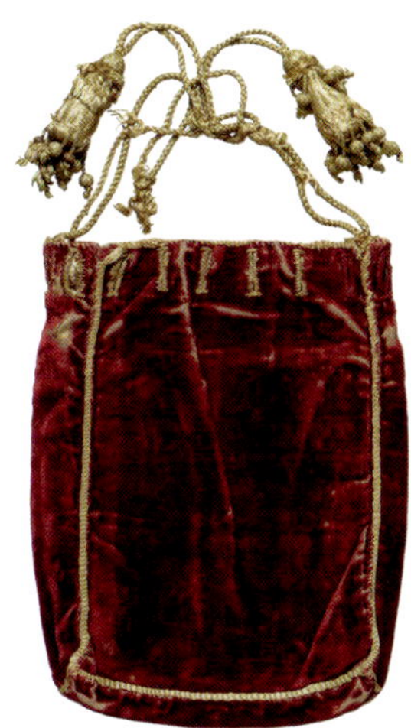

THIS PORTRAIT DIPTYCH survives intact with its red velvet carrying pouch, which if not original is certainly very old.[1] The pair represented are René I d'Anjou (1409–1480) and his second wife, Jeanne de Laval (1433–1498). In addition to being duke of Anjou and count of Provence, René I was duke of Lorraine and the titular king of Naples and Sicily, Hungary, and Jerusalem. Dressed soberly here in black, he wears a chain of gold scallop shells with a pendant of the Order of Saint Michael. He holds a rosary of large wooden cylinders that reappears in trompe l'oeil on the frame's base, where it ends with the Cross of Lorraine. Jeanne, also unpretentiously attired in black, became René's second wife at twenty-one in 1454, her husband then twice her age.

The identity of the couple is based on several other portraits, including those as donor figures on the left and right wings of Nicolas Froment's monumental *Burning Bush Altarpiece*, dated 1476 and housed in the Cathedral of Saint-Sauveur, Aix-en-Provence. Their likenesses are also well known from several portrait medals, two by Francesco Laurana of Jeanne de Laval and of René and Jeanne together, and another by Pietro da Milano of the couple.[2]

On the reverse of each portrait is the device of Jean de Matheron, a jeweled crown above a stalk of lilies, painted over a field of fleurs-de-lis on a blue ground. Swirling through the center on a banderole is Matheron's motto *DIDAT SERVATA FIDES* (Loyalty enriches).[3] Although Jean's father, Michel, was secretary to René and later counselor in 1453, his son was apparently intended as the recipient of the diptych. Jean was master of the accounts and counselor in 1470 and is said to have been by the king's side at his death in 1480. Supporting the legend that this portrait diptych was René's gift to Jean Matheron is its ownership for generations by the Matheron family, until its sale in 1872.[4] Such portraits were often given to favored assistants and confidants by rulers. In this case, it appears to have been a more personal and intimate gesture than one intended for propagandistic aims.[5]

Nicolas Froment worked for René I from 1475 to 1479, just prior to the duke's death. However, there is no unanimity concerning the authorship of the portrait diptych to Froment. Grete Ring attributed it to the workshop.[6] Françoise Robin accepted it as autograph but with the caveats that its looser brushwork when compared to that of the *Burning Bush Altarpiece* is explained by the vast difference in size of the two works and that the diptych portraits are from 1479–80, that is, several years after the 1476 altarpiece.[7] Regardless of its authorship, this diptych is a remarkable testament to a friendship, evidenced by a precious memento of portraits on one side and the recipient's insignia on the other. The fidelity expressed in the latter signals the nature of Matheron's relationship to those on the obverse.

MWA

SELECTED REFERENCES: Hill 1930, no. 952, p. 253, pl. 155; Ring 1949, no. 217, p. 226; Robin 1985, pp. 211–13; Dülberg 1990, pp. 77–78, 230 nos. 174, 175, pls. 49–51 figs. 112–14; De Winter 1996; Hand et al. 2006, cat. 10, pp. 82–87; Marie-Claude Léonelli, cat. 18, in Bresc-Bautier et al. 2010, pp. 89–90.

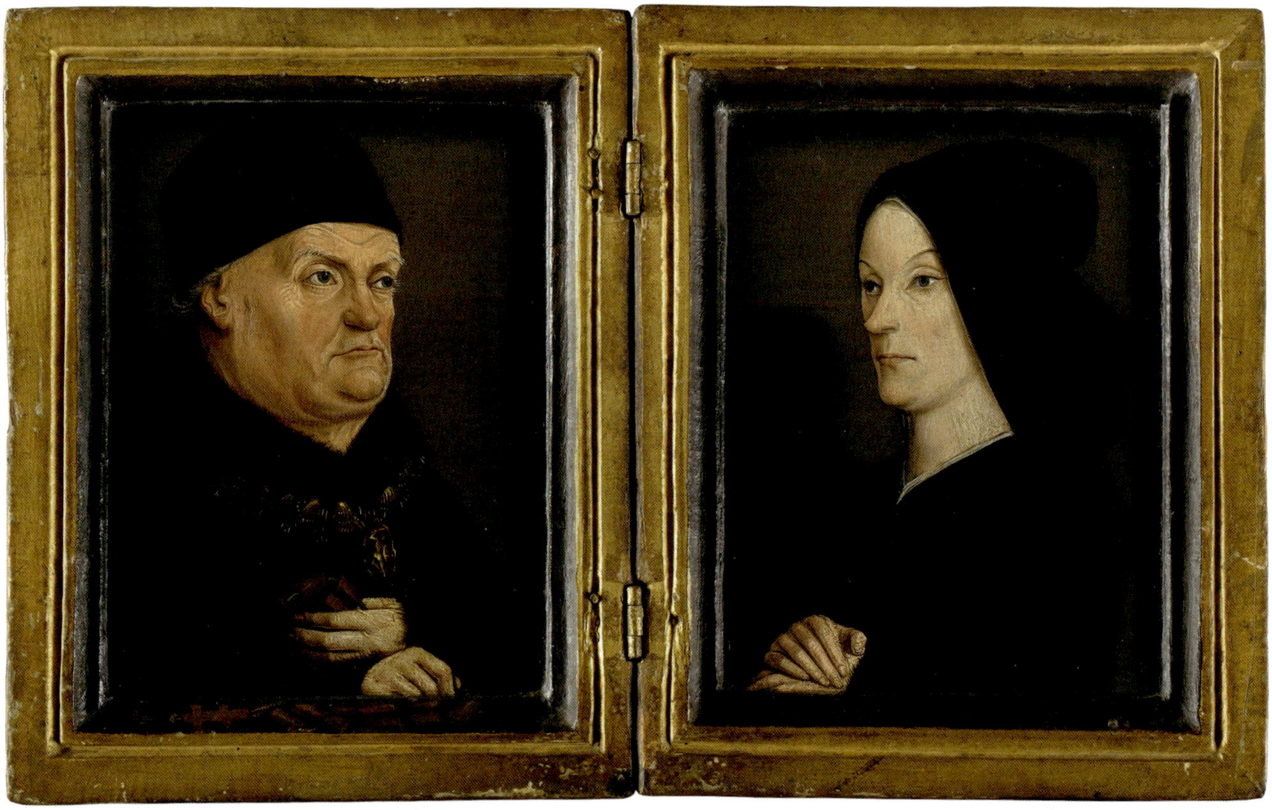

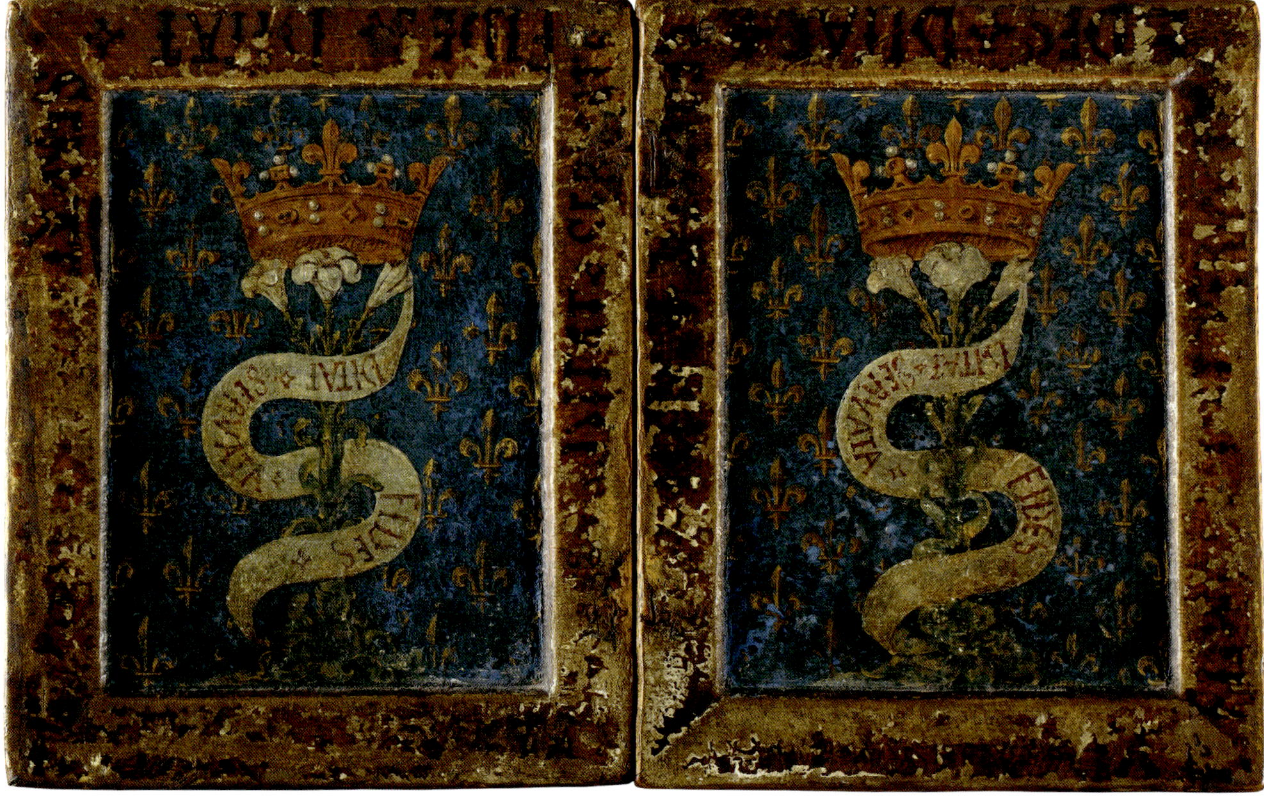

CAT. 13

WOLFGANG BEURER (MASTER WB)

German, Middle Rhine, active ca. 1480–1500

Johann von Rückingen (recto); *Wild Man with von Rückingen Coat of Arms* (verso), 1487

Oil on wood panel, overall, including original frame: 19¼ × 15⅜ × 2⅛ in. (48.8 × 39.1 × 5.3 cm); painted surface: 14¾ × 10⅞ in. (37.3 × 27.5 cm)

Inscribed (on recto): (on frame, at bottom) *1487 DIE 24 MENS*[*I*]*Z APRIL*[*IS*] (1487, the 24th day of the month of April); (on frame, at left), [insignia of Order of the Holy Sepulcher]; (on frame, at right), [insignia of Cyprian Order of the Sword, with motto] *POVR LOIAVLITE MAINTENIR* (To maintain loyalty); (on side of sitter's signet ring) *R*

Museo Nacional Thyssen-Bornemisza, Madrid (271.a [1934.15.a; recto]; 271.b [1934.15.b; verso])

JOHANN VON RÜCKINGEN (died 1509) was a merchant patrician in Frankfurt who was ennobled in 1468 and is documented as having made a pilgrimage to Jerusalem in 1487.[1] This portrait appears to have been painted shortly before that trip, as the original frame bears the date of April 24 of that year. While the precise date of von Rückingen's departure remains unknown, he is recorded as having arrived back in Frankfurt in January 1488.[2] The vertical moldings of the frame are marked with the insignia of two chivalric orders that Johann joined during the pilgrimage: the Order of the Holy Sepulcher and the Cyprian Order of the Sword. Those details must have been added after his return.

This portrait was probably accompanied by a likeness of von Rückingen's wife, Agathe Monis (1461–1502), whom he married in 1477. The background scene showing couples in a garden would be consistent with such a pairing, and the piece of jewelry in Johann's hand may represent a gift to his wife. A nearly identical accessory appears in Wolfgang Beurer's portrait of a couple in Frankfurt (ca. 1490, Städel Museum, Frankfurt am Main), although there it is held by the woman. On the present work, two holes in the right edge of the frame suggest a hinged attachment and thus a folding diptych.[3] Johann's impending journey to the Holy Land, fraught with potential hazards, likely motivated the couple to have both their appearances documented for posterity.

The von Rückingen family coat of arms on the reverse was displayed when the diptych was closed.[4] The escutcheon is held by a so-called Wild Man, a legendary woodland figure commonly used as a heraldic bearer (see cats. 16 and 37).[5] Now in a compromised state of preservation, the depiction shows remnants of a different stage of the composition, visible as a man's legs clad in red. The reasons for the change are unknown.[6]

Von Rückingen entered the historical record mainly for having violated Frankfurt's sumptuary laws soon after his return from Jerusalem.[7] For his membership in the Order of the Sword, he had acquired a velvet doublet and a gold neck chain hung with the order's insignia. Yet Frankfurt forbade its citizens, patricians included, from wearing velvet clothing and gold neck chains in public.[8] The intention was to keep social distinctions in check. As early as February 1488, the city council began issuing warnings to Johann. For more than a year, he repeatedly defied them. His relentless disobedience ultimately prompted the city to jail him for seven weeks in late 1489, until he signed an oath to dress according to code. This episode underscores the great importance Johann associated with the outward signs of his pilgrimage, as is also suggested by the addition of the insignia to the portrait's frame.

The artist responsible for this and several other unsigned paintings also produced four portrait engravings, two of which are signed with the monogram *WB*. Scholars have proposed his identification as "Wolfgang Beurer" based on a stylistically related drawing owned by Albrecht Dürer, which the Nuremberg master noted as having been made in 1484 by a draftsman of that name (in Dürer's dialect, "wo[l]fgang pewrer").[9] Beurer is thought to have been active from about 1480 to 1500 in Frankfurt and elsewhere in the Middle Rhine region.

JPW

SELECTED REFERENCES: Buchner 1953, no. 33, pp. 47–48, 190, fig. 31; Dülberg 1990, pp. 114–15, 213 no. 128, pl. 232 figs. 600, 601; Lübbeke 1991, no. 34, pp. 150–55; Bodo Brinkmann, cat. 53, in Budde and Krischel 2001, pp. 358–59; Schedl 2016, p. 332, no. 83, pp. 334–38, 566–68, figs. 153, 154.

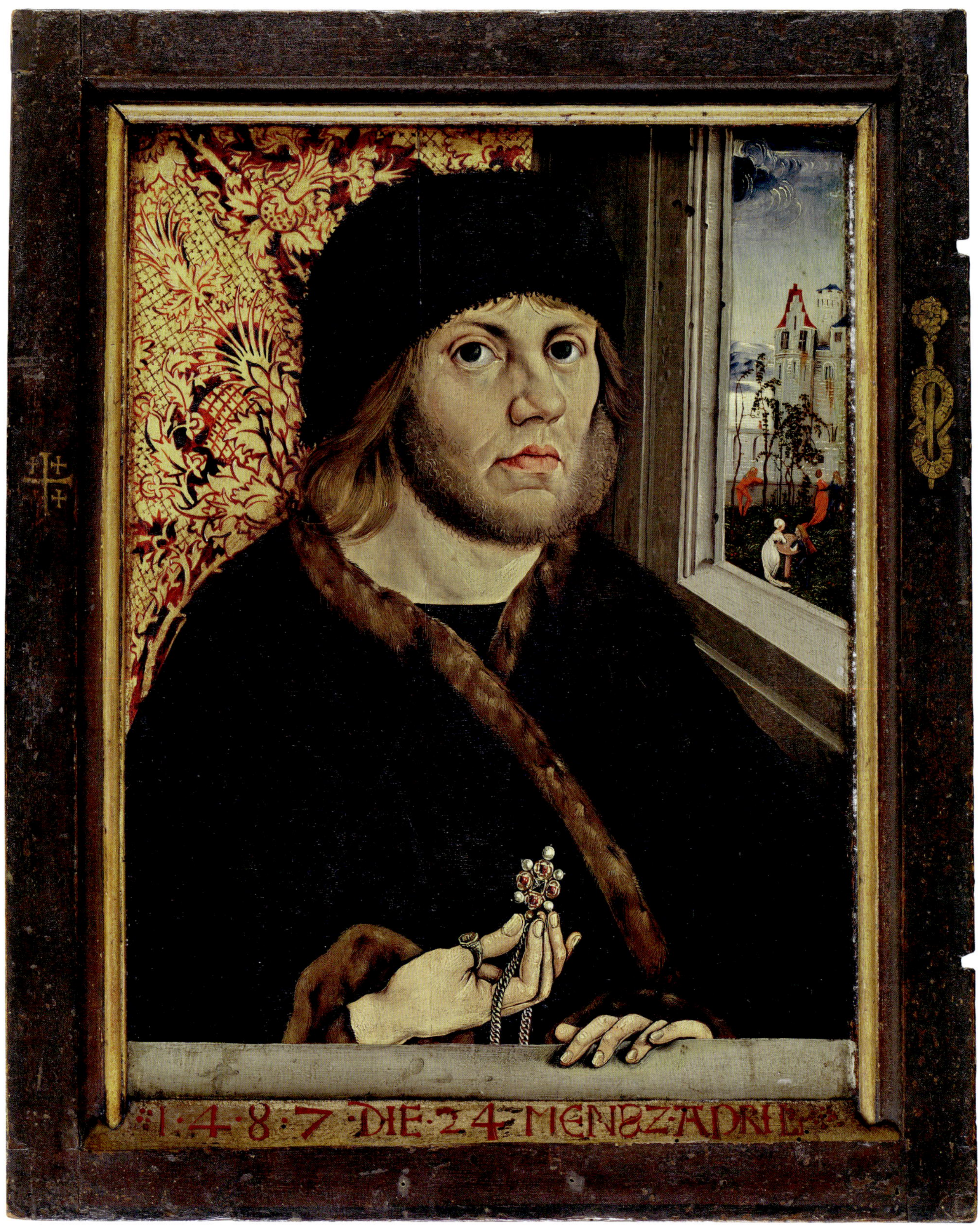
1·4·8·7·DIE·24·MENSZ·APRIL

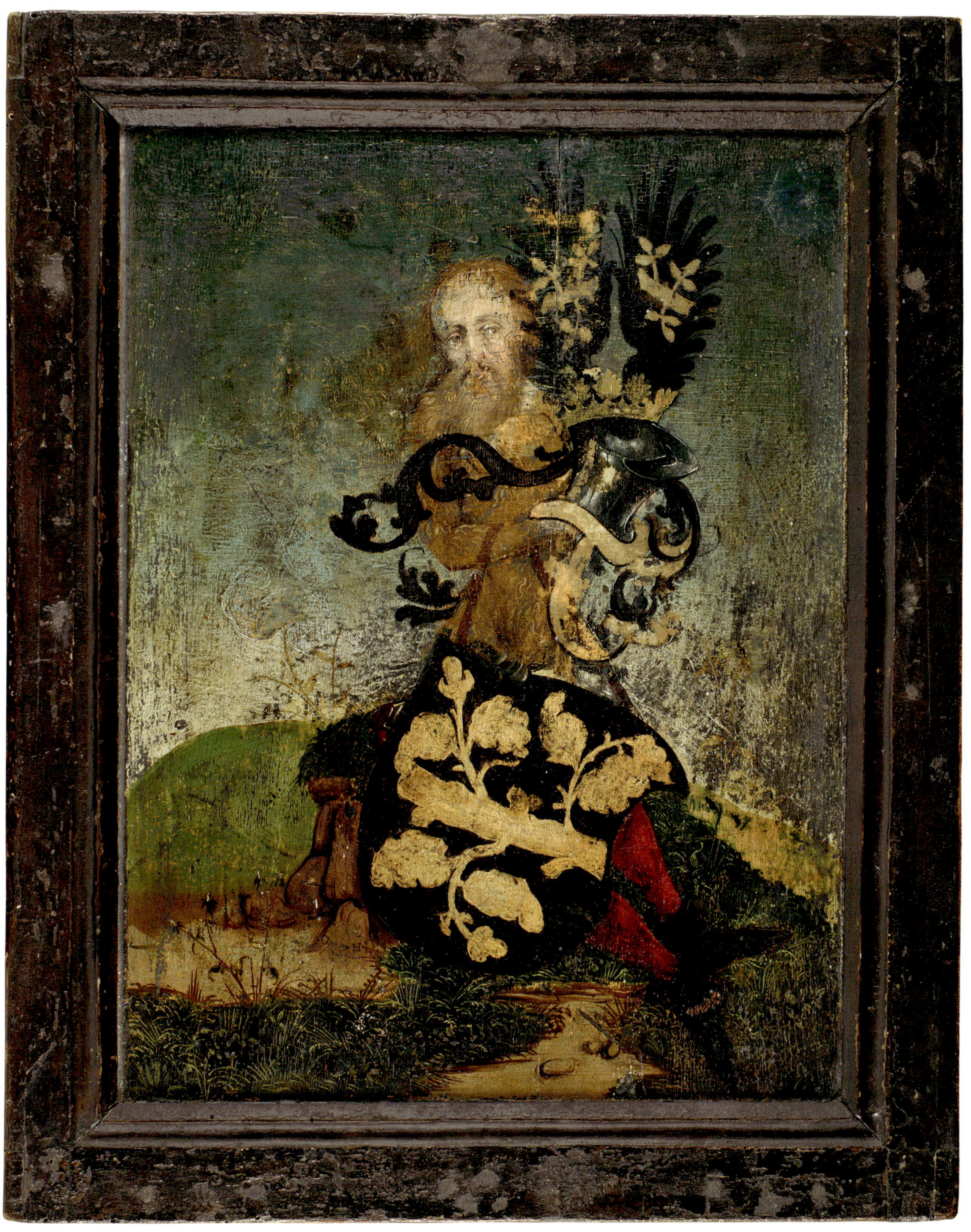

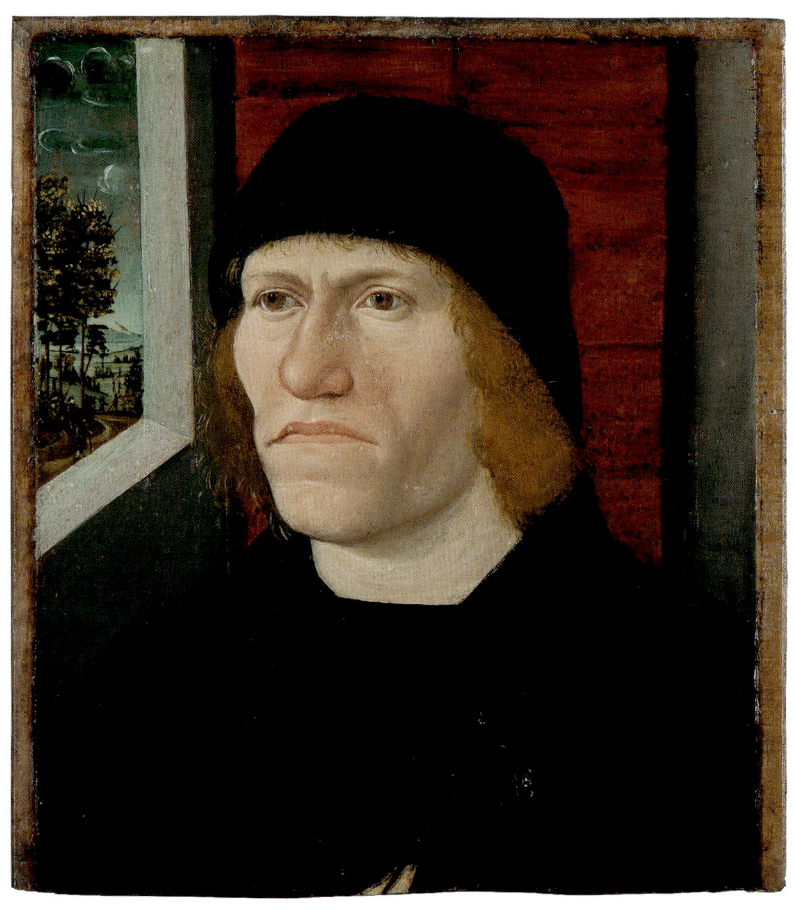

CAT. 14

UNKNOWN ARTIST

German, Frankfurt, active late 15th century
Friedrich Faut von Monsperg (recto); *Faut von Monsperg Coat of Arms* (verso), 1485

Oil on walnut panel, 10¼ × 8⅞ in. (26 × 22.5 cm)
Historisches Museum, Frankfurt am Main (B0633)

THE COAT OF ARMS on the back of this panel identifies the young male sitter as a member of the Frankfurt patrician family Faut von Monsperg.[1] The painting's date was recorded in an inscription formerly on the reverse, which read, in translation, "Herr von Monsprug [*sic*] was painted in the year 1485."[2] Although that inscription was not original to the picture (it lay atop a later, now-removed coat of gray paint), its content had likely been transferred from the initial, lost frame.[3] Knowledge of the date and the family tree allows an identification of the individual in this portrait: he is probably Friedrich Faut von Monsperg, a merchant who died in 1516.[4]

The sitter is shown in three-quarter view to the left, wearing a fur cap, doublet, and coat, all black. The likeness has a resolute, somewhat stern character, owing to the slightly knit brow, the downturned corners of the mouth, and the prominent chin. The blue flowers held by the sitter resemble forget-me-nots. At the lower edge, only the tips of the fingers clutching the stem are visible. That is because, sometime before the panel passed into museum ownership, the bottom end was cut by several centimeters, probably to fit a new frame. Behind the sitter is a room with gray walls and a red cloth hanging with green borders. A window offers a view into a landscape traversed by several wanderers. Without the original frame, it is impossible to say whether the panel was once fitted with a cover.

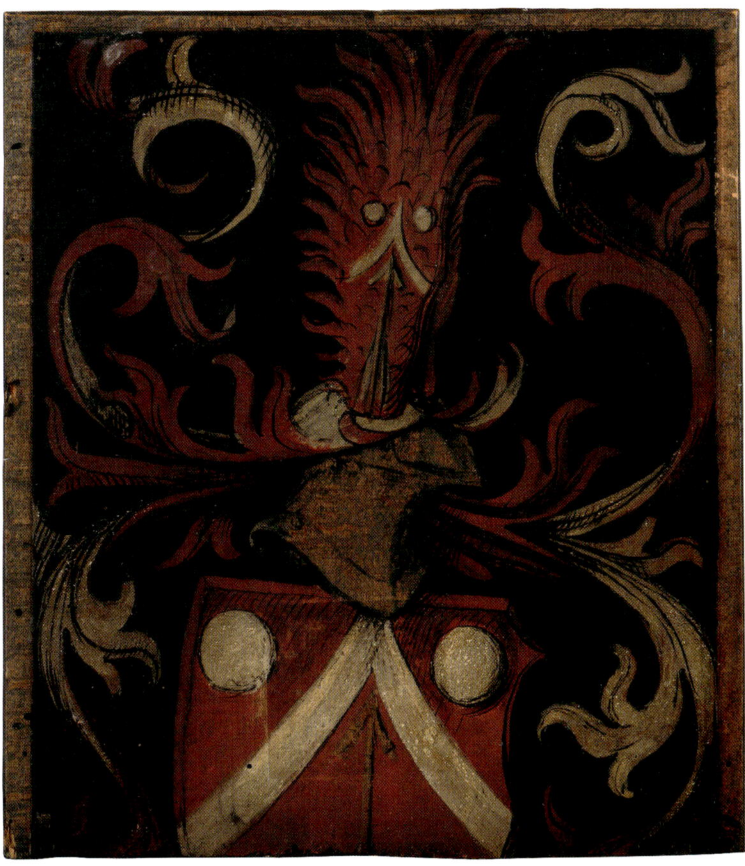

Friedrich Faut von Monsperg had several potential reasons for marking the year 1485 with a portrait. For one thing, he became a member of the politically powerful Zum Frauenstein association, one of Frankfurt's patrician societies. For another, he suffered and recovered from a serious, unspecified illness and, as a result, prepared a will. Furthermore, the death of his only brother, Hans, left Friedrich as the last in the family's male lineage.[5] Thus, while the portrait may commemorate the sitter's social and professional advancement of that year, it could also have arisen from a concern for remembrance in the face of mortality.

Friedrich was still a bachelor at the time of the portrait. Five years later, he married Margareta Cämmerer von Fulda (died 1509). Because their only son died in infancy, Friedrich's death in 1516 extinguished the male line of the Faut von Monsperg family.

The painter responsible for this portrait remains unidentified, and no other works by the same hand are known.[6] A general resemblance to the style of Wolfgang Beurer (see cat. 13) may indicate that the two artists, both apparently active in Frankfurt, were acquainted.[7]

The background of this work is one of the earliest in German portraits to show a room pierced by a window. The motif arose in the Netherlands, the earliest dated example being the 1462 *Portrait of a Man* by Dieric Bouts (National Gallery, London). This compositional device provided an effective means to establish spatial depth, represent a natural light source, and introduce a contrast between an interior and a landscape background.

JPW

SELECTED REFERENCES: Buchner 1953, no. 31, pp. 46, 190, fig. 32; Prinz 1957, pp. 162–63; Stange 1970, p. 47, no. 147; Dülberg 1990, p. 203 no. 93, pl. 174 figs. 407, 408; Schedl 2016, no. 81, pp. 325–28, 562–64, figs. 149, 150.

CAT. 15A,B

UNKNOWN ARTIST

German, Frankfurt, active late 15th century

15A Portrait: *Heinrich zum Jungen* (recto); *Inscriptions* (verso), 1477

15B *Cover with zum Jungen Coat of Arms* (recto); *Vine Scroll Decoration* (verso), 1477

Portrait: mixed media(?) on parchment, laid down on spruce panel, overall, with frame: 13¾ × 10⅜ in. (34.8 × 26.2 cm); painted surface: 11¾ × 8⅜ in. (29.8 × 21.2 cm)

Cover: distemper on canvas, laid down on wood panel: 13⅞ × 10¼ in. (35 × 26 cm)

Inscribed (on portrait panel): (on recto, at top, on cartellino) *Do ich waß xxxiiii jor alt do / was ich allso gestaltt* (When I was 34 years old, I looked like this); (on recto, at upper right, inscribed by a later hand), *Henrich zum / Jungen Ortens / Conrads Daniel*[*ens*] */ Karlens und An / thony zum / Jungen gebruder / anher*[1] (Heinrich zum Jungen, ancestor of the brothers Ort, Conrad, Daniel, Karl, and Anthony zum Jungen); (on reverse, at upper center), [genealogical details and provenance information by Johann Maximilian zum Jungen (1596–1649)]; (on reverse, at lower center, on paper, in nineteenth-century hand) [further related notes][2]

Historisches Museum, Frankfurt am Main (B0904)

THE PRESENT WORK, painted by an unknown artist in 1477, probably in Frankfurt, is one of the earliest portraits to survive together with its cover.[3] Within the general development of portraiture in Germany, this picture belongs to the first decades in which independent, secular portraits of civic elites began to emerge alongside the older tradition of princely portraiture. Furthermore, the work has local significance as the oldest extant portrait from Frankfurt, a city whose flourishing merchant and patrician families would increasingly turn to portraiture as a means of documentation and memorialization (see cats. 14 and 35A,B). Those functions were also served not only by an individual's likeness but also, as in this work, by his or her coat of arms; indeed, heraldic motifs are the most common type of decoration found on portrait versos and covers.

The sitter is Heinrich zum Jungen (1443–1482), a merchant and first-generation citizen of Frankfurt. His father, Ort, had fled from nearby Mainz because of a craft guild revolt against the city's patrician class, to which he belonged.

Below: Verso, cat. 15A

Opposite: Recto, cat. 15A

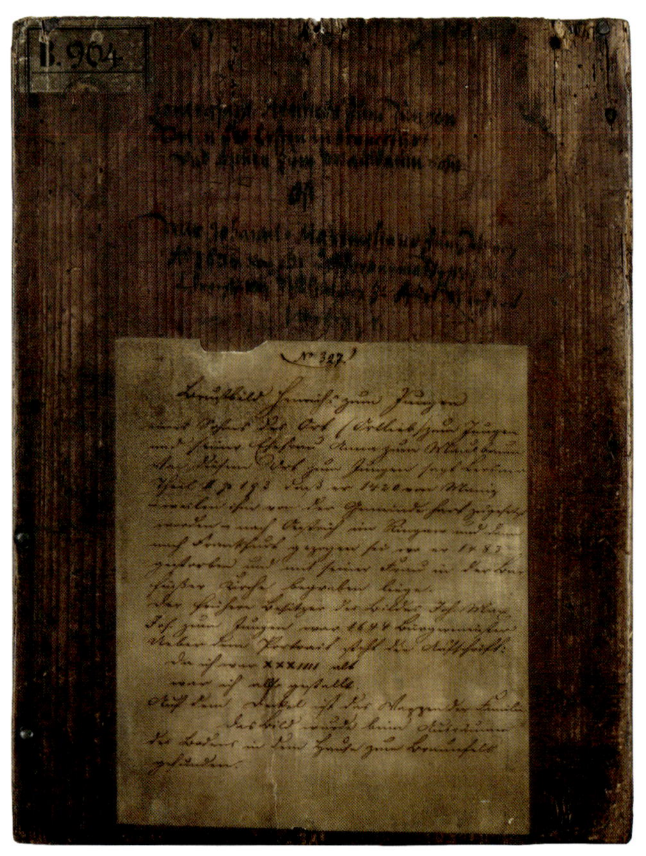

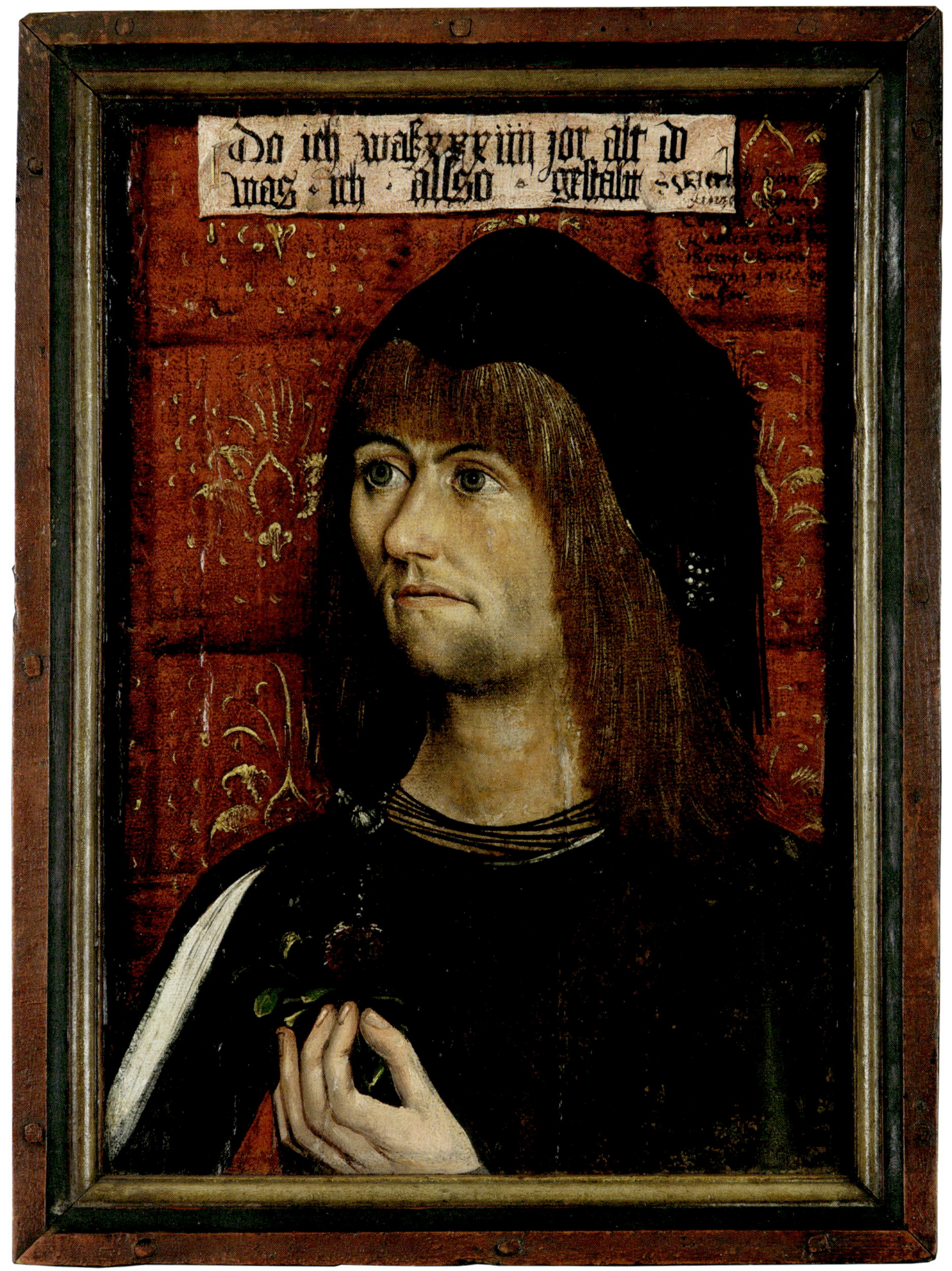
Do ich was xxxiiii jor alt do
was · ich · also · gestalt

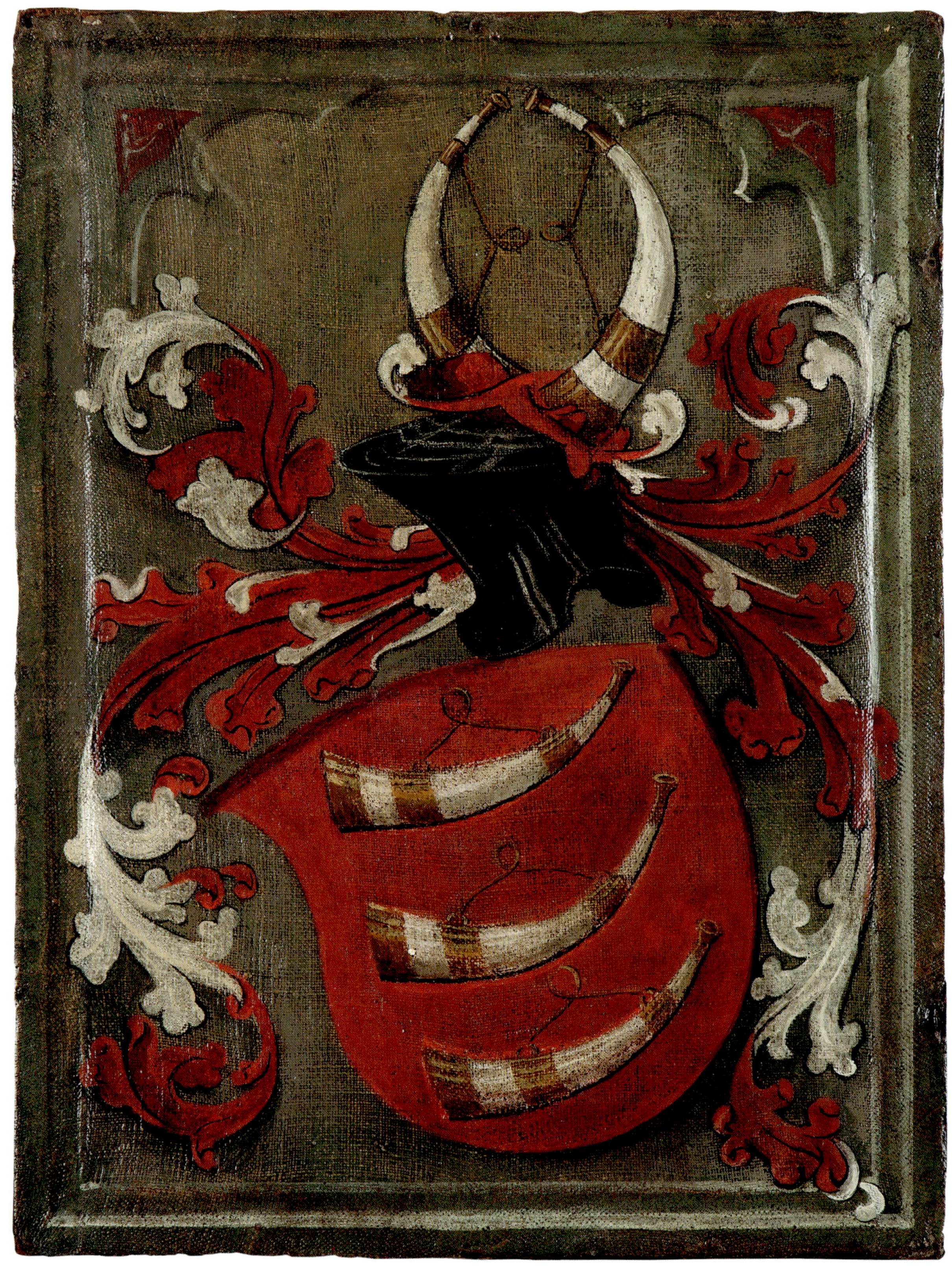

Opposite: Recto, cat. 15B

Above: Verso, cat. 15B

In Frankfurt, he gained admission to the local patriciate and prospered as a trader of cloth, fur, and spices.[4] Heinrich joined him in the profession. As was common for merchants of the period, they had far-flung dealings; for example, Heinrich is documented as having traveled as far as Naples in 1460–61.[5] He married Margarete von Glauburg in 1467, and the couple had four children. He died in 1482 and was buried in the family tomb in the Chapel of Our Lady at Frankfurt's Barfüsserkirche.[6]

The identification of the sitter is based on the family coat of arms on the cover and on early inscriptions added to the front and back of the portrait panel, which name him as the person depicted.[7] The original inscription on the cartellino at the top gives Heinrich's age as thirty-four, which renders a date of 1477 for the painting.

The heraldic panel is thought to have been attached with hinges at the right edge of the portrait.[8] When the panels were folded together, the coat of arms was on display; when they were opened, the portrait was at the left, adjacent to the reverse of the cover. That surface, painted in red tones, is adorned with an ornamental vine pattern.[9]

Heinrich wears a black cap adorned with a hanging bundle of cords, a black doublet slit along the sleeves, and a bluish-green cloak draped across his chest and left side. In his left hand, he holds a red flower. Although flowers often appear in conjugal portraits, Heinrich's marriage predates this work by ten years, making it unlikely to have been a factor in the commission.[10] However, in the year of the portrait's creation, a significant family event did occur: Heinrich's father established the previously mentioned hereditary burial site.[11] Concerns about death, legacy, and remembrance must therefore have been especially acute for both him and Heinrich at the time, and these could well have prompted a portrait commission. With that in mind, it bears mentioning that flowers, fated to wilt, were a common symbol of life's transience.

JPW

SELECTED REFERENCES: Schönberger 1933; Buchner 1953, no. 30, pp. 45, 189–90, fig. 30; Stange 1970, p. 114, no. 516; Dülberg 1990, pp. 202–3 no. 92, pl. 174 figs. 405, 406; Schedl 2016, no. 80, pp. 322–25, 560–62, figs. 145–48.

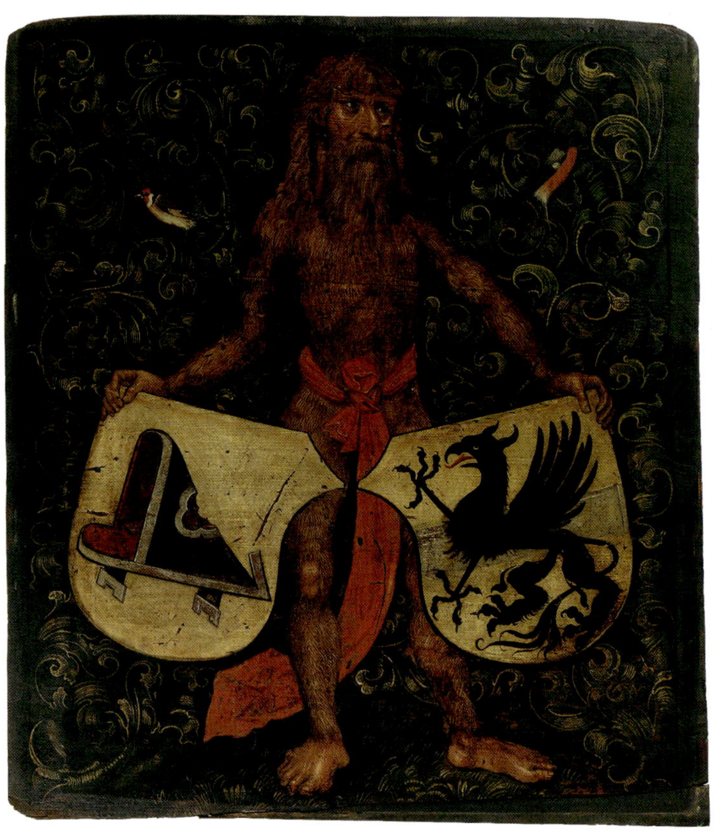

CAT. 16

JAKOB ELSNER OR WORKSHOP

Elsner: German, ca. 1460–1517

Portrait Cover with a Wild Man (recto); *Inscription* (verso), 1497

Oil on limewood panel, 18 × 15⅝ in. (45.7 × 39.5 cm)

Inscribed (on verso): *Tausent-vierhundert-lxxxxvii • / • Lazarus • holtczschuhers • gestalt • / • Als • er • was • Im • funffundzwan(n)cz= / = igsten • jar •* (One thousand-four hundred-lxxxxvii / Lazarus Holtczschuher [*sic*] figure / As he was in [his] twenty-fifth / year)

Germanisches Nationalmuseum, Nuremberg, Freiherrlich Loeffelholz von Colbergsche Familienstiftung, Hans Friedrichsche Linie (Gm2438)

AS AN INSCRIPTION on the upper half of the verso indicates, this panel was originally a sliding lid for a lost portrait of Lazarus Holzschuher. On the recto, centered in a near-frontal pose before a dense background of green leaves is a bearded Wild Man, with a knotted red loincloth hanging from his hirsute body. In either hand he bears the heraldic devices of Holzschuher and his wife, Katharina Bühl (or Buehlin). Three songbirds are perched in the green arabesque, which is meant to represent the forest, the Wild Man's true environment: a goldfinch and a bullfinch, in the upper half, and a dun-colored nightingale in the lower left-hand corner.[1]

The birds could be read as secular symbols of love and virtue. The goldfinch is also a sign of fertility,[2] just as the Wild Man symbolizes power and fruitfulness. His task as bearer of the family coat of arms ultimately guarantees the endurance of the family line.[3] He represents the *Neue Minne* (a new form of love), which, unlike the *Hohe Minne* (lofty love), is free from religious and societal pressures: he is driven only by his instincts and thus perfectly suited to portraits commissioned for weddings. Albrecht Dürer's 1499 portrait of Oswolt Krel (Alte Pinakothek, Munich), displaying on its hinged covers Wild Men carrying the coat of arms of Krel and his wife, Agathe von Esendorf, was painted for just such an occasion.[4]

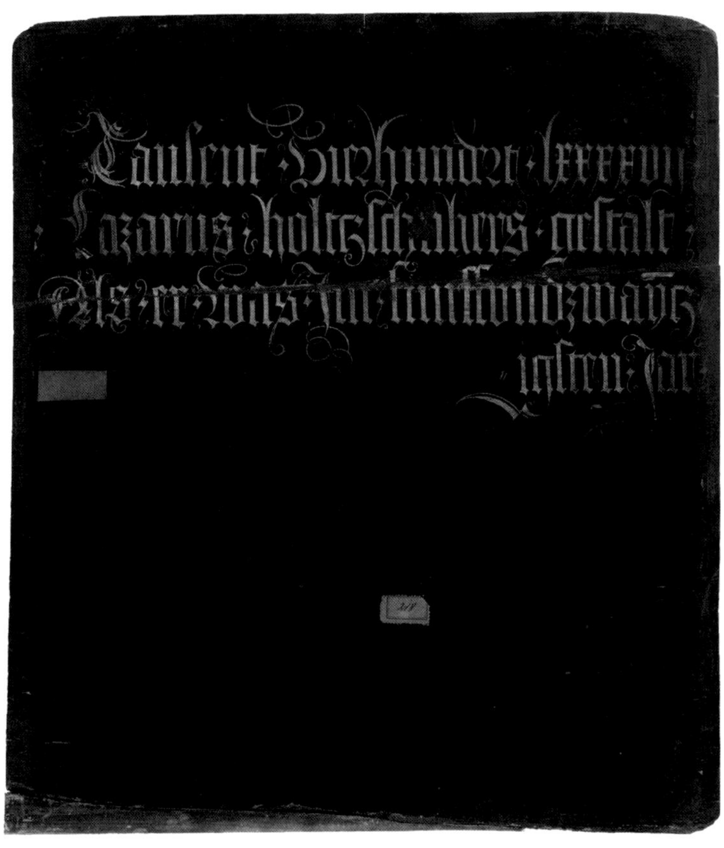

Lazarus Holzschuher, born into one of Nuremberg's oldest patrician families, was an established member of the city's elite. According to marriage records, in 1496 he married Katharina Bühl, daughter of Margaretha Haller and Johann Bühl of Landshut, who was the personal physician of the duke of Bavaria-Landshut. An etching by Johann Alexander Böner may be a reproduction of the original, now-lost portrait of Holzschuher done shortly after his wedding, although Böner mentioned the year of Holzschuher's death, 1523, in the inscription.[5]

Clearly beveled side edges with abrasion marks show that the cover was inserted from below into a groove between the inner and outer frames of Holzschuher's portrait. Dürer's 1526 portrait of the elder Holzschuher brother, Hieronymus (see fig. 16), retains its original double frame with its sliding mechanism as well as the sliding cover with the arms of alliance. There, the lid slides into the grooves from the right to cover the portrait. The right edge of the lid is wider, so that when fully inserted, it fits snugly behind the outer frame and vanishes from sight. When the lid is in place, the portrait becomes a closed box. This would have been the case for Lazarus's portrait as well, but the original, wider piece along the bottom edge has unfortunately been broken.[6]

These sealed portrait boxes were probably treated as family documents and stored safely in coffers.[7]

AD

SELECTED REFERENCES: Dülberg 1990, pp. 115, 213 no. 129, pl. 233 fig. 602; Hentschel 2018, pp. 3–7, fig. 1; Beate Fücker and Judith Hentschel, no. 54, in Hess et al. 2019, vol. 2, pp. 796–805, figs. 1–4; Mayr 2019, https://www.rdklabor.de/w/?oldid=111022#15._Jh.

CAT. 17

HANS MEMLING

Netherlandish, active by 1465–1494

Portrait of a Man (recto); *Flowers in a Jug* (verso), late 1480s

Oil on panel, 11½ × 8⅞ in. (29.2 × 22.5 cm)

Museo Nacional Thyssen-Bornemisza, Madrid (284.a [1938.1.a], 284.b [1938.1.b])

IN THE LAST QUARTER of the fifteenth century, Hans Memling was unrivaled as Bruges's foremost painter of portraits, which constitute one-third of his extant oeuvre. Memling was sought after not only by local residents but also by the significant number of wealthy Italian and Spanish merchants who had settled in the city. This led to the artist's considerable fame and influence abroad, as his foreign clients transported portraits back to their homelands.[1]

The Thyssen-Bornemisza *Portrait of a Man* in fact has been identified as a depiction of both a Spaniard and an Italian. Colin Eisler based the former assumption on an old, lost inscription on the back of the panel,[2] while Dirk De Vos suggested the latter based on the type, costume, and hairstyle of the sitter.[3] Lorne Campbell and Till-Holger Borchert favored a Spaniard, citing parallels in costume.[4] Given the prominently placed carpets on both sides of the panel, Borchert wondered whether the sitter was involved in the Spanish wool and textile industry, which featured prominently in Bruges's late fifteenth-century commerce.[5]

Irrespective of his country of origin, the man is portrayed in devotion to a holy image, probably a Virgin and Child, that was in a now-lost panel at the right. He is situated in the corner of a loggia; behind him are a red marble column and a carpet-covered balustrade that opens on to a wooded landscape. Another Memling work, namely the *Triptych of Benedetto Portinari* (see figs. 19 and 36), provides a model for the possible reconstruction of a triptych that would include the Thyssen-Bornemisza portrait.[6] Here the Virgin and Child take center stage, flanked by Saint Benedict at the left and Benedetto Portinari at the right. All the figures appear in the same interior loggia with a unified landscape beyond. In keeping with the conventions of hierarchy in Netherlandish marital triptychs, the holy figures in the reconstructed triptych would have taken the center position, while the Thyssen-Bornemisza man would be at the left and

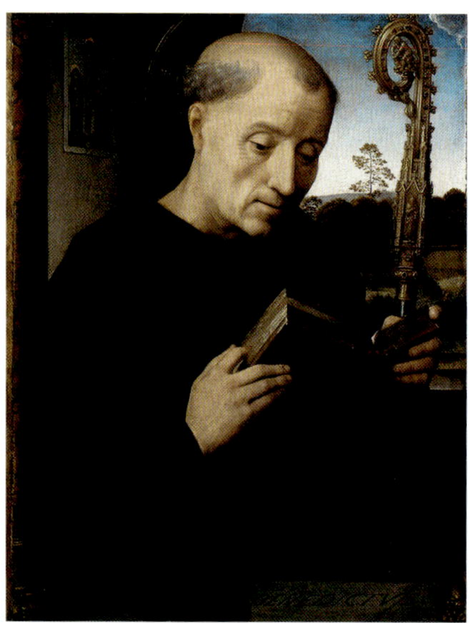

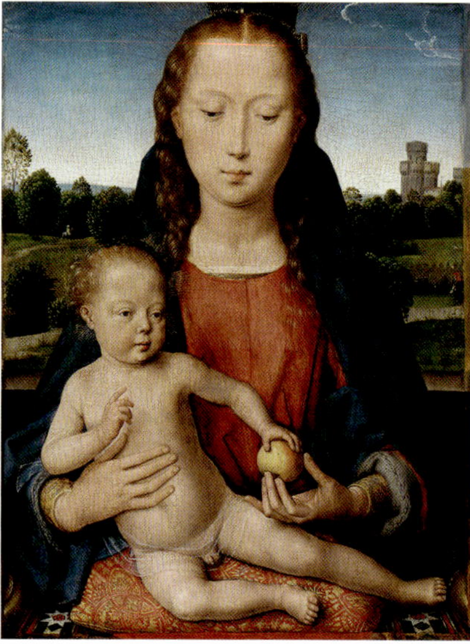

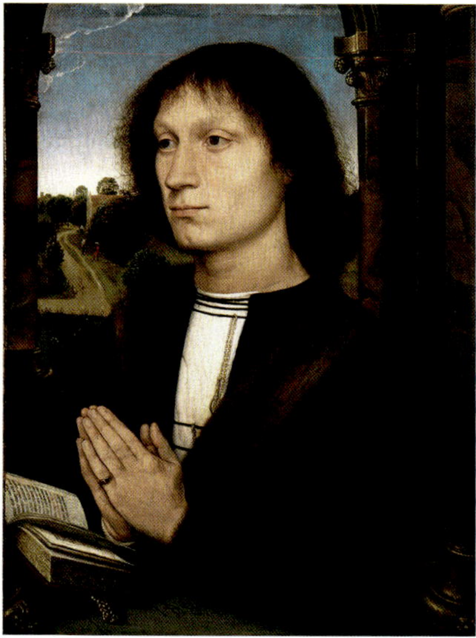

Fig. 36. Hans Memling. *Triptych of Benedetto Portinari (Saint Benedict, Virgin and Child, Benedetto Portinari)*, 1487. Oil on oak panel, left wing: 18 × 13⅝ in. (45.5 × 34.5 cm); central panel, 16⅜ × 12⅜ in. (41.5 × 31.4 cm); right wing: 17 × 13⅜ in. (43.2 × 34 cm). Central panel: Staatliche Museen zu Berlin–Preussischer Kulturbesitz, Gemäldegalerie; left and right wings: Gallerie degli Uffizi, Florence

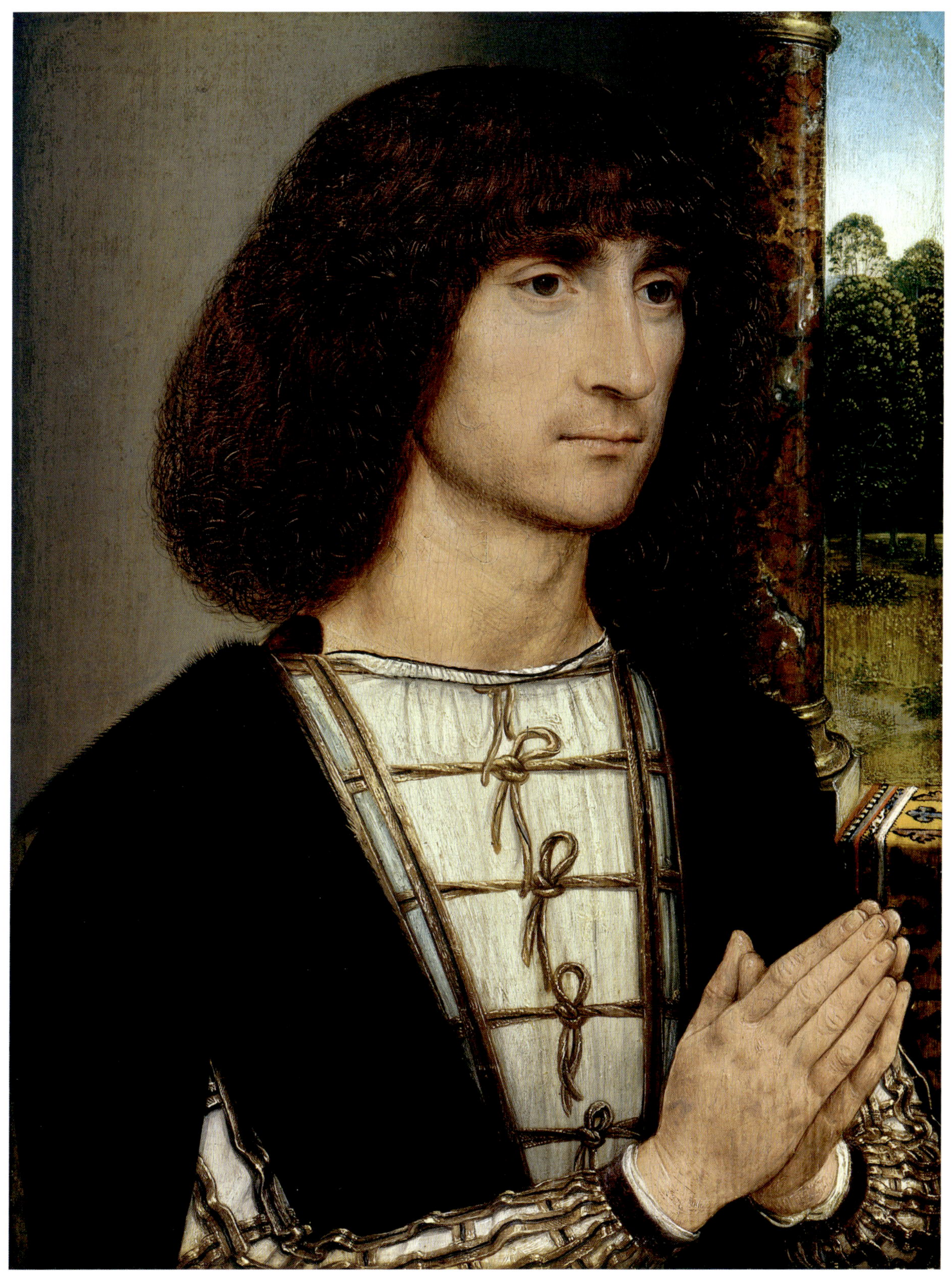

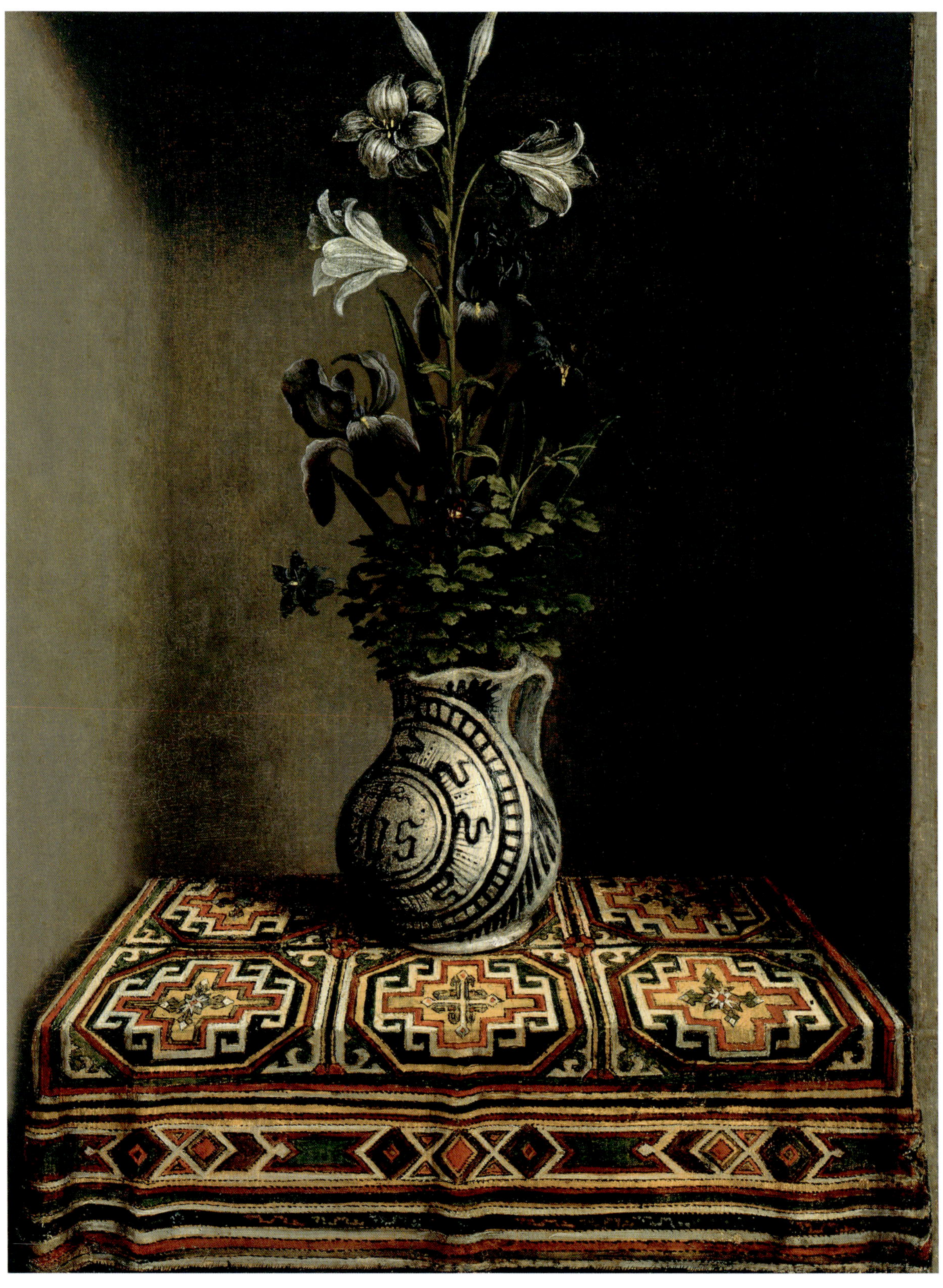

his wife at the right. This would conform to the configuration of other Memling triptychs, such as the one from about 1470 including the portraits of Tommaso and Maria Portinari (The Metropolitan Museum of Art, New York) with the *Virgin and Child* (National Gallery, London)[7] and that of Willem Moreel and Barbara van Vlaenderberch (1482, Musées Royaux des Beaux-Arts de Belgique, Brussels), the latter for which the centerpiece has been lost.[8]

Assuming that the Thyssen-Bornemisza portrait was the left wing of a triptych, then—when closed—the portrait of the man's wife would have folded over the Virgin and Child at the center, and the man's portrait would have folded over that of his wife.[9] Alternatively, as the Thyssen-Bornemisza panel is narrower in relationship to its height than most Memling portraits, the panels of the man and his wife could both have folded over the centerpiece of the Virgin and Child. In this scenario, the panel representing the holy figures would be twice the width of the portraits, and the reverse of the wife's portrait would have shown perhaps a coat of arms or even a skull as a memento mori.

In the triptych's closed position, the reverse of the man's portrait, an exquisite still-life painting of flowers in a maiolica jug on an oriental carpet—all beautifully arranged on a table in the niche of a wall—would have protected the portrait and been viewed on most occasions. Victor Stoichita has pointed out that this image would have appeared to be an integral part of the wall, essentially straddling the line between fiction and reality.[10] The bouquet, a precursor of the genre of still-life painting in the later sixteenth and seventeenth centuries,[11] comprises stems of columbine, iris, and lily, all symbolic of the Virgin. Columbine refers to her steadfastness in belief, the iris (sword lily) to her compassion, and the lily to her purity.[12] The maiolica jug holding the flowers is painted with the letters *YHS*, the monogram of Christ. As Angelica Dühlberg proposed, the flowers also represent the Christian virtues for which the sitter on the obverse strived, and the monogram signals Jesus's sacrificial death, which guaranteed everlasting life for humankind.[13] As such, the still life is emblematic of the likely image of the lost Virgin and Child centerpiece and corresponds to the fervent devotion expressed by the man portrayed on the obverse.

This exquisite example of Memling's consummate execution and handling dates to the late 1480s. The reconstructed triptych compares closely to the *Triptych of Benedetto Portinari* of 1487, discussed above. With its masterful loose, spontaneous, but highly descriptive brushwork, it relates best to the artist's other late portraits, such as the *Portrait of a Man with a Pink* (ca. 1485, Morgan Library and Museum, New York) and *Maarten Nieuwenhove* (1487, Sint-Janshospitaal, Memlingmuseum, Bruges).[14]

MWA

SELECTED REFERENCES: Pächt 1948, p. 54n23; Friedländer 1967–76, vol. 6, pt. 2, suppl. 232, p. 110, pl. 235; Rosenbaum 1979, cat. 25, pp. 42, 115–17; Eisler 1989, no. 10, pp. 106–15; Dülberg 1990, pp. 163, 260 no. 237, pl. 143 fig. 303, 304; De Vos 1994, no. 72, pp. 262–63; Stoichita 1997, p. 20; Reindert L. Falkenburg, "The Scent of Holyness: Notes on the Interpretation of Botanical Symbolism in the Paintings by Hans Memling," in Verougstraete et al. 1997, pp. 149–61; Till-Holger Borchert, cat. 25, in Borchert 2005, pp. 175–76; Hélène Verougstraete, "Diptychs with Instructions for Use," in Hand and Spronk 2006, p. 162; Lane 2009, pp. 108–9, 289–90 no. 43.

CAT. 18

HANS MEMLING

Netherlandish, active by 1465–1494
Allegory of Chastity, 1479–80

Oil on oak panel, 15⅛ × 12⅝ in. (38.3 × 31.9 cm)
Institut de France, Musée Jacquemart-André, Paris (MJAP-P 857)

A YOUNG, BEAUTIFULLY dressed maiden, her dark hair cascading down her back, emerges from an amethyst mountain before a tranquil landscape, the upper portion of which is restoration and not part of the original concept. Demurely gazing downward, she crosses her hands over her lap in a gesture of modesty. A lion with a golden shield on its back stands guard on rocks to either side of a stream that carries gemstones and coral as it flows from the base of the mountain. Lacking any sign of heraldry, the lions' shields serve a protective function, enhanced by the menacing glower of the beasts toward the viewer.

Various sources and interpretations have been offered for the combined elements of the painting, most notably by Micheline Comblen-Sonkes.[1] She sees in the blue color of the amethyst rock a relationship to the violet flower, emblematic of humility and a symbol of virginity that must be protected by the vigilant lions. The clear, flowing water signals the purity of the maiden, and the precious stones in it refer to the Garden of Eden. The moralizing message here, Comblen-Sonkes suggests, may be a religious one in which the virtue of virginity leads to rewards in paradise.

The challenge in arriving at a convincing solution to this enigmatic presentation is that very few allegories exist in Northern Renaissance painting at this early date (see cat. 42). The oeuvre of Hans Memling, to whom the painting is attributed, includes only two other examples: an *Allegory of True Love* of about 1485–90, which comprises two separated panels, *Young Woman with a Pink* (The Metropolitan Museum of Art, New York) and *Two Horses and a Monkey* (Museum Boijmans Van Beuningen, Rotterdam), and the *Triptych of Earthly Vanity and Divine Salvation* of about 1485 or later (Musée des Beaux-Arts, Strasbourg).[2]

The panel is extremely thin and has been cradled. This presents the possibility that it was once separated from an image on its reverse, which Friedrich Winkler proposed might have been a portrait.[3] Noting the nearly square shape of the panel, Philippe Lorentz concurred and suggested that the present painting might represent Saint Barbara, around whom a rock grew to protect her from her father's wrath over her conversion to Christianity. The portrait on the reverse of the panel would then have represented a woman named Barbara who wished to associate herself with the virtuous nature of her patron saint.[4] Alternatively, the *Allegory of Chastity* may have been intended to highlight the pure virtues of any woman shown in the related female portrait. Whether the allegory was a sliding panel over a portrait or functioned as the separate exterior in diptych form cannot be determined from the existing material evidence.

The allegory has been accepted as a Memling by Max Friedländer, Comblen-Sonkes, and Dirk De Vos and given an early date, around 1470–75, by the former two and a later one, 1479–80, by the latter.[5] The later date would correspond with those of other allegories in Memling's oeuvre. Lorne Campbell and Barbara Lane are less positive about the attribution, citing weaknesses in execution found in the painting, whose subject matter remains enigmatic as well.[6]
MWA

SELECTED REFERENCES: Winkler 1928; Friedländer 1967–76, vol. 6, pt. 1, no. 96, p. 57, pl. 124; Comblen-Sonkes 1988, no. 157, pp. 77–86; Campbell 1990a; Dülberg 1990, p. 288 no. 313, pl. 67 fig. 146; De Vos 1994, no. 34, pp. 164–65; Campbell 1995; Lorentz 1995, p. 75; Barbara Baert, "The *Allegory with a Virgin*: Contributions to the Solution of an Iconographical Enigma," in Verougstraete et al. 1997, pp. 195–210; Lane 2009, no. B11, p. 330; Brückle 2013.

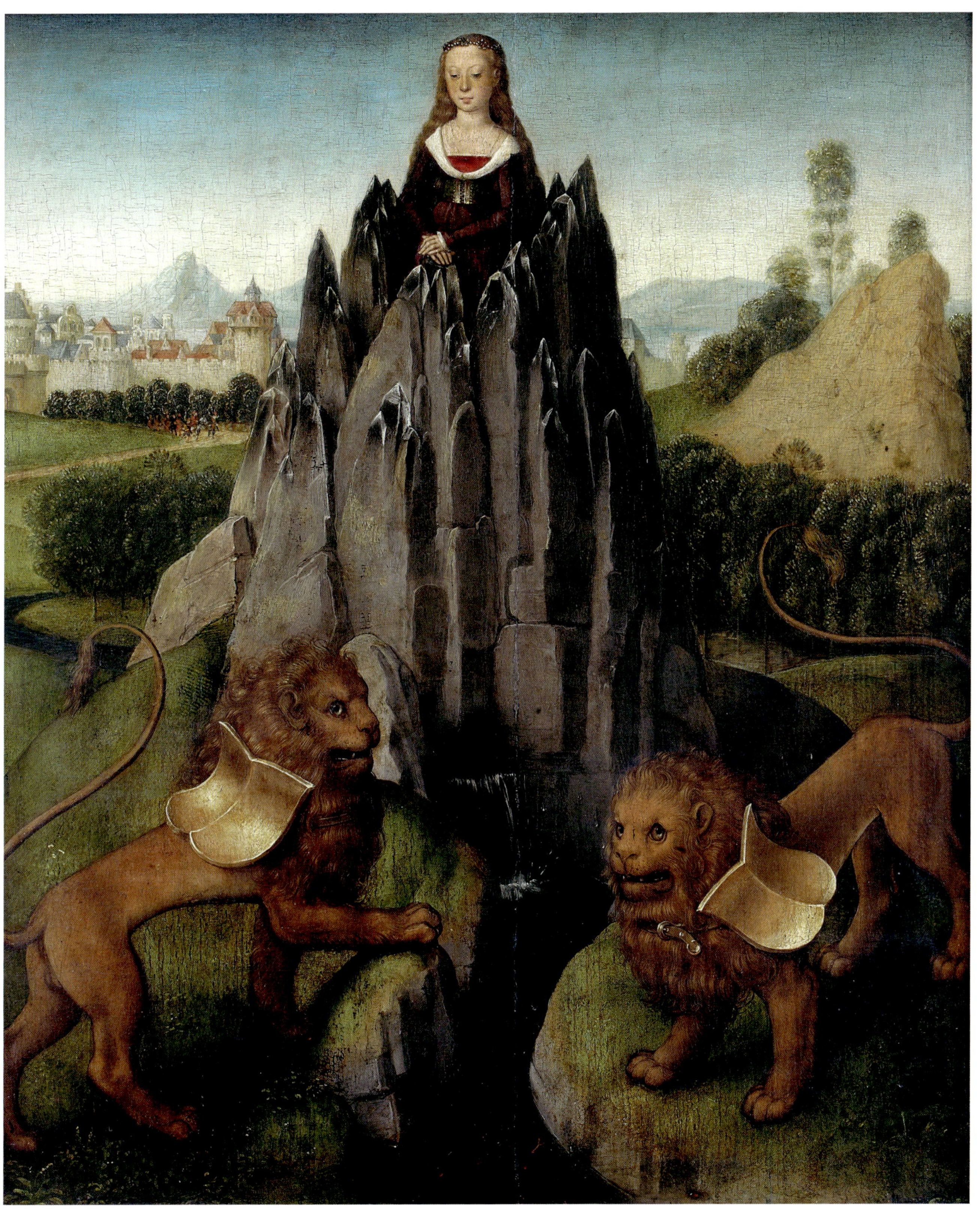

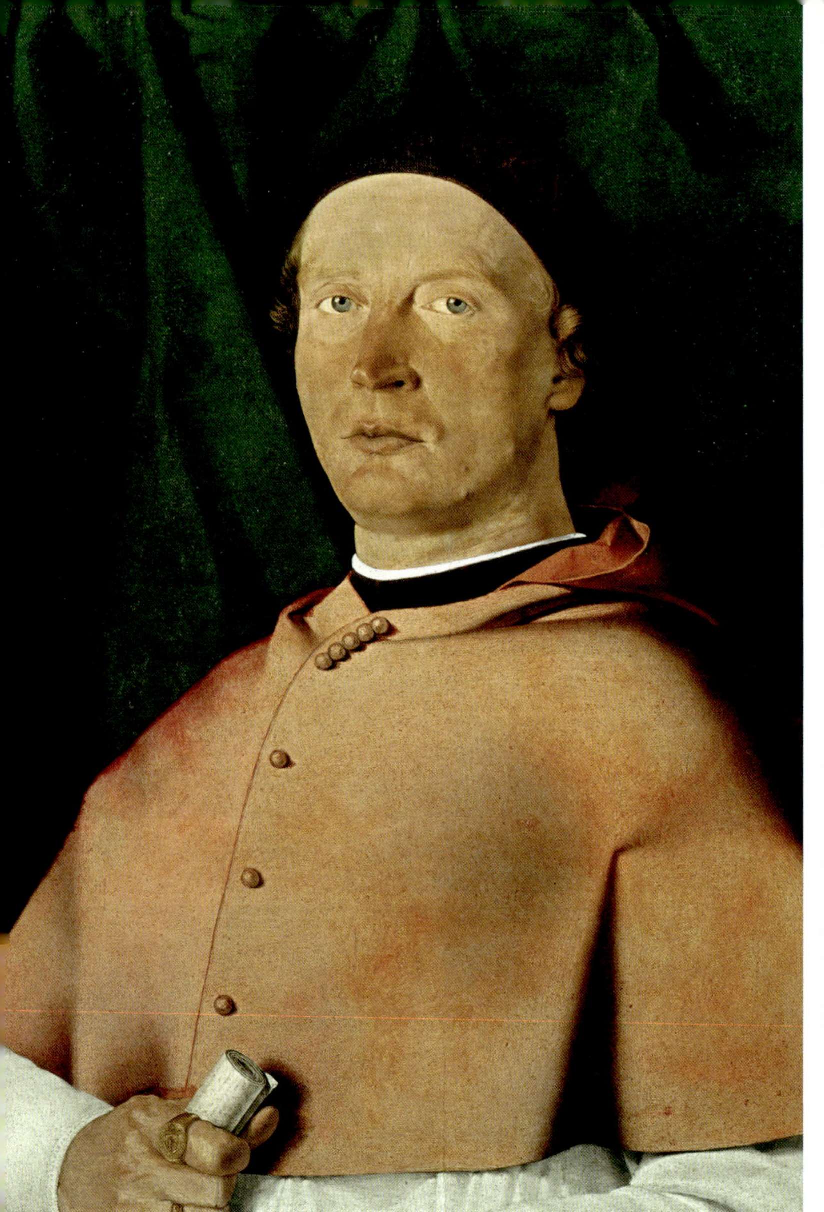

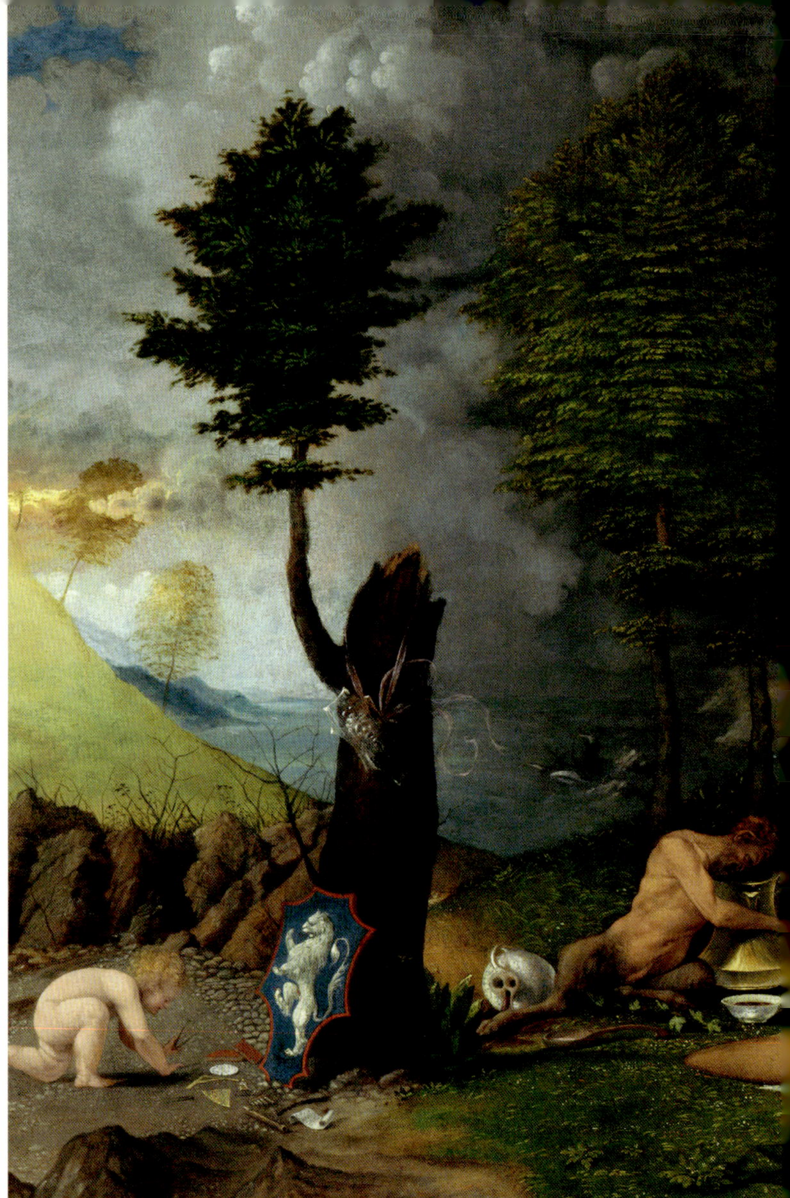

COVERED PORTRAITS IN ITALY, 1475–1550

CATHERINE WHISTLER

When a portrait is paired with a painted reverse or a cover, each gains in significance and in attraction through a play of concealment and revelation that involves both the hands and the imagination. Hidden images may seem eccentric in a culture such as ours, in which pictures are on open display, but this practice was already unfamiliar by 1602, when a Venetian notary needed to explain the term *timpano* as meaning a cover.[1] In Venice at that time, as in other centers, the idea of the "gallery" as a grandly sociable space with an ensemble of paintings and sculptures was taking shape.

Painted reverses and covers belong to the earlier Renaissance culture of the *studiolo*, where significant objects, from medals to small sculptures and paintings, could be removed from cabinets and decorated boxes or unveiled for companionable viewing. The concept of "virtuous riches," of accumulating antiquities and works of art as a sign of civility, good judgment, and self-awareness, prevailed in this culture, which allowed individuals as varied as merchants and statesmen to delight in the tranquil sustenance their collections brought them.[2] The pleasures of anticipation and the ingenuity involved in decoding the relationship between a painting and what lay concealed were part of the experience of visiting a collection, mirroring the shared enjoyment of the memory games and puzzles that were becoming a feature of social life beyond courtly circles.[3]

These intellectual and tactile pleasures relate both to elite appreciation of luxury objects such as portrait medals, with their conjunction of prestigious representation and personalized imagery, and to communal experiences such as the unveiling of altarpieces and relics as part of regular devotional practices in Italian churches.[4] Medals, promising fame and permanence, kindled the fashion for small portraits with painted reverses that featured similar impresa-type imagery, where fictive porphyry might also be used to suggest prestige and durability. Beyond elite collections, habits of concealment embraced domestic devotional images (usually of the Madonna and Child), which acted as a focus for prayer and sanctified the home: out of respect and decorum, paintings were furnished with decorated shutters, curtains, or painted covers.[5]

In Venice, as in Florence, the prosperous home and the aristocratic palazzo were spaces for sensory encounters with juxtaposed paintings. Chests with vividly painted stories were essential furnishings, and birth trays with bespoke imagery on front and back were familiar. A variety of images were handled with anticipation, as decorated caskets and gaming boards were opened and musical instruments were enhanced by painted lids.[6] Enjoyment in gradual unveiling is implicit in the long panel that accompanied the Morelli-Nerli wedding chests, commissioned in Florence in 1472 (The Courtauld Gallery, London), where fictive embroidered curtains are drawn back to reveal scenes from Roman history.[7] Similarly, the sequential viewing of paintings that decorated doors or screens—often with unusual or innovative imagery—reveals the sophisticated visual culture of prosperous Venetian households in the 1490s and 1500s.[8] The increasing profile of northern European paintings and prints in Venetian and Florentine homes, including portraits with painted versos or emblematic imagery as well as naturalistic landscapes, rounds out this picture of cosmopolitan viewing.

Few extant covers can be securely associated with their original paintings, which might have had a variety of subjects, but those for which there is compelling evidence are portraits.[9] That portable paintings other than the devotional should require veiling may partly have arisen from the same sense of respect for the power or status of an image, especially when portraits were linked to transformational

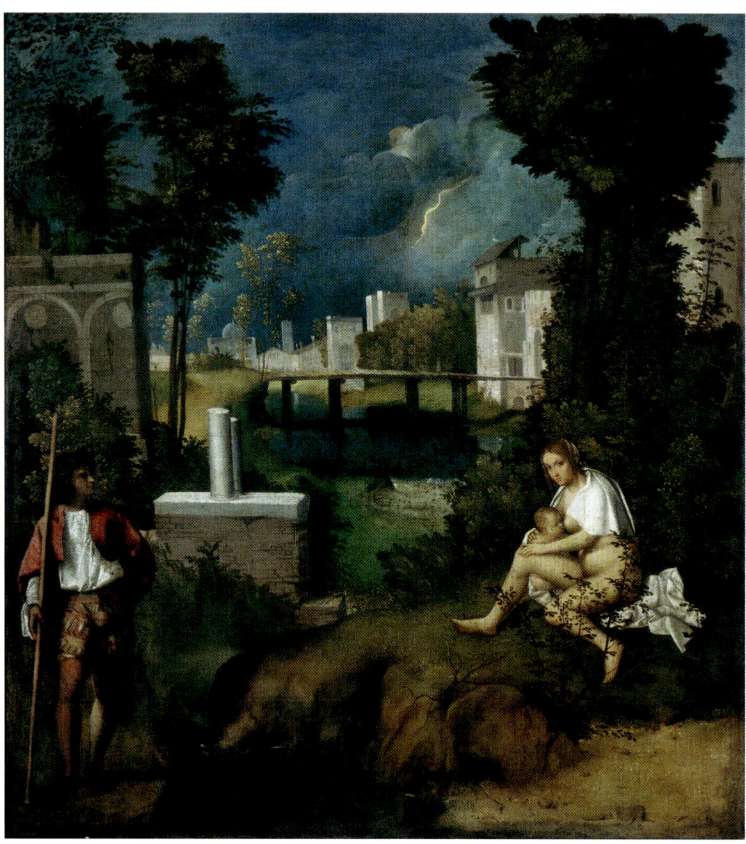

Fig. 37. Giorgione (Italian, 1477/78–1510). *The Tempest*, ca. 1504. Oil on canvas, 32⅜ × 28¾ in. (82 × 73 cm). Gallerie dell'Accademia, Venice (915)

events—betrothal, bereavement, victory over adversity—or marked significant relationships such as friendship. Praise for painted portraits commonly extolled the illusion of living presence, recalling their commemorative nature.[10] The practice of covering them was widespread. In a charming courtly anecdote from 1471 Milan, the toddler Gian Galeazzo Maria Sforza wanted to hug his father's portrait when it was uncovered.[11] Comparisons to mirrors might be invoked, with implications of truth and revelation, while mirrors sometimes concealed paintings or could be covered by them (see cat. 43). Fra Sabba da Castiglione told a vivid tale that hinged on the uncovering of a juxtaposed female portrait and mirror.[12]

That the fashion for painted covers and reverses was particularly strong in Venice seems reflected in the balance of paintings in this volume. This is supported by the richness of Venetian documentary evidence, notably the specific descriptions relating to Gabriele Vendramin's collection, which featured many *timpani*, including one for Giorgione's *La Vecchia* (see fig. 3) that portrayed a man clad in black; the term recurs in Venetian inventories, and Lorenzo Lotto's records of expenses refer to *timpani* and other covers.[13] Although information is lacking on how canvas *timpani* were attached to frames in Venice (possibly as lids), they could, being lightweight, accompany relatively large paintings, unlike the panels favored in Florence, where the term *tirella*, meaning something that could be moved to one side, implies strong sliding or hanging mechanisms.[14]

Moreover, the allegorical nature of the covers' imagery chimed with Venetian explorations of the poetic landscape in the 1500s, as typified by Giorgione's *Tempest* (fig. 37) and Titian's *Pastoral Concert* (perhaps ca. 1511, Musée du Louvre, Paris), with their open-ended subject matter. There are affinities, too, with the opportunities for iconographic experimentation afforded by Venice's thriving print culture. Busy trade routes across the Alps no doubt encouraged the taste for, and acquaintance with, northern European paintings and prints in Venice, including the use of the painted reverse and cover. Jacometto's captivating double-sided portraits, for example, amplify Northern prototypes (cats. 19, 20A,B, and 23).

Were painted covers in fact more prevalent in Venice than elsewhere? Our knowledge is limited by problems of survival and identification in other Italian centers. The impact of northern European art was equally strong in many places, including Florence and Urbino, while the *studiolo* culture that privileged painted reverses and covers flourished throughout Italy. Instances from Raphael's career alone—the allegorical reverses of the portraits of Angelo and Maddalena Doni (ca. 1506–7, Gallerie degli Uffizi, Florence); his reference in 1508 to a *tavoleta* in Urbino that acted as a cover for a Madonna and Child; or the *Small Holy Family* for Cardinal Bibbiena with its allegorical cover of about 1517–18 (the latter two paintings in the Louvre)—indicate wide engagement with these practices.[15] In addition, Giorgio Vasari's matter-of-fact statement identifying Bronzino's *Pygmalion and Galatea* (see fig. 5) as the cover for a portrait by Pontormo suggests familiarity with this type of production.[16]

Other tantalizing questions remain on the character of hidden images. Modern scholars have emphasized the private, even secretive nature of covers, especially in relation to portraits of lovers, yet these works would have been routinely visible to the household and visitors.[17] Moreover, painted covers offered the repeated experience of revelation for the owner's friends and family, with an aura of playfulness around their notional secrecy. Renaissance literary comparisons (*paragone*) of painting and poetry, in which the painter's talent lies in representing the externals of the body, but the poet delves beyond, into the subject's immaterial soul, can be illuminating.[18] However, against the construal of the allegorical cover as a spiritual portrait that accompanies a physical portrayal stand Renaissance fictions of the personal. Covers and painted reverses, albeit bespoke, encode ambitions and admonitions in keeping with broader cultural frameworks—aspirations toward fame, dynastic or personal; dedication to virtuous pursuits; and warnings about submission to fortune, the preservation of honor, and the power of true love.

Above all, their qualities of ingenuity and inventiveness made painted covers attractive, and their liminal status as objects that functioned as lids and screens meant that expectations surrounding religious and historical subjects did not prevail. Painters could be remarkably innovative, especially when relations with a patron were fruitful, as Lotto found with Bernardo de' Rossi (cat. 30A) and his circle, and Titian with Gabriele Vendramin (see cat. 33). Some, like Giorgione and Bronzino, took the opportunity to reflect on the nature and significance of their art.[19] Recalling the *paragone*, painters could demonstrate how, like poets, they were able to conjure representations of allusion and enchantment within which the imagination might wander. Ultimately, it was the beauty and originality of many painted covers that ensured their continuing afterlife as independent works of art.

CAT. 19

JACOMETTO VENEZIANO

Italian, active by ca. 1472–before 1498
Portrait of a Boy (recto); *Pseudo-porphyry* (verso), ca. 1475–80

Tempera and oil on wood panel, 9 × 7¾ in. (22.9 × 19.7 cm)
The National Gallery, London Salting Bequest, 1910 (NG2509)

A CELEBRATED PAINTER and illuminator in late fifteenth-century Venice, Jacometto Veneziano specialized in small-scale, multisided portraits (cats. 20A,B and 23), a genre that would continue to flourish in the lagoon during the early sixteenth century under Lorenzo Lotto (cats. 29A,B and 30A,B), Giorgione, and Titian. Jacometto has been described as the first Italian artist to "consistently adopt" the Netherlandish tradition of adorning the reverses and covers of portraits.[1]

While Jacometto's preeminence as an artist is evidenced in documents, it remains difficult to define his identity and the full scope of his activities, especially his role as a manuscript illuminator, for which he was celebrated as being "the best in the world."[2] He was also a musician, whose skill in playing the lyre and composing verse was celebrated by Girolama Corsi in a poem she dedicated to him.[3] The seminal source on Jacometto, *Notizia d'opere di disegno* (*Notes on Pictures and Works of Art*), was written in 1543 by the Venetian connoisseur Marcantonio Michiel, who recorded portraits, drawings, and manuscript illuminations by the artist in several patrician houses of the Veneto.

Among Jacometto's patrons was the humanist and diplomat Bernardo Bembo. In 1472 and 1481, Jacometto painted the likenesses (now lost) of Bembo's two young sons, Carlo and Pietro (see discussion under cat. 23).[4] Around 1475, Giovanni Bellini also depicted the son of a distinguished Venetian in his *Portrait of a Boy* (see fig. 26), which formed the door of an inheritance chest containing the sculpted bust of the youth's deceased father, the diplomat Angelo Probi.[5] While the identity of the boy in the present portrait is unknown, the work likely belongs to the same tradition and period, from the mid to late 1470s. The youth's idealized face is rendered with crystalline precision and dramatically illuminated, highlighting the bright clarity of his pale eyes and the smooth texture of his hair and skin.

The portrait vividly demonstrates the influence of Antonello da Messina, the Sicilian master whose Venetian sojourn in 1474–75 was formative to Jacometto's style and to Venetian art as a whole. Both artists were profoundly indebted to Netherlandish portraiture in style and format, but Jacometto's work also reflects another characteristic of many Northern examples: their multisided structure. Like Jacometto's *Alvise Contarini* (cat. 20A) and the *Portrait of a Woman, Possibly a Novice of San Secondo* (see fig. 42), the present work is painted on its reverse with pseudo-porphyry, the form of decoration most frequently found on the reverses of Netherlandish portraits since the 1430s under Jan van Eyck. A precious and durable stone with imperial and funerary associations, porphyry signaled the wealth, status, and antiquarian tastes of the patron or sitter as well as the portrait's function of preserving his or her image for posterity.[6] The contrast between the sitter's transience and the primordial, immutable nature of stone—and the particularly enduring quality of porphyry—served as a form of memento mori, a theme often depicted allegorically on portrait reverses.
AMN

SELECTED REFERENCES: Antonio Mazzotta, cat. 32, in Sallay et al. 2009, pp. 186–87; Angelini 2012, pp. 134 fig. 7, 137, 142; Mazzotta 2012, p. 150, fig. 1A; Eveline Baseggio Omiccioli, "A New Interpretation of Jacometto's 'Most Perfect Work': Parallels in Portraits by Giovanni Bellini and Leonardo da Vinci," in Wilson 2015, pp. 143, 148 fig. 5; Mazzotta 2017, p. 75.

Verso, cat. 19

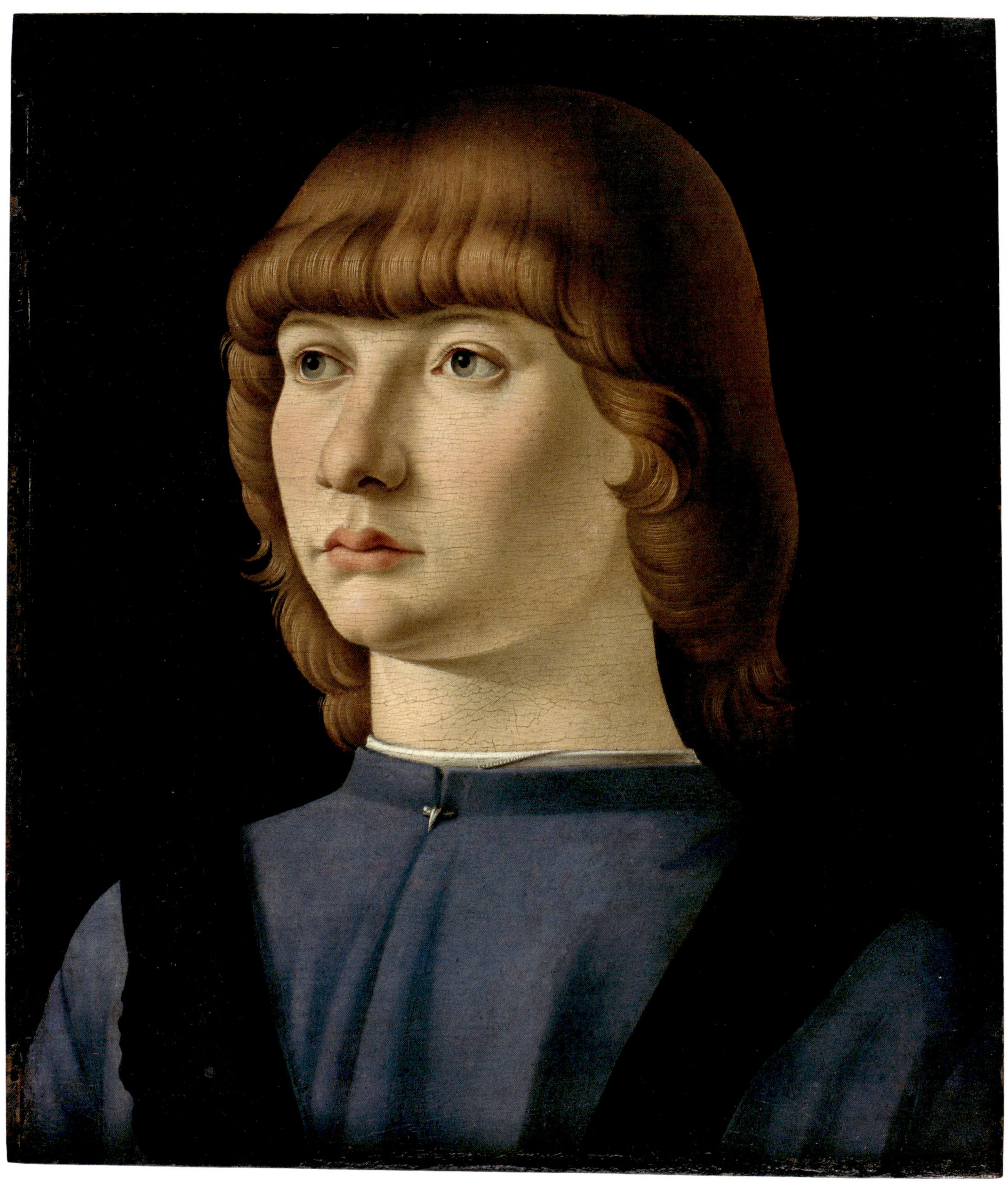

CAT. 20A

JACOMETTO VENEZIANO

Italian, active by ca. 1472–before 1498
A Tethered Roebuck (recto); *Alvise Contarini* (verso), ca. 1485–95

Oil on wood panel, 4⅝ × 3⅜ in. (11.7 × 8.6 cm)
Inscribed, in Greek (on recto): *AIEI* (Forever)
The Metropolitan Museum of Art, New York, Robert Lehman Collection, 1975 (1975.1.86)

CAT. 20B

JACOMETTO VENEZIANO

Portrait of a Woman (Daria Querini?) (recto); *Orpheus and Charon* (verso), ca. 1485–95

Oil on wood panel, 4 × 2⅞ in. (10.2 × 7.3 cm)
The Metropolitan Museum of Art, New York, Robert Lehman Collection, 1975 (1975.1.85)

THIS PAIR OF DIMINUTIVE double-sided portraits was described in 1543 by the Venetian connoisseur Marcantonio Michiel in his *Notizie d'opere del disegno*, a seminal source on private art collections throughout northern Italy. Providing invaluable details about the portraits' authorship, sitters, original covered structure, and protective case, he noted, "There is a little portrait of M(esser) Alvixe Contarini, son of M(esser) . . . who died some years ago, and a portrait across from it on the same panel of a nun of San Secondo, and on the cover of these portraits a little deer in a landscape, while its leather case has foliage of stamped gold. This most perfect work is by the hand of Jacometto."[1] Michiel viewed these works in the residence of the collector Michele Contarini, who, like Alvise, the portrait sitter, and Taddeo Contarini, Giorgione's patron, belonged to the same branch of the powerful Venetian family.[2]

Discrepancies in the size and preparation of the two panels (now separated) suggest that they were not originally joined as a diptych but were fitted into a boxlike structure with a sliding cover.[3] According to Michiel, the deer appeared on the lid's exterior, meaning that Alvise's image occupied its underside, and the panel's unpainted (lower) edge served as a handle, reflecting the design of other sliding portrait covers (see cat. 27B). The female portrait appeared face up on the box's interior, while the grisaille scene on its reverse formed the bottom exterior. Jacometto's box belongs to a tradition of integrating painted, illuminated, and carved portraits within encasements of various sizes, media, and functions (see cats. 44–49); however, these panels represent a unique extant example of such a complex decorative scheme.[4]

New interpretations regarding the imagery on the reverses of the two portraits propose that Jacometto's box, like the cabinet of Angelo Probi painted around 1474 by Giovanni Bellini (see "Uncovering Renaissance Portraits" in this volume), was commissioned in a funerary context, probably by Alvise Contarini as the bereaved widower of Daria Querini, whom he married in 1481 and who appears here as his painted companion.[5] Michiel's (potentially mistaken) identification of the female sitter as a nun is difficult to reconcile with her low neckline, prompting proposals that she is Alvise's wife, platonic muse, or widow-turned-tertiary.[6]

The key to resolving many questions surrounding the Lehman panels is the abraded and previously unidentified grisaille scene painted on the female portrait's reverse. The figure seated on the ground represents Orpheus playing a stringed instrument, echoing the lute player's pose in Cornelis Cort's allegory *Hearing* (1561, National Gallery of Art, Washington, D.C.), while Charon, the ferryman of the River Styx, is faintly visible standing in a gondola (fig. 38).[7] The composition recalls that of an early sixteenth-century maiolica plate by Nicola da Urbino (fig. 39).[8]

In book 10 of Ovid's *Metamorphoses*, the anguished Orpheus, unable to retrieve his wife, Eurydice, from the underworld, pleads with Charon to grant him access a second time, singing of his despair on the banks of the River Styx: "Orpheus wanted to cross the Styx for a second time, / but his pleas were in vain and the ferryman pushed him away from the bank. / So he sat there in rags for a week, without eating a morsel of food; / his anguish, his grief and his tears were all that kept him alive."[9] Ovid's account of the following episode, in which Orpheus's music enchants a deer with "a collar . . . resting his weary limbs on the grassy turf," probably inspired the reclining roebuck on the reverse of Alvise's portrait.[10] This animal was also a traditional symbol of love, fidelity, and Christian salvation in sources

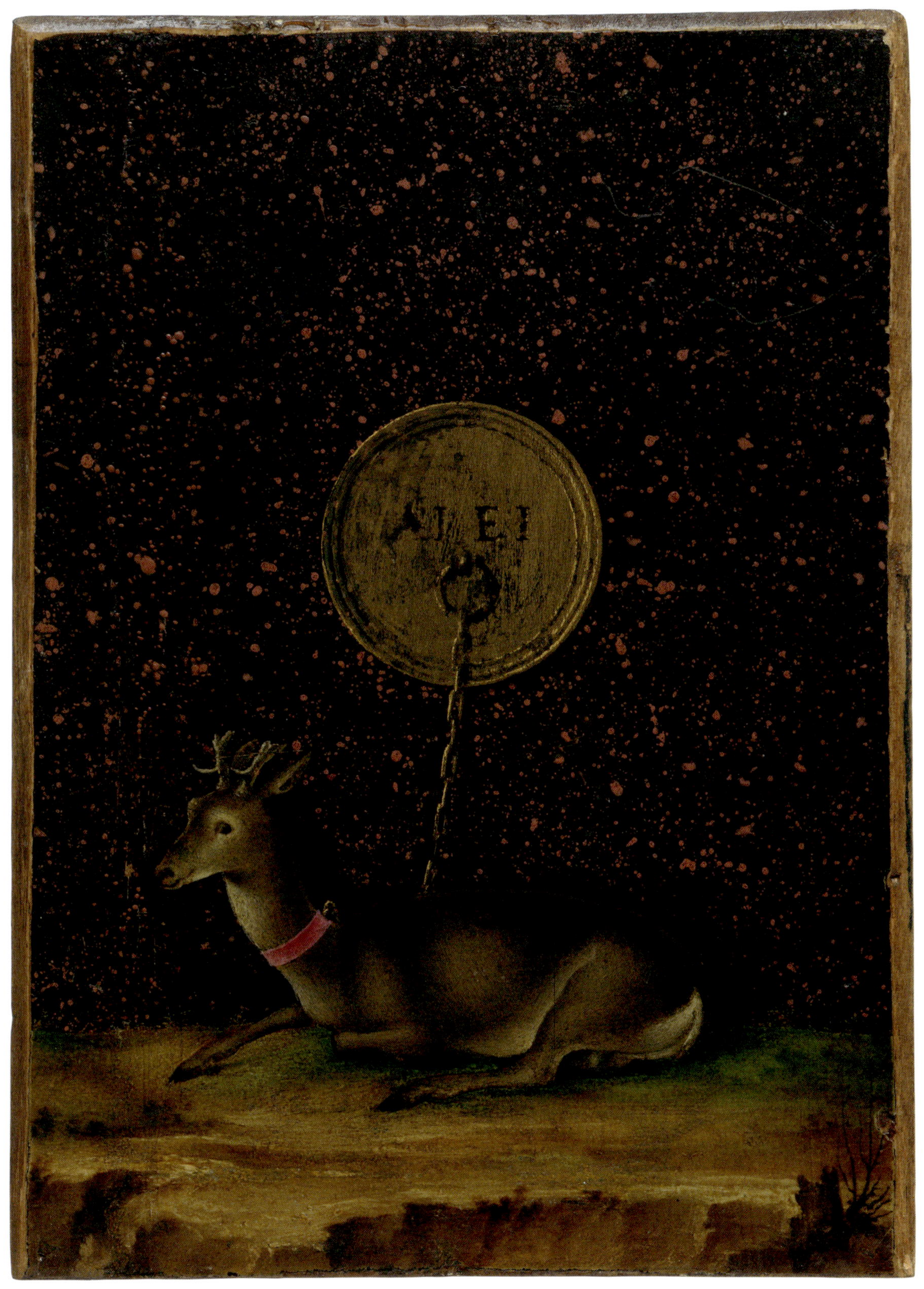
AIEI

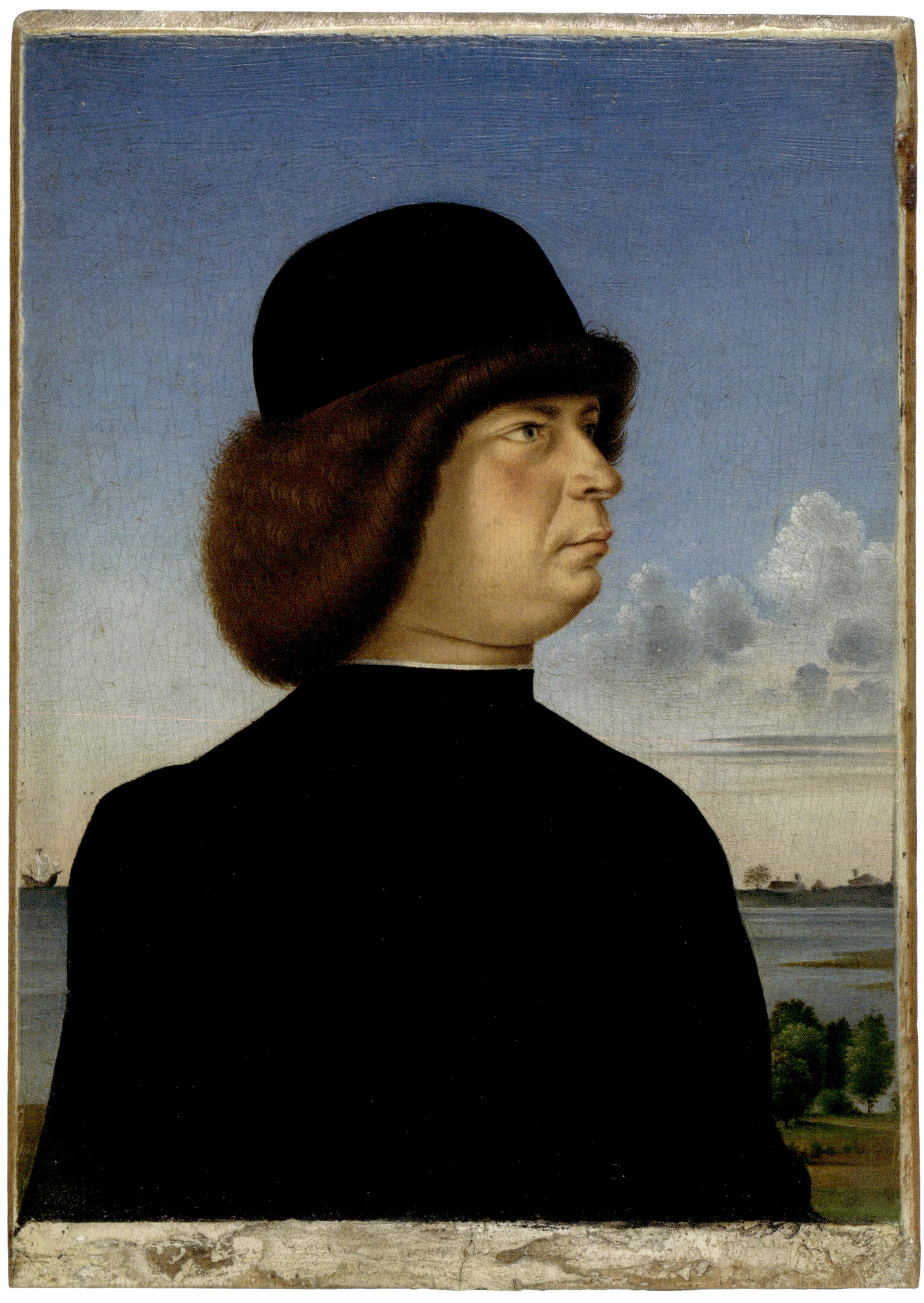

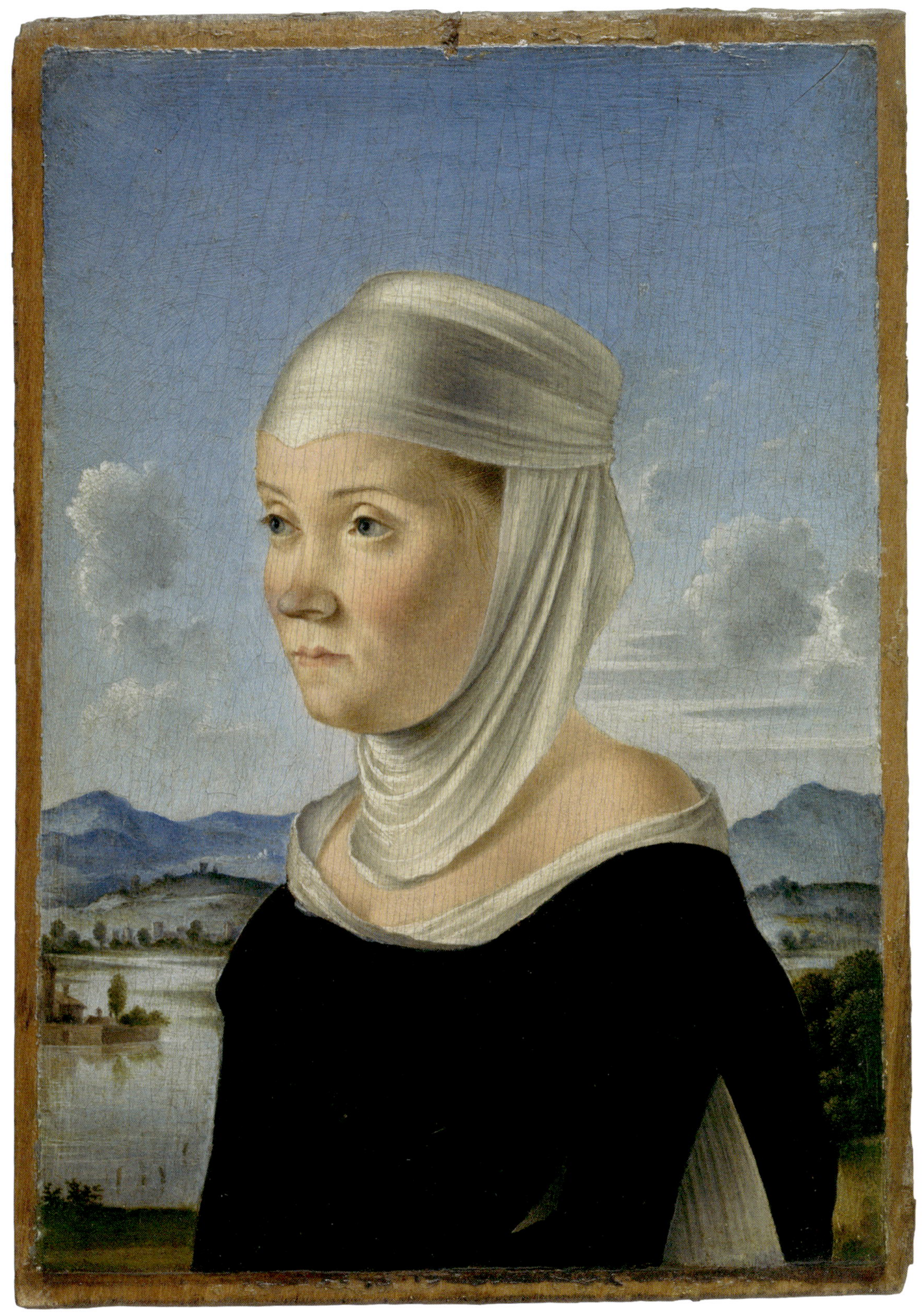

ranging from the Song of Solomon to chivalric romances and love poetry, including, above all, Petrarch's sonnets.[11]

Deer frequently appeared in heraldic devices and imprese (see fig. 15 and cat. 21), a genre that employed various types of wordplay.[12] The inscription *AIEI* (meaning "forever" in Greek), carved in the roundel chained to a slab of porphyry—a durable stone with funerary associations—seems to function as an epitaph on various levels.[13] The uneven spacing of the four letters, with a marked gap between *AI* and *EI*, separates them into two distinct pairs, like initials, following a visual and literary tradition of wordplays on personal names.[14] Similar to a telestich, the four letters represent not the first but the last letters of the sitters' two names (Daria Querini and Alvise Contarini), so that the couple are, metaphorically, forever bound through the inscription's dual meanings. Together with the accompanying image of Orpheus grieving Eurydice's death, the stone slab represents Daria's tomb, to which the deer, symbolizing Alvise, is eternally devoted.[15] Through the figure of Orpheus, Alvise proclaimed himself not only as a bereaved husband but also as a cultured lover of music and poetry.

Upon Alvise's death, the portrait box may have passed to his son Marco or his cousin Pietro, and then, in 1527, to the latter's son Michele Contarini, in whose residence Michiel saw it in 1543.[16] The portraits were among the works given in 1550 by Michele Contarini to the renowned collector Gabriele Vendramin, who also owned dozens of covered portraits by Venetian masters (see cat. 33) as well as a grisaille portrait by Jacometto.[17]

AMN

SELECTED REFERENCES: Pope-Hennessy 1987, cats. 96, 97, pp. 240-43; Dülberg 1990, pp. 36, 236–37 nos. 183, 184, pls. 30–34 figs. 75–80; D. Brown 2001, cat. 19, pp. 154–57; Lucco 2006, cats. 69, 70, pp. 334–35; Nancy Edwards, cats. 123a, 123b, in Bayer 2008, pp. 265–68; Bolzoni 2010, pp. 267–70; Andrea Bayer, cats. 152a, 152b, in Christiansen and Weppelmann 2011, pp. 346–49; Whistler 2012, pp. 229, 231 fig. 6, 232 fig. 6v; Evelyn Baseggio Omiccioli, "A New Interpretation of Jacometto's 'Most Perfect Work': Parallels in Portraits by Giovanni Bellini and Leonardo da Vinci," in Wilson 2015, pp. 143–67; Nogueira forthcoming.

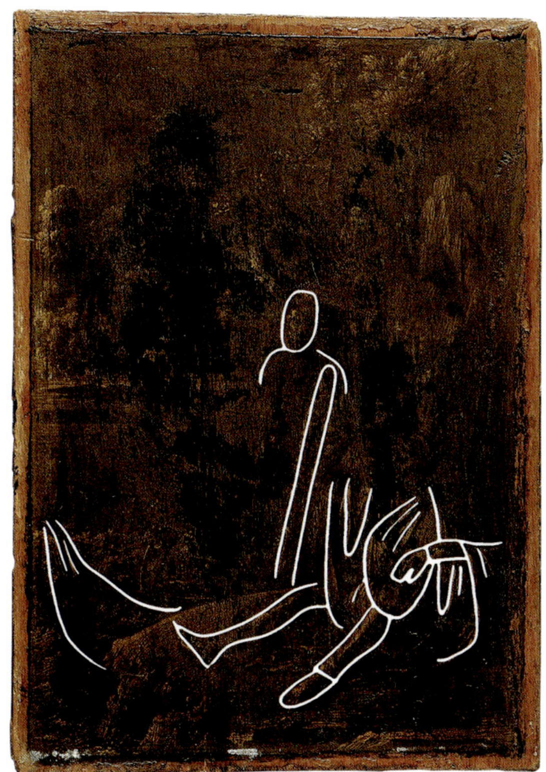

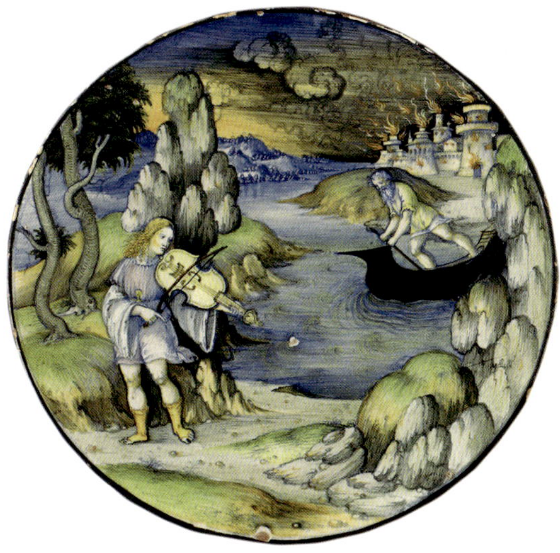

Fig. 38. Rendering of figural outlines in Jacometto Veneziano's *Orpheus and Charon* (reverse of cat. 20B)

Fig. 39. Nicola da Urbino (Italian, ca. 1480–1537/38). Plate with *Orpheus and Charon*, ca. 1515. Maiolica, Diam. 11 1/16 in. (28.2 cm). Museo Correr, Venice (Cl. IV N. 13)

CAT. 21

GABRIELE SYMEONI

Italian, 1509–1575
"Esto tiene su remedio y non yo"
("This Has Its Remedy, I Do Not"), 1574

From *Le imprese heroiche et morali*, fol. 198; published by Guillaume Rouille, Lyon, 1574

Text in letterpress, woodcut illustrations, 7 5/16 × 4 15/16 in. (18.5 × 12.5 cm)

The Metropolitan Museum of Art, New York, Museum Accession, transferred from the Library (21.36.6)

FROM 1543, the merchant-publisher Guillaume Rouille was based in Lyon, an important junction of trade routes to nearby Switzerland, Italy, and Spain. Accordingly, he invested in publications by authors of various nationalities, offering editions in French, Italian, Latin, and Spanish.[1] In 1549, for example, Rouille published a new French commentary on Andrea Alciato's popular emblems (cat. 34) as well as its first translation into Spanish. Ten years later, in 1559, he jointly published two related books containing imprese, one composed by the Italian scholars Paolo Giovio (see cat. 6) and Lodovico Domenichi, the other by Gabriele Symeoni. The latter's *Le imprese heroiche et morali* (*Heroic and Moral Imprese*) appears to have been conceived for Rouille as a direct response to the collection of imprese of important historical and contemporaneous figures found in Giovio and Domenichi's *Dialogo dell'imprese militari et amorose* (*Dialogue on Military and Amorous Imprese*).

An impresa consists of a symbolic image combined with a motto, but unlike Alciato's emblems, it does not include an explanatory verse. The device was widely taken up as a means of self-expression and could be embroidered onto clothing and flags or otherwise applied to decorate one's residence and belongings.[2] In the *Dialogo*, Giovio offered guidelines for the successful formulation of an impresa. He argued for a good balance between image and motto. The meaning should not be too difficult to understand, nor be too easily deciphered. Accordingly, he suggested presenting the motto in a foreign language, and keeping it concise. The imagery could be made compelling through the inclusion of strange animals, natural elements, or mechanical instruments, while avoiding the human figure.[3]

The authors of both books further underscored the inherently personal nature of the impresa, suggesting that beyond a simple means of identification, the chosen imagery and words should grant access to the very core of one's being. Symeoni, in particular, emphasized this point. His introduction opened by invoking Saint Augustine's statement that nothing is more difficult than to truly come to know the wishes, thoughts, and spirit of another person. As a remedy, Symeoni advised not to trust in words or actions but, instead, to pay attention to the way someone dresses and to closely study his or her chosen impresa because, with it, "naturally, anyone would seek to demonstrate and evoke a reaction to that which they carry in their heart."[4]

This impresa underscores Symeoni's sentiment. It consists of a deer, wounded by an arrow while chewing on the aphrodisiacal herb dittany of Crete, paired with the phrase "This Has Its Remedy, I Do Not," written in Spanish per Giovio's instructions. According to Symeoni, the impresa was designed by a lovesick man who wished to demonstrate to his lady that his love for her was an affliction that could not be cured.[5] A comparison with the imagery on the reverse of Jacometto's portrait of Alvise Contarini (cat. 20A) emphasizes that the meanings of imprese were often hidden in the details. Each composition shows a deer to signify the concept of love, but the precise condition—love for a deceased partner versus a vow to a living, possibly unrequited love—is revealed through the context in which it is depicted. These images therefore required close reading and foreknowledge of iconographic details, which explains why books like this edition by Rouille became popular items in early modern humanist libraries across Europe.

FS

SELECTED REFERENCES: Grässe 1859–69, vol. 3 pp. 490–91, vol. 6 pp. 408–9; Brunet 1860–65, vol. 3 cols. 582–84, vol. 5 cols. 392–93; Brun 1930, p. 304; Landwehr 1976, no. 345, p. 98; Adams et al. 1999–2002, vol. 1, no. F.270, pp. 518–20.

mente à nostri tempi M. Antonio da Prato gran Cancelliere e Legato di Francia.

VN' AMICO INNAMORATO.

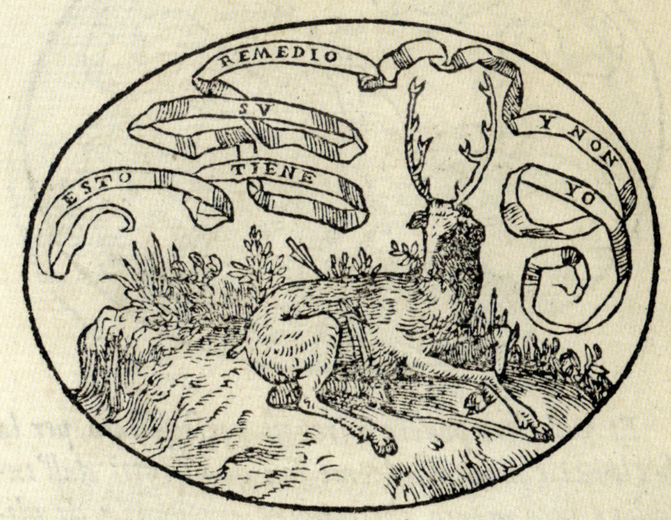

Vn' altr' Amico mi contò vn giorno d'vna impresa, che vn' innamorato haueua fatta per vna sua Dama, la quale era, volendo mostrare che'l suo male era senza rimedio, vn Ceruio ferito d'vna freccia con vna herba in bocca chiamata Dittamo, che nasce abondantemente nell' Isola di Candia, con la quale il Ceruio mangiandola si guarisce, e le parole dell' impresa eran tali, ESTO TIENE SV REMEDIO Y NON YO. imitando in questo quel verso d' Ouidio nelle Metamorfosi in persona

CAT. 22

UNKNOWN MAKER

Italian

Book Box, 15th century

Tooled leather, 6 × 6½ × 2¾ in. (15 × 16.5 × 6.8 cm)

The Metropolitan Museum of Art, New York, Rogers Fund, 1951 (51.116a, b)

THIS WELL-PRESERVED leather box was once used as a protective carrying case for a small book. Tooled leather was an attractive option for such cases, as it was durable, relatively inexpensive, and easily decorated. Holes in the attachments on either side suggest it may have had straps to secure the lid and to allow the book to be easily carried and perhaps worn against the body on journeys. This arrangement echoes the practice of Christian missionaries who carried Gospel Books across vast distances in the early Middle Ages. It also recalls the activities of mendicant preachers from the thirteenth century onward, when the production of single-volume Bibles in small script greatly increased the portability of the sacred text.[1] Although few early book boxes survive, several are known from the fifteenth century, during which flourishing urban workshops combined with the rise of the printing press to allow for books to be produced in greater numbers.[2]

A large, blank escutcheon surrounded by flowers on swirling, leafy vines decorates either side of the box. Although these plant motifs are too generic to identify the type of book once kept in the box, similar floral designs adorn the margins of many late medieval books, with contents ranging from prayers to poetry. It is likewise impossible to know if the escutcheons were once painted with the coat of arms of a specific patron; it is also quite likely that they were left blank and simply used as a popular design motif denoting luxury in a generalized sense. Nevertheless, even if the box betrays very little sense of its original contents or intended owner, it survives as a touching reflection of the personal commodities of its time.

Books, like various types of devotional works and painted portraits, were carried by their owners on their travels, whether locally or internationally. According to a sixteenth-century source, Jacometto's diminutive pair of painted portraits (cat. 20A,B), which were originally joined in the form of a box, originally had a tooled leather carrying case that probably resembled the present box.[3] Nicolas Froment's diptych bearing portraits of René d'Anjou and Jeanne de Laval was transported in a velvet bag (cat. 12C), while the miniature wax portrait of Paulus Praun had a leather pouch (cat. 51C). Carrying cases protected these precious belongings and made them easier to keep close at hand, whether for frequent use or simply as reminders of the importance of their contents.

SF

SELECTED REFERENCES: unpublished.

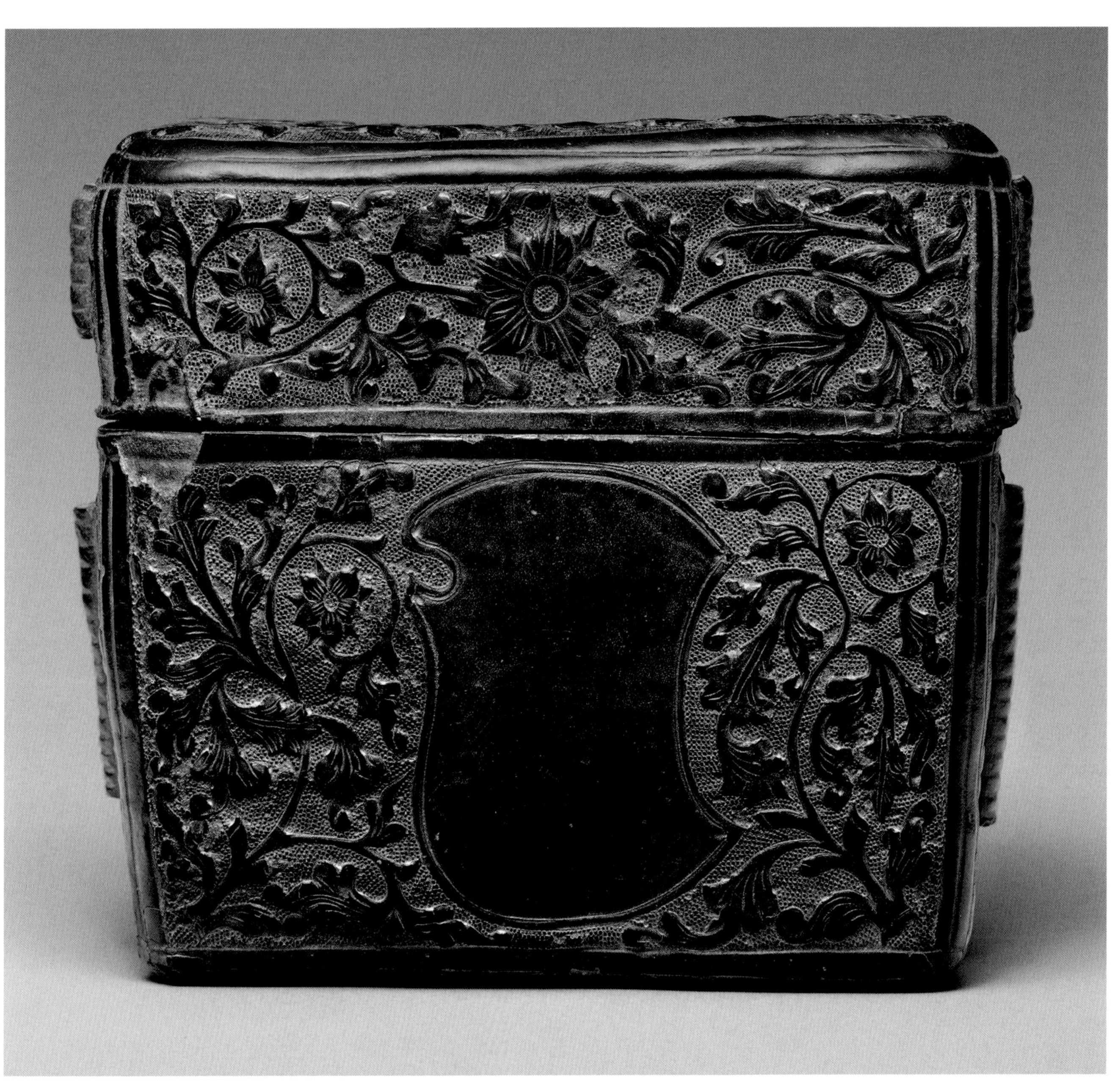

CAT. 23

JACOMETTO VENEZIANO

Italian, active by ca. 1472–before 1498
Portrait of a Man (possibly Pietro Bembo) (recto);
Inscription with a Verse by Horace and Tied Laurel Branches (verso), mid-1490s

Tempera and oil on wood panel, 10¼ × 7½ in. (26 × 19 cm)

Inscribed (on verso): *Felices ter et amplius / quos / irrupta tenet copula* (Happy three times and more are those for whom love holds unbroken bonds)

The National Gallery, London, Layard Bequest, 1916 (NG3121)

THE ESTEEMED VENETIAN scholar and diplomat Bernardo Bembo was among the humanist patrons who collected portraits, illuminations, and other small-scale works by the late fifteenth-century master Jacometto Veneziano (see cats. 19 and 20A,B). The artist was commissioned by Bernardo to paint the portraits (now lost) of his two young sons: one of the infant Carlo in 1472, and the other of his elder son, Pietro, in 1481, at the age of eleven.[1] In the 1490s, Pietro Bembo would establish himself as a distinguished humanist, poet, and philologist, composing *Gli asolani* (*The People of Asolo,* 1505), a vernacular dialogue on platonic love dedicated to his lover, Lucrezia Borgia.

Celebrated in later stages of life as a papal secretary, historian, patron, and cardinal, Pietro was the subject of numerous portraits, including two by Titian (figs. 40 and 41), who captured his highly distinctive aquiline nose, pointing sharply downward at the tip, large nostrils, and dark, deeply set eyes.[2] It has been previously unnoticed that the same unique facial features (albeit those of a younger, fleshier man) characterize the sitter in the present portrait, which may well represent Pietro portrayed by Jacometto on a second occasion, this time as a man in his twenties. The likeness, probably a late work by the artist (when Antonello da Messina's influence was not as dominant as in the prior decade), could have been painted following Pietro's return to the Veneto from Sicily in 1494.

The identification of the sitter as a scholar and poet is suggested both by his blue garment (*vesta*) and by the reverse of the painting, which bears two crossed laurel branches (symbolizing literary achievement) as well as a verse derived from Horace's *Odes* (1.13), a series of approximately one hundred lyric poems written by the Roman author in the first century BCE.[3] That Pietro was intimately familiar and engaged with the *Odes* is evidenced by his marginal notations in two manuscript copies of Horace's literary works commissioned by his father in the 1470s and 1480s, which both contain marginal annotations by father and son (although not on *Ode* 1.13 specifically).[4] Further connecting the portrait's reverse with the Bembo family is a later Horatian manuscript, datable around 1485, which has an illuminated frontispiece bearing Bernardo's motto (*Virtus et honore*) and impresa (the laurel and palm branches).[5] The two crossed and knotted laurel branches on the reverse of the London panel simultaneously call to mind Bernardo's similar emblem and equate Pietro's poetic triumphs with those of Horace. Yet the other symbolic meanings of laurel—as an allusion to eternal and unrequited love—also relate specifically to the amorous poem quoted in the inscription and the function of the portrait.

Horace's verse "Felices ter et amplius / quos irrupta tenet copula" (Happy three times and more are those for whom love holds unbroken bonds) occurs in the last stanza of a poem in which the poet, ensnared in a love triangle, attempts to convince his beloved that the enduring love he offers is more desirable than the erratic affections of his rival.[6] The verse has been interpreted as a reference to conjugal fidelity, and the painting's function as a nuptial portrait.[7] However, when considered within the overall context of Horace's poem, it clearly expresses the passionate plea of a jealous lover.

Pietro may have commissioned the portrait in the mid-1490s as a gift for his beloved Costanza Fregoso, whom he lauded in a poem with distinct parallels to the verse and the knotted branches on the panel's reverse: "Let nothing proceed any longer as was wont / Since the knot has been loosened with which was held / [That] which nothing but death ought to have undone."[8] According to Mauro Lucco, Raphael painted a portrait of Costanza for Bembo in 1507–8, when the two reignited their relationship; in exchange for that portrait, Costanza received a likeness of the humanist.[9] Following a well-established tradition canonized by Petrarch, Bembo exchanged portraits (now lost) with lovers on two other occasions: with Maria Savorgnan, whose portrait was

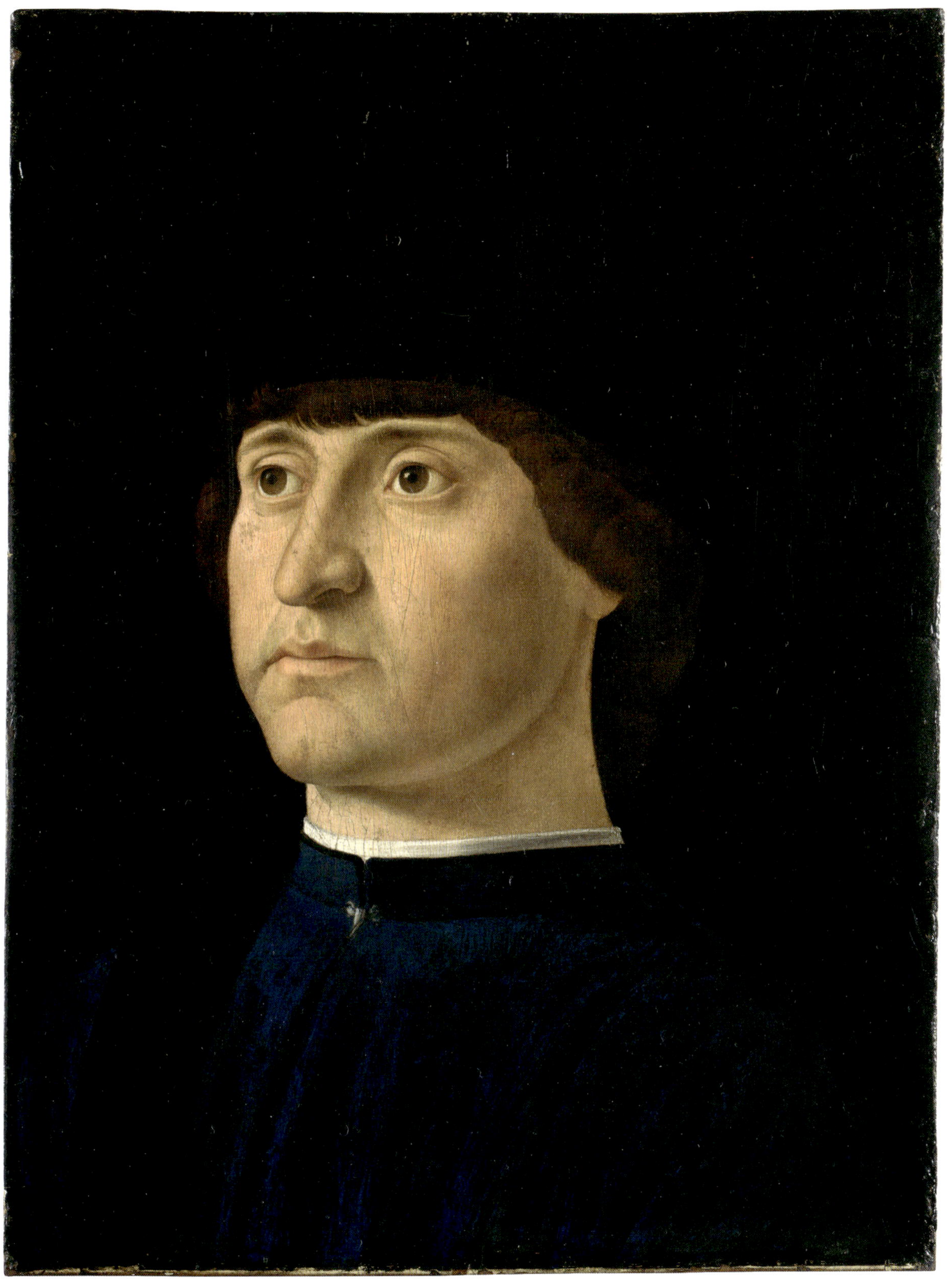

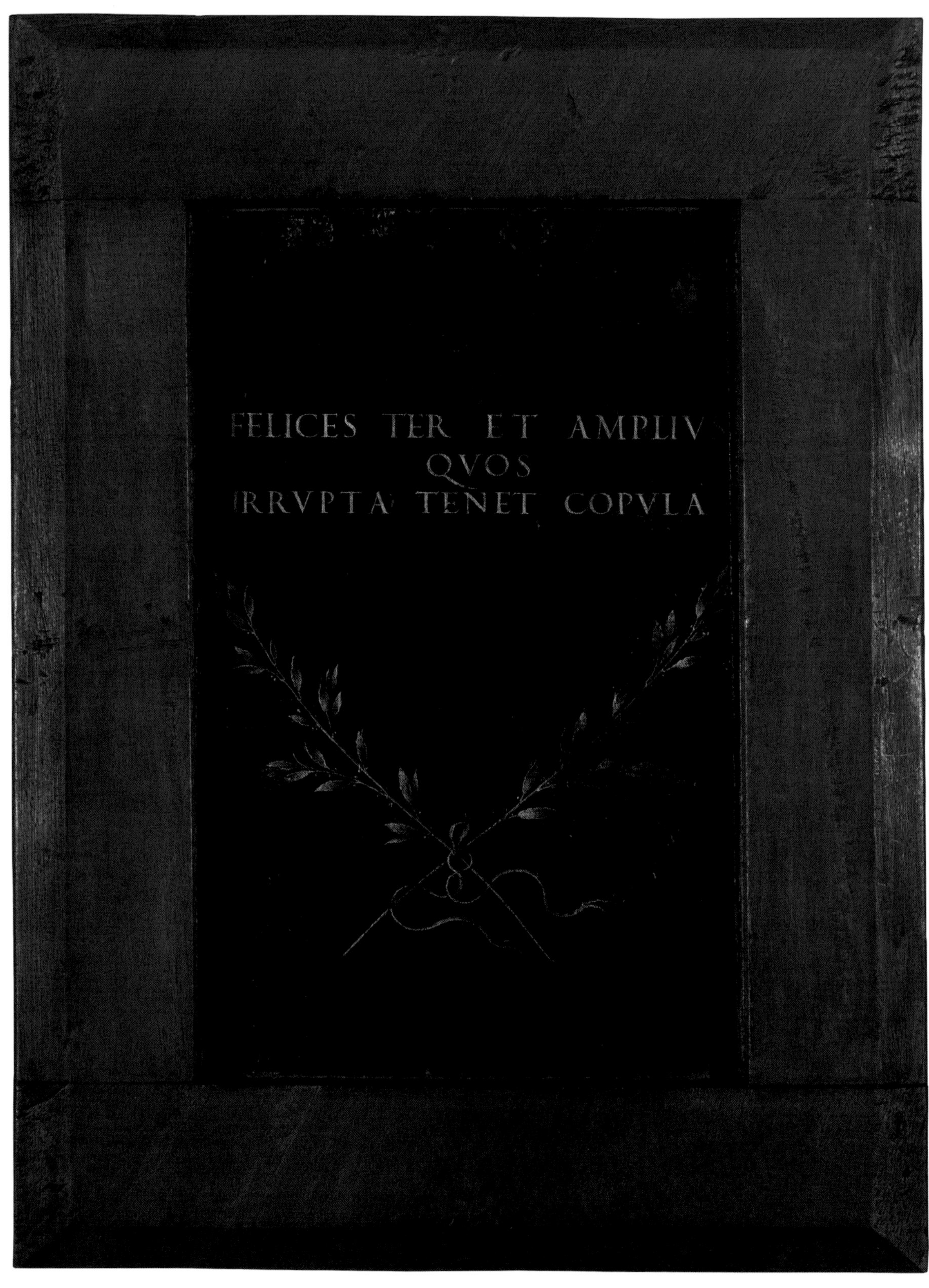
FELICES TER ET AMPLIVS
QVOS
IRRVPTA TENET COPVLA

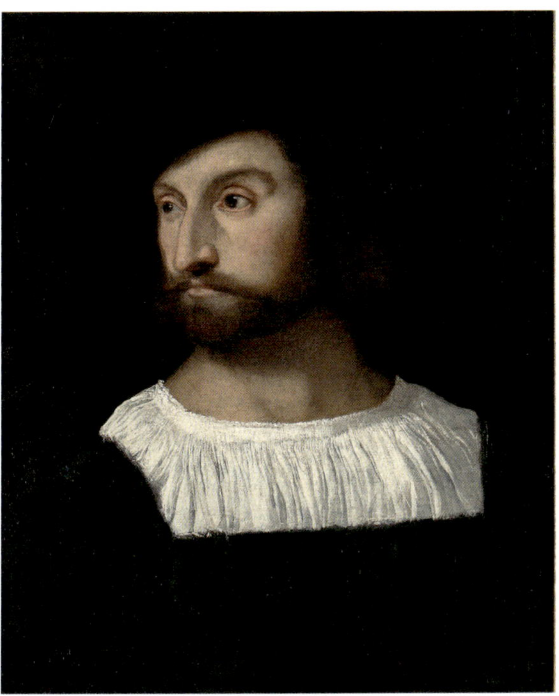

Fig. 40. Attributed to Titian (Tiziano Vecellio; Italian, 1485/90?–1576). *Pietro Bembo*, 1515/20. Oil on canvas, 23⅝ × 18¼ in. (60 × 46.2 cm). Musée des Beaux-Arts et d'Archéologie, Besançon (896.1.327)

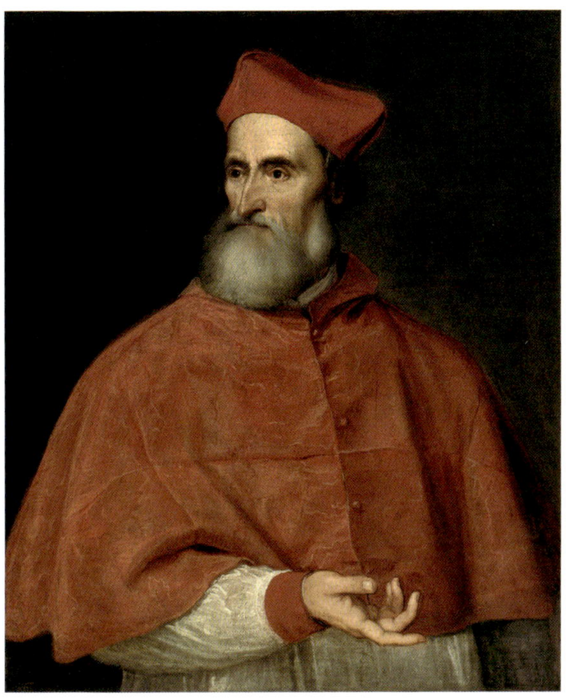

Fig. 41. Titian. *Cardinal Pietro Bembo*, 1539–40. Oil on canvas, 37¼ × 30⅛ in. (94.5 × 76.5 cm). National Gallery of Art, Washington, D.C., Samuel H. Kress Collection (1952.5.28)

painted in 1500 by Giovanni Bellini, and with Elisabetta Querini, whose image Titian captured in 1543. A portrait of Querini by Titian (either the copy made for Bembo or another version) originally had a cover depicting the Triumph of Love (cat. 33).[10]

Given Jacometto's documented history as a portraitist for the Bembo family and the similarity of the sitter's distinctive features to those of Pietro Bembo, who owned and annotated two copies of Horace's literary works and repeatedly exchanged portraits as amorous gifts, it is plausible that the London portrait was commissioned by the poet to win his beloved's affection. The reverse of the portrait, with its classicizing laurel branches and Roman majuscule script (see cat. 24) for the Horatian verse, closely recalls ancient numismatic models and thus embodies Bembo's humanist ideals.

AMN

SELECTED REFERENCES: Dülberg 1990, pp. 38–39, 88, 111, 131, 228 no. 168, pls. 54, 55 figs. 121–23; Dunkerton et al. 1991, pp. 100, 102 figs. 133, 134; D. Brown 2001, cat. 20, pp. 158–59; Angelini 2012, pp. 137 fig. 10, 140, 142; Sergio Momesso, cat. 37, in Beltramini and Gasparotto 2016, 235–37, 240; Eveline Baseggio Omiccioli, "A New Interpretation of Jacometto's 'Most Perfect Work': Parallels in Portraits by Giovanni Bellini and Leonardo da Vinci," in Wilson 2015, pp. 143, 150 figs. 8, 9; Mazzotta 2017, pp. 75, 76 fig. 11, 78, 82, 85 fig. 24.

CAT. 24

CIRCLE OF JACOMETTO VENEZIANO

Jacometto: Italian, active by ca. 1472–before 1498
Portrait of a Lady (recto); *Pseudo-marble with Inscription* (verso), 1470s

Oil on panel, 13⅜ × 10⅞ in. (34 × 27.5 cm)

Inscribed (on verso): *V LLLL F / DELITIIS ANIMUM / EXPLE / POST MORTEM / NULLA VOLUP / TAS* (V LLLL F Satisfy the soul with delights[,] for after death there is no pleasure)

Philadelphia Museum of Art, John G. Johnson Collection, 1917 (243)

THIS UNCOMPROMISING female portrait shares certain features with the works of the late fifteenth-century Venetian artist Jacometto, both in the sitter's headdress and the panel's fictive marble reverse, inscribed in Latin with gilded Roman majuscules (see cats. 20A,B and 23). While the panel has been attributed to Jacometto with varying degrees of certainty, stylistically it does not reflect the same crystalline technique and dramatic play of light and shadow that the artist adopted from Antonello da Messina.[1] Instead, it appears closer to the oeuvre traditionally ascribed to Jacopo de' Barbari, a Venetian painter and printmaker whose identity has been conflated with Jacometto's by certain scholars.[2]

The headdress, which hangs down on the right side of the sitter's face and neck, may represent the same wimple-like style depicted in two female portraits by Jacometto (cat. 20B and fig. 42) but portrayed here as yellow (rather than white) and in an undone state. A comparison of the three headdresses reveals that they were worn with vastly different types of garments, ranging from the habit of a Dominican nun (fig. 42) to the present sitter's distinctly secular garb.[3] Moreover, the serpentine extension of the present headdress, resembling a scarf, is conspicuously tucked into this woman's laced bodice, forming a focal point of the image and directing the viewer's gaze toward her décolletage.

According to Elfreide Knauer, the yellow scarf indicates the sitter's status as a prostitute.[4] A Venetian decree of 1421 (still in effect in the late fifteenth century) states, "When the prostitutes who live in some segregated quarters of Venice as well as the procuresses go into the city of Venice, they must wear over their outer garments a yellow scarf slung around their necks in such a way that it is visible and not hidden, under penalty."[5] Diaphanous yellow scarves appear in several early sixteenth-century Venetian portraits, including Titian's *La Bella* (1536, Galleria Palatina, Palazzo Pitti, Florence), where they are woven into the female sitter's blond hair and therefore are much more subtle in appearance.[6]

Knauer argues that the Latin inscription on the panel's reverse further evokes the sitter's compromised moral and social standing, interpreting the acronym of the first line, in the style of ancient Roman dedications, as follows: "V[otum] L[uxuriae] L[icentiae] L[asciviae] L[upa] F[ecit] (The whore dedicated herself to wantonness, license, lewdness)."[7] She asserts that the remaining lines derive from the legendary Greek epigram, known widely in the fifteenth century, on the tomb of Sardanapalus, the Assyrian king infamous for his licentiousness: "Though knowing full well that thou art but mortal, indulge thy desire, find joy in thy feasts. Dead, thou shalt have no delight."[8]

Eveline Baseggio Omiccioli, emphasizing that the inscription adheres to the epicurean nature and dedicatory format of those on Roman funerary stelae, offers another

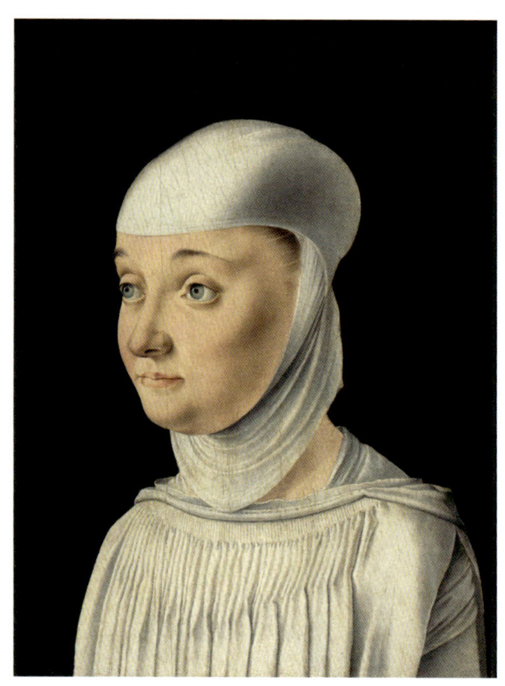

Fig. 42. Jacometto Veneziano. *Portrait of a Woman, Possibly a Novice of San Secondo*, ca. 1490. Oil on wood panel, 9½ × 6⅛ in. (24 × 15.5 cm). Cleveland Museum of Art, Mr. and Mrs. William H. Marlatt Fund (1976.9)

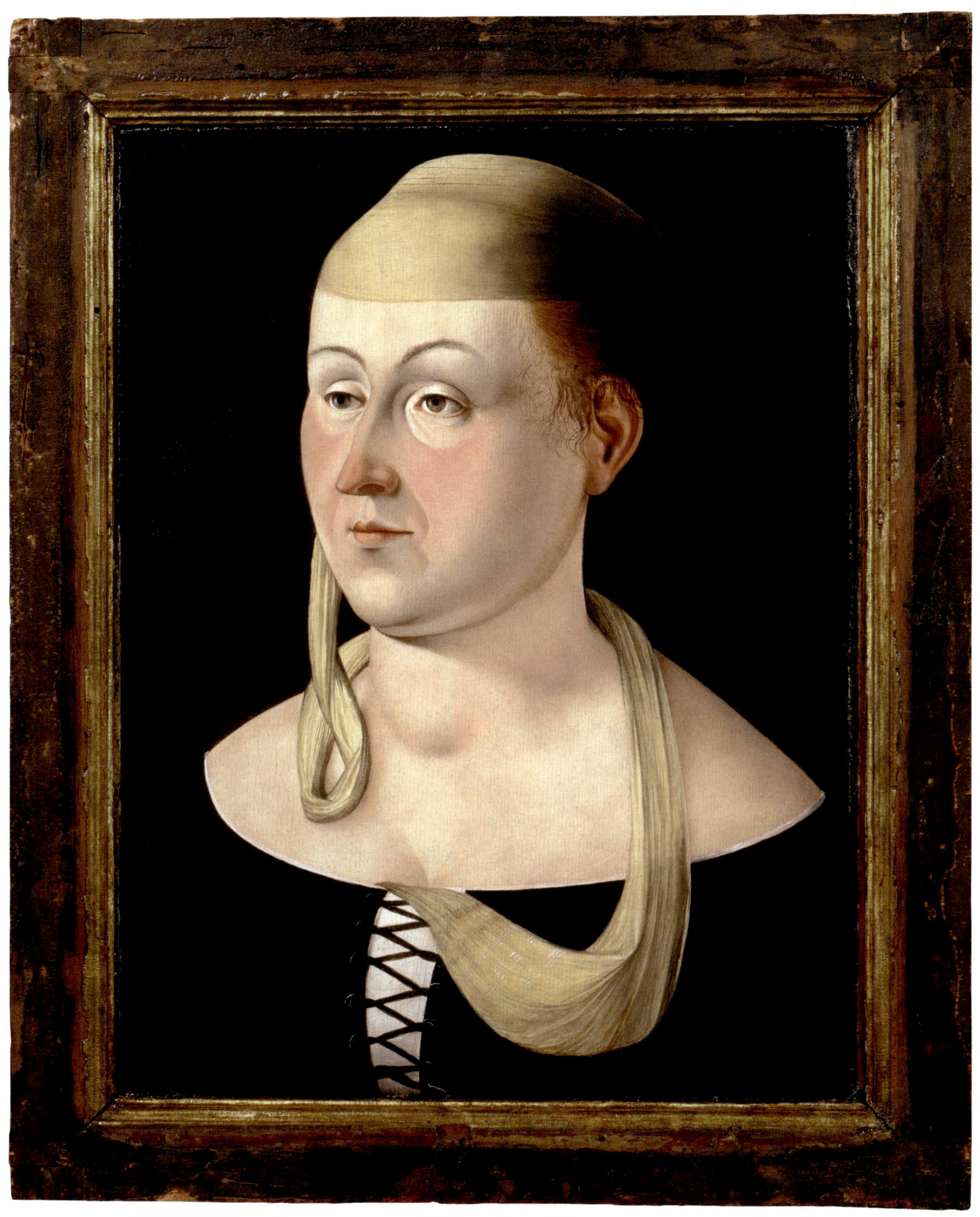

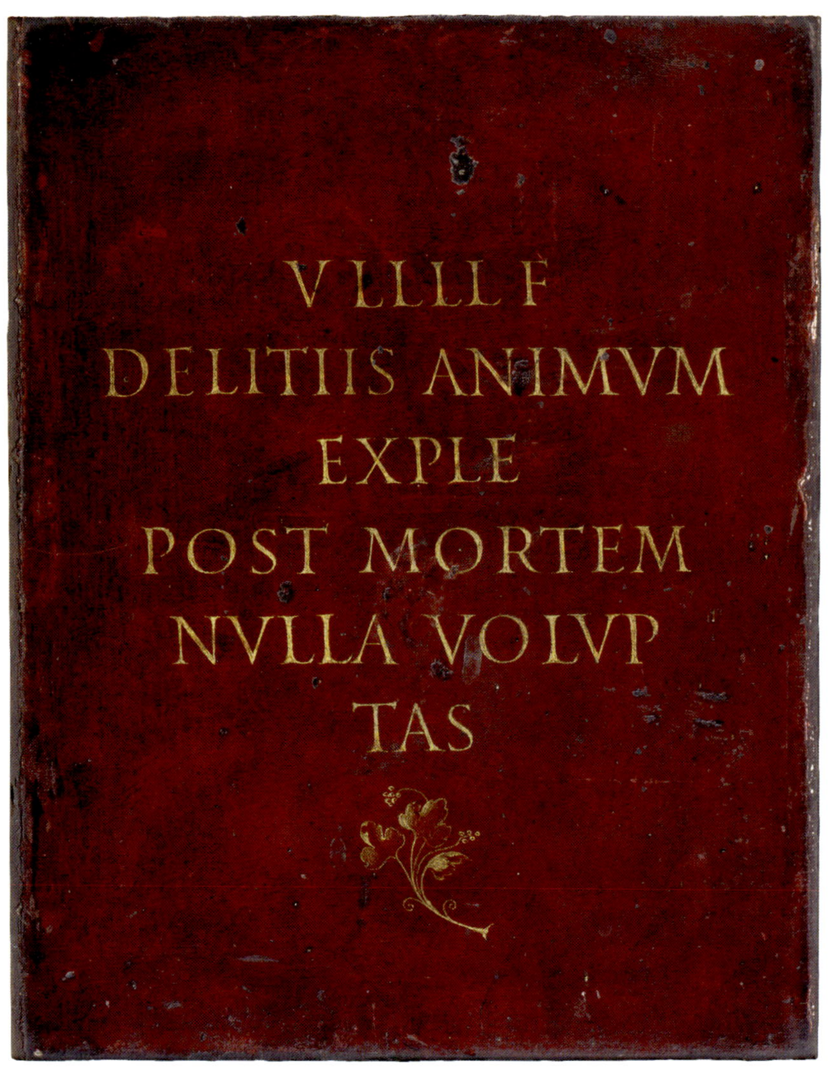

interpretation, *V*[*otum*] *L*[*aetus*] *L*[*ibens*] *L*[first name] *L*[last name] *F*[*ecit*], translated as "He willingly and gladly made a vow to LL."[9] The combination of the Roman majuscule script with the female portrait calls to mind marble funerary stelae that feature the deceased's sculpted effigy with his or her inscribed epitaph.

The Latin abbreviation *V LLLL F* may have held multiple meanings and served as a conversation piece for viewers. Baldassare Castiglione recounts in his *Libro del cortegiano* (*Book of the Courtier*, 1528) that Renaissance patrons and their guests entertained themselves by variously interpreting Latin abbreviations, especially in a malevolent manner.[10]

AMN

SELECTED REFERENCES: Sweeny 1966, no. 243, pp. 39–40; Dülberg 1990, pp. 57–58, 131–32, 153, 228 no. 167, pl. 53 figs. 119, 120; Bernard Aikema and Beverly Louise Brown, cat. 66, in Aikema and Brown 1999, pp. 326–27; D. Brown 2001, cat. 21, pp. 160–61; Knauer 2002; DePrano 2008, pp. 627–29, figs. 6a, 6b; Mazzotta 2012, pp. 152 fig. 4, 155; Eveline Baseggio Omiccioli, "A New Interpretation of Jacometto's 'Most Perfect Work': Parallels in Portraits by Giovanni Bellini and Leonardo da Vinci," in Wilson 2015, pp. 149, 151 figs. 10, 11, 152.

CAT. 25

UNKNOWN ARTIST

Venetian

Portrait of a Man (Giulio Mellini?) (recto); *Allegorical Landscape* (verso), late 15th century

Oil on wood panel, 12⅛ × 9⅛ in. (30.8 × 23 cm), original; 14¼ × 9⅞ in. (36 × 25 cm), with additions at all sides

Musée du Louvre, Paris, Département des Peintures (RF 1345)

THIS IMPOSING double-sided depiction of a young man with a complex landscape on the verso is an important example of the creative expansion of portraiture imagery found in works in Venice and northern Italy during the decades around 1500. The sitter is dressed in a red damask jacket beneath a fur-lined cloak and wears a distinctive red hat recognizable from many works by Vittore Carpaccio (but with a particularly distinctive brim). The long bangs curling from under the cap and the sweep of the hair almost to the shoulder, a style sometimes called a *zazzera*, are features seen in many portraits from the very end of the century. The figure is set behind an illusionistically painted frame—most frequently seen in portraits from northern Europe—whose depth is indicated by highlights suggesting the fall of light, which also illuminates the figure from the left.

An extensive landscape, suggestive of the Venetian lagoon and including a walled group of buildings extending into the water (a once-recognizable church complex?), opens out on the reverse. The foreground is dominated by a marble urn in which an orange tree grows, its trunk supporting two shields, one with a visible coat of arms, the other turned away from the viewer. Two putti lean against the planter, and the surrounding ground is populated by numerous birds and animals, including a peacock, a partridge, rabbits, an ox, and a deer.

The identifications of both the artist and the sitter are still open to debate. The work entered the Louvre in 1902 with an attribution to Vincenzo Catena, but other early authors suggested instead Marco Marziale, who was active in Venice between about 1492 and 1507. Subsequent attributions have widened the field, including, most recently, to Jacometto Veneziano, based on the similarity of the landscape elements of the verso here to those found in his portraits in the Robert Lehman Collection (see cat. 20A,B) and to miniatures believed to be by him.[1] The mobility of the sitter's features and glance, rather unlike the more fixed, smoothly modeled heads of the portraits firmly attributed to Jacometto, casts some doubt on this attractive theory.

From the time of the work's entry into the Louvre, most authors identified the sitter as Giulio Mellini, or, in one case, Pierre-Paul Millini, purportedly on the basis of research done by an unidentified "vicomte d'Agiout," who is cited as having read the coat of arms.[2] The Mellini family had a greater presence farther south on the Italian peninsula, although there was a Venetian branch, which, according to Giovanni Battista di Crollalanza's *Dizionario* of Italian heraldry, had arms divided in two halves, one half including a fleur-de-lis and the other three bands of gold. It is difficult to interpret the arms seen here as containing these elements.[3]

It seems certain that the painting was done to commemorate a betrothal or marriage, either as a freestanding work or part of a diptych now missing the figure of the bride. Many of the details on the reverse have meanings of relevance to marriage and the arrival of children: the oranges as wedding gifts, with allusions to both "chastity" within marriage and fecundity; the rabbits or hares as belonging to the realm of Venus; the long-antlered deer as associated with sensual love; and the marbled urn as a symbol of durability.[4] If the clues were all legible to the viewer, then reading front and back together would provide insight into this patrician sitter's place in the world and his hopes for his marriage. Just a few years later, in an evolution of this approach to representation, the great Venetian artist Lorenzo Lotto would create "covers" for portraits that both complicated the allegory depicted and moved it off the verso, continuing to deepen the possibilities for presenting fundamental narratives about the sitter (see cats. 29B and 30B).

AB

SELECTED REFERENCES: Ricci 1913, no. 1252a, p. 44; Dominique Thiébaut, "XIIIe–XVe Siècle," in Foucart-Walter 2007, p. 57; Angelini 2012, pp. 140–42, figs. 14, 15, 145 fig. 18; Mazzotta 2017, pp. 75, 78, 79 fig. 15, 80 fig. 16.

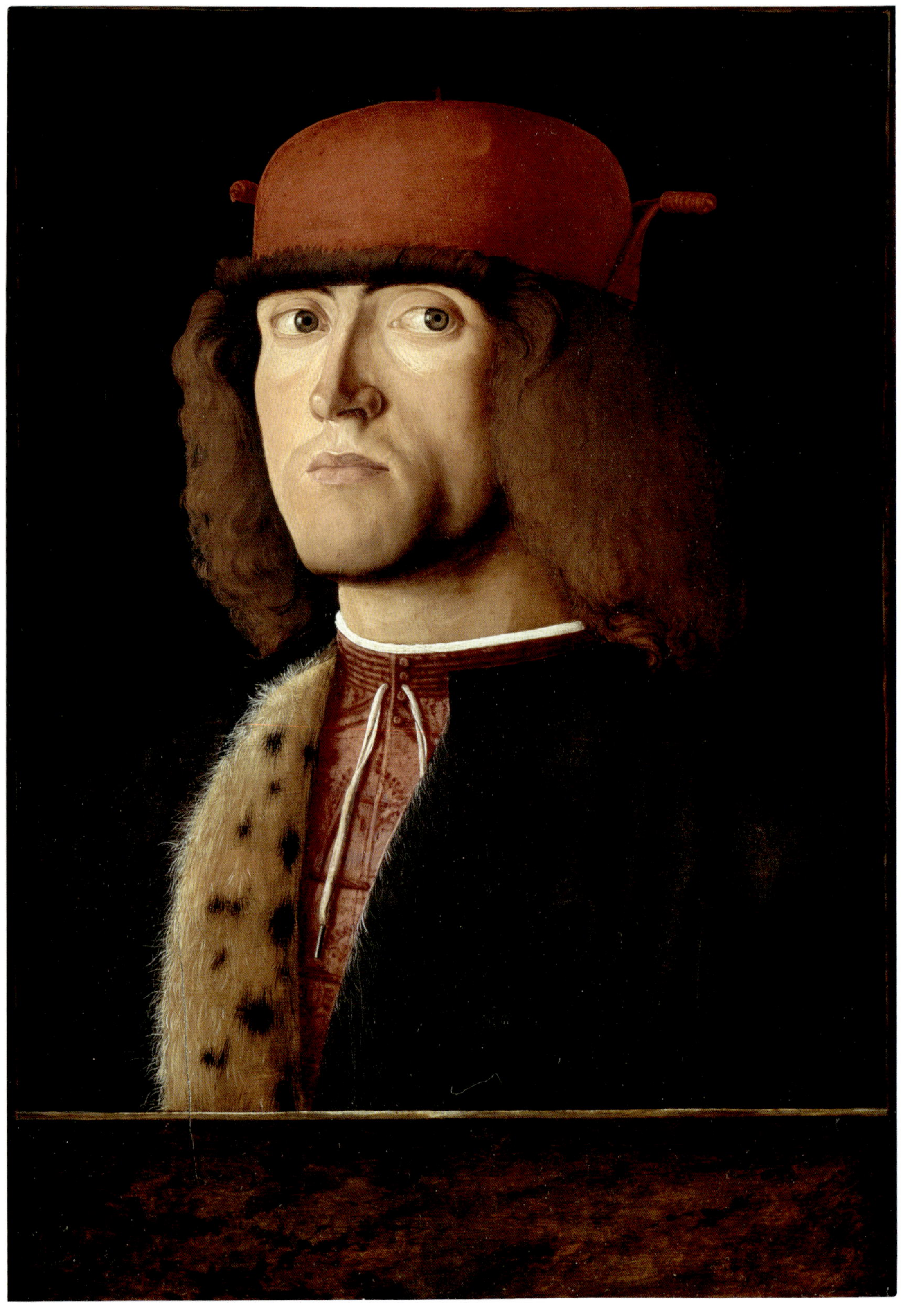

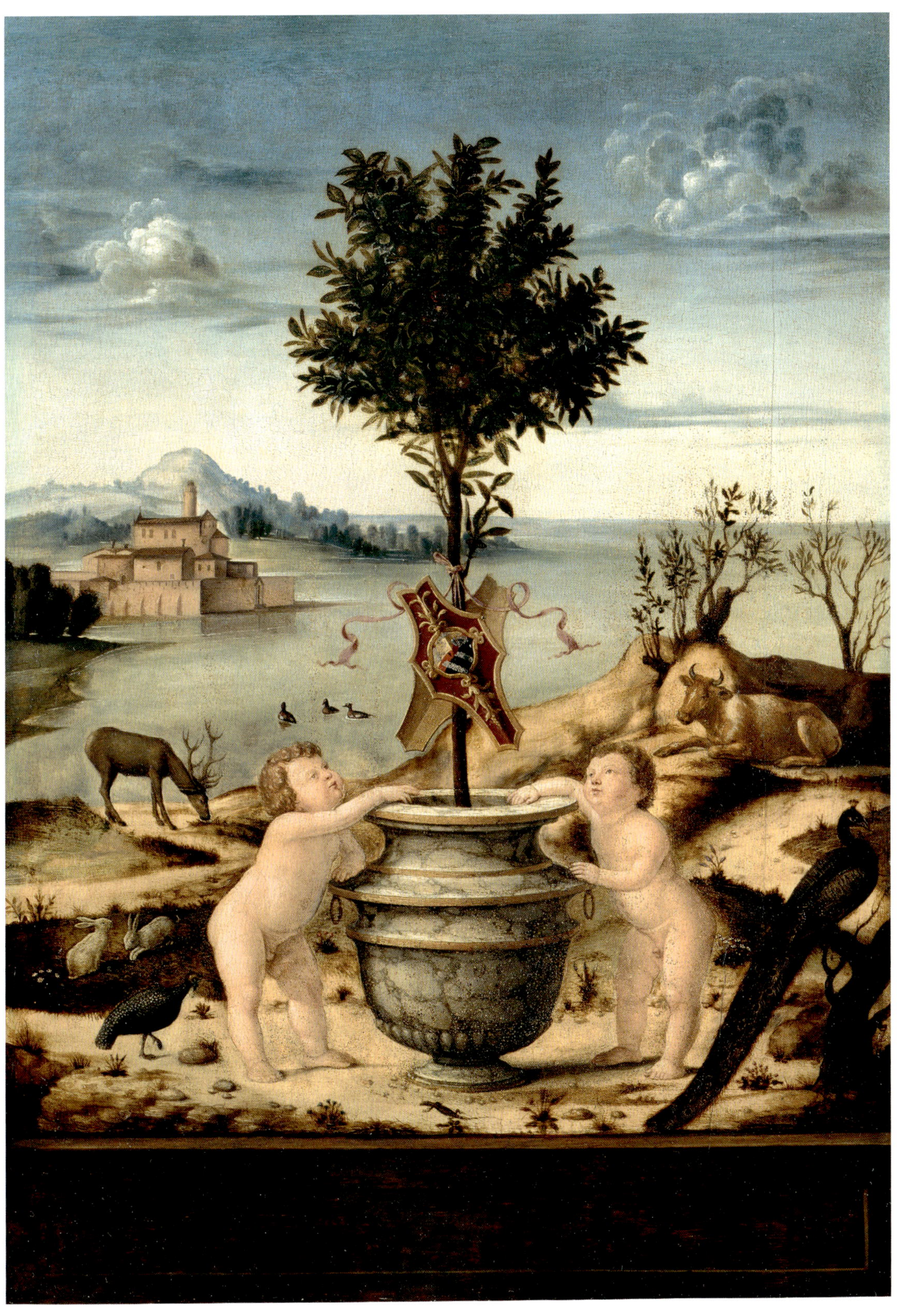

CAT. 26

ATTRIBUTED TO JACOPO DE' BARBARI

Italian, active by 1497–died by 1516
Portrait of a Man ("The German") (recto);
Interior with Two Nudes (verso), ca. 1500

Oil on poplar panel, 23⅞ × 17⅞ in. (60.5 × 45.5 cm)
Staatliche Museen zu Berlin–Preussischer Kulturbesitz, Gemäldegalerie (1664)
Not exhibited

ALMOST EVERY ASPECT of this brilliant and imposing double-sided portrait has been open to multiple interpretations and hypotheses: the identity of the artist (or artists), where and for whom it was painted, and the meaning of the scene on the verso. The sitter for now remains anonymous, but he is most often thought to be a German, although perhaps one resident in Venice around 1500. As became increasingly common at that moment in paintings both north and south of the Alps, the man is shown to the waist and his hand appears to rest on the edge or "frame" of the painting (unfortunately, the small banderole he holds includes neither a signature nor an identification). He wears a heavy, fur-lined coat over an elaborately embroidered chemise (as in some portraits by Albrecht Dürer), and his shoulder-length hair is held in place by a black hat with a curved brim recognizable in many Venetian portraits from the end of the previous century. A majestic landscape appears through the window at his right, with an extensive townscape perched on hills before a lofty Alpine range and towering clouds above. Although the town is described in some detail, it has not yet been identified.

The verso shows a man and woman, nude except for some fluttering veils; he embraces her from behind as she looks into a small mirror. They are in an austerely empty room, pierced by windows at the left, with a half-open door at the rear leading to a street where some houses are visible. Despite the lack of furniture, this is surely a bedroom, with a high bed reached by a step and partially closed off by a red curtain at the right; comparable beds can be seen in works by Carpaccio, such as *The Birth of the Virgin* (1504–8; Accademia Carrara, Bergamo). In a feat of virtuoso painting, a single laurel branch is set in a glass of water on a sill directly beyond the viewer's reach but not within the couple's space. The exactitude of its observation, including the optical illusion created by the refraction of its stem, denotes the hand of an artist for whom such accuracy was important.

Is this a marriage portrait, or one part of a diptych celebrating a couple? If so, the imagery on the verso is remarkably personal and complex. A range of meanings has been assigned to the various elements, each with ambiguous connotations.[1] The composition of the two figures, with the man embracing the woman while standing behind her, strongly suggests the iconography of Adam and Eve, as often found in fifteenth- and sixteenth-century visual imagery, but also that of more threatening groupings alluding to the dangers posed by sexuality, such as Death and the Maiden, well known from Northern prints of about this time. The woman gazes into a mirror, which is often a symbol of vanitas, and thus the fleetingness of pleasure, but can be a reference to the allegorical figure of Veritas or Prudence as well. The detail of the half-open door has reminded some viewers of the imagery of ancient sarcophagi, in which such a door represented the boundary between one world and the next. Finally, the prominent laurel branch in its thin, transparent glass could continue an allusion to the fragility of life and love, but it is also key to many paintings that refer to marriage.[2]

Some readings of the scene in its entirety have leaned harder on the aspects referring to marriage, even suggesting that it may be a visual epithalamium, or marriage poem,[3] or in a harsher view, may be focused more on the elements referring to the passage of time and to death. For a fifteenth- or sixteenth-century viewer, the two might well have gone hand in hand. In addition, Ulrich Pfisterer has noted that the emphasis on the senses on this side of the painting may add another level to the complex allegory.[4]

Who painted this work? Several scholars believe that the recto and verso are so distinct that the portrait must be by a German artist and the reverse by an Italian;[5] these would have to account for the fact that the wooden support has been identified as poplar, which means that it was most likely prepared in Italy. Recently, several authors have argued that both sides were painted by Jacometto Veneziano (see cats. 19, 20A,B, and 23), but it is difficult to see this challenging work in the context of that artist's known oeuvre.[6]

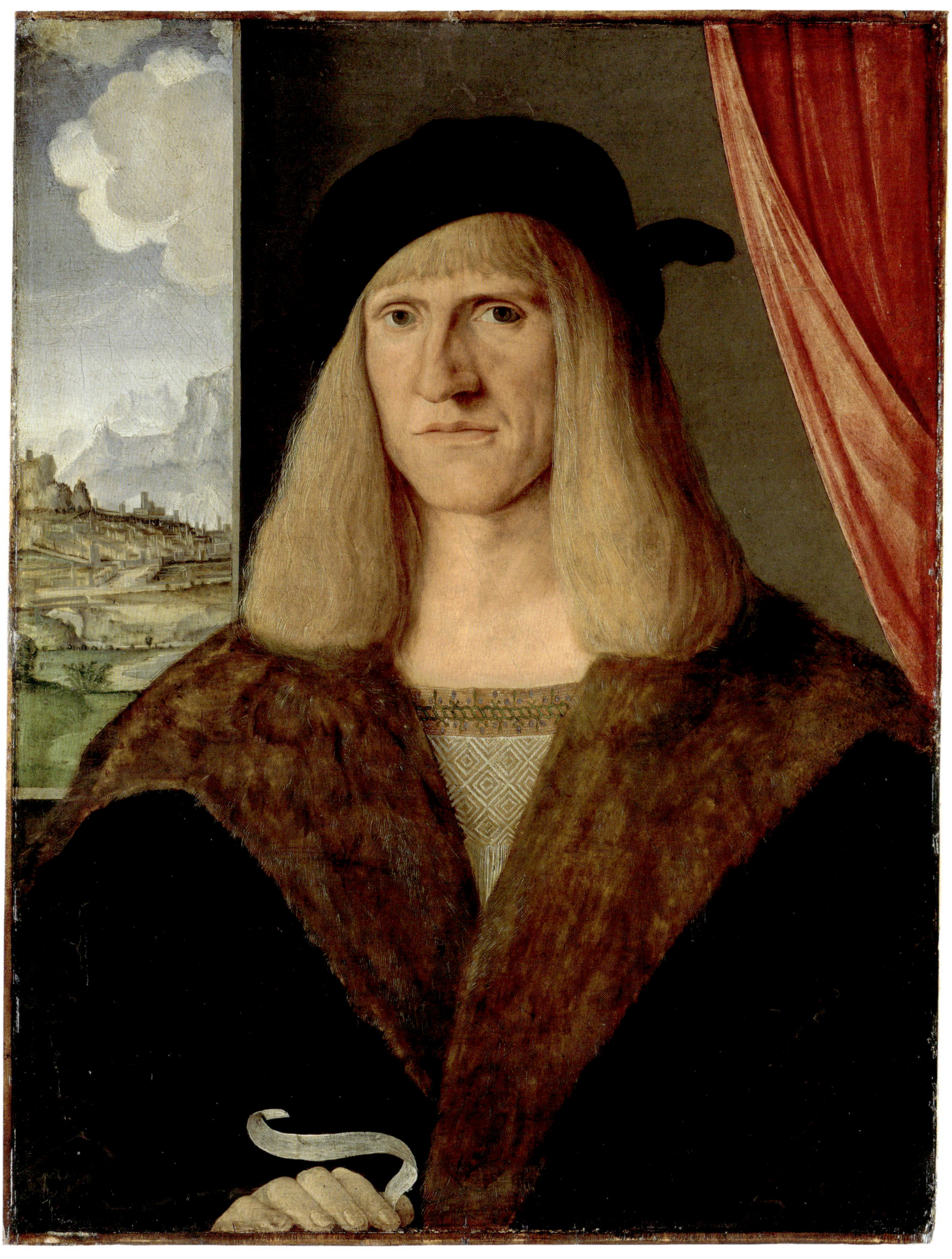

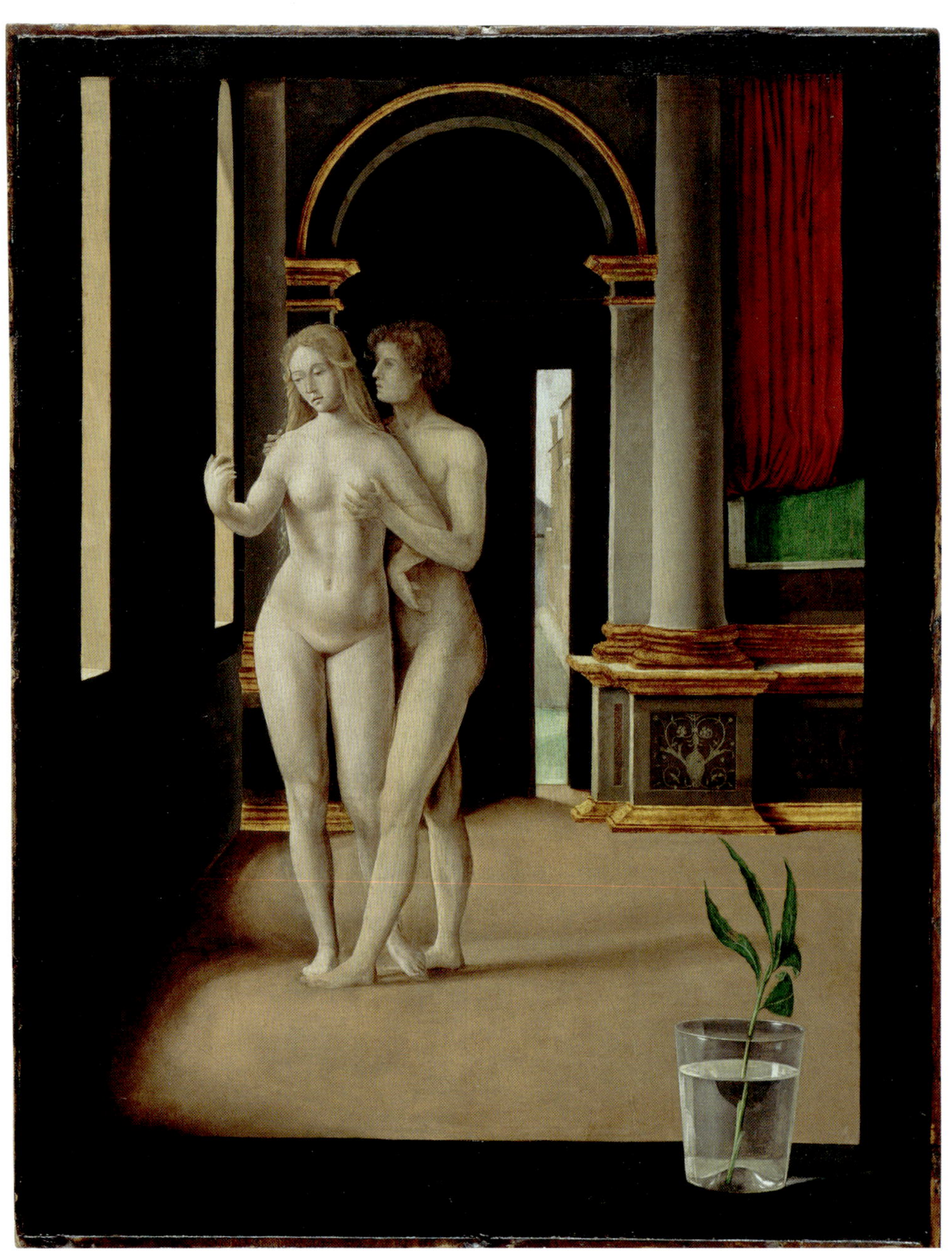

The more traditional attribution to Jacopo de' Barbari—active in both Venice and the North and known for his brilliant depictions of complex objects in space—continues to seem the most likely. As the artist himself wrote, painting made "visible what in nature is both palpable and visible," a statement that should be kept in mind while gazing at that sprig of laurel in a glass.[7]

AB

SELECTED REFERENCES: Dülberg 1990, pp. 161–63, 249 no. 211, pl. 139 figs. 295, 296; Bernard Aikema, cat. 26, in Aikema and Brown 1999, pp. 234–35; Lüdemann 2010; Dagmar Korbacher, cat. 168, in Christiansen and Weppelmann 2011, pp. 374–76; Ulrich Pfisterer, cat. 98, in Kren 2018, pp. 330–31.

CAT. 27A

ATTRIBUTED TO RIDOLFO GHIRLANDAIO

Italian, 1483–1561

Cover with a Mask, Grotteschi, *and Inscription*, ca. 1510

Oil on wood panel, 28¾ × 19⅞ in. (73 × 50.3 cm)
Inscribed: *SVA CVIQVE / PERSONA* (To each his own mask)
Gallerie degli Uffizi, Florence (1890 n. 6042)

CAT. 27B

ATTRIBUTED TO RIDOLFO GHIRLANDAIO

Portrait of a Woman (*La Monaca*), ca. 1510

Oil on wood panel, 25⅝ × 18⅞ in. (65.1 × 47.9 cm)
Gallerie degli Uffizi, Florence (1890 n. 8380)

ATTRIBUTED TO THE early sixteenth-century Florentine master Ridolfo Ghirlandaio, the *Portrait of a Woman* was originally concealed by the sliding panel embellished with imagery and an inscription that poignantly express, in a highly self-referential manner, the dual role of portrait covers in masking and revealing the sitter's identity.[1] Classicizing ornamental and zoomorphic motifs (*grotteschi*), painted in grisaille to resemble stone relief, surround a mask animated by illumination and flesh-toned features. Two additional masks are balanced beneath the feline paws of the chimeric creatures, symbols of the duality of the self, which further evoke the notion of multifaceted identities. In addition to their theatrical functions, masks also served to preserve the features of the deceased, reinforcing the funerary associations of the dolphins (symbols of the soul's journey after death), the oil lamp (signifying eternal life), and the bucranium (ox's head) that were frequently associated with sepulchral monuments.[2]

The fictive tablet is inscribed with a Latin phrase meaning "to each his own mask," known from two first-century Roman texts by the philosopher Seneca and the rhetorician Quintilian, respectively.[3] The inscription also recalls a passage in Cicero's *De officiis* (*On Duties*) asserting that nature provides humans with four masks: one universal, one specific to the individual, one situational, and one self-chosen.[4] The panel's inscription is not only a moralizing statement about the human condition but also a commentary on both the artifice of portraiture and the function of portrait covers to bridge the private and public realms.

Masks representing Virtue and Vice, accompanied by inscriptions and an oil lamp, appear in the grisaille background of Giorgio Vasari's *Lorenzo de' Medici* (ca. 1534, Gallerie degli Uffizi, Florence).[5] Just as outward beauty was perceived as reflecting inner virtue, the idealized mask on the cover of the woman's portrait signifies her esteemed character.

The inextricable connections between the painted portrait and its cover, as well as between the female sitter and her mask, are highlighted here by physiognomic parallels: the delicate, arched eyebrows, the pronounced philtrum, and the shape of the nose. Through its mirrored features, the mask does not simply conceal the sitter's face but reflects and embodies her.

Serving as a handle, the cover has a wide, unpainted upper margin that indicates it was removed by sliding it upward (rather than from the side), when, momentarily, the mask would have been poised above the sitter's face. Markings on the cover's reverse, which correspond with strips applied to the portrait's reverse, have been interpreted as evidence that the layered structure may have been embedded into wall paneling that possibly echoed the trompe l'oeil *grotteschi* on the cover.[6]

The sitter's pose, in three-quarter view with her head subtly rotated toward the viewer, echoes the innovative formulas for female portraiture established by Leonardo and closely reflected in Raphael.[7] While the present portrait was ascribed to Leonardo in the early nineteenth century, it has also been variously attributed to Raphael and several early sixteenth-century Florentine artists, including Mariotto Albertinelli and Giuliano Bugiardini.[8] Most recently, Antonio Natali has advanced the theory that both the portrait and cover are by Ridolfo Ghirlandaio, who had close ties to Raphael and is also known as a painter of *grotteschi*.[9]

Holding a book of prayers while seemingly resting her other hand on the picture frame, the woman is seated in a loggia overlooking a view of Florence depicted with topographical accuracy: on the right, is the Dominican Convent of San Jacopo di Ripoli, on the left, the Ospedale di San Paolo. The Church of Santo Spirito, visible behind the Ospedale, appears without the bell tower designed by Fra Bartolomeo and erected between 1512 and 1518, thereby

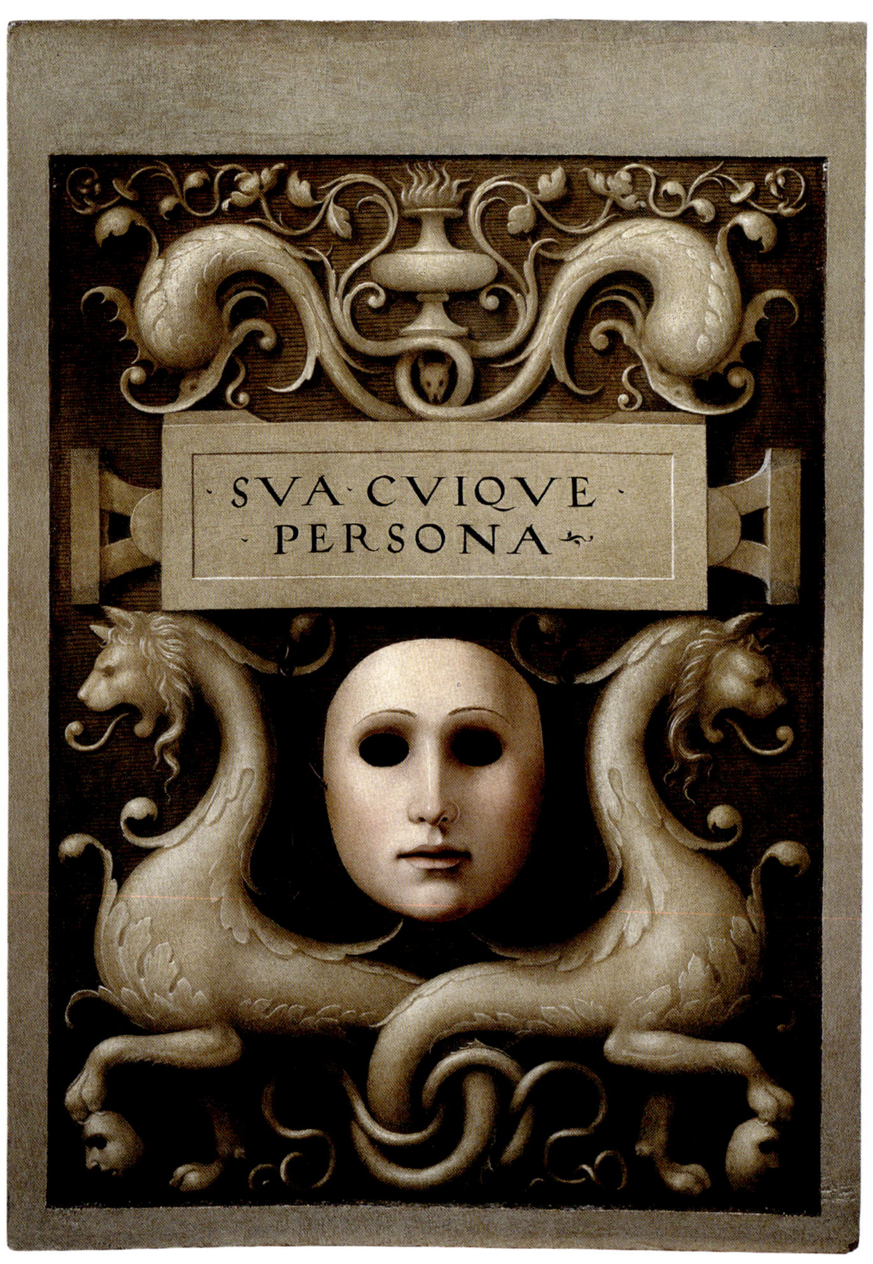

providing a plausible terminus ante quem for the painting.[10] The relative positions of these three Florentine sites, shown from a viewpoint looking southwest, suggest that the sitter was (or was intended to be) positioned in a palazzo slightly to the north of the Church of Santa Maria Novella, perhaps in the vicinity of the former Villino Strozzi.

While the sitter's identity remains unknown, her attire, including the low neckline of her *gamurra*, suggests that she is a Florentine patrician (rather than a nun, as formerly thought), whose unadorned fashion is in keeping with early sixteenth-century sumptuary laws.[11] According to Natali, she could be Caterina Antinori, the widowed and ailing daughter of Niccolò di Tommaso Antinori, who lived at San Jacopo di Ripoli, where her father had commissioned two altarpieces from Ridolfo Ghirlandaio.[12]

AMN

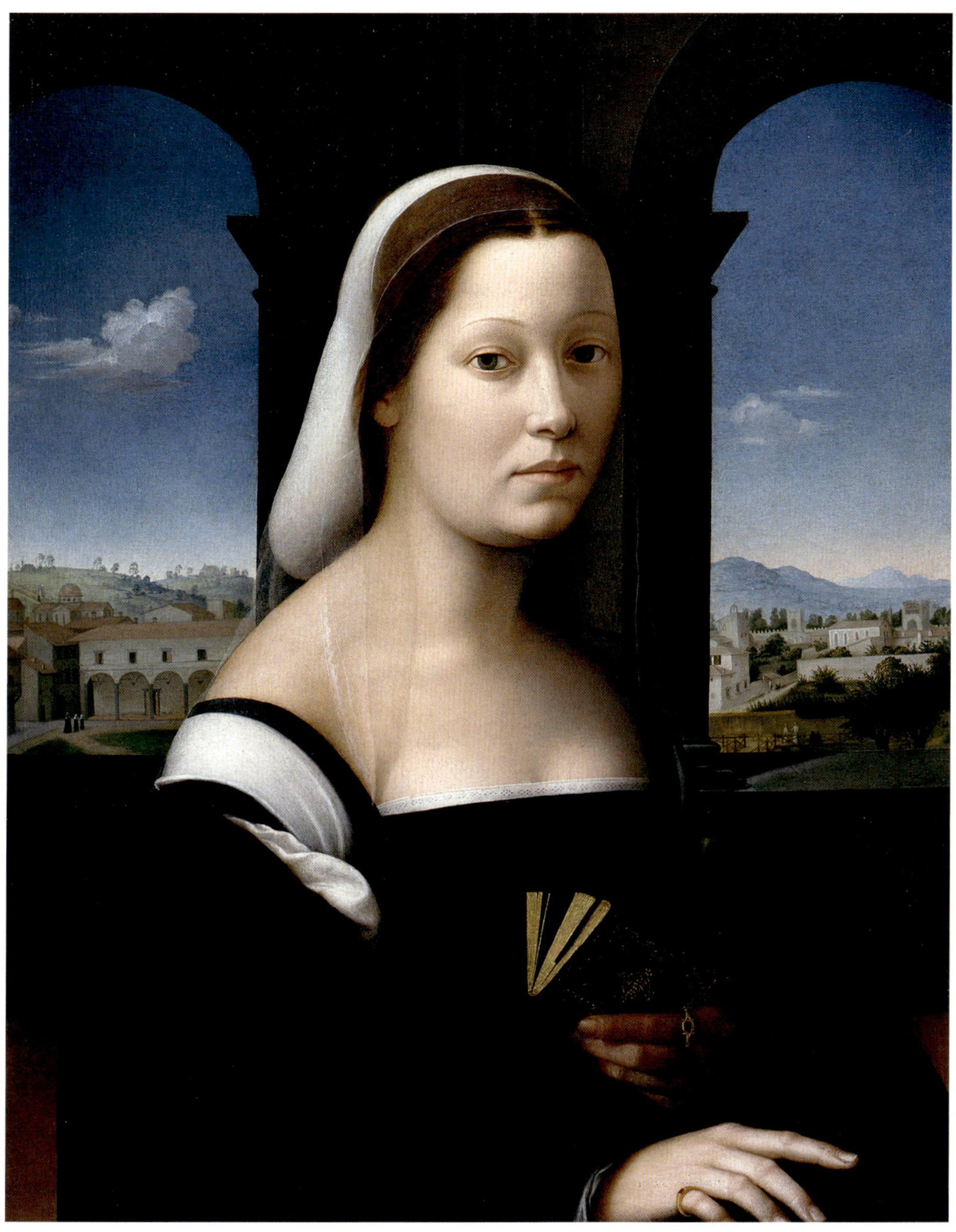

SELECTED REFERENCES: Pagnotta 1987, cat. 25, pp. 201–2, color pl. 1; Dülberg 1990, pp. 92, 130–31, 229 no. 172, pl. 57 fig. 126; Antonio Natali, "La coperta della Monaca," in Natali 1995, pp. 116–37; Antonio Natali, cats. 31, 31a, in Cecchi and Natali 1996, pp. 134–35; Hannah Baader, "Anonym: 'Sua cuique Persona'; Maske, Rolle, Porträt (um 1520)," in Preimesberger et al. 1999, pp. 239–46; D. Brown 2001, cat. 36, pp. 208–13; Antonio Natali, "Madonne fiorentine: Raffaello, di Ridolfo," in Ciatti and Natali 2008, pp. 30, 32, 34, 35, 36, 37; Carlo Falciani, cats. 3, 4, in Ciatti and Natali 2008, pp. 81–89; Sylvia Ferino-Pagden, cat. 1.16, in Ferino-Pagden 2009, pp. 82–84; Gaylord Brouhot, cats. 2, 3, in Falciani 2015, pp. 76–79; Antonio Natali, "Florentine Painters and Raphael at the Beginning of the Sixteenth Century," in Falciani 2015, pp. 36–43; Belting 2017, pp. 94–96; Spinelli 2018.

CAT. 28

AGNOLO DI DOMENICO DI DONNINO DEL MAZZIERE (MASTER OF SANTO SPIRITO)

Italian, 1465–1513

Portrait of a Young Woman (recto); *Laurel Wreath, Shield, Ornamental Ribbons, and Poetic Inscriptions* (verso), ca. 1490

Oil on poplar panel, 19 × 12⅝ in. (48.1 × 32.1 cm)

Inscribed (by the artist): (on recto, along bottom border) • *NOLI ME TANGERE* • [design] (Touch me not [John 20:17]); (on verso, around all four borders, read in the intended direction, at top) • *TIMORE DINFAMIA* • *E/* • *SOLO DISIO DONORE* • (Fear of infamy and only desire of honor); (at left border) • *FV CHE IDIO VOLLE* • (It was God's will); (at right border) • *SARA CHE IDIO VORRA* • (it shall be God's will); (at bottom) • *PIANSI GIA* • / • *QVELLO CHIO VOLLI* • / • *POI CHIO LEBBI* • (I wept for what I wanted, then later possessed) [design]

Staatliche Museen zu Berlin–Preussischer Kulturbesitz, Gemäldegalerie (80)

THIS PORTRAIT of a young woman in a serene landscape alludes to the ideal virtues of married life and reminds us that marriage among the well-to-do and the aristocracy in medieval and Renaissance Florence was an economic transaction with political and dynastic dimensions.[1]

The inscription in epigraphic letters on the portrait, painted along the parapet that serves as the bottom border for the figure, *NOLI ME TANGERE* (Touch me not), represents the words uttered by the resurrected Christ to Mary Magdalen in the garden (John 20:17).[2] It provides the basis for my suggestion that this otherwise anonymous young Florentine woman was almost certainly named Maddalena. Female portraits of the time often contained symbolic signifiers of identity that could take various forms, and in the present case the inscription, rather than an object or insignia, would assume this function. An example, to stand in for others, is Leonardo's *Ginevra de' Benci* (see fig. 24), in which the young woman is seen against a background landscape with a prominent juniper tree (*ginepro*), an allusion to her baptismal name.

For a long time misattributed, this portrait was eventually identified by Everett Fahy as part of a group of paintings and drawings of relatively homogeneous style by the anonymous Florentine Master of Santo Spirito, who produced altarpieces in the eponymous church in Florence.[3] Further archival research revealed a more precise identity for this artist among the works by the Del Mazziere brothers, Donnino (1459–after 1520s) and Agnolo (1465–1513), who were the sons of the painter Domenico di Donnino del Mazziere and who inherited his painting practice, as was often traditional among artists and artisans of this period. The Del Mazziere brothers continued to run the workshop together in Florence.[4] The younger Agnolo del Mazziere, the author of the present portrait and a prolific draftsman, is deemed the more skilled and "modern" painter of the two brothers. Agnolo befriended the painter Cosimo Rosselli, with whom he may have studied (according to Vasari in 1568).[5]

The back of the painting bears several intriguing inscriptions in epigraphic letters, with political overtones.[6] The upper border quotes a line from Petrarch's *Trionfi* (*Triumphs*, 1351), translated as "fear of infamy and only desire of honor," that celebrates the Triumph of Chastity and provides an apt accompaniment for the virginal bride in the portrait.[7] On the side borders, the words at left and right, when read as a continuous phrase, form an age-old Florentine aphorism, "It was God's will, it shall be God's will," emphasizing that God's will inexorably commands Fate (*fortuna*). The verse at the bottom border, meaning "I wept for what I wanted,

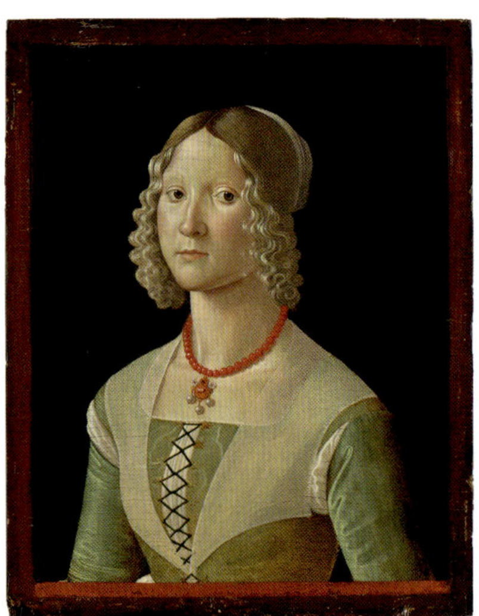

Fig. 43. Davide Ghirlandaio (David Bigordi; Italian, 1452–1525). *Selvaggia Sassetti (Born 1470)*, ca. 1487–88. Tempera on wood panel, 22½ × 17⅜ in. (57.2 × 44.1 cm). The Metropolitan Museum of Art, New York, The Friedsam Collection, Bequest of Michael Friedsam, 1931 (32.100.71)

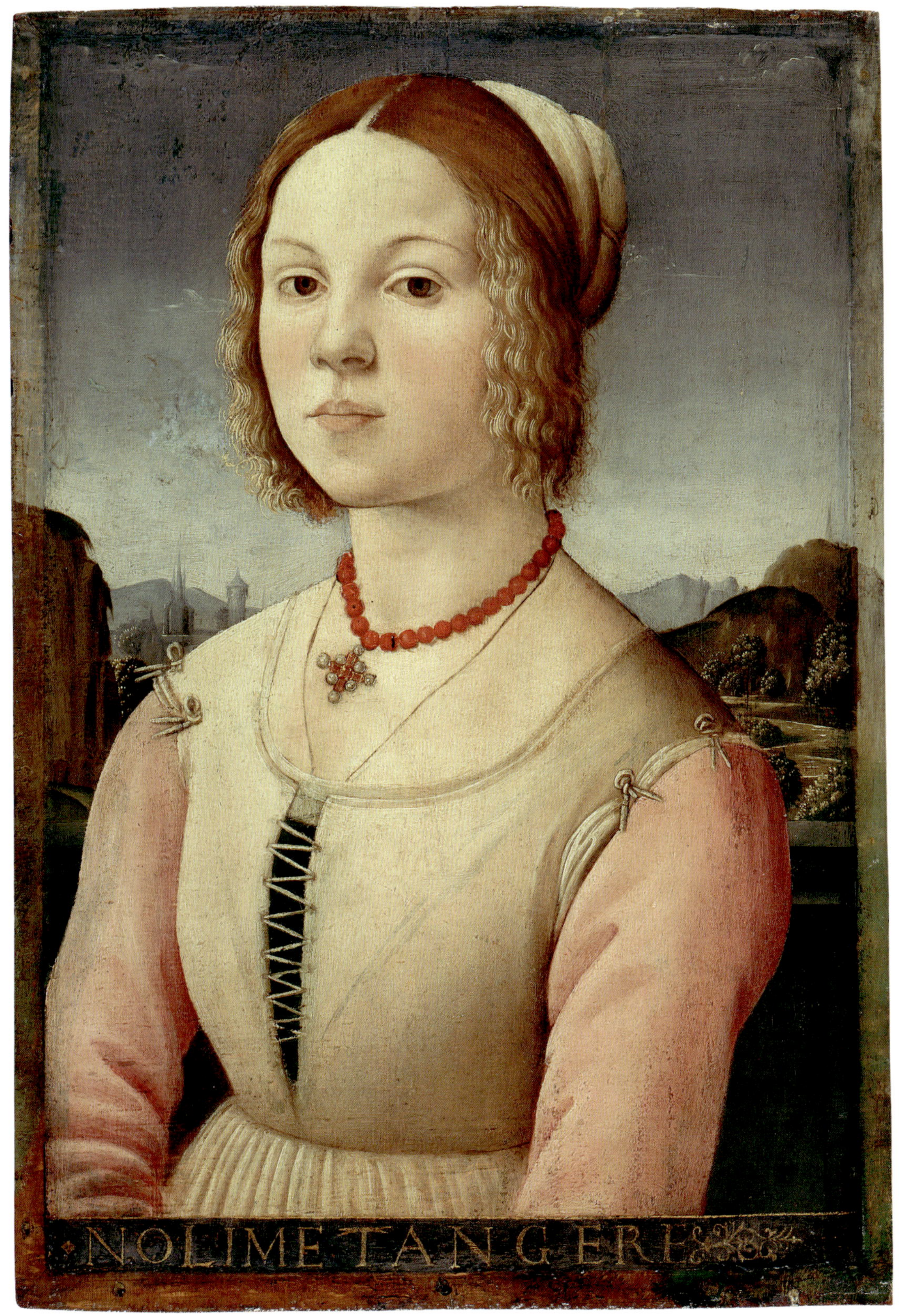
NOLIME TANGERE

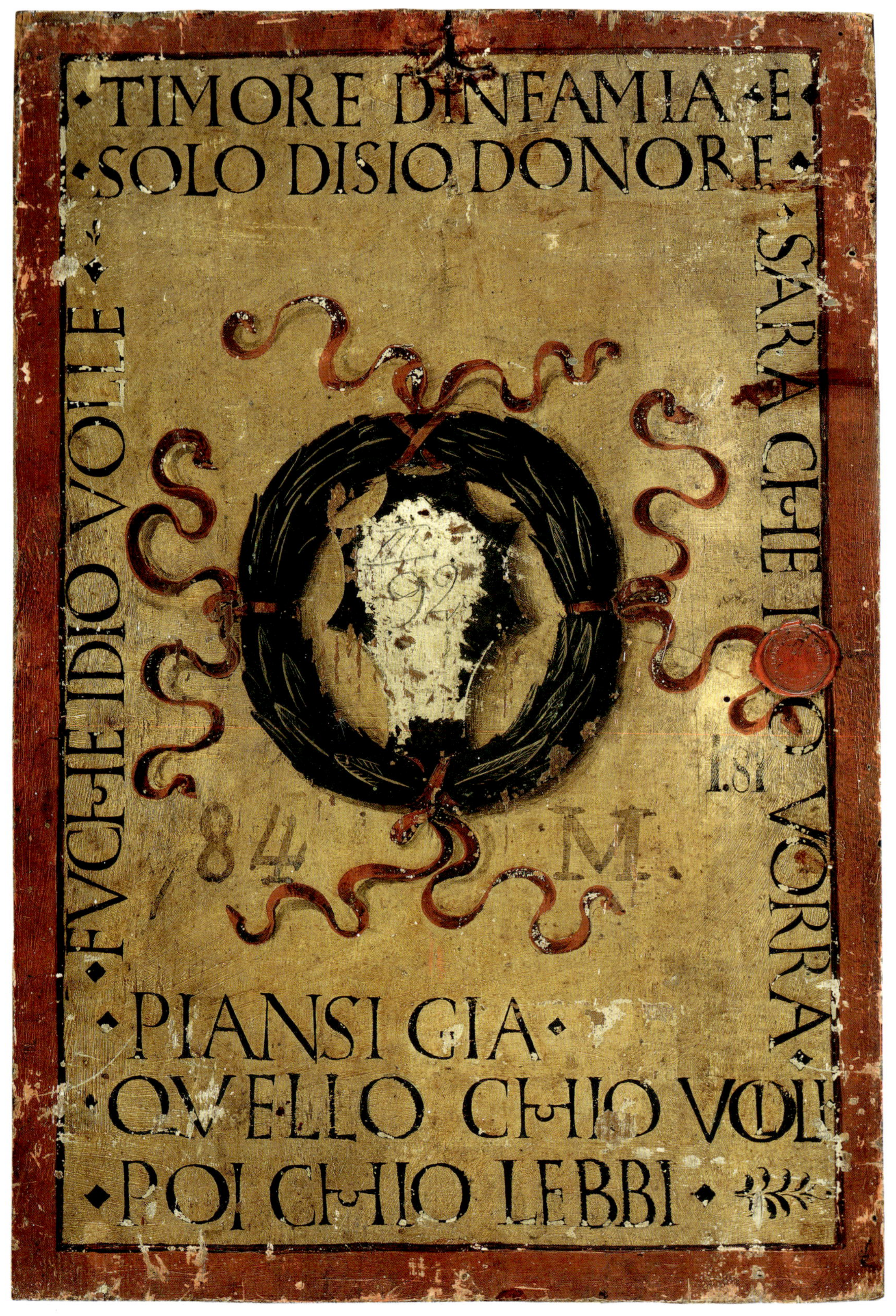
TIMORE DINFAMIA E
SOLO DISIO DONORE
FVCHE IDIO VOLLE
SARA CHE I
VORRA
PIANSI GIA
QVELLO CHIO VOLI
POI CHIO LEBBI
784
M.
I.81

then later possessed," is from a sonnet by the poet Antonio di Matteo di Meglio (1384–1448) on the vicissitudes of love.[8] Di Meglio was the most important and famous herald (*araldo*) of the Signoria of Florence, a prominent ceremonial government post in the city-state from 1350 to 1532.[9]

The Berlin painting is in a traditional style of engagement or marriage portraits of aristocratic young women in late fifteenth-century Florence. The compositional type may be compared to that of Davide Ghirlandaio's portrait of Selvaggia ("Vaggia") Sassetti, now in The Metropolitan Museum of Art (fig. 43), although the latter is a less ambitious painting.[10] Selvaggia, born in 1470, was the fifth of the seven daughters of the Florentine banker Francesco Sassetti and his wife, Nera Corsi. She married Simone d'Amerigo Carnesecchi in 1488, and this would have been the occasion for her portrait, which accords well with the independent evidence of painting style. A prominent art patron, Francesco Sassetti commissioned the fresco cycle on the life of Saint Francis in the Church of Santa Trinita in Florence from Davide's famous elder brother, Domenico Ghirlandaio (1448–1494), who completed the fresco cycle for Sassetti in December 1485 and who was a brilliant portrait painter himself. Although painted by different artists, both the Berlin and Met portraits represent a young woman in three-quarter view, slightly below the waist and facing left, with remarkable graphic precision and in very similar attire and hairstyles. The Met's Selvaggia is seen against a plain dark background (originally discolored azurite), which possibly once contained a landscape. The painting surface of the Berlin portrait has suffered some losses, especially in the shield on the verso, and once included a translucent veil over the young woman's shoulders, covering the front of her bodice and fastened near her waist (the vestiges painted in white hues are still visible), just like that worn by Selvaggia in The Met's portrait.

Despite the prominent landscape in the Berlin painting, which recedes in atmospheric perspective into the far distance, and despite the young woman's gaze, which partly engages the viewer, certain subtle illusionistic details reveal that she inhabits an enclosure, between the ledge at the very bottom in the foreground with the inscription *NOLI ME TANGERE*, which runs below her waist, and a low wall behind her, as if she were sitting within a balcony or loggia. She is the "not to be touched" maiden, a virginal pawn in the aristocratic marriage market. In the background landscape, mountains at the left cradle a town, while a winding path at the right, with trees in a valley edged by mounds and mountains, helps lead the spectator's eye from the middle ground to the background in a continuous depth of space.

The use of the landscape here—as a compositional device in a portrait with the female figure seen in three-quarter view—was still relatively new in late fifteenth-century Florentine painting. In most female portraits during the second half of the century, the figure was depicted in strict profile with a landscape behind, which renders an interaction between the sitter and the background remote or nonexistent. In later portraits of the female figure in three-quarter view, the woman appears enclosed in her domestic realm: whether a landscape is depicted or not beyond the view of a window (or balcony), the interior of the architectural setting predominates and even oppresses her.[11] Here, although domesticity is implicit to Maddalena's role as a future wife, she is seen in as free a context as possible, given her status as a marriageable young woman.

The elaborate (restored) historical frame is not original to the portrait and seems to have accommodated a sliding cover.[12] Its lintel, inscribed with an allusion to Christ, should not overly affect our understanding of the original inscriptions painted on the recto and verso of the portrait itself, as here discussed.[13]

CCB

SELECTED REFERENCES: Cartwright 1902, p. 276 (Lorenzo di Credi); Gemäldegalerie Berlin 1975, no. 80 (Lorenzo di Credi), p. 122; Fahy 1976, p. 192 (Master of Santo Spirito); Covi 1986, pp. 164, 164n27, 467 no. 164 (Lorenzo di Credi[?]); *Gemäldegalerie Berlin* 1986, pp. 51, 424 fig. 1169 no. 80; Dülberg 1990, pp. 228–29, no. 169 (Lorenzo di Credi?); *Gemäldegalerie Berlin* 1996–98, vol. 2, pp. 82, 471 fig. 2164, 582 no. 80; Roberta Orsi Landini and Mary Westermann Bulgarella, "Costume in Fifteenth-Century Florentine Portraits of Women," in D. Brown 2001, pp. 90–91, fig. 2; Stephan Weppelmann, "Some Thoughts on Likeness in Italian Early Renaissance Portraits," in Christiansen and Weppelmann 2011, pp. 67, 384–85n21; Monbeig Goguel 2015, pp. 68, 331n16; Rowley and Völlnagel 2020, pp. 77, 80 fig. 35, 99 no. 6, 107 cat. 16; Bambach forthcoming.

CAT. 29A

LORENZO LOTTO

Italian, ca. 1480–1556

Portrait of a Woman, ca. 1505

Oil on wood panel, 14¼ × 11⅛ in. (36 × 28 cm)
Musée des Beaux-Arts, Dijon (CA T 52)

CAT. 29B

LORENZO LOTTO

Portrait Cover with an Allegory, ca. 1505

Oil on wood panel, 16⅞ × 13¼ in. (42.9 × 33.7 cm)
National Gallery of Art, Washington, D.C., Samuel H. Kress Collection (1939.1.147)

A DIGNIFIED WOMAN is presented against the folds of a curtain; her contemplative gaze, directed slightly to the right, conveys an air of self-assured detachment (A). Her static pose implies that she may be seated. Light falling from the left accentuates her plump chin and the slight bags under her eyes. Soberly yet richly dressed, with her gold-brown hair caught in a finely worked net under a transparent coif, she wears a silken, scarf-like *fazuolo* around her shoulders. The crisp white fabric of a chemise is pulled through the capacious slashed sleeves of her black dress, a fashionable look in the early 1500s.

The painting is bare of details, such as the jewelry or ornaments associated with marriage, that might give clues to the woman's identity. Stylistically close to Lotto's *Bishop Bernardo de' Rossi* (cat. 30A), the portrait was made in Treviso probably in late 1505.[1] The attractive theory that the sitter is the bishop's widowed sister, Giovanna Malaspina, part of his household from 1493 until her death in 1502, is not supported by any documentary evidence.[2] Balancing another idea, that her cap and *fazuolo* suggest those of a *balia*, or wet nurse, is the costume (and lack of jewelry) of an older patrician woman in a group portrait by Bernardino Licinio (ca. 1520, State Hermitage Museum, St Petersburg).[3] Autonomous Venetian female portraits from 1500 to 1505 present distinctly unidealized types, and possibly the plain, matronly representation seen in Gentile Bellini's portrayal of Queen Caterina Cornaro (ca. 1500, Szépművészeti Múzeum, Budapest) was fashionable for a time.[4] Lotto adapts this grave approach for his Trevisan sitter, aiming for a naturalistic air that is also inflected by Albrecht Dürer's works, which he would have seen on trips to Venice.[5]

Lotto's painting is remarkable not only for its play of light and dark, both in luminosity and the near-monochrome palette, but also for its design. The slight turn of the figure conveys a sense of volume and space, yet there is no fictive parapet, black background, or illusionistic landscape to denote her separation from the viewer. Instead, while maintaining the conviction of an authentic presence, Lotto creates this essential distance through the green curtain that places the woman in a private space. The fabric recalls the *spalliere,* or hangings placed at shoulder level in households, as seen in the bedchamber in Vittore Carpaccio's *Dream of Saint Ursula* (1495, Accademia, Venice). There, green drapery hanging from high above a long bench is lifted to reveal a cabinet with precious books and objects. The curtain in this portrait may refer to domestic *spalliera* hangings or to drapes used to protect images, suggesting the privilege accorded to the viewer.

In the *Allegory* (B), a glorious sunrise illuminates a verdant landscape with clumps of tall trees and wooded hills rising toward rocky mountains. Soft grass in the foreground is dotted with flowers, and a silvery stream runs past the meditative figure of a young woman, clad in white and gold, who reclines against a cut tree from which a laurel bough springs. This is an enchanted place where a winged boy (*amorino*), borne on a flowery cloud, sends a cascade of blossoms through the brightening air to fall upon the wide-eyed woman. The groves are inhabited by the companions of Pan, unruly god of nature: a male satyr with an empty drinking vessel reclining in a pool bordered by rocks, and a female satyr peeping from behind a tree trunk who laughs at him.

Lotto's extraordinary inventiveness and pictorial skills are evident, as they are in his portrait cover with an allegory, also in Washington (cat. 30B), to which the painting is close stylistically.[6] But instead of creating an atmospheric landscape that binds a litany of impresa-like motifs in harmony, here Lotto depicts a numinous place, redolent of the sylvan landscapes of classical and chivalric traditions. Both works were stimulated by northern European art, including prints by Dürer, and by the developing Venetian genre of the poetic

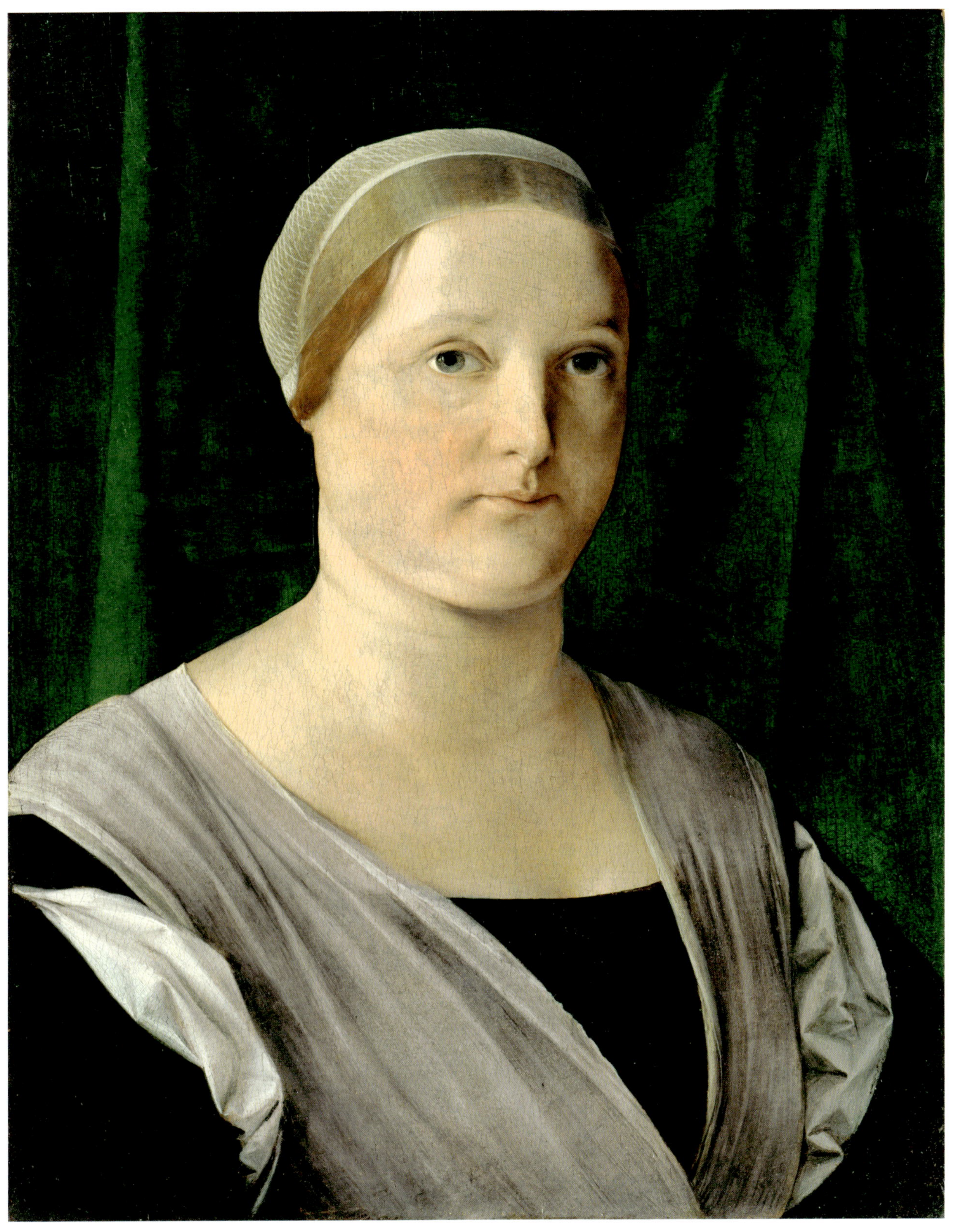

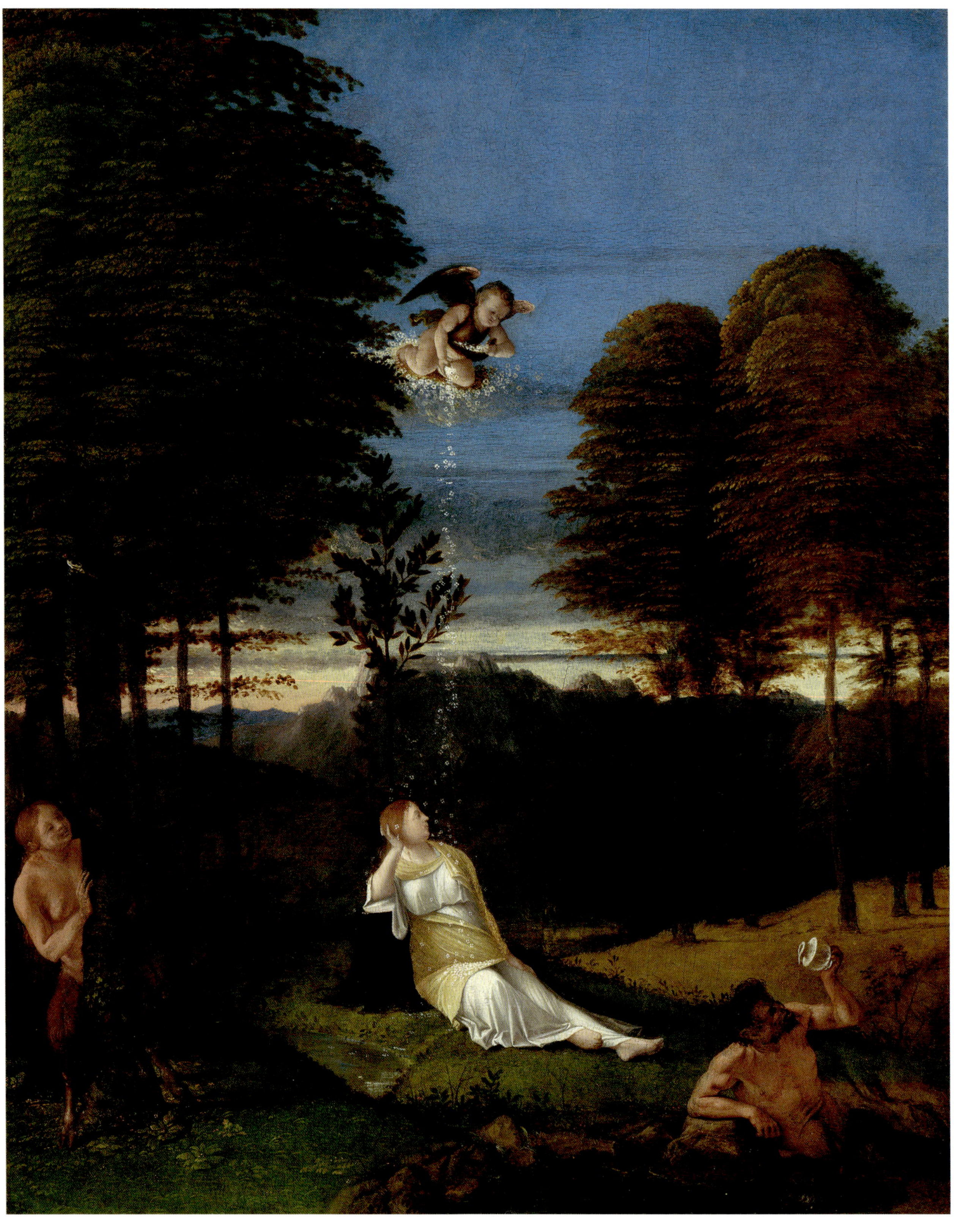

landscape, notably seen in Giorgione's *Tempest* (see fig. 37), to which Lotto's Washington allegories are often compared. While a pairing with the *Portrait of a Woman* has long been presumed—sometimes reinforced by the interpretation of the subject as a celebration of chastity—there is no documentary evidence for the association.[7]

As an allegory, Lotto's painting captures the imaginative world of Venetian poets and intellectuals, particularly that of the brilliant circle around Bernardo de' Rossi, including Giovanni Aurelio Augurello, whose portrait with its accompanying cover Lotto was commissioned to paint.[8] This flourishing of humanism in Treviso had seen the composition of the antiquarian romance *Hypnerotomachia Poliphili*, published in 1499 by Aldus Manutius with vivid woodcut illustrations (its jokey classical title translating as *Poliphilus's Struggle for Love in a Dream*). Inventiveness, wit, and erudition were prized in this culture, to which Lotto creatively responded.

Like the cover for De' Rossi's portrait, the *Allegory* has a number of possible interpretations that enrich the experience of repeated viewing. References to poetry would instantly have come to mind, since Petrarch's *Canzoniere* 126 evokes a vision of the golden-haired Laura in a woodland setting with flowers and cool water, where she bathes and reclines against a laurel tree (though here the satyr is enjoying the pool). Other references to the familiar theme of the nymph, or beautiful girl, of the fountain, whose sleep in nature must not be disturbed, can be teased out (the nymph becomes nude Nature, unveiled by a satyr, in the *Hypnerotomachia Poliphili*; fig. 44).[9]

In no sense is Lotto illustrating a text; rather, the painting evolved as the result of dialogue with the patron. Technical examination revealed that the artist first painted a seated male figure, plausibly Hercules, the mythological hero whose choice between virtue and vice, or rather responsibility over hedonism, was emblematic.[10] Whether Lotto reused an existing panel or the first idea was adapted is unknown. The intemperate, instinctive character of the satyrs is strikingly contrasted with the profound stillness of the woman, singled out by Love, who rains down white flowers that embody her virtuous thoughts, as though sanctifying the space.[11] Perhaps the allegory concerns a vision of landscape as a site where poetic fantasy can thrive, later taken up by Valerio Belli on Pietro Bembo's portrait medal of 1532; if so, the painting would have been appropriate as a cover for the portrait of a poet like Augurello.[12] In Venice in 1545, Lotto was asked to provide a copy of Augurello's portrait and its cover, a reminder that covers, as innovative paintings, had an afterlife by which their imagery was disseminated.[13]

CW

SELECTED REFERENCES: Dülberg 1990, pp. 144–45, 293 no. 329, pl. 79 fig. 167; David Alan Brown, cats. 4, 5, in Brown et al. 1997, pp. 81–87; Humfrey 1997, p. 12; Sylvia Ferino-Pagden, "Pictures of Women—Pictures of Love," cats. 36, 37, in Brown and Ferino-Pagden 2006, pp. 200–207; Margaret Binotto, cat. 51, in Villa 2011, pp. 266–69; Dal Pozzolo 2021, nos. I.8, I.9, pp. 112–15.

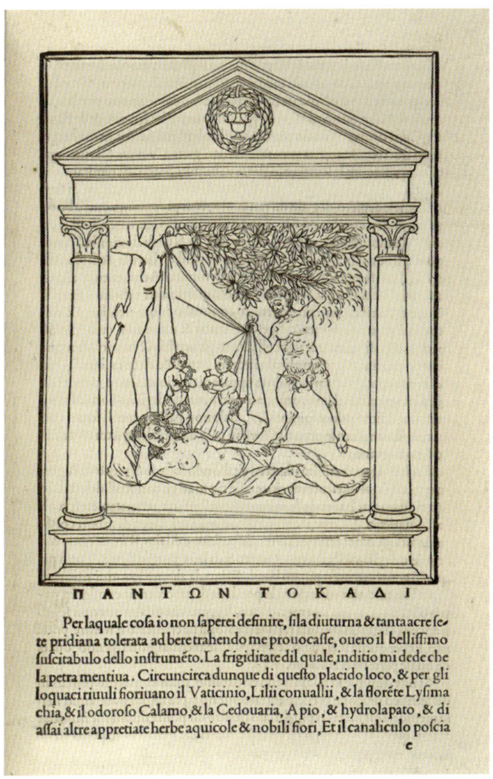

ΠΑΝΤΩΝ ΤΟΚΑΔΙ

Per laquale cosa io non saperei definire, sila diuturna & tanta acre sete pridiana tolerata ad bere trahendo me prouocasse, ouero il bellissimo suscitabulo dello instruméto. La frigiditate dil quale, inditio mi dede che la petra mentiua. Circuncirca dunque di questo placido loco, & per gli loquaci riuuli fioriuano il Vaticinio, Lilii conuallii, & la floréte Lysimachia, & il odoroso Calamo, & la Cedouaria, Apio, & hydrolapato, & di assai altre appretiate herbe aquicole & nobili fiori, Et il canaliculo poscia

c

Fig. 44. Attributed to Benedetto Bordone (Italian, ca. 1455/60–1530). *Nymph Discovered by a Satyr.* From *Hypnerotomachia Poliphili* (*Poliphilus's Struggle for Love in a Dream*), attributed to Francesco Colonna. Book printed by Aldus Manutius, Venice, 1499. Woodcut; bound volume: 11 3/8 × 8 1/2 in. (29 × 21.5 cm). The Morgan Library and Museum, New York (PML 373, E1 recto)

CAT. 30A

LORENZO LOTTO

Italian, ca. 1480–1556

Bishop Bernardo de' Rossi, 1505

Oil on wood panel, 21⅝ × 16¼ in. (54.7 × 41.3 cm)

Museo Nazionale di Capodimonte, Naples (259)

Not exhibited

CAT. 30B

LORENZO LOTTO

Portrait Cover with an Allegory, 1505

Oil on wood panel, 22¼ × 16⅝ in. (56.5 × 42.2 cm)

Inscribed (formerly, on verso): *BERNARD. RVBEVS / BERCETI COM. PONT / TARVIS. NAT. / ANN. XXXVI. MENS. X. D. V. / LAVRENT. LOTVS P. CAL. / IVL. M. D. V.* (Bernardo Rossi of Berceta, Papal Count [Bishop] of Treviso, age 36 years, 10 months, 5 days, Painted by Lorenzo Lotto, July 1, 1505)

National Gallery of Art, Washington, D.C., Samuel H. Kress Collection (1939.1.156)

CAT. 30C

FOLLOWER OF FRANCESCO FRANCIA

Francia: Italian, ca. 1450–1517

Portrait Medal of Bernardo de' Rossi (obverse); *Allegory of Virtue* (reverse), ca. 1520; cast possibly 17th century

Bronze, Diam. 2 9/16 in. (6.5 cm), weight 1 oz. (127.96g)

Inscribed: (on obverse, around circumference) *BER[nardus] RV[beus] CO[mes] B[erceti] EP[iscopu]S TAR[visinus] LE[gatus] BO[noniae] VIC[arius] GV[bernator] ET PRAE[fectus]* (Bernardo Rossi, count of Berceto, bishop of Treviso, legate of Bologna, vicar-general, and prefect); (on reverse, around circumference) *OB VIRTVTES IN FLAMINIAM RESTITVTAS* (The restitution of the virtues in Romagna)

The Metropolitan Museum of Art, New York, Robert Lehman Collection, 1975 (1975.1.1275)

LOTTO MAY HAVE already been in Treviso when Bernardo de' Rossi (1468–1527) arrived as its bishop in August 1499.[1] Forceful in diocesan reforms, covetous with the diocese's patrimony, and favoring associates from his native Parma, De' Rossi raised the ire of powerful local interests to the extent of an assassination attempt in 1503. By then, Lotto had caught the bishop's attention as a brilliantly talented artist. Intellectually and doubtlessly politically alert, Lotto knew that his portrait had to assert the authority, power, and dignity of the sitter.

The painting has a commanding presence (A). Lotto extended its ostensible size by suggesting the blue sky above the green curtain and by showing part of De' Rossi's beringed hand, brandishing a document. Visual conventions in portraiture were evolving from Netherlandish bust-length types, with parapets and dark backgrounds, to more expansive portrayals, sometimes against landscapes.[2] However, instead of the clear demarcation of fictive space seen in portraits made in Venice in the 1490s by artists such as Pietro Perugino, Alvise Vivarini, or Andrea Solario, Lotto presents De' Rossi in a narrow field, as though sharing the viewer's actual space. The bishop seems caught in an eloquent moment of address, the result of his turning pose, frank gaze, and pursed lips. This lifelike, immediate air is accentuated by the warmth of the flesh tones and the lack of idealization in the facial features.

Yet, balancing this illusionism is the admission of representation, as Lotto alludes to other pictorial modes. Unlike the tactile treatment of the features and curtain, the bishop's body beneath its rose-colored cape (*mozzetta*) is presented as a broad, polished form that evokes the solidity and durability of sculpture, while the gold-embroidered fabric behind him suggests a sacred space. This material does not hang from a curtain rail but is thrown over a screen, its folds unevenly ruched.[3] Specifically recalling the green-curtained enclosures in devotional paintings, such as the altarpiece by Alvise Vivarini of about 1480 in San Francesco, Treviso, it appears in the same form in Lotto's painting of the Virgin and Child with saints, which features a landscape opening beyond (ca. 1505, Scottish National Gallery, Edinburgh).[4] This association of a screen with divinely endowed authority is appropriate for the portrait of a controversial bishop. Lotto altered the motif in his *Portrait of a Woman* (cat. 29A), depicting the green fabric in an indeterminate manner.[5] In later works, he would employ curtains in portraiture in adventurous ways, but the nuanced use here is particularly remarkable.

Bernardo's likeness is known through later images in which his face has thickened, as in the present portrait

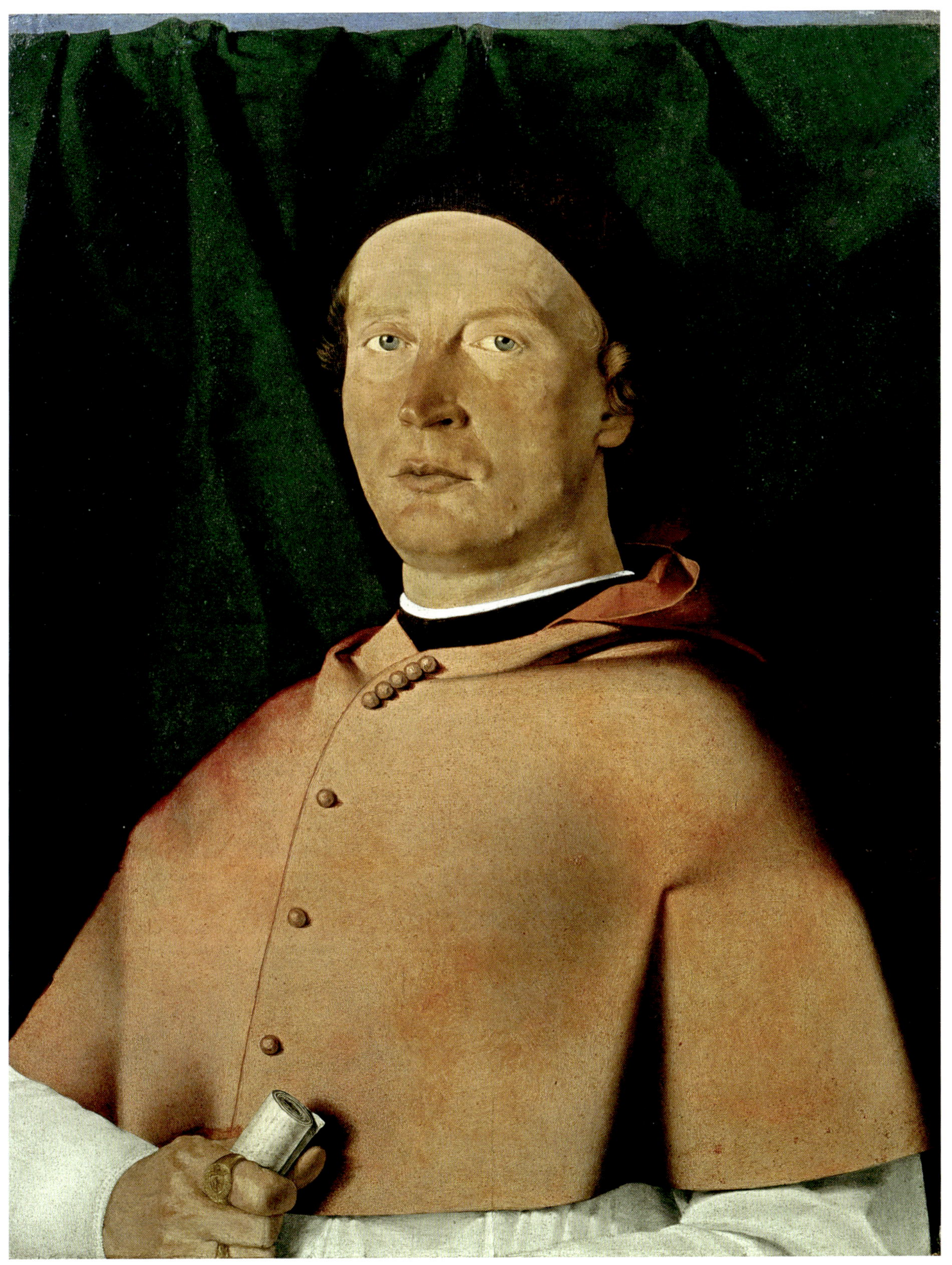

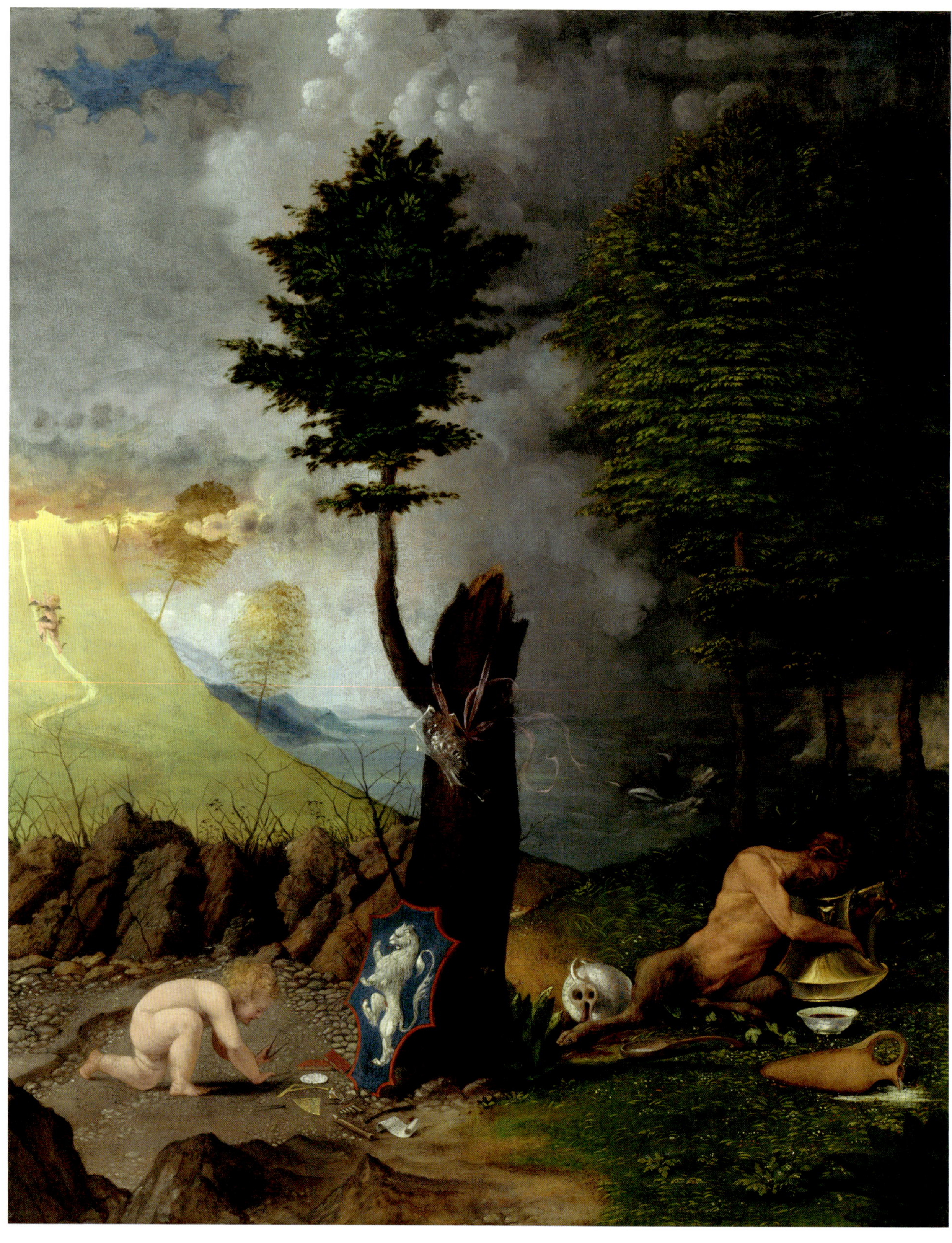

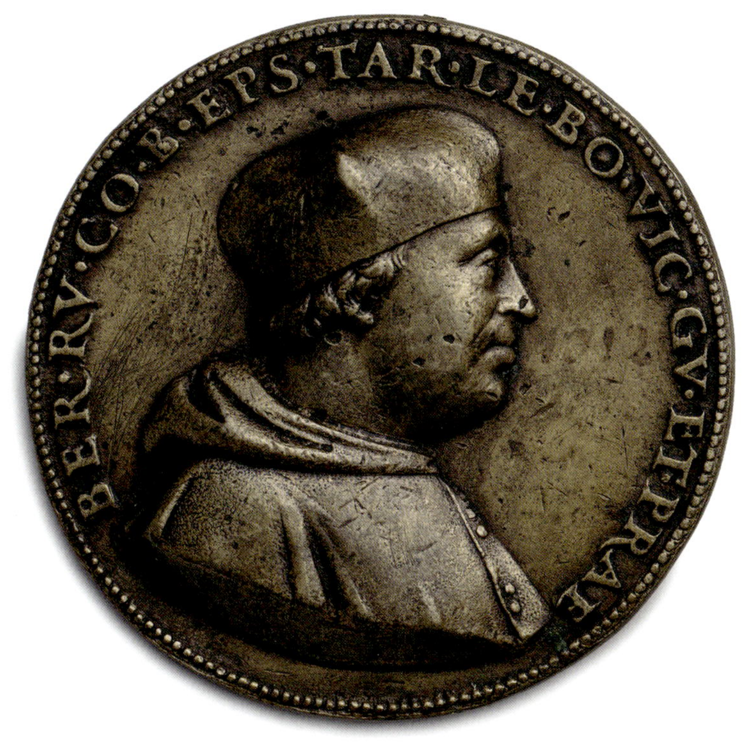
BER·RV·RV·CO·B·EPS·TAR·LE·BO·VIC·GV·ET·PRAE

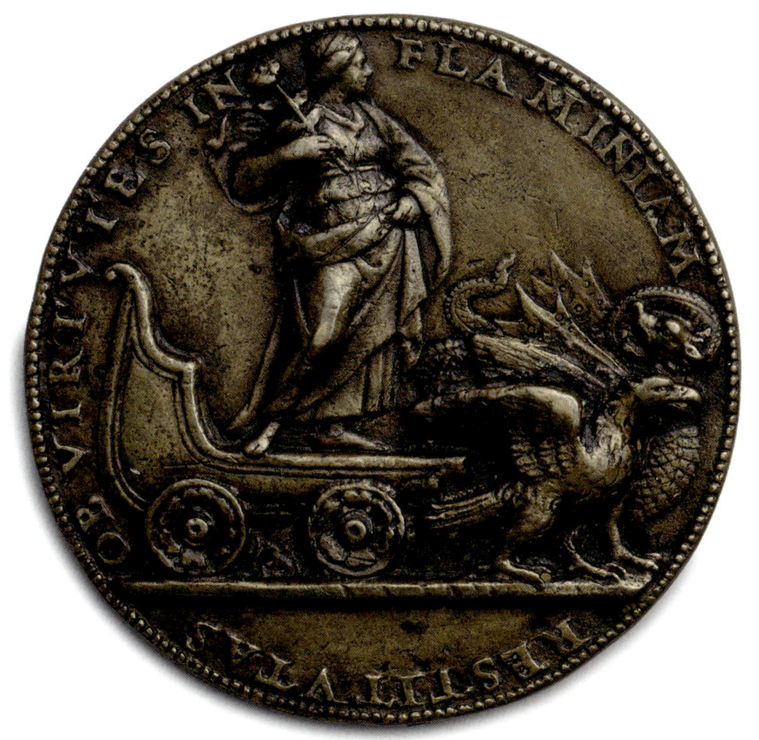
OB VIRTVTES IN FLAMINIAM
RESTITVTAS

medal (C) and the terracotta bust of about 1523–24 in the Cappella Malchiostro in the Duomo at Treviso.[6] De' Rossi's desire to impress his persona on both contemporaries and posterity is attested by this handsome medal, commissioned from a follower of Francesco Francia after the bishop's appointment as papal legate to Bologna in 1519. Shown in canonical profile form, the portrait carries an inscription that summarizes the prelate's high-level career.[7] The allegory on the reverse celebrates victory and peace. A resolute female figure, seemingly with military dress beneath her mantle, holds a flower, while her triumphal chariot, drawn by a winged dragon and an eagle, runs on wheels that incorporate flowers. Clearly the viewer was meant to appreciate "the restitution of the virtues in Romagna," as the inscription states, although Bernardo's hard-line approach to governance won him few friends. The familiar conjunction of likeness and allegory on the medal, intended to be turned over in the hand, is a reminder of the intimate relation between portrait and associated image, seen also in De' Rossi's painted portrait and its cover.

That the cover (B) was always intended as a companion piece is evidenced by an early inscription formerly on its reverse, recorded in the scholarly literature. This gave the identity of the sitter, his age of thirty-six years and ten months, and the artist's name together with the date of July 1, 1505, in a Latin form that doubtless had an ornamental as well as a documentary function. The panel was almost certainly set into the molding of the painting's frame so as to slide across and gradually reveal the portrait beneath; it is described as a "*coverta*" (cover) in a 1510 inventory.[8]

No doubt De' Rossi was closely involved in devising the imagery: his coat of arms with a rampant lion is prominent (the heraldic lion recalls his signet ring in the portrait). The complexity of the allegory reflects the erudition and wit of the bishop and the poets and writers in his orbit in Treviso.[9] Elite taste for intellectual puzzles and for the ingeniously compressed figurations of emblems lies behind the painting, in which the artist's task was to unify diverse motifs into a visually persuasive composition.

The sheer beauty of the painting of the tumultuous sky and vivid landscape, with its contrasting elements of fertile grass and stony ground, of stormy sea and sunlit mountain, demonstrates Lotto's virtuosity. The various vignettes—a shipwreck; a satiated satyr with his empty or spilled vessels of milk and wine; the blasted tree (perhaps a holm oak) with its new growth; the crouching boy who picks up a compass from an array of objects redolent of humanist interests; and the distant, eight-winged boy who races up a steep path—are like arresting metaphors in poetry that can be unpicked in conversation. Together, these elements yield commentaries on the soul's journey toward salvation through earthly life with its sensuous and intellectual pleasures. They reflect ideas in philosophical, literary, and theological texts familiar to the widely read De' Rossi and the close friends who viewed his portrait and its accompanying allegory.[10] All the motifs are delightfully open to layered interpretations, especially with repeated viewing.

The bishop's coat of arms faces the musical, mathematical, and learned elements—and Lotto surely emphasized delight in *disegno*, as the boy draws in the dust. Prominent above is a transparent shield with Medusa's head, an evanescent yet conspicuous motif denoting the presiding divinity, Minerva, goddess of wisdom and protector of peace and the arts. The satyr belongs to the realm of Pan, god of nature, as do the musical pipes, a world of pleasure explored in contemporaneous poetry and painting that is understood as suffused with merits as much as with temptation.[11] The dangers of excess in either realm are clear; Minerva's prudence and love of virtue open the path toward illumination.

The painting's esoteric and essentially poetic nature defies prosaic explanation. However, rather than presenting a binary opposition of virtue and vice as is often assumed, the allegory counsels judicious choices, based on shared values. There must have been exchanges between De' Rossi and Lotto in refining its invention and realization, particularly as technical investigation showed that the mountain with its fiery light, redolent of divine revelation, was a late addition, painted over a continuation of the blue mountain range.[12]
CW

SELECTED REFERENCES: Dülberg 1990, pp. 143–44, 238–39 no. 187, pls. 77, 78 figs. 165, 166; David Alan Brown, cats. 2, 3, in Brown et al. 1997, pp. 73–80; Humfrey 1997, pp. 9–12; Pollard 2007, vol. 1, no. 209, p. 224; Enrico Maria Dal Pozzolo, cats. 3, 4, in Dal Pozzolo and Falomir 2018, pp. 189–95; Dal Pozzolo 2021, no. I.6, pp. 106–9.

CAT. 31

TITIAN (TIZIANO VECELLIO)

Italian, ca. 1485/90?–1576

Two Satyrs in a Landscape, ca. 1509–15

Pen and brown ink, highlighted with white gouache on fine, off-white laid paper, 8½ × 5 15/16 in. (21.6 × 15.1 cm)

The Metropolitan Museum of Art, New York, Rogers Fund, 1999 (1999.28)

THE MET'S *Two Satyrs* by Titian exemplifies a new idiom in Venetian art—of figures set in a pastoral landscape—that resonated in European art until the late nineteenth century. Still influenced by Giorgione's style and subject matter, Titian's drawing is roughly contemporary with his *Concert Champêtre* (Musée du Louvre, Paris), painted in 1509–10 in a nearly square format,[1] and evokes a similar mood of an idyllic remote past of undisturbed nature, inspired by the poetry of classical and contemporary authors of his time. Titian's use of the pen-and-ink technique is exquisitely pictorial, with varied, freely applied strokes and small dabs of luminous white gouache, lending movement, texture, and tonal unity to the scene. His superb mastery of the pen is everywhere apparent, from the foreground figures built with broadly sculptural chiaroscuro effects to the background landscape, in which the forms of architecture and nature ineffably dissolve in the distant haze of the horizon. The poetic quality of the drawing is achieved through this subtlety of technique and a certain elusiveness of mood.

Titian brought sensuous form, poetic expression, and astrological allusion into harmony here, creating one of the greatest and rarest examples of Venetian Renaissance drawing. Although he was a tirelessly prolific painter, only thirty-five to forty extant drawings are attributable to him. He conceived this enigmatic composition in an unusually vertical format. The two male satyrs exhibit few physical traits evidencing their mythical part-animal appearance and recline nearly conjoined in the foreground, one facing the other. The satyr seen from the back at center gently leans to hold a celestial disk or sphere inscribed with a horoscope. It includes the crescent moon, the sun, six concentric circles representing orbits of planets, three small squares for the positions of the planets, and two still-undeciphered words. Beyond the satyrs stretches a bucolic landscape. Here, with a few deft strokes, Titian indicated a town with a bell tower close to the left border of the paper, and nearer in the pictorial space, toward the center right, he sketched a more detailed complex of buildings, some modestly rural, others with towers, turrets, and the oblique view of the facade of a church, indicating a monastic site and town.

All the elements of the composition seem complete, from the modeling of the sky with horizontal parallel strokes of the pen and curving hatched strokes defining the gathering clouds to the shrubs and foliage between the satyrs and the group of buildings at right. This degree of finish suggests a drawing done for presentation to a patron or friend (of unknown identity). If my hypotheses are correct—that this idyllic scene alludes to an individual's destiny as foretold by the stars (whether it can be read precisely as a horoscope is open to question)[2] and that the twin satyrs in the foreground perhaps wittily allude to Gemini—the drawing could have served as an idea for the painted cover of a portrait. The unusual (portrait-like) verticality of the composition may support this theory, and Titian was not above humorous subversions of classical imagery.[3]

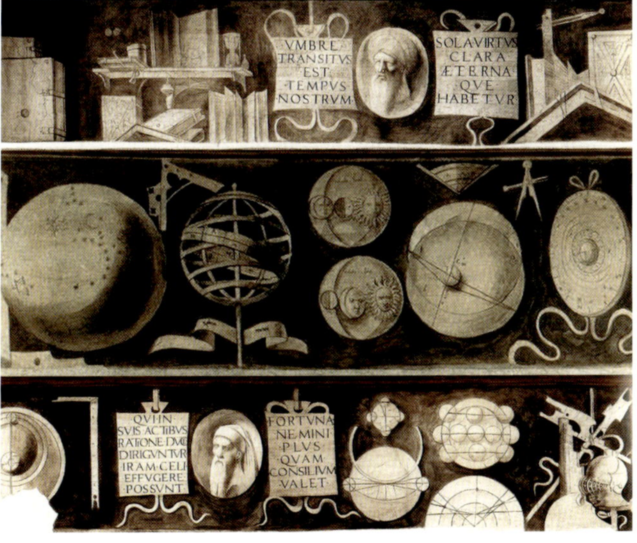

Fig. 45. Giorgione (Italian, 1477/78–1510). Frieze painted in fresco with detail of the attributes and instruments of the Liberal Arts and Mechanical Arts, ca. 1502–3. Casa Marta-Pellizzari (now Museo Casa Giorgione), Castelfranco, Italy

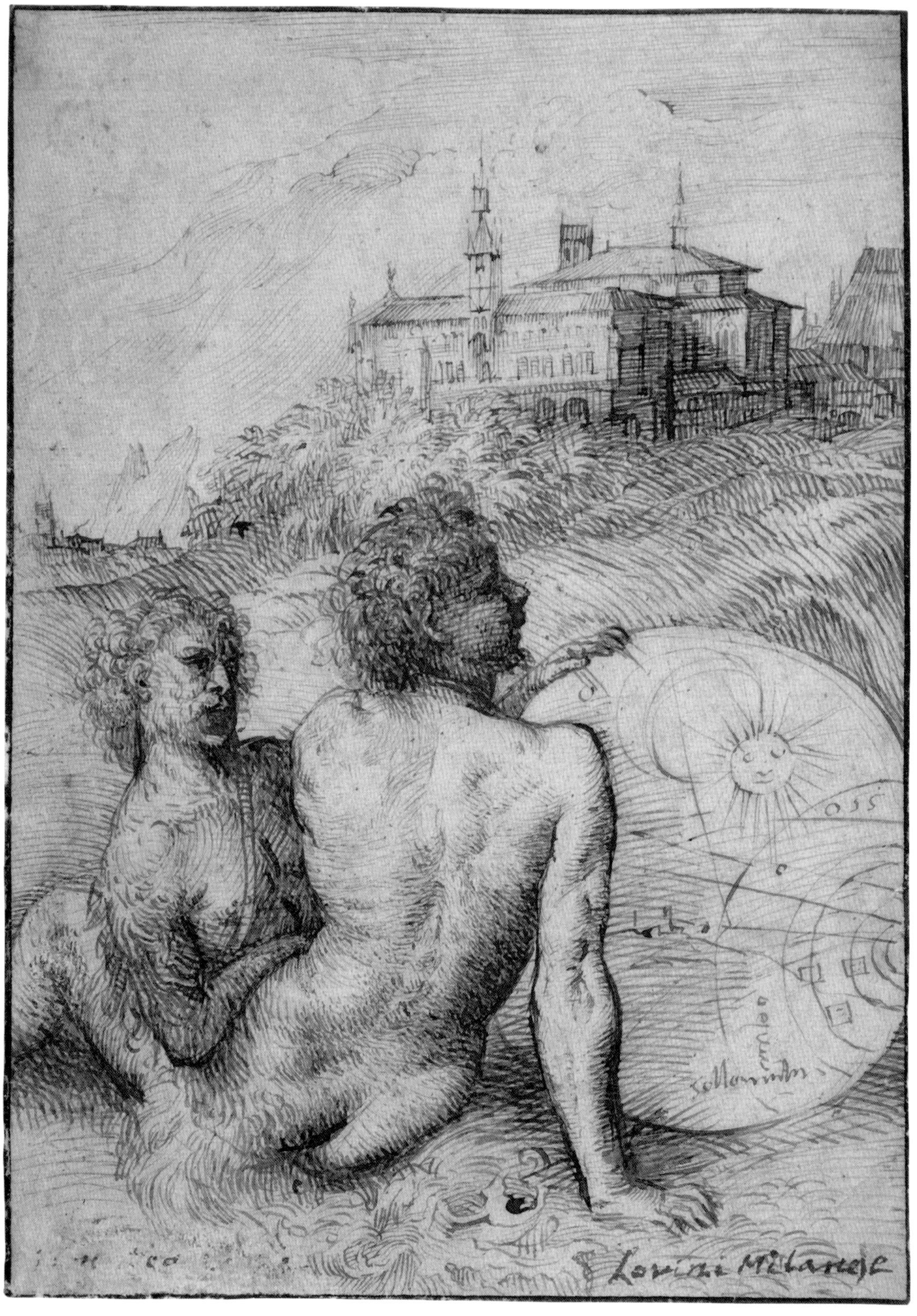

Titian produced this allusive imagery in a climate of renewed scientific debate in Italy about the validity of astrology in relation to astronomy. In the 1490s to early 1500s, Venice (the capital of the Italian book printing industry) and the Veneto region offered a more sympathetic culture for the study of astrology. Some reflections of this arise in Giorgione's and Girolamo Campagnola's art, in works that are nearly contemporary with Titian's *Two Satyrs*. The theorist Giovan Battista Abioso wrote his treatise as a dialogue in defense of astrology (entitled *Dialogus in astrologiae defensionem* and published in Venice in 1494), with erudite arguments invoking the authority of Ptolemy, Albumasar (Abu Ma'shar al-Balkhi), and Albertus Magnus. He noted astrology was a "supreme science" and "divine wisdom" guiding humanity to foresee the future, whether fortunate or calamitous.[4] In 1496 Abioso settled in Treviso (north of Venice), where he formed a school of astrology, not far from Castelfranco, Giorgione's hometown.[5]

The frescoes by Giorgione in ocher monochrome on the long frieze of the main room in the Casa Marta-Pellizzari (now Museo Casa Giorgione) depict the attributes and instruments of the Liberal Arts and Mechanical Arts.[6] A portion of the frieze includes portraits, inscriptions, astronomical-astrological instruments, and disks with eclipses of the sun and moon (fig. 45). Based on Abiaso's *Dialogus*, the imagery purports to foreshadow the nefarious results of a planetary conjunction of Saturn, Jupiter, and Mars in Cancer in 1503 that would lead to a total eclipse of the moon.[7] The bearded astrologer at extreme right in Giorgione's celebrated painting *The Three Philosophers* (ca. 1506–9, Kunsthistorisches Museum, Vienna) holds a sheet of lunar computations.[8]

In Giulio Campagnola's engraving, dated 1509, a recumbent astrologer on an island leans on a celestial disk or globe much like that in Titian's *Satyrs* (fig. 46). The landscape with an architectural complex of buildings on the opposite shore in Campagnola's engraving also resembles the background in the *Satyrs*, but there the seething monster at right looks ominously at a skull and bones in an otherwise idyllic scene.[9] The engraving and a poem by Campagnola with astrological imagery have been connected to a reading that predicted the dramatic defeat of Venetian forces in the Battle of Agnadello on May 14, 1509, during the War of the League of Cambrai (1508–16).[10]

CCB

SELECTED REFERENCES: Zafran 1985, cat. 3, pp. 20–21 (with bibliography); Wethey 1987, pp. 18, 151, 159, 167–68 no. 54; Konrad Oberhuber, cat. 99, in Laclotte 1993, p. 510; Bambach 1999; Hans Aurenhammer, cat. 19, in Eclercy and Aurenhammer 2019, pp. 81–83.

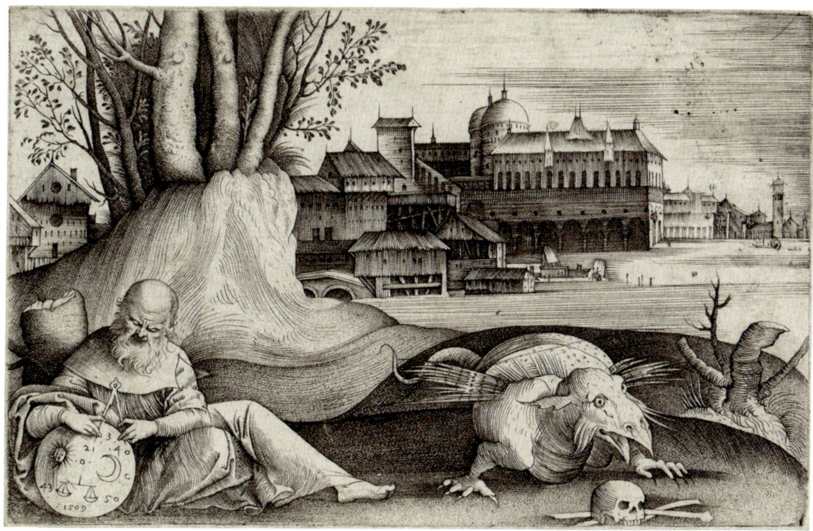

Fig. 46. Giulio Campagnola (Italian, ca. 1482–after 1515). *The Astrologer*, 1509. Engraving with stippling (second state), 4 × 6⅛ in. (10 × 15.3 cm). British Museum, London, Purchase W. & G. Smith (1845,0825.771)

CAT. 32

TITIAN (TIZIANO VECELLIO)

Italian, 1485/90?–1576

Cupid and the Wheel of Fortune, ca. 1520

Oil on canvas, 26 × 21¾ in. (65.9 × 55.3 cm)

National Gallery of Art, Washington, D.C., Samuel H. Kress Collection (1939.1.213)

A WINGED *amorino*, or cupid, buffeted by winds, resolutely holds on to a large wheel, his feet firmly planted on a stone ledge; behind him are the antique motifs of an animal skull (bucranium), tied to a tree with ribbons, and a hanging mask. Painted with a near-monochrome (*grisaille*) palette, this is an inventive response to classical sculptural reliefs with boys as protagonists. Ancient Roman sarcophagi featuring a variety of activities enacted by children, from hunting scenes to mythological episodes, gave impetus to Renaissance artists; the ledge-type motif seen here also appears in these works.

Titian incorporated fictive reliefs of animated boys into some paintings, such as *Sacred and Profane Love* (1515–16, Galleria Borghese, Rome) and *Clarice Strozzi* (1542, Staatliche Museen zu Berlin, Gemäldegalerie), the latter with its wrestling putti.[1] Here the imagery relates to the power of Love to arrest the movement of the wheel of fortune (Fortune, or Fate, in classical art familiarly appears with her foot on a wheel). Scholarly debate about the precise subject serves to highlight the poetic nature of this type of imagery, which viewers' conversations could illuminate with new meanings.[2] The wheel may also represent the inexorable course of time, leading onward to death. A recent interpretation links this image to the emblematic theme of a Roman fifteenth-century plaquette, in which an *amorino* pulls at the wheel of Bacchus and Ariadne's chariot; such objects were widely collected.[3] References to the inevitable passing of time and the brevity of life are also here in the tree and in the beribboned skull, which recalls sacrifice and death, while the grinning mask may allude to the ephemeral theater of life. The idea that Love's strength will overcome time and fate is uplifting and consoling.

This striking work is unusual for Titian, but its rarity may be merely a question of survival. His early monochrome frescoes at the Fondaco dei Tedeschi involved cupids and *all'antica* imagery. While Andrea Mantegna had pioneered a mode of *grisaille* allegorical or narrative paintings in the form of illusionistic sculpture, Titian did not produce that type of autonomous painting, nor did he seek to render the actuality of marble or bronze. However, an inventory reference to *timpani* by Titian that were set at a high level in Gabriele Vendramin's *camerino d'anticaglie*, the treasure house of his collection, is tantalizing in its implication that those lost canvases might have presented imagery of a kind found in painted covers, suitable for pairing with antique-style objects.[4] A likely function for the *Cupid and the Wheel of Fortune* is that of a *timpano*, or cover, especially given its freedom of handling; it probably dates from about 1520.[5] Its affinity with the imagery of small bronze plaquettes is appropriate in evoking the type of object that the elite sitter of a related portrait would have known and handled. The portrait it likely covered must have been relatively small, but whether it was of a male or female sitter is open to speculation.

CW

SELECTED REFERENCES: Shapley 1979, vol. 1 pp. 481–82, vol. 2 pls. 342, 342A; Dülberg 1990, pp. 55–58, 295–96 no. 336, pl. 140 fig. 298; Peter Humfrey, "Titian / Cupid with the Wheel of Time / c. 1515/1520," in *Italian Paintings*, https://purl.org/nga/collection/artobject/354.

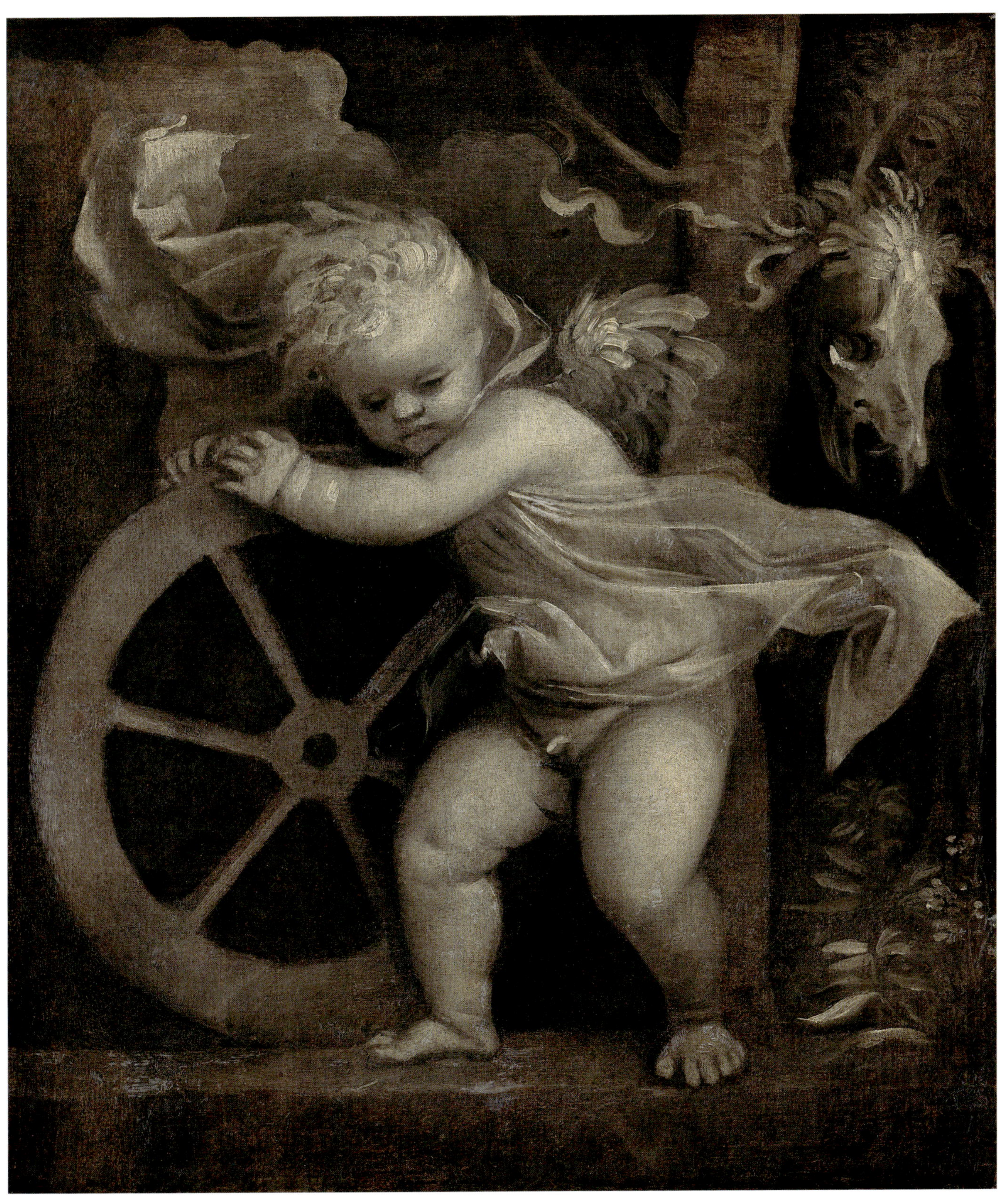

CAT. 33

TITIAN (TIZIANO VECELLIO)

Italian, 1485/90?–1576

The Triumph of Love, ca. 1543–46

Oil on canvas, mounted on panel, Diam. 34¾ in. (88.3 cm)

Ashmolean Museum of Art and Archaeology, University of Oxford. Accepted by HM Government in lieu of Inheritance Tax and allocated to the Ashmolean Museum, and purchased with the assistance of the Art Fund (with a contribution from the Wolfson Foundation), Daniel Katz Ltd, the Friends of the Ashmolean, the Tradescant Group, the Elias Ashmole Group, Mr. Michael Barclay, the Highfield family, the late Mrs. Yvonne Carey, the late Mrs. Felicity Rhodes (Virtue-Tebbs, Madan and Russell Funds), and other private donations, 2008 (WA2008.89)

A DELIGHTFULLY INVENTIVE work, this painting shows Cupid, god of love, preparing to fire an arrow from his bow while insouciantly, if precariously, balanced on the back of a roaring lion. The group is placed in a garden before a screen of foliage fronting a view of a lagoon in which distant Veneto buildings recede toward the craggy Dolomite Mountains. This scene is observed through an oculus, or round window: indeed, the fearsome lion, who rests his front paws on the curved ledge, seems about to spring into the viewer's space. Once rectangular in form, the canvas was cut to a roundel and laid on panel, probably in the late seventeenth century.[1] It is a rare survivor as a documented cover (*timpano*) for a now-lost portrait of a Venetian noblewoman, also by Titian, in the collection of Gabriele Vendramin.[2]

Titian took the familiar classical subject of Love Conquers All and personalized it for his patron and friend. The idea of true or virtuous love subjugating the wilder passions, from Virgil's *Eclogues*, was often represented as Cupid seated on a tamed lion or in a chariot drawn by lions (see cat. 34). However, Titian alluded here to a prized sculpture group in Vendramin's celebrated *camerino d'anticaglie* showing Cupid trampling on a lion. Recalling his visit there, the writer Anton Francesco Doni described a conversation he and Vendramin enjoyed while examining the bronze group and its pleasing invention.[3] In creating a circular composition, Titian also referred to the imagery on the reverses of medals that feature naturalistic elements breaking through the molded borders; Vendramin was proud of his substantial holdings of medals. The original illusionistic effect of the painting must have been striking.

As a cover for a female portrait, this allegory gave pause for thought, in anticipation of revelation. Titian painted few portraits of Venetian noblewomen. Since the collection inventory recording the portrait provides a description of the sitter's stance and costume, the lost work was almost certainly a version of one of his portraits of Elisabetta Querini Massola (died ca. 1559).[4] The first, completed by December 1543, was for her intimate friend, Pietro Bembo (see cat. 23), with whom Elisabetta shared interests in art and antiquities. A copy, presumably of that portrait, was owned by Bembo's friend Carlo Gualteruzzi, while a new portrait was painted by Titian in 1545 for the papal nuncio in Venice, Giovanni della Casa. Vendramin's version, probably by Titian's studio, was one of four paintings attributed to the artist hanging in a *camera*, perhaps a bedroom, together with a Byzantine-style Madonna.[5] Yet the *Triumph* is an autograph work and an utterly creative one, evidencing changes of mind in the underdrawing and great freedom of handling, with quick touches such as a stroke of white paint on Cupid's calf to give a sense of tension and energy.[6] Stylistically, it belongs to about 1543–46.

While the allusions to Vendramin's sculpture and medal collection are clear, in the imagery of the Venetian lagoon and the flight of Cupid's arrows, Titian was additionally referring to the sitter of the portrait beneath. Poetry in honor of Elisabetta by Bembo and Pietro Aretino appeared in the late 1530s and early 1540s, while a Petrarchan-style sonnet that Giovanni Della Casa wrote in early 1545 in praise of her beauty and virtue presented her as a goddess arising from the Adriatic, whose gaze alone had more power than Cupid's arrows to ignite love. The nexus of friendship, literary interests, and Titian patronage involving Aretino, Bembo, and Della Casa has long been investigated by scholars, but the role of Elisabetta Querini as a patron has only recently been appraised, demonstrating her distinctive influence in this arena.[7] Della Casa felt the force of her personality as Elisabetta impatiently awaited his sonnets in her honor, and the commission to Titian for her first portrait may have come from her, as a gift to Bembo.[8] Titian was aware of the conventions of poetry in praise of female beauty, and his painted cover is a refreshingly witty image for a portrait of

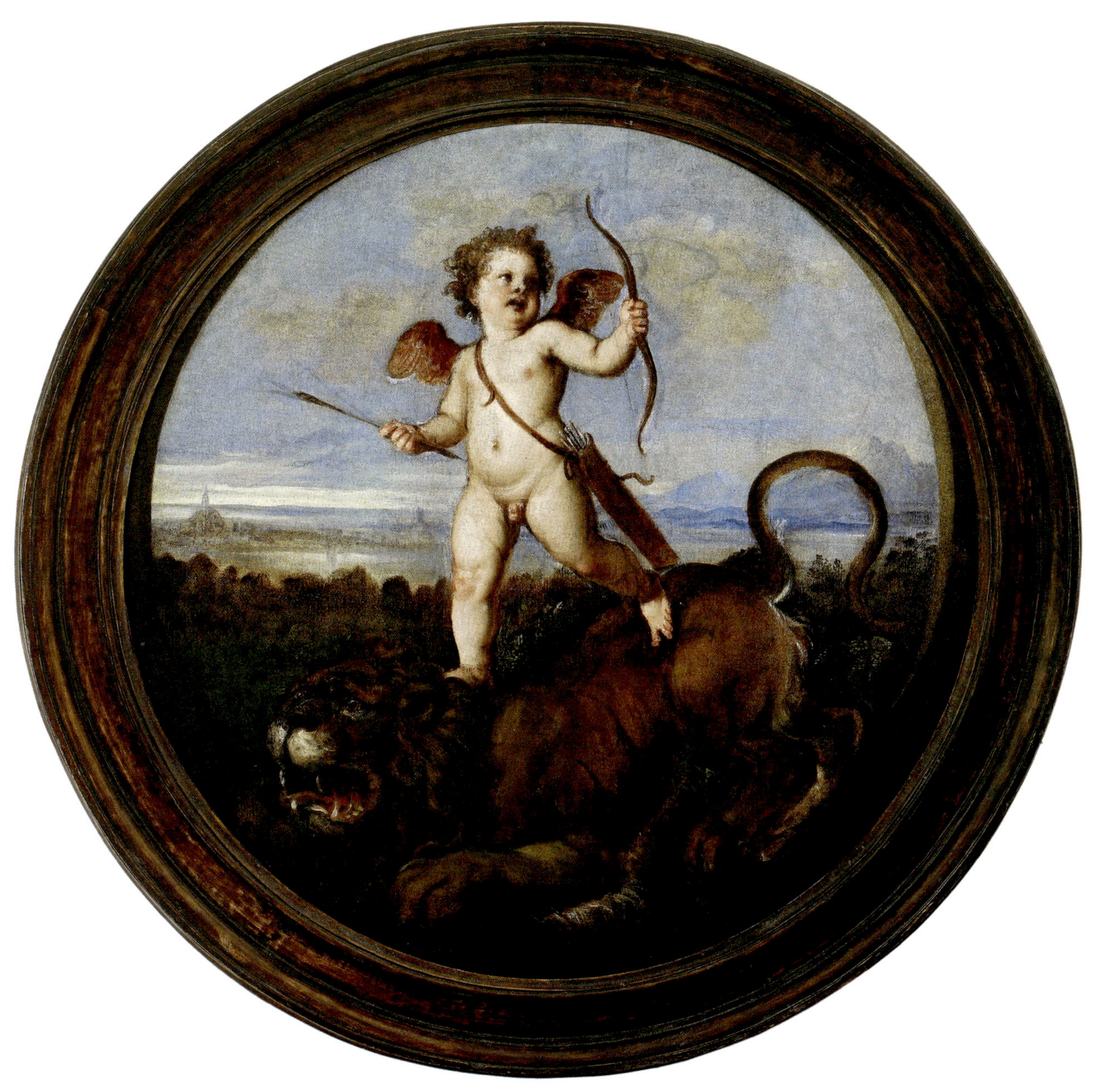

a mature noblewoman, whom Vendramin would also have known. Vendramin surely commissioned the cover not only to add to his collection of Titian's paintings but also to celebrate Elisabetta as a renowned literary muse.
CW

SELECTED REFERENCES: Whistler 2009; Whistler 2012; Dunkerton and Spring 2013.

CAT. 34

ANDREA ALCIATO AND JEAN LEFÈVRE

Alciato: Italian, 1492–1550, Lefèvre: French, 1493–1563
"Potentissimus affectus Amor"/*Amour affection tres puissante*
("Love, a Most Powerful Passion"), 1536

From *Livret des emblemes de maistre Andre Alciat* [. . .] (*Booklet of the Emblems of Master Andrea Alciato* [. . .]) published by Chrestien Wechel, Paris, 1536

Text in letterpress, woodcut illustrations, 6⅜ × 4¼ × ⅝ in. (16.2 × 10.8 × 1.6 cm)

The Metropolitan Museum of Art, New York, Harris Brisbane Dick Fund, 1937 (37.37.7)

IN DISCUSSING TITIAN'S *Triumph of Love*, Catherine Whistler writes that painted covers often provided a playful or erudite gloss on the picture hidden beneath.[1] During the sixteenth century, in particular, the number of resources available to inspire such imagery grew exponentially. These included illustrated publications of fables and emblems, both of which relied on symbolic imagery accompanied by short passages of text to convey their hidden, deeper meaning. While fables such as Aesop's had been collected since antiquity, the emblem or emblem book was a product of the Renaissance. Some of the heraldic elements (imprese) of the emblem were already employed in the fifteenth century, appearing, for instance, on the reverses of medals and painted portraits, but the Italian humanist Andrea Alciato (also Alciatus or Alciati) is generally credited with the official codification of the new genre.

Alciato's collection of emblems (1531), the first ever to be published in book form, was the product of a lifelong interest in history, poetry, epigraphy, and Egyptian hieroglyphs. He combined these interests in his emblems, which consisted of a symbolic image, a title or motto, and a short text explaining the meaning or moral behind the imagery. Alciato had developed the concept as early as 1522, when, according to a letter to the printer-publisher Francesco Calvo, he had fashioned a booklet of emblems (now lost) in manuscript version: "During this Saturnalia, at the behest of the illustrious Ambrogio Visconti, I composed a little booklet of epigrams, which I entitled Emblems: in separate epigrams I describe something which, from history or from nature, has some elegant significance, after which painters, goldsmiths, and founders [metalworkers] could fashion the kind of thing we call badges and which we fasten on hats, or use as trade-marks, like the anchor of Aldus, the dove of Froben, and the elephant of Calvo, long pregnant, but producing nothing."[2]

The sources for many of Alciato's emblems can be traced back to antiquity. For example, the Latin verse accompanying "Love, a Most Powerful Passion" derives from the Greek poet Marcus Argentarius (active 1st century BCE or 1st century CE). His epigrams were known in the sixteenth century through the so-called *Planudean Anthology*, a collection of epigrams from around 500 BCE to 800 CE compiled by the Byzantine monk and scholar Maximus Planudes.[3] Alciato paraphrases one of Argentarius's epigrams in which the latter seems to describe the decorations of a signet ring incised with an image of Eros taming one or several lions. A number of contemporaneous gemstones survive that match this description,[4] and the subject is also found in various iterations in other Greek and Roman works of art. Although often equated with the positive expression "Omnia vincit amor" (Love Conquers All), derived from Virgil's *Eclogues*, Argentarius's and Alciato's texts both contain a slightly more duplicitous message that urges the reader to be wary of love. Their verses end with the ominous realization that, if Eros can tame something as wild as a lion, a mere mortal human stands no chance against him: "Would one who has the power to conquer such a beast leave us unharmed?"[5]
FS

SELECTED REFERENCES: Grässe 1859–69, vol. 1, pp. 62–63; Brunet 1860–65, vol. 1, cols. 147–49; Brun 1930, p. 139; Landwehr 1976, no. 17, p. 26; Daly 1985, vol. 1 no. 106, vol. 2 no. 106; Adams et al. 1999–2002, vol. 1, no. F.006, pp. 16–17.

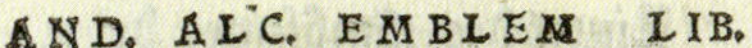
AND. ALC. EMBLEM LIB.

Potentißimus affectus Amor.

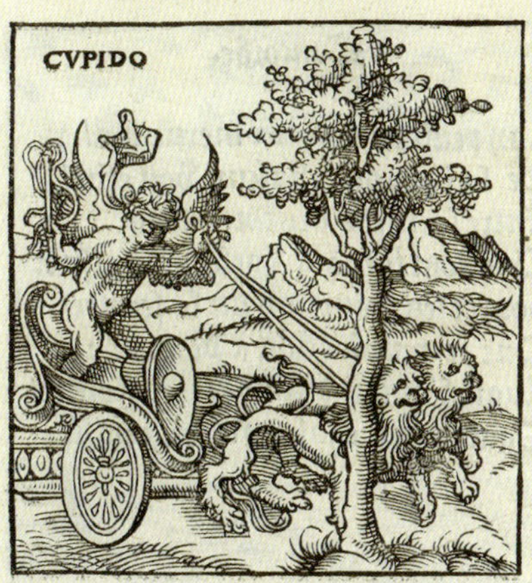

Aspice ut inuictus uires auriga leonis
Expressus gemma pusio uincat Amor.
Vtq; manu hac scuticam teneat, hac flectat habenas,
Vtq; sit in pueri plurimus ore decor.
Dira lues procul esto, feram qui uincere talem
Est potis, à nobis temperet an ne manus?

Liuret des Emblemes de
Andre Alciat.

Amour affection trespuissante.

Pensez a ce petit chartier
Qui scait mettre au ioug les lyons/
Nous pourra il point chastier:
Et ouurer sur ce que voulions/
Noz cueurs: dōt fault que allieurs pliōs:
Car sil est puissant pour telles bestes/
Pensez vous que nous en allions/
Sans quil nous lie cueurs & testes?

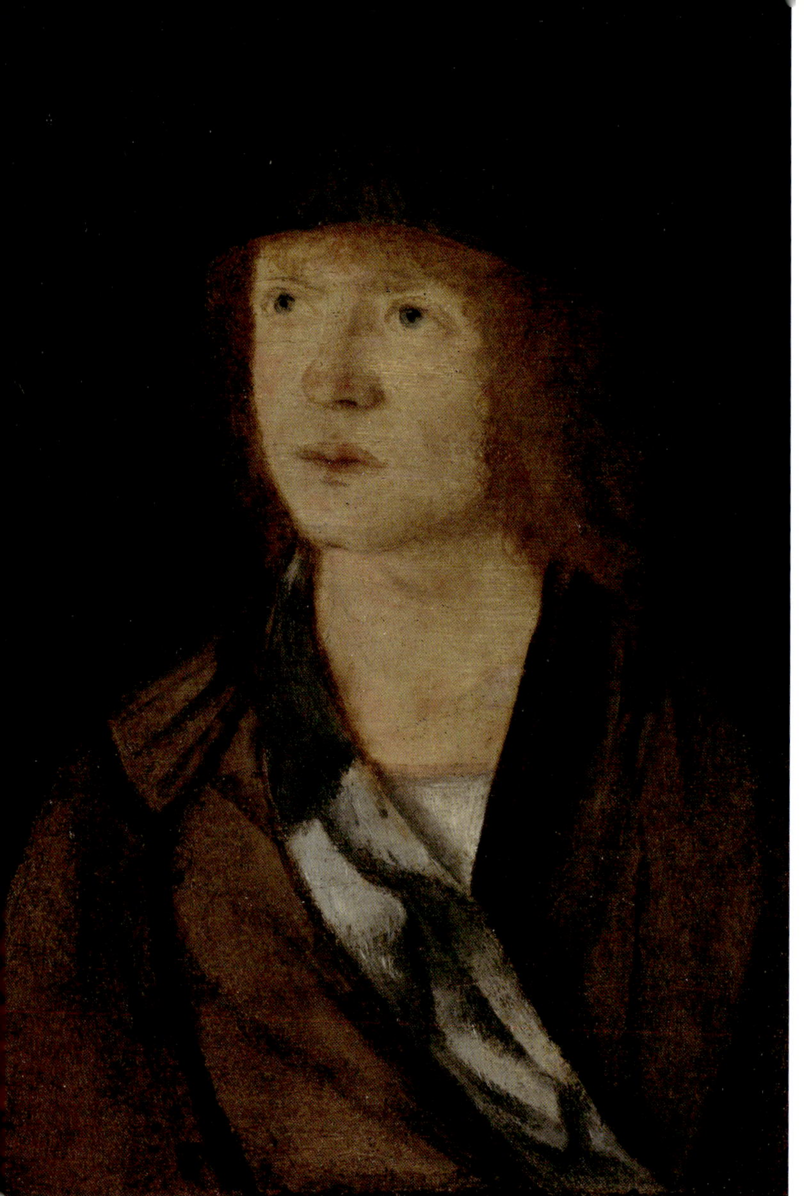

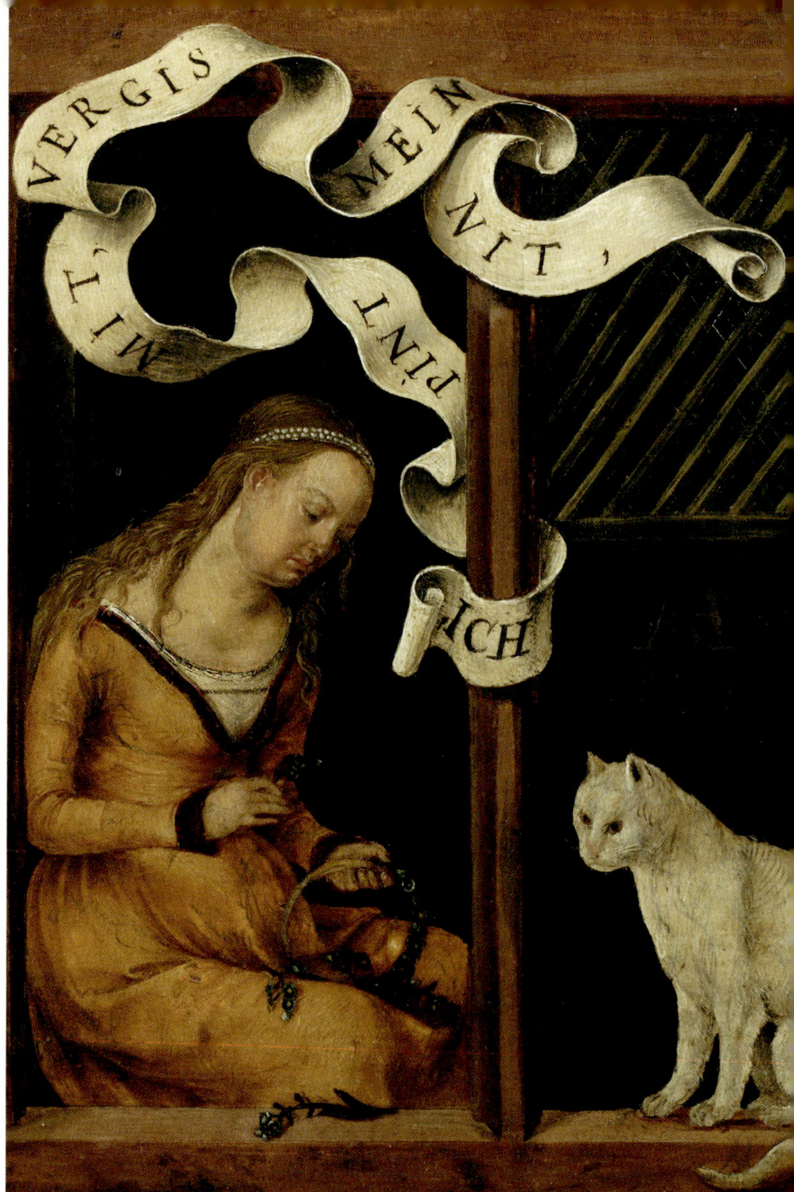

COVERED PORTRAITS IN NORTHERN EUROPE, 1500–1550

JOSHUA P. WATERMAN

The double-sided and covered portraits produced in northern Europe during the first half of the sixteenth century share many characteristics with those of the preceding decades.[1] Coats of arms, which also appeared prominently in contemporaneous manuscript illumination and prints (cats. 36 and 37), remained the principal accompaniment to such portraits. They were far more common than vanitas motifs and allegories of love and virtue, the other main subjects. The latter two categories did, however, receive greater attention than before, appearing more often and with more variety. In general, the period is marked by a greater quantity of production. Within that increase, portrait diptychs of married couples especially proliferated.

The sixteenth-century growth in portrait commissions was driven largely by demand among prosperous merchants, entrepreneurs, and bankers in the major centers of commerce. In the Low Countries, Antwerp became the leading commercial and artistic hub, having supplanted Bruges in that distinction. In the German-speaking lands, the bulk of production was concentrated in the so-called free imperial cities, such as Nuremberg, Augsburg, Frankfurt, and Cologne. At the same time, the princely court remained a significant source of commissions, not just for state portraits meant for permanent display but also for likenesses of a private nature. In the sacred sphere, devotional portraits on diptych and triptych wings, by nature double-sided, continued to be made for both clerical and lay patrons; however, the Protestant Reformation's criticism of image veneration caused a decline in that portrait type.

The enduring prevalence of heraldic decorations is represented in this section by Martin Caldenbach's 1506 portrait of Jakob Stralenberg, shown together with its original sliding cover (cat. 35A,B), and by Bernhard Strigel's 1527 diptych of Margarethe Vöhlin and Hans Roth (cat. 40A,B).[2] In both instances, the family coats of arms were displayed when the works were closed, on the cover of the Strahlenberg portrait and on the respective reverses of the Vöhlin and Roth likenesses.

Whereas the Vöhlin–Roth panels retain their original frames and are thus in a remarkably complete state of preservation, the fragmentary condition of the Stralenberg portrait and cover is more typical. Separation and dispersal eventually befell most double-sided or covered portraits. For a work once fitted with a sliding cover, the removal of the original frame represented a particularly acute loss of context, since the procedure eliminated a distinctive identifying feature: the grooves into which the cover was inserted.

In light of the great rarity of intact survivals,[3] the small portrait of a woman attributed to Ludger tom Ring the Younger (cat. 41) provides a near-unique opportunity to study an example that retains its original frame and sliding cover. A comparably rare instance is Albrecht Dürer's 1526 portrait of Hieronymus Holzschuher, whose extant heraldic cover can still be slotted into the original frame (see fig. 16).

Devotional art also provided a setting for portraits that were mostly kept concealed, to be opened and viewed during celebrations of the Mass or for private devotions.[4] Lucas Cranach the Elder's *Portrait of a Man with a Rosary* of about 1508 (cat. 39) reflects the ongoing currency of such works. Bearing a grisaille image of a male saint on the reverse, the panel originally formed the left folding wing of a small triptych. The man's wife and a grisaille female saint appeared on either side of the opposite wing. A sacred subject, now lost, occupied the center. The closed triptych, with the wings folded over the center, displayed the two saints side by side; in their muted, gray tonality, they were meant to evoke stone sculpture. Painted imitations of statues were common on triptych exteriors in the Low Countries, where Cranach likely

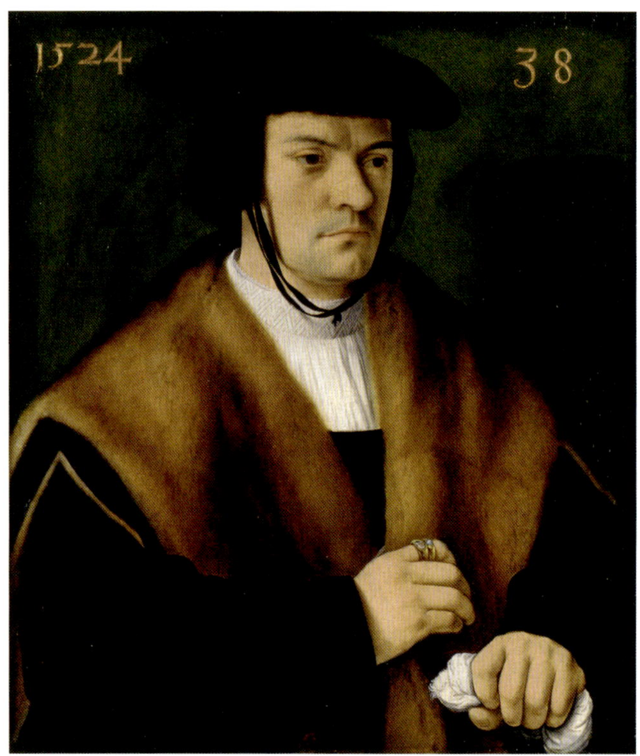

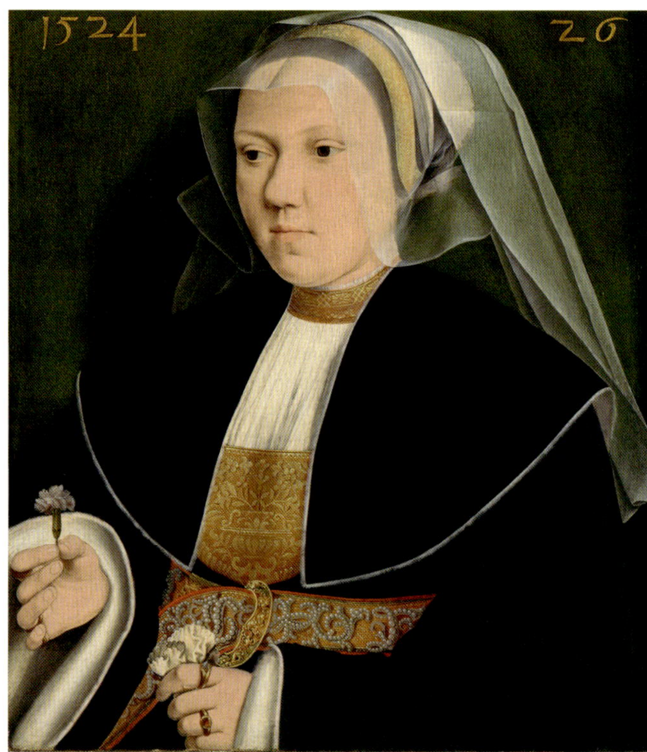

created these panels. Opening the triptych increased the visual splendor: the portraits of the man and woman, rendered in lifelike colors, came into view to the left and right of a religious painting or sculpture. Turned toward the center, the couple appeared to be praying for their future salvation.

Devotional and secular portraits shared a common concern for what lay beyond an individual's brief time in this world—on the one hand, the afterlife, and on the other, remembrance by posterity. Vanitas symbols, which refer to life's transience, make explicit the longing for remembrance inherent in every portrait.[5] Skulls, skeletons, and decaying corpses were this subject's most common motifs. In sixteenth-century northern Europe, vanitas-themed portrait versos gained new prominence, thanks in large part to the extraordinary concentration of examples produced in Cologne.[6] The reverses of numerous panels by Bartholomäus Bruyn the Elder, the city's most prolific portraitist, display a skull in a niche (figs. 47–49).

As happened with vanitas symbols, allegorical depictions also became more common in the North during the sixteenth century.[7] This was likely owing to Northerners' ever-increasing knowledge of Italian portraiture, in which the use of allegory was well established by the turn of the century. The examples associated with portraits mainly concerned conjugal love and personal virtue. A portrait of a young man by Hans Süss von Kulmbach, dated 1508, bears on its reverse a scene of a woman making a wreath of forget-me-nots (cat. 38). Together with the panel's small size, the verso image indicates that the work was likely intended as a courtship or betrothal gift. The forget-me-nots symbolize the man's aspirations of faithfulness and devotion in the relationship.

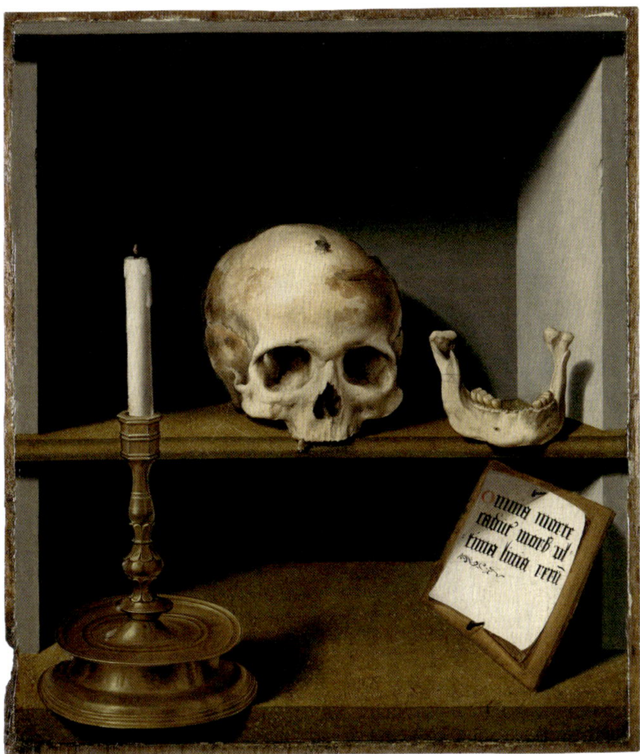

Opposite: **Fig. 47.** Bartholomäus Bruyn the Elder (German, 1493–1555). *Gerhard von Westerberg*, 1524. Oil on wood panel, 24 5/8 × 20 5/8 in. (62.3 × 52.4). Compton Verney, Warwickshire (CVCSC:0385.N)

Fig. 48. Bartholomäus Bruyn the Elder. *Margaretha von Mochau*, 1524. Oil on wood panel, 24 × 20 1/8 in. (61 × 51 cm). Kröller-Müller Museum, Otterlo (KM 102.025)

This page: **Fig. 49.** Bartholomäus Bruyn the Elder. *Vanitas* (reverse of fig. 48)

The 1548 *Allegory of Virtue* by Lucas Cranach the Younger (cat. 42), which is thought to have been a portrait cover, presents a case of the broadening of allegory into the religio-political domain: its iconography may well allude to the Schmalkaldic War (1546–47), a conflict between Catholic imperial forces and a league of Protestant princes. The conjectured accompanying portrait could have represented a key personality of the war, for example, Johann Friedrich I of Saxony, the leader of the Protestant forces. Moreover, because the 1548 allegory exists in more than one version, any associated likeness would also have been made in multiples. Serial production was a relatively new, Reformation-era development in the genre of the covered portrait, one inaugurated by the marriage portraits of Martin Luther and Katharina von Bora (cat. 44A,B).

CAT. 35A

MARTIN CALDENBACH

German, ca. 1480–1518

Jakob Stralenberg, 1506

Oil on linden panel, overall: 16⅛ × 11⅛ in. (40.8 × 28.1 cm); painted surface: 15⅝ × 10¾ in. (39.5 × 27.2 cm)

Städel Museum, Frankfurt am Main (1739)

CAT. 35B

MARTIN CALDENBACH

Sliding Cover with Stralenberg Coat of Arms, 1506

Oil on linden panel, 11¼ × 11 in. (28.6 × 27.7 cm), excluding ¼ in. (0.7 cm) strip added to left side

Inscribed (at upper center): *Jacob Stralnburger war also gestalt/Do er was xxxvii jar alt/ANNO M D VI* (Jacob Stralnburger [*sic*] looked like this when he was 37 years old, in the year 1506)

Historisches Museum, Frankfurt am Main (X03330)

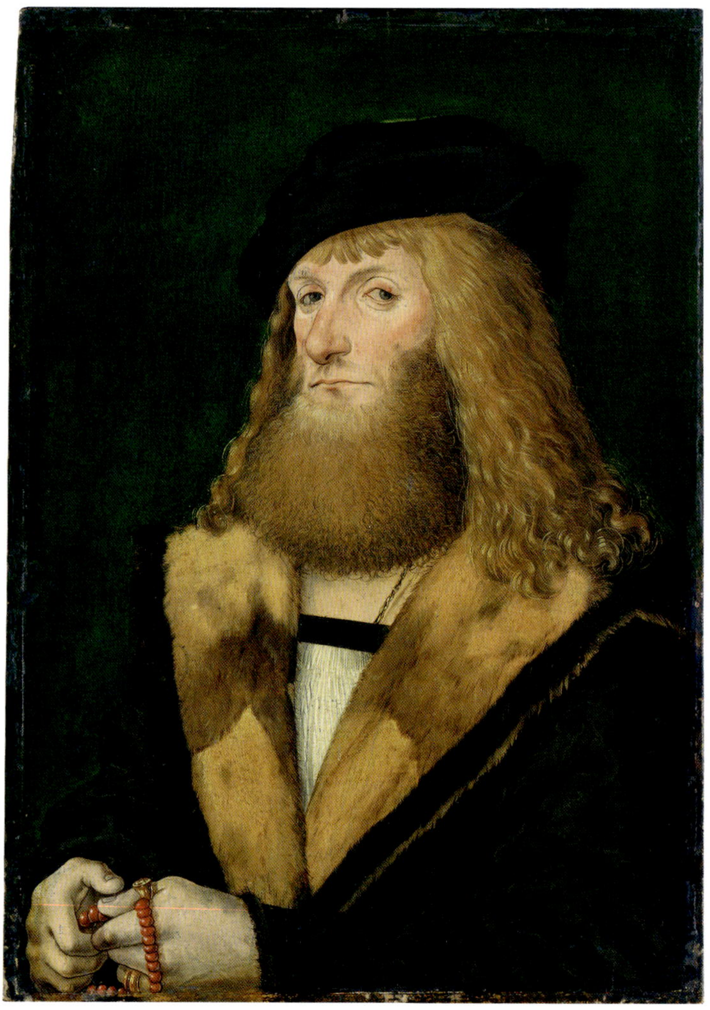

THIS WORK IS the only independent portrait securely attributed to Martin Caldenbach, one of the leading painters in Frankfurt at the beginning of the sixteenth century. Trained in the workshop of his father, Hans, Martin became a sought-after painter of altarpieces.[1] Most of his preserved paintings are religious panels. His artistic skill and judgment were esteemed by none other than Albrecht Dürer, with whom he was personally acquainted.[2]

The sitter, Jakob Stralenberg (1469/70–1516), was a Frankfurt patrician active in the local government. He became a member of the city council in 1499, served as a lay jurist (*Schöffe*) in 1505, and twice held mayoral posts (1503, 1510).[3] Stralenberg is identifiable in this portrait thanks to the cover panel, which bears his family coat of arms[4] and an inscription that states his name, his age of thirty-seven, and the 1506 date of the depiction. The inclusion of a string of rosary beads indicates that Stralenberg must have wished to emphasize his piety. He married in 1508, but it seems unlikely that this work served a courtship function, in which a flower would be the usual attribute.

Whereas the portrait retains its original dimensions, the cover has been cut down (mainly at the top and bottom edges), resulting in a nearly square shape.[5] That the two belong together is supported by several factors: the similar widths; the style of the script and curled ornaments on the cover, which relate to corresponding elements in Caldenbach's drawings and a woodcut by him; and the similar mossy green tone found in both the heraldic medallion and the portrait's original background, the latter now darkened by the addition of a bluish layer.[6]

The heraldic panel is thought to have functioned most likely as a sliding cover. Nevertheless, a hinged attachment, in the manner of a diptych's, remains a possibility because crucial material evidence has been lost, namely, the original frame or frames and the surfaces of both panel reverses, which have been planed down.[7] One configuration is impossible: the two depictions could not have formed the front and back of a single panel, later split apart, since the wooden supports differ in their board counts.[8]

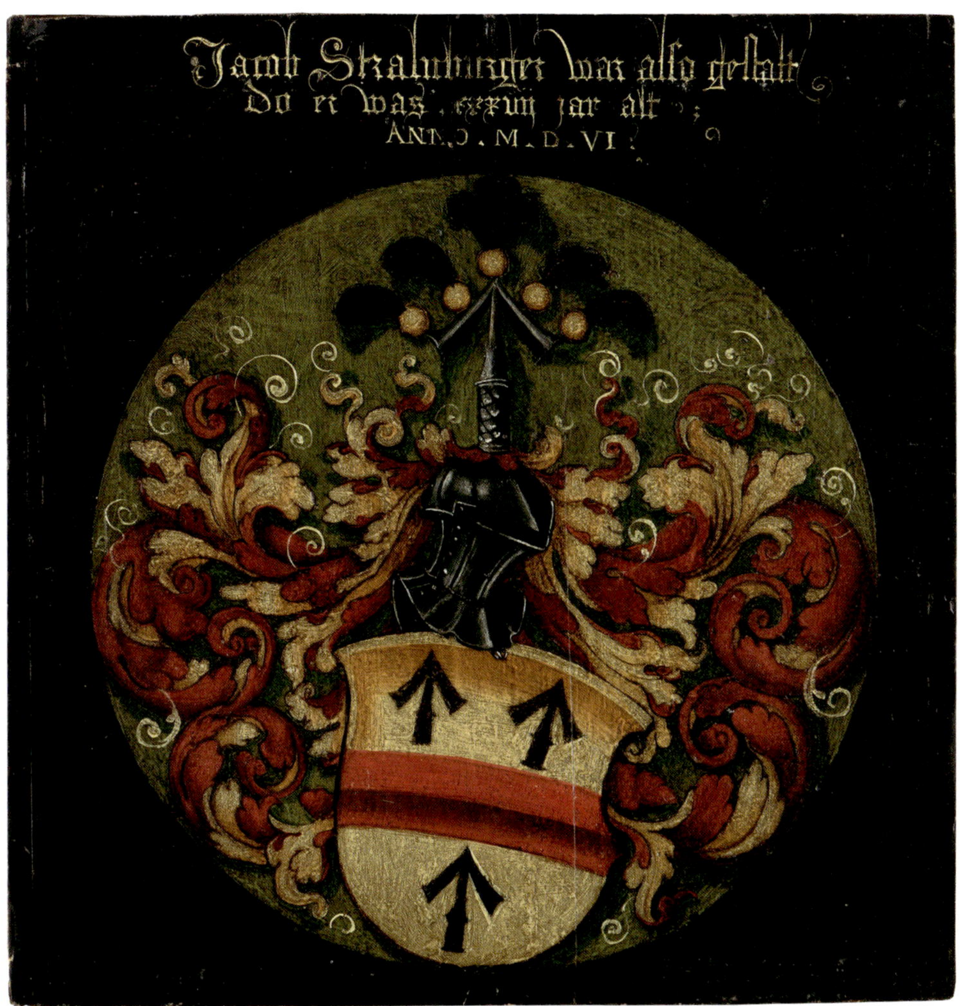

Caldenbach's likeness of Stralenberg is striking in its combination of realism and refinement. The sixteenth-century viewer, having removed the portrait's cover, encountered a calm, confident, somewhat stern character. While the depiction is frank—with droopy eyelids, thin lips, ruddy patches in the skin, and a wart on the cheek—the execution exudes elegance, especially in the graceful quality of line throughout the facial contours and in the hair and beard.

Like all the other paintings associated with Caldenbach, this one lacks a signature. Yet because of its outstanding quality and general resemblance to Dürer's early portraits, the present work played a key role in the early twentieth-century rediscovery and assembly of Caldenbach's oeuvre, which includes drawings signed with the monogram *MC*.[9] A telltale detail of Caldenbach's authorship is the presence of X-like crossed veins on the back of Stralenberg's hand, a feature that appears in many of the artist's paintings and drawings.[10]
JPW

SELECTED REFERENCES: Buchner 1953, no. 40, pp. 54–55, 192, fig. 38; Hüneke 1965, pp. 133–37, 207–8, no. 13; Dülberg 1990, p. 197, no. 71, pl. 178 figs. 422, 423; Bodo Brinkmann, in Brinkmann and Kemperdick 2005, pp. 142–52, figs. 109, 112; Schedl 2016, no. 72, pp. 306–8, 543–44, figs. 127, 128.

CAT. 36

UNKNOWN ARTIST

South Netherlandish

Manuscript Leaf with Coat of Arms, from a Book of Hours, ca. 1500

Tempera, ink, and shell gold on parchment, sheet: 6 5/16 × 4 11/16 in. (16 × 11.9 cm); illumination: 5 7/16 × 3 11/16 in. (13.8 × 9.4 cm)

Inscribed (on *bas-de-page*): *God zij uns holt, lucke valt menich folt* (God be kind to us, as luck fails every so often) [love knot with *S*, *T*, and *A*]

The Metropolitan Museum of Art, New York, The Friedsam Collection, Bequest of Michael Friedsam, 1931 (32.100.475a)

THIS RICHLY DECORATED parchment page is from a set of eight detached manuscript leaves that entered the collection of The Metropolitan Museum of Art in 1931. Texts on the other leaves identify the original manuscript as a book of hours, a type of lay prayer book popular across Europe at the end of the Middle Ages. By the time this manuscript was made, printed books of hours were being mass-produced and ranged from plain editions intended for buyers of modest means to lavishly illustrated examples for wealthy patrons. To compete with the cheaper printed books, workshops adapted to these new circumstances by creating highly individualized manuscripts with lively decorations influenced by the latest fashions. In a time when books were becoming affordable for almost everyone, expensive manuscripts retained their appeal as luxurious commodities and bespoke status symbols.

This combination of extravagance and personalization is exemplified in the present page, which showcases the coat of arms of an unidentified Flemish family. The azure arms bear a silver star with a red rose at the center, supported by fierce griffins. The helm is crowned with a silver coronet, mantled in azure, argent (silver), and gules (red) and crested with a bearded man in an elaborate hat. The arms are contained in a coral-pink frame, its inner and outer borders formed by branches (*Astwerk*), a rustic decorative motif popular in the Gothic architecture of the period.[1] Scattered on the frame are pearls and gemstones in golden settings that form pendants and hang from finely wrought chains. The *bas-de-page* features a round pendant hanging from the inner border and containing the motto "God be kind to us, as luck fails every so often" in Flemish on a banderole that is draped over a crown and a love knot with the letters *S*, *T*, and *A*.

Three other leaves in the set are decorated with coats of arms in the *bas-de-page*, and all of these show the arms impaled with three turrets of gold on an azure ground.[2] This implies that the book of hours was made for a couple, perhaps on the occasion of their marriage; the arms on the present page would have belonged to the husband, and the impaled arms to his wife.

Clearly an impressive commission, the manuscript was an effective display of great affluence, and yet its wealthy patrons were probably not aristocrats. Their arms and motto are not easily identified in the surviving sources, and although bright and attractive, the manuscript's illuminations have a sketchy quality that suggests the artists were working quickly, producing luxury commodities for patrons whose budgets were expansive but not unlimited. What the manuscript and its flamboyant heraldry reflect instead is a moment in northern European history when a wide array of well-to-do middle-class families were claiming elite status, using their newfound wealth derived from commerce and urbanization to participate in forms of conspicuous consumption that had once been the sole purview of the landed aristocracy.

SF

SELECTED REFERENCES: unpublished.

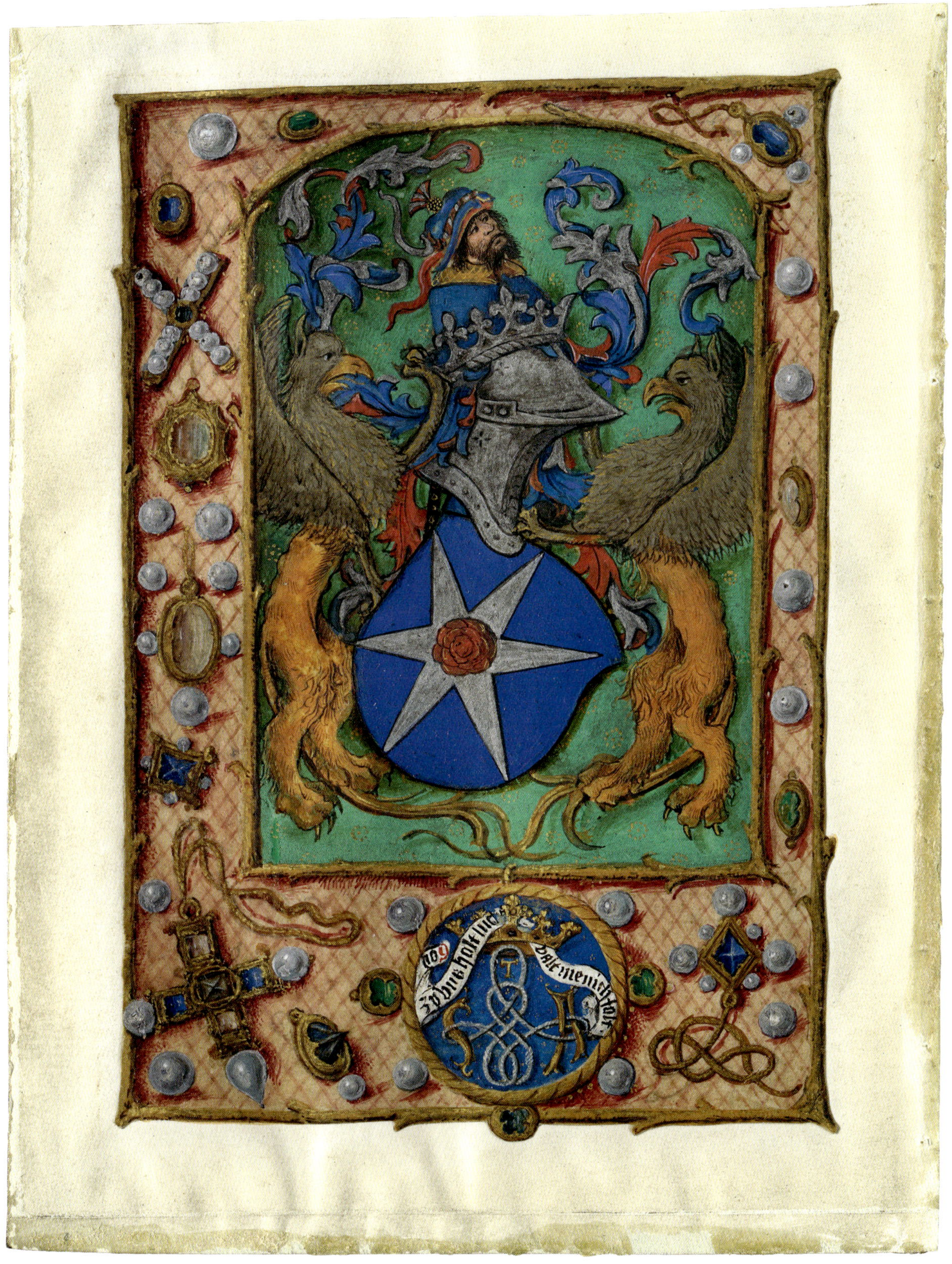

CAT. 37

ALBRECHT DÜRER

German, 1471–1528

Coat of Arms with Skull, 1503

Engraving on antique laid paper, plate: 8 11/16 × 6 3/16 in. (22.1 × 15.8 cm); sheet: 9 9/16 × 7 1/16 in. (24.3 × 17.9 cm)

Signed and dated in the plate (at bottom center): *AD* [monogram] / *1503*

The Metropolitan Museum of Art, New York, Fletcher Fund, 1919 (19.73.113)

IN THIS ENGRAVING, Albrecht Dürer creatively reconfigures the elements of a heraldic display, known as an "achievement": a shield; a helmet crested by angel's wings; and two supporting figures, a bride and a Wild Man. A mythical creature from Germanic folklore, the Wild Man frequently appeared in medieval and Renaissance art as a bearer and protector of coats of arms.[1] Dürer deploys this well-established visual trope to create an allegory centered around themes of love and death, emphasizing the Wild Man's associations with virility, lust, and marriage and depicting on his shield not an armorial design but a human skull. The presence of the Wild Man and the combination of allegory and heraldry have distinct parallels with the pictorial language of Renaissance portrait covers and reverses (see cats. 13 and 16).

Scholars have frequently interpreted this print as a memento mori in which the bride—a symbol of youth, beauty, and love—is the unwitting victim of Lust and Death.[2] Yet Dürer may have intended to accord the woman greater agency. Her manner is completely unlike that of the imperiled, clearly distressed females in Dürer's *Young Woman Attacked by Death* (also known as *The Ravisher*) and *Abduction of Proserpina*.[3] So, too, does she differ from the seemingly unmoved figure in his *Promenade*, in which a youthful couple strolls outdoors, oblivious to Death lurking in the background.[4] Instead, this woman evokes the heroines (or antiheroines) connected to the so-called Power of Women theme. Her subtle smile and tilted head recall, for example, fifteenth- and early sixteenth-century depictions of the seductress Phyllis riding a besotted and subdued Aristotle.[5] Dürer's figure casts a knowing glance toward her left hand, which gently grasps the strap from which shield and helmet hang. While the Wild Man holds the forked staff, the placement of her hand near the buckle strongly suggests that she wields some measure of control.

Dürer's identification of the woman as a bride, by virtue of her very particular, precisely rendered headdress, further inflects the meaning of the print. The power of a beautiful maiden's love to tame the Wild Man was a highly popular theme in the period, appearing frequently on objects connected to marriage and courtship.[6] A love coffret from the first half of the fifteenth century, for example, portrays a woman leading a Wild Man on a rope or leash (Historisches Museum, Basel).[7] Its inscription, reading *ZAM • VND • WILD • MACHT • MICH • AIN • BILD* (A woman makes me tame and wild), refers both to monogamy and to passion.[8] Dürer's engraving, with its bride and Wild Man groom, similarly points to this dual nature of marriage.

The skull on the shield, then, could refer to the fleeting nature of earthly love. In the context of an image overtly alluding to familial arms, however, the marital (and implied physical) union of bride and groom chiefly brings to mind one thing—children, or succession, the hereditary line through which a family name lives on, in a sense overcoming death. Whether Dürer's intention was to celebrate marriage and succession in this way or, conversely, to suggest that even family dynasties eventually fall victim to time, is not clear, although the foliate ornamentation swirling around the helmet is likely a stylized representation of acanthus leaves, long associated with immortality. The angelic wings, while sometimes featuring in personifications of Death, could also represent glory or fame. With this in mind, we might return to the woman's hand on the strap and imagine her unbuckling it, allowing the helmet either to be held aloft by the strength of the wings or brought down by the weight of the shield.

JSS

SELECTED REFERENCES: Koehler 1897, no. 30, p. 30; Meder 1932, no. 98, p. 109; Hollstein 1962, no. 98, p. 89; Strauss 1977, no. 40, pp. 122–23; Husband 1980, cat. 58, pp. 193–96, fig. 129; Schoch et al. 2001, no. 37, pp. 105–7; Spira 2016, no. 57, p. 91.

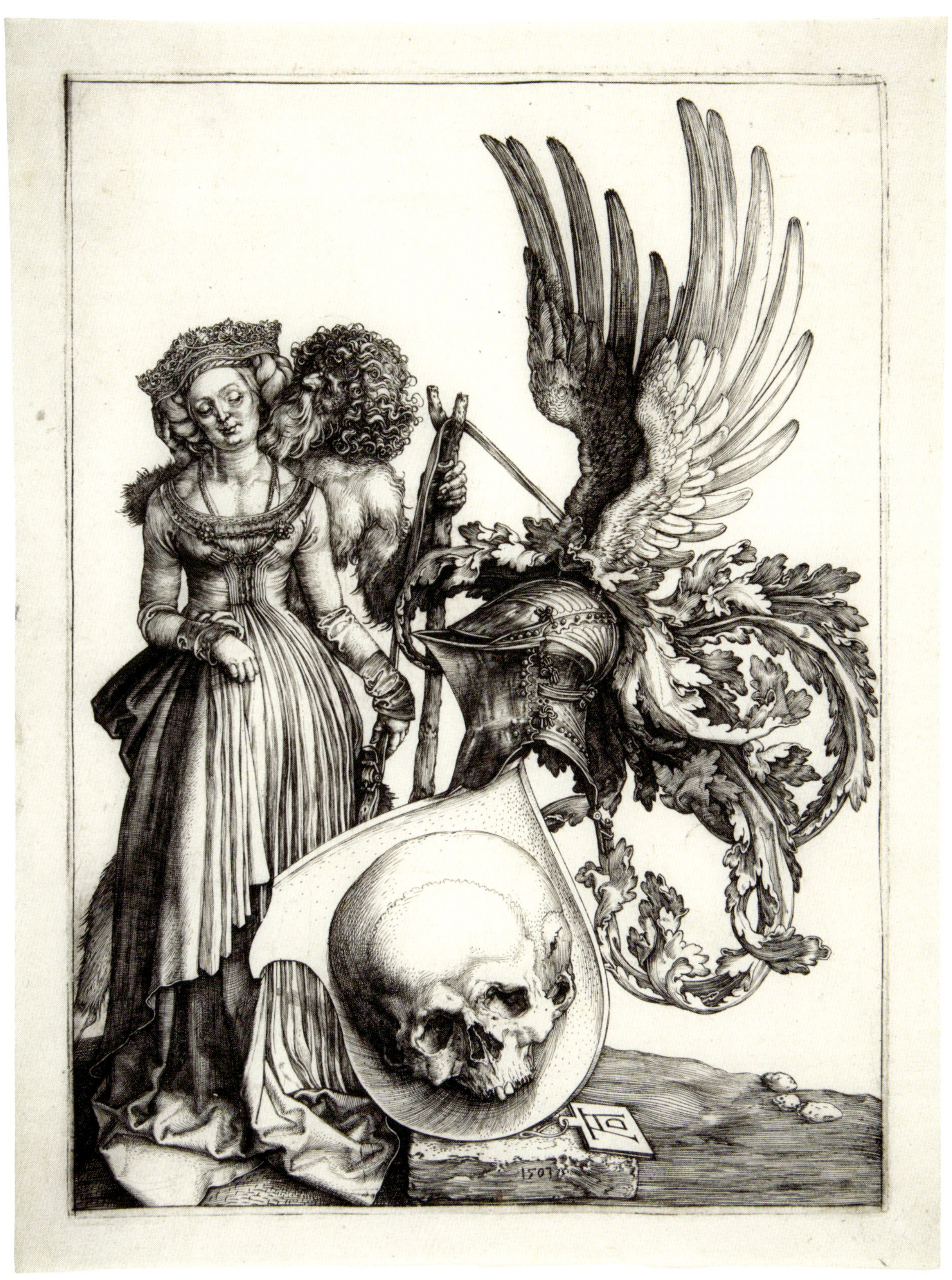

CAT. 38

HANS SÜSS VON KULMBACH

German, ca. 1480/85–1522

Portrait of a Young Man (recto); *Girl Making a Garland* (verso), ca. 1508

Oil on poplar panel, overall: 7½ × 6⅛ in. (19 × 15.6 cm); painted surface: 7⅜ × 5¾ in. (18.7 × 14.5 cm)

Inscribed (on verso): (on scroll) *ICH PINT MIT, VERGIS MEIN NIT.* (I bind with forget-me-nots.); (at right center) [signed, falsely, with initials of Albrecht Dürer, and dated] *AD* [monogram] *1508*

The Metropolitan Museum of Art, New York, Gift of J. Pierpont Morgan, 1917 (17.190.21)

THIS DOUBLED-SIDED portrait panel is the work of Hans Süss von Kulmbach, who was an associate and occasional collaborator of Albrecht Dürer in Nuremberg.[1] The artist most probably arrived in the city several years before he was awarded citizenship there in 1511. Up until his untimely death in 1522, Kulmbach was one of the most in-demand painters in Nuremberg.[2]

The portrait of an unidentified young man on the front of the panel is remarkable in its subtlety of pose and characterization. Despite the loss of detail in the abraded surface, the likeness conveys a sense of movement and inner life, achieved by orienting the sitter's torso frontally but turning his head slightly to the side and directing his pensive gaze upward.

The scene on the reverse suggests that the portrait was created in the context of courtship or betrothal, as a gift for the man's beloved. A young woman, seated at a window and watched by a cat, binds a garland of forget-me-nots. A "speaking" inscription, in the first person, describes her activity (*Ich pint mit, vergis mein nit*). The legend evokes a line of sung verse, both in its internal rhyme (*mit... nit*) and in the way it unfurls along the twists and turns of a floating banderole. The forget-me-not, as its name implies, connotes faithfulness and devotion. Moreover, floral garlands, like the one being made here, were commonly donned at weddings by bride and groom alike. The woman's unbound hair, not concealed beneath a bonnet, is a sign of her unwed status, and the band of pearls she wears stands for purity and

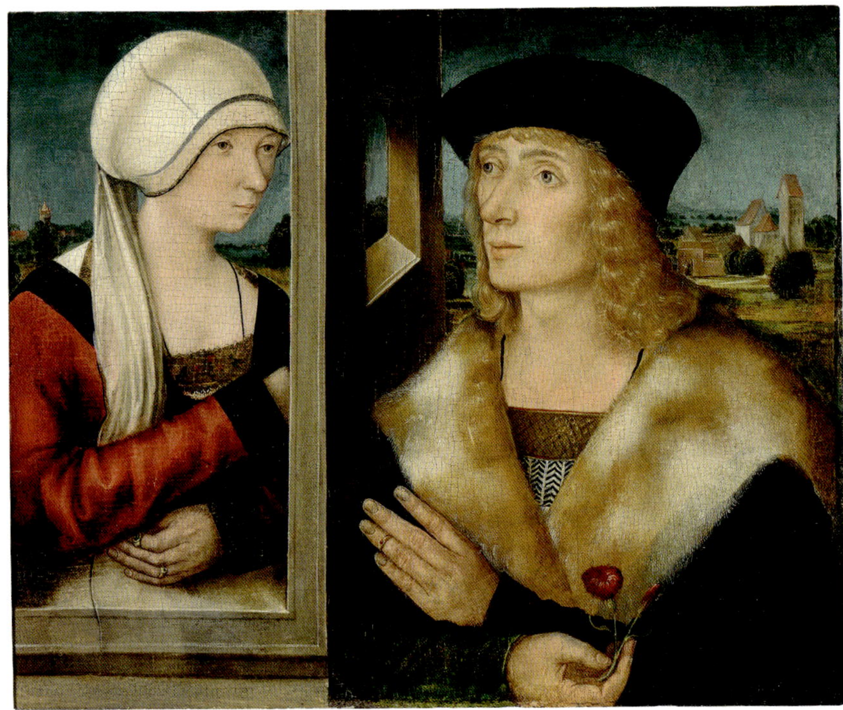

Fig. 50. Unknown artist (German, active early 16th century). *Double Portrait of an Engaged Couple*, ca. 1500–1510. Oil on wood panel, 17¹¹⁄₁₆ × 21⅝ in. (45 × 55 cm). Private collection

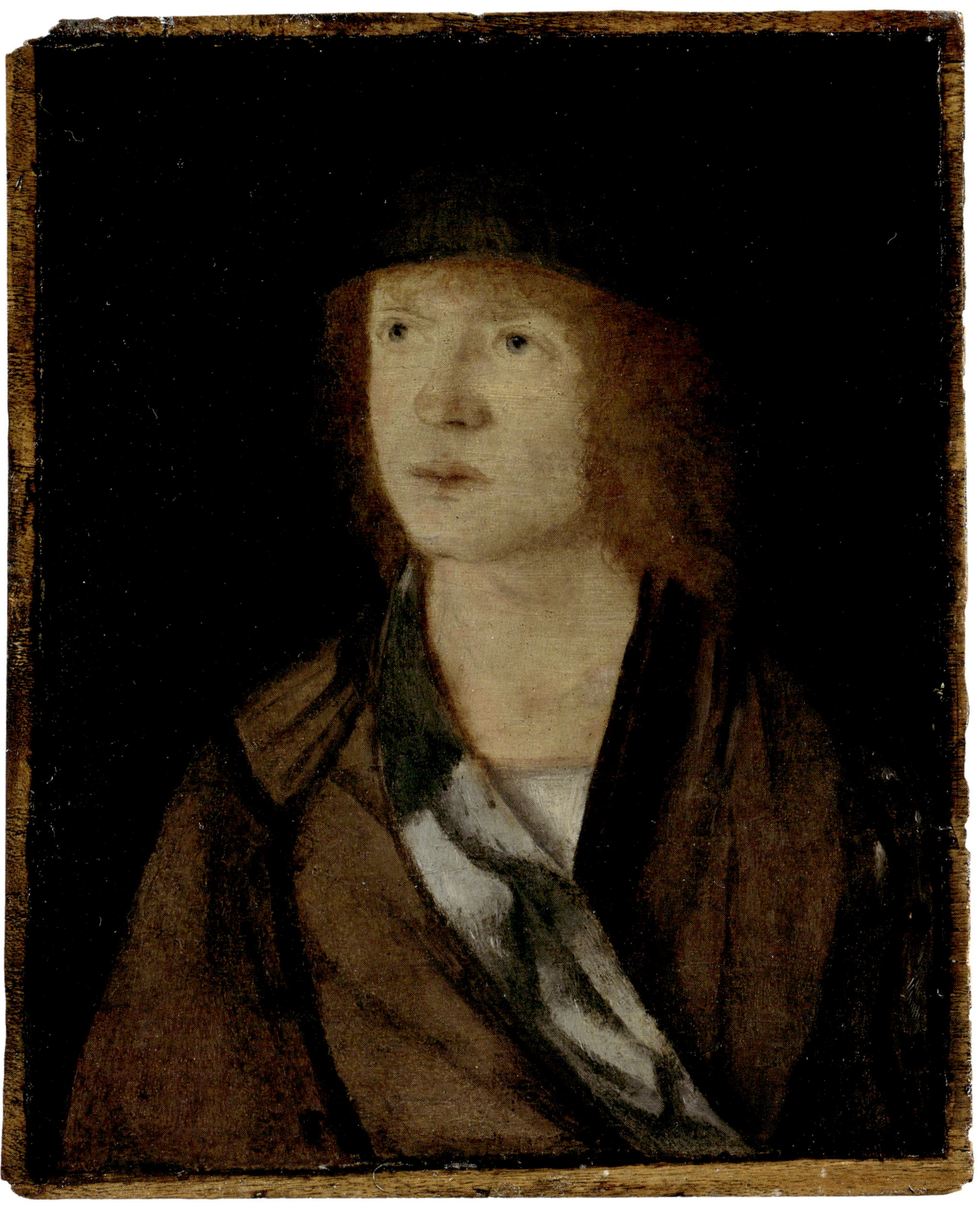

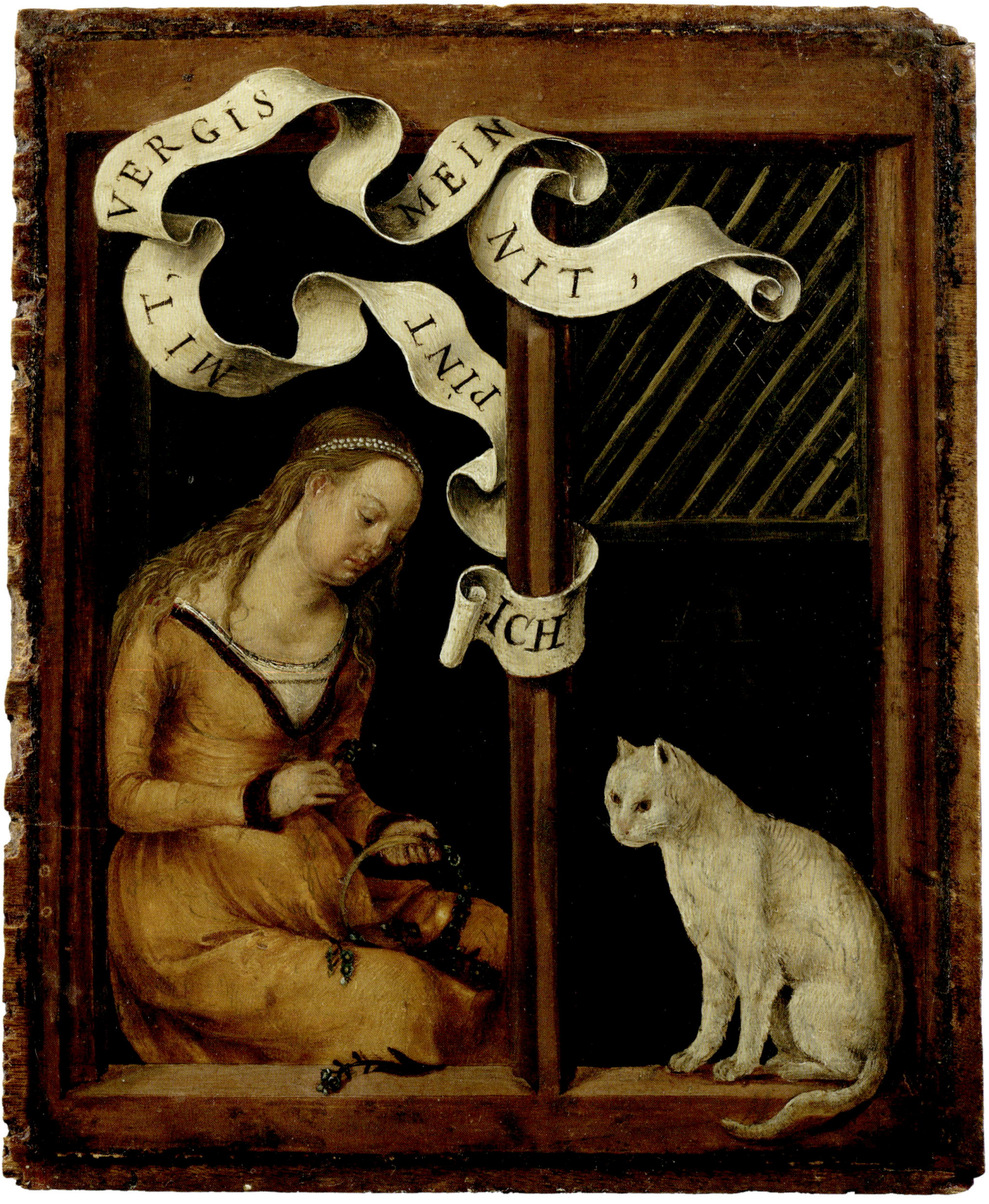
VERGIS MEIN NIT,
MIT,
ICH

virtue. Cats had both positive and negative associations; this one may symbolize domesticity.[3]

Although the female figure is allegorical and lacks the character of a portrait, much of the picture's charm lies in its evocation of a plausible scene from everyday life. Furthermore, the implied scenario—a woman at a window, above street level, observed by her suitor below—lends purpose to the upturned gaze of the man on the other side. While the imagery on a portrait's verso often reflected the sitter's thoughts, aspirations, or imagination, the present panel's combination of two sides into a narrative-like episode represents an unusual and innovative use of the double-sided format.

The window setting, as both a barrier and an opening, calls to mind the state of betrothal as a threshold between a couple's former apartness and future togetherness. Window metaphors informed other portraits of couples in the period: one by Fra Filippo Lippi (ca. 1440, The Metropolitan Museum of Art, New York) and another by a Swabian painter of the early sixteenth century (fig. 50).[4] The motif has an early precedent in a verse of the Song of Solomon (2:9): "Behold, [the bridegroom] standeth behind our wall, he looketh forth at the windows, shewing himself through the lattice."

The false *AD* monogram on the verso represents a later attempt to mark the painting as a work by Dürer, surely long after Kulmbach had fallen into obscurity. While the date of 1508 belongs to that same, later intervention, it may have been transferred from the lost frame and thus could be correct. If so, this picture counts among Kulmbach's earliest-known works.

Small and light, the portrait is easily held in the hand. It is unknown whether the work had a cover, either sliding or hinged. Given the support's astonishing thinness (only .16 centimeter [1⁄16 inch]), storage in a case for protection is conceivable.[5] The presumed courtship or betrothal context would rule out a pendant; even so, the addition of a companion piece after marriage remains a possibility.[6]

JPW

SELECTED REFERENCES: Stadler 1936, pp. 54, 129 nos. 118a, b, pl. 58; Butts 1985, pp. 76–78, figs. 57, 58; Kurt Löcher, cat. 162, in *Gothic and Renaissance Art in Nuremberg* 1986, pp. 343–44; Dülberg 1990, pp. 16, 148, 243 no. 196, pl. 98 figs. 198, 199; Strieder 1993, pp. 131–32, 250 no. 124; Maryan W. Ainsworth, no. 40, in Ainsworth and Waterman 2013, pp. 166–71, 308–9.

CAT. 39
LUCAS CRANACH THE ELDER

German, 1472–1553

Portrait of a Man with a Rosary (recto); *Male Saint* (verso), probably 1508

Oil on oak panel, overall: 18¾ × 14 (47.4 × 35.6 cm); painted surface: (recto) 18¾ × 13¾ in. (47.6 × 34.9 cm), (verso) 18⅜ × 13⅜ in. (46.5 × 34 cm)

The Metropolitan Museum of Art, New York, H. O. Havemeyer Collection, Bequest of Mrs. H. O. Havemeyer, 1929 (29.100.24)

THIS UNSIGNED, UNDATED portrait is decorated on the reverse with the figure of a saint, possibly the apostle Peter, placed in a niche and represented in monochrome gray, in imitation of a statue. Ever since this work was first published in 1916, it has, with little exception, been attributed to Lucas Cranach the Elder, court painter to the electors of Saxony in Wittenberg.[1] Its pendant painting shows a woman facing left, her hands folded in prayer, also before a dark green background (fig. 51).[2] The figure of Saint Catherine of Alexandria on the reverse of the pendant is likewise in grisaille and occupies a matching niche. The dimensions of both panels are consistent, except for about five centimeters missing at the bottom of the female portrait.

These panels must have formed the folding wings of a devotional triptych, with a centerpiece twice the width of the portraits. In the closed state, the grisaille saints were visible side by side. Opening the triptych revealed the man and the woman at either side, directing their prayers toward a sacred subject at the center, for example, a Virgin and Child. The central image need not have been Cranach's work—it could have preexisted—nor must it have been a painting (a sculpted relief is another possibility).

The two panels occupy a key position in Cranach's artistic biography, since material and iconographic evidence

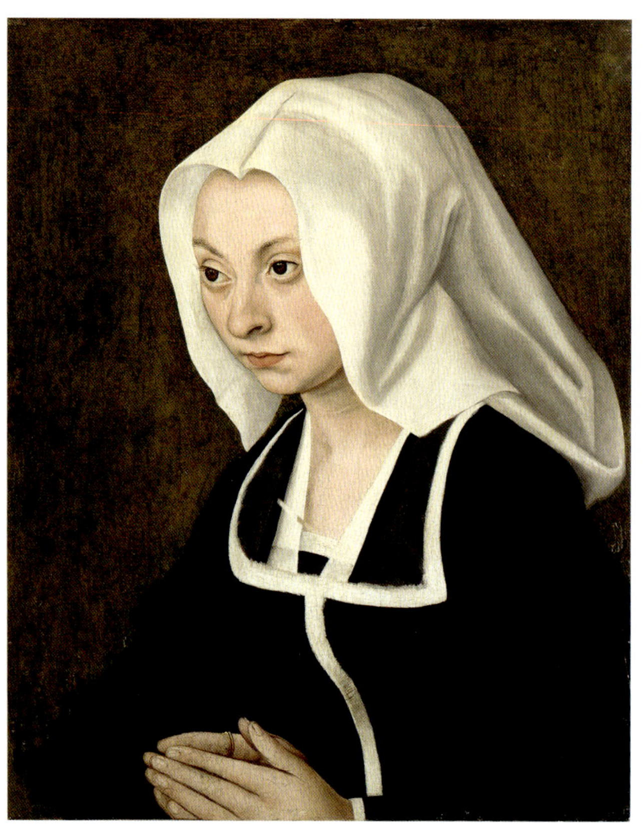

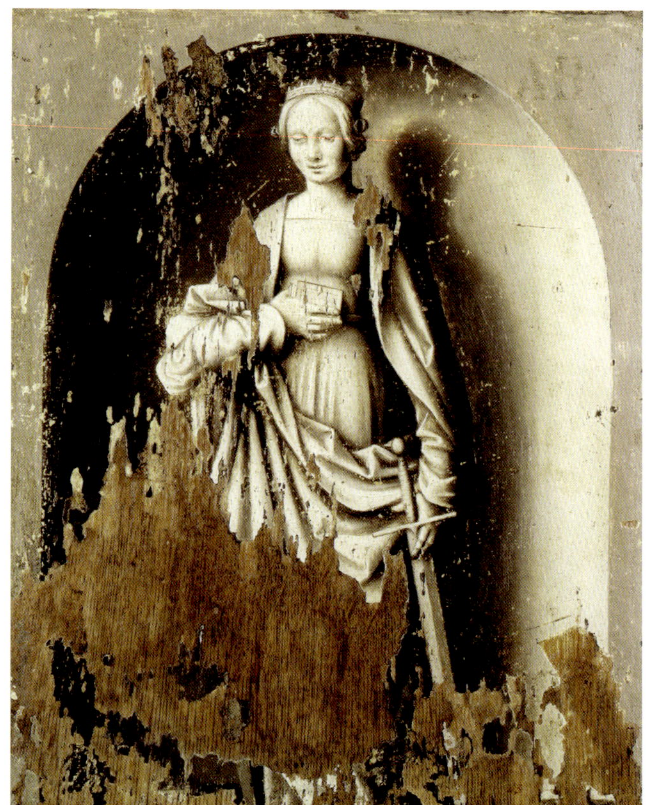

Fig. 51. Lucas Cranach the Elder. *Portrait of a Woman in Prayer* (recto) and *Saint Catherine of Alexandria* (verso), ca. 1508. Oil on oak panel, 16⅞ × 13¼ in. (42.6 × 33.7 cm). Kunsthaus Zürich, Donated by August Abegg, 1925 (1643). On long-term loan to the Kunstmuseum Basel

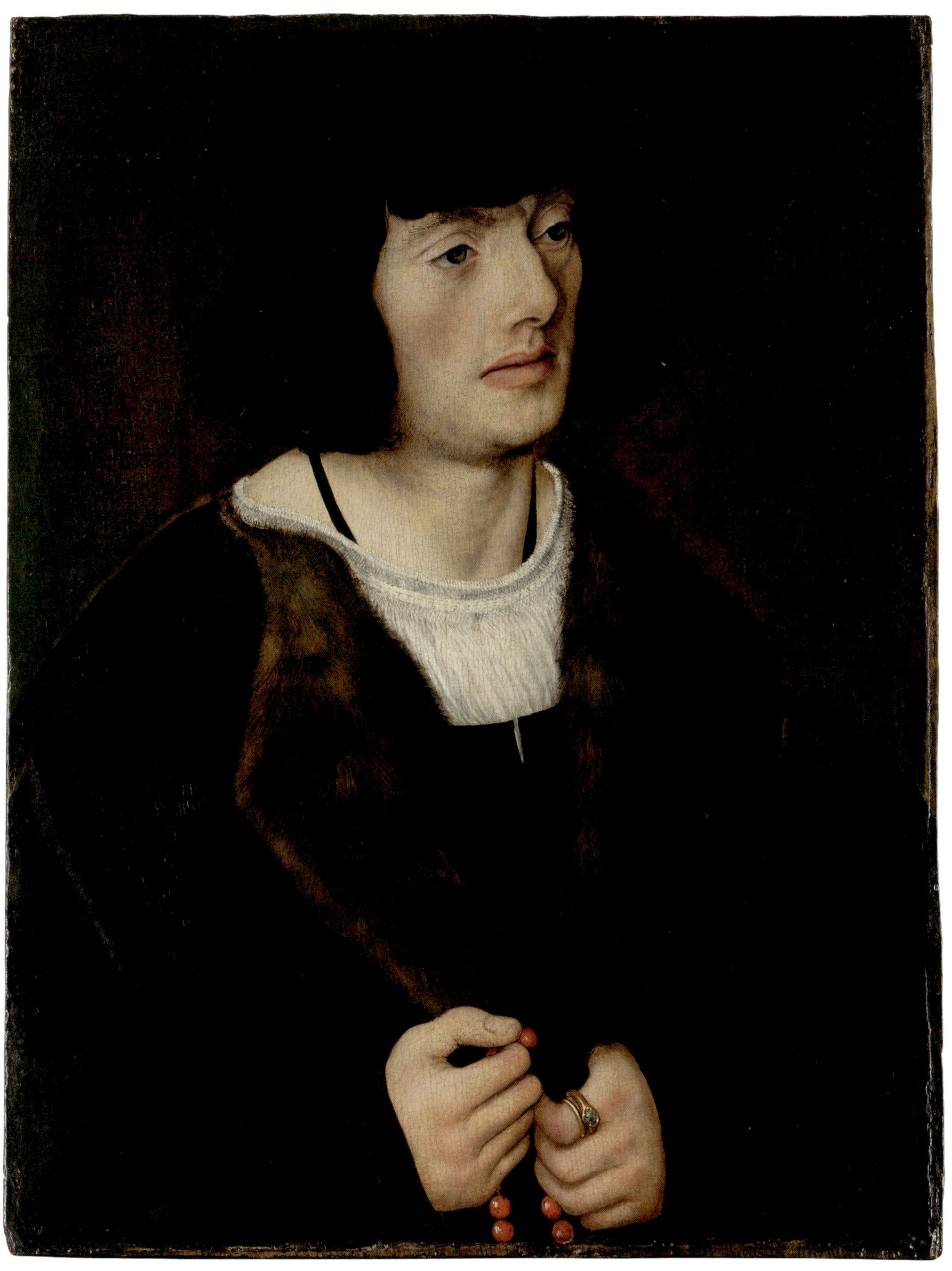

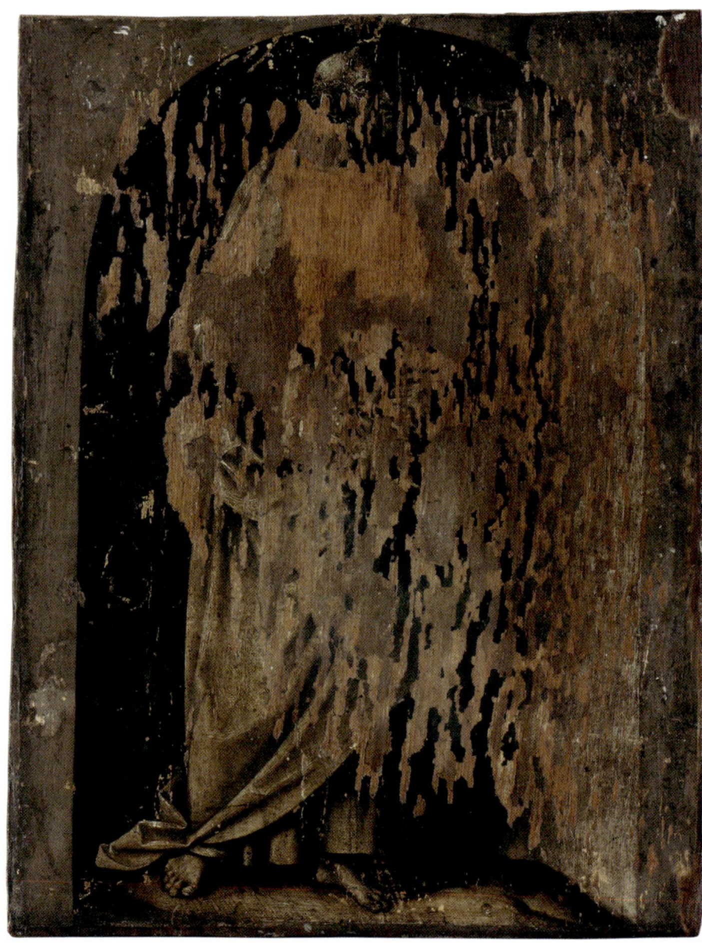

Verso, cat. 39

indicates that they were probably created during a significant trip that he made to the southern Netherlands between July and November 1508.[3] The wooden supports of the portraits consist of oak, a rarity in Cranach's oeuvre but nearly ubiquitous in Netherlandish painting. Moreover, dendrochronological analysis of the New York panel indicated that the oak originated in the Baltic region, as was characteristic of oak planks used in the Low Countries but not of those obtainable in Saxony.[4] The same analysis yielded 1508 as a plausible date by which this board could have been available for use, which accords with the time of Cranach's journey. In addition, the woman's hood type is typical of the Low Countries. Crucially, the man's signet ring displays the coat of arms of the Six family, first documented in the area of Lille, in French Flanders.[5]

Cranach was probably sent to the Netherlands by his employer, Elector Friedrich III. He is documented as having worked in Malines for Margaret of Austria, regent of the Netherlands, and having visited Antwerp.[6] The concrete occasion for the trip and the full extent of Cranach's travels are unknown. While the journey may have served the political aims of Friedrich, it was also probably intended to advertise the artist's talents abroad and to allow him to meet Flemish colleagues and study their works.

In the decades before Cranach's visit, small devotional diptychs and triptychs with half-length donor portraits had gained popularity in the Low Countries, most notably in the works of Hans Memling (see cat. 17).[7] Both in that formal aspect and in the use of trompe l'oeil statues on the wing exteriors, Cranach was accommodating his Netherlandish patrons' tastes and expectations. Upon Cranach's return to Saxony, forms and motifs inspired by the Netherlandish journey appeared in his new works, including, for example, the *Altarpiece of the Holy Kinship* of 1509 (Städel Museum, Frankfurt am Main).[8]

JPW

SELECTED REFERENCES: Dieter Koepplin, in Koepplin and Falk 1974–76, vol. 2, p. 682, under cat. 595, figs. 333, 335; Dülberg 1990, pp. 85, 261 no. 241, pl. 152 figs. 328, 331; Bodo Brinkmann, cat. 12, in Brinkmann 2007, pp. 138–39; Maryan W. Ainsworth, no. 8, in Ainsworth and Waterman 2013, pp. 44–46, 284; Hofbauer 2021, passim, figs. 1, 3 no. 1.

CAT. 40A
BERNHARD STRIGEL
German, 1460–1528

Margarethe Vöhlin (recto); *Vöhlin Coat of Arms* (versos), 1527

Oil on linden panel, poplar frame, with frame: 19½ × 14⅝ in. (49.6 × 37 cm); visible surface: 16⅞ × 11⅞ in. (43 × 30 cm)

Inscribed (at bottom, on frame): *Tausent vnd funfhundert iar Auch siben vnd zwaintzge das is war / Zallt man, do hett ich zwaintzg iar wol, Am tag Margrethe ich sagen sol* (In the year one thousand five hundred, also seven and twenty, that is true, as one counts, I was twenty years old, on [Saint] Margaret's Day [i.e., July 20] I should say)

National Gallery of Art, Washington, D.C., Ralph and Mary Booth Collection (1947.6.5.a–b)

CAT. 40B
BERNHARD STRIGEL
Hans Roth (recto); *Roth Coat of Arms* (verso), 1527

Oil on linden panel, poplar frame, with frame: 19½ × 14⅝ in. (49.6 × 37 cm); painted surface: 16¾ × 11⅞ in. (42.6 × 30 cm)

Inscribed (at bottom, on frame): *Gleich in gemeldtem iar a[u]ch ich, do liess ich Conterfeten mich 1527 / Vnd ward Octobris sechtzehn tag. Alt sechsundzwaintzg iar wie ich sag* (In the same year, 1527, I too had myself portrayed. And, on the sixteenth day of October, I turned twenty-six years old, as I say); (on sitter's signet ring) *HR* [in mirror image] [Roth family coat of arms]

National Gallery of Art, Washington, D.C., Ralph and Mary Booth Collection (1947.6.4.a–b)

BERNHARD STRIGEL of Memmingen in southern Germany was a prolific and sought-after painter of altarpieces and portraits. As a court artist to Emperor Maximilian I, he enjoyed patronage at the highest level. This portrait pair of a young couple, made in 1527, the year before Strigel's death, is one of the artist's last dated works. Its completeness is remarkable: both the original inscribed frames and the heraldic depictions on the reverses are intact.

The coats of arms are those of the Vöhlin and Roth families, merchant patricians based in Memmingen and Ulm, respectively, and both having strong ties to Augsburg, among other commercial centers.[1] The inscriptions, which are fashioned as first-person couplets, as is typical of German portraits of the period, supply the date of 1527 and note the sitters' respective ages and birthdays: the woman was twenty on Saint Margaret's Day (July 20) of that year, and the man turned twenty-six on October 16. The male sitter's signet ring provides one last, crucial clue to identification: it shows the Roth coat of arms and the initials *HR* in mirror image (as is appropriate for a signet design meant to be pressed into wax seals).[2] Taken together, this evidence has made it possible to identify the sitters as Hans Roth (died 1573) and Margarethe Vöhlin (died 1582), who married in Augsburg on February 5, 1526.[3] Roth was involved in long-distance trade and banking; Vöhlin's family was the most powerful and commercially successful in Memmingen.

Presumably the two panels would originally have been attached with hinges to form a folding diptych. When the diptych was closed, the coats of arms would have been visible on either side. Shadows painted around the coats of arms make them appear as if slightly elevated above the imitation-stone red background. In the portraits, Strigel used similar slim shadows to convey a sense of depth.

On the right panel, the orange that Roth holds and the falconer on horseback in the background refer to love and marriage. While the fruit was a conjugal symbol associated with the golden apples featured in the Labors of Hercules and the Judgment of Paris, the falconer and his bird was a courtly love motif, the falcon representing the beloved.[4]

Contrary to custom, Vöhlin is situated on the left, the side of greater importance (the heraldic dexter), normally reserved for the husband. Such an exception to the usual arrangement might be explained by the male portrait's having been created independently and only later supplemented with a female likeness.[5] Yet that situation does not apply to the present pair, given that both portraits are dated in the same year and that the couple's marriage took place the year before. It has been proposed that Vöhlin's twentieth birthday was possibly the occasion for the commission and the reason for putting her in the place of honor.[6]

JPW

SELECTED REFERENCES: Otto 1964, pp. 78–79 (color pls.), 81, 106–7 no. 87, figs. 154, 155; Stange 1970, p. 221, no. 966; Dülberg 1990, pp. 23, 127, 208–9 nos. 114, 115, pl. 194 figs. 467–70; Hand 1993, pp. 167–73; Michael Niekel, cats. 167, 168, in Haag et al. 2011, pp. 260–61.

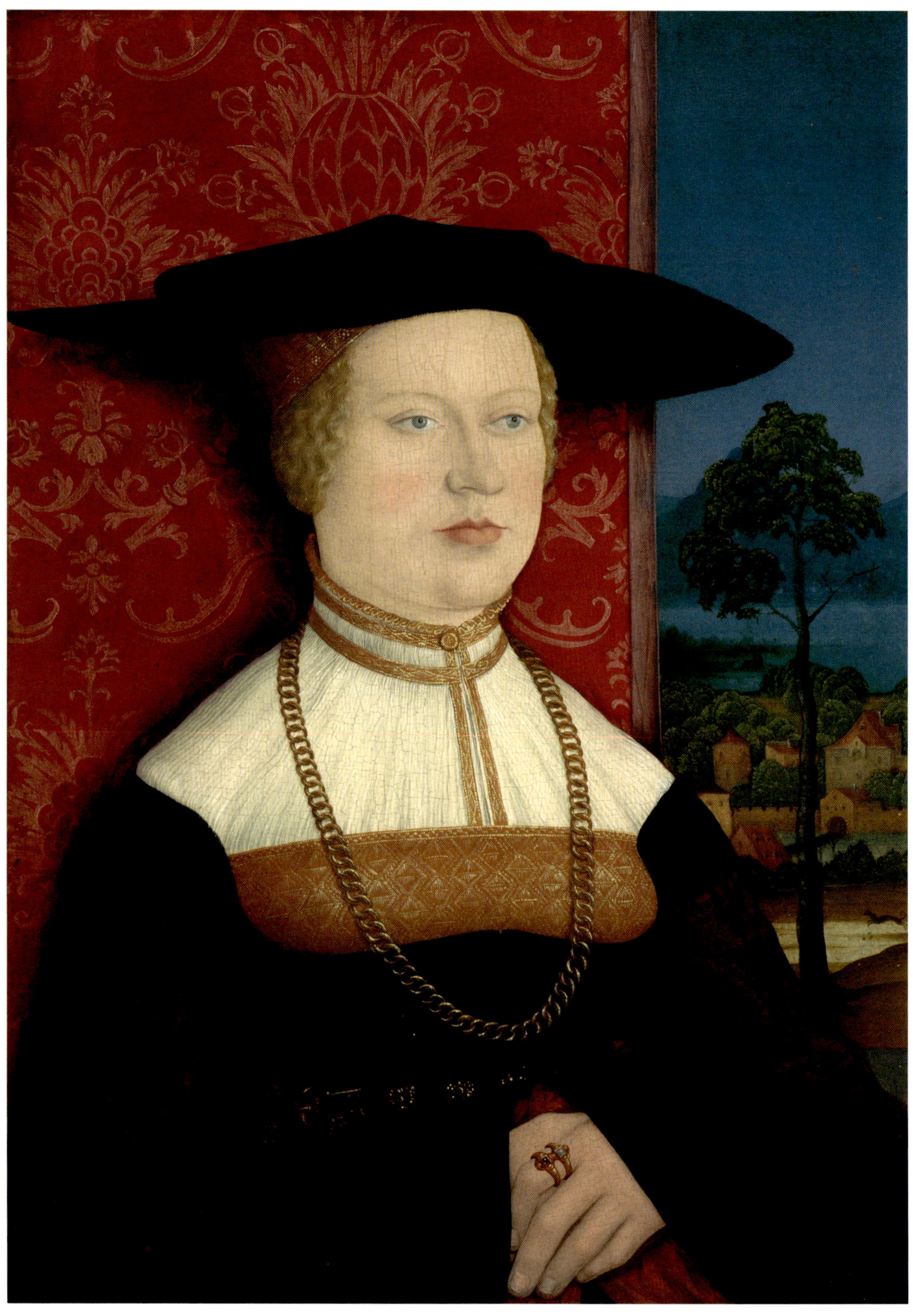

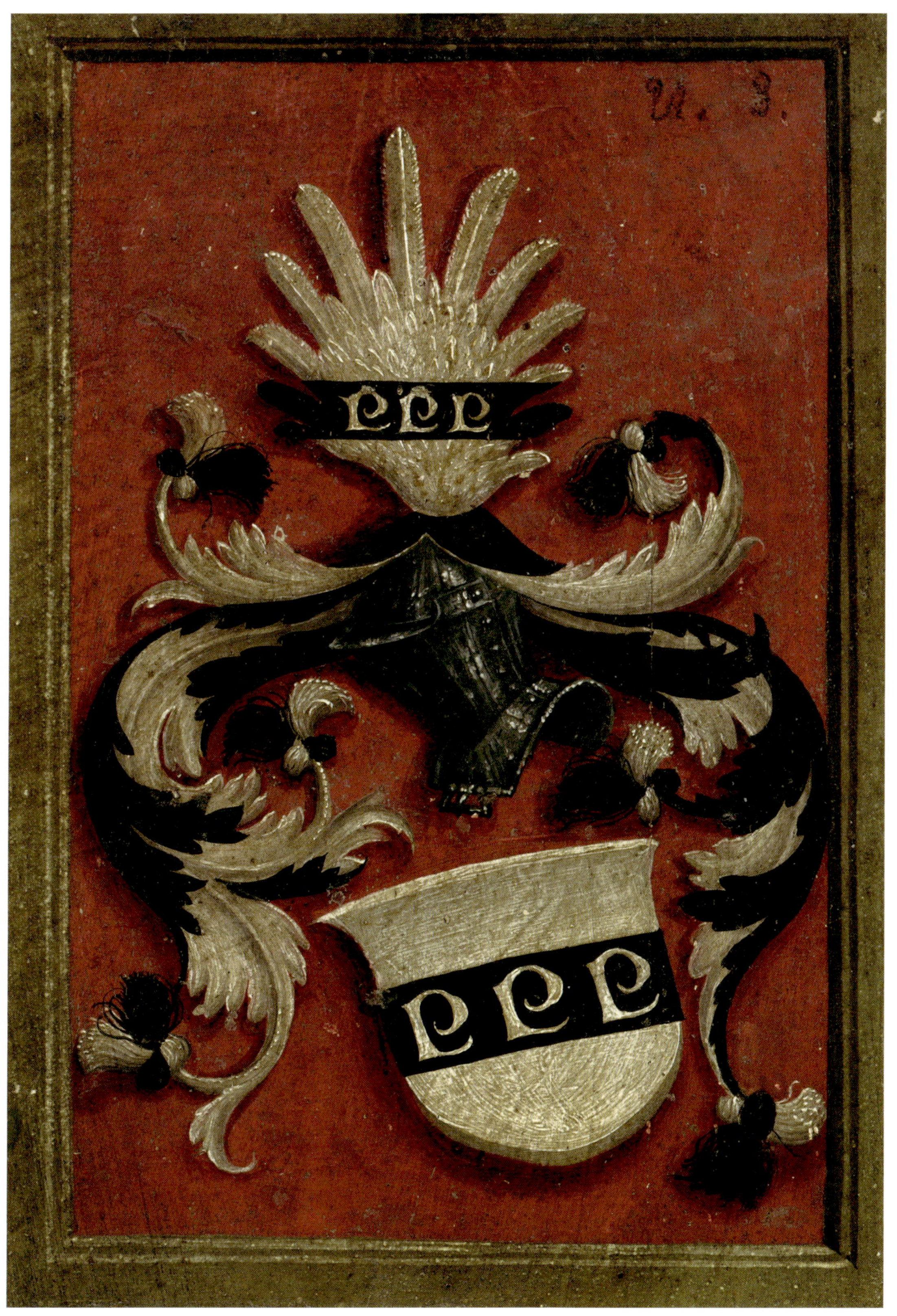

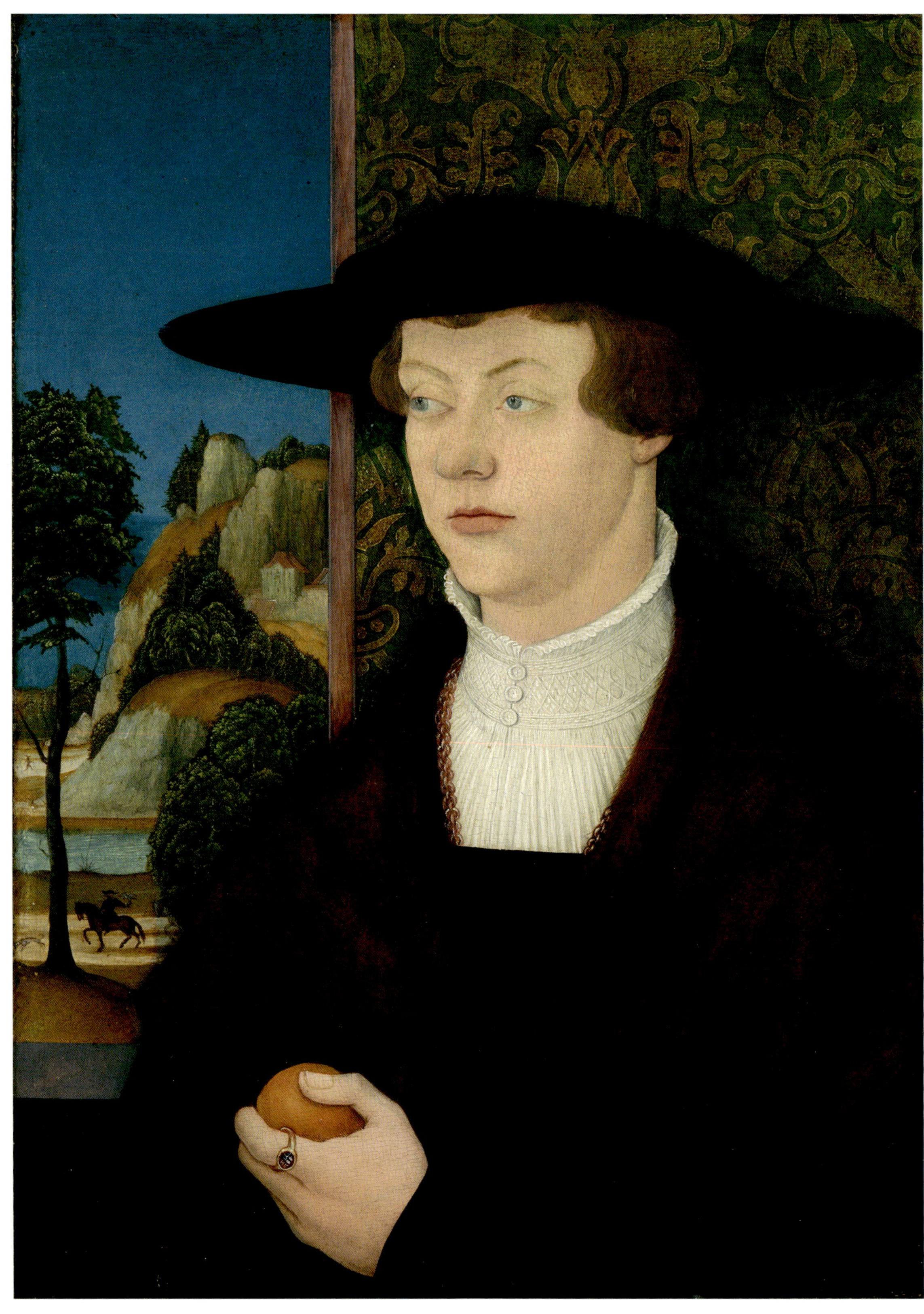

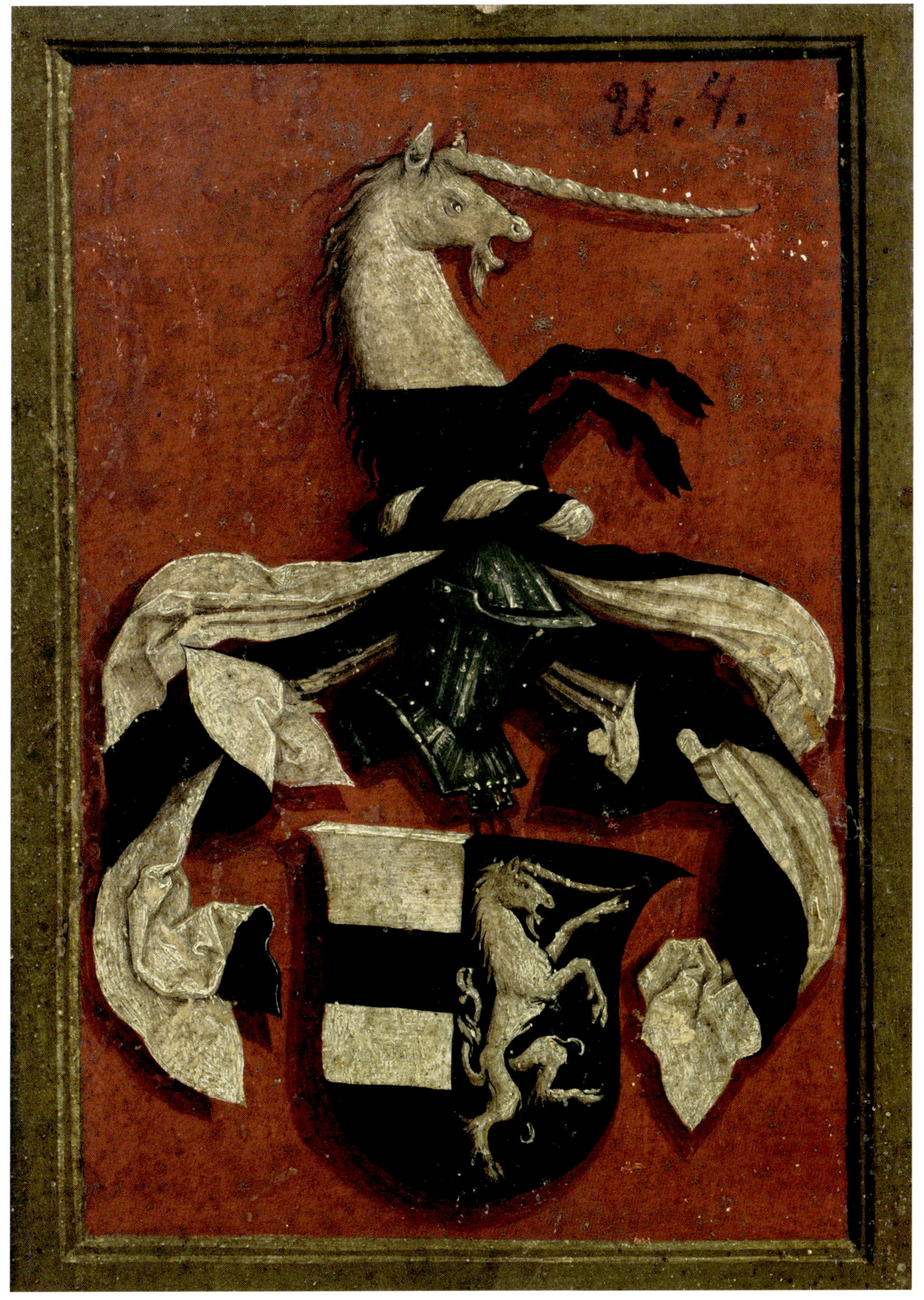

CAT. 41

ATTRIBUTED TO LUDGER TOM RING THE YOUNGER(?)

German, 1522–1584

Portrait of a Woman; Sliding Portrait Cover with Inscription,
ca. 1560

Oil on copper panel, 4⅛ × 3¼ in. (10.5 × 8 cm)

Inscribed (on cover): *Syr. VI / Ein trewer Freund ist / ein starcker Schutz, wer den / hat, der hat einen grosen Schaz / und ist mit keinem geldt / noch gut zu bezahlen* (Sir. VI / A faithfull friend is a strong defence: and he that hath found such an one hath found a treasure. Nothing doth countervail a faithful friend, and his excellency is invaluable)

Suermondt-Ludwig-Museum, Aachen (GK 431)

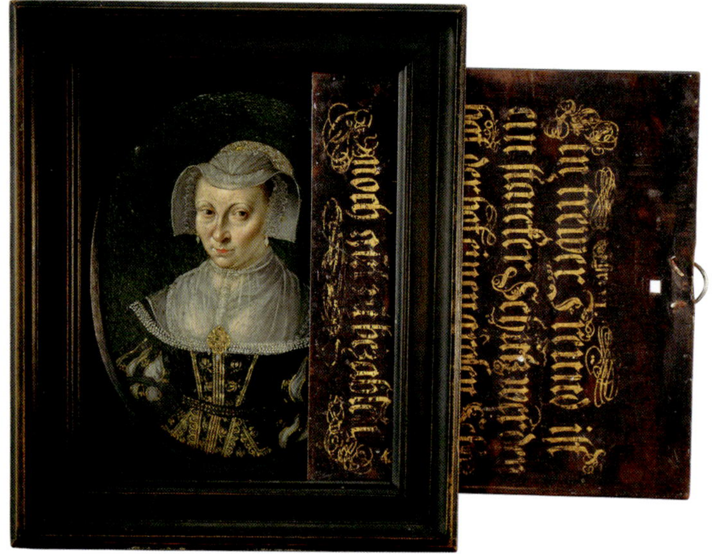

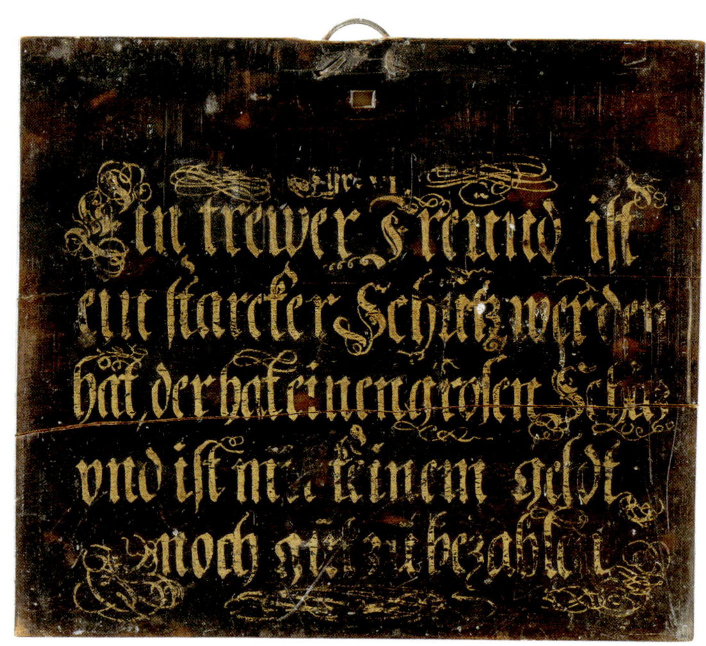

THIS FRONTAL PORTRAIT of a middle-aged woman before a green background is painted on an oval copper panel. The subject, angled slightly to the left, wears a black dress with slashed sleeves and a white collar that is covered by a large, diaphanous shawl secured at the chest with a heavy brooch. The dress is richly embroidered in silver and gold, as is the woman's hood.[1]

The panel sits in a smooth, rectangular frame behind a second, outer frame furnished with grooves that allow a cover to be slid into place over the portrait. The cover is extremely thin (just under 2 millimeters), and since it is not reinforced by the structure of a frame, it has snapped lengthwise twice during handling, damages that have been inexpertly repaired with adhesive tape.[2] The sliding lid is inscribed with gold lettering quoting a passage from the Book of Sirach (6: 14–15) on the value of true friendship. Originally the portrait and its sliding lid would have been a very personal gift to a good friend.[3]

The former attribution to Ludger tom Ring the Younger has been called into question. Surprisingly, the work has been thought to have been painted around 1700 under Dutch influence.[4]

AD

SELECTED REFERENCES: Riewerts and Pieper 1955, no. 155, p. 128, fig. 140; Dülberg 1990, pp. 91–92, 229–30 no. 173, pls. 60, 61 figs. 131–33; Lorenz 1996, vol. 2, no. 217, p. 649; Herklotz 2000, pp. 256 fig. 9, 258; Herklotz 2001, p. 110.

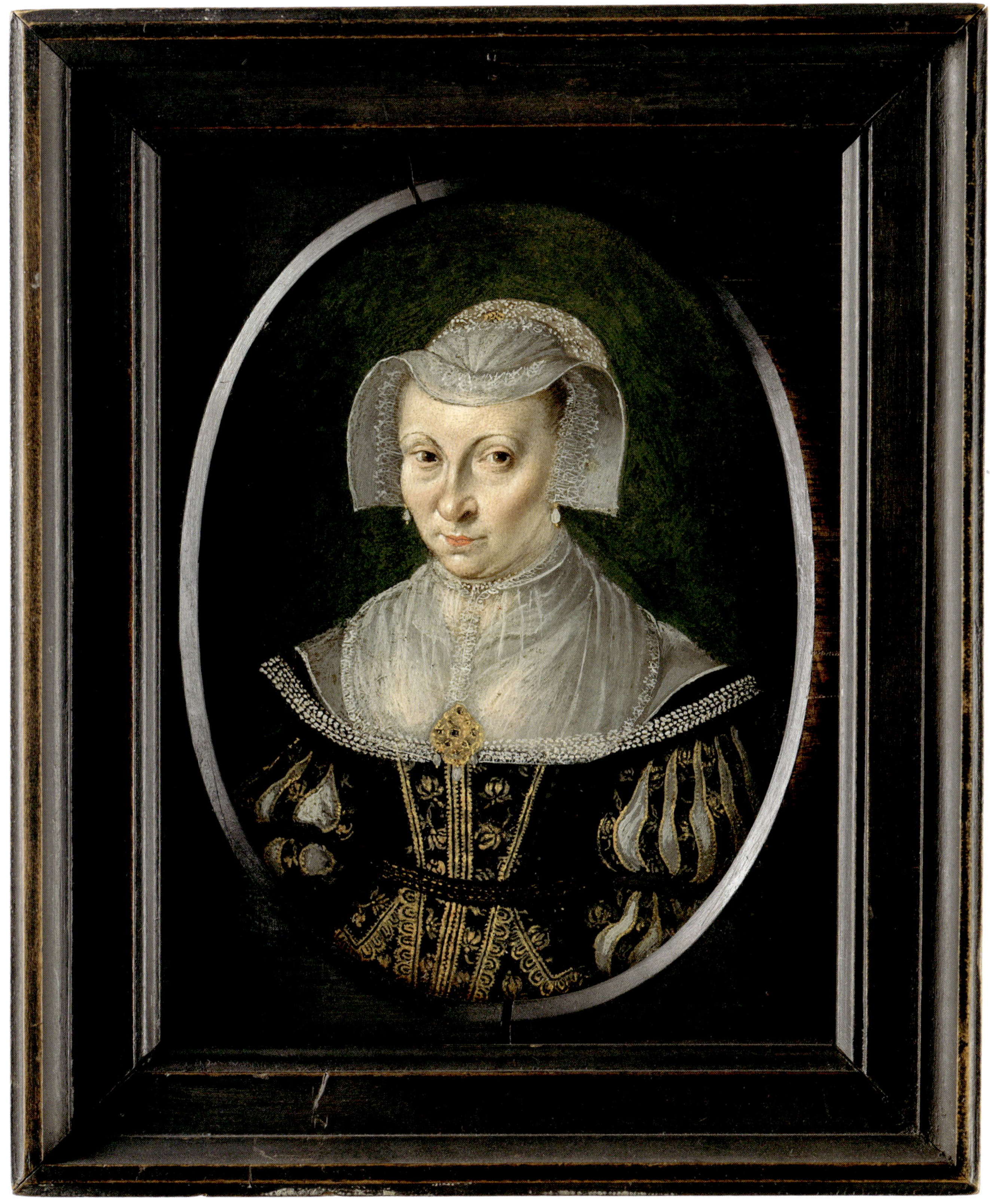

CAT. 42

LUCAS CRANACH THE YOUNGER

German, 1515–1586

Allegory of Virtue, 1548

Oil on poplar panel, 12¾ × 8⅝ in. (32.3 × 21.8 cm), without added wooden strips at edges

Inscribed (on recto): (at upper center) *DEO ET VIRTVTE* [*DVCE*(?)] ([Led?] by God and virtue);[1] (at upper right) *VIRTVS* (Virtue); (at lower center) *DVRATE* (Persevere); (at lower right, inscribed, dated, and signed) *VIA ARDVA / EST SED MA / NET IN ACVMI / NE IN EXTIMA / BILE PRAEMIVM* (The path is arduous, but an invaluable prize awaits at the summit) */ 1548 /* [winged-serpent mark, wings lowered]

Kunsthistorisches Museum, Vienna, Gemäldegalerie (6080)

THE WINGED-SERPENT insignia at the lower right indicates an origin in the workshop of Lucas Cranach the Elder in Wittenberg. The style of the painting has most often been associated with Cranach's son of the same name.[2] By 1548, the date of this work, Lucas the Younger was in his early thirties and a highly experienced member of the shop.

In its dimensions, format, and subject matter, the painting is suggestive of a portrait cover.[3] The theme concerns virtue, both the difficulty of its attainment and the immeasurable value of its rewards. A jagged, tower-like rock formation represents the *mons virtutis* (mountain of virtue), familiar from the Renaissance iconography of Hercules, who was admired for his choice of virtue over vice.[4] The oversized figure in armor at the lower right can therefore be identified as that mythical hero.[5] The inscription on his large plaque refers to virtue's path and rewards. Pointing upward, toward the summit, Hercules urges the painting's protagonists to follow his example.

Virtue is personified by the fashionably dressed young woman near the top of the cliff. She beckons with her left hand to a man scaling the nearly vertical path, while pointing with her right to what awaits at the top: a laurel wreath and a gold neck chain suspended from a palm tree, which together allude variously to victory, fame, and immortality. The inscription on the banderole around the tree names both God and virtue as guides in life.

Failure in the pursuit of virtue is exemplified by the man in red who plummets from the path. Like the more fortunate climber above, he too carries both a sword and a book, thus referring to the union of arms and letters in those who pursue virtue. The inscription above the portal at the base of the mountain (*Durate*) encourages perseverance.

This painting possibly alludes to the political and religious struggles in Germany during the late 1540s.[6] The main clue to its contemporary topical significance lies in the small foreground figures, which evoke themes of secular conflict and ecclesiastical authority. One of these figures, a ruler on horseback wearing gold armor and bearing a war hammer, approaches the threshold to virtue's path. He is conducted by guards armed with halberds and two clerics carrying large books. In 1548 the most notable recent conflict was the Schmalkaldic War (1546–47), which had culminated in the victory of Emperor Charles V's Catholic forces over a league of Protestant princes. Among the war's outcomes was the imprisonment from 1547 to 1552 of Elector Johann Friedrich of Saxony, the Cranachs' main patron. Furthermore, in June 1548, Charles declared the Augsburg Interim, a controversial new law on religion. It is therefore conceivable that the painting concerns virtuous leadership in the war's aftermath.

This composition exists in a little-known, same-size variant, also dated 1548 and of similar style (fig. 52).[7] The

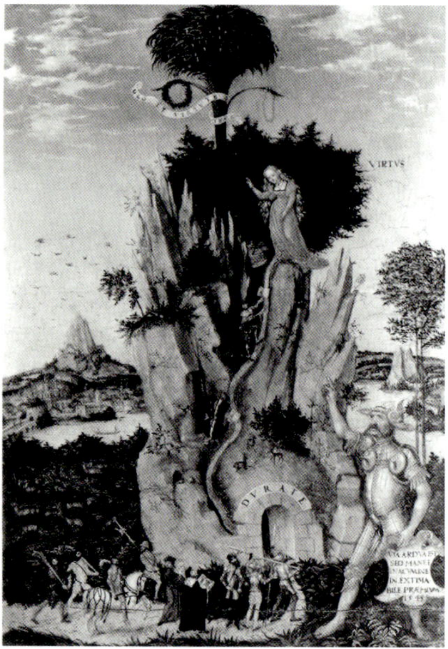

Fig. 52. Attributed to Lucas Cranach the Younger. *Allegory of Virtue*, 1548. Oil on wood panel, 12⅝ × 8½ in. (32 × 21.5 cm). Private collection

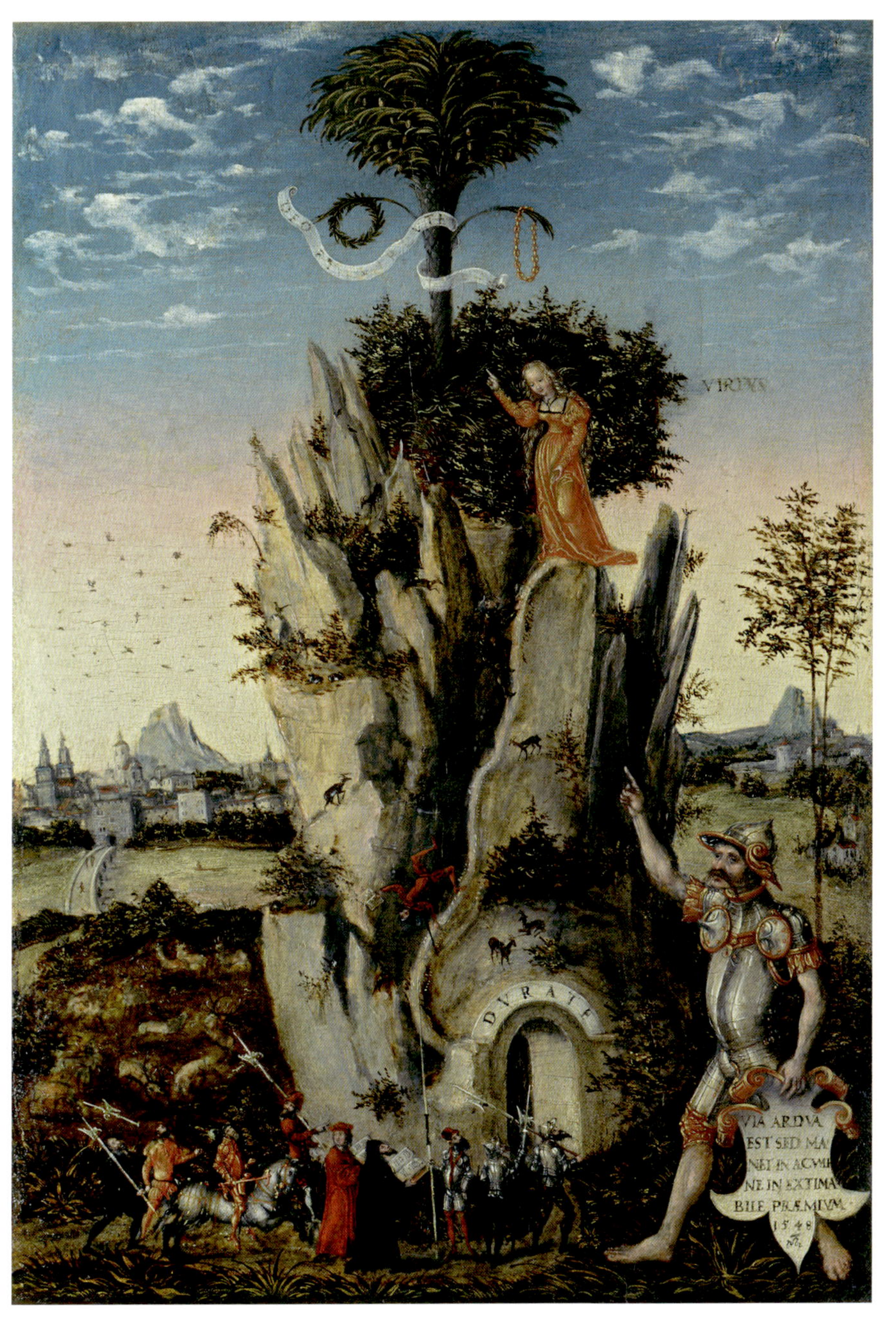

existence of multiples casts new light on the type of portrait that may have accompanied it. Namely, the variant raises the possibility of a series of ruler portraits made for propagandistic or diplomatic purposes.

JPW

SELECTED REFERENCES: Schütz 1972, cat. 26, pp. 32–33, fig. 26; Dülberg 1990, p. 300 no. 350; Koepplin 2006, pp. 139–41, 168 fig. 1; Hoppe-Harnoncourt 2015, pp. 156, 162–65, fig. 6; Susanne Wegmann, cat. 3/38, in Enke et al. 2015, pp. 368–69.

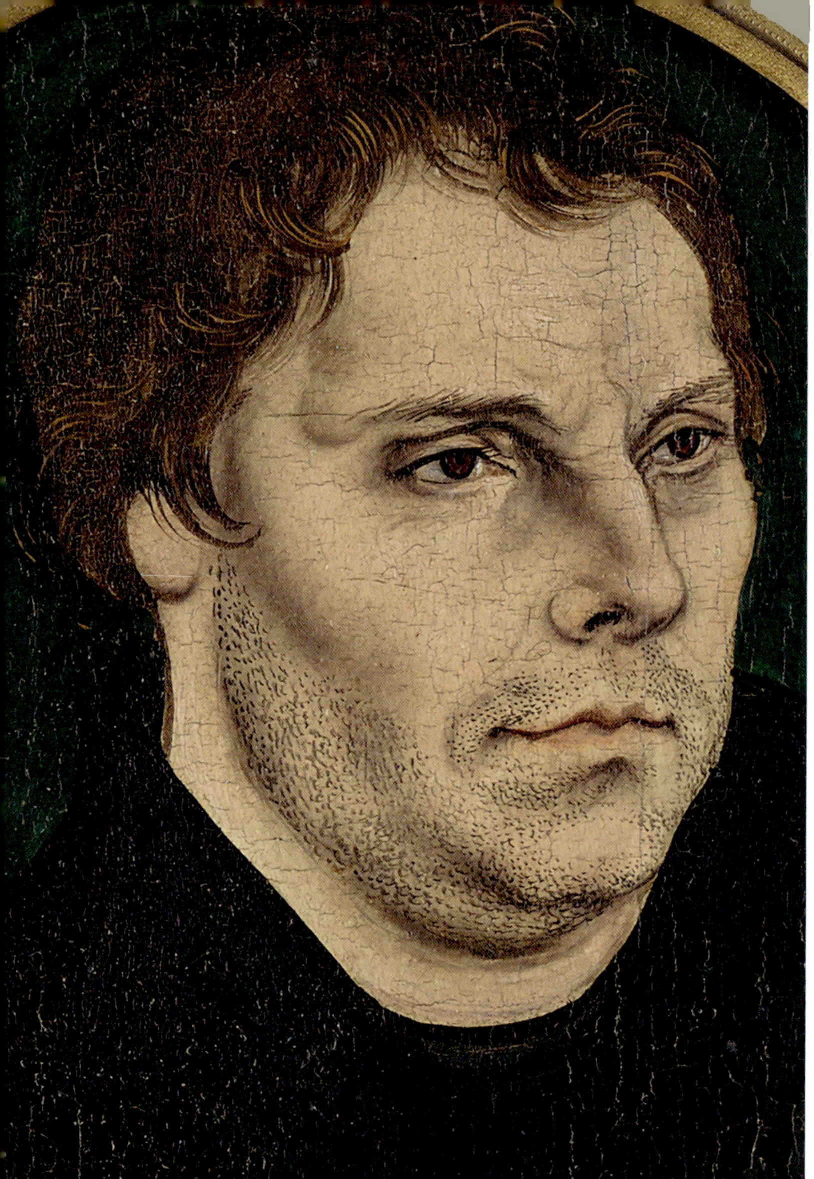

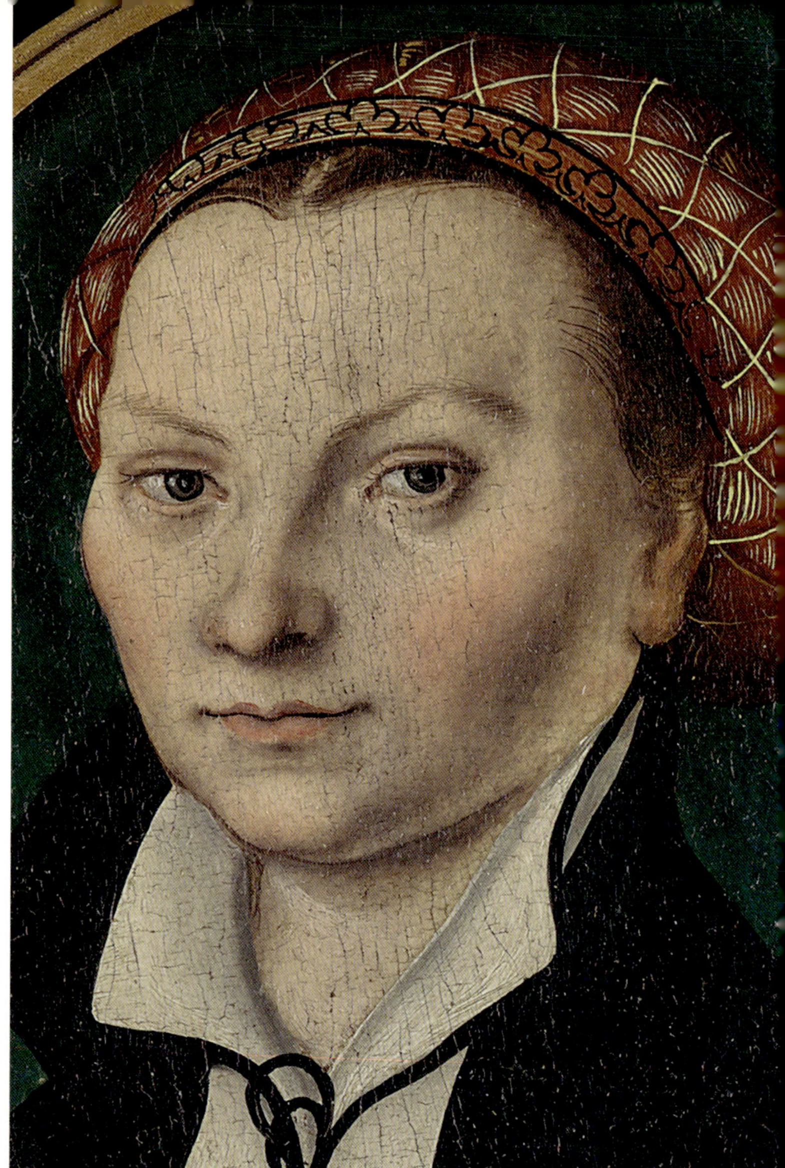

PORTABLE PORTRAITS, 1520–1650

ANGELICA DÜLBERG

Small-scale portraits decorated with allegorical images, either on the reverse or on sliding or hinged lids, were often kept in lavish cases or sachets for added protection. These intimate, personal documents of the sitters were popular as engagement or wedding gifts and as mementos for one's descendants and friends. Most notably, they also served to spread propaganda during the Reformation.

Toward the end of the sixteenth century, the Venetian noblewoman Bianca Cappello had her reasons for reviving the familiar, if "outdated," custom of adorning portraits with attributive allegorical figures (fig. 53).[1] She had been the mistress of Francesco I de' Medici for many years, and after the death of the grand duke's wife, he married her. Bianca's change in station is reflected in the painting on the reverse of her portrait—a copy of Michelangelo's drawing *Il Sogno* (*The Dream*)—as what was once a depraved carnal union has been chastened, awakened by the divine genius, and transformed into a pure, virtuous love. Cappello's portrait was intended to legitimize her son, Don Antonio, and according to his estate of 1621, was kept safe inside a walnut box.[2]

Evidence of another very personal and intimate love affair can be found in the relief portraits, concealed inside a pair of walnut canisters, of Elector Friedrich the Wise of Saxony and his mistress, Anna Rasper (or Dornle) (cat. 47A,B).[3] The couple lived together for many years and are reported to have had four illegitimate children, three of whom the elector included in his will before his death in 1525. The canister reverses feature wooden reliefs, one of a centaur and the other of a mythical female hybrid, which symbolize the human subjects' romantic relationship.

Another special type of portraiture consisted of small-scale paintings on round wooden panels that could be closed—either by a companion picture or by a thematically matched lid—to form a small capsule. Most of these can be traced back to the artistic circles around Lucas Cranach the Elder, Hans Holbein the Younger, and Bartholomäus Bruyn the Elder and were probably inspired by medals or medallions. They were especially popular under Elector Friedrich the Wise of Saxony for propagandistic purposes. Similarly, Reformation princes and reformers used the painted roundels to convey their messages. Some of the roundels were reproduced in vast numbers and disseminated as gifts to further a cause. Cranach's encapsulated portraits of Martin Luther and Katharina von Bora (cat. 44A,B), for instance, were copied a thousand times on the occasion of their marriage in 1525.[4] The portraits' original circular frames were shaped in such a way that the two fit together precisely to create a small black box.[5]

Often the reverses were simply painted black and decorated with turned concentric grooves as, for instance, in the case of Holbein's portrait of a young man in a red cap and livery, the latter embroidered in black with the initials *HR* (*Henricus Rex*), indicating that he served in the court of Henry VIII (cat. 45). That this portrait was probably paired with one of the man's wife is suggested by another Holbein painting of a Tudor court official housed at the Kunsthistorisches Museum in Vienna.[6] Alternatively, it may have had a painted lid that closed to create a capsule, similar to that for the picture of Philipp Melanchthon at the Niedersächsisches Landesmuseum Hannover, Landesgalerie (cat. 46A,B).[7]

In late sixteenth-century Italy, the custom of painting portraits on roundels was adopted for wedding gifts. The portraitist Lavinia Fontana, in particular, frequently created such small pieces. Her portrait of a young nobleman from Bologna is slightly larger than that of his intended, and the reverse sides of both have embossed decorations (cat. 49A,B)—details indicating that the pictures probably originally fit

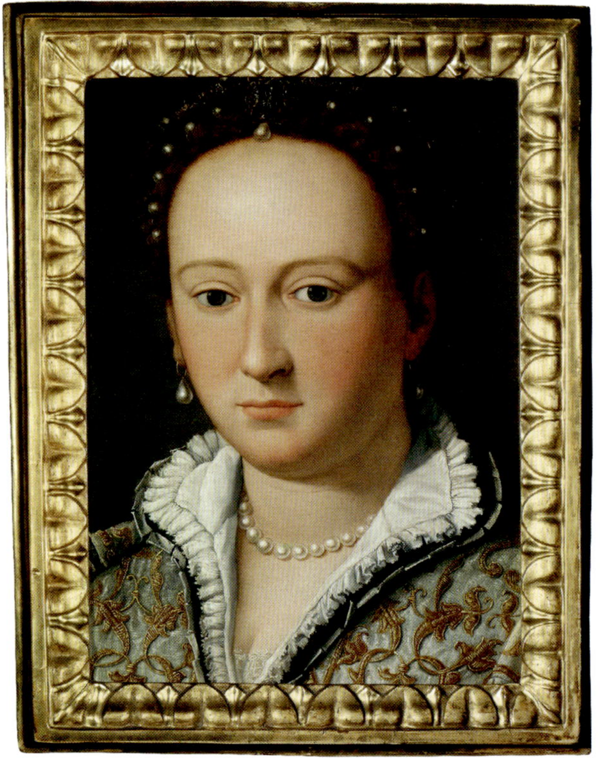

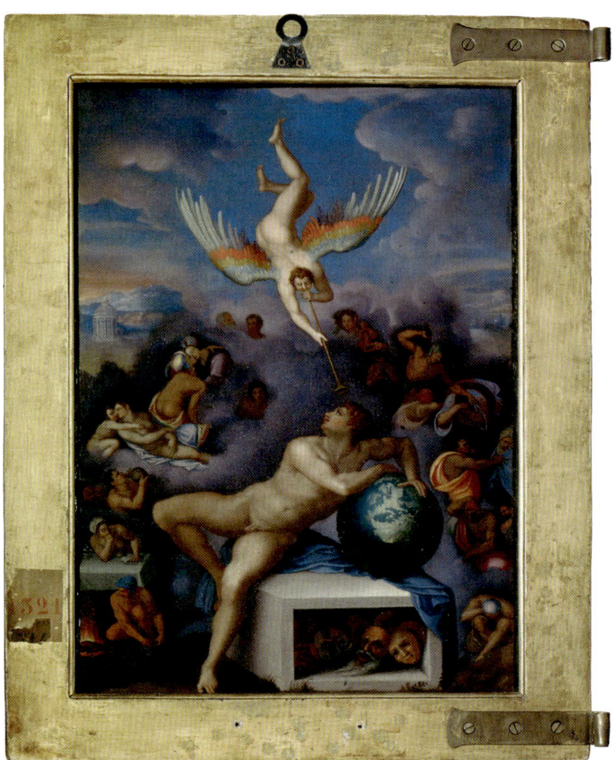

Fig. 53. Alessandro Allori (Italian, 1535–1607). *Bianca Cappello* (recto); *The Dream, after Michelangelo* (verso), early 1570s. Oil on copper panel, 14⅝ × 10⅝ in. (37 × 27 cm). Gallerie degli Uffizi, Florence

together to form a capsule, like those from the North. The bride's wedding dress is the traditional red of Bologna, and the bridegroom's upturned collar is accordingly trimmed in red.

Further examples from Italy in the late 1500s include the two wax reliefs of a woman and a man in profile (cat. 50A,B). The images are clearly paired, given the sitters' garb (their simple, single-layer ruffs in particular) and the frames, which have the same dimensions and partial gilding. What is unusual, however, is that the figures do not face each other but are instead both shown from the right. Another relief portrait in wax depicts a noble lady in profile, facing left, inside an oval locket of gilded copper (cat. 52). The frame is embellished with strapwork, fruits, and leaves, while the back is decorated with an eagle with wings spread standing on a plinth, baroque scrollwork, and bundles of fruit. The lid features a landscape inside a strapwork cartouche, masks, small birds, and vases.

Many wax portraits were produced in Nuremberg in the decades around 1600, including that of Paulus Praun in profile, facing right (cat. 51A–C). The portrait, crafted on a piece of slate, is fitted inside an oval wooden capsule with a lid. For additional protection, the capsule was stored in a yellow leather pouch, which has survived.

The wax portrait of Nuremberg philanthropist Elisabeth Krauss, on the other hand, was kept safe behind a sliding lid inserted from above (cat. 54). Krauss was a popular personage, given her philanthropic activities and the foundation she started. A great many replicas of her portrait, based on a model from 1632, were produced from the time the foundation was launched in 1639/40. Protective sliding lids were not limited to small works but were used for much larger portraits as well, including those of Lazarus Holzschuher (cat. 16) and his brother Hieronymus (see fig. 16).

Renaissance mirrors were usually protected by sliding lids, which is why Italian sources noted the phrase "*a uso di specchio*" (used as a mirror) in describing covered portraits.[8] A Florentine mirror from the mid-1500s (cat. 43) even has two covers. The second cover, hidden beneath an exterior one, presumably contained a "forbidden" image, either the portrait of a mistress or an erotic display.

Apart from portrait medals, which were frequently given as gifts, such as the one depicting George the Bearded, Duke of Saxony (1537, The Metropolitan Museum of Art, Robert Lehman Collection), coin boxes (*Schraubtaler*) were popular as presents for friends or other persons of note. Above all, they were used as engagement gifts to the bridegroom or the bride. When screwed together, the hollowed-out and threaded coins formed small silver boxes containing a portrait of the young woman or man (cat. 48).

A portrait of Louis Hesselin is even concealed inside an elaborate watch decorated with miniature copies in enamel of allegorical paintings by Simon Vouet (cat. 53).

CAT. 43

ATTRIBUTED TO GIORGIO VASARI AND WORKSHOP

Vasari: Italian, 1511–1574

Tabernacle Mirror Frame with Two Sliding Covers, ca. 1572

Walnut and glass, 16⅜ × 15⅛ in. (41.5 × 38.5 cm)

The Metropolitan Museum of Art, New York, Robert Lehman Collection, 1975 (1975.1.2090)

LIKE PAINTED PORTRAITS, Renaissance mirrors often had protective covers adorned with emblems and allegories that enhanced the likeness concealed below—namely, the beholder's transient reflection.[1] A mid-sixteenth-century Florentine mirror was furnished with a cover depicting an *Allegory of Prudence* that would have conveyed a moralizing admonition to the viewer poised to confront his or her own image beneath (fig. 54).[2] Jan van der Straet's *Allegory of Vanity* portrays a seated woman gazing at her image in a mirror, whose sliding cover (opened by a circular handle) bears a skull that echoes her own visage (see fig. 2). Vividly evoking the inevitable passage of time, the message of this memento mori is underscored by the fleeting nature of her reflection and by the hourglass above.[3] According to literary topoi dating back to antiquity, mirrors were both closely associated with portraiture and symbolic of love. Socrates, for example, asserts that the lover is the mirror in which the beloved beholds him or herself.[4]

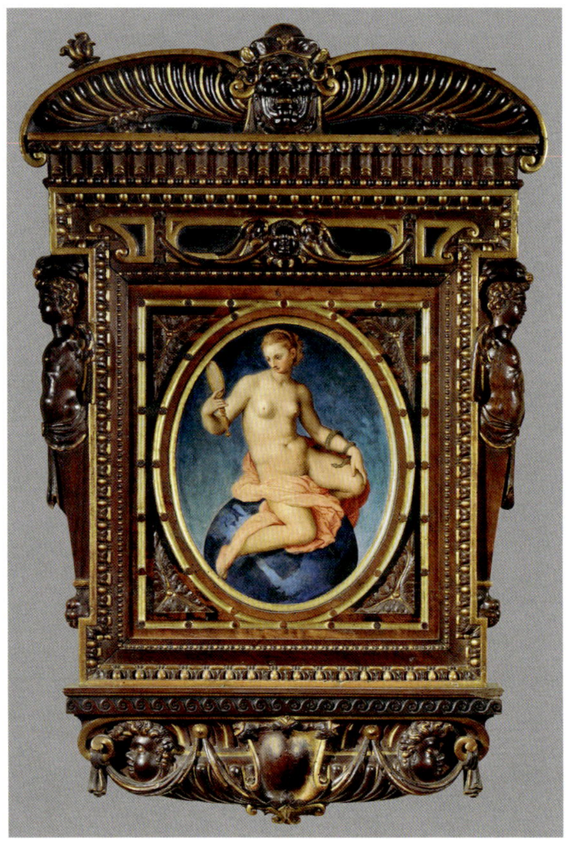

Mirrors could also serve as covers for painted portraits, a format frequently employed for amorous gifts because it could conceal a beloved's identity and, when opened and gazed upon by its owner, form a clandestine double portrait of the couple.[5] The sixteenth-century Venetian sculptor Alessandro Vittoria owned a mirror with a small portrait of a lady by Titian, which he kept in his study.[6] Among the most intriguing accounts of a mirror concealing the likeness of a beloved is the portrait of Elisabetta Gonzaga, duchess of Urbino, owned by the courtier and writer Baldassare Castiglione (ca. 1502, possibly by Raphael and now in the Uffizi).[7] In 1606 Castiglione's biographer Antonio Beffa Negrini described the work as "the portrait of the beautiful and esteemed Signora, by the hand of Raphael of Urbino . . . behind a large and beautiful mirror that could be opened and closed by those who knew the artifice" and which also concealed two love poems Castiglione dedicated to Elisabetta known as *sonetti del specchio* (mirror sonnets).[8]

A rare and elaborate example of this tradition, the present tabernacle mirror frame has three oval rebates and two sliding shutters that originally created a complex layered structure of reflective surfaces and concealable painted images. Stylistic parallels with frames designed by the artist and historian Giorgio Vasari and his workshop during the early 1570s suggest that this mirror frame was produced in the same context.[9] Modifications to the frame in the late nineteenth century included the replacement and repositioning of the two shutters, whereby they now slide open from opposite sides using the shell-and-volute handles. Originally, however, both shutters opened to the right, and

Fig. 54. *Mirror with Cover Depicting an Allegory of Prudence*. Florentine, mid-16th century. Oil on wood panel, 17 × 16⅜ in. (43 × 41.5 cm). Casa Vasari, Arezzo

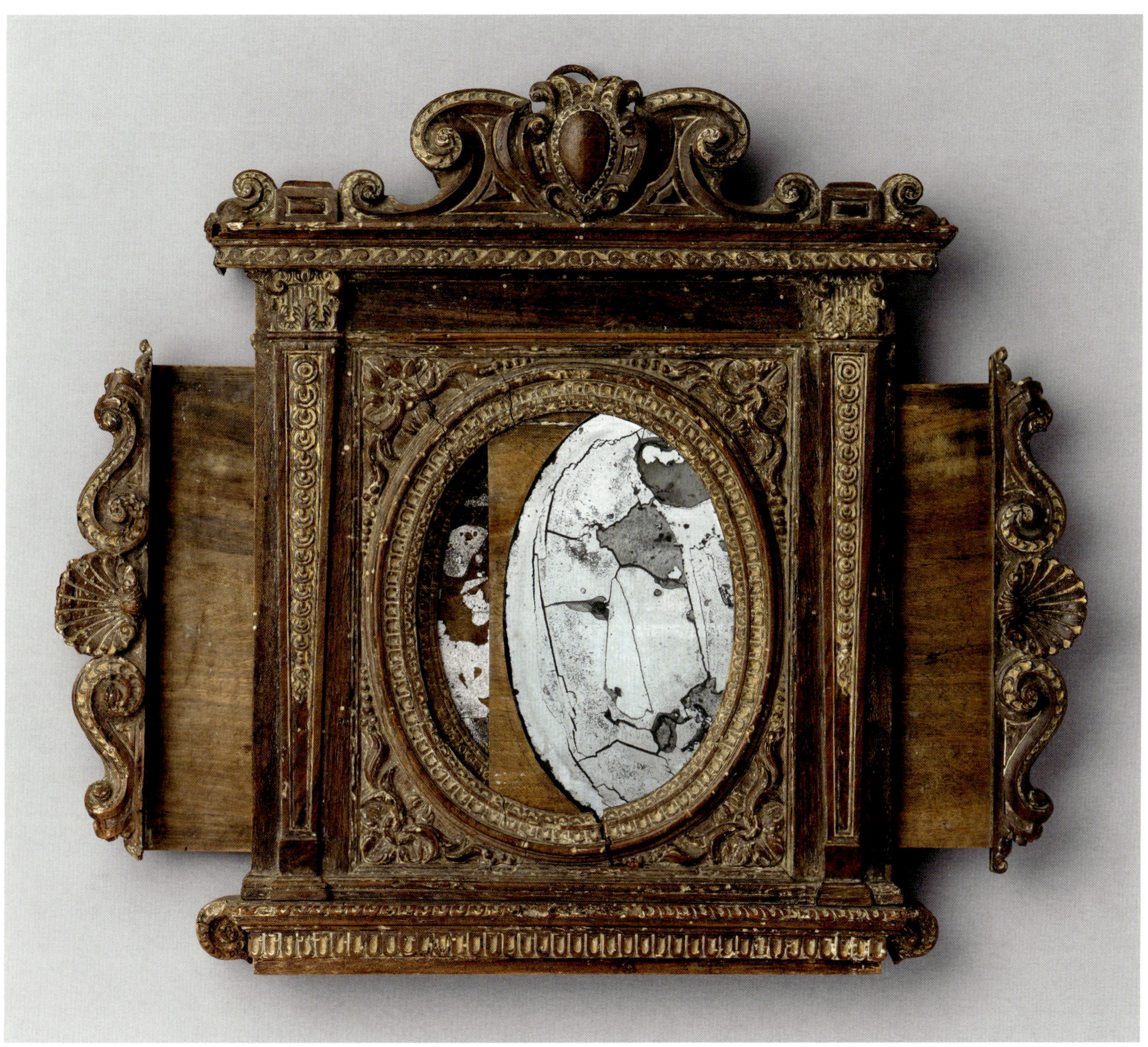

only the upper one was furnished with a handle.[10] In its former configuration, the uppermost rebate bore a mirror that may well have been made of polished metal.[11] This mirror concealed the sliding panel beneath it, which was probably adorned with a painting (perhaps an allegory) and, because it lacked a handle, could remain disguised to unknowing eyes. Beneath this sliding panel was a second painting (perhaps a portrait) produced on a thin support, such as copper, as indicated by the narrow space allocated for it.[12] The presence of the mirrored cover and the absence of a handle on the original second shutter suggest that the object was designed for discretion in an amorous context.[13]

AMN

SELECTED REFERENCES: Timothy J. Newbery and Laurence B. Kanter, cat. 26, in Newbery et al. 1990, pp. 54–55; Newbery 2007, no. 31, pp. 56–57; Deborah L. Krohn and Linda Wolk-Simon, cat. 115, in Bayer 2008, pp. 225–26; Bolzoni 2010, p. 210, fig. 24.

CAT. 44A,B

LUCAS CRANACH THE ELDER

German, 1472–1553

Martin Luther and *Katharina von Bora*, 1525

Each: Oil on wood panel, Diam., vertical, 4 3/16 in. (10.6 cm), horizontal, 4 1/8 in. (10.5 cm); thickness, 3/16 in. (.5 cm)

Inscribed: (at left of Luther portrait, signed and dated) [winged-serpent mark (wings raised)] *1525*; (at right of von Bora portrait) [same mark in reverse]

The Morgan Library and Museum, New York,Purchased by Pierpont Morgan, 1909 (AZ038)

THIS PORTRAIT PAIR belongs to a series of small roundels that Lucas Cranach the Elder and his workshop made in 1525 to commemorate the marriage of Protestant reformer and theology professor Martin Luther to Katharina von Bora, which took place in Wittenberg on June 13 of that year. Cranach augmented the series with rectangular pairs, some of which date from 1526. The original total must have been considerable, for at least thirteen pairs are still extant, along with several individual panels whose pendants are lost.[1]

Cranach, a friend of Luther, was the main producer of images in service of the Protestant Reformation.[2] He was also a witness to the marriage of Luther and von Bora. Probably first distributed as gifts, these portraits transcended visual documentation and verged on propaganda.[3] The marriage was controversial, an act of Reformation polemics in the domestic sphere. It represented a rejection of the Catholic practice of clerical celibacy and came to stand as a model for Protestant family life.

Luther (1483–1546), a former Augustinian monk, had been ordained as a priest in 1507, while von Bora (1499–1552) was an ex-nun whose escape from a Cistercian convent in 1523 Luther had facilitated. The very fact of their marriage thus called to mind the breaking of priestly, monastic, and conventual vows. In his writings of the time, Luther argued that the church tradition of placing celibacy on a higher spiritual level than marriage should be overturned. Moreover, he rejected the notion of marriage as a sacrament of the Christian faith.[4] Especially in this early, formative phase of the Reformation, the marriage portraits of Luther and von Bora were laden with provocative ideological significance.

Recent technical examination of the 1525–26 marriage portraits, both round and rectangular, reveals that Cranach must have transferred the designs to the panels by tracing cartoons—same-scale drawings—with a stylus.[5] The contours of the forms correspond almost exactly on the roundels, except for a pair in Basel with smaller-scale figures (1525, Kunstmuseum Basel). Cranach used the same cartoons for several of the rectangular pairs. Concerning the division of labor at the paint stage, it is notable that the New York roundels differ somewhat from one another in the refinement of their brushwork. The likeness of von Bora appears more finely painted than that of Luther, which is generally harder, more reliant on linear description, and heightened in contrast.[6] Comparable small differences are found within other serially produced portrait pairs from the Cranach workshop.[7] This phenomenon suggests the involvement of multiple hands up to the final stages of execution, even within discrete couplings in a given series.

Although the original frames of the New York roundels are lost, the intact frames of the Basel pair demonstrate that their profiles were shaped to interlock with one another, creating a "capsule." The Basel examples also show that, as was typical for Cranach, the frame and support were fashioned separately and glued together rather than having been turned from a single piece of wood.[8]

The use of a roundel format for painted portraits was a sixteenth-century innovation, and Cranach appears to have been its initiator. Only after his experiments of 1525–27 did this format spread to Hans Holbein the Younger in Basel and London (cats. 45 and 46A,B) and Bartholomäus Bruyn the Elder in Cologne (see figs. 47 and 48).[9] The main inspiration came from portrait medals and circular plaquettes, both Italian and German, which in turn ultimately derived from ancient coins.[10] A parallel phenomenon is found in German tondos in wooden relief (cat. 47A,B).

JPW

SELECTED REFERENCES: Kuhn 1936, p. 44, no. 142, pl. XXV; Dieter Koepplin, in Koepplin and Falk 1974–76, vol. 1, p. 295, under cats. 177, 178; Friedländer and Rosenberg 1978, p. 107, nos. 189–90E; Allmuth Schuttwolf and Werner Schade, in Schuttwolf et al. 1994, p. 50; John T. McQuillen, cat. 223, in *Martin Luther* 2016, catalogue vol., pp. 234–35.

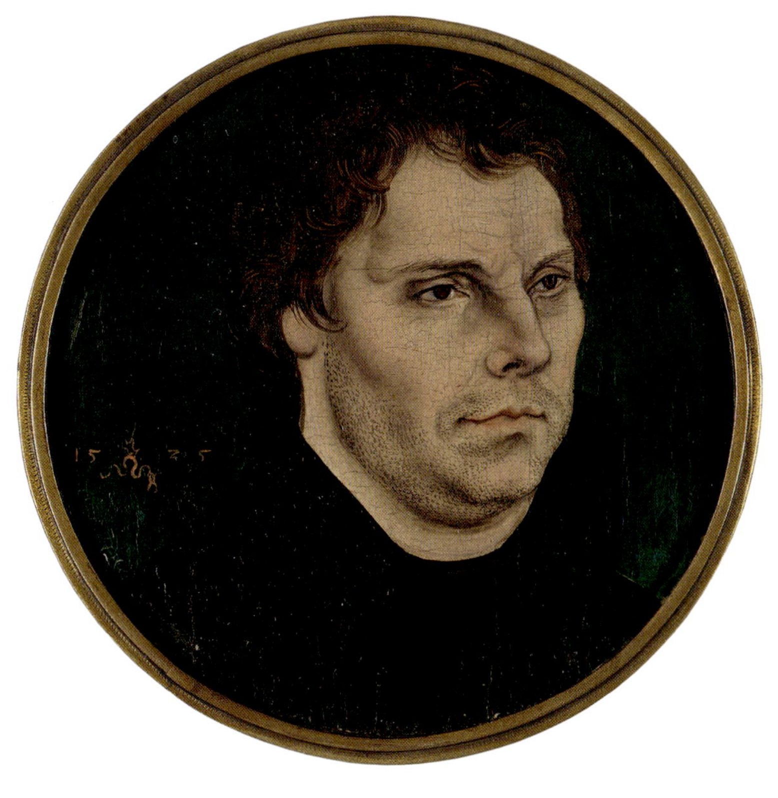

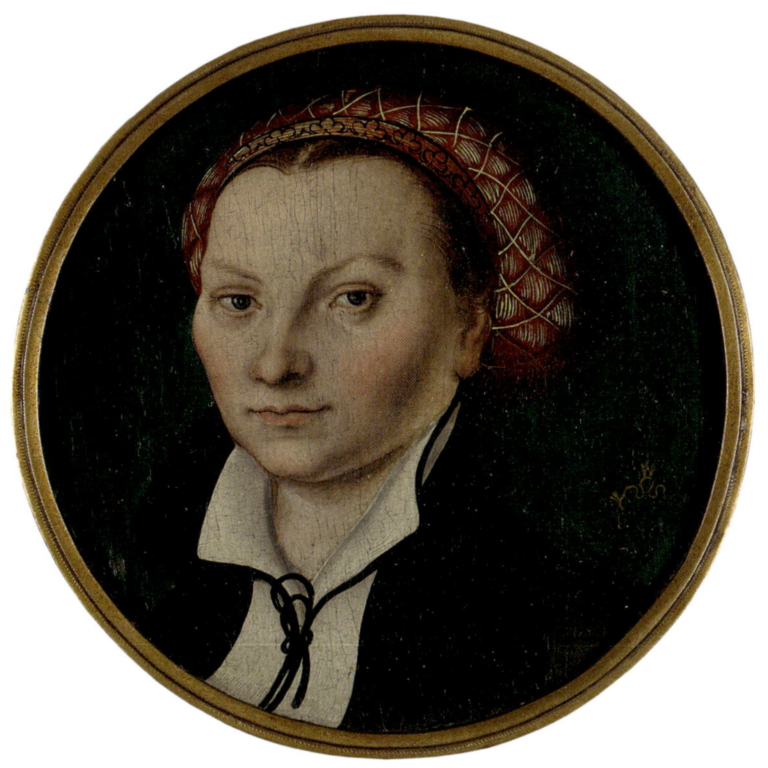

CAT. 45

HANS HOLBEIN THE YOUNGER

German, 1497/98–1543

Portrait of a Man in Royal Livery, 1532–35

Oil and gold on vellum, laid down on linden panel, overall, with engaged frame: Diam. 5 in. (12.7 cm); painted surface: Diam. 3¾ in. (9.5 cm)

The Metropolitan Museum of Art, New York, Bequest of Mary Stillman Harkness, 1950 (50.145.24)

HANS HOLBEIN THE YOUNGER was born in Augsburg, Germany, and trained there with his father, a noted painter of religious art and portraits. Initially, he worked in Basel, but in 1526 he traveled to England, where he was employed for two years by members of the humanist circle surrounding Thomas More, a well-connected jurist and social philosopher. After a hiatus in Basel, Holbein resumed his career in London in 1532, eventually becoming King's Painter to Henry VIII in 1535 (see cat. 46A,B). It is there that he gained his reputation as one of the greatest portraitists of the early sixteenth century. Holbein's paintings visually chronicle the history of court life, from the highest royal personages to those who functioned in various lesser capacities, whether in the sphere of religion, politics, diplomacy, or culture and entertainment.

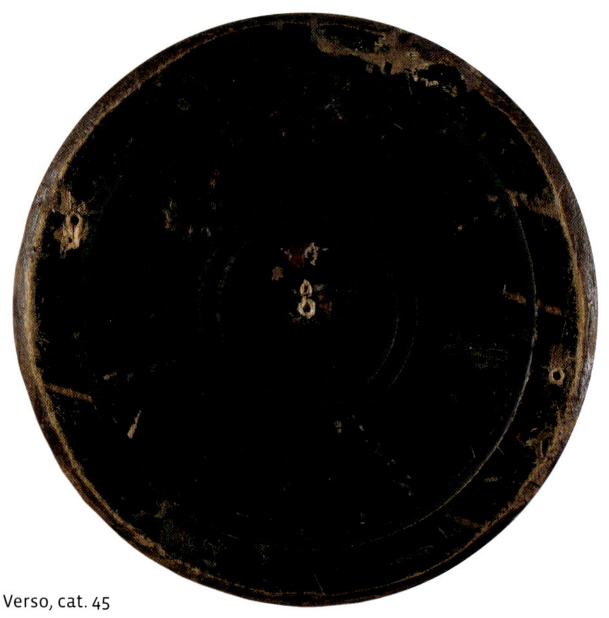

Verso, cat. 45

Although the man in The Met painting has not been identified, he clearly worked in some role at the court of Henry VIII since he wears royal livery. Not of noble birth, he would have been a craftsman or attendant.[1] His attire—a coat of red broadcloth embroidered with the king's initials, *HR* (*Henricus Rex*)—not only associates him with life at court but also signifies his loyalty to his sovereign.[2] A pair of portraits by Holbein from 1534 (Kunsthistorisches Museum, Vienna) shows a woman and a man, the latter wearing attire similar to the sitter's in The Met portrait. These two have been identified tentatively as the artist Susanna Horenbout and her husband, John Parker, or as Serjeant-Painter Andrew Wright and his wife. Additionally, The Met sitter has been related to Lucas Horenbout, brother of Susanna and painter in service to the king.[3] Proof is lacking for these suggestions, however, and the specific service that these individuals performed is not known.[4]

This exquisite portrait and its original engaged gold frame are both beautifully preserved. They immediately recall Holbein's portrait miniatures in watercolor on vellum, such as those of William and Margaret Roper in The Met collection.[5] Yet the present example was made in oil on vellum and laid down on linden wood. It joins a group of portrait roundels that emerged at the beginning of the sixteenth century as a new art form, probably initiated by Lucas Cranach the Elder (see cat. 44), which ultimately derived from portrait medals and ancient coins. Only five inches in diameter (12.7 centimeters), The Met portrait could have been handheld for personal contemplation and enjoyment. Its excellent condition implies that it once had a protective cover, such as the one that survives for Holbein's portrait of Philipp Melanchthon (cat. 46A,B). The purportedly lost cover may have carried an inscription identifying the sitter or showing his motto or device. The panel was turned on a lathe, and three decorative concentric circles were engraved into the verso, which was painted black.
MWA

SELECTED REFERENCES: Ganz 1912, pp. 115, 241–42; Chamberlain 1913, vol. 2, pp. 71, 353; Ganz 1921, pp. 263–66, 268; Rowlands 1985, pp. 96, 141 no. 52, pl. 82; Foister 2004, p. 15; Foister 2006, cat. 43, pp. 41, 50, 175; Maryan W. Ainsworth, no. 31, in Ainsworth and Waterman 2013, pp. 138–39; Adam Eaker, cat. 86, in Cleland and Eaker 2022, pp. 221–22.

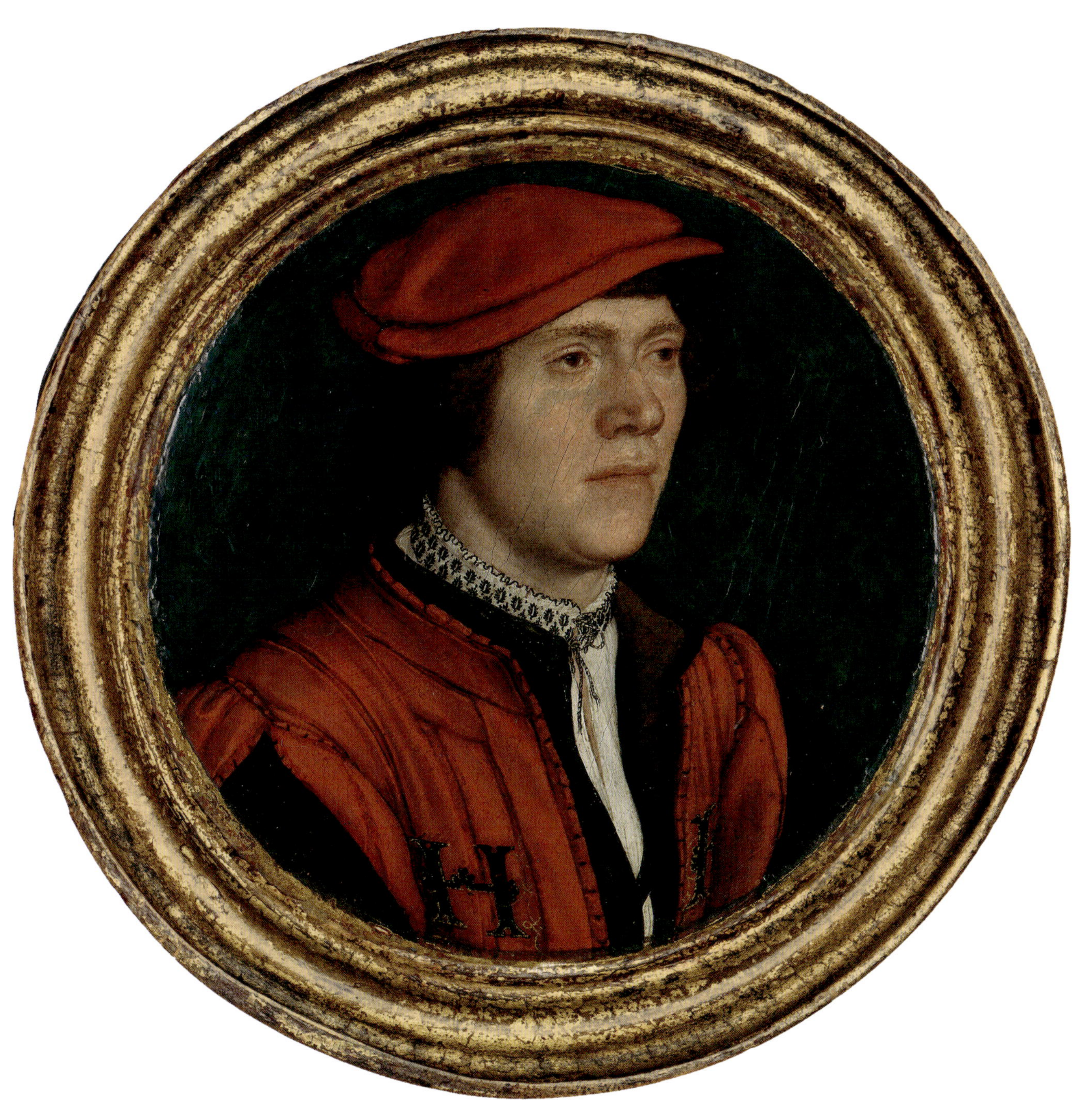

CAT. 46A,B

HANS HOLBEIN THE YOUNGER

German, 1497/98–1543

Philipp Melanchthon; *Portrait Cover with* Grotteschi *and Inscription*, 1535

Oil on oak panel, gold-painted engaged frame, Diam. 3⅝ in. (9 cm), 4¾ in. (12 cm) with lid

Inscribed (on cartouche of lid): *QVI CERNIS TANTVM NON, VIVA MELANTHONIS ORA, / HOLBINVS RARA DEXTERITATE DEDIT.* (Behold Melan[ch]thon's features, almost as if alive, Holbein has captured them, with the utmost skill.)

Niedersächisches Landesmuseum Hannover, Landesgalerie (PAM 798)

Not exhibited

THIS PORTRAIT OF one of the leading proponents of the Reformation, Philipp Schwarzerdt, known as Melanchthon (1497–1560), survives with its highly ornate lid and laudatory inscription. The subdued demeanor of the sitter belies the turbulent times in which it was made. It was painted by Hans Holbein the Younger sometime after the *Portrait of a Man in Royal Livery* (cat. 45), during the artist's second period in England, when he was engaged with portraying members of Henry VIII's court as well as noted intellectuals and German merchants in London.

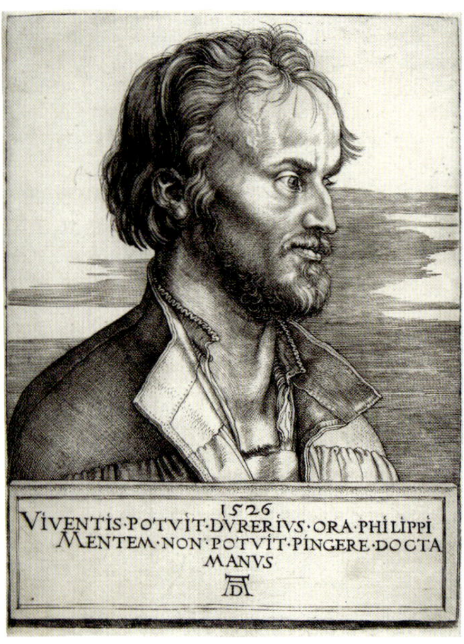

After Henry annulled his marriage to Katherine of Aragon in favor of Anne Boleyn in 1533, he subsequently changed the rules of succession to suit the new arrangement. Henry was recognized as head of the Church of England in 1534, formally breaking with Rome. Those previously favored at court who refused to support the king's new directions were censured or worse. Thomas More, a close friend of Holbein (the artist had lived with him during his first English period) and lord chancellor from 1529 to 1532, was convicted of treason and beheaded in 1535. During this tumultuous period, Holbein negotiated between opposing alliances, managing to thrive as a painter of religious themes and portraits.

It was also the time of the rise of the Protestant Reformation. In 1518 Melanchthon, a professor of Greek at the University of Wittenberg at the young age of twenty-one, met Martin Luther and embraced his reformist movement. With Luther's approval, he drafted the Augsburg Confession, a statement of Lutheran doctrine that was presented to Charles V at the Diet of Augsburg in 1530. Melanchthon's seminal work of 1521, the *Loci Communes* (*Commonplaces*), the initial elucidation of Lutheran doctrine, appeared in 1535 in a revised version dedicated to Henry VIII and sent to the king in August of that year.[1]

For the image of the Lutheran activist, Holbein fashioned a shell portrait that could be handheld and easily transported, the owner perhaps taking the opportunity to show it to like-minded adherents of the reformist movement.[2] When opened, the covering lid reveals a Latin text separating *grotteschi* that include satyrs, dolphins, and cornucopias painted in white. In translation it reads, "Behold Melan[ch]thon's features, almost as if alive, Holbein has captured them, with the utmost skill."[3] In this interaction of text and image, a comparison is made between two famous men, a religious reformer and the king's painter; the living presence of the former was replicated by the unparalleled painting skill of the latter. It is highly debatable that Holbein ever met Melanchthon, who spent his entire life in Germany, and the artist therefore may have relied on portraits by Cranach or Dürer for his physiognomy.[4] Unlike the inscription

Fig. 55. Albrecht Dürer (German, 1471–1528). *Philipp Melanchthon*, 1526. Engraving, sheet: 6¹⁵⁄₁₆ × 5 in. (17.7 × 12.7 cm), fair margin. The Metropolitan Museum of Art, New York, Fletcher Fund, 1919 (19.73.117)

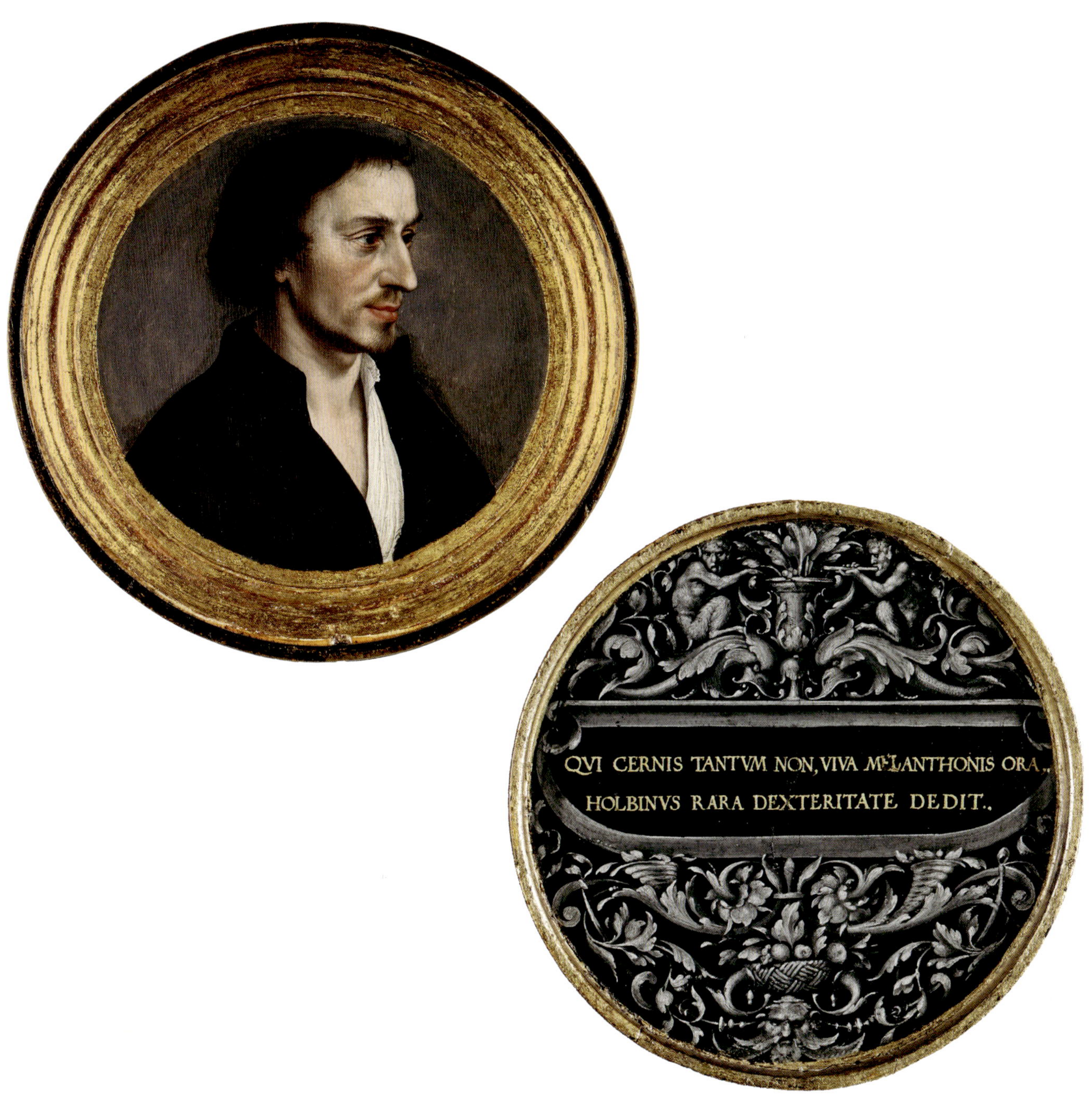

beneath Dürer's 1526 engraved portrait of Melanchthon (fig. 55)—*Viventis Potvit Durerivs ora Philippi* [. . .] *Manus / AD* (Dürer can picture the features of the living Philip but lacks the skill to depict his mind)—the emphasis here is solely on Holbein's achievement.

MWA

SELECTED REFERENCES: Rowlands 1985, pp. 94–95, 143–44 no. 60, color pls. 30, 31, pls. 96, 97; Dülberg 1990, pp. 95–96, 166, 272–73 no. 269, pls. 250–52 figs. 650–55; Peter van der Ploeg, cat. 20, in Buck et al. 2003, pp. 102–3; Foister 2004, pp. 111, 163; Woollett 2021, pp. 15, 114–15 cat. 23.

CAT. 47A

MEISTER DER DOSENKÖPFE

German, active 1525

Elector Friedrich the Wise of Saxony; *Cover with a Centaur*, 1525

Portrait: wood, pearwood; canister bottom: walnut, partially painted, Diam. 8¾ in. (22 cm)

Inscribed and dated (on raised rim of canister): *HERCZOG • FRIDRICH • CVRFVRST • IN • SASEN • 1 • 5 • 2 • 5* (*Duke Friedrich, Elector of Saxony, 1525*)

Kunsthistorisches Museum, Vienna, Kunstkammer (KK 3878, 3879)

CAT. 47B

MEISTER DER DOSENKÖPFE

Anna Rasper or Anna Dornle(?); *Cover with a Siren*, 1525

Portrait: [same as cat. 47A]

Inscribed and dated (on raised rim of canister): *ANNA • RASPER • DORNLE • STIEF • TOCHTER • 1 • 5 • 2 • 5* (*Anna Rasper Dornle Stepdaughter 1525*)

Kunsthistorisches Museum, Vienna, Kunstkammer (KK 3893, 3894)

THESE RELIEF PORTRAITS, each forming the base of a walnut canister, represent a unique as well as very intimate and personal token of the love affair between Elector Friedrich the Wise of Saxony (1463–1525) and his mistress, Anna Rasper (or Dornle). The raised rim of the canister with the portrait of Friedrich, slightly facing left, bears a gilt inscription giving his name and the date of the work. In her portrait, the lady inclines her head slightly to the right and is accompanied by an inscription giving similar information.[1]

The wood-carver seems to have modeled Friedrich's portrait either on an inverted copperplate engraving by Albrecht Dürer from 1524 or on the artist's silverpoint drawing that preceded it, likely made on the occasion of Friedrich's visit to the Imperial Diet in Nuremberg in 1523 (École des Beaux-Arts, Paris).[2] Dürer's bust portrait, in two-thirds view, deliberately omits any attributes of worldly might. Given the round format of the relief, the wood-carver reduced the bust to a head and raised the elector's face, smoothing his wrinkles and lending him a more boyish appearance.

Dürer may have drawn Anna Rasper as well, and the artist modeled the canister relief on that image. Also rendered in pearwood, hers is another youthful visage, with soft chin, full lips in a faint smile, slim nose, and alert, almond-shaped eyes under delicate curved brows. Anna is depicted neither as a married wife with a veiled bonnet nor as a maiden with long, loose hair. Instead, she has short, wavy tresses and wears a beret-like headdress, by no means conventional at the time and denoting an outsider status.[3]

The unwed elector lived for many years in close companionship with his commoner mistress Anna. Various sources confirm that they had four illegitimate children, three of whom were still alive when, in the hours before his death in 1525, Friedrich dictated his last will and testament to Georg Spalatin.[4] To avoid naming his lover, Friedrich resorted to code in addition to using the nicknames of his sons, Friedrich and Sebastian: *Fritzn vnd Bastls muter sollen 200 gulden gegeben vnnd zugeschickt werden* (Fritz's and Bastl's mother should be provided with 200 gulden). The sons each received 500 gulden annually from interest income, while the daughter, then thirteen years old, inherited a lump sum of 500 gulden.[5]

Although Martin Luther reported that Anna and her daughter were expelled from court, presumably because of tightening bans on concubinage, Friedrich's will suggests that the relationship continued in one form or another after the expulsion. Anna herself later said that she did not believe Friedrich would marry anyone else as long as she lived.[6]

Like the wooden faces, the reliefs carved on the canister lids are oriented facing each other: a rearing centaur, armed with lance and shield, and another hybrid creature, a winged form with a woman's head and torso, talons, and coiled serpentine tail. Whereas the centaur could allude to the mythical abduction of women, the siren-like figure could symbolize the unfulfilled longing for sensual pleasure.[7]
AD

SELECTED REFERENCES: Bange 1928, pp. 34–35, pls. 25, 26; Koepplin and Falk 1974–76, vol. 1, pp. 275–78, figs. 137, 138; Alfred Schädler, cats. 515, 516, in *Welt im Umbruch* 1980–81, vol. 2, pp. 161–62; Dülberg 1990, p. 93, pl. 247 figs. 639, 640; Eser 1996, nos. 47, 48, pp. 297–301, figs. 88, 89; Ritschel 2006, pp. 326–41, figs. 15, 16; Thomas Kuster, cats. 123, 124, in Haag et al. 2011, pp. 207–9.

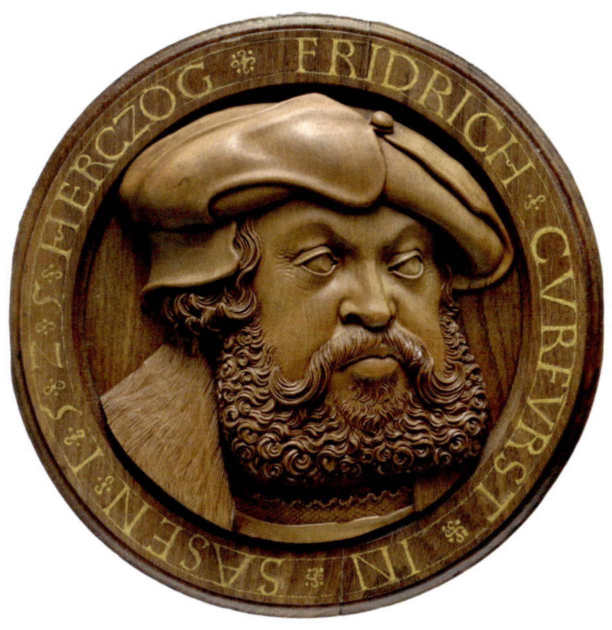
HERCZOG FRIDRICH CVRFVRST IN SASEN

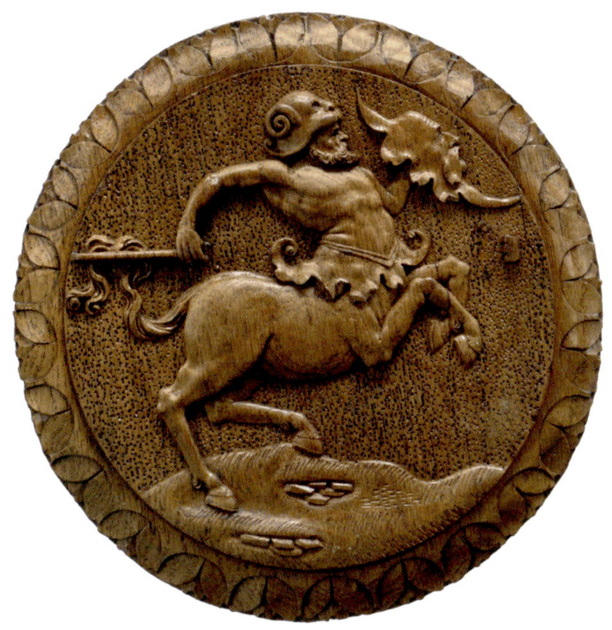

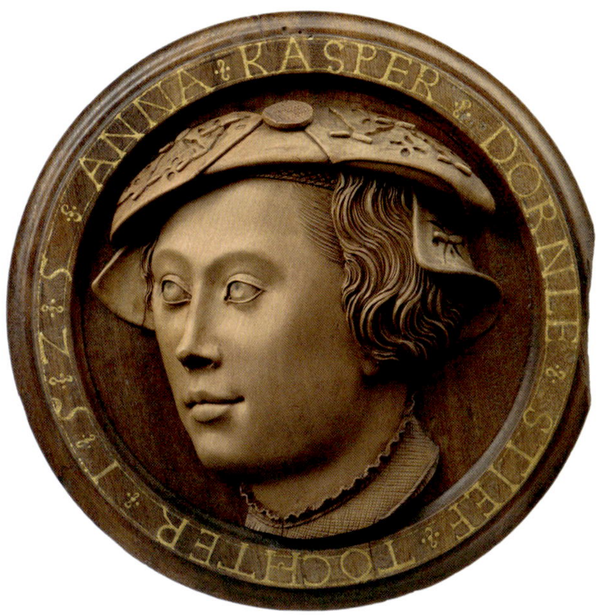
ANNA KASPER DORNLE
TOCHTER

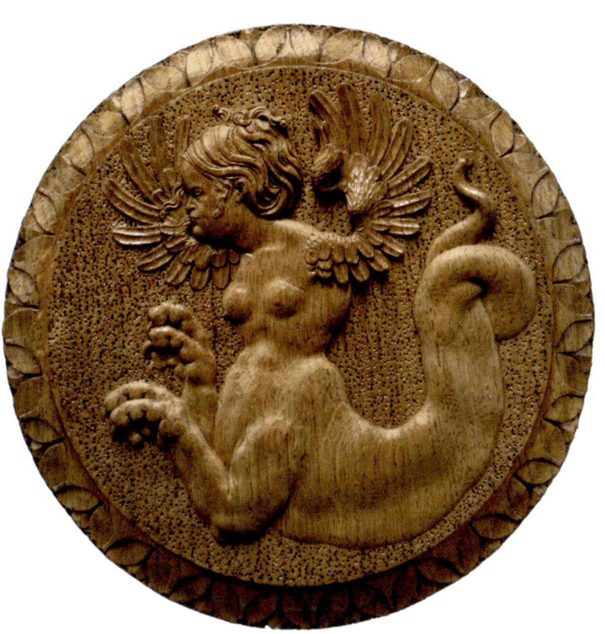

CAT. 48

UNKNOWN MAKER

German

Coin Box (Schraubtaler) *of Heinrich Julius, Duke of Brunswick-Lüneburg-Wolfenbüttel: Wild Man* and *Portrait of Ferdinand II* (obverses); *Portrait of a Lady* (interior), 17th century

Coins: silver; portrait: gouache on vellum (?), Diam. 1½ in. (4 cm)

Inscribed (on Wild Man coin): *HONESTVM • PRO • PATRIA • 1604* (Honor for one's country); (on portrait of Ferdinand) *FERDINANDVS • II • D:G • R • IM • S • A • G • H • B • REX* [*FERDINANDVS II, DEI GRATIA, ROMANORVM IMPERATOR, SEMPER AVGVSTVS, GERMANIAE, HUNGARIAE, BOHEMIAE, REX*] (Ferdinand II, by the grace of God, Roman emperor, always Augustus, king of Germany, Hungary, Bohemia)

Niedersächsisches Landesmuseum Hannover, Münzkabinett (91:000:001)

THIS BOX IS MADE of two different thalers, the first from the Duchy of Brunswick-Wolfenbüttel depicting a Wild Man,[1] the other from Bohemia with a full-figure portrait of Ferdinand II, Holy Roman Emperor. *Schraubtaler* (screw-thalers or screw-coins) were fashioned out of real currency as showpieces for admirers. They typically consisted of two thalers, hollowed out and smoothed on one side, then provided with a thread and a counter thread. When screwed together, the coins formed a small silver box suitable for carrying on the person.[2] If the coins came from different countries or periods, the boxes were known as *Zwitter-Schraubtaler* (hybrid coin boxes).[3]

Initially, the interiors of the boxes contained elaborate engravings or small oil portraits, followed after a time by watercolor or gouache paintings on parchment. They were intended as presents for friends or other deserving persons. Often they were given as engagement gifts to the bridegroom or bride, since most contain portraits of young men or women.[4]

During his reign, Duke Heinrich Julius (1564–1613) ordered the mint in the town of Zellerfeld, located in the Harz area, to produce coins and medals featuring the image of the Wild Man, who was considered a symbol of the Harz Mountains. The silver coins usually depict the colossal mountain spirit freestanding in a frontal, full-figure pose with a torn-out tree trunk or fir tree in his right hand. The giant's vigorous body is covered with hair, and he has a long, thick, pointed beard. He wears only a loincloth of fir or spruce, although sometimes an oak wreath serves the purpose instead. His hat is made of moss.[5]

Mintmaster Heinrich Oeckeler minted the Wild Man found on this coin box in Zellerfeld in 1604 with the above-mentioned motto of Heinrich Julius. The coin with its full-figure portrait of Ferdinand II was probably minted around 1624 in Prague, following his election as Holy Roman Emperor in September 1619. He appears in armor, imperial crown on his head and sword angled to the left in its sheath. He grips the scepter in his right hand, the imperial orb in his left. The inscription encircling him confirms his state positions.

Inside the box, on a round piece of parchment, is the full-figure depiction of a young woman. She wears an ornate red-and-black dress, with a large, round lace collar and lace cuffs, and a red cup covering her braided and pinned-up hair. A green plant trails from the architectural feature beside her, and in the background is an open landscape. The lady's costume and style of headdress date the painting later than the hybrid coin box,[6] whose two thalers were no longer in circulation. This suggests that the little box was commissioned for personal reasons such as an upcoming wedding. AD

SELECTED REFERENCES: unpublished.

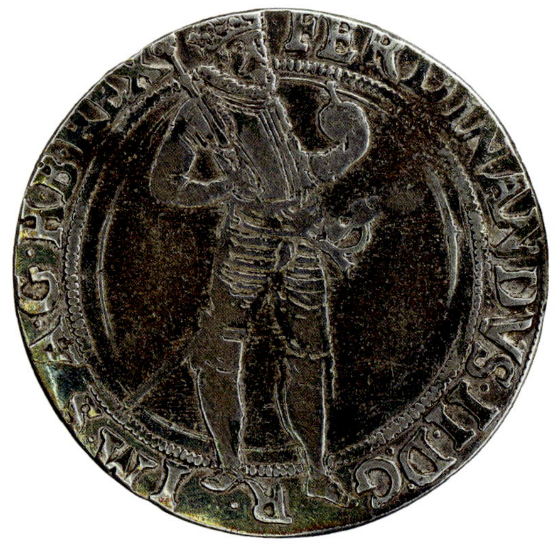

Thaler with Emperor Ferdinand II

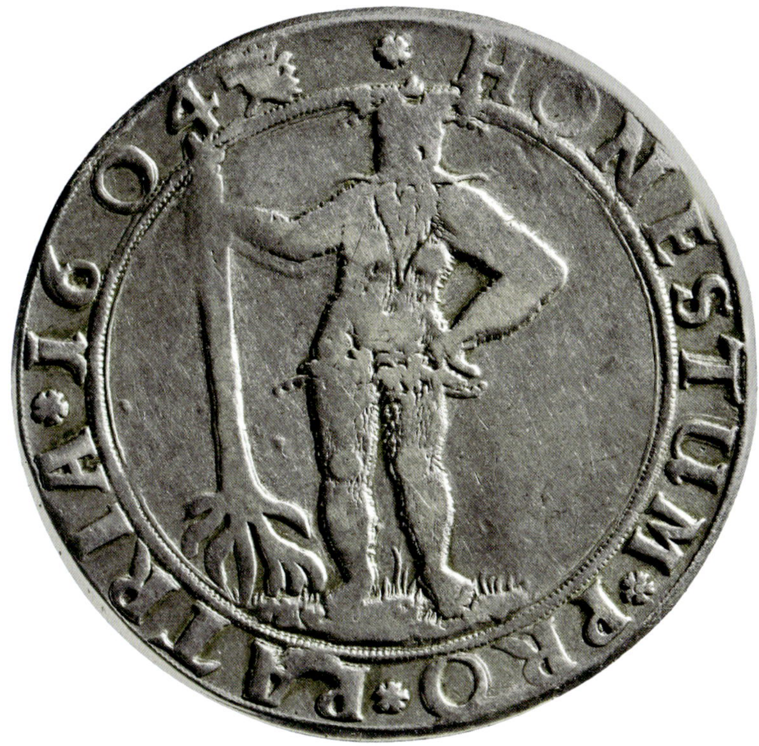

Thaler with Wild Man

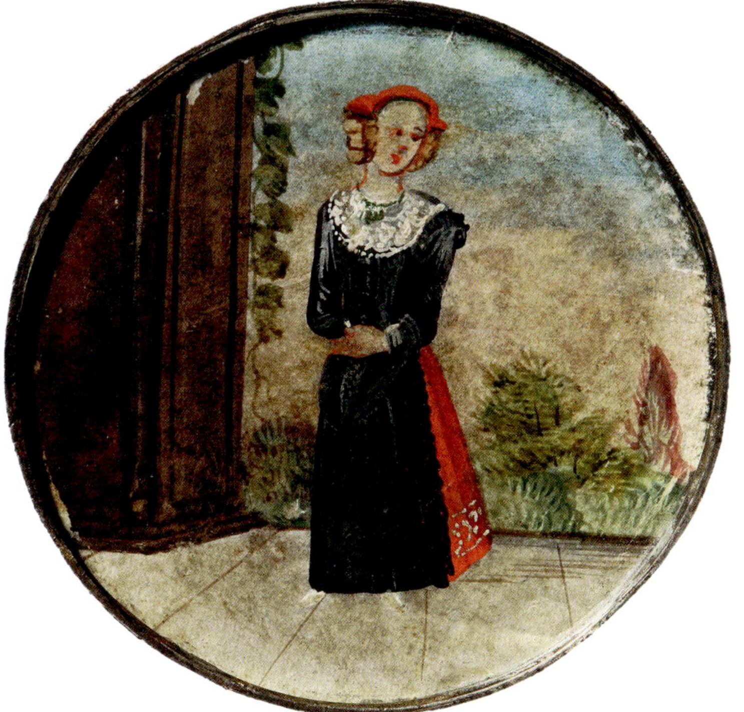

Portrait of a Lady

CAT. 49A,B

LAVINIA FONTANA

Italian, 1552–1614

Portrait of a Woman and *Portrait of a Man*, possibly late 1570s or early 1580s

Oil on wood panel, male portrait: Diam. 3 15/16 in. (10 cm); female portrait: Diam. 3 13/16 in. (9.7 cm)

Smith College Museum of Art, Northampton, Massachusetts, Purchased with the Dr. Robert A. and Minna Flynn Johnson, class of 1936, Acquisition Fund (SC 2019.14.1,.2)

WORKING UNDER THE guidance of her father, Prospero, the Bolognese artist Lavinia Fontana began producing modestly scaled, finely executed paintings on various supports in the second half of the 1570s. These include several remarkable self-portraits, one probably executed to mark her betrothal to Gian Paolo Zappi in 1577 (Accademia di San Luca, Rome) and another, a roundel on copper, painted for the Spanish Dominican antiquarian Alfonso Chacón in 1579 (Gallerie degli Uffizi, Florence).[1] The latter shows the height of her ambitions and skills as she places herself among her own collection of statuettes and antique copies painted with precision and a sensitivity to the flicker of light over various surfaces.

Portraiture remained fundamental to Fontana's practice over the next decades, and she captured a broad spectrum of Bolognese society in works ranging in scale from miniature to life-sized. Some of the most remarkable of these celebrated betrothals or marriages and captured women in elaborate dresses with significant jewels and other accessories that were recognizable in that context. This recently rediscovered, intimate portrait pair, each about four inches in diameter, was attributed to the artist by Babette Bohn; it would almost certainly have been painted as a private celebration of marriage for this unidentified young couple.[2]

The young woman wears a variation on the garments seen both in Fontana's own *Self-Portrait at a Spinet* of 1577, mentioned above, and in her portraits of Bologna's noble brides, such as the *Young Noblewoman* (ca. 1580, National Museum of Women in the Arts, Washington, D.C.), in which the sitter also wears a red overdress and a heavy gold pendant necklace with a hanging pearl, her hair held back with a gold band. The combination of red and white probably alludes to the Petrarchan colors of love, and the local tradition of red nuptial gowns is confirmed in documents, as when a "dress of red embroidered grosgrain silk" appears in account books relating to the marriage of Camilla Paleotti and Salustio Gozzadini (both from important Bolognese families) in 1578.[3] There is less gold embroidery and elaborate jewelry on view here than in some of Fontana's more substantial, formal portraits, and this may suggest a bride from a less affluent family. The portrayal of the fresh-faced, bearded young man is unusual in that—unlike the sitters in all of Lavinia's known male portraits—he is not wearing black, but a light-colored jacket shot through with rosy tones and, with his collar rimmed with the same red as the bride's gown, thus continues the Petrarchan motif.

Portrait pairs such as this are rare in the artist's oeuvre. Another recently attributed example unusually shows the couple twice as the front and back of the same small copper support (ca. 1577, Museo de Zaragoza, on loan from the Real Academia de Nobles y Bellas Artes de San Luis).[4] In the present pair, the format is even more personal and unexpected. They form the top and bottom of a small box, with the male portrait painted on the reverse of a carefully turned lid that fits over the marginally larger base with the woman's portrait. Perhaps the closest comparisons in formal terms are with Northern works, such as Cranach's portrait

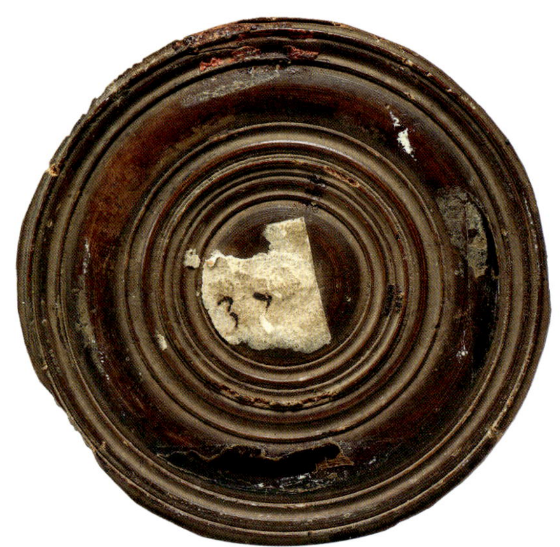

Reverse, male portrait

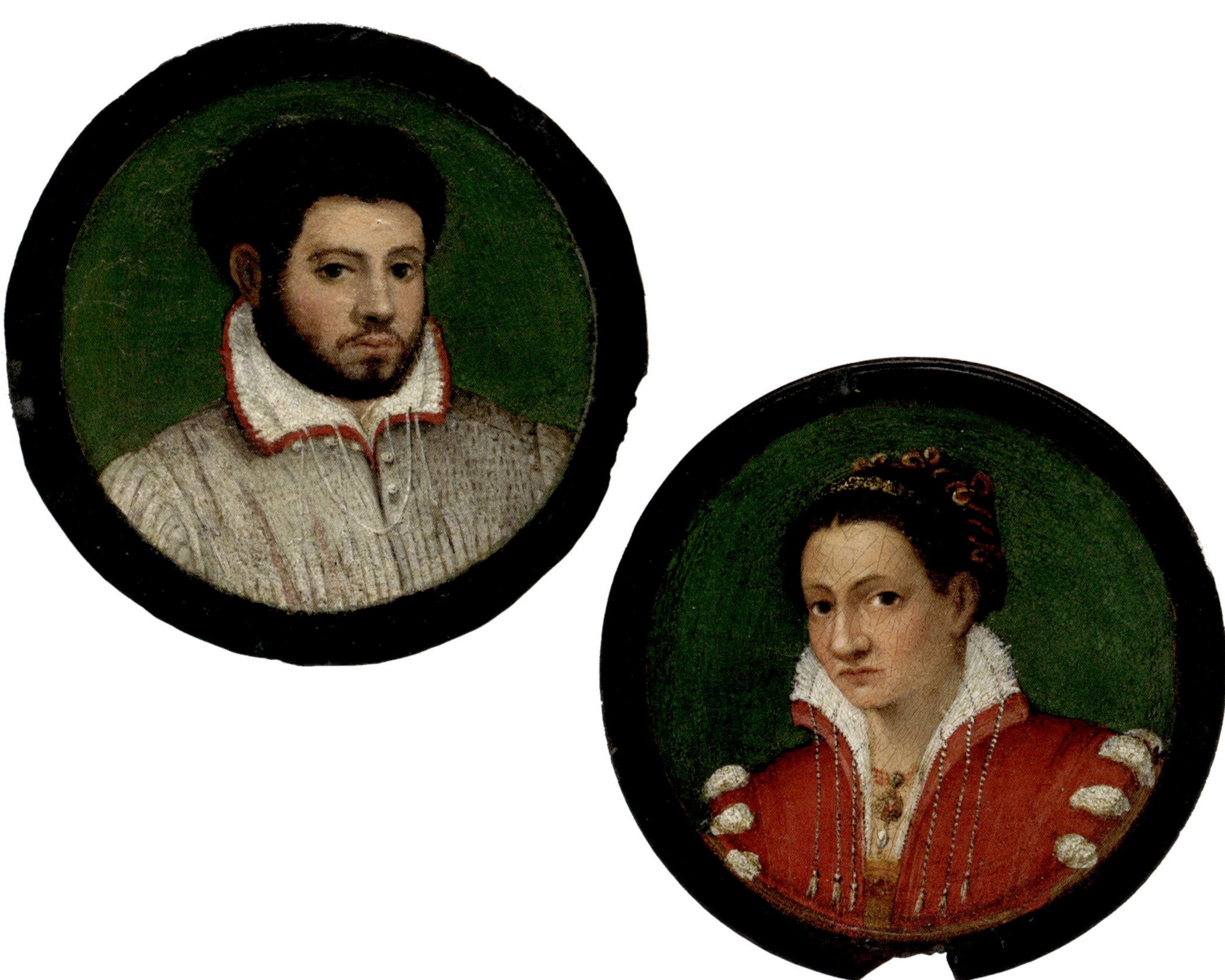

pair of Martin Luther and his wife, Katharina von Bora, in 1525 (cat. 44A,B). In German these are often called *Kapsel* (capsule) portraits.[5] Fontana's portrait pair is closely related to another group of small paintings by the artist, known as *ritrattini*, that are now in the Uffizi and were probably part of the collection of such works famously assembled by Leopoldo de' Medici, many of which came from Bologna.[6] One, a female portrait on copper with an early attribution to Fontana and dated by Maria Teresa Cantaro to around 1583–84, shares many characteristics with the depiction of this young bride.[7]

When the Cremonese artist Sofonisba Anguissola painted the renowned miniaturist Giulio Clovio, she showed him holding a portrait of a similar format, which he may be in the process of completing (1556, private collection, Rome); Giorgio Vasari confirmed that various people owned "in little cases most beautiful portraits by his hand, of various lords, their friends, or ladies loved by them."[8] These roughly contemporary references and depictions of miniature portraits help to contextualize Lavinia's young pair, but the more intimate suggestion of two figures interlocked recalls even more vividly the pair painted by Jacometto a century earlier (cat. 20A,B). Although they gaze outward toward the viewer when side by side, they speak to each other through composition, color, and the carefully crafted support they share.
AB

SELECTED REFERENCES: Carrabino 2019.

CAT. 50A,B

UNKNOWN ARTIST

Italian, probably Florence

Portrait of a Gentleman and *Portrait of a Lady*, 1565–85

Pigmented wax, black glass, seed pearls, gilding; mounted under glass with gilded and black wood frame, Diam. 2¾ in. (7 cm)

The Metropolitan Museum of Art, New York, Gift of J. Pierpont Morgan, 1917 (17.190.463,.464)

THIS PAIR OF miniature roundels portrays an elegantly dressed couple in profile. Both figures are facing right and hold a white cloth in the left hand, hers concealed from view and his extended in an authoritative gesture. The woman wears a deep blue zimarra textured with gold brocade. Her white chemise, including the goffered ruffs at the wrist and neck, is enriched throughout with gold embroidery. The gold-patterned lace veil caps a sheer forehead cloth secured by jeweled hair ornaments. Hanging over her bodice is a long gold chain rendered in low relief and inset with seed pearls. Her earrings also combine real pearls with painted gold and silver detail.

The woman's male companion wears a black doublet, slashed and pinked to reveal a deep yellow lining, with gold buttons down the front. His white shirt has starched lace and goffered trim at the neck and cuffs. A cloak of deep blue is draped over one shoulder and pulled across his body in an aristocratic manner. His hair is closely cropped, and he has a short mustache. Both figures have delicately rendered flesh, with a pink tint to their lips and ears.

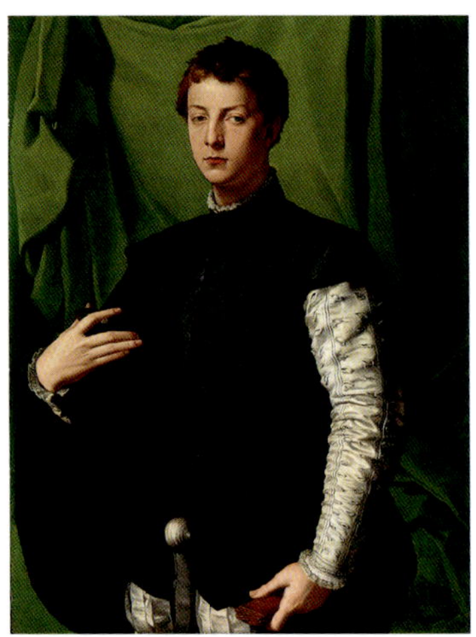

In the late fifteenth century, the use of unpigmented wax in low relief was a preliminary stage in the design of cameos and medallions. The pliable medium allowed the artist to render precise details and texture. By the early sixteenth century in Italy, medalists experimented with pigmented wax to produce miniature colored-wax portraits as finished works of art.[1] In *On Technique*, his introduction to the 1550 publication of his famous *Lives of the Artists*, Giorgio Vasari noted that these innovative wax portraits appeared so lifelike that they lacked only "the spirit and the power of speech."[2] This new vogue in portraiture is often attributed to the northern Italian medalist Antonio Abondio, although Vasari singles out the Florentine Pastorino de' Pastorini as the genre's most accomplished artist. These naturalistic wax portrayals, enhanced with precious gems, seed pearls, and gold, conjured the illusion of life in miniature.

It is difficult to firmly attribute the present roundels or to establish the identity of the couple. That the reliefs are executed on opaque black glass rather than on slate suggests an Italian origin for the pair. However, the popularity of colored-wax miniatures quickly spread across Europe, no doubt initiated by the peripatetic employment of Abondio by the Hapsburg courts. The same is true of prevailing aristocratic fashion trends, which are difficult to locate within a specific European court. Nevertheless, considerations of material and dress make it probable that these portrait roundels were produced in Tuscany from 1565 to 1585.

Such miniature portraits were popular gifts, intended to be held and viewed in private for an intimate rapport with the sitter. Agnolo Bronzino's life-size painted portrait of Lodovico Capponi conveys the demeanor of the recipient, who displays a wax portrait roundel in his hand while covering its subject with his finger (fig. 56).[3] The guarded pose intentionally restricts access to the sitter's identity—an inclination toward concealment that is a major aspect of sixteenth-century habits of viewing these miniature portraits.

SL

SELECTED REFERENCES: O'Shaughnessy n.d.

Fig. 56. Agnolo Bronzino (Agnolo di Cosimo di Mariano; Italian, 1503–1572). *Lodovico Capponi*, 1550–55. Oil on panel, 45⅞ × 33¾ in. (116.5 × 85.7 cm). The Frick Collection, New York, Henry Clay Frick Bequest (1915.1.19)

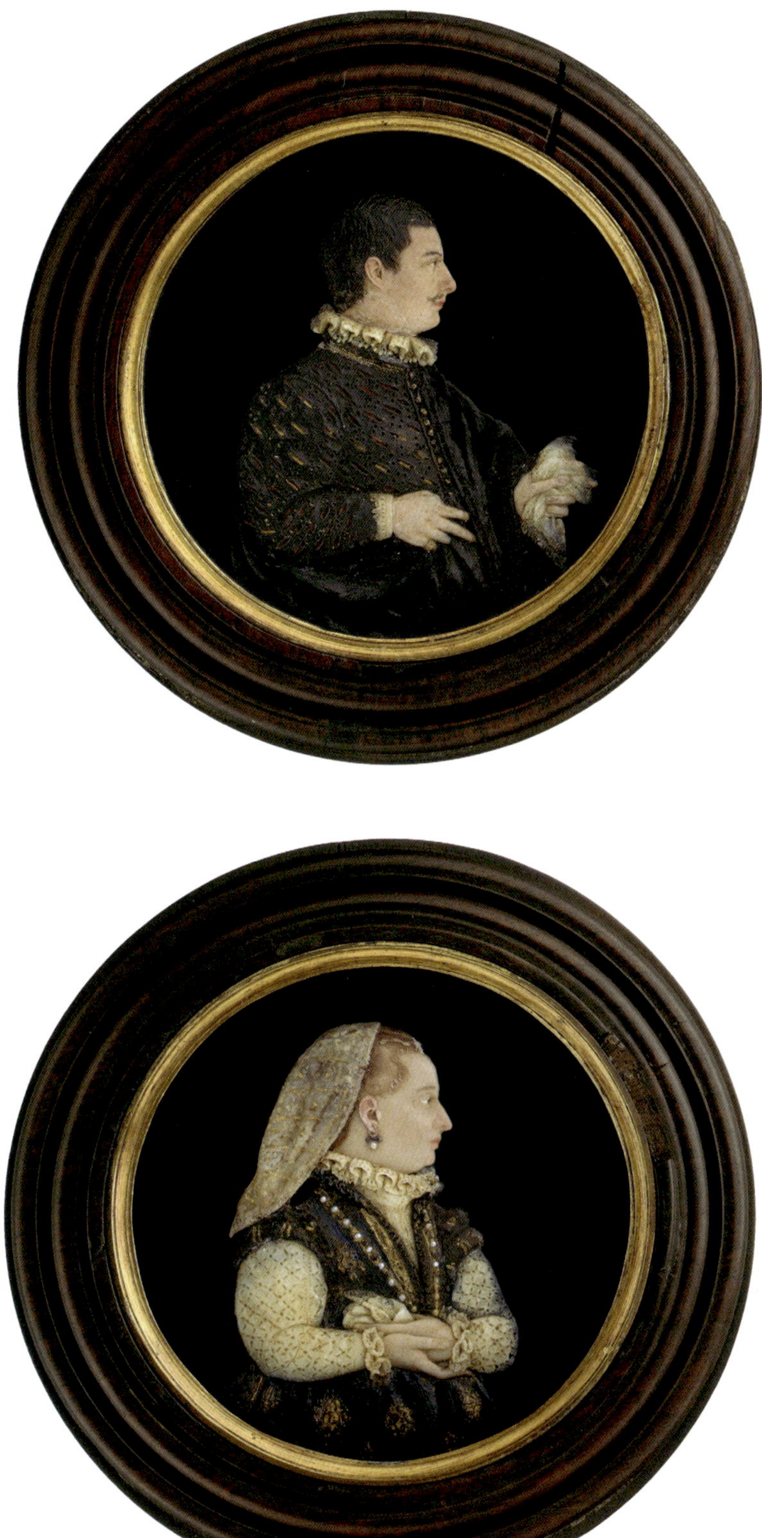

CAT. 51A–C
MATTHÄUS CARL

German, active ca. 1584–1609

Portrait of Paulus Praun, Cover, and Carrying Case, 1584

Portrait: colored wax, 2⅝ × 2 in. (6.5 × 5 cm); capsule: wood, slate; case: leather

Inscribed: (on portrait, on either side of head) *PAVLVS / PRAVN*; (on note on reverse) *Paulus Prauns Seel. Bildtnus Anno 1584 / von Jeremias Imhoff verehrt / worden* (Paulus Praun's portrait from 1584 / honored by Jeremias Imhoff)

Germanisches Nationalmuseum, Nuremberg, Friedrich von Praun'schen Familienstiftung (Med8995)

INSIDE A GLAZED wooden capsule is the bust profile, facing right, of Paulus Praun (1548–1616), executed in colored wax and fitted on an oval of shiny black roof slate. Praun's distinctive bald pate is bordered by loose, dark curls. His beard and mustache are also slightly wavy, and his dark vest is finished with a millstone collar. The words *PAVLVS / PRAVN* appear in wax along the upper edge of the image field, to either side of his head. On the reverse, a note has been glued in place that reads in translation, "Paulus Praun's portrait from 1584 / honored by Jeremias Imhoff." The inscription must have been added after quite some time, as its wording indicates that Praun has already died. It was presumably written by Jeremias I Imhoff, a member of one of the eldest patrician families of Nuremberg, who passed the portrait on to the Praun family.[1]

This wax medallion (A) appears to have been the model for a medal, also crafted by Matthäus Carl in 1584. On the medal, the initials *MC* appearing on Praun's arm allow the medallion to be attributed to Carl as well. The artist was born around 1550 in Augsburg, where he also received his training. Records place him from 1584 in Nuremberg, where he attained master status in the goldsmith guild and became a citizen in 1585. His citizenship documents describe him as a "*goldarbeiter und conterfetter in wachs*" (goldworker and portraitist in wax).[2]

The wax medallion itself is based on two painted terracotta relief portraits of Praun fashioned by the Netherlandish sculptor Johann Gregor van der Schardt in 1580 (Landesmuseum Württemberg, Stuttgart, and Germanisches Nationalmuseum, Nuremberg).[3]

Accompanying the wax medallion is a cover (B) decorated on either side with crisscrossed, ovoid shapes delineated by double parallel grooves. The two pieces can be joined together to form a closed capsule, which was put in a yellow leather pouch for safekeeping (C).[4] Capsule portraits and small-format portraits painted on wood with hinged covers were often kept in protective sachets like this one; very few of these have survived (we have learned of their use primarily through written sources).[5] Another rare example—the portraits of René of Anjou and Jeanne de Laval, which folded together to form a portrait box that was stored in a red velvet sack—is housed at the Louvre (cat. 12A–C).[6]

The patrician Paulus Praun, born in Nuremberg, took over his father's German-Italian silk trading business together with his brothers Hans and Jakob as equal partners. He lived primarily in Nuremberg until 1589, when he moved to Bologna (where he is buried) and ran that branch of the family business from the palazzo of Senator Francesco Sampieri.[7] Praun's tremendous wealth allowed him to pursue his love of collecting from a young age, and he amassed one of the sixteenth century's largest private art collections north of the Alps. His collection, known as the Praun'sches Kabinett, included German and Italian works, but its focus was classical art forms: paintings, with drawings and prints, as well as sculptures, to which Praun added coins, gems, and books.[8]

AD

SELECTED REFERENCES: Bott 1985, pp. 155 fig. 126, 458–59 cat. 679; Achilles-Syndram 1994, no. 70, pp. 190–91; Bernd Mayer, cat. 188, in Mayer and Achilles-Syndram 1994, pp. 367–68; Kammel and Lorenz 2008, p. 86, fig. 5; Hess and Hirschfelder 2010, no. 22, p. 389.

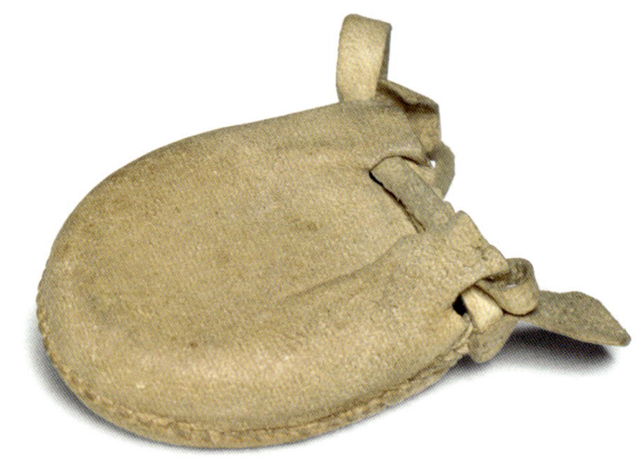

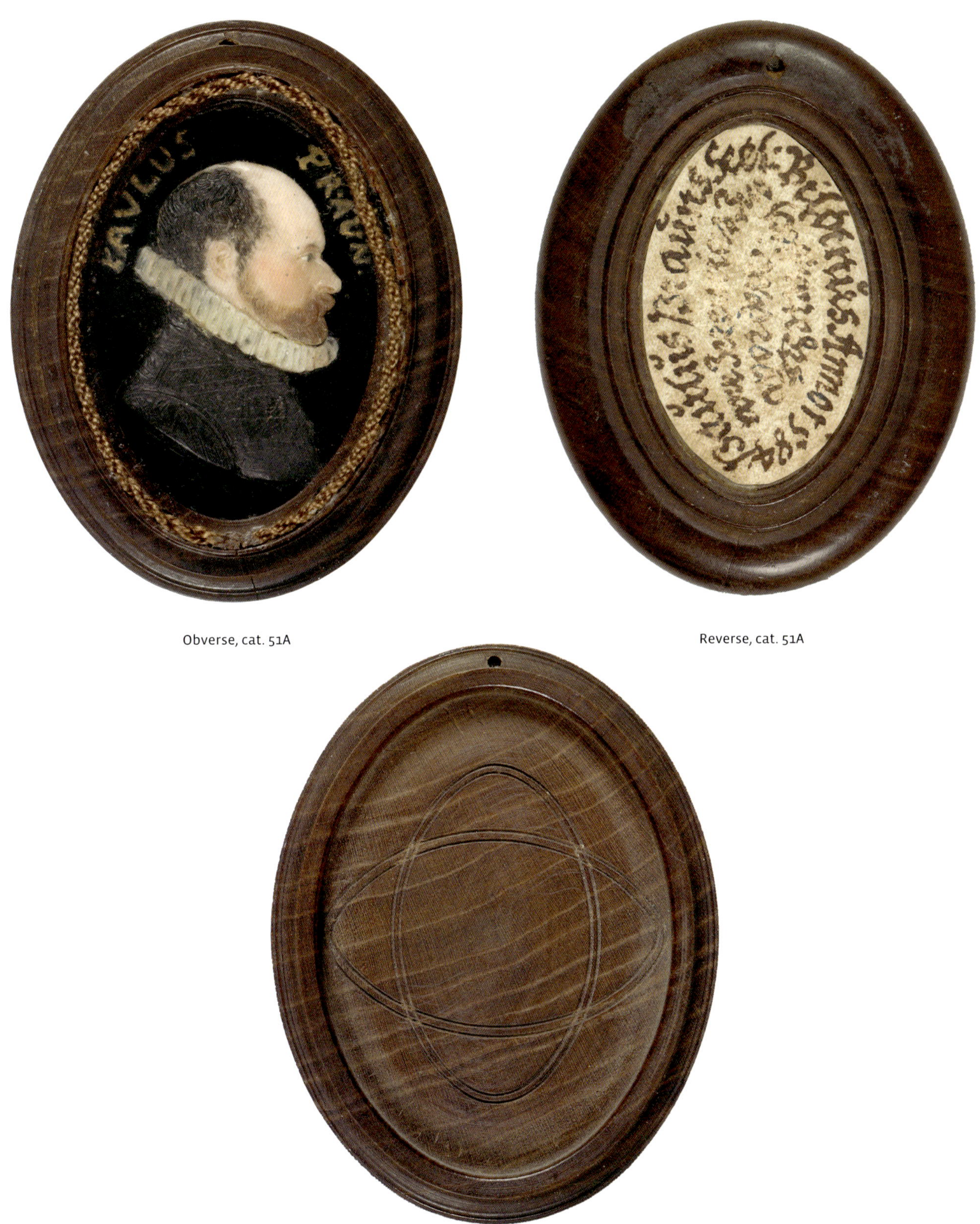

Obverse, cat. 51A

Reverse, cat. 51A

Cover, cat. 51B

CAT. 52

UNKNOWN MAKER

Wax: probably French; case: probably southern German or northern Italian

Portrait of a Lady, 1560–80 (wax); late 16th century (case)

Pigmented wax, seed pearls, emerald, ruby, linen, metal thread, gilded-copper or brass alloy, glass, 5 3/8 × 3 1/8 in. (13.7 x 7.9 cm)

The Metropolitan Museum of Art, New York, Gift of J. Pierpont Morgan, 1917 (17.190.911a, b)

MOUNTED ON BLUE GLASS, this wax profile of a lady is embellished with a long pearl necklace, buttons with a tiny ruby and emerald cabochons, and a pearl earring. The woman's braided hair is adorned with a band of jewel-studded gold links securing a hairnet. A linen band ornamented with gilded-thread embroidery hangs from her chignon. Her gown, complemented by a tight ruff around the neck, has remarkable protruding epaulettes; similar shoulder ornaments were popular courtly fashion in Valois France and northern Italy around 1560–90.[1] That such attention has been lavished on a tiny portrait demonstrates the considerable pains taken by the artist to capture the personality behind the sitter's facade.

The rim of the gilded-copper oval case is topped with a swiveling suspension ring and marked with four bulging scrollwork clasps that seem to secure it but are purely ornamental. In addition to hiding the portrait from unwanted eyes, the case would have protected the wax from bleaching by the sun. The design of the front cover combines details from the ornamental prints of Hans Vredeman de Vries and Theodore Bang.[2] A phoenix struggling with an elongated scrollwork spray in its beak balances above an elevated brazier with darting sparks. This mythological bird, dying in flames and reborn from ashes, was a symbol of resurrection and the Christian faith.

Centered on the back of the case is an oval framed by bold strapwork. Two crooked trees stand before fortified structures on the left and a village on the right. This composition derives from a 1530–40 plaquette by Peter Flötner, although Flötner's central vanitas symbol (a putto and skull) is missing here.[3] The oval is surrounded by fruits and two ewers filled with palm sprays, the latter alluding to Christ.

Given the extensive reach of the early modern luxury trade, the production of such cases by specialists in southern Germany or by artisans trained there working in northern Italy cannot be excluded. That empty cases may have been furnished with wax portraits made elsewhere is suggested by the lower positions of the bustlines of many examples, including this one, which do not accord with the contour of their frames. Several dozen works of this type have survived. The variation in their quality may be attributed to the wealth of those who commissioned them, and the best are a few that were likely made for princely patrons.[4]

Only a few waxes are attributed to artists from southern Germany. One, part of the Salton Bequest at The Metropolitan Museum of Art, possibly depicts the Nuremberg patrician Hans II Praun; it is associated with the wax-and-medal artists Georg Holdermann and Johann Philipp von der Pütt.[5] Most waxes are attributed to the circle of the Italians Antonio Abondio and Francesco Segala, including works at the Cleveland Museum of Art and the Philadelphia Museum of Art that are comparable to the present one.[6] The Ringling Museum in Sarasota preserves several important examples, while The Met has a copy by Alfred André from late nineteenth-century Paris that adapted sixteenth-century French ornamental prints.[7]

WK

SELECTED REFERENCES: *Collection du Baron Albert Oppenheim* 1904, no. 118, p. 49; Williamson 1910, no. 38, pp. 55–56, pl. XXII.

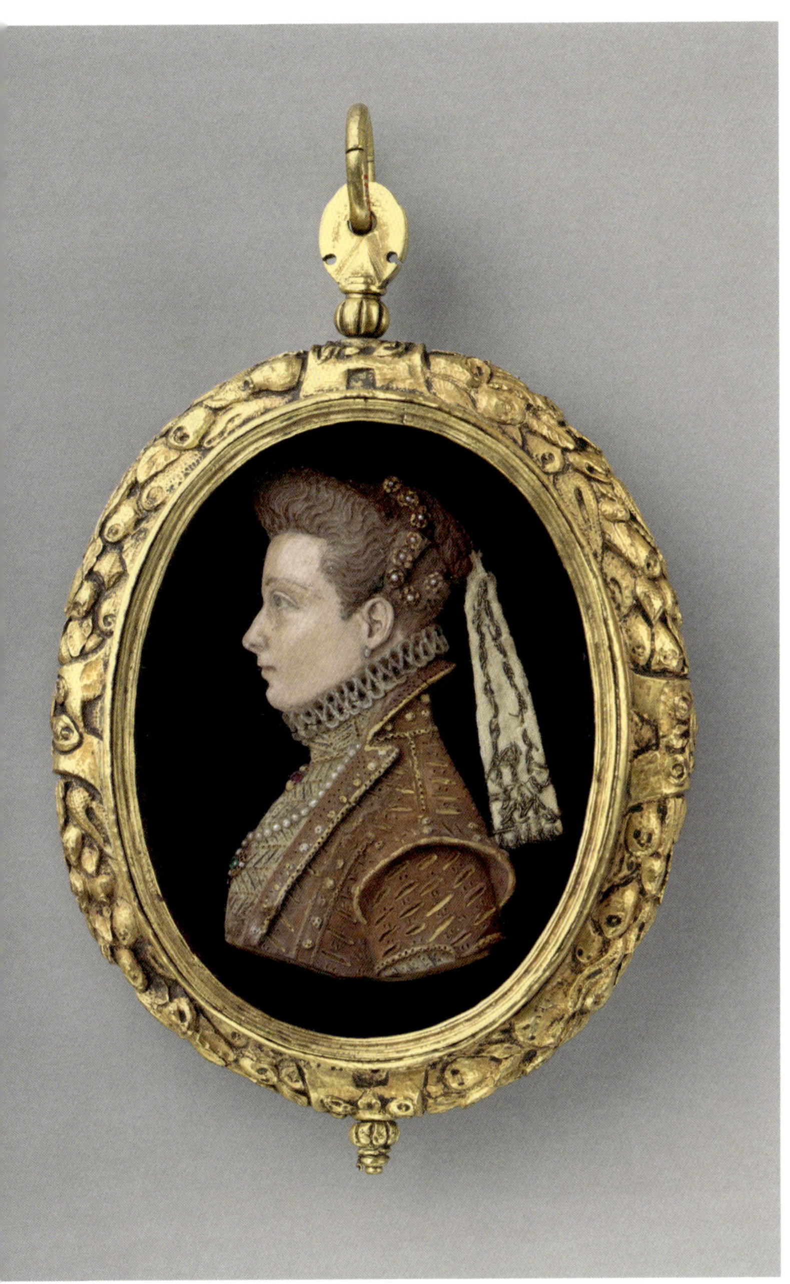

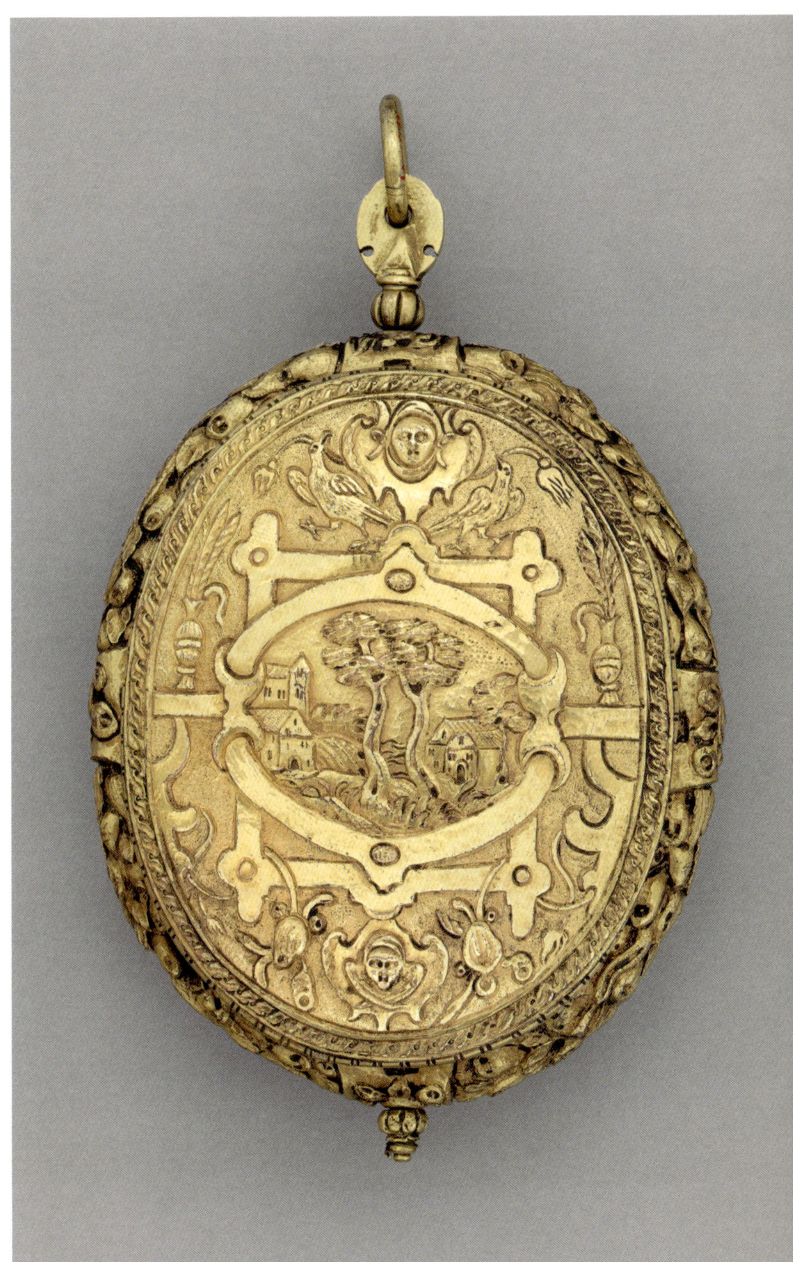

CAT. 53
LAMBERTUS VRYTHOFF, WATCHMAKER; CASE DECORATION AFTER SIMON VOUET

Vrythoff: Dutch, recorded 1724–69; Vouet: French, 1590–1649

Watch Depicting the Rape of Europa *and* Mercury and the Three Graces, ca. 1645 (case), ca. 1750 (movement)

Case: polychrome enamel on gold; Movement: gilded brass and steel, partly blued, Diam. 2⅛ in. (5.4 cm)

The Metropolitan Museum of Art, Gift of J. Pierpont Morgan, 1917 (17.190.1413)

MET CURATOR EMERITA Clare Vincent and her late husband, John H. Leopold, restored this intriguing watch to its rightful place as a high point in the histories of watchmaking and the art of enameling on gold in seventeenth-century France. They identified the object in the estate inventory of Monsieur Louis Hesselin (1602–1662), King Louis XIV's superintendent of entertainments, the patron being confirmed by the arms emblazoned on the dial.[1]

As the petals of a flower must be unfolded to reveal its interior, the hinged backplate covering the movement cage must be lifted to reveal Hesselin's otherwise "hidden" face, which is glorified by background ornamentation in enamel and gold. The likeness is painted after a print by Robert Nanteuil, one of the superior portraitists of the French court. Located at the bottom of the case, the picture literally faces the pierced gilded-brass plate covering the movement, which is an eighteenth-century replacement. The portrait's confrontation with an instrument able to measure and display time would have reminded the courtier of the brevity of life and "the ultimate futility of pursuing earthly goods and pleasures" every time he admired his watch.[2]

Timepieces small enough to be worn became esteemed collector's items during the Renaissance. Their lavish decoration, which often employed gold, the ultimate precious metal, became an ideal way to display wealth and social status. Often the case designers and enamel artists were more appreciated for their virtuosity than the watchmakers. Watches needed skillful maintenance, and after a generation or less, new owners wanted a modernized movement since they either found it too time-consuming to service the original or lacked the knowledge to repair it.[3]

Monsieur Hesselin was famous for amassing a substantial art collection, consisting mostly of Italian Renaissance paintings but also containing the works of more contemporaneous masters like Claude Lorrain, Poussin, Charles Le Brun, and Simon Vouet.[4] The exterior cover of this watchcase reflects the collector's passions, for the image on the enamel closely resembles Vouet's painting *Europa and the Bull* (early 1640s, Museo Nacional Thyssen-Bornemiza, Madrid), a widely admired composition publicized through a 1642 engraving by Michel Dorigny.[5] The enamel roundel on the back presents *Mercury and the Three Graces*, also after a painting by Vouet that was documented through a 1642 Dorigny engraving.[6] When the watch is opened, the iconographic subjects and applied style change as a battle scene, after designs by Jacques Courtois, is illustrated.[7]

Significantly, Hesselin kept this beloved item until his death, possibly because its "hidden" face continued to show him in the prime of life, no matter how fast time flew.
WK

SELECTED REFERENCES: Leopold and Vincent 1993; Vincent 2002, p. 90, fig. 1.

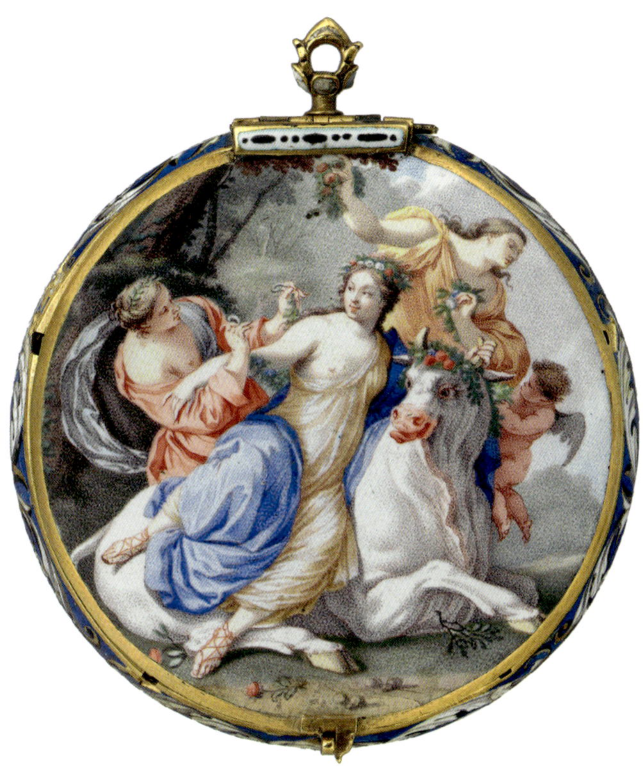

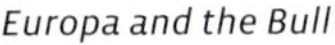

Europa and the Bull

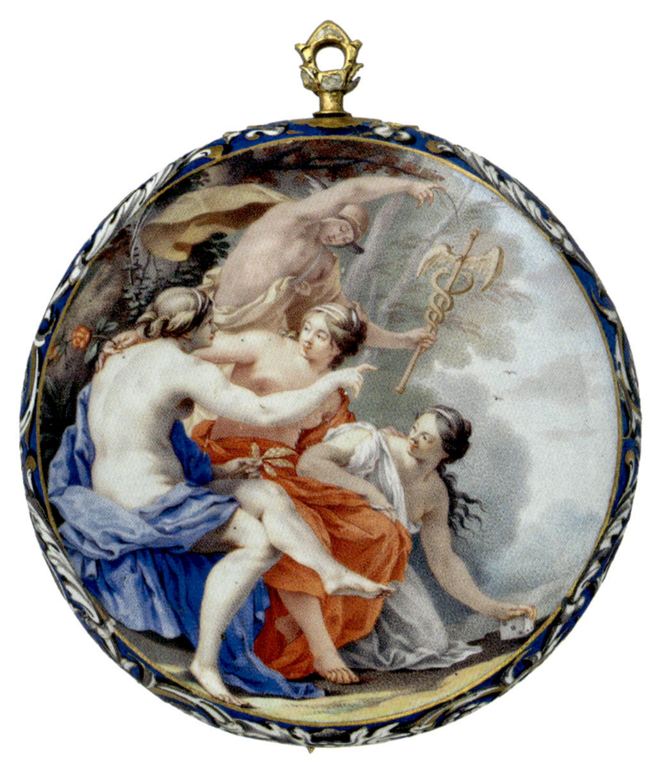

Mercury and the Three Graces

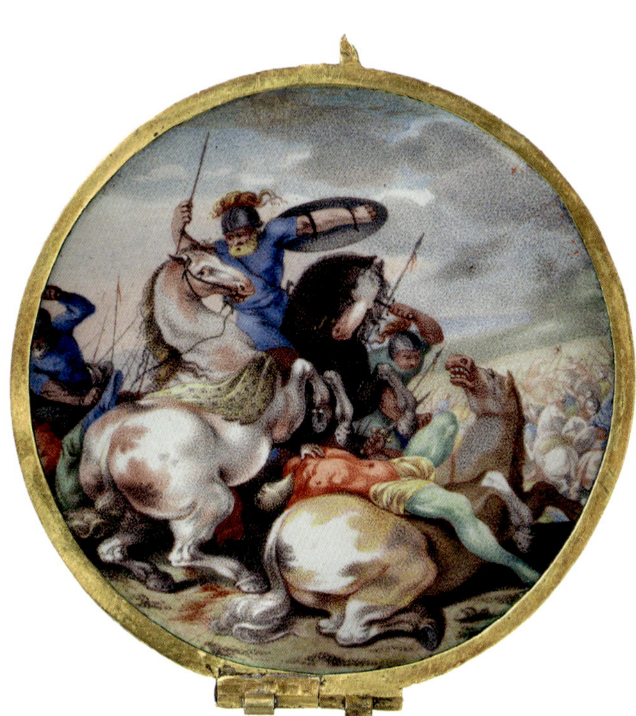

Battle Scene

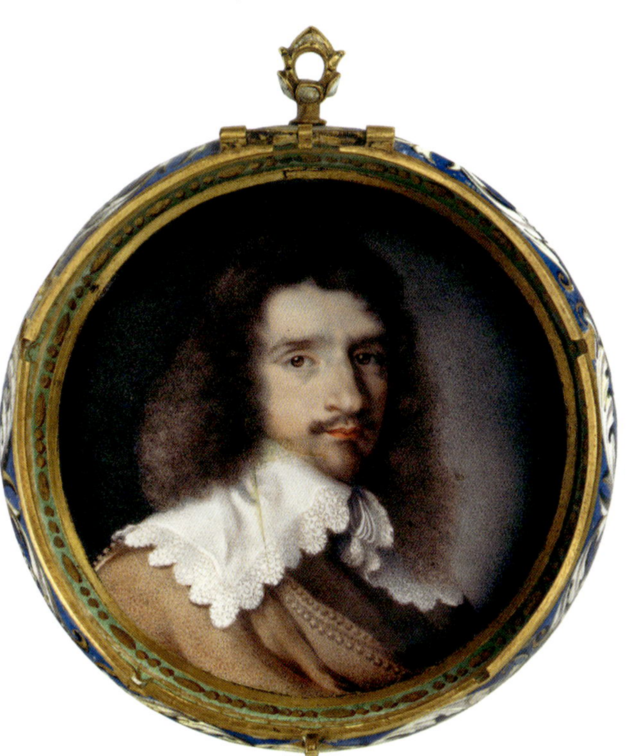

Lambertus Vrythoff

CAT. 54

UNKNOWN ARTIST

German, Nuremberg

Portrait of Elisabeth Krauss with Sliding Cover, ca. 1639/40(?)

Colored wax and wood, 5⅜ × 4⅞ in. (13.5 × 12.2 cm)

Inscribed (on wooden panel): (at upper right) *ELISABETHA KRAUSINN/N...1...* (*Elisabeth Krauss/B[orn]...1...*); (at lower left) *HOLDER.../FEC....* (*Holder[mann].../made...*)

Germanisches Nationalmuseum, Nuremberg, Museen der Stadt Nürnberg, Kunstsammlungen (Pl.O.2808)

THIS WAX PORTRAIT is on a black wooden panel in a box with a dual frame. The top frame features a groove, into which a sliding cover can be inserted from above. The colored-wax relief was cast in a mold, then scarified, pressed, and punched in places, as evident in the stippled pattern of the black dress and the braided embellishment on its shoulders. The millstone collar and cuffs are made of bleached wax. According to the Germanisches Nationalmuseum inventory, the wooden panel was inscribed in the upper right-hand corner with the name and birth date of the sitter and in the bottom left-hand corner with spurious information regarding the creation of the work.[1]

Elisabeth Krauss (1569–1639) is depicted in three-quarter profile to the left, her arms bent at waist height, her hands clasped. She wears a tight black doublet with long sleeves and light-colored cuffs over a voluminous pleated skirt, cut off around the hips. A large white millstone collar girds her neck, while her hair is covered by a close-fitting fur hood.[2]

Krauss was born the daughter of peasants Hans and Elisabeth Streit in Bronnamberg, in the Middle Franconia region, near Cadolzburg. When she was only ten years old, after her father died, Elisabeth was sent to the economic metropolis of Nuremberg to earn her living as a maid. By her own account, she performed her tasks with such diligence and honesty that her employer, Konrad Krauss—a merchant's apprentice originally from Kitzingen who was seven years younger—married her in 1598. The couple had three children, all of whom died young. Konrad made his fortune in trading foodstuffs, textiles, and metalware. He was appointed to the Grand Council and in 1624 ennobled by Emperor Ferdinand II. He succumbed to a raging epidemic in 1632.[3]

During her lifetime, Elisabeth became known for her philanthropy, donating most of her wealth to orphans and the indigent. Her fame endured for centuries through one of the most important and best endowed civic foundations, which she established in her will in 1639. In addition to creating twelve annual scholarships for students of theology, Elisabeth earmarked aid for foundling hospitals and feeding the poor. The foundation ran through the end of World War II.[4]

Given her high profile and the tremendous popularity of her foundation, a relatively large number of portraits of Elisabeth Krauss exist. The oldest in a broad range of portrait types is represented by the Nuremberg wax relief. Several replicas dated 1632 have survived, but their stylistic and qualitative differences suggest that they were modeled after the original when the foundation was created in 1639/40.

The wax embosser Georg Holdermann's name appears on all but one of the wax reliefs, including this one, although he cannot have been the craftsman, having died in 1629. His Nuremberg workshop was presumably taken over after his death by his brother-in-law, Heinrich Kramer, who carried on operations under Holdermann's name. Kramer himself died in 1632, meaning the later replicas were fabricated in a different, unknown embossing workshop. It seems the reliefs served primarily as gifts for individuals involved in running the foundation.

Of the surviving wax portraits of Elisabeth Krauss, the Bayrisches Nationalmuseum in Munich houses the best copy, one that also reflects Kramer's techniques in rendering clothing. That piece is inscribed with *ELISABETHA KRAUSIN/NAT 1569* and *HOLDERMANN FEC 1632*.[5] The present copy, from Nuremberg, is probably one of the replicas from 1639/40, as it lacks the expressive power of the portrait in Munich.[6]

AD

SELECTED REFERENCES: Maué 1997, no. 14, pp. 65–68; Bernhard Ebneth, "Elisabeth und Konrad Krauß," in Korn et al. 2014, p. 157–64; Moritz and Ebneth 2016.

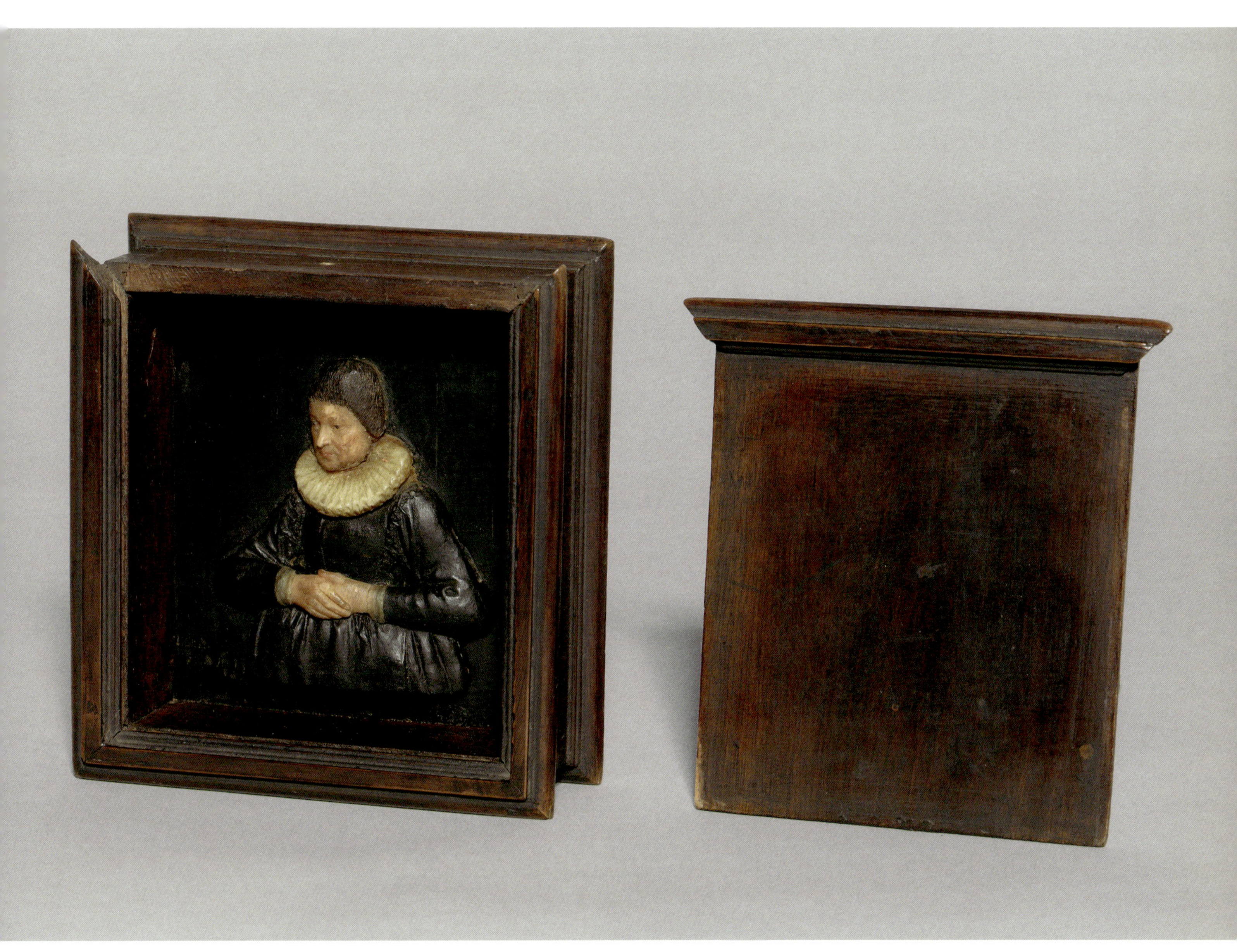

NOTES

Uncovering Renaissance Portraits

1 The most comprehensive examination of this material is Dülberg 1990, esp. pp. 9, 30–31, 60–70. See also L. Campbell 1990b, pp. 65–67; Hélène Verougstraete and Roger Van Schoute, "Cadres et supports chez Memling," in Verougstraete et al. 1997, pp. 269–70; Smith 1998, p. 35; V. Schmidt 2005, pp. 95–101; Simons 2011, pp. 37–49; Rutherglen 2016; Koos 2018.

2 "una tavola di Nostra Donna in uno tabernacolo con due sportelli dipinti con uno vello di seta innanzi" (a panel of Our Lady in a tabernacle with two painted shutters with a silk veil in front); Victor M. Schmidt, "Curtains, *Revelatio*, and Pictorial Reality in Late Medieval and Renaissance Italy," in Rudy and Baert 2007, pp. 192–93, citing Lydecker 1987, p. 210n3.

3 The *Saint Jerome* is possibly identifiable as that in the Detroit Institute of Arts (25.4). See Dülberg 1990, pp. 41–42n214; Spallanzani and Gaeta Bertelà 1992, p. 52; V. Schmidt 2005, p. 99; Simons 2011, p. 38.

4 "daer het den lichten dagh, en den Const-hongerigen oogen, maer te veel in een kist"; van Mander 1906, p. 184; cited (in German) in Krause 2016, p. 165; Dülberg 1990, pp. 60–61n337. For a larger discussion of the storage of portraits, see Dülberg 1990, pp. 9, 60–65.

5 V. Schmidt, "Curtains, *Revelatio*, and Pictorial Reality in Late Medieval and Renaissance Italy," in Rudy and Baert 2007, pp. 195–97.

6 L. Campbell 1990b, pp. 65–67, 254n121; Dülberg 1990, pp. 35–40, 90–91; Cranston 2000, pp. 18–30; Whistler 2009; Whistler 2012, esp. pp. 224–27; Verougstraete 2015, pp. 85–87; Miguel Falomir and Ana González Mozo, "Lotto's Portraits: Their Conception and Execution," in Dal Pozzolo and Falomir 2018, pp. 76–78.

7 For mirrors with or as covers, see Dami 1921; Dülberg 1990, pp. 38–39; D. Thornton 1997, p. 172; Bolzoni 2008, pp. 221–22; Whistler 2012, p. 223. For *timpani*, see Dülberg 1990, pp. 45–58; Penny 2004–8, vol. 1, "Portrait of Giovanni della Volta with His Wife and Children," appendix I, pp. 99–101; Whistler 2009, p. 539; Whistler 2012, p. 224; Sylvia Ferino-Pagden, "I 'timpani' o 'coperti,'" in Ferino-Pagden et al. 2022, pp. 189–93.

8 Veca 1981, pp. 48–59; Stoichita 2015, pp. 55–65.

9 In 1404 Antoine of Burgundy, duke of Brabant, obtained a chain and hook for this purpose; L. Campbell 1990b, p. 66.

10 See Billinge et al. 1997, pp. 19–20.

11 L. Campbell 1990b, pp. 66, 254n121. For paintings protected by curtains in Henry VIII's collection at the Palace of Westminster, see Simon 1996, pp. 13–14. For portraits in the collection of Queen Isabella of Castile stored in cases or boxes, see Manso Porto 2006, p. 65. For portraits stored in Charles V's collection in Yuste, see Madrazo 1884, p. 38.

12 For Octavian Secundus Fugger's paintings with sliding covers, see Lieb 1980, no. 1445, p. 296; Dülberg 1990, p. 35. For the collection of Ferdinand of Tyrol, see Lieb 1980, pp. 156–58. For the covered portraits in Margaret of Austria's collection, see Finot 1895, pp. 210–11; L. Campbell 1990b, pp. 65–67, 254n121; Eichberger 1996.

13 L. Campbell 1998, p. 174.

14 Dülberg 1990, p. 40; L. Campbell 1998, p. 202.

15 For the Vendramin collection, see Ravà 1920; Anderson 1979, esp. p. 647; Dülberg 1990, p. 35; Lauber 2002b; Whistler 2009; Whistler 2012, pp. 227–33. For Giorgione's *Tempest* as a portrait cover, see Schmitter 2022, pp. 206–22.

16 Brown and Oberhuber 1978, pp. 48, 78–79n144.

17 Dülberg 1990, pp. 18–24.

18 V. Schmidt, "Curtains, *Revelatio*, and Pictorial Reality in Late Medieval and Renaissance Italy," in Rudy and Baert 2007, pp. 212–13; Hills 2010.

19 For cassoni lids, see Randolph 2014, pp. 151–67. For Courbet, see Elsner 2015, pp. 220–26; Koos 2018, pp. 41–42. For the proposal that numerous Italian portraits of seminude female sitters had covers depicting the sitter clothed, see Bertelli 2002, pp. 65–112; Bertelli 2007.

20 Cropper 1997; Lingo 2016; Elizabeth Pilliod, cat. 8, in Edelstein and Gasparotto 2018, p. 129.

21 "La yimagine de la nostra Donna di debba tenere coperta com velo o vero com veli sottili e gentili di seta"; Cassidy 1992, p. 189n33; Hills 2010, p. 9.

22 Cassidy 1992, pp. 186, 188–90.

23 Elsner 2015, pp. 240–41.

24 Quoted in Simons 2011, pp. 37–38, where quoted from Trexler 1991, p. 98.

25 Quoted in Simons 2011, p. 38.

26 V. Schmidt, "Curtains, *Revelatio*, and Pictorial Reality in Late Medieval and Renaissance Italy," in Rudy and Baert 2007, pp. 191–99; Blümle and Wismer 2016.

27 Pausanias, *Description of Greece*, 5.12.4.

28 See Eberlein 1982; Nova 1994, pp. 179–99; Muthesius 1997, pp. 124–26; V. Schmidt, "Curtains, *Revelatio*, and Pictorial Reality in Late Medieval and Renaissance Italy," in Rudy and Baert 2007, pp. 199–206; Krischel 2013; Evangelatou 2019; Vryzidis and Papastavrou 2021; Exodus, 26:31–35, 27:21, 30:6, 35:12; Matthew 27:51; Mark 15:38; Luke 23:45.

29 Drpić 2016, p. 246. Bissera Pentcheva (2007, p. 126) argues that "as the silk curtain covers and protects the icon, so too the donor imagines the protection of the Virgin."

30 Parani 2018, p. 25.

31 Hilsdale 2014, p. 50.

32 Eberlein 1982; Nova 1994, pp. 180–82.

33 Fucci 2015.

34 Dülberg 1990, p. 16n39.

35 Linda Wolk-Simon, "'Rapture to the Greedy Eyes': Profane Love in the Renaissance," in Bayer 2008, p. 45.

36 Fucci 2015, p. 149.

37 Ibid.

38 Poussin 1989, p. 91; Simons 2011, p. 43.

39 Ibid.

40 Mancini 1956–57, vol. 1, p. 146.

41 Tiziana Scarpa, cat. 33, in Spinosa 2006, pp. 170–71; Whistler 2009, p. 539.

42 For a discussion of the act of revealing the illuminations in the Copenhagen Psalter as a "devotional experience," see De Hamel 2016, p. 326. For book curtains, see Christine Sciacca, "Raising the Curtain on the Use of Textiles in Manuscripts," in Rudy and Baert 2007, pp. 161–90.

43 See, for example, the textile cover for a miniature of the Ascension from a thirteenth-century Gospel Book produced in Turkey (J. Paul Getty Museum, Los Angeles, MS Ludwig II 5 [83.MB.69], fol. 188).

44 For *Tutte le dame del re*, see Buck 2008. For Bertelli, see Suzanne Karr Schmidt, "Liftable Skirts and Deadly Secrets," in S. Schmidt 2018, pp. 353–91.

45 Depictions of triptychs in Roman frescoes reveal that this format was also employed in antiquity for narrative painting; see, for example, wall of cubiculum B, Casa della Farnesina (Roman, ca. 20 BCE, Museo Nazionale Romano, Palazzo Massimo alle Terme).

46 As described in Polybius *Histories* 6.53–54; Pliny *Natural History* 35.6; Flower 1996, pp. 7, 8, 206–9; Ackers 2019, pp. 136–37; Bartůněk 2019, p. 33.

47 See Flower 1996, p. 202; Fejfer 2008, p. 107.

48 Flower 1996, pp. 7–9. See, for example, the *Funerary Relief for Aemilius Aristomachus and Aemilia Hilara* (Roman, 51–50 BCE, National Museum of Denmark, Copenhagen, 1187) and the *Tomb of Maria Auxesis* (early 2nd century CE, Museo Nazionale Romano, Rome).

49 In his *Ricordanze*, dated to 1473, the Florentine artist Neri di Bicci records that he painted two altar curtains with images of Christ; V. Schmidt, "Curtains, *Revelatio*, and Pictorial Reality in Late Medieval and Renaissance Italy," in Rudy and Baert 2007, p. 193.

50 Jacobs 2012, p. 5.

51 V. Schmidt 2005, p. 54; Lynn F. Jacobs, "The Thresholds of the Winged Altarpiece: Altarpiece Exteriors as Liminal Spaces," in Ganz and Rimmele 2016, pp. 210–15.

52 For the relationship between icons and portraits, see Alexander Nagel, "Iconos y retratos / Icons and Early Modern Portraits," in Falomir 2008, pp. 41–53, 421–25. For icons with sliding lids, see Weitzmann 1976, pp. 9, 31–32 no. B.10 (pls. xiii, lvi), 38–40 no. B.15 (pl. lxi).

53 Jannic Durand, "Precious-Metal Icon Revetments," in H. Evans 2004, pp. 243–51.

54 Noreen 2010, pp. 120, 129.

55 Weitzmann 1976, pp. 77 no. B.47 (pl. cii), 77–78 no. B.48 (pl. CIII); Gerstel 2006; Rodriguez 2018.

56 V. Schmidt 2005, pp. 50, 54.

57 For a double-sided Fayum portrait, see the *Portrait of a Man* (2nd century CE, Manchester Museum, 5381).

58 Grisebach 2015, p. 189.

59 Gardner 1983; Dülberg 1990, pp. 116–26; Cranston 2000, p. 23; Verougstraete and Van Schoute 2000, pp. 110–11; V. Schmidt 2005, pp. 44–58; Borgers 2022.

60 V. Schmidt 2005, p. 44.

61 See Mundy 1988; Dülberg 1990, pp. 116–27; Verougstraete and Van Schoute 1998; Victor M. Schmidt, "Portable Polyptychs with Narratives Scenes: Fourteenth-Century *De luxe* Objects between Italian Painting and French *Arts somptuaires*," in V. Schmidt 2002, pp. 395–419; V. Schmidt 2005, pp. 46, 48–49; Kemperdick and Lammertse 2012, pp. 91–92; Dunlop 2015, pp. 68–73; Eveline Baseggio Omiccioli,

"A New Interpretation of Jacometto's 'Most Perfect Work': Parallels in Portraits by Giovanni Bellini and Leonardo da Vinci," in Wilson 2015, pp. 143, 149; Fricke 2020, pp. 231–38; Mills 2021; Kozlowski 2022, pp. 31–32, 91–104, 119–22, 127–49.

62 Kozlowski 2022, pp. 147–49.

63 Dülberg 1990, p. 120.

64 Gamboni 2002, p. 29; Barry 2020, pp. 192–93. For Pliny's discussion of porphyry, see Mundy 1988, pp. 38–39.

65 Flood 2016, pp. 182, 213n42; quoting Albertus Magnus 1967, p. 128.

66 Flood 2016, pp. 193–94, fig. 23.

67 For the argument that they are jasper, see Verougstraete and Van Schoute 2000, pp. 110–11. See also Borgers 2022.

68 Kozlowski 2018, pp. 23, 29n90; citing Cennino Cennini 2015, chap. 36.

69 See Del Bufalo 2012.

70 Mundy 1988, p. 37.

71 D. Brown 2001, cat. 4, pp. 110–11. See also Stefan Weppelmann, cat. 7, in Christiansen and Weppelmann 2012, p. 100.

72 For the relation between coats of arms and portraiture, see Dülberg 1990, pp. 107–16.

73 For the Orsini polyptych, see V. Schmidt 2005, pp. 256–60, 276–77 pls. xxi, xxii, 281–93.

74 Three panels from the ensemble are in The Met (1975.1.12, 1975.1.13, 41.100.23), while the fifth is in the Museo Nacional Thyssen-Bornemisza, Madrid, Carmen Thyssen Collection (CTB.1997.20).

75 Kozlowski 2022, pp. 44 fig. 2.5, 48, 52.

76 Machtelt Brüggen Israëls, cat. 5, in Silver 2022, pp. 217–20, fig. 98.

77 For other examples of heraldic painters, see Dülberg 1990, pp. 30–31; Hablot 2018, p. 119.

78 Gordon 2015, pp. 40–44.

79 Perkinson 2009, p. 253.

80 Ibid., p. 136; Belting 2001, pp. 62–83; Pastoureau 1987, p. 112.

81 Along with emblems and allegories, heraldry frequently adorned Italian double-sided birth trays, as in an example with Medici and Tournabuoni arms and devices (ca. 1448, The Metropolitan Museum of Art, 1995.7); see Jacqueline Marie Musacchio, cat. 70, in Bayer 2008, pp. 154–56.

82 See, for example, the Shield of Edward IV, attributed to Pierre Coustain (ca. 1481, Rijksmuseum, Amsterdam, SK-A-4641).

83 Belting 2001, p. 72.

84 Ibid., p. 64.

85 "Covers ... were far more common both north and south of the Alps than one might suppose from the number that survive today"; Bernard Aikema and Beverly Louise Brown, cat. 66, in Aikema and Brown 1999, p. 326, citing L. Campbell 1990b, pp. 65–67.

86 Thompson 1982, pp. 8–10; Dülberg 1990, pp. 26–27.

87 Thompson 1982, p. 8.

88 See, for example, Adriaen van der Spelt and Frans van Mieris the Elder's *Trompe l'Oeil Still Life with Flower Garland and Curtain* (fig. 8), Rembrandt's *Holy Family* (1646, Museum Schloss Wilhelmshöhe, Kassel), and Gerard Dou's *Man Smoking a Pipe* (1650, Rijksmuseum, Amsterdam).

89 For an example of emblems used as political propaganda, see Hablot 2004.

90 For ancient sources of Renaissance medals, see Glass 2015.

91 Kristen Lippincott, "'*Un Gran Pelago*': The Impresa and the Medal Reverse in Fifteenth-Century Italy," in Scher 2000, pp. 76–78.

92 Orvieto 2009, pp. 216–17.

93 Lippincott, "*Un Gran Pelago*," in Scher 2000, p. 77.

94 Lorne Campbell, "Diptychs with Portraits," in Hand and Spronk 2006, pp. 32–45; Victor M. Schmidt, "Diptychs and Supplicants: Precedents and Contexts of Fifteenth-Century Devotional Diptychs," in ibid., pp. 14–31.

95 The *Bembo Diptych* (Alte Pinakothek, Munich, and National Gallery of Art, Washington, D.C.) and the *Tripych of Earthly Vanity and Divine Salvation* (Musée des Beaux-Arts, Strasbourg). For the latter, see Till-Holger Borchert, cat. 25, in Borchert 2014, pp. 158–59.

96 For Boltraffio's portrait, see Veca 1981, p. 43, pl. 41 (reverse); Fiorio 2000, no. A7, pp. 91–93; Belting 2001, p. 77. For Previtali's portrait, whose upside-down orientation suggests it may have been housed in a rotating frame, see Mauro Natali, no. 122, in *Museo Poldi Pezzoli* 1982, pp. 125–26, 326–27 pls. 256, 257; Zanchi 2001, pp. 8–10, figs. 5, 6, 10.

97 Mauro Natale, no. 194, in *Museo Poldi Pezzoli* 1982, pp. 156, 400 pl. 344, 488 pl. 472.

98 Dülberg 1990, p. 290, no. 321; see also Zöllner 2015, nos. 8a, 8b, p. 188.

99 On Dürer's *Saint Jerome*, see Andrew John Martin, cat. 3/1, in Aikema 2018, pp. 222–23, 352.

100 Cunnally 1999, pp. 35–37; Syson and Thornton 2001, p. 13.

101 Jonathan J. G. Alexander, cat. 41, in Alexander 1993, pp. 106–8; Syson and Thornton 2001, pp. 17–18.

102 An example of this coin is in the British Museum (R.6379).

103 Zöllner 2005, p. 40.

104 Ibid.

105 Dülberg 1990, pp. 133–67.

106 The significance of chastity as the foremost female virtue is reflected in Alberti's *Della famiglia* (*On the family*, 1433–40), in which a groom reminds his young bride, "Nothing is so important for yourself, so acceptable to God, so pleasing to me ... as your chastity"; Alberti 1969, p. 213.

107 For alternate theories on this matter, see "Covered Portraits in Italy, 1475–1550" by Catherine Whistler in this volume.

108 For the diptych, see Hand et al. 2006, cat. 25, pp. 170–77; John Oliver Hand, cats. 1.5, 1.6, in Beltramini et al. 2013, pp. 78–81 figs. 1.5, 1.6, 100–101. For Memling's portrait of Bernardo Bembo, see Borchert 2005, pp. 78–82, 124 pl. 11, 160 cat. 10; Lorne Campbell and Luke Syson, cat. 11, in Campbell et al. 2008, pp. 102–3; Dagmar Korbacher, cat. 145, in Christiansen and Weppelmann 2011, pp. 330–32. For Bembo's ownership of Memling's paintings, see L. Campbell 1981, p. 471; Paula Nuttall, "Memling and the European Renaissance Portrait," in Borchert 2005, pp. 78–83; Lina Bolzoni, "I ritratti e la comunità degli amici fra Venezia, Firenze e Roma," in Beltramini et al. 2013, pp. 210–15.

109 David Alan Brown, "Ginevra de' Benci," in Boskovits and Brown 2003, pp. 367–68n63; Jobst 2017, pp. 235–37.

110 "Un quadro de una Donna Vecchia ... il coperto del detto quadro depento con un'homo con una vesta di pella negra" (A painting of an Old Woman ... the cover for this painting painted with a man dressed in black fur); Anderson 1979, p. 643. For *La Vecchia*, see Bernard Aikema, cat. 6/20, in Aikema and Martin 2018, pp. 315, 381–82. For the connection between the two and comparable dating, see Bernard Aikema, "Giorgione: I rapporti con il nord e una nuova lettura della Vecchia e della Tempesta," in Nepi Scirè and Rossi 2003, pp. 76–80; Simone Facchinetti, cat. 29, in Facchinetti and Galansino 2016, p. 137; Bernard Aikema, "'La vecchia' di Giorgione," in Ferino-Pagden et al. 2022, pp. 337–39.

111 See note 15 above. The Vendramin inventory included a portrait of Bellini with a cover depicting his student Vittore Belliniano: "quadreto con il retrato d Zuan Belin e de Vetor suo dixipulo nel cop[er]chio" (a small painting with the portrait of Giovani Bellini and of his student Vittore on the cover); Whistler 2012, p. 229; Windows 2012, p. 36.

112 "Un quadretto con sua cassa de un giovene sbarbato de man de Zuan Belin a guazo.... Una casseta con un quadro dento de un zovan sbarbato con capuzo a guazo de man de Zuan Bedin [*sic*]" (A small panel with its own case of a beardless youth by Giovanni Bellini in gouache.... A box with a small painting inside depicting a young beardless youth with a hat in gouache by Giovanni Bellini); Ravà 1920, p. 170; Dulberg 1990, p. 42. See also Andrea Bayer, cats. 152a, 152b, in Christiansen and Weppelmann 2011, p. 347; Omiccioli, "A New Interpretation of Jacometto's 'Most Perfect Work,'" in Wilson 2015, p. 150.

113 Benedicenti 1992, p. 6; Peter Humfrey, "The Portrait in Fifteenth-Century Venice," in Christiansen and Weppelmann 2011, p. 57; Omiccioli, "A New Interpretation of Jacometto's 'Most Perfect Work,'" in Wilson 2015, pp. 149–51, 155 fig. 14.

114 Parronchi 1965; Omiccioli, "A New Interpretation of Jacometto's 'Most Perfect Work,'" in Wilson 2015, pp. 149–51, 156 fig. 16.

115 Falomir and González Mozo, "Lotto's Portraits," in Dal Pozzolo and Falomir 2018, pp. 76–78; Christiansen 2019.

116 The account book mentions covers, for both portraits and other works, on folios 2v, 16v, 17r, 31v, 33r, 52v, 60v, 61v, 68v, 83v, 127v, 151r, 152r, 159r; Lotto 2017.

117 In 1545 Lorenzo Lotto was commissioned to copy "un retrato de misser Joan Aurelio Augurello con il roverso et coperto come stava el proprio originale" (a portrait of Giovanni Aurelio Augurello with the reverse and cover as they were in the original). See Lotto 1969, p. 102.

118 The contract of June 16, 1524, states that "quali picture di dette tavolete siano di quella coresponenza in significato a li altri quadri sopra quali se ponerano respectivamente"; Galis 1980, pp. 363–64. See also Zanchi 2016.

119 In a letter dated February 10, 1528, Lotto wrote, "Circha li disegni de li coperti, sapiate che son cose che non essendo scritte, bisogna che la imaginatione

le porti a luce"; Galis 1980, p. 364. See Whistler 2012, p. 225.

120 For Titian's *timpani*, see Ost 1992, pp. 55–79; Whistler 2009; Whistler 2012; Ferino-Pagden, "I 'timpani' o 'coperti,'" in Ferino-Pagden et al. 2022, pp. 189–93. For the *Allegory of Prudence* (ca. 1550, National Gallery, London), see Dülberg 1990, pp. 52–56; Luisa Attardi, cat. 38, in Villa 2013, p. 237.

121 Dülberg 1990, pp. 42–44; P. Thornton 1991, p. 204; Jennifer Fletcher, "The Renaissance Portrait: Functions, Uses and Display," in Campbell et al. 2008, pp. 58–59; Rutherglen 2012, pp. 98–106; Knight Powell 2018. For sacred works, see Hill 1905, pp. 59–60; Dülberg 1990, pp. 58, 279–80 nos. 282, 284; Spallanzani and Gaeta Bertelà 1992, pp. 27, 53, 72, 107, 133; V. Schmidt 2005, pp. 95–101; Simons 2011, p. 38.

122 Sara van Dijk, "Learned: Portraits of Humanists," in van Dijk and Ubl 2021, pp. 200–201. For portrait miniatures as gifts, see Fumerton 1986; Friso Lammertse, "Authority: Portraits of Power," in van Dijk and Ubl 2021, p. 99; Adam Eaker, "The Tudor Art of the Gift," in Cleland and Eaker 2022, pp. 112–13.

123 For the circulation of early panel portraits and their diplomatic function, see Miguel Falomir, "The Court Portrait," in Campbell et al. 2008, pp. 66–68; Larner 1971, p. 319; V. Schmidt, "Diptychs and Supplicants: Precedents and Contexts of Fifteenth-Century Devotional Diptychs," in Hand and Spronk 2006, p. 15; Kozlowski 2018, pp. 27–28n54. For portrait miniatures with silk pouches in ivory boxes, see Koos 2014; Koos 2018, pp. 39–40.

124 Oliver Tostmann, "The Advantages of Painting Small: Italian Women Artists and the Matter of Scale," in Straussman-Pflanzer and Tostmann 2021, p. 36.

125 Dülberg 1990, p. 42; Musacchio 2007, pp. 487–88; Jacqueline Marie Musacchio, cat. 126a, in Bayer 2008 pp. 36, 272–74.

126 Quoted in M. Evans 2020, p. 160; quoting Vasari 1996, vol. 2, p. 856.

127 Baxandall 1963, p. 326; M. Evans 2020, p. 159.

128 These include small, round wooden boxes with carved lids, such as the *Elector Friedrich the Wise of Saxony*, attributed to the Meister der Dosenköpfe (cat. 47A). For capsule portraits and miniatures, see Dülberg 1990, pp. 41, 90–93; M. Evans 2005, pp. 244–47; Maryan W. Ainsworth, no. 31, in Ainsworth and Waterman 2013, pp. 138–39; Koos 2018; M. Evans 2020, pp. 160–99; van Dijk, "Learned: Portraits of Humanists," in van Dijk and Ubl 2021, pp. 200–201; Eaker, "The Tudor Art of the Gift," in Cleland and Eaker 2022, p. 112.

129 Strong 1983, cat. 30, pp. 48–49; Foister 2006, p. 102.

130 Strong 1983, p. 48.

131 Lammertse, "Authority: Portraits of Power," in van Dijk and Ubl 2021, pp. 99–100; Sara van Dijk, "Cherish Me: Portraits and Marriage," in ibid., pp. 169, 173.

132 Lammertse, "Authority: Portraits of Power," in ibid., pp. 98–99.

133 See Scarisbrick 2011, pp. 8–77; Koos 2018; Tostmann, "The Advantages of Painting Small," in Straussman-Pflanzer and Tostmann 2021, p. 36; Eaker, "The Tudor Art of the Gift," in Cleland and Eaker 2022, pp. 112–13.

134 Möbius 1949.

135 For the Heneage Jewel, see Strong 1983, cat. 208, pp. 129–30; Adam Eaker, cat. 58, in Cleland and Eaker 2022, pp. 158–59. The Drake jewel is worn by its recipient, Sir Francis Drake, in a portrait painted in 1591 (National Maritime Museum, Greenwich, London, Caird Collection).

136 Eaker, cat. 58, in Cleland and Eaker 2022, pp. 158–59.

Coining Multisided Portraits: Precedents and Parallels

1 For Petrarch's numismatic collection and those of other fourteenth-century collectors in the Veneto, see Karet 2014, pp. 107–9. See also Cunnally 1999, pp. 34–39; Syson and Gordon 2001, p. 109.

2 Letter of February 25, 1355, to Lello di Pietro Stefano dei Tosetti, a Roman nobleman: "Aliquot sibi aureas argenteasque nostrorum principum effigies minutissimis ac veteribus literis inscriptas, quas in delitiis habebam, dono dedi, in quibus et Augusti Cesaris vultus erat pene spirans. 'Et ecce' inquam, 'Cesar, quibus successisti; ecce quos imitari studeas et mirari, ad quorum formulam atque imaginem te componas'"; Francesco Petrarca, *Le familiari*, edited by Vittorio Rossi (Florence: Casa Editrice Le Lettere, 1933–68), vol. 3, p. 315; as quoted in Nicholas Mann, "Petrarch and Portraits," in Mann and Syson 1998, p. 16.

3 Zanker 1988, pp. 95–97.

4 For the interrelation of the obverse and reverse on Roman coins, see Wallace-Hadrill 1986, p. 69.

5 For the influence of Petrarch and Roman coins on the earliest Renaissance medals, commissioned in 1390 by Francesco II da Carrara of Padua, see Stephen K. Scher, "An Introduction to the Renaissance Portrait Medal," in Scher 2000, pp. 3–4. See also Luke Syson, "Circulating a Likeness? Coin Portraits in Late Fifteenth Century Italy," in Mann and Syson 1998, pp. 113–25; Joanna Woods-Marsden, "Portrait of the Lady, 1430–1520," in D. Brown 2001, p. 82; Stahl 2013.

6 Jonathan J. G. Alexander, cat. 74, in Alexander 1994, pp. 157–58; Cunnally 1999, p. 35; De la Mare and Nuvoloni 2009, no. 57, p. 226; Beard 2021, pp. 92–93, fig 3.8. For Pietro Bembo's numismatic interests, see Davide Gasparotto, cat. 5.27, in Beltramini et al. 2013, p. 337.

7 Paula Nuttall, "Memling and the European Renaissance Portrait," in Borchert 2005, pp. 78–82; Till-Holger Borchert, cat. 10, in ibid., pp. 124 pl. 11, 160; Lorne Campbell and Luke Syson, cat. 11, in Campbell et al. 2008, pp. 102–3; Lorne Campbell, cat. 17, in Falomir 2008, pp. 192–93, 466–67; Luke Syson, cat. 18, in ibid., pp. 194–95; Dagmar Korbacher, cat. 145, in Christiansen and Weppelmann 2011, pp. 330–32; Till-Holger Borchert, cat. 41, in Borchert 2014, pp. 204–5; Vincent Delieuvin, "Léonard, apprenti peintre chez Andrea del Verrocchio," in Delieuvin and Frank 2019, p. 85; Delieuvin, cat. 23, in ibid., p. 399; Beard 2021, pp. 78–80.

8 Inv. nos. 652 and 1952.5.46a, b, respectively. For the diptych, see Hand et al. 2006, cat. 25, pp. 170–77; John Oliver Hand, cats. 1.5, 1.6, in Beltramini et al. 2013, pp. 78–81 figs. 1.5, 1.6, 100–101. For Bembo and Memling, see L. Campbell 1981, p. 471; Nuttall, "Memling and the European Renaissance Portrait," in Borchert 2005, pp. 78–83; Lina Bolzoni, "I ritratti e la comunità degli amici fra Venezia, Firenze, e Roma," in Beltramini et al. 2013, pp. 210–15.

9 Bembo's motto, *Virtus et honor*, originally painted on the reverse of the *Ginevra*, was replaced by *Virtutem forma decorat*. For *Ginevra de' Benci*, see Fletcher 1989; D. Brown 2001, cat. 16, pp. 142–46; David Alan Brown, "Ginevra de' Benci," in Boskovits and Brown 2003, pp. 357–69; Eveline Baseggio Omiccioli, "A New Interpretation of Jacometto's 'Most Perfect Work': Parallels in Portraits by Giovanni Bellini and Leonardo da Vinci," in Wilson 2015, pp. 161–63; Bambach 2019, vol. 1, pp. 113–23; Delieuvin and Frank 2019, pp. 79–87, 399 cat. 23.

10 For the influence of Petrarch on the laurel and palm branches, see Delieuvin and Frank 2019, p. 86.

11 British Museum 1867, 0101.587.

12 British Museum G3, RUnc.4. Dülberg 1990, pp. 134–36; Dunkerton et al. 1991, pp. 100–101, figs. 129, 130; Zöllner 2015, nos. 41a, 41b, pp. 215–16.

13 While there were several significant prototypes, Pisanello's numerous portrait medals of contemporary rulers and their court members codified the formula. For Pisanello's drawings of Roman coins, see Syson and Gordon 2001, p. 91, fig. 3.6; Glass 2015. For the earliest medals, see Stahl and Waldman 1993–94; Alan M. Stahl, "Mint and Medal in the Renaissance," in Scher 2000, pp. 137–38. For the relationship between medals and double-sided portraits, see Dülberg 1990, p. 104.

14 For personal emblems used by members of the French and Burgundian courts, see Hablot 2004.

15 See, for instance, Museum of Fine Arts, Boston, 69.403.

16 British Museum, London, C.2774.

17 For example, on the reverse of Hans Maler's *Portrait of Anton Fugger*, see Krause 2016, p. 160, figs. 4a, 4b.

18 Dülberg 1990, pp. 116–27; V. Schmidt 2005, pp. 45–50.

19 Dülberg 1990, p. 120.

20 Dunlop 2015, pp. 68–70.

21 Mundy 1988.

22 For the mosaic in San Clemente, Rome, as well as the tomb of Giovanni and Piero de' Medici, see Butterfield 1997, p. 54.

23 Timothy B. Husband, cat. 59, in Ainsworth and Waterman 2013, p. 256.

Cat. 1

1 *Roman Imperial Coinage* 1, pp. 25–26 (regarding Spanish mints). For a close silver parallel, see ibid., p. 45, no. 52a; *Coins of the Roman Empire in the British Museum* 1, p. 63, no. 353, pl. 7.7.

2 For the development of the imagery on Greek coins, see Holloway 1998, pp. 3–24.

3 Pollini 1990, pp. 8–9; Zanker 1990, pp. 98–100.

4 See Zanker 1990, pp. 92–98, for a thorough discussion of the laurels and the *clipeus virtutis* in Augustan art.

5 *Res gestae divi Augusti* 34. See also Sutherland 1987, pp. 7–10.

6 Wallace-Hadrill 1981, p. 300; Welch 2019.

7 Wallace-Hadrill 1981, pp. 298, 308, 317; Eiland 2019, pp. 39–40.
8 Weiss 1988, pp. 167–79; Bruni 2022, pp. 52–53, figs. 1–4.

Cat. 2

1 This coin is actually an aureus quinarius, that is, a half-aureus weighing about 3 grams, instead of 6 grams (a standard aureus).
2 *Roman Imperial Coinage* 5.2, pp. 220 no. 12 (example of a similar obverse), 225 nos. 43–46 (examples of a similar reverse).
3 Ibid., p. 214.
4 Burnett 1987, pp. 142–43; Bowman 2005, pp. 69–71.
5 Burnett 1987, p. 143, see pl. 18; Bowman 2005, p. 67.

Cat. 3

1 Lee 2017, p. 150.
2 Lee 2017, pp. 143, 147, 149–50; see also Mertens 1985, pp. 43–44.
3 Frontisi-Ducroux 1997, pp. 77–78.
4 Ibid., p. 59; Lee 2017, pp. 144, 154–59.
5 Frontisi-Ducroux 1997, pp. 58–59; Lee 2017, p. 165.

Cat. 4

1 Eleanora Luciano, cat. 87, in Christiansen and Weppelmann 2011, pp. 231–32; citing Eleanora Luciano, cat. 7, in Brown 2001, p. 120n3.
2 Luciano, in Brown 2001, p. 119.
3 Stephen K. Scher, in Scher 1994, p. 52.
4 Pollard 2007, vol. 1, p. 30.
5 Scher, in Scher 1994, p. 53.
6 Luciano, in Brown 2001, p. 119.
7 Ibid., p. 120; Scher, in Scher 1994, p. 53.
8 Bambach 2019, vol. 1, pp. 120–23, figs. 2.31–2.35.

Cat. 5

1 Stephen K. Scher, cat. 8a, in Scher 1994, p. 54; Stephen K. Scher, cat. 88, in Christiansen and Weppelmann 2011, p. 232.
2 Scher, in Christiansen and Weppelmann 2011, p. 233.
3 Scher, in Scher 1994, p. 54.
4 *Vespasiano Memoirs* 1926, pp. 412–13.
5 Pisanello painted two now-lost portraits of Vittorino, one of which depicted the scholar accompanied by ancient philosophers and a phoenix; see Pollard 2007, vol. 1, p. 28.
6 Scher, in Christiansen and Weppelmann 2011, p. 233.
7 Syson and Gordon 2001, p. 119.

Cat. 6

1 The Met's specimen is a good-quality, possibly contemporaneous cast.
2 Catalogues of Giovio's medal have overlooked most important aspects of his biography. Among others, see Zimmermann 1995; Vasari 1997, pp. 431–32 (under "Giovio, Paolo"); Giovio 1999; Zimmermann 2001; Agosti 2008; Bambach 2019, vol. 1 pp. 13, 21–28, 481–83, vol. 2 pp. 244–45, 293, 364, vol. 3 pp. 321, 344, 498–500, 544, vol. 4 pp. 45–46nn, 144–51; Bambach 2022, pp. 28–32, 68–70.
3 Agosti 2008, p. 42, on Giovio's becoming Vasari's friend (1532); on his rapport and editorial work on Vasari's *Vite* (in 1546 and later), ibid., pp. 34–96.
4 Paolo Giovio's letter to Cosimo de' Medici, cited by Vasari, is dated November 12, 1551: Gaetano Milanesi, in Vasari 1906, vol. 3, pp. 10–12; Vasari 1966–87, vol. 3, pp. 368–69. Vasari's *Vite* refer to Pisanello with the wrong baptismal name, Vittore, rather than Antonio.
5 Joseph R. Bliss et al., cats. 3–76, in Scher 1994, pp. 41–200; Stephen K. Scher, "An Introduction to the Renaissance Portrait Medal," in Scher 2000, pp. 1–25; Raymond B. Waddington, "Pisanello's *Paragoni*," in ibid, pp. 27–45; Kristen Lippincott, "'*Un Gran Pelago*': The Impresa and the Medal Reverse in Fifteenth-Century Italy," in ibid., pp. 75–96; Louis Alexander Waldman. "'The Modern Lysippus': A Roman Quattrocento Medalist in Context," in ibid., pp. 97–107; J. Graham. Pollard, "Text and Image," in ibid., pp. 149–64.
6 Zimmermann 2001.
7 Especially Bambach 2022, on Giovio's three unpublished biographies and the probable act of self-censorship.
8 Lazarus himself had no agency in the miracle of his resurrection by Christ, and he was traditionally depicted either fully wrapped in funerary bindings, as in Giotto's fresco in the Arena Chapel, Padua (ca. 1303–5), or with partially shed funerary cloths, as in Sebastiano del Piombo's painting (ca. 1517–19, The National Gallery, London), but never entirely nude as on the verso of Giovio's medal.

Cat. 7

1 Timothy B. Husband, no. 59, in Ainsworth and Waterman 2013, p. 256.
2 Gelfand 2020, pp. 46–47.

Cat. 8

1 For Margaret's emblems across various media, see Wilson 2004; Till-Holger Borchert, cat. 6, in Marti et al. 2009, p. 177; Hugo van der Velden, cat. 73, in ibid., p. 260, pl. 51.
2 In particular, Nicolas Finet's *Benois seront les misericordieux* (1468–77, Koninklijke Bibliotheek, Brussels, MS 9269) contains eight portraits, approximately seventy monograms attached by love knots (a device used by Charles to a much lesser degree), 130 white roses, thirty daisies, and eight coats of arms; see Normore 2015, p. 186. For the use of marguerites as a symbol, see Ashdown-Hill 2007, pp. 64–65. For Margaret's manuscript commissions, see Kurt Barstow, "The Library of Margaret of York and Some Related Books," in Kren 1992, pp. 258–62; Smeyers 1999, pp. 374–91, esp. figs. 28, 29, 31–33, 36–38.
3 For Marmion's oeuvre, see Maryan W. Ainsworth, "New Observations on the Working Technique in Simon Marmion's Panel Paintings," in Kren 1992, pp. 243–55; Thomas Kren, "Simon Marmion," in Kren and McKendrick 2003, p. 98. Marmion illuminated the following three manuscripts for Margaret: *Les visions du chevalier Tondal* (1475, J. Paul Getty Museum, MS 30; see Kren and Wieck 1990; Thomas Kren, cat. 14, in Kren and McKendrick 2003, pp. 112–16); *La vision de l'âme de Guy de Thorno* (1475, Getty, MS 31; see Thomas Kren, cat. 13, in Kren and McKendrick 2003, pp. 111–12); and Jean Miélot's *Vie de Sainte Catherine d'Alexandrie* (1475, Bibliothèque Nationale de France, Paris, Département des Manuscrits, NAF 28650). For Marmion's Breviary for Philip the Good, begun in 1467 and completed in 1470 for Charles and Margaret, see Sarah Hindman, no. 8, in Hindman et al. 1997, pp. 61–72; Hindman 2023.
4 Charles Sterling and Maryan W. Ainsworth, no. 1, in Sterling et al. 1998, p. 6; Maryan W. Ainsworth, cat. 11, in Kren and McKendrick 2003, p. 107.
5 For a discussion of *The Lamentation*'s attribution and dating, as well as the related drawing in the Fogg Art Museum, see Sterling and Ainsworth, no. 1, in Sterling et al. 1998, pp. 4–6.
6 According to Ainsworth, the panel's recto and verso are contemporaneous; Sterling and Ainsworth, no. 1, in Sterling et al. 1998, p. 5.
7 For example, the arms of Cardinal Antonio Casini on the reverse of Masaccio's *Madonna and Child* (Gallerie degli Uffizi, Florence), painted around 1426.
8 For love knots, see Freeman 1976, pp. 167–74; Kirsch 1991, p. 22. My thanks to Tim Caster, who identified the knot as a jury mast knot, which is similar in form to a love knot.
9 *La vision de l'âme de Guy de Thurno* (Getty, MS 31), fols. 7, 17, where several marguerites also appear (see Kren and Wieck 1990, p. 32, fig. 19; Kren, cat. 14, in Kren and McKendrick 2003, p. 113–14); *Les visions du chevalier Tondal* (Getty, MS 30), fol. 24v (Kren and Wieck 1990, p. 48, pl. 10), and also fols. 13v, 24v, 29, 38.
10 See, for example, *Les visions du chevalier Tondal* (Getty, MS 30, fols. 7, 17; Kren and Wieck 1990, pp. 39 pl. 1, 45 pl. 7); the Boussu Hours (early 1490s, Bibliothèque de l'Arsenal, Paris, MS 1185, fol. 54); and *Le livre des échecs amoreux moralisés* (Bibliothèque Nationale de France, MS fr. 9197, fol. 202), attributed to the Master of Antoine Rolin, Marmion's pupil (see Kren 1992, pp. 210 fig. 184, 214 fig. 194).
11 *Les visions du chevalier Tondal* (Getty MS 30), fol. 34v (Kren and Wieck 1990, p. 54, pl. 15), as well as fols. 20, 30v, 43v.
12 Sterling and Ainsworth, no. 1, in Sterling et al. 1998, p. 4.
13 Ibid.
14 Ainsworth, cat. 11, in Kren and McKendrick 2003, p. 108.

Covered Portraits in Northern Europe, 1430–1500

1 For more on this, see "Uncovering Renaissance Portraits" by Alison Manges Nogueira in this volume.
2 See, for example, the *Virgin and Child and Three Donors*, attributed to the Master of the Legend of Saint Ursula, or the *Virgin and Child with Willem van Bibaut* by the Master of the Magdalen Legend in Hand et al. 2006, cat. 24, pp. 164–69, and cat. 23, pp. 156–63, respectively.
3 On marble imitation related to portraits, see Dülberg 1990, pp. 116–27; for the Van Eyck portrait, ibid., no. 143, p. 219. This painting once had a pendant, a self-portrait of Van Eyck, which has been stolen. In diptych form, the reverse of Margareta's portrait, the painted stone, would have been seen most often.
4 L. Campbell 1998, pp. 174–211.
5 Held 1957, p. 83. See also Hensick 2003.
6 See Dülberg 1990, pp. 133–53, for various allegories related to portraiture.
7 https://www.metmuseum.org/art/collection/search/437059.
8 Falque 2012.

9 Rogier van der Weyden seems also to have been the first to focus on representations of memento mori imagery in devotional triptychs. See the *Triptych of Jean Braque* (ca. 1452/53, Musée du Louvre, Paris), discussed in Hindriks 2022.
10 Dülberg 1990, pp. 107–16.
11 See De Vos 1999, no. 25, pp. 298–301. See also Lorne Campbell, cat. 19a,b, in Campbell and Stock 2009, pp. 315–19; Martha Wolff, cat. 20a,b, in ibid., pp. 320–25.
12 Dülberg 1990, pp. 163 no. 237, 260.
13 For such enhanced experiences regarding memento mori imagery in the fifteenth and sixteenth centuries, see Hindriks 2022. See Reindert L. Falkenburg, "The Scent of Holyness: Notes on the Interpretation of Botanical Symbolism in Paintings by Hans Memling," in Verougstraete et al. 1997, pp. 149–61, for further thoughts on the evocation of physical sensations and the interpretation of botanical symbolism in Memling's paintings.

Cat. 9

1 Lorne Campbell (1998, p. 432n19) noted a parallel instance of a Virgin and Child in the style of Dieric Bouts that adorns the verso of a *Portrait of a Man*, which was exhibited in "Paintings from the Lulworth Castle Gallery," Russell-Cotes Art Gallery and Museum, Bournemouth, in 1967 (cat. 82). Furthermore, a document concerning works at the Hôtel-Dieu in Beaune in 1501 lists an image of "Our Lady and St. Bernard on one side and on the other side the portrait of my lord the late duke Philip" (that is, Philip the Good); see L. Campbell 1998, p. 432n20, citing J.-B.-C. Boudrot, "Inventaire de l'Hôtel-Dieu de Beaune (1501)," *Société d'histoire, d'archéologie et de littérature de l'arrondissement de Beaune: Mémoires* 1 (1874), pp. 117–204.
2 Various unconvincing suggestions have been made for the identity of the London portrait as well as a highly unlikely proposal for a pendant of a *Portrait of a Man*, possibly of the van Themseke family; see L. Campbell 1998, p. 430.
3 For the manner in which intact diptychs were intended to be unfolded and used in the fifteenth and early sixteenth centuries, see Hélène Verougstraete, "Diptychs with Instructions for Use," in Hand and Spronk 2006, pp. 156–71.
4 See Verougstraete, "Diptychs with Instructions for Use," in Hand and Spronk 2006, pp. 158–63, and figs. 1, 2 for examples that, however, involve portraits linked to religious images. For further on portrait diptychs, see Lorne Campbell, "Diptychs with Portraits," in Hand and Spronk 2006, pp. 32–45; Till-Holger Borchert, "Innovation, Reconstruction, and Deconstruction: Early Netherlandish Diptychs in the Mirror of Their Reception," in Hand and Spronk 2006, pp. 172–99.
5 As a result of the stylistic similarity to Rogier's works, the London painting was assigned early on to Rogier himself by Max Friedländer, Georges Hulin de Loo, Friedrich Winkler, and Martin Davies (the latter with some reservation). See L. Campbell 1998, pp. 430–31.
6 For a detailed comparison of the London and Washington portraits, see L. Campbell 1998, pp. 430–31. See also Davies 1968, pp. 170–71; Davies 1972, pp. 221–22; De Vos 1999, p. 406.
7 L. Campbell 1998, p. 432.

Cat. 10

1 Fry 1911, pp. 20–202.
2 Kantorowicz 1940.
3 Walsh 2005, p. 289; Keith Christiansen, cat. 71, in Christiansen and Weppelmann 2011, pp. 208–10.
4 Lorne Campbell, cats. 12, 16, in Campbell and Stock 2009, pp. 289–91, 300–302.
5 The *Portrait of a Fat Man, So-Called Robert de Masmines*, attributed to Rogier (1440s, versions in the Gemäldegalerie, Staatliche Museen zu Berlin, and the Museo Nacional Thyssen-Bornemisza, Madrid), also shows a white background, as does the *Portrait of a Man* (ca. 1440–50, Borromeo Collection, Isola Bella). For a discussion of these issues, see Stephan Kemperdick, cats. 16, 17, in Kemperdick and Sander 2009, pp. 265–71; Jochen Sander, cat. 18, in ibid., pp. 272–73.
6 Armstrong 1977, p. 72.
7 De Vos 1999, nos. 25, 27, pp. 298–301, 305–7; Campbell, cat. 19a,b, in Campbell and Stock 2009, pp. 315–19; Martha Wolff, cat. 20a,b, in ibid., pp. 320–25.

Cat. 11

1 My sincere thanks to Tim Newbery for sharing with me his examination report of the frame for the Courtauld Gallery; email exchange with the author, April 14, 2023. This provides a revision of the information concerning the frame in L. Campbell 1990b, p. 66; Lorne Campbell, cat. 22, in Campbell and Stock 2009, p. 329.
2 Scharf 1950, no. XXXI, pp. 74–77 ; Panofsky 1953, vol. 1, pp. 292, 477–78n5.
3 Davies 1972, p. 227. Campbell (cat. 22, in Campbell and Stock 2009, p. 331) is rather more supportive of the identification of this portrait with Guillaume Fillastre.
4 Davies 1972, p. 227; De Vos 1999, p. 409; Stephan Kemperdick, cat. 41, in Kemperdick and Sander 2009, p. 368.
5 Lüttenberg 2000. For previous, unconvincing suggestions regarding the translation and meaning of the motto, see Dülberg 1990, pp. 127–28, 223 no. 153; De Vos 1999, no. C9, p. 409.
6 Winkler 1950, pp. 215–16; Davies 1972, p. 227; Friedländer 1967–76, vol. 2, suppl. 134, p. 89, pl. 139.
7 Kemperdick, cat. 41, in Kemperdick and Sander 2009, p. 370.
8 De Vos 1999, pp. 311 fig. 29a, 409.
9 L. Campbell 1990, pp. 65–66, 96, 98; L. Campbell 1996, pp. 131–32; Campbell, cat. 22, in Campbell and Stock 2009, p. 331.

Cat. 12A–C

1 Angelica Dülberg (1990, pp. 77–78, 230 nos. 174, 175) has emphasized the rarity of this diptych's survival in its velvet pouch.
2 See Inès Villela-Petit, cats. 19, 20, 22, in Bresc-Bautier et al. 2010, pp. 91–92.
3 Confirmation of this identification comes from a medal attributed to Niccolò Fiorentino that shows Matheron's portrait on the obverse and his motto on the reverse. Hill 1930, no. 952, p. 253, pl. 155. See also Hand et al. 2006, cat. 10, pp. 82–83.
4 What is known of the Matheron family has been researched by Marie-Claude Léonelli; see Léonelli, cat. 18, in Bresc-Bautier et al. 2010, pp. 89–90.
5 Dülberg (1990, pp. 77–78, 230 nos. 174, 175) stressed the intimate, private character of this diptych. The well-known commission of Elector Johann Friedrich I of Saxony to Lucas Cranach the Elder for sixty pendant portraits of Friedrich III the Wise, his father, and Johann the Steadfast of Saxony, his uncle, is an example of propagandistic aims.
6 Ring 1949, no. 217, p. 226.
7 Robin 1985, p. 212. See also De Winter 1996, p. 799; Hand et al. 2006, cat. 10, p. 83.

Cat. 13

1 The identification of the sitter is recent, first made by Schedl 2016, pp. 336–37. Further biographical information appears there and in Kriegk 1871, pp. 182–85; Bock 2001, pp. 422–23n1257.
2 See Kriegk 1871, pp. 182, 185.
3 Lübbeke 1991, pp. 150, 152.
4 On black, a gold oak branch, horizontal, with three twigs.
5 On this subject, see Husband 1980, esp. Gloria Gilmore-House, cats. 51, 52, 58, and Timothy Husband, cats. 53–57, pp. 179–96.
6 See Dülberg 1990, pp. 114–15; Lübbeke 1991, p. 152; Schedl 2016, p. 336. The von Rückingen coat of arms, even if reworked, is original to the picture. This is corroborated by the sitter's signet ring, which is marked with the letter *R* and whose charge, though indistinct, appears to represent the same oak branch motif.
7 Bock 2001, pp. 422–23n1257; Schedl 2016, pp. 336–37. For a detailed account of the episode, see Kriegk 1871, pp. 182–85.
8 See Bock 2001, pp. 421–22.
9 See the overview of the literature in Schedl 2016, pp. 328–33.

Cat. 14

1 On red, a silver (white) chevron flanked by two silver (white) balls; an arrow beneath.
2 "Herr von Monsprug wurde gemalt Ao 1485"; quoted from Schedl 2016, p. 325, citing Prinz 1957, p. 162.
3 The inscription and gray coating were removed during a restoration in 1930; see Schedl 2016, p. 563.
4 Ibid., p. 325. The identification was made in Prinz 1957, p. 162. A date of birth is not recorded.
5 See Schedl 2016, p. 326.
6 See ibid., pp. 326–28, for a review of the literature.
7 For a discussion of the similarities, see Bodo Brinkmann, "Wolfgang Beurer (Meister WB)," in Brinkmann and Kemperdick 2002, p. 351. The suggestion in Stange 1955, p. 30, that the painter of the present portrait was active on the Upper Rhine, in Strasbourg, has rightly been rejected.

Cat. 15A,B

1 The transcription is from Schedl 2016, p. 560, citing Schönberger 1933, p. 13.
2 See ibid., pp. 323–24.
3 Dülberg 1990, p. 108n659. An earlier German example, though devotional in nature, is Hans Pleydenwurff's diptych of Georg Graf von Löwenstein of about 1456,

now split between Nuremberg (Germanisches Nationalmuseum) and Basel (Kunstmuseum), for which see Dagmar Hirschfelder and Oliver Mack, no. 24, in Hess et al. 2019, vol. 1, pp. 337–49.

4 Körner 2003, s.v. "zum Jungen, Ort," p. 239.

5 For this and the other biographical details here about Heinrich zum Jungen, see Schedl 2016, p. 324.

6 The church was demolished in the eighteenth century; the site is now occupied by the Paulskirche (built 1789–1833).

7 On red, three silver-and-gold (white-and-yellow) hunting horns. For the recto inscriptions, see above; for the early verso inscription, see Schedl 2016, p. 324.

8 Schedl 2016, pp. 324–25, 560–61. Buchner (1953, p. 190, under no. 30) referred to it as a sliding cover.

9 While the canvas underlayer and distemper medium of the heraldic panel are unusual for a work of this type, the parchment support on the portrait panel is a feature not wholly uncommon in Northern portraiture of the period. On intermediary supports of parchment or paper for portrait paintings, see Ainsworth 2017, pp. 29–32; Hirschfelder and Mack, no. 24, in Hess et al. 2019, vol. 1, pp. 337–38, with references to earlier literature in both.

10 This is noted in Schedl 2016, p. 324.

11 The year of the tomb's endowment is noted in Florian 1706–34, vol. 1, p. 60.

Cat. 16

1 Dülberg 1990, pp. 114–16, 213 no. 129, pl. 233 fig. 602; Hentschel 2018, pp. 3–7, fig. 1; Beate Fücker and Judith Hentschel, no. 54, in Hess et al. 2019, vol. 2, pp. 796–805, figs. 1–4.

2 Roth-Bojadzhiev 1985, pp. 23–30; Lurker 1991, pp. 513, 710.

3 Bernheimer 1952, pp. 176–85; Bischoff "Wilder Mann mit Keule," cat. 29, in Bischoff and Gagel 1977, pp. 161–66; Dülberg 1990, p. 115; Lurker 1991, p. 834; Mayr 2019, https://www.rdklabor.de/w/?oldid=111022#15._Jh.

4 Dülberg 1990, p. 115; Mayr 2019, https://www.rdklabor.de/w/?oldid=111022#15._Jh.

5 Hentschel 2018, pp. 3–7, fig. 2; Fücker and Hentschel, no. 54, in Hess et al. 2019, vol. 2, pp. 796–805, fig. 5.

6 Dülberg 1990, pp. 91–92, 190–91 no. 47, pls. 184, 185 figs. 441–44.

7 Dülberg 1990, pp. 18, 60–61, 63, 77–89.

Cat. 17

1 Paula Nuttall, "Memling and the European Renaissance Portrait," in Borchert 2005, pp. 69–91.

2 An old label, inscribed "del Maestra de (?) Orbens (?)," was removed along with the numbers 86 and XXI by Arthur Kay (1939, pp. 156–60) before 1933; Eisler 1989, p. 108.

3 De Vos 1999, p. 262.

4 Lorne Campbell, "Memling and the Netherlandish Portrait Tradition," in Borchert 2005, pp. 54, 67n28; Till-Holger Borchert, cat. 25, in Borchert 2005, p. 176. See also Lane 2009, p. 289.

5 Borchert, cat. 25, in Borchert 2005, p. 176.

6 Some scholars assumed that the Thyssen-Bornemisza portrait is the left half of a diptych; Friedländer 1967–76, vol. 6, pt. 2, suppl. 232, p. 110, pl. 235; Pächt 1948, p. 54n23. However, this would go against the conventions of dextrality of sitters and holy figures in Netherlandish diptychs. See Hugo van der Velden, "Diptych Altarpieces and the Principle of Dextrality," in Hand and Spronk 2006, pp. 124–55. Concurring with the reconstruction as a triptych are Rosenbaum 1979, cat. 25, pp. 115–17; Eisler 1989, no. 10, pp. 106–15; Dülberg 1990, pp. 163, 260; De Vos 1994, no. 72, p. 262; Borchert, cat. 25, in Borchert 2005, pp. 175–76; Lane 2009, p. 289.

7 See Maryan W. Ainsworth, "Tommaso di Folco Portinari (1428–1501); Maria Portinari (Maria Maddalena Baroncelli, born 1456): Catalogue Entry," https://www.metmuseum.org/art/collection/search/437056.

8 De Vos 1999, no. 22, pp. 131–33; Borchert, cat. 18, in Borchert 2005, pp. 168–69.

9 Extended hinges would have been necessary to allow for the extra width of a closure over two panels. Hélène Verougstraete ("Diptychs with Instructions for Use," in Hand and Spronk 2006, p. 162) imagines the Thyssen-Bornemisza portrait as part of a diptych rather than a triptych with a different way of closing. The frame of the Thyssen-Bornemisza painting is not original and therefore can offer no further clues to the way the painting was opened or closed; see Hélène Verougstraete and Roger Van Schoute, "Cadres et supports chez Memling," in Verougstraete et al. 1997, p. 280. For this and other examples of sequential closing of a triptych, see Lane 2009, p. 290.

10 Stoichita 2015, p. 55.

11 Pächt 1948, p. 54n23.

12 For the flowers in Memling's paintings as evocative of fragrant smells during the contemplation of devotional images, see Reindert L. Falkenburg, "The Scent of Holyness: Notes on the Interpretation of Botanical Symbolism in the Paintings by Hans Memling," in Verougstraete et al. 1997, pp. 149–61. See also Bergström 1955; De Vos 1994, no. 72, p. 262.

13 Dülberg 1990, p. 163.

14 Maryan W. Ainsworth, "Minimal Means, Remarkable Results: Memling's Portrait Painting Technique," in Borchert 2005, p. 104. All Memling scholars concur with this late dating.

Cat. 18

1 Comblen-Sonkes 1988, no. 157, pp. 77–86, with extensive bibliography. Barbara Baert challenges this interpretation, looking more broadly at medieval literature and culture; Baert, "The *Allegory with a Virgin*: Contributions to the Solution of an Iconographical Enigma," in Verougstraete et al. 1997, pp. 195–210. An unlikely suggestion posits that this image resembles a *mystère* that was shown on the occasion of the Feast of the Pheasant in Lille in 1454. Although also guarded by two lions, the woman there was naked and had wine pouring from her breasts; Brückle 2013.

2 See Maryan Ainsworth, "Young Woman with a Pink," https://www.metmuseum.org/art/collection/search/437059; De Vos 1994, nos. 64, 73, pp. 245–47, 264–67.

3 Winkler 1928, p. 12. Comblen-Sonkes (1988, p. 82), Dülberg (1990, p. 288 no. 313), and Campbell (1990a) also agreed with this proposal.

4 Lorentz 1995, p. 75. The rarely represented episode from the saint's life is shown again in the name painting by the Master of the Legend of Saint Barbara (1480, Musées Royaux des Beaux-Arts de Belgique, Brussels).

5 Friedländer 1967–76, vol. 6, pt. 1, no. 96, p. 57; Comblen-Sonkes 1988, p. 84; De Vos 1994, no. 34, p. 164.

6 Campbell 1995, p. 253; Lane 2009, p. 330.

Covered Portraits in Italy, 1475–1550

1 Rosella Lauber, "Memoria, visione e attesa: Tempi e spazi del collezionismo artistico nel primo Rinascimento veneziano," in Hochmann et al. 2008, p. 69, and Paola Benussi, ed., "Appendice documentaria," in ibid, pp. 373–74; Whistler 2009, p. 536.

2 D. Thornton 1997, pp. 113–14; Schmitter 2004.

3 D'Ascia 1998; Nuttall 2010; Wood 2017.

4 Humfrey 1993, pp. 50–53; Nova 1994; Victor M. Schmidt, "Curtains, *Revelatio*, and Pictorial Reality in Late Medieval and Renaissance Italy," in Rudy and Baert 2007, pp. 191–213.

5 Musacchio 2000; Donal Cooper, "Devotion," in Ajmar-Wollheim and Dennis 2006, pp. 190–203, esp. p. 192; Morse 2007.

6 Randolph 2014. On musical instruments, see Flora Dennis, "Music," in Ajmar-Wollheim and Dennis 2006, pp. 228–43, esp. p. 233.

7 Campbell 2009, p. 74.

8 Rutherglen 2016; see also Henry 2021.

9 Dülberg 1990 provides an important catalogue and documentation.

10 See Luke Syson, "Witnessing Faces, Remembering Souls," in Campbell et al. 2008, pp. 14–31; Elizabeth Perkins, "Giovanni Bellini, Antonello da Messina and the 'Signs of Men's Character,'" in Wilson 2015, pp. 127–41, with further references.

11 Welch 1990, p. 166.

12 Whistler 2012, p. 223nn22–24, with further references. For Fra Sabba da Castiglione (1480–1554), see Barocchi 1971–77, vol. 3, p. 2935.

13 Dülberg 1990, pp. 45–58; Penny 2004–8, vol. 1, pp. 99–101, with additional inventory evidence. For more on Lotto, see Christiansen 2019, and on Vendramin's *timpani*, Schmitter 2022, pp. 207–22.

14 D. Brown 2001, cat. 36, p. 209.

15 See, respectively, Alessandro Cecchi, cats. 8, 9, in *Raffaello a Firenze* 1984, pp. 105–18; Shearman 2003, vol. 1, pp. 112–14; Henry and Joannides 2012, cat. 68, pp. 252–57; Reiss 2022, p. 270.

16 On Bronzino and Pontormo, see Cropper 1997.

17 See Simons 2013, esp. pp. 25–26.

18 Löhr 2003; Zöllner 2005; Bolzoni 2010.

19 On *La Vecchia* and its *timpano*, see Settis 2008; on Bronzino, Bastian Eclercy, cats. 77, 78, in Eclercy 2016, pp. 186–89.

Cat. 19

1 David Alan Brown, "Ginevra de' Benci," in Boskovits and Brown 2003, pp. 367–68n63.

2 Lauber 2005, pp. 97, 113n180; Dillon Bussi 2014.

3 Lauber 2005, p. 99; Angelini 2012, p. 148n70.

4 Michiel 1884, p. 52; Eveline Baseggio Omiccioli, "A New Interpretation of Jacometto's 'Most Perfect Work': Parallels in Portraits by Giovanni Bellini and Leonardo da Vinci," in Wilson 2015, p. 162.

5 Omiccioli, "A New Interpretation of Jacometto's 'Most Perfect Work,'" in Wilson 2015, pp. 149–51, 155 fig. 14, 156 fig. 16; Peter Humfrey, "The Portrait in Fifteenth-Century Venice," in Christiansen and Weppelmann 2011, pp. 56–57.
6 Mundy 1988, p. 37.

Cat. 20A,B

1 Andrea Bayer, cats. 152a, 152b, in Christiansen and Weppelmann 2012, p. 346. For a reinterpreted transcription of Michiel's text, see Lauber 2005, p. 98: "Vi è uno ritratto piccolo de M(esser) Alxise Contarini q(uondam) M(esser) . . . che morse già anni, et ne l'instesso quadretto un ritratto a l'incontro d'una monacha da San Segondo, et sopra la coperta de detti ritratti una cervetta in un paese, et nella coperta de cuoro de detto quadretto fogliami di oro maxenato, di mano di Iacometto, opera perfettissima." For a summary of the various transcriptions/translations of this text, see Evelyn Baseggio Omiccioli, "A New Interpretation of Jacometto's 'Most Perfect Work': Parallels in Portraits by Giovanni Bellini and Leonardo da Vinci," in Wilson 2015, p. 165n24. For a dissenting view on the identification of the Lehman portraits with Michiel's passage, see Dillon Bussi 1995, pp. 34–36, fig. 15. For the copy of the portrait of Alvise Contarini in the collection of the Duke of Buccleuch and Queensberry, see Peter Humfrey, cat. 6, in Humfrey et al. 2004, pp. 68–69.
2 For Taddeo Contarini, see Anderson 1997, pp. 148–60; Lauber 2005, pp. 100–101.
3 Bayer, in Christiansen and Weppelmann 2012, pp. 346–47. The female portrait is (and always was) smaller, and its edges of ungessoed wood suggest that it may have fit into some form of framework. Technical examination undertaken in 2009 by Luuk Hoogstede, Dorothy Mahon, and George Bisacca, described in Examination Record: Jacometto Veneziano, October 2009, Paintings Conservation Department, The Metropolitan Museum of Art.
4 Nogueira forthcoming.
5 Ibid.
6 For a summary of these interpretations, see Everett Fahy, "The Marriage Portrait in the Renaissance, or Some Women Named Ginevra," in Bayer 2008, pp. 17–27; Bayer, in Christiansen and Weppelmann 2012, pp. 347–48. For the woman's headdress, see D. Brown 2001, p. 154; Lauber 2005, pp. 98–99; Nancy Edwards, in Bayer 2008, p. 266; Bayer, in Christiansen and Weppelmann 2012, p. 348; Omiccioli, "A New Interpretation of Jacometto's 'Most Perfect Work,'" in Wilson 2015, pp. 152–61; Periti 2016, pp. 57–60.
7 Nogueira forthcoming. I thank Manus Gallagher for sharing his sketch of the composition made from close-hand examination of the panel in 1996, which, in revealing the outline of a figure standing in the boat, provided a key element in deciphering the subject matter of the scene. Although Angelica Dülberg (1990, p. 26) was unaware of Charon's presence, describing the boat as "empty," she correctly identified its owner: "the empty boat on the shore may be that of Charon, who ferries the soul of the deceased into the hereafter."
8 Timothy Wilson, "Le service du Museo Correr," in Barbe and Crépin-Leblond 2011, pp. 164, 170, fig. B. For the myth of Orpheus and its representations in the Renaissance, see Nogueira forthcoming.
9 Ovid *Metamorphoses* 10.72–75; Ovid, *Metamorphoses: A New Verse Translation*, trans. David Raeburn (London: Penguin, 2004), p. 385.
10 Ovid *Metamorphoses* 10.112, 10.127; Ovid, *Metamorphoses*, trans. David Raeburn, pp. 387, 388.
11 Mundy 1988, p. 39; Bath 1992, pp. 219–33, 275–316; Emison 1997, pp. 126–39, fig. 28; Lauber 2005, p. 99; Cohen 2008, pp. 142–50; Edwards, in Bayer 2008, p. 266; Bayer, in Christiansen and Weppelmann 2012, p. 348.
12 See Nogueira forthcoming. For a box adorned with a similar image of a stag reclining in the grass, see Jacqueline Marie Musacchio, cat. 38b, in Bayer 2008, pp. 107–8.
13 Nogueira forthcoming.
14 Lotto's Lucina Brembati (ca. 1508, Accademia Carrara, Bergamo) contains a rebus alluding to the sitter's name. For wordplays in classical literature, see Robinson 2019.
15 Mundy 1988, pp. 37–38; V. Schmidt 2005, pp. 44–58.
16 For the wills of Pietro and Michele Contarini, see Battilotti and Franco 1978, pp. 83–84.
17 Lauber 2005, pp. 99, 115n197, citing Ravà 1920, p. 170; Omiccioli, "A New Interpretation of Jacometto's 'Most Perfect Work,'" in Wilson 2018, p. 162; Schmitter 2002, pp. 215 figs. 16–19, 216. For the relationship among members of the Contarini family, see Battilotti and Franco 1978, p. 86; Lauber 2002b, pp. 53–54; Whistler 2009, p. 541; Whistler 2012, pp. 227–32; Nogueira forthcoming.

Cat. 21

1 Davis 1966, pp. 74–77.
2 For clothing and flags, see Paolo Giovio, *Dialogo dell'imprese militari et amorose* (Lyon: Guillaume Rouille, 1574), fol. 8. For interior decoration and belongings, see Davis 1966, pp. 92–93.
3 Free translation by the author, from Giovio, *Dialogo*, fol. 12.
4 Gabriele Symeoni, *Le imprese heroiche et morali*, printed and bound with Giovio, *Dialogo* (The Metropolitan Museum of Art, 21.36.6), fols. 171–73.
5 Symeoni, *Le imprese*, fols. 198–99.

Cat. 22

1 A typical example is the Parisian Bible from about 1235 in The Met collection (31.134.9), which measures just 6½ × 3¾ × 3⅛ inches (16.5 × 9.5 × 7.9 cm) when closed and is thus easily portable.
2 Examples in The Met collection include an Italian box for a medical text (52.131a, b), a French case for a missal (24.135.2), and a northern European box with a coat of arms for a bishop (51.117).
3 Andrea Bayer, cat. 152a, b, in Christiansen and Weppelmann 2012, p. 346. See cat. 20A,B, n. 1, in this catalogue for more on the transcription of this source.

Cat. 23

1 Michiel 1884, pp. 46 (Pietro), 52 (Carlo); Peter Humfrey, "The Portrait in Fifteenth-Century Venice," in Christiansen and Weppelmann 2011, pp. 56–57.
2 For the Besançon portrait (fig. 40), see Davide Gasparotto, cat. 3.19, in Beltramini et al. 2013, pp. 187, 208–9; Wencke Deiters, "Umanisti e poeti, letterate, poetesse e cortigiane," in Ferino-Pagden et al. 2022, pp. 260–61, cat. 50. For the National Gallery portrait (fig. 41), see Marsel Grosso, cat. 6.1, in Beltramini et al. 2013, pp. 353, 368–69; Peter Humfrey, "Titian/*Cardinal Pietro Bembo*/1539/1540," *Italian Paintings of the Sixteenth Century*, NGA Online Editions, https://purl.org/nga/collection/artobject/41638/2019-03-21. For the proposed portrait of Pietro Bembo by Giovanni Bellini (Royal Collection, Hampton Court Palace, London), see Pincus 2008.
3 For an identification of the blue robe, see Dagmar Korbacher, cat. 166, in Christiansen and Weppelmann 2011, p. 371; Peter Humfrey, "The Portrait in Fifteenth-Century Venice," in ibid., p. 56; Sergio Momesso, cat. 37, in Beltramini and Gasparotto 2016, pp. 235–37, 240.
4 De la Mare and Nuvoloni 2009, no. 64 pp. 240–41, no. 82 pp. 282–83; Laura Nuvoloni, cat. 36, in Beltramini and Gasparotto 2016, pp. 234–35.
5 The manuscript was written by Bartolomeo Sanvito in the mid-1480s (King's College, Cambridge, MS 34, fol. 1).
6 Horace *Odes* 1.13.17–18; Segal 1973; Sutherland 2005, pp. 75–77.
7 Nancy Edwards, in Bayer 2008, pp. 266–67.
8 Pietro Bembo, *Rime* XLVI, ll. 10–11: "poi che quel nodo è sciolto, ond'io fui preso,/ che'altro che morte, scogliere non devea"; Bembo 1966, p. 28. Costanza Fregoso is referred to in three ways in Bembo's letters: as Madonna C, Gostanza, and MG; Lucco 2000, p. 53; Kidwell 2004, pp. 24–25 (for the English translation); Williams 2017, pp. 170–72.
9 Lucco 2000, p. 68. In a letter of 1508, Bembo noted that he was consumed by jealousy of Costanza's flirtation with another; ibid., p. 52.
10 Walter and Zapperi 2006, pp. 31–44, 59–68; Catherine Whistler, cat. 34, in Eclercy and Aurenhammer 2019, pp. 114–15.

Cat. 24

1 For questions of attribution, see Manca 1992, pp. 34–35, 186–87 no. R36; Bernard Aikema and Beverly Louise Brown, cat. 66, in Aikema and Brown 1999, pp. 326–27; D. Brown 2001, cat. 21, pp. 160–61; Mazzotta 2012, pp. 152 fig. 4, 155.
2 For the attribution to Jacopo de' Barbari, see Aikema and Brown, cat. 66, in Aikema and Brown 1999, pp. 326–27. For the conflation of Jacometto's and Jacopo de' Barbari's identities, see Angelini 2012.
3 Nogueira forthcoming.
4 Knauer 2002; Knauer 2009, pp. 6–8, fig. 2.
5 Knauer 2002, p. 99n21; Clarke 2015, p. 427.
6 Knauer 2002, p. 113n71.
7 Ibid., p. 105. For Roman inscriptions on Venetian portraits, see De Grummond 1975.
8 Knauer 2002, pp. 104–5.
9 Eveline Baseggio Omiccioli, "A New Interpretation of Jacometto's 'Most Perfect Work': Parallels in Portraits by Giovanni Bellini and Leonardo da Vinci," in Wilson 2015, pp. 149, 164n7, also 164n5.
10 Knauer 2002, p. 105n48.

Cat. 25

1 Dominique Thiébaut, "XIIIe–XVe Siècle," in Foucart-Walter 2007, p. 57, for a partial overview to that date; Angelini 2012, pp. 140–42 figs. 14, 15,

145 fig. 18; Mazzotta 2017, pp. 75, 78, 79 fig. 15, 80 fig. 16.

2 Guiffrey 1902, p. 19, as "Pierre-Paul Millini"; see Ricci 1913, no. 1252a, p. 44, with other earlier bibliography and the shift to an identification as "Giulio Mellini."

3 Crollalanza 1886–90, vol. 2, p. 124. Documents in the Département des Peintures, Musée du Louvre, include exchanges with Giorgio Ferrari, Director, Biblioteca Nazionale Marciana, Venice (1970–71), and with Bertrand Jestaz, Conservateur, Département des Objets d'Art, Louvre (1973), in which Ferrari reported that no historical evidence of a "Giulio Mellini" had been found, and both questioned the identification of the family's coat of arms based on examination and drawings. The author thanks Stéphane Loire for his assistance with this research.

4 Beverly Louise Brown, "Picturing the Perfect Marriage: The Equilibrium of Sense and Sensibility in Titian's 'Sacred and Profane Love,'" in Bayer 2008, p. 243; Nancy Edwards, cats. 121a, 121b, 123a, 123b, in ibid., pp. 261–62, 266; Bolzoni 2010, pp. 272–73; Angelini 2012, pp. 140–42.

Cat. 26

1 See Dülberg 1990, pp. 161–63, 249 no. 211; Bernard Aikema, cat. 26, in Aikema and Brown 1999, pp. 234–35; Bolzoni 2010, pp. 266–67; Lüdemann 2010; Dagmar Korbacher, cat. 168, in Christiansen and Weppelmann 2011, pp. 374–76; Mazzotta 2017, pp. 78, 82, fig. 19; Ulrich Pfisterer, cat. 98, in Kren 2018, pp. 330–31.

2 Dal Pozzolo 1993.

3 Lüdemann 2010.

4 Pfisterer, cat. 98, in Kren 2018, pp. 330–31.

5 See, for example, Aikema, cat. 26, in Aikema and Brown 1999, pp. 234–35.

6 Mazzotta 2017, pp. 78, 82; Pfisterer, cat. 98, in Kren 2018, pp. 330–31.

7 As quoted by Korbacher, cat. 168, in Christiansen and Weppelmann 2011, p. 376.

Cat. 27A,B

1 For technical evidence of the relationship between the two panels, see Carlo Falciani, cat. 4, in Ciatti and Natali 2008, pp. 86, 88; Sylvia Ferino-Pagden, cat. 1.16, in Ferino-Pagden 2009, p. 84.

2 Falciani, cat. 4, in Ciatti and Natali 2008, p. 89. For a discussion of this work within the larger context of masks, see Richard Weihe, "Person und Mask: 'Sua cuique persona' als Schema der Maskierung," in Ferino-Pagden 2009, pp. 21–27.

3 Seneca (*De beneficiis*, 2.17) and Quintillian (*De institutione oratoria*, 5.12). Seneca, *Moral Essays*, trans. John W. Basore (Cambridge, Mass.: Harvard University Press, 1975), vol. 3, pp. 82–83: "Adspicienda ergo non minus sua cuique persona est quam eius, de quo iuvando quis cogitat" (It is, then, every man's duty to consider not less his own character than the character of the man to whom he is planning to give assistance). Antonio Natali, cats. 31, 31a, in Cecchi and Natali 1996, pp. 134; Gaylord Brouhot, cat. 3, in Falciani 2015, p. 78; Gianeselli 2017, p. 361.

4 Belting 2017, p. 94; De Lacy 1977, pp. 163–65. Masks were a frequent motif in the writings of early sixteenth-century authors, such as Machiavelli, Castiglione, Guicciardini, and Erasmus; see Ferino-Pagden, cat. 1.16, in Ferino-Pagden 2009, pp. 83–84.

5 Hannah Baader, "Anonym: 'Sua cuique Persona'; Maske, Rolle, Porträt (um 1520)," in Preimesberger et al. 1999, p. 245.

6 Ferino-Pagden, cat. 1.16, in Ferino-Pagden 2009, p. 83; Falciani, cats. 3, 4, in Ciatti and Natali 2008, pp. 83, 86, 88.

7 Mina Gregori ("Raffaello fino a Firenze e oltre," in *Raffaello a Firenze* 1984, p. 32) argues that the cover was painted by Raphael and relates to one of the Doni portraits. See also Antonio Natali, "La coperta della Monaca," in Natali 1995, p. 127.

8 Natali, "La coperta della Monaca," in Natali 1995, pp. 117–37.

9 Ibid.; Brouhot, cat. 2, in Falciani 2015, p. 77. For the association of the portrait and cover in a nineteenth-century document, see Natali, "La coperta della Monaca," in Natali 1995, p. 126.

10 Brouhot, cat. 2, in Falciani 2015, p. 77.

11 Ibid.

12 Antonio Natali, "Madonne fiorentine: Raffaello, amico di Ridolfo," in Ciatti and Natali 2008, pp. 36, 38; Ferino-Pagden, cat. 1.16, in Ferino-Pagden 2009, p. 84. Palazzo Antinori is southeast of Santa Maria Novella.

Cat. 28

1 On marriage in Florence during this period, see especially these studies based on documents: Klapisch-Zuber 1985; Chabot et al. 2006; Chabot 2011; Klapisch-Zuber 2020.

2 *Biblia Sacra juxta Vulgatam Clementinam*, edited by Michael Tweedale (London, 2005), p. 1365; https://www.wilbourhall.org/pdfs/vulgate.pdf: "Dicit ei Jesus: Noli me tangere, nondum enim ascendi ad Patrem meum: vade autem ad fratres meos" (Jesus saith unto her, Touch me not; for I am not yet ascended to my Father).

3 Zeri 1962, pp. 218, 236; Fahy 1976, pp. 192–95. Some attributions of drawings and paintings to this master are open to question.

4 Compare especially Padoa Rizzo 1988; Padoa Rizzo 1991; Anna Padoa Rizzo, "I Del Mazziere," in Gregori et al. 1992, pp. 114–15; Nesi 2022, pp. 1–4.

5 Vasari 1966–87, vol. 3, p. 447, under Cosimo Rosselli.

6 For further discussion, see Bambach forthcoming.

7 Petrarch, "*Triumphus Pudicitie / Trionfo della Pudicizia*," line 87; *Trionfi*, edited by Guido Bezzola, Letteratura Italiana Einaudi (Milan: Rizzoli, 1957); http://www.letteraturaitaliana.net/pdf/Volume_2/t44.pdf.

8 Uzielli 1884, p. 32, offering the ironic comment, "sola prova del genio poetico di Leonardo" (the one and single proof of Leonardo's poetic genius), and providing the most authoritative transcription of this sonnet's text, pp. 93–95. Uzielli included the biography of "messer Antonio di Matteo di Meglio cavaliere Araldo della Magnifica Signoria di Firenze" [Antonio di Matteo di Meglio, lord herald of the magnificent Republic of Florence] and catalogued Antonio's manuscripts of poetry with collation notes.

9 Uzielli 1884; Branciforte 1995; Pallini 2002 (all with citations of archival documents). Although Antonio di Meglio's functions were those of a herald, and although he would have been called an "*araldo*" in very early sources, his actual titles in documents were "*Miles curialis*" and "*Sindicus et referendarius*" of the Florentine Republic; Pallini 2002, p. 8.

10 Everett Fahy (cat. 17, in Christiansen and Weppelmann 2011, pp. 117–18) catalogued The Met's painted portrait by Davide Ghirlandaio (22½ × 17⅜ in. [57.2 × 44.1 cm]) and convincingly identified Selvaggia Sassetti as the sitter.

11 Patricia Simons (1988) makes similar points in her discussion of profile portraits of women in Italian paintings.

12 Dülberg 1990, p. 229, no. 169, inscribed on the lintel, "*SPECIOSVS FORMA PRE FILIIS HOMINVM*" (Attractive in form before the sons of men).

13 Owing to its fragility, this frame will not accompany the portrait in The Met's exhibition and will be replaced by a travel frame.

Cat. 29A,B

1 David Alan Brown, cats. 4, 5, in Brown et al. 1997, pp. 81–87; Dal Pozzolo 2021, nos. I.8, I. 9, pp. 112–15.

2 See Gentili 1985, pp. 90–91, and the discussions in Brown, cats. 4, 5, in Brown et al. 1997, pp. 81–87; Sylvia Ferino-Pagden, "Pictures of Women—Pictures of Love," cats. 36, 37, in Brown and Ferino-Pagden 2006, pp. 200–207; Dal Pozzolo 2021, nos. I.8, I.9, pp. 112–15.

3 See Doretta Davanzo Poli, "Fashion in Lotto's Paintings and Documents," in Dal Pozzolo and Falomir 2018, pp. 112–13. For the Licinio group portrait, see Artemieva 2001, cat. 15, pp. 78–79.

4 This was argued by Beverly Louise Brown in cat. 57, in Aikema and Brown 1999, p. 328, citing the portrait currently attributed to Marco Basaiti at the Worcester Art Museum; see additionally Carpaccio's *Woman with a Book* (1500–1505, Denver Art Museum); Peter Humfrey, cat. 47, in Humfrey et al. 2022, p. 221. For Gentile Bellini's portrait, see Dagmar Korbacher, cat. 163, in Christiansen and Weppelmann 2011, pp. 364–65.

5 Humfrey 1997, pp. 10–12; Dal Pozzolo 2021, nos. I.8, I.9, pp. 112–15.

6 For the history of attribution and detailed scholarly interpretation, see Margaret Binotto, cat. 51, in Villa 2011, pp. 266–69; Dal Pozzolo 2021, nos. I.8, I.9, pp. 112–15.

7 This pairing was first proposed by Gentili 1985, pp. 87–91, and followed with further proposals on the subject matter by many scholars; see Binotto, cat. 51, in Villa 2011, pp. 266–69; Dal Pozzolo 2021, nos. I.8, I.9, pp. 112–15.

8 Giuseppe Gullino, "Lotto's Social Milieu: 1. Venice and Treviso," in Dal Pozzolo and Falomir 2018, pp. 119–37, with references; identifying these works today can only be speculative. Dal Pozzolo 2021, no. I.3, pp. 100–101, summarizes arguments for a possible identification of Augurello's portrait together with the possibility that its cover might have been the Washington *Allegory* (cat. 29B).

9 See Baert 2018; Holberton 2021, vol. 1, pp. 200–209, 266.

10 Brown, cat. 5, in Brown et al. 1997, pp. 86–87.

11 See Cortesi Bosco 1992 for an interpretation as an allegory of the vigilance of the soul, perhaps identifiable with a painting in Lotto's possession in 1550.
12 For Bembo's medal, see Pollard 2007, vol. 1, no. 441, p. 450. On Augurello, see Soranzo 2020, pp. 72–77; Dal Pozzolo 2021, p. 100.
13 Soranzo 2020, p. 73.

Cat. 30A–C
1 Dal Pozzolo 2021, p. 24; Raffaella Poltronieri, "Regesto biografico," in ibid., p. 66.
2 For comparisons, see David Alan Brown, cat. 2, in Brown et al. 1997, p. 74; Humfrey 1997, pp. 9–11.
3 For examples of curtain rails, see Victor M. Schmidt, "Curtains, *Revelatio*, and Pictorial Reality in Late Medieval and Renaissance Italy," in Rudy and Baert 2007, pp. 191–213.
4 See David Alan Brown, cat. 1, in Brown et al. 1997, pp. 70–72.
5 It was similarly deployed in Lotto's portrait of a Dominican friar (ca. 1505, The National Trust, Upton House, Warwickshire); see Dal Pozzolo 2021, no. I.7, pp. 110–11.
6 Reproduced in Enrico Maria Dal Pozzolo, cats. 3, 4, in Dal Pozzolo and Falomir 2018, fig. 3.1, p. 190.
7 See Pollard 2007, vol. 1, no. 210, p. 225, for translations.
8 Dal Pozzolo, cats. 3, 4, in Dal Pozzolo and Falomir 2018, p. 190; and see Miguel Falomir and Ana González Mozo, "Lotto's Portraits: Their Conception and Execution," in ibid., p. 74, fig. 31, for a re-creation of this and an alternative diptych format.
9 See Giuseppe Gullino, "Lotto's Social Milieu. 1: Venice and Treviso," in Dal Pozzolo and Falomir 2018, pp. 119–37, on Trevisan humanist circles, with references.
10 See Gentili 1985, pp. 76–82; Cortese Bosco 1987, vol. 1, pp. 346–48, for a detailed reading based on the theology of Jean Gerson; Margaret Binotto, "Lotto al bivio: La dialettica di *virtus* e *voluptas* nella pittura profana," in Villa 2011, pp. 249–59; Dal Pozzolo 2021, no. I.6, pp. 106–9, for a summary.
11 Holberton 2019.
12 David Alan Brown, cat. 3, in Brown et al. 1997, p. 79.

Cat. 31
1 Musée du Louvre, Département des Peintures (71 [MR 251]), oil on canvas, 41⅜ × 54 in. (105 × 137 cm). The attribution to Titian is now widely accepted, but see Anderson 1997, pp. 308–9, with an unconvincing attribution to Giorgione and earlier literature.
2 Harold Wethey (1997, no. 54, p. 167) reports a suggestion by Islamic scholar Eric Schroeder that the disk represents a horoscope drawn between January 20 and 21 and April 8 and 9, 1513.
3 A famous example is Titian's caricature of the *Laocoön*, unearthed in 1506, showing the antique sculptural group in the form of apes in a landscape, known from the woodcut by Niccolò Boldrini of about 1540–45 (an impression is British Museum W,5.74).
4 Giovanni Battista Abioso, *Dialogus in astrologiae defensionem cum vaticinio a diluvio usque ad Christi annos 1702* (Venice: Franciscus Lapicida, 1494), Bayerische Staatsbibliothek, Munich (4 Inc.c.a 1052—BSB-Ink A-2, 1). See Rizzo 2014. Also Gandolfi 2013; De Santis 2018.
5 Rizzo 2014.
6 Catalogued in Pignatti 1971, nos. 16a, 16b, pp. 103–4, pls. 57–73.
7 Abioso, *Dialogus in astrologiae defensionem*, n.p. (image 60). See De Santis 2018.
8 Anderson 1997, pp. 86–91, 152–55, 298–99.
9 See most recently Brooke 2022, on Campagnola's engraving and its relationship to astrology and the artist's poetry.
10 Brooke 2022, pp. 261–63.

Cat. 32
1 See Brown 2019.
2 Shapley 1979, vol. 1, pp. 481–82; Dülberg 1990, pp. 55–58, 295–96 no. 336; Brown 1996, p. 230, pl. 254.
3 An unpublished discussion by Douglas Lewis of a plaquette in the National Gallery of Art, Washington, D.C. (1957.14.150), is noted in Peter Humfrey, "Titian/Cupid with the Wheel of Time/c. 1515/1520," in *Italian Paintings*, https://purl.org/nga/collection/artobject/354, entry note 9.
4 Schmitter 2022, pp. 214–19, with references.
5 Humfrey, "Titian / Cupid with the Wheel of Time /c. 1515/1520," in *Italian Paintings*, https://purl.org/nga/collection/artobject/354.

Cat. 33
1 Jill Dunkerton, "Appendix: The Conservation of the 'Triumph of Love,'" in Whistler 2009, p. 542; Whistler 2012, with the correct reconstruction.
2 On *timpani* in the Vendramin collection, see also Schmitter 2022.
3 Anton Francesco Doni, *I marmi* (Venice: Francesco Marcolini, 1552), pt. 3, fol. 40–41; see Whistler 2012, p. 222n14.
4 Wethey 1971, L.26, p. 204.
5 On Titian and Vendramin's collection, see Penny 2004–8, vol. 2, pp. 225–27; Whistler 2012.
6 Dunkerton and Spring 2013.
7 Sherman 2013.
8 Whistler 2012, p. 235; Sherman 2013, p. 45.

Cat. 34
1 Whistler 2009, p. 539. See also cat. 33 in this volume.
2 Translation quoted from V[irginia] W. C[allahan], "The Life of Andreas Alciatus and Its Relation to His Emblems," in Daly 1985, vol. 1, p. [xx].
3 Temple 2018, p. 54; Enenkel 2019, pp. 55–58.
4 See, for example, the carved Roman gemstones in the British Museum, London (1890,0601.37 and 1867,0507.221).
5 "Est potis, a nobis temperet an ne manus?" Translation of Alciato's text quoted from Enenkel 2019, pp. 58, 59.

Covered Portraits in Northern Europe, 1500–1550
1 This essay is broadly indebted to Angelica Dülberg's foundational study, *Privatporträts: Geschichte und Ikonologie einer Gattung im 15. und 16. Jahrhundert* (Dülberg 1990). For general surveys of portraiture in the German-speaking lands and the Low Countries from 1500 to 1550, see Haag et al. 2011 and Borchert and Jonckheere 2015, respectively, and for portrait types and functions, with emphasis on northern European examples, see van Dijk and Ubl 2021, each with references to earlier literature.
2 On the topic of heraldry on portrait reverses and covers, see Dülberg 1990, pp. 107–16.
3 See ibid., pp. 91–92.
4 Ibid., pp. 83–85, 163–64.
5 Ibid., pp. 153–63.
6 Ibid., pp. 81, 107.
7 Ibid., pp. 107, 133–53.

Cat. 35A, B
1 On Hans and Martin Caldenbach, see Schedl 2016, pp. 292–317, 531–54 nos. 65–76.
2 See Dürer's comments in two letters of 1509 to the Frankfurt patrician Jakob Heller; Schedl 2017.
3 Bodo Brinkmann, in Brinkmann and Kemperdick 2005, p. 147; for the dates of the mayoral posts, see Kriegk 1868, pp. 489–90.
4 On silver (white), a red fess accompanied by three black broad arrows; on the helmet, a broad arrow of natural color topped with five gold (yellow) balls with black plumes of feathers.
5 Approximately four centimeters (1⅝ inches) are missing from the top and eight centimeters (3⅛ inches) from the bottom; see Brinkmann, in Brinkmann and Kemperdick 2005, p. 148.
6 Ibid., pp. 149–50.
7 On the states of the versos, see the notes in Brinkmann, in Brinkmann and Kemperdick 2005, p. 142; Schedl 2016, no. 72, pp. 543–44.
8 The portrait panel is made up of one board, the heraldic panel of three; see Schedl 2016, pp. 307n1880, 543.
9 See Schedl 2017.
10 See Brinkmann, in Brinkmann and Kemperdick 2005, p. 149; Schedl 2016, p. 294.

Cat. 36
1 Crossley 1993; Kavaler 2005, p. 239.
2 The leaves are also in the collection of The Met (32.100.475c, e, and f).

Cat. 37
1 Husband 1980, pp. 185–96. For another engraving by Dürer of an imaginary coat of arms, see Strauss 1977, no. 31, pp. 96–97.
2 See, for example, Bartrum 1995, p. 35; Andrew John Martin and Christof Metzger, "Costumes and Roles," in Metzger 2019, p. 183.
3 For these prints, see Strauss 1977, nos. 2, 84, pp. 24–25, 236–37. For two recent alternative discussions of the print, see Schaurte 2022 and Rothwell Hughes 2023.
4 See Strauss 1977, no. 20, pp. 66–68.
5 See depictions of this medieval tale by the Master of the Housebook in Filedt Kok 1985, cat. 54, p. 148; and by Hans Baldung in Bernhard 1978, p. 317. Other notable precedents include *Solomon's Idolatry* by the Master of the Housebook: see Filedt Kok 1985, cat. 7, p. 97; and *Samson and Delilah* by Master E.S.: see Shestack 1967, cat. 56, n.p.
6 Bernheimer 1952, pp. 123, 125–26; Husband 1980, pp. 9, 114; Colin 1999, p. 8. For other discussions of the association of Wild Men not only with lust but with marriage and domestic harmony, see Silver 1983; Kaufmann 1984, pp. 32–34.

7 Husband 1980, cat. 17, pp. 89–91, fig. 53.
8 Ibid., p. 91.

Cat. 38

1 Friedländer (1906, p. 587) was the first to make the attribution.
2 See Butts 2006, pp. 127–58; Manuel Teget-Welz, "Hans von Kulmbach: Ein Nürnberger Maler macht Karriere," in Teget-Welz and Dickel 2022, pp. 31–47; Matthias Weniger, "Das malerische Schaffen des Hans von Kulmbach: Versuch einer Würdigung," in Teget-Welz and Dickel 2022, pp. 49–67.
3 On the symbolism discussed here, see Dülberg 1990, p. 148; Maryan W. Ainsworth, in Ainsworth and Waterman 2013, p. 169.
4 Baldwin 1986, passim. See also Dülberg 1990, p. 148; Nancy Edwards, in Bayer 2008, p. 256, under cat. 118.
5 Dülberg (1990, p. 243, no. 196) proposes a protective case or bag.
6 Dülberg (ibid.) argues against a pendant, while Kurt Löcher (in *Gothic and Renaissance Art in Nuremberg* 1986, cat. 162, pp. 343–44) and van Dijk and Ubl (2021, p. 8) are in favor of one.

Cat. 39

1 Friedländer (1916, col. 132) and all later references concur in this attribution, except Hofbauer (2021, esp. pp. 107–10), who considers the picture Netherlandish and tentatively ascribes it to Joos van Cleve.
2 This painting was identified as the pendant by Dieter Koepplin, in Koepplin and Falk 1974–76, vol. 2, p. 682, under cat. 595.
3 Ibid.
4 See Maryan W. Ainsworth, no. 8, in Ainsworth and Waterman 2013, pp. 45, 284n1 (analysis by Peter Klein).
5 On blue, a star and two crescents. See Wehle and Salinger 1947, p. 200, with reference to the later, Dutch branch of the family. For the Lille period, ca. 1500, see Hofbauer 2021, pp. 100–101.
6 Schade 1980, pp. 28, 30; Borchert 2010, pp. 26–29; Messling 2014, pp. 363–64, with references to earlier literature.
7 On this topic, see Dülberg 1990, pp. 83–85; Jacobs 2012, pp. 151, 164, 166.
8 See Bodo Brinkmann, cat. 19, in Brinkmann 2007, pp. 154–58. For other relevant Cranach works, see Schade 1980, pp. 28, 30; Werner Schade, "Cranach's Contact with the Netherlands: Pointers from a Journey Observed," in Brinkmann 2007, pp. 91–97; Borchert 2010, pp. 26–29.

Cat. 40A,B

1 Vöhlin: on silver, a black fess bearing three letters *P*. Roth: divided vertically; on the proper right (dexter), on black, a silver unicorn rampant; on the proper left (sinister), four horizontal stripes, silver and black (here, the shield reversed to face the sinister for heraldic *courtoisie*); on the helmet, a demi-unicorn divided horizontally, silver and black.
2 In actual, functional colored signet rings, the design was carved in a piece of rock crystal, beneath which the tincture was applied.
3 For a full documentation of the identification, see Hand 1993, pp. 170–72, 172–73nn10–13.
4 On the symbolism of the orange, see Dülberg 1990, pp. 142–43, 149. On falconry as a symbol, see Friedman 1989. For the occurrence of both motifs in an Italian Renaissance portrait pair at The Met (1975.1.95, .96), see Nancy Edwards, cats. 121a, 121b, in Bayer 2008, pp. 261–63.
5 Examples include Hiller and Vey 1969, pp. 32–34, figs. 32, 33; Dülberg 1990, pp. 244–45 no. 199, pls. 102–3 figs. 207–9; Dagmar Hirschfelder, cats. 7, 8, in Hess and Eser 2012, pp. 272–73.
6 Hand (1993, pp. 172, 173n15) cites an unpublished proposal by Charles Talbot.

Cat. 41

1 Riewerts and Pieper 1955, no. 155, p. 128, fig. 140; Lorenz 1996, vol. 2, no. 217, p. 649.
2 Dülberg 1990, pp. 91–92, 229–30 no. 173, pls. 60, 61 figs. 131–33.
3 Herklotz 2000, pp. 256 fig. 9, 258; Herklotz 2001, p. 110.
4 Lorenz 1996, vol. 2, no. 217, p. 649.

Cat. 42

1 The missing *DVCE* in the section before the tree trunk can be inferred from the inscription in fig. 52.
2 Werner Schade, however, assigns the work to Lucas the Elder; see unpublished opinion cited in Koepplin 2006, pp. 140–41.
3 See Glück 1910, p. 221; Dülberg 1990, p. 300, no. 350; Koepplin 2006, p. 139; Hoppe-Harnoncourt 2015, p. 163; Susanne Wegmann, cat. 3/38, in Enke et al. 2015, p. 368. It remains unresolved whether the cover would have been hinged or sliding; the verso of the panel is concealed, and the original edges are not preserved.
4 On the theme of Hercules at the Crossroads, see Panofsky 1930, passim.
5 This identification was first made in Schütz 1972, cat. 26, pp. 32–33.
6 Ibid., p. 33. See also Schade 1980, p. 91; Koepplin 2006, pp. 139–40; Hoppe-Harnoncourt 2015, p. 163; Susanne Wegmann, in Enke et al. 2015, p. 368, no. 3/38; Guido Messling, "Allegory of Virtue," in Haag and Sharp 2016, n.p.
7 Formerly in the Rothschild-Halphen collection, Paris; confiscated during World War II and transferred to the collection of Hermann Göring; returned to France in 1945. See Alford 2012, "Appendix C: Paintings and Sculpture, by Artist," p. 199, no. 7390.

Portable Portraits, 1520–1650

1 Dülberg 1990, pp. 42–43, 56, 146–48, 242 no. 193.
2 "Uno scatolino di noce con ritratto in rame di Bianca Cappello, alto braccia ½" (A box of walnut with the portrait on copper of Bianca Cappello, height ca. 30 cm); Langedijk 1981–87, vol. 1, no. 12,8, p. 314.
3 Dülberg 1990, p. 93; Eser 1996, nos. 47, 48, pp. 297–301; Ritschel 2006, pp. 326–41; Thomas Kuster, cats. 123, 124, in Haag et al. 2011, pp. 207–9.
4 Koepplin and Falk 1974–76, vol. 1, p. 278, cats. 177, 178, color pl. 9; Dülberg 1990, pp. 94–95.
5 Dülberg 1990, pp. 94–95, 274 no. 270, pl. 248 figs. 641–43.
6 Ibid., p. 277 no. 278, pl. 249 figs. 648, 649; Foister 2004, pp. 15–16, figs. 10, 11.
7 Dülberg 1990, pp. 95, 272–73 no. 269, pls. 250–52 figs. 650–55.
8 Ibid., pp. 38–39, pl. 269 figs. 706–9.

Cat. 43

1 For mirrors with or as covers, see Dami 1921; D. Thornton 1997, p. 172; Bolzoni 2008, pp. 221–22; Whistler 2012, p. 223. For mirrors covered with curtains, see P. Thornton 1991, p. 237. For other formats that combined mirrors and portraits, see Wijnands 2019.
2 Dülberg 1990, pp. 38–39, pl. 269 figs. 708, 709.
3 Baroni Vannucci 1997, no. 261, pp. 233–34; see also ibid., no. 263, p. 234, for the related drawing in The Met's collection (50.605.31). Another shuttered mirror in the Robert Lehman Collection bears an inscription, "Not Beauty but Truth is to be admired"; see Timothy J. Newbery and Laurence B. Kanter, cat. 19, in Newbery et al. 1990, p. 49.
4 Plato *Phaedrus* 255d.
5 For Lotto's commissions in this format, see Lotto 1969, pp. 48, 78, 233; Lotto 2017, pp. 151, 320. See also Fletcher 1973, p. 385n30.
6 "Testamento di Alessandro Vittoria, Codicillo, Inventario," in Giovanelli 1858, p. 131: "Un Retratto piccolo di donna, di mano di Titiano, in forma di specchio."
7 Shearman 1992, pp. 136–37; Barbara Maria Savy, cat. 3.12, in Beltramini et al. 2013, p. 202.
8 Cranston 2000, pp. 163–67; Bolzoni 2008, p. 221; Bolzoni 2010, pp. 209–10.
9 Timothy Newbery, written communication to Alison M. Nogueira, August 2020, object files, Robert Lehman Collection, The Metropolitan Museum of Art: updated catalogue entry to Newbery 2007, no. 31, pp. 56–77.
10 Newbery and Kanter, cat. 26, in Newbery et al. 1990, p. 54.
11 Newbery, written communication to Alison M. Nogueira, August 2020, as in note 9 above: updated catalogue entry to Newbery 2007, no. 31, pp. 56–57.
12 Newbery and Kanter, cat. 26, in Newbery et al., 1990, p. 54.
13 Deborah L. Krohn and Linda Wolk-Simon, cat. 115, in Bayer 2008, p. 226.

Cat. 44A,B

1 For this tally, see Daniel Görres, Amalie Hänsch, Thomas Klinke, Wibke Ottweiler, and Aline Sindel, with Vincent Christlein, "Hochzeitsbildnisse Martin Luthers und Katharina von Boras (1525–1526)," in Schubert et al. 2022, https://lucascranach.org/index.php/luther/portrait-3. On Cranach's portraits of Luther in general, see Holste 2004, pp. 165–91; Schuchardt 2015; Schubert et al. 2022.
2 See Timo Trümper, "Art in the Service of Politics: Cranach and the Reformation," in *Martin Luther* 2016, essay vol., pp. 231–39, with references to earlier literature.
3 Dieter Koepplin, in Koepplin and Falk 1974–76, vol. 1, p. 278.
4 For an overview of these issues, see Safley 1996, esp. pp. 18–21.
5 Görres et al., in Schubert et al. 2022, https://lucascranach.org/index.php/luther/portrait-3.

6 As observed during technical examination undertaken by Maryan Ainsworth, Michael Gallagher, Kristen Holder, and Evan Read in the Department of Paintings Conservation at The Metropolitan Museum of Art, June 2023.
7 As in the pair of the Saxon electors Fredrich III and Johann I at The Metropolitan Museum of Art (46.179.1, .2); see Joshua P. Waterman, cats. 17A, 17B, in Ainsworth and Waterman 2013, p. 84.
8 For the Basel examples, see Dülberg 1990, p. 274 no. 270; Görres et al., in Schubert et al. 2022, https://lucascranach.org/index.php/luther/portrait-3. For the practice in Cranach's work, see Gunnar Heydenreich, "'that you paint with such wonderful speed': Virtuosity and Efficiency in the Artistic Practice of Lucas Cranach the Elder," in Brinkmann 2007, p. 35; Heydenreich 2007, pp. 76–89.
9 Dieter Koepplin, in Koepplin and Falk 1974–76, vol. 1, pp. 276, 278; Dülberg 1990, pp. 93–94. For Bruyn's earliest examples, likely from about 1530 (not about 1520, as previously believed), see Zehnder 1990, nos. 246, 247, pp. 45–46, figs. 18–21.
10 Dieter Koepplin, in Koepplin and Falk 1974–76, vol. 1 pp. 276, 278, vol. 2 p. 654 under cat. 566; Schwarz-Hermanns 2007, pp. 128–30.

Cat. 45
1 Foister 2004, p. 15.
2 Paul Ganz (1912, pp. 241–42) first made the connection of the sitter with the court of Henry VIII. For further agreement on and amplification of this proposal, see Maryan W. Ainsworth, no. 31, in Ainsworth and Waterman 2013, pp. 138–39, 302; https://www.metmuseum.org/art/collection/search/436660.
3 The purported identities of the sitters were first suggested by Chamberlain (1913, vol. 2, pp. 71, 353). Ganz (1921) agreed with Chamberlain and proposed that The Met sitter may be Lucas Horenbout. For further on the question of the identities of these sitters, see Ainsworth, no. 31, in Ainsworth and Waterman 2013, pp. 139, 302nn14–19.
4 Foister 2006, cats. 39, 40, p. 47. See also Ainsworth, no. 31, in Ainsworth and Waterman 2013, pp. 138–39.
5 See, for example, MMA50.69.1, "William Roper (1493/94–1578)," https://www.metmuseum.org/art/collection/search/436661; MMA50.69.2, "Margaret Roper (Margaret More, 1505–1544)," https://www.metmuseum.org/art/collection/search/436662; Adam Eaker, cats. 87, 88, in Cleland and Eaker 2022, pp. 222–23.

Cat. 46A,B
1 Foister 2004, p. 163.
2 Susan Foister (2004, pp. 163–65) proposed that Holbein's Melanchthon portrait was intended to be presented to Henry VIII along with the *Loci Communes*. John Rowlands (1985, p. 94) alternatively suggested Thomas Cromwell and Thomas Cranmer, archbishop of Canterbury, as possible recipients of the portrait. See also Anne T. Woollett, "The Pictorial Eloquence of Hans Holbein the Younger," in Woollett 2021, p. 15.
3 Foister (2004, pp. 164–65) asserts that John Leland, English poet, antiquary, and Henry VIII's court librarian, was responsible for the verses inscribed on the lid.
4 Peter van der Ploeg, cat. 20, in Buck et al. 2003, p. 102. For a different opinion on this matter, see Woollett, "The Pictorial Eloquence of Hans Holbein the Younger," in Woollett 2021, p. 15.

Cat. 47A,B
1 Bange 1928, pp. 34–35, pls. 25, 26; Koepplin and Falk 1974–76, vol. 1, pp. 275–78, figs. 137, 138; Alfred Schädler, cats. 515, 516, in *Welt im Umbruch* 1980–81, vol. 2, pp. 161–62; Dülberg 1990, p. 93, pl. 247 figs. 639, 640; Eser 1996, nos. 47, 48, pp. 297–301, figs. 88, 89; Thomas Kuster, cats. 123, 124, in Haag et al. 2011, pp. 207–9.
2 Achim Riether, cat. 53, in Haag et al. 2011, pp. 104–5.
3 Ritschel 2006, pp. 339–40.
4 Ludolphy 2006, p. 49.
5 Ibid., pp. 49–50; Ritschel 2006, pp. 336–37.
6 Ludolphy 2006, p. 48.
7 Eder 1996, no. 47, p. 297; Ritschel 2006, pp. 338–39 figs. 15, 16, 341; Kuster, cats. 123, 124, in Haag et al. 2011, pp. 207–9.

Cat. 48
1 Gutbrod 1992, p. 3.
2 Förschner 1978, pp. 3, 5; Pressler 2000, p. 13.
3 Pressler 2000, p. 14.
4 Ibid., pp. 14, 15.
5 Gutbrod 1992, p. 1.
6 See Förschner 1978, no. 13 p. 42, no. 16 p. 45; Pressler 2000, no. 641, p. 218.

Cat. 49A,B
1 Accademia di San Luca, 743; Uffizi, 1890.4013. Maria Teresa Cantaro, cats. 7, 8, in Ruiz Gómez 2019, pp. 104–7; Bohn 2021, pp. 157–60; Brady 2023, pp. 40–41, 46.
2 Reported by Bohn to Robert Simon Fine Art, New York, December 2012.
3 Woods-Marsden 1998, p. 216; document cited in Murphy 2003, p. 111.
4 Leticia Ruiz Gómez, cat. 35, in Ruiz Gómez 2019, pp. 168–69.
5 Dülberg 1990, p. 274, no. 270; Carrabino 2019.
6 Cantaro 1989, nos. 4a.56a–e, pp. 142–44.
7 Uffizi, 1890, n. 8844; Cantaro 1989, no. 4a.56a, p. 142.
8 Javier Docampo, cat. 16, in Ruiz Gómez 2019, pp. 122–23; Vasari 1996, vol. 2, p. 856.

Cat. 50A,B
1 Daninos 2008; O'Shaughnessy n.d.
2 Vasari 1960, pp. 149, 188–90.
3 Mendelsohn and Ng 2023, with bibliography.

Cat. 51A–C
1 Bott 1985, pp. 155 fig. 126, 458–59 cat. 679; Achilles-Syndram 1994, no. 70, pp. 190–91; Bernd Mayer, cat. 188, in Mayer and Achilles-Syndram 1994, pp. 367–68; Kammel and Lorenz 2008, pp. 85 fig. 5, 86–87; Hess and Hirschfelder, no. 22, p. 389.
2 Mayer, cat. 188, in Mayer and Achilles-Syndram 1994, pp. 367–68.
3 Ibid., p. 367; Kammel and Lorenz 2008, p. 87, fig. 8.
4 Mayer, cat. 188, in Mayer and Achilles-Syndram 1994, p. 368.
5 Dülberg 1990, pp. 41–42.
6 Ibid., pp. 77–78, 230 nos. 174, 175.
7 Achilles-Syndram 2001, pp. 678–79.
8 Ibid., p. 678.

Cat. 52
1 Cleland and Wieseman 2018, pp. 32–37, figs. 24–29. I thank Elizabeth Cleland for her kind advice.
2 Berliner and Egger 1981, vol. 1, pp. 69–70, 78.
3 Weber 1975, vol. 1, p. 68, no. 48, pl. 13.
4 Jolly 2011, pp. 40–57, figs. 16–26.
5 The Mark and Lottie Salton Collection, bequest of Lottie Salton, 2021.
6 Jolly 2011, p. 51, fig. 22; PMA 30-1-59.
7 See https://emuseum.ringling.org/search/portrait%20wax and MMA 17.190.997.

Cat. 53
1 Leopold and Vincent 1993.
2 Ana Matissse Donefer-Hickie, cat. 9, in Koeppe 2019, p. 67.
3 Vincent and Leopold 2015, pp. 98–103, 124–27, nos. 20, 26.
4 Leopold and Vincent 1993, pp. 109, 117n27; citing Wildenstein 1957.
5 This observation is based on a note in the object files in the Department of European Sculpture and Decorative Arts, The Metropolitan Museum of Art, by Eugen Gschwind, of Basel, Switzerland, who examined the object on September 14, 1959.
6 Leopold and Vincent 1993, p. 107, fig. 9.
7 Ibid., pp. 109, 117n.27; citing Wildenstein 1957.

Cat. 54
1 Diemer 1979, p. 135; Maué 1997, no. 14, p. 65.
2 Maué 1997, no. 14, p. 65.
3 Hirschmann 1985; Maué 1997, no. 14, p. 65; Bernhard Ebneth, "Elisabeth und Konrad Krauß," in Korn et al. 2014, p. 157–64; Moritz and Ebneth 2016.
4 Maué 1997, no. 14, p. 65; Moritz and Ebneth 2016.
5 BNM München, R 1611; Maué 1997, no. 14, pp. 66–67, 67–68n8.
6 Ibid., no. 14, p. 67.

WORKS CITED

Achilles-Syndram 1994
Katrin Achilles-Syndram, ed. *Die Kunstsammlung des Paulus Praun: Die Inventare von 1616 und 1719*. Nuremberg: Im Selbstverlag des Stadtrats zu Nürnberg, 1994.

Achilles-Syndram 2001
Katrin Achilles-Syndram. "Praun, Paulus." *Neue Deutsche Biographie*, vol. 20, pp. 678–79. Berlin: Duncker & Humblot, 2001. https://www.deutsche-biographie.de/pnd119159236.html#ndbcontent.

Ackers 2019
Helen I. Ackers. "The Face of the Deceased: Portrait Busts in Roman Tombs." In *The Materiality of Mourning: Cross-Disciplinary Perspectives*, edited by Zahra Newby and Ruth E. Toulson, pp. 121–47. London: Routledge, 2019.

Adams et al. 1999–2002
Alison Adams, Stephen Rawles, and Alison Saunders. *A Bibliography of French Emblem Books of the Sixteenth and Seventeenth Centuries*. 2 vols. Geneva: Librairie Droz, 1999–2002.

Agosti 2008
Barbara Agosti. *Paolo Giovio: Uno storico lombardo nella cultura artistica del Cinquecento*. Florence: Leo S. Olschki, 2008.

Aikema 2018
Bernard Aikema, ed., in collaboration with Andrew John Martin. *Dürer e il Rinascimento tra Germania e Italia*. Exh. cat., Palazzo Reale, Milan. Milan: 24 Ore Cultura, 2018.

Aikema and Brown 1999
Bernard Aikema and Beverly Louise Brown, eds. *Renaissance Venice and the North: Crosscurrents in the Time of Bellini, Dürer and Titian*. Exh. cat., Palazzo Grassi, Venice. Milan: Bompiani, 1999.

Ainsworth 2017
Maryan W. Ainsworth. "Hugo van der Goes and Portraiture." In *The Primacy of the Image in Northern European Art, 1400–1700: Essays in Honor of Larry Silver*, edited by Debra Taylor Cashion, Henry Luttikhuizen, and Ashley D. West, pp. 27–38. Brill's Studies in Intellectual History 271; Brill's Studies on Art, Art History, and Intellectual History 22. Leiden: Brill, 2017.

Ainsworth and Christiansen 1998
Maryan W. Ainsworth and Keith Christiansen, eds. *From Van Eyck to Bruegel: Early Netherlandish Painting in The Metropolitan Museum of Art*. Exh. cat. New York: The Metropolitan Museum of Art. 1998.

Ainsworth and Waterman 2013
Maryan W. Ainsworth and Joshua P. Waterman. *German Paintings in The Metropolitan Museum of Art, 1350–1600*. New York: The Metropolitan Museum of Art, 2013.

Ajmar-Wollheim and Dennis 2006
Marta Ajmar-Wollheim and Flora Dennis, eds. *At Home in Renaissance Italy*. Exh. cat. London: Victoria and Albert Museum, 2006.

Alberti 1969
Leon Battista Alberti. *The Family in Renaissance Florence*. Translated by Renée Neu Watkins. Columbia: University of South Carolina Press, 1969.

Albertus Magnus 1967
Albertus Magnus. *Book of Minerals of Albertus Magnus*. Translated by Dorothy Wyckoff. Oxford: Clarendon Press, 1967.

Alexander 1994
Jonathan J. G. Alexander, ed. *The Painted Page: Italian Renaissance Book Illumination, 1450–1550*. Exh. cat., Royal Academy of Arts, London; Pierpont Morgan Library, New York. Munich: Prestel, 1994.

Alford 2012
Kenneth D. Alford. *Herman Göring and the Nazi Art Collection: The Looting of Europe's Art Treasures and Their Dispersal after World War II*. Jefferson, N.C.: McFarland & Co., 2012.

Anderson 1979
Jaynie Anderson. "A Further Inventory of Gabriel Vendramin's Collection." *Burlington Magazine* 121, no. 919 (October 1979), pp. 639–48.

Anderson 1997
Jaynie Anderson. *Giorgione: The Painter of "Poetic Brevity"; including Catalogue Raisonné*. Paris: Flammarion, 1997.

Angelini 2012
Alessandro Angelini. "Jacometto Veneziano e gli umanisti: Proposta per il 'Ritratto di Luca Pacioli e di Guidobaldo da Montefeltro' del Museo di Capodimonte." *Prospettiva*, no. 147/148 (July–October 2012), pp. 126–49.

Armand 1883–87
Alfred Armand. *Les médailleurs italiens des quinzième et seizième siècles*. 3 vols. 2nd ed., rev. Paris: E. Plon et Cie., 1883–87.

Armstrong 1977
C. A. J. Armstrong. "The Golden Age of Burgundy: Dukes that Outdid Kings." In *The Courts of Europe: Politics, Patronage and Royalty 1400–1800*, edited by A. G. Dickens, pp. 55–75. London: Thames & Hudson, 1977.

Artemieva 2001
Irina Artemieva, ed. *Cinquecento veneto: Dipinti dall'Ermitage*. Exh. cat., Museo Civico, Bassano del Grappa; Museu Nacional d'Art, Barcelona. Milan: Skira, 2001.

Ashdown-Hill 2007
John Ashdown-Hill. "'Al ful of fresshe floures whyte and reede': The Jewellery of Margaret of York and Its Meaning." *The Ricardian* 17 (2007), pp. 56–72.

Attwood 2003
Philip Attwood. *Italian Medals c. 1530–160, in British Public Collections*. 2 vols. London: British Museum Press, 2003.

Baert 2018
Barbara Baert. "The Sleeping Nymph Revisited: Ekphrasis, *Genius Loci* and Silence." In *The Figure of the Nymph in Early Modern Culture*, edited by Karl A. E. Enenkel and Anita Traninger, pp. 149–76. Leiden: Brill, 2018.

Baldwin 1986
Robert Baldwin. "A Window from the Song of Songs in Conjugal Portraits by Fra Filippo Lippi and Bartholomäus Zeitblom." *Source: Notes in the History of Art* 5, no. 2 (Winter 1986), pp. 7–14.

Bambach 1999
Carmen C. Bambach. "Titian . . . Two Satyrs in a Landscape." In "Recent Acquisitions: A Selection 1998–1999." *The Metropolitan Museum of Art Bulletin* 57, no. 2 (Autumn 1999), p. 26.

Bambach 2019
Carmen C. Bambach. *Leonardo da Vinci Rediscovered*. 4 vols. New Haven: Yale University Press, 2019.

Bambach 2022
Carmen C. Bambach. "Leonardo and His Circle: *Disegno* and the Education of Painters." In *Leonardo and His Circle: Painting Technique in the Light of Restorations and Scientific Studies (Rome, 29–30 November 2019)*, edited by Antonio Sgamelloti and Brunetto Giovanni Brunetti, pp. 17–78. Atti dei Convegni Lincei 347. Rome: Bardi Edizioni, 2022.

Bambach forthcoming
Carmen C. Bambach. "The Berlin Portrait of a Young Woman and the Politics of Her Marriage." *Artibus et Historiae* 45, no. 89 (forthcoming).

Bange 1928
Ernst Friedrich Bange. *Die Kleinplastik der deutschen Renaissance in Holz und Stein*. Florence: Pantheon Casa Editrice; Munich: Kurt Wolff Verlag, 1928.

Barbe and Crépin-Leblond 2011
Françoise Barbe and Thierry Crépin-Leblond, eds. *Majolique: La faïence italienne au temps des humanistes, 1480–1530*. Exh. cat., Musée National de la Renaissance, Château d'Ecouen. Paris: Réunion des Musées Nationaux–Grand Palais, 2011.

Barocchi 1971–77
Paola Barocchi, ed. *Scritti d'arte del Cinquecento*. 3 vols. Milan: Riccardo Ricciardi, 1971–77.

Baroni Vannucci 1997
Alessandra Baroni Vannucci. *Jan Van Der Straet detto Giovanni Stradano: Flandrus pictor et inventor*. Milan: Jandi Sapi, 1997.

Barry 2020
Fabio Barry. *Painting in Stone: Architecture and the Poetics of Marble from Antiquity to the Enlightenment*. New Haven: Yale University Press, 2020. https://aaeportal-com.metlibrary.idm.oclc.org/?id=-22080.

Bartrum 1995
Giulia Bartrum. *German Renaissance Prints, 1490–1550*. London: British Museum Press, 1995.

Bartůněk 2019
Jiří Bartůněk "Imagines Maiorum and Posthumous Masks of Ancient Civilizations." In *Colloquia Classica*, edited by Martin Trefný, pp. 32–50. Roudnice nad Laben, Czech Republic: Podřipské Muzeum, 2019.

Bath 1992
Michael Bath. *The Image of the Stag: Iconographic Themes in Western Art*. Baden-Baden: Verlag Valentin Koerner, 1992.

Battilotti and Franco 1978
Donata Battilotti and Maria Teresa Franco. "Regesti di committenti e dei primi collezionisti di Giorgione." *Antichità Viva* 17, nos. 4–5 (1978), pp. 58–86.

Baxandall 1963
Michael Baxandall. "A Dialogue on Art from the Court of Leonello d'Este: Angelo Decembrio's *De Politia Litteraria* Pars LXVIII." *Journal of the Warburg and Courtauld Institutes* 26, no. 3/4 (1963), pp. 304–26.

Bayer 2008
Andrea Bayer, ed. *Art and Love in Renaissance Italy*. Exh. cat., The Metropolitan Museum of Art, New York; Kimbell Art Museum, Fort Worth. New York: The Metropolitan Museum of Art; New Haven: Yale University Press, 2008.

Beard 2021
Mary Beard. *The Twelve Caesars: Images of Power from the Ancient World to the Modern*. Princeton, N.J.: Princeton University Press, 2021.

Belting 2001
Hans Belting. *An Anthropology of Images: Picture, Medium, Body*. Translated by Thomas Dunlap. Princeton, N.J.: Princeton University Press, 2001.

Belting 2017
Hans Belting. *Face and Mask: A Double History*. Translated by Thomas S. Hansen and Abby J. Hansen. Princeton, N.J.: Princeton University Press, 2017.

Beltramini and Gasparotto 2016
Guido Beltramini and Davide Gasparotto, eds. *Aldo Manuzio: Renaissance in Venice*. Exh. cat., Gallerie dell'Accademia, Venice. Venice: Marsilio, 2016.

Beltramini et al. 2013
Guido Beltramini, Davide Gasparotto, and Adolfo Tura, eds. *Pietro Bembo e l'invenzione del Rinascimento*. Exh. cat., Palazzo del Monte di Pietà, Padua. Venice: Marsilio, 2013.

Bembo 1966
Pietro Bembo. *Prose della volgar lingua: Gli Asolani, Rime*. Edited by Carlo Dionisotti. Turin: TEA Editori Associati, 1966.

Benedicenti 1992
Giovanbattista Benedicenti. "Per Giovanni Bellini: Una nuova lettura del ritratto di Birmingham." *Paragone* 43, no. 513 (November 1992), pp. 3–9.

Bergström 1955
Ingvar Bergström. "Disguised Symbolism in 'Madonna' Pictures and Still Life: I." *Burlington Magazine* 97, no. 631 (October 1955), pp. 303–8.

Berliner and Egger 1981
Rudolf Berliner and Gerhart Egger. *Ornamentale Vorlagenblätter des 15. bis 19. Jahrhunderts*. 3 vols. 2nd ed. Munich: Klinkhardt & Biermann, 1981.

Bernhard 1978
Marianne Bernhard, ed. *Hans Baldung Grien: Handzeichnungen, Druckgraphik.* Munich: Südwest Verlag, 1978.

Bernheimer 1952
Richard Bernheimer. *Wild Men in the Middle Ages: A Study in Art, Sentiment, and Demonology*. Cambridge, Mass.: Harvard University Press, 1952.

Bertelli 2002
Sergio Bertelli. *Il re, la Vergine, la sposa: Eros, maternità e potere nella cultura figurativa europea*. Rome: Donzelli Editore, 2002.

Bertelli 2007
Sergio Bertelli. "Giulia Farnese come Madonna, in un dipinto di Pinturicchio per Alessandro VI Borgia: Iconografia 'nuziale' nella pittura del XVI secolo." *Rivista di Engramma* 59 (November 2007), pp. 327–37.

Billinge et al. 1997
Rachel Billinge, Lorne Campbell, Jill Dunkerton, Susan Foister, Jo Kirby, Jennie Pilc, Ashok Roy, Marika Spring, and Raymond White. "The Methods and Materials of Northern European Painting, 1400–1550." *National Gallery Technical Bulletin* 18 (1997), pp. 6–55.

Bischoff and Gagel 1977
Ulrich Bischoff and Hanna Gagel. *Der Mensch um 1500: Werke aus Kirchen und Kunstkammern*. Exh. cat., Skulpturengalerie der Staatlichen Museen Preussischer Kulturbesitz, Berlin. Berlin: Felgentreff & Goebel, 1977.

Blümle and Wismer 2016
Claudia Blümle and Beat Wismer, eds. *Hinter dem Vorhang: Verhüllung und Enthüllung seit der Renaissance—von Tizian bis Christo*. Exh. cat. Munich: Hirmer; Düsseldorf: Museum Kunstpalast, 2016.

Bock 2001
Hartmut Bock. *Die Chronik Eisenberger: Edition und Kommentar; Bebilderte Geschichte einer Beamtenfamilie der deutschen Renaissance—Aufstieg in den Wetterauer Niederadel und das Frankfurter Patriziat*. Schriften des Historischen Museums Frankfurt am Main 22. Frankfurt am Main: Historisches Museum, 2001.

Bohn 2021
Babette Bohn. *Women Artists, Their Patrons, and Their Publics in Early Modern Bologna.* University Park: Pennsylvania State University Press, 2021.

Bol 2004
Peter C. Bol, ed. *Die Geschichte der antiken Bildhauerkunst*. Vol. 2, *Klassische Plastik*. Mainz: Philipp von Zabern, 2004.

Bolzoni 2008
Lina Bolzoni. *Poesia e ritratto nel Rinascimento*. Edited by Federica Pich. Rome: Laterza, 2008.

Bolzoni 2010
Lina Bolzoni. *Il cuore di cristallo: Ragionamenti d'amore, poesia e ritratto nel Rinascimento*. Turin: Giulio Einaudi, 2010.

Borchert 2005
Till-Holger Borchert, with contributions by Maryan W. Ainsworth, Lorne Campbell, and Paula Nuttall. *Memling's Portraits*. Exh. cat., Museo Thyssen-Bornemisza, Madrid; Groeningemuseum, Bruges; Frick Collection, New York. London: Thames & Hudson, 2005.

Borchert 2010
Till-Holger Borchert. "Cranach der Ältere in den Niederlanden." In *Die Welt des Lucas Cranach: Ein Künstler im Zeitalter von Dürer, Tizian und Metsys*, edited by Guido Messling, pp. 26–29. Exh. cat., Palais des Beaux-Arts/Paleis voor Schone Kunsten, Brussels; Musée du Luxembourg, Paris. Tielt, Belgium: Lannoo, 2010.

Borchert 2014
Till-Holger Borchert, ed. *Memling: Rinascimento fiammingo*. Exh. cat., Scuderie del Quirinale, Rome. Milan: Skira, 2014.

Borchert and Jonckheere 2015
Till-Holger Borchert and Koenraad Jonckheere, eds. *Portraits de la Renaissance aux Pays-Bas*. Exh. cat., Bozar, Palais des Beaux-Arts, Brussels. Lichtervelde, Belgium: Hannibal; Brussels: Bozar Books, 2015.

Borgers 2022
Kathrin Borgers. "Recto and Verso: The Pictorial Fronts and the Marbled Reverses of Two Flemish Panel Paintings." *Arts* 11, no. 1 (2022). https://doi.org/10.3390/arts11010010.

Boskovits and Brown 2003
Miklós Boskovits and David Alan Brown. *Italian Paintings of the Fifteenth Century*. Washington, D.C.: National Gallery of Art, 2003.

Bott 1985
Gerhard Bott, ed. *Wenzel Jamnitzer und die Nürnberger Goldschmiedekunst 1500–1700: Goldschmiedearbeiten: Entwürfe, Modelle, Medaillen, Ornamentstiche, Schmuck, Porträts*. Exh. cat., Germanisches Nationalmuseum, Nuremberg. Munich: Klinkhardt & Biermann, 1985.

Bowman 2005
Alan K. Bowman. "Diocletian and the First Tetrarchy, A.D. 284–305." In *The Cambridge Ancient History*. 2nd ed. Vol. 12, *The Crisis of Empire, A.D. 193–337*, edited by Alan K. Bowman, Peter Garnsey, and Averil Cameron, pp. 67–89. Cambridge: Cambridge University Press, 2005.

Brady 2023
Aoife Brady. *Lavinia Fontana: Trailblazer, Rulebreaker.* Exh. cat. Dublin: National Gallery of Ireland, 2023.

Branciforte 1995
Suzanne Branciforte. "Antonio Di Meglio, Dante, and Cosimo De' Medici." *Italian Studies* 50, no. 1 (1995), pp. 9–23.

Bresc-Bautier et al. 2010
Geneviève Bresc-Bautier, Thierry Crépin-Leblond, and Elisabeth Taburet-Delahaye, eds. *France 1500: Entre Moyen Âge et Renaissance*. Exh. cat., Galeries Nationales du Grand Palais, Paris. Paris: Editions de la Réunion des Musées Nationaux, 2010.

Brinkmann 2007
Bodo Brinkmann, ed. *Cranach*. Exh. cat., Städel Museum, Frankfurt am Main; Royal Academy of Arts, London. London: Royal Academy of Arts, 2007.

Brinkmann and Kemperdick 2002
Bodo Brinkmann and Stephan Kemperdick. *Deutsche Gemälde im Städel, 1300–1500*. Kataloge der Gemälde im Städelschen Kunstinstitut Frankfurt am Main 4. Mainz: Philipp von Zabern, 2002.

Brinkmann and Kemperdick 2005
Bodo Brinkmann and Stephan Kemperdick. *Deutsche Gemälde im Städel, 1500–1550*. Kataloge der Gemälde im Städelschen Kunstinstitut Frankfurt am Main 5. Mainz: Philipp von Zabern, 2005.

Brooke 2022
Irene Brooke. "A Poetic Prognostication by Giulio Campagnola and Its Relationship to His *Astrologer*." *Print Quarterly* 39, no. 3 (September 2022), pp. 251–63.

B. Brown 2019
Beverly Louise Brown. "Sugar and Spice and All Things Nice? Titian's Portrait of Clarice Strozzi." *Artibus et Historiae* 40, no. 80 (2019), pp. 177–213.

D. Brown 2001
David Alan Brown. *Virtue and Beauty: Leonardo's* Ginevra de' Benci *and Renaissance Portraits of Women*. Exh. cat. Washington, D.C.: National Gallery of Art, 2001.

P. Brown 1996
Patricia Fortini Brown. *Venice and Antiquity: The Venetian Sense of the Past*. New Haven: Yale University Press, 1996.

Brown and Ferino-Pagden 2006
David Alan Brown and Sylvia Ferino-Pagden, with Jaynie Anderson, Deborah Howard, Peter Humfrey, and Mauro Lucco. *Bellini, Giorgione, Titian and the Renaissance of Venetian Painting*. Exh. cat. Washington, D.C.: National Gallery of Art; Vienna: Kunsthistorisches Museum, in association with Yale University Press, New Haven, 2006.

Brown and Oberhuber 1978
David Alan Brown and Konrad Oberhuber. "*Monna Vanna* and *Fornarina*: Leonardo and Raphael in Rome." In *Essays Presented to Myron P. Gilmore*, edited by Sergio Bertelli and Gloria Ramakus, vol. 2, pp. 25–86. Florence: La Nuova Italia, 1978.

Brown et al. 1997
David Alan Brown, Peter Humfrey, and Mauro Lucco. *Lorenzo Lotto: Rediscovered Master of the Renaissance*. Exh. cat., National Gallery of Art, Washington, D.C.; Accademia Carrara di Belle Arti, Bergamo; Galeries Nationales du Grand Palais, Paris. Washington, D.C.: National Gallery of Art; New Haven: Yale University Press, 1997.

Brückle 2013
Wolfgang Brückle. "Political Allegory at the Court of Charles the Bold: Pageantry, an Enigmatic Portrait, and the Limits of Interpretation." In *Staging the Court of Burgundy: Proceedings of the Conference "The Splendour of Burgundy,"* edited by Wim Blockmans, Till-Holger Borchert, Nele Gabriëls, Johan Oosterman, and Anne van Oosterwijk, pp. 121–32. London: Harvey Miller Publishers, 2013.

Brun 1930
Robert Brun. *Le livre illustré en France au XVIe siècle*. Paris: Librairie Félix Alcan, 1930.

Brunet 1860–65
Jacques-Charles Brunet. *Manuel du libraire et l'amateur de livres*. . . . 6 vols. Paris: Firmin Didot frères, fils et Cie., 1860–65.

Bruni 2022
Stefano Bruni. "Resti di relitti antichi nel Tesoro di Lorenzo il Magnifico." In *Taxidia: Scritti per Fede Berti*, edited by Francesca Curti and Alessandra Parrini, pp. 49–56. Pisa: Edizioni ETS, 2022.
Buchner 1953
Ernst Buchner. *Das deutsche Bildnis der Spätgotik und der frühen Dürerzeit*. Berlin: Deutscher Verein für Kunstwissenschaft, 1953.
Buck 2008
Stephanie Buck. "Beauty and Virtue for Francis I: Iohannes Ambrosius Nucetus and the Early Portrait Miniature." *Journal of the Warburg and Courtauld Institutes* 71 (2008), pp. 191–210.
Buck et al. 2003
Stephanie Buck, Jochen Sander, Ariane van Suchtelen, Quentin Buvelot, and Peter van der Ploeg. *Hans Holbein the Younger, 1497/98–1543: Portraitist of the Renaissance.* Exh. cat. Zwolle, The Netherlands: Waanders; The Hague: Royal Cabinet of Paintings Mauritshuis, 2003.
Budde and Krischel 2001
Rainer Budde and Roland Krischel, eds. *Genie ohne Namen: Der Meister des Bartholomäus-Altars*. Exh. cat., Wallraf-Richartz-Museum, Fondation Corboud, Cologne. Cologne: DuMont, 2001.
Burnett 1987
Andrew Burnett. *Coinage in the Roman World*. London: Seaby, 1987.
Butterfield 1997
Andrew Butterfield. *The Sculptures of Andrea del Verrocchio*. New Haven: Yale University Press, 1997.
Butts 1985
Barbara Rosalyn Butts. "'Dürerschüler' Hans Süss von Kulmbach." PhD diss., Harvard University, Cambridge, Mass., 1985.
Butts 2006
Barbara Butts. "The Drawings of Hans Süss von Kulmbach." *Master Drawings* 44, no. 2 (Summer 2006), pp. 127–212.
C. Campbell 2009
Caroline Campbell, with contributions by Graeme Barraclough and Tilly Schmidt. *Love and Marriage in Renaissance Florence: The Courtauld Wedding Chests*. London: Courtauld Gallery, in association with Paul Holberton Publishing, 2009.
L. Campbell 1981
Lorne Campbell. "Notes on Netherlandish Pictures in the Veneto in the Fifteenth and Sixteenth Centuries." *Burlington Magazine* 123, no. 941 (August 1981), pp. 467–73.
L. Campbell 1990a
Lorne Campbell. "Book Review: *Les primitifs flamands, I. Corpus de la peinture des anciens Pays-Bas méridionaux au quinzième siècle, 15, Les Musées de l'Institut de France: Musées Jacquemart-André et Marmottan à Paris, Musée Condé à Chantilly* by Micheline Comblen-Sonkes." *Burlington Magazine* 132, no. 1049 (August 1990), pp. 577–78.
L. Campbell 1990b
Lorne Campbell. *Renaissance Portraits: European Portrait-Painting in the 14th, 15th and 16th Centuries*. New Haven: Yale University Press, 1990.
L. Campbell 1995
Lorne Campbell. "Book Review: *Hans Memling, The Complete Works* by Dirk De Vos." *Burlington Magazine* 137, no. 1105 (April 1995), pp. 253–54.
L. Campbell 1996
Lorne Campbell. "Campin's Portraits." In *Robert Campin: New Directions in Scholarship*, edited by Susan Foister and Susie Nash, pp. 123–35. Turnhout, Belgium: Brepols, 1996.
L. Campbell 1998
Lorne Campbell. *The Fifteenth Century Netherlandish Paintings.* National Gallery Company. London: National Gallery Publications, 1998.
Campbell and Stock 2009
Lorne Campbell and Jan van der Stock. *Rogier van der Weyden, 1400–1464: Master of Passions.* Exh. cat., M Leuven, Belgium. Zwolle, The Netherlands: Waanders; Leuven: Davidsfonds, 2009.
Campbell et al. 2008
Lorne Campbell, Miguel Falomir, Jennifer Fletcher, and Luke Syson. *Renaissance Faces: Van Eyck to Titian*. Exh. cat., National Gallery, London. London: National Gallery Company, 2008.
Cantaro 1989
Maria Teresa Cantaro. *Lavinia Fontana, bolognese: "pittora singolare" 1552–1614*. Milan: Jandi Sapi Editore, 1989.
Carrabino 2019
Danielle Carrabino. "Lavinia Fontana: Renaissance Artist" (2019). https://scma.smith.edu/blog/lavinia-fontana-renaissance-artist.
Cartwright 1902
Julia Cartwright (Mrs. Ady, pseud.). *The Painters of Florence from the Thirteenth to the Sixteenth Century*. London: John Murray, 1902.
Cassidy 1992
Brendan Cassidy. "Orcagna's Tabernacle in Florence: Design and Function." *Zeitschrift für Kunstgeschichte* 55, no. 2 (1992), pp. 180–211.
Cecchi and Natali 1996
Alessandro Cecchi and Antonio Natali, eds. *L'officina della maniera: Varietà e fierezza nell'arte fiorentina del Cinquecento fra le due repubbliche (1494–1530)*. Exh. cat., Galleria degli Uffizi, Florence. Florence: Giunta Ragionale Toscana; Venice: Marsilio, 1996.
Cennino Cennini 2015
Cennino Cennini's Il libro dell'arte. Translated by Lara Broecke. London: Archetype Publications, 2015.
Chabot 2011
Isabelle Chabot. *La dette des familles: Femmes, lignage et patrimoine à Florence aux XIVe et XVe siècles*. Rome: Ecole Francaise de Rome, 2011.
Chabot et al. 2006
Isabelle Chabot, Jérôme Hayez, and Didier Lett, eds. *La famille, les femmes et le quotidien (XIVe–XVIIIe siècle): Textes offerts à Christiane Klapisch-Zuber*. Paris: Publications de la Sorbonne, 2006.
Chamberlain 1913
Arthur B. Chamberlain. *Hans Holbein the Younger*. 2 vols. London: George Allen & Co., 1913.
Christiansen 2019
Keith Christiansen. "Thoughts Regarding Two Lost Portrait Covers by Lorenzo Lotto." *Artibus et Historiae* 40, no. 80 (2019), pp. 160–68.
Christiansen and Weppelmann 2011
Keith Christiansen and Stefan Weppelmann, eds. *The Renaissance Portrait: From Donatello to Bellini*. Exh. cat., Bode-Museum, Berlin; The Metropolitan Museum of Art, New York. New York: The Metropolitan Museum of Art, 2011.
Ciatti and Natali 2008
Marco Ciatti and Antonio Natali, eds. *L'amore, l'arte e la grazia: Raffaello, la* Madonna del Cardellino *restaurata*. Exh. cat., Palazzo Medici Riccardi, Florence. Florence: Mandragora, 2008.
Clarke 2015
Paula C. Clarke. "The Business of Prostitution in Early Renaissance Venice." *Renaissance Quarterly* 68, no. 2 (Summer 2015), pp. 419–64.
Cleland and Eaker 2022
Elizabeth Cleland and Adam Eaker. *The Tudors: Art and Majesty in Renaissance England*. Exh. cat., The Metropolitan Museum of Art. New York; Cleveland Museum of Art; Legion of Honor, San Francisco. New York: The Metropolitan Museum of Art, 2022.
Cleland and Wieseman 2018
Elizabeth Cleland and Marjorie E. Wieseman. *Renaissance Splendor: Catherine de' Medici's Valois Tapestries*. Exh. cat. Cleveland: Cleveland Museum of Art; New Haven: Yale University Press, 2018.
Cohen 2008
Simona Cohen. *Animals as Disguised Symbols in Renaissance Art*. Brill's Studies in Intellectual History 169; Brill's Studies on Art, Art History, and Intellectual History 2. Leiden: Brill, 2008.
Coins of the Roman Empire in the British Museum 1
Coins of the Roman Empire in the British Museum. Vol. 1, *Augustus to Vitellius*, by Harold Mattingly. London: Printed by order of the Trustees of the British Museum, 1923.
Cole 2000
Merrill Cole. "Admiration's Double Labor: Phaedrus in the Mirror." *American Imago* 57, no. 2 (Summer 2000), pp. 121–40.
Colin 1999
Susi Colin. "The Wild Man and the Indian in Early 16th Century Book Illustration." In *Indians and Europe: An Interdisciplinary Collection of Essays*, edited by Christian F. Feest, pp. 5–35. Lincoln: University of Nebraska Press, 1999.
***Collection du Baron Albert Oppenheim* 1904**
Collection du Baron Albert Oppenheim: Tableaux et objets d'art. Paris: Librairie Centrale des Beaux Arts, 1904.
Comblen-Sonkes 1988
Micheline Comblen-Sonkes, with Ignace Vandevivere. *Les Musées de l'Institut de France: Musées Jacquemart-André et Marmottan à Paris, Musée Condé à Chantilly.* Les Primitifs flamands 1; Corpus de la peinture des anciens Pays-Bas Méridionaux au quinzième siècle 15. Brussels: Centre National de Recherches "Primitifs flamands" et A.C.L., Ministère de l'Education Nationale, 1988.
Cortesi Bosco 1987
Francesca Cortesi Bosco. *Il coro intarsiato di Lotto e Capoferri per Santa Maria Maggiore in Bergamo*. 2 vols. Cinisello Balsamo, Milan: Edizioni Amilcare Pizzi, 1987.
Cortesi Bosco 1992
Francesca Cortesi Bosco "*Divina vigilia*: Il sonno vigilante dell'Anima nel dipinto di Lorenzo Lotto K 291 della National Gallery di Washington." *Notizie da Palazzo Albani* 21, no. 1 (1992), pp. 25–49.
Covi 1986
Dario A. Covi. *The Inscription in Fifteenth Century Florentine Painting*. New York: Garland Publishing, 1986.
Cranston 2000
Jodi Cranston. *The Poetics of Portraiture in the Italian Renaissance*. Cambridge: Cambridge University Press, 2000.
Crollalanza 1886–90
Giovanni Battista di Crollalanza. *Dizionario storico-blasonico delle famiglie nobili e notabili italiane estinte e fioranti.* 3 vols. Pisa: Presso la Direzione de Giornale Araldico, 1886–90.

Cropper 1997
Elizabeth Cropper. *Pontormo: Portrait of a Halberdier*. Los Angeles: Getty Museum, 1997.
Crossley 1993
Paul Crossley. "The Return to the Forest: Natural Architecture and the German Past in the Age of Dürer." In *Künstlerischer Austausch / Artistic Exchange: Akten des XXVIII. Internationalen Kongresses für Kunstgeschichte, Berlin, 15.–20. Juli 1992*, edited by Thomas W. Gaehtgens, vol. 2, pp. 71–80. Berlin: Akademie Verlag, 1993.
Cunnally 1999
John Cunnally. *Images of the Illustrious: The Numismatic Presence in the Renaissance*. Princeton, N.J.: Princeton University Press, 1999.
Dal Pozzolo 1993
Enrico Maria Dal Pozzolo. "Il lauro di Laura e delle 'maritate veneziane.'" *Mitteilungen des Kunsthistorischen Institutes in Florenz* 37, no. 2/3 (1993), pp. 257–92.
Dal Pozzolo 2021
Enrico Maria Dal Pozzolo. *Lorenzo Lotto: Catalogo generale dei dipinti*. Milan: Skira, 2021.
Dal Pozzolo and Falomir 2018
Enrico Maria Dal Pozzolo and Miguel Falomir, eds. *Lorenzo Lotto: Portraits*. Exh. cat., Museo Nacional del Prado; National Gallery, London. Madrid: Museo Nacional del Prado, 2018.
Daly 1985
Peter M. Daly, ed., with Virginia W. Callahan, assisted by Simon Cuttler. *Andrea Alciatus*. Vol. 1, *The Latin Emblems: Indexes and Lists*. Vol. 2, *Emblems in Translation*. Index Emblematicus. Toronto: University of Toronto Press, 1985.
Dami 1921
Luigi Dami. "Cornici da specchio del cinquecento." *Dedalo: Rassegna d'arte* 1, no. 3 (1921), pp. 625–42.
Daninos 2008
Andrea Daninos. "Qualche novità sulla scultura in cerra fra Cinquecento e Settecento." *Prospettiva*, no. 132 (October 2008), pp. 88–99.
D'Ascia 1998
Luca D'Ascia. "Humanistic Culture and Literary Invention in Ferrara at the Time of the Dossi." In *Dosso's Fate: Painting and Court Culture in Renaissance Italy*, edited by Luisa Ciammitti, Steven F. Ostrow, and Salvatore Settis, pp. 309–32. Los Angeles: Getty Research Institute for the History of Art and the Humanities, 1998.
Davies 1968
Martin Davies. *Early Netherlandish School*. National Gallery Catalogues. 3rd ed., rev. London: National Gallery, 1968.
Davies 1972
Martin Davies. *Rogier van der Weyden: An Essay, with a Critical Catalogue of Paintings Assigned to Him and to Robert Campin*. London: Phaidon, 1972.
Davis 1966
Natalie Zemon Davis. "Publisher Guillaume Rouillé, Businessman and Humanist." In *Editing Sixteenth-Century Texts: Papers Given at the Editorial Conference, University of Toronto, October 1965*, edited by Richard J. Schoeck, pp. 72–112. Toronto: University of Toronto Press, 1966.
De Grummond 1975
Nancy Thomson de Grummond. "VV and Related Inscriptions in Giorgione, Titian, and Dürer." *Art Bulletin* 57, no. 3 (September 1975), pp. 346–56.
De Hamel 2016
Christopher De Hamel. *Meetings with Remarkable Manuscripts*. London: Allen Lane, 2016.
De Lacy 1977
Phillip H. De Lacy. "The Four Stoic *Personae*." *Illinois Classical Studies* 2 (1977), pp. 163–72.
De la Mare and Nuvoloni 2009
A. C. de la Mare and Laura Nuvoloni. *Bartolomeo Sanvito: The Life and Work of a Renaissance Scribe*. Edited by Anthony Hobson and Christopher De Hamel. Handwriting of the Italian Humanists 2. Paris: Association Internationale de Bibliophilie, 2009.
Del Bufalo 2012
Dario Del Bufalo. *Porphyry: Red Imperial Porphyry: Power and Religion*. English ed. Turin: Umberto Allemandi & C., 2012.
Delieuvin and Frank 2019
Vincent Delieuvin and Louis Frank, eds. *Léonard de Vinci*. Exh. cat., Musée du Louvre, Paris. Paris: Louvre Éditions; Hazan, 2019.
DePrano 2008
Maria DePrano. "'No painting on earth would be more beautiful': An Analysis of Giovanna degli Albizzi's Portrait Inscription." *Renaissance Studies* 22, no. 5 (November 2008), pp. 617–41.
De Santis 2018
Francesco De Santis. "Astrologia, Storia e *Virtus* in Giorgione e Gliulio Campagnola." *Bollettino Telematico dell'Arte*, November 21, 2018. http://www.bta.it/txt/a0/08/bta00859.html.
De Vos 1994
Dirk De Vos. *Hans Memling: The Complete Works*. Ghent: Ludion Press, 1994.
De Vos 1999
Dirk De Vos. *Rogier van der Weyden: The Complete Works*. New York: Harry N. Abrams, 1999.
De Winter 1996
Patrick M. De Winter. "Froment, Nicolas." *The Dictionary of Art*, edited by Jane Turner, vol. 11, pp. 799–800. New York: Grove, 1996.
Diemer 1979
Claudia Diemer. "Georg Holdermann und Heinrich Kramer: Zu Nürnberger Wachsreliefs des frühen 17. Jahrhunderts." *Anzeiger des Germanischen Nationalmuseums* 1979, pp. 121–40.
van Dijk and Ubl 2021
Sara van Dijk and Matthias Ubl. *Remember Me: Renaissance Portraits*. Exh. cat. Amsterdam: Rijksmuseum, 2021.
Dillon Bussi 1995
Angela Dillon Bussi. "Due ritratti di Raffaele Zovenzoni: E alcune ipotesi sul Maestro degli Uffici di Montecassino, il Maestro delle Sette Virtù, Jacometto e Lauro Padovano." *Libri e documenti*, Archivio Storico Civico e Biblioteca Trivulziana 21, no. 1 (1995), pp. 24–42.
Drpić 2016
Ivan Drpić. *Epigram, Art, and Devotion in Later Byzantium*. Cambridge: Cambridge University Press, 2016.
Dülberg 1990
Angelica Dülberg. *Privatporträts: Geschichte und Ikonologie einer Gattung im 15. und 16. Jahrhundert*. Berlin: Gebrüder Mann Verlag, 1990.
Dunkerton and Spring 2013
Jill Dunkerton and Marika Spring, with contributions from Rachel Billinge, Kamilla Kalinina, Rachel Morrison, Gabriella Macaro, David Peggie, and Ashok Roy. "Cat. 13: *The Triumph of Love*." In "Titian's Painting Technique before 1540." *National Gallery Technical Bulletin* 34 (2013), pp. 100–105.
Dunkerton et al. 1991
Jill Dunkerton, Susan Foister, Dillian Gordon, and Nicholas Penny. *Giotto to Dürer: Early Renaissance Painting in the National Gallery*. New Haven: Yale University Press, in association with National Gallery Publications, London, 1991.
Dunlop 2015
Anne Dunlop. "On the Origins of European Painting Materials, Real and Imagined." In *The Matter of Art: Materials, Practices, Cultural Logics, c. 1250–1750*, edited by Christy Anderson, Anne Dunlop, and Pamela H. Smith, pp. 68–96. Manchester: Manchester University Press, 2015.
Eberlein 1982
Johann Konrad Eberlein. *Apparitio regis—revelatio veritatis: Studien zur Darstellung des Vorhangs in der bildenden Kunst von der Spätantike bis zum Ende des Mittelalters*. Wiesbaden: Ludwig Reichert Verlag, 1982.
Eclercy 2016
Bastian Eclercy, ed. *Maniera: Pontormo, Bronzino and Medici Florence*. Exh.cat., Städel Museum, Frankfurt am Main. Munich: Prestel, 2016.
Eclercy and Aurenhammer 2019
Bastian Eclercy and Hans Aurenhammer, eds. *Titian and the Renaissance in Venice*. Exh. cat., Städel Museum, Frankfurt am Main. Munich: Prestel, 2019.
Edelstein and Gasparotto 2018
Bruce Edelstein and Davide Gasparotto, eds. *Miraculous Encounters: Pontormo from Drawing to Painting*. Exh. cat., Galerie degli Uffizi, Florence; Morgan Library and Museum, New York; J. Paul Getty Museum, Los Angeles. Florence: Giunti; Los Angeles: J. Paul Getty Museum, 2018.
Eichberger 1996
Dagmar Eichberger. "Margaret of Austria's Portrait Collection: Female Patronage in the Light of Dynastic Ambitions and Artistic Quality." *Renaissance Studies* 10, no. 2 (June 1996), pp. 259–79.
Eiland 2019
Murray Eiland. "Roman Gold Coins: The Art of Spin." *Antiquus* 1, no. 1 (January 2019), pp. 39–41.
Eisler 1989
Colin Eisler. *Early Netherlandish Painting: The Thyssen-Bornemisza Collection*. London: Sotheby's Publications, 1989.
Elsner 2015
Jaś Elsner. "Green Curtains and Picture Covers: Towards an Archaeology of the Pictorial Closet." In *Inter-disciplinary Encounters: Hidden and Visible Explorations of the Work of Adrian Rifkin*, edited by Dana Arnold, pp. 219–58. London: I. B. Tauris, 2015.
Emison 1997
Patricia Emison. *Low and High Style in Italian Renaissance Art*. New York: Garland Publishing, 1997.
Enenkel 2019
Karl A. E. Enenkel. *The Invention of the Emblem Book and the Transmission of Knowledge, ca. 1510–1610*. Brill's Studies in Intellectual History 295; Brill's Studies on Art, Art History, and Intellectual History 36. Leiden: Brill, 2019.
Enke et al. 2015
Roland Enke, Katja Schneider, and Jutta Strehle, eds. *Lucas Cranach der Jüngere: Entdeckung eines Meisters*. Exh. cat., Augusteum, Lutherstadt Wittenberg. Munich: Hirmer, 2015.
Eser 1996
Thomas Eser. *Hans Daucher: Augsburger Kleinplastik der Renaissance*. Munich: Deutscher Kunstverlag, 1996.
Evangelatou 2019
Maria Evangelatou. "Textile Mediation in Late Byzantine Visual Culture: Unveiling Layers of Meaning through the Fabrics of the Chora Monastery." In *Catalogue of*

the Textiles in the Dumbarton Oaks Byzantine Collection, edited by Gudrun Bühl and Elizabeth Dospěl Williams. Washington, D.C.: Dumbarton Oaks Research Library and Collection, 2019. https://www.doaks.org/resources/textiles/essays/evangelatou.

H. Evans 2004

Helen C. Evans. *Byzantium: Faith and Power (1271–1577)*. Exh. cat. New York: The Metropolitan Museum of Art; New Haven: Yale University Press, 2004.

M. Evans 2005

Mark Evans. "The Pedigree of the Portrait Miniature: European Sources of an English Genre." In *Hans Holbein und der Wandel in der Kunst des frühen 16. Jahrhunderts*, edited by Bodo Brinkmann and Wolfgang Schmid, pp. 229–52. Turnhout, Belgium: Brepols, 2005.

M. Evans 2020

Mark Evans, with Elania Pieragostini. *Renaissance Watercolours: From Dürer to Van Dyck*. Exh. cat., Victoria and Albert Museum, London. London: V&A Publishing, 2020.

Facchinetti and Galansino 2016

Simone Facchinetti and Arturo Galansino. *In the Age of Giorgione*. Exh. cat. London: Royal Academy of Arts, 2016.

Fahy 1976

Everett Fahy. *Some Followers of Domenico Ghirlandaio*. New York: Garland Publishing, 1976.

Falciani 2015

Carlo Falciani. *Florence: Portraits at the Medici Court*. Exh. cat., Musée Jacquemart-André, Paris. Brussels: Mercatorfonds, 2015.

Falomir 2008

Miguel Falomir, ed. *El retrato del Renacimiento*. Exh. cat., Museo Nacional del Prado, Madrid; National Gallery, London. Madrid: Museo Nacional del Prado, 2008.

Falque 2012

Ingrid Falque. "*Ung petit tableau fermant a deux fuilletz:* Notes sur l'évolution formelle et les voies de diffusion du diptych dévotionnel dans les anciens Pays-Bas (XVe–XVIe siècles)." *Le Moyen-Age: Review d'Histoire et de Philologie* 118, no. 1 (2012), pp. 89–127.

Fejfer 2008

Jane Fejfer. *Roman Portraits in Context*. Image and Context 2. Berlin: Walter de Gruyter, 2008.

Ferino-Pagden 2009

Sylvia Ferino-Pagden, ed. *Wir sind Maske*. Exh. cat., Museum für Völkerkunde, Vienna. Cinisello Balsamo, Milan: Silvana, 2009.

Ferino-Pagden et al. 2022

Sylvia Ferino-Pagden, Francesca Del Torre Scheuch, and Wencke Deiters, eds. *Tiziano e l'immagine della donna nel Cinquecento veneziano*. Exh. cat., Palazzo Reale, Milan. Milan: Skira, 2022.

Filedt Kok 1985

J. P. Filedt Kok. *The Master of the Amsterdam Cabinet, or the Housebook Master, ca. 1470–1500*. Exh. cat. Amsterdam: Rijksprentenkabinet/Rijksmuseum, in association with Princeton University Press, Princeton, N.J., 1985.

Finot 1895

Jules Finot. *Inventaire-sommaire des archives départementales antérieures à 1790: Nord; Archives civiles—série B*. Vol. 8. Lille: L. Danel, 1895.

Fiorio 2000

Maria Teresa Fiorio. *Giovanni Antonio Boltraffio: Un pittore milanese nel lume di Leonardo*. Milan: Jandi Sapi, 2000.

Fletcher 1973

Jennifer Fletcher. "Notes: Marcantonio Michiel's Collection." *Journal of the Warburg and Courtauld Institutes* 36 (1973), pp. 382–85.

Fletcher 1989

Jennifer Fletcher. "Bernardo Bembo and Leonardo's Portrait of Ginevra de' Benci." *Burlington Magazine* 131, no. 1041 (December 1989), pp. 811–16.

Flood 2016

Finbarr Barry Flood. "'God's Wonder': Marble as Medium and the Natural Image in Mosques and Modernism." *West 86th: A Journal of Decorative Arts, Design History, and Material Culture* 23, no. 2 (Fall–Winter 2016), pp. 168–219.

Florian 1706–34

Gebhard Florian. *Der Weit-berühmten Freyen Reichs- Wahl- und Handels-Stadt Franckfurt am Mayn Chronica*. Edited by Achilles August von Lersner. 2 vols. Frankfurt, 1706–34.

Flower 1996

Harriet I. Flower. *Ancestor Masks and Aristocratic Power in Roman Culture*. Oxford: Clarendon Press; New York: Oxford University Press, 1996.

Foister 2004

Susan Foister. *Holbein and England*. New Haven: Yale University Press, 2004.

Foister 2006

Susan Foister, with contributions by Tim Batchelor. *Holbein in England*. Exh. cat., Tate Britain, London. London: Tate, 2006.

Förschner 1978

Gisela Förschner. *Kleinkunst in Silber: Schraubtaler und Schraub-Medaillen; eine Ausstellung des Münzkabinetts*. Frankfurt am Main: Historisches Museum Frankfurt am Main, 1978.

Foucart-Walter 2007

Elisabeth Foucart-Walter, ed. *Catalogue des peintures italiennes du musée du Louvre: Catalogue sommaire*. Paris: Gallimard; Musée du Louvre, 2007.

Fowlkes-Childs and Seymour 2019

Blair Fowlkes-Childs and Michael Seymour. *The World Between Empires: Art and Identity in the Ancient Middle East*. Exh. cat. New York: The Metropolitan Museum of Art, 2019.

Freeman 1976

Margaret B. Freeman. *The Unicorn Tapestries*. New York: The Metropolitan Museum of Art; E. P. Dutton, Inc., 1976.

Fricke 2020

Beate Fricke. "At the Threshold of Painting: The Man of Sorrows by Albrecht Dürer." In *Renaissance Metapainting*, edited by Péter Bokody and Alexander Nagel, pp. 209–38. London: Harvery Miller Publishers, 2020.

Friedländer 1906

[Max J.] Friedländer. "Ausstellungen: Die Ausstellung altdeutscher Kunst im Burlington Fine Arts Club zu London—Sommer 1906." *Repertorium für Kunstwissenschaft* 29 (1906), pp. 582–89.

Friedländer 1916

Max J. Friedländer. "Gemäldegalerie: Ein neu erworbenes Porträt Cranachs." *Amtliche Berichte aus den Königlichen Kunstsammlungen* 37, no. 7 (April 1916), cols. 129–36.

Friedländer 1967–76

Max J. Friedländer. *Early Netherlandish Painting*. Comments and notes by Nicole Veronee-Verhaegen; translated by Heinz Norden. New York: Praeger Publishers, 1967–76.

Friedländer and Rosenberg 1978

Max J. Friedländer and Jakob Rosenberg. *The Paintings of Lucas Cranach*. Rev. ed. Translated by Heinz Norden and Ronald Taylor. Ithaca, N.Y.: Cornell University Press, 1978.

Friedman 1989

Mira Friedman. "The Falcon and the Hunt: Symbolic Love Imagery in Medieval and Renaissance Art." In *Poetics of Love in the Middle Ages: Texts and Contexts*, edited by Moshé Lazar and Norris J. Lacy, pp. 157–83. Fairfax, Va.: George Mason University Press, 1989.

Frontisi-Ducroux 1997

Françoise Frontisi-Ducroux. "L'œil et le miroir." In *Dans l'œil du miroir*, by Françoise Frontisi-Ducroux and Jean-Pierre Vernant, pp. 51–250. Paris: Odile Jacob, 1997.

Fry 1911

Roger Fry. "A Portrait of Leonello d'Este by Roger van der Weyden." *Burlington Magazine* 18, no. 94 (January 1911), pp. 200–202.

Fucci 2015

Robert Fucci. "Parrhasius and the Art of Display: The Illusionistic Curtain in Seventeenth-Century Dutch Painting." *Nederlands Kunsthistorisch Jaarboek / Netherlands Yearbook for History of Art* 65 (2015), pp. 144–75.

Fumerton 1986

Patricia Fumerton. "'Secret' Arts: Elizabethan Miniatures and Sonnets." *Representations*, no. 15 (Summer 1986), pp. 57–97.

Galis 1980

Diana Galis. "Concealed Wisdom: Renaissance Hieroglyphic and Lorenzo Lotto's Bergamo *Intarsie*." *Art Bulletin* 62, no. 3 (September 1980), pp. 363–75.

Gamboni 2002

Dario Gamboni. *Potential Images: Ambiguity and Indeterminacy in Modern Art*. London: Reaktion, 2002.

Gandolfi 2013

Giangiacomo Gandolfi. "Realismo e verosimiglianza nel contenuto astronomico di opere d'arte rinascimentali: Parte 1: Il caso del fregio giorgionesco di Casa Marta a Castelfranco." In ResearchGate, November 2013, pp. 155–69. https://www.researchgate.net/publication/315787379.

Ganz 1912

Paul Ganz, ed. *Hans Holbein d. J.: Des Meisters Gemälde in 252 Abbildungen*. Stuttgart: Deutsche Verlags-Anstalt, 1912.

Ganz 1921

Paul Ganz. "Les portraits-miniature de Hans Holbein le jeune: À propos du 'Holbein' de la collection Engel-Gros." *La Revue de l'Art Ancien et Moderne* 39, no. 225 (April 1921), pp. 263–69.

Ganz and Rimmele 2016

David Ganz and Marius Rimmele, eds. *Klappeffekte: Faltbare Bildträger in der Vormoderne*. Berlin: Reimer, 2016.

Gardner 1983

Julian Gardner. "Fronts and Backs: Setting and Structure." In *La pittura nel XIV e XV secolo: Il contributo dell'analisi tecnica alla storia dell'arte*, edited by H. W. van Os and J. R. J. van Asperen de Boer, pp. 297–322. Bologna: C.L.U.E.B., 1983.

Gelfand 2020

Laura D. Gelfand. "Mimesis and Rivalry: Representing Stone in 15th-Century Paintings." In *Paintings on Stone: Science and the Sacred 1530–1800*, edited by Judith W. Mann, pp. 43–49. Exh. cat. Saint Louis, Mo.: Saint Louis Art Museum; Munich: Hirmer, 2020.

Gemäldegalerie Berlin 1975

Katalog der ausgestellten Gemälde des 13.–18. Jahrhunderts. Berlin-Dahlem: Gemäldegalerie, Staatliche Museen zu Berlin–Preussischer Kulturbesitz, 1975.

***Gemäldegalerie Berlin* 1986**
The Complete Catalogue of the Gemäldegalerie, Berlin. New York: Harry N. Abrams, 1986.
***Gemäldegalerie Berlin* 1996–98**
Gemäldegalerie Berlin. 2 vols. Berlin: Staatliche Museen zu Berlin–Preussischer Kulturbesitz, Ars Nicolai, 1996–98.
Gentili 1985
Augusto Gentili, with the collaboration of Marco Lattanzi and Flavia Polignano. *I giardini di contemplazione: Lorenzo Lotto, 1503/1512*. Rome: Bulzoni, 1985.
Gerstel 2006
Sharon E. J. Gerstel. "An Alternative View of the Late Byzantine Sanctuary Screen." In *Thresholds of the Sacred: Architectural, Art Historical, Liturgical, and Theological Perspectives on Religious Screens, East and West*, edited by Sharon E. J. Gerstel, pp. 135–61. Washington, D.C.: Dumbarton Oaks Research Library and Collection, 2006.
Gianeselli 2017
Matteo Gianeselli. "The Reverse of Giuliano Bugiardini's 'Portrait of a Lady' in Paris." *Burlington Magazine* 159, no. 1370 (May 2017), pp. 360–63.
Giovanelli 1858
Benedetto Giovanelli. *Vita di Alessandro Vittoria: Scultore trantino*. Edited by Tommaso Gar. Trento: Monauni, 1858.
Giovio 1574
Paolo Giovio. *Dialogo dell'imprese militari et amorose*. Lyon: Guillaume Rouille, 1574.
Giovio 1999
Paolo Giovio. *Scritti d'arti: Lessico ed ecfrasi*. Edited by Sonia Maffei. Strumenti e testi 5. Pisa: Scuola Normale Superiore, 1999.
Glass 2015
Robert Glass. "Filarete and the Invention of the Renaissance Medal." *Medal* 66 (2015), pp. 26–37.
Glück 1910
Gustav Glück. "Ein neugefundenes Jugendwerk Lorenzo Lottos." *Kunstgeschichtliches Jahrbuch der k. k. Zentral-Kommission für die Erforschung und Erhaltung der Kunst- und Historischen Denkmale* 4 (1910), pp. 212–27.
Gordon 2015
Dillian Gordon. *The Wilton Diptych*. London: National Gallery Company, 2015.
***Gothic and Renaissance Art in Nuremberg* 1986**
Gothic and Renaissance Art in Nuremberg, 1300–1550. Exh. cat. New York: The Metropolitan Museum of Art; Nuremberg: Germanisches Nationalmuseum; Munich: Prestel, 1986.
Grässe 1859–69
Johann Georg Theodor Grässe. *Trésor de livres rares et précieux; ou Nouveau dictionnaire bibliographique....* 7 vols. Dresden: Rudolf Kuntze, 1859–69.
Gregori et al. 1992
Mina Gregori, Antonio Paolucci, and Cristina Acidini Luchinat, eds. *Maestri e botteghe: Pittura a Firenze alla fine del Quattrocento*. Exh. cat., Palazzo Strozzi, Florence. Cinisello Balsamo, Milan: Silvana, 1992.
Grisebach 2015
Lucius Grisebach. "The Integrity of the Work." In *Der doppelte Kirchner: Die zwei Seiten der Leinwand*, edited by Inge Herold, Ulrike Lorenz, and Thorsten Sadowsky, pp. 187–92. Exh. cat., Kunsthalle, Mannheim; Kirchner Museum, Davos. Mannheim: Kunsthalle Mannheim; Cologne: Wienand, 2015.
Guiffrey 1902
Jean Guiffrey. "Les accroissements des musées: Musée du Louvre." *Les Arts* 1, no. 12 (December 1902), pp. 13–19.
Gutbrod 1992
Werner Gutbrod. "Der Wilde Mann: Ein Münzbild aus dem Harz." *Geldgeschichtliche Nachrichten* 27, no. 147 (1992), pp. 7–10.
Haag and Sharp 2016
Sabine Haag and Jasper Sharp, eds. *Edmund de Waal: During the Night*. Exh. cat. Vienna: Kunsthistorisches Museum, 2016.
Haag et al. 2011
Sabine Haag, Christiane Lange, Christof Metzger, and Karl Schütz, eds. *Dürer, Cranach, Holbein: Die Entdeckung des Menschen; das deutsche Porträt um 1500*. Exh. cat. Vienna: Kunsthistorisches Museum; Munich: Kunsthalle der Hypo-Kulturstiftung; Hirmer, 2011.
Hablot 2004
Laurent Hablot. "The Use of Emblems by Philip the Bold and John the Fearless." In *Art from the Court of Burgundy 1364–1419*, pp. 81–83. Exh. cat. Dijon: Musée des Beaux-Arts de Dijon; Cleveland: Cleveland Museum of Art; Paris: Réunion des Musées Nationaux, 2004.
Hablot 2018
Laurent Hablot. "The Van Lymborch Brothers: Heraldic Painters? The Position of Heraldry and Emblematic Motifs in the Art of the Van Lymborch Brothers." *Maelwael Van Limborch Studies 1*, edited by André Stufkens and Clemens Verhoeven, pp. 112–29. Turnhout, Belgium: Brepols, 2018.
Hand 1993
John Oliver Hand, with the assistance of Sally E. Mansfield. *German Paintings of the Fifteenth through Seventeenth Centuries*. The Collections of the National Gallery of Art, Systematic Catalogue. Washington, D.C.: National Gallery of Art; Cambridge: Cambridge University Press, 1993.
Hand and Spronk 2006
John Oliver Hand and Ron Spronk, eds. *Essays in Context: Unfolding the Netherlandish Diptych*. Cambridge, Mass.: Harvard University Art Museums; New Haven: Yale University Press, 2006.
Hand et al. 2006
John Oliver Hand, Catherine A. Metzger, and Ron Spronk, eds. *Prayers and Portraits: Unfolding the Netherlandish Diptych.* Exh. cat. Washington, D.C.: National Gallery of Art; Antwerp: Koninklijk Museum voor Schone Kunsten; in association with Harvard University Art Museums, Cambridge, Mass., and Yale University Press, New Haven, 2006.
Held 1957
Julius S. Held. "Artis Pictoriae Amator: An Antwerp Art Patron and His Collection." *Gazette des Beaux-Arts* 50 (July 1957), pp. 53–84.
Henry 2021
Chriscinda Henry. *Playful Pictures: Art, Leisure, and Entertainment in the Venetian Renaissance Home*. University Park: Pennsylvania State University Press, 2021.
Henry and Joannides 2012
Tom Henry and Paul Joannides, eds. *Late Raphael*. Exh. cat., Museo Nacional del Prado, Madrid; Musée du Louvre, Paris. Madrid: Museo Nacional del Prado, 2012.
Hensick 2003
Teri Hensick. "The Fogg's Copy after a Lost Van Eyck: Conservation History, Recent Treatment, and Technical Examination of the *Woman at Her Toilet*." In *Recent Developments in the Technical Examination of Early Netherlandish Painting: Methodology, Limitations & Perspectives*, edited by Molly Faries and Ron Spronk, pp. 83–95. Cambridge, Mass.: Harvard University Art Museums; Turnhout, Belgium: Brepols, 2003.
Hentschel 2018
Judith Hentschel. "Porträtdeckel mit Wildem Mann: Schiebedeckel zu einem verschollenen Porträt des Lazarus I. Holzschuher aus der Werkstatt Jakob Elsners." *Kulturgut*, 2nd quarter (2018), pp. 3–7.
Herklotz 2000
Ingo Herklotz. "Zwei Selbstbildnisse von Nicolas Poussin und die Funktionen der Porträtmalerei." *Marburger Jahrbuch für Kunstwissenschaft* 27 (2000), pp. 243–68.
Herklotz 2001
Ingo Herklotz. "Zwei Selbstbildnisse von Nicolas Poussin und die Funktionen der Porträtmalerei." In *Meisterwerke der Malerei: Von Rogier van der Weyden bis Andy Warhol*, edited by Reinhard Brandt, pp. 88–114. Leipzig: Reclam, 2001.
Hess and Eser 2012
Daniel Hess and Thomas Eser, eds. *The Early Dürer*. Exh. cat., Germanisches Nationalmuseum Nürnberg. Nuremberg: Verlag des Germanischen Nationalmuseums, in association with Thames & Hudson, London, 2012.
Hess and Hirschfelder 2010
Daniel Hess and Dagmar Hirschfelder, eds. *Renaissance, Barock, Aufklärung: Kunst und Kultur vom 16. bis zum 18. Jahrhundert*. Nuremberg: Verlag des Germanischen Nationalmuseums, 2010.
Hess et al. 2019
Daniel Hess, Dagmar Hirschfelder, and Katja von Baum, eds. *Die Gemälde des Spätmittelalters im Germanischen Nationalmuseum: Franken 1*. 2 vols. Regensburg, Switzerland: Schnell & Steiner, 2019.
Heydenreich 2007
Gunnar Heydenreich. *Lucas Cranach, the Elder: Painting Materials, Techniques and Workshop Practice*. Amsterdam: Amsterdam University Press, 2007.
Hill 1905
George Francis Hill. *Pisanello*. London: Duckworth and Co.; New York: Charles Scribner's Sons, 1905.
Hill 1930
George Francis Hill. *A Corpus of Italian Medals of the Renaissance before Cellini*. Vol. 1, *Text*. Vol. 2, *Plates*. London: British Museum, Printed by order of the Trustees, 1930.
Hiller and Vey 1969
Irmgard Hiller and Horst Vey. *Katalog der deutschen und niederländischen Gemälde bis 1550 (mit Ausnahme der Kölner Malerei) im Wallraf-Richartz-Museum und im Kunstgewerbemuseum der Stadt Köln*. Kataloge des Wallraf-Richartz-Museums 5. Cologne: Wallraf-Richartz-Museum, 1969.
Hills 2010
Paul Hills. *The Renaissance Image Unveiled: From Madonna to Venus*. Watson Gordon Lecture 2009. Edinburgh: National Galleries of Scotland, in association with the University of Edinburgh and varie, 2010.
Hilsdale 2014
Cecily J. Hilsdale. *Byzantine Art and Diplomacy in an Age of Decline*. Cambridge: Cambridge University Press, 2014.
Hindman 2023
Sandra Hindman. "The Case for Simon Marmion—Once Again." In *Collectors, Commissioners, Curators: Studies*

in Medieval Art for Stephen N. Fliegel, edited by Elina Gertsman, pp. 213–32. Berlin: De Gruyter; Kalamazoo, Mich.: Medieval Institute Publications, 2023.

Hindman et al. 1997
Sandra Hindman, Mirella Levi D'Ancona, Pia Palladino, and Maria Francesca Saffiotti. *Illuminations*. Robert Lehman Collection 4. New York: The Metropolitan Museum of Art, in association with Princeton University Press, Princeton, N.J., 1997.

Hindriks 2022
Sandra Hindriks. "*Vanitas* and *Trompe-l'œil*: Pictorial Illusion as a Visual Strategy of the *Memento Mori*." *Netherlands Yearbook for History of Art / Nederlands Kunsthistorisch Jaarboek* 72, no. 1 (November 2022), pp. 58–93.

Hirschmann 1985
Gerhard Hirschmann. "Elisabeth Krauss (1569–1639)." In *Frauengestalten in Franken: Eine Sammlung von Lebensbildern*, edited by Inge Meidinger-Geise, pp. 72–74. Würzburg: Weidlich, 1985.

Hochmann et al. 2008
Michel Hochmann, Rosella Lauber, and Stefania Mason, eds. *Il collezionismo d'arte a Venezia.* Vol. 2, *Dalle origini al Cinquecento*. Venice: Fondazione di Venezia, Marsilio, 2008.

Hofbauer 2021
Michael Hofbauer. "Neue Überlegungen zu den Bildnissen des Herrn Six und seiner Gattin—Werke von Joos van Cleve?" In *Cranach: Parerga und Paralipomena; Neues zu Lucas Cranach und seinen Söhnen*, pp. 93–110. Heidelberg: arthistoricum.net, 2021. https://doi.org/10.11588/arthistoricum.722.c12361.

Holberton 2019
Paul Holberton. "'Honesta voluptas': The Renaissance Justification for Enjoyment of the Natural World." In *Green Worlds in Early Modern Italy: Art and the Verdant Earth*, edited by Karen Hope Goodchild, April Oettinger, and Leopoldine Prosperetti, pp. 69–86. Amsterdam: Amsterdam University Press, 2019.

Holberton 2021
Paul Holberton. *A History of Arcadia in Art and Literature: The Quest for Secular Human Happiness Revealed in the Pastoral: Fortunato in Terra*. 2 vols. London: Ad Ilissvm, 2021.

Holloway 1998
R. Ross Holloway. *Ancient Greek Coins: Catalogue of the Classical Collection, Museum of Art, Rhode Island School of Design*. Archaeologica Transatlantica 15. Providence, R.I.: Center for Old World Archaeology and Art, Brown University; Louvain-la-Neuve, Belgium: Département d'Archéologie et d'Histoire ce l'Art, College Erasme, 1998.

Hollstein 1962
F. W. H. Hollstein. *German Engravings, Etchings, and Woodcuts, ca. 1400–1700*. Vol. 7, *Albrecht and Hans Dürer.* Edited by K. G. Boon and R. W. Scheller. Amsterdam: Menno Hertzberger, 1962.

Holste 2004
Tanja Holste. "Die Porträtkunst Lucas Cranachs d. Ä." PhD diss., Christian-Albrechts-Universität, Kiel, Germany, 2004. https://nbn-resolving.org/urn:nbn:de:gbv:8-diss-13833.

Hoppe-Harnoncourt 2015
Alice Hoppe-Harnoncourt. "Lucas Cranach der Jüngere? Überlegungen zu zwei datierten Werken aus dem Kunsthistorischen Museum in Wien." In *Lucas Cranach der Jüngere und die Reformation der Bilder*, edited by Elke Anna Werner, Anne Eusterschulte, and Gunnar Heydenreich, pp. 154–67. Munich: Hirmer, 2015.

Humfrey 1993
Peter Humfrey. *The Altarpiece in Renaissance Venice*. New Haven: Yale University Press, 1993.

Humfrey 1997
Peter Humfrey. *Lorenzo Lotto*. New Haven: Yale University Press, 1997.

Humfrey et al. 2004
Peter Humfrey, Timothy Clifford, Aiden Weston-Lewis, and Michael Bury. *The Age of Titian: Venetian Renaissance Art from Scottish Collections*. Exh. cat., Royal Scottish Academy Building, Edinburgh. Edinburgh: National Galleries of Scotland, 2004.

Humfrey et al. 2022
Peter Humfrey, Susannah Rutherglen, Sara Menato, Deborah Howard, Catherine Whistler, Joanna Dunn, Linda Borean, Andrea Bellieni. *Vittore Carpaccio: Master Storyteller of Renaissance Venice*. Exh. cat., National Gallery of Art, Washington, D.C.; Fondazione Musei Civici, Palazzo Ducale, Venice. New Haven: Yale University Press, 2022.

Hüneke 1965
Ursula Hüneke. *Der Maler Martin Caldenbach: Ein Beitrag zur Frankfurter Kunst um 1500*. Bonn: Rheinische Friedrich-Wilhelms-Universität, 1965.

Husband 1980
Timothy Husband, with Gloria Gilmore-House. *The Wild Man: Medieval Myth and Symbolism*. Exh. cat. New York: The Metropolitan Museum of Art, 1980.

Italian Paintings
Italian Paintings of the Sixteenth Century. NGA Online Editions. https://www.nga.gov/research/online-editions/italian-paintings-of-the-sixteenth-century.html.

Jacobs 2012
Lynn F. Jacobs. *Opening Doors: The Early Netherlandish Triptych Reinterpreted*. University Park: Pennsylvania State University Press, 2012.

Jobst 2017
Christoph Jobst. "Symbols and Devices in Fifteenth-Century Italian and Netherlandish Art." In *Emblems and Impact: Von Zentrum und Peripherie der Emblematik; Selected Proceedings of the 10th International Conference of the Society for Emblem Studies*, edited by Ingrid Hoepel and Simon McKeown, vol. 2, pp. 233–44. Newcastle upon Tyne, U.K.: Cambridge Scholars Publishing, 2017.

Jolly 2011
Anna Jolly. *Wachsbildnisse eines Fürstenpaares von Antonio Abondio*. Monographien der Abegg-Stiftung 17. Riggisberg, Switzerland: Abegg-Stiftung, 2011.

Kammel and Lorenz 2008
Frank Matthias Kammel and Anke Lorenz. "Faszination der Präsenz: Die Wachsbüste des Johann Wilhelm Loeffelholz." In *Enthüllungen: Restaurierte Kunstwerke von Riemenschneider bis Kremser Schmidt*, edited by Christine Kupper, pp. 82–93. Exh. cat., Germanisches Nationalmuseum, Nuremberg. Nuremberg: Verlag des Germanischen Nationalmuseums, 2008.

Kantorowicz 1940
Ernst Kantorowicz. "The Este Portrait by Roger van der Weyden." *Journal of the Warburg and Courtauld Institutes* 3, no. 3/4 (April–July 1940), pp. 165–80.

Karet 2014
Evelyn Karet. "The Origins of Northern Italian Collecting: Humanist Collections." In *The* Antonio II Badile *Album of Drawings: The Origins of Collecting Drawings in Early Modern Northern Italy*, by Evelyn Karet, pp. 107–31. Farnham, U.K.: Ashgate Publishing Limited, 2014.

Kaufmann 1984
Lynn Frier Kaufmann. *The Noble Savage: Satyrs and Satyr Families in Renaissance Art*. Studies in Renaissance Art History 2. Ann Arbor, Mich.: UMI Research Press, 1984.

Kavaler 2005
Ethan Matt Kavaler. "Nature and the Chapel Vaults at Ingolstadt: Structuralist and Other Perspectives." *Art Bulletin* 87, no. 2 (June 2005), pp. 230–48.

Kay 1939
Arthur Kay. *Treasure Trove in Art*. Edinburgh: Oliver and Boyd, 1939.

Kemperdick and Lammertse 2012
Stephan Kemperdick and Friso Lammertse. "Painting around 1400 and Jan van Eyck's Early Work." In *The Road to Van Eyck*, edited by Stephan Kemperdick and Friso Lammertse, pp. 89–108. Exh. cat. Rotterdam: Museum Boymans van Beuningen, 2012.

Kemperdick and Sander 2009
Stephan Kemperdick and Jochen Sander, eds. *The Master of Flémalle and Rogier van der Weyden*. Exh. cat., Städel Museum, Frankfurt am Main; Gemäldegalerie, Staatliche Museen zu Berlin. Ostfildern, Germany: Hatje Cantz Verlag, 2009.

Kidwell 2004
Carol Kidwell. *Pietro Bembo: Lover, Linguist, Cardinal*. Montreal: McGill-Queen's University Press, 2004.

Kirsch 1991
Edith W. Kirsch. *Five Illuminated Manuscripts of Giangaleazzo Visconti*. University Park: Published for College Art Association by the Pennsylvania State University Press, 1991.

Klapisch-Zuber 1985
Christiane Klapisch-Zuber. *Women, Family, and Ritual in Renaissance Italy*. Translated by Lydia Cochrane. Chicago: University of Chicago Press, 1985.

Klapisch-Zuber 2020
Christiane Klapisch-Zuber. *Mariages à la florentine: Femmes et vie de famille à Florence (XIVe–XVe siècle)*. Paris: EHESS; Gallimard; Seuil, 2020.

Knauer 2002
Elfriede Regina Knauer. "Portrait of a Lady? Some Reflections on Images of Prostitutes from the Later Fifteenth Century." *Memoirs of the American Academy in Rome* 47 (2002), pp. 95–117.

Knauer 2009
Elfriede R. Knauer. "Leonardo da Vinci's Gioconda and the Yellow Shawl: Observations on Female Portraits in the Renaissance." *Raccolta Vinciana* 33 (2009), pp. 1–79.

Knight Powell 2018
Amy Knight Powell. "A Short History of the Picture as a Box." *Representations* 141, no. 1 (Winter 2018), pp. 95–130.

Koehler 1897
S. R. Koehler. *A Chronological Catalogue of the Engravings, Dry-Points and Etchings of Albrecht Dürer as Exhibited at the Grolier Club*. New York: Grolier Club, 1897.

Koeppe 2019
Wolfram Koeppe, ed. *Making Marvels: Science and Splendor at the Courts of Europe*. Exh. cat. New York: The Metropolitan Museum of Art, 2019.

Koepplin 2006
Dieter Koepplin. "Wie erklärt sich eine von Cranach gemalte Maria-Ekklesia 'in der Sonne' aus der Situation um 1550?" In *Politik und Bekenntnis: Die Reaktionen auf das Interim von 1548*, edited by Irene Dingel and Günther Wartenberg, pp. 139–76. Leipzig: Evangelische Verlagsanstalt, 2006.

Koepplin and Falk 1974–76
Dieter Koepplin and Tilman Falk. *Lukas Cranach: Gemälde, Zeichnungen, Druckgraphik*. Exh. cat., Kunstmuseum Basel. 2 vols. Basel: Birkhäuser, 1974–76.

Koos 2014
Marianne Koos. "Wandering Things: Agency and Embodiment in Late Sixteenth-Century English Miniature Portraits." *Art History* 37, no. 5 (November 2014), pp. 836–85.

Koos 2018
Marianne Koos. "Concealing and Revealing Pictures 'in Small Volumes': Portrait Miniatures and Their Envelopes." In "Wearing Images," edited by Diane H. Bodart. Special issue, *Espacio, Tiempo y Forma*, ser. 7, no. 6 (2018), pp. 33–54. http://dx.doi.org/10.5944/etfvii.6.2018.

Korn et al. 2014
Brigitte Korn, Michael Diefenbacher, and Steven M. Zahlaus, eds. *Von nah und fern: Zuwanderer in die Reichsstadt Nürnberg*. Exh. cat. Nuremberg: Stadtmuseum Fembohaus, Museen der Stadt Nürnberg; Petersberg, Germany: Michael Imhof, 2014.

Körner 2003
Hans Körner. *Frankfurter Patrizier: Historisch-genealogisches Handbuch der Adeligen Ganerbschaft des Hauses Alten-Limpurg zu Frankfurt am Main*. 2nd ed., rev. by Andreas Hansert. Neustadt an der Aisch, Germany: Degener, 2003.

Kozlowski 2018
Sarah K. Kozlowski. "Toward a History of the Trecento Diptych: Format, Materiality, and Mobility in a Corpus of Diptychs from Angevin Naples." *Zeitschrift für Kunstgeschichte* 81, no. 1 (2018), pp. 3–29.

Kozlowski 2022
Sarah K. Kozlowski. *Portable Panel Paintings at the Angevin Court of Naples: Mobility and Materiality in the Trecento Mediterranean*. Trecento Forum 4. Turnhout, Belgium: Brepols, 2022.

Krause 2016
Stefan Krause. "Die Porträts des Malers Hans Maler: Spiegelbild der Tiroler Wirtschaft um 1520; Praktische Verwendung von Bildnissen in der Renaissance." In *Nur Gesichter? Porträts der Renaissance*, edited by Wolfgang Meighörner, pp. 156–72. Exh. cat., Tiroler Landesmuseum Ferdinandeum, Innsbruck. Innsbruck: Tiroler Landesmuseen-Betriebsgesellschaft m.b.H., 2016.

Kren 1992
Thomas Kren, ed. *Margaret of York, Simon Marmion, and the Visions of Tondal*. Malibu, Calif.: J. Paul Getty Museum, 1992.

Kren 2018
Thomas Kren, with Jill Burke and Stephen J. Campbell, eds. *The Renaissance Nude*. Exh. cat., J. Paul Getty Museum, Los Angeles; Royal Academy of Arts, London. Los Angeles: J. Paul Getty Museum, 2018.

Kren and McKendrick 2003
Thomas Kren and Scot McKendrick. *Illuminating the Renaissance: The Triumph of Flemish Manuscript Painting in Europe*. Exh. cat., J. Paul Getty Museum, Los Angeles; Royal Academy of Arts, London. Los Angeles: J. Paul Getty Museum, 2003.

Kren and Wieck 1990
Thomas Kren and Roger S. Wieck. *The Visions of Tondal from the Library of Margaret of York*. Malibu, Calif.: J. Paul Getty Museum, 1990.

Kriegk 1868
Georg Ludwig Kriegk. *Deutsches Bürgerthum im Mittelalter: Nach urkundlichen Forschungen und mit besonderer Beziehung auf Frankfurt a.M.* Vol. 1. Frankfurt am Main: Literarische Anstalt (Rütten & Löning), 1868.

Kriegk 1871
Georg Ludwig Kriegk. *Geschichte von Frankfurt am Main in ausgewählten Darstellungen: Nach Urkunden und Acten*. Frankfurt am Main: Heyder und Zimmer, 1871.

Krischel 2013
Roland Krischel. "Cloths in and on Paintings: From Curtain to Shutter and Back Again." In *Setting the Scene: European Painted Cloths from the Fourteenth to the Twenty First Century*, edited by Nicola Costaras and Christina Young, pp. 1–10. London: Archetype Publications, 2013.

Kuhn 1936
Charles L. Kuhn. *A Catalogue of German Paintings of the Middle Ages and Renaissance in American Collections*. Germanic Museum Studies 1. Cambridge, Mass.: Harvard University Press, 1936.

Laclotte 1993
Michel Laclotte, ed. *Le siècle de Titien: L'âge d'or de la peinture à Venise*. Exh. cat., Galeries Nationales du Grand Palais, Paris. Paris: Réunion des Musées Nationaux, 1993.

Landwehr 1976
John Landwehr. *French, Italian, Spanish, and Portuguese Books of Devices and Emblems 1534–1827: A Bibliography*. Utrecht: Haentjens, Dekker & Gumbert, 1976.

Lane 2009
Barbara G. Lane. *Hans Memling: Master Painter in Fifteenth-Century Bruges*. London: Harvey Miller Publishers, 2009.

Langedijk 1981–87
Karla Langedijk. *The Portraits of the Medici: 15th–18th Centuries*. 3 vols. Florence: Studio per Edizioni Scelte, 1981–87.

Larner 1971
John Larner. *Culture and Society in Italy, 1290–1420*. New York: Charles Scribner's Sons, 1971.

Lauber 2002a
Rosella Lauber. "Et è il nudo che ho io in pittura de l'istesso Zorzi: Per Giorgione e Marcantonio Michiel." *Arte Veneta* 59 (2002), pp. 98–115.

Lauber 2002b
Rosella Lauber. "Per un ritratto di Gabriele Vendramin: Nuovi contribute." In *Figure di collezionisti a Venezia tra Cinque e Seicento*, edited by Linda Borean and Stefania Mason, pp. 25–71. Udine: Forum, 2002.

Lauber 2005
Rosella Lauber. "'Opera perfettissima': Marcantonio Michiel e la *Notizia d'opere di disegno*." In *Il collezionismo a Venezia e nel Veneto ai tempi della Serenissima*, edited by Bernard Aikema, Max Seidel, and Rosella Lauber, pp. 77–116. Collana del Kunsthistorisches Institut in Florenz, Max-Planck-Institut 10. Venice: Marsilio, 2005.

Lee 2017
Mireille M. Lee. "The Gendered Economics of Greek Bronze Mirrors: Reflections on Reciprocity and Feminine Agency." *Arethusa* 50, no. 2 (Spring 2017), pp. 143–68.

Leonardo da Vinci 1989
Leonardo da Vinci. *Leonardo on Painting: An Anthology of Writings by Leonardo da Vinci with a Selection of Documents Relating to His Career as an Artist*. Edited by Martin Kemp. Selected and translated by Martin Kemp and Margaret Walker. New Haven: Yale University Press, 1989.

Leopold and Vincent 1993
J. H. Leopold and Clare Vincent. "A Watch for Monsieur Hesselin." *Metropolitan Museum Journal* 28 (1993), pp. 103–19.

***Lexicon Iconographicum Mythologiae Classicae* 1981–99**
Lexicon Iconographicum Mythologiae Classicae. 9 vols. Zurich: Artemis Verlag, 1981–99.

Lieb 1980
Norbert Lieb. *Octavian Secundus Fugger (1549–1600) und die Kunst*. Tübingen, Germany: J. C. B. Mohr (Paul Siebeck), 1980.

Lingo 2016
Stuart Lingo. "Agnolo Bronzino's *Pygmalion and the Statue* and the Dawn of Art." *Art History* 39, no. 5 (November 2016), pp. 868–95.

Löhr 2003
Wolf-Dietrich Löhr. "'e nuovi Omeri, e Plati': Painted Characters in Portraits by Andrea del Sarto and Agnolo Bronzino." In *Poetry on Art: Renaissance to Romanticism*, edited by Thomas Frangenberg, pp. 48–100. Donnington, U.K.: Shaun Tyas, 2003.

Lorentz 1995
Philippe Lorentz. *Hans Memling au Louvre*. Exh. cat., Musée du Louvre, Paris. Paris: Réunion des Musées Nationaux, 1995.

Lorenz 1996
Angelika Lorenz, ed. *Die Maler tom Ring*. Vol. 1, *Aufsätze*. Vol. 2, *Katalog, Werkverzeichnis*. Exh. cat. Münster: Westfälisches Landesmuseum für Kunst und Kulturgeschichte, 1996.

Lotto 1969
Lorenzo Lotto. *Il "libro di spese diverse" con aggiunta di lettere e d'altri documenti*. Edited by Pietro Zampetti. Venice: Istituto per la Collaborazione Culturale, 1969.

Lotto 2017
Lorenzo Lotto. *Il libro di spese diverse*. Edited by Francesco De Carolis. Richerche e documenti d'arte 1. Trieste: EUT, Edizioni Università di Trieste, 2017, pp. 151.

Lübbeke 1991
Isolde Lübbeke. *Early German Painting, 1350–1550: The Thyssen-Bornemisza Collection*. Translated by Margaret Thomas Will. London: Sotheby's Publications, 1991.

Lucco 2000
Mauro Lucco. "A New Portrait by Raphael and its Historical Context." *Artibus et Historiae* 21, no. 41 (2000), pp. 49–73.

Lucco 2006
Mauro Lucco, ed. *Antonello da Messina: L'opera completa*. Exh. cat., Scuderie del Quirinale, Rome. Cinisello Balsamo, Milan: Silvana, 2006.

Lüdemann 2010
Peter Lüdemann. "Ikonographische Beobachtungen zur Rüseite von Jacopo de' Barbaris Porträt eines Mannes ("Bidnis eines Deutschen") in den Staatlichen Museen." *Jahrbuch der Berliner Museen* 52 (2010 [2012]), pp. 7–17.

Ludolphy 2006
Ingetraut Ludolphy. *Friedrich der Weise: Kurfürst von Sachsen 1463–1525*. 1984; repr. Leipzig: Leipziger Universitätsverlag, 2006.

Lurker 1991
Manfred Lurker. *Wörterbuch der Symbolik*. 5th ed. Stuttgart: A. Kröner Verlag, 1991.

Lüttenberg 2000
Thomas Lüttenberg. "'Je he ce que mord': Die Bedeutung von Motto und Emblem auf einem Rogier van der

Weyden zugeschriebenen Porträt." *Zeitschrift für Kunstgeschichte* 63, no. 4 (2000), pp. 558–61.

Lydecker 1987

John Kent Lydecker. "Il patriziato fiorentino e la committenza artistica per la casa." In *I ceti dirigenti nella Toscana del Quattrocento: Atti del V e VI Convegno: Firenze 10–11 dicembre 1982, 2–3 dicembre 1983*, edited by Donatella Rugiadini, pp. 209–21. Monte Oriolo, Italy: Francesco Papafava, 1987.

Madrazo 1884

Pedro de Madrazo. *Viaje artístico de tres siglos por las colecciones de cuadros de los reyes de España, desde Isabel la Católica hasta la formación del Real museo del Prado de Madrid*. Madrid: Daniel Corteza y Ca., 1884.

Manca 1992

Joseph Manca. *The Art of Ercole de' Roberti*. Cambridge: Cambridge University Press, 1992.

Mancini 1956–57

Giulio Mancini. *Considerazioni sulla pittura*. Edited by Adriana Marucchi. 2 vols. Rome: Accademia Nazionale dei Lincei, 1956–57.

van Mander 1906

Carel van Mander. *Das Leben der niederländischen und deutschen Maler / Het leven der doorluchtighe Nederlandtsche en Hooghduytsche schhilders*. Translated by Hanns Floerke. Munich: G. Müller, 1906.

Mann and Syson 1998

Nicolas Mann and Luke Syson, eds. *The Image of the Individual: Portraits in the Renaissance*. London: Published for the Trustees of the British Museum by British Museum Press, 1998.

Manso Porto 2006

Carmen Manso Porto, ed. *Isabel la Católica y el arte*. Madrid: Real Academia de la Historia, Marquesa viuda de Arriluce de Ybarra, 2006.

Marti et al. 2009

Susan Marti, Till-Holger Borchert, Gabriele Keck, eds. *Splendour of the Burgundian Court: Charles the Bold (1433–1477)*. Exh. cat., Historisches Museum, Berne; Bruggemuseum and Groeningemuseum, Bruges; Kunsthistorisches Museum, Vienna. Antwerp: Mercatorfonds, 2009.

***Martin Luther* 2016**

Martin Luther. Essay vol., *And the Reformation*. Catalogue vol.: *Treasures of the Reformation*. Exh. cat., State Office for Heritage Management and Archaeology Saxony-Anhalt—State Museum of Prehistory; Luther Memorials Foundation of Saxony-Anhalt; Stiftung Deutsches Historisches Museum; Foundation Schloss Friedenstein Gotha; Minneapolis Institute of Art; Morgan Library and Museum, New York; Pitts Theology Library of the Candler School of Theology at Emory University, Atlanta. Dresden: Sandstein Verlag, 2016.

Maué 1997

Claudia Maué. *Die Bildwerke des 17. und 18. Jahrhunderts im Germanischen Nationalmuseum*. Pt. 1, *Franken*. Mainz: Philipp von Zabern, 1997.

Mayer and Achilles-Syndram 1994

Bernd Mayer and Katrin Achilles-Syndram, eds. *Kunst des Sammelns: Das Praunsche Kabinett: Meisterwerke von Dürer bis Caracci*. Exh. cat. Nuremberg: Verlag des Germanischen Nationalmuseums, 1994.

Mayr 2019

Vincent Mayr. "Wilde Leute (2019)." *RDK Labor*. https://www.rdklabor.de/w/?oldid=111022.

Mazzotta 2012

Antonio Mazzotta. "'Ritratti' veneziani per Jacometto, Marco Basaiti e Andrea Previtali." *Prospettiva*, no. 147/148 (July–October 2012), pp. 150–58.

Mazzotta 2017

Antonio Mazzotta. "Altri 'ritratti' veneziani per Antonello, Jacometto e Andrea Previtali." *Prospettiva*, no. 165/166 (January–April 2017), pp. 69–91.

Meder 1932

Joseph Meder. *Dürer-Katalog: Ein Handbuch über Albrecht Dürers Stiche, Radierungen, Holzschnitte, deren Zustände, Ausgaben und Wasserzeichen*. Vienna: Gilhofer & Ranschburg, 1932.

Mendelsohn and Ng 2023

Daniel Mendelsohn and Aimee Ng. *Bronzino's Ludovico Capponi*. Frick Diptych 12. New York: Frick Collection, in association with D. Giles Ltd., 2023.

Mertens 1985

Joan R. Mertens. "Greek Bronzes in the Metropolitan Museum of Art." *The Metropolitan Museum of Art Bulletin* 43, no. 2 (Autumn 1985), pp. 5–64.

Messling 2014

Guido Messling. "Cranach in den Niederlanden." In *Dialog—Transfer—Konflikt: Künstlerische Wechselbeziehungen im Mittelalter und in der Frühen Neuzeit*, edited by Wolfgang Augustyn and Ulrich Söding, pp. 363–84. Veröffentlichungen des Zentralinstituts für Kunstgeschichte in München 33. Passau, Germany: Dietmar Klinger Verlag, 2014.

Metzger 2019

Christof Metzger, ed. *Albrecht Dürer*. Exh. cat. Vienna: Albertina; Munich: Prestel, 2019.

Michiel 1884

Anonymous [Marcantonio Michiel]. *Notizie d'opere del disegno pubblicate ed illustrate da D. Jacopo Morelli*. 2nd ed., revised and enlarged by Gustavo Frizzoni. Bologna: Nicola Zanaichelli, 1884.

Mills 2021

Robert Mills. "Back-to-Front: Abstraction and Figuration in Bosch's Visions of the Hereafter Abstraction." *Abstraction in Medieval Art: Beyond the Ornament*, edited by Elina Gertsman, pp. 115–38. Amsterdam: Amsterdam University Press, 2021. https://doi.org/10.2307/j.ctv1g13jk5.8.

Mitsis and Ziogas 2016

Phillip Mitsis and Ioannis Ziogas, eds. *Wordplay and Powerplay in Latin Poetry*. Trends in Classics—Supplementary Volumes 36. Berlin: De Gruyter, 2016.

Möbius 1949

Hans Möbius. "Wachsmedaillons und Silbermedaillen aus der Zeit des Landgrafen Carl von Hessen-Kassel (1670–1730)." *Marburger Jahrbuch für Kunstwissenschaft* 14 (1949), pp. 225–33.

Monbeig Goguel 2015

Catherine Monbeig Goguel. "For Agnolo di Donnino del Mazziere, the Maestro di Santo Spirito." In *Rethinking Renaissance Drawings: Essays in Honour of David McTavish*, edited by Una Roman D'Elia, pp. 64–69, 331–32. Montreal: McGill-Queen's University Press, 2015.

Moritz and Ebneth 2016

Gabriele Moritz and Bernhard Ebneth. "Elisabeth Krauß: Wie ein Dienstmädchen zur reichsten und sozial engagiertesten Frau Nürnbergs wurde." *Museenblog Nürnberg* 2016. https://museenblog-nuernberg.de/2016/06/22/elisabeth-krauss/.

Morse 2007

Margaret A. Morse. "Creating Sacred Space: The Religious Visual Culture of the Renaissance Venice *Casa*." *Renaissance Studies* 21, no. 2 (April 2007), pp. 151–84.

Mundy 1988

E. James Mundy. "Porphyry and the 'Posthumous' Fifteenth Century Portrait." *Pantheon* 46 (1988), pp. 37–43.

Murphy 2003

Caroline P. Murphy. *Lavinia Fontana: A Painter and Her Patrons in Sixteenth-Century Bologna*. New Haven: Yale University Press, 2003.

Musacchio 2000

Jacqueline Marie Musacchio. "The Madonna and Child, a Host of Saints, and Domestic Devotion in Renaissance Florence." In *Revaluing Renaissance Art*, edited by Gabriele Neher and Rupert Shepherd, pp. 147–64. Aldershot, U.K.: Ashgate, 2000.

Musacchio 2007

Jacqueline Marie Musacchio. "Objects and Identity: Antonio de' Medici and the Casino at San Marco in Florence." In *The Renaissance World*, edited by John Jeffries Martin, pp. 481–500. New York: Routledge, 2007.

***Museo Poldi Pezzoli* 1982**

Museo Poldi Pezzoli. Vol. 1, *Dipinti*. Musei e gallerie di Milano. Milan: Electa, 1982.

Muthesius 1997

Anna Muthesius. *Byzantine Silk Weaving: AD 400 to AD 1200*. Edited by Ewald Kislinger and Johannes Koder. Vienna: Verlag Fassbaender, 1997.

Natali 1995

Antonio Natali. *La piscina di Betsaida: Movimenti nell'arte fiorentina del Cinquecento*. Florence: Maschietto & Musolino, 1995.

Nepi Scirè and Rossi 2003

Giovanna Nepi Scirè and Sandra Rossi, eds. *Giorgione: "le maraviglie dell'arte."* Exh. cat., Gallerie dell'Accademia, Venice. Venice: Marsilio, 2003.

Nesi 2022

Alessandro Nesi. "Precisazioni, conferme e proposte per Donnino e Agnolo del Mazziere." *Quaderni di Maniera*, October 2022, pp. 1–8. https://issuu.com/quaderni__di__maniera/docs/quaderno__mazziere__bassa__web.

Newbery 2007

Timothy Newbery. *Frames*. Robert Lehman Collection 13. New York: The Metropolitan Museum of Art, in association with Princeton University Press, Princeton, N.J., 2007.

Newbery et al. 1990

Timothy J. Newbery, George Bisacca, and Laurence B. Kanter. *Italian Renaissance Frames*. Exh. cat. New York: The Metropolitan Museum of Art, New York, 1990.

Nixon 2004

Virginia Nixon. *Mary's Mother: Saint Anne in Late Medieval Europe*. University Park: Pennsylvania State University Press, 2004.

Nogueira forthcoming

Alison Manges Nogueira. "Concealing Portraits in Renaissance Venice: The Myth of Jacometto's Painted Box Uncovered." *Burlington Magazine* 166, no. 1451 (forthcoming).

Noreen 2010

Kirstin Noreen. "Re-Covering Christ in late Medieval Rome: The Icon of Christ in the Sancta Sanctorum." *Gesta* 49, no. 2 (January 2010), pp. 117–35.

Normore 2015

Christina Normore. *A Feast for the Eyes: Art, Performance, and the Late Medieval Banquet*. Chicago: University of Chicago Press, 2015.

Nova 1994
Alessandro Nova. "Hangings, Curtains, and Shutters of Sixteenth-Century Lombard Altarpieces." In *Italian Altarpieces 1250–1550: Function and Design*, edited by Eve Borsook and Fiorella Superbi Gioffredi, pp. 177–99. Oxford: Clarendon Press, 1994.

Nuttall 2010
Paula Nuttall. "Dancing, Love and the 'Beautiful Game': A New Interpretation of a Group of Fifteenth-Century 'Gaming' Boxes." "Re-Thinking Renaissance Objects: Design, Function and Meaning." Special issue, *Renaissance Studies* 24, no. 1 (February 2010), pp. 118–41.

***O'Hagan Coin Collection* 1908**
The O'Hagan Coin Collection: Catalogue of the Collection of Roman Coins in Gold, Silver and Bronze, Formed by H. Osborne O'Hagan, Esq. Roman Coins. Sale cat. Sotheby, Wilkinson & Hodge, London, July 13–22, 1908.

Orvieto 2009
Paolo Orvieto. *Poliziano e l'ambiente mediceo*. Rome: Salerno Editrice, 2009.

O'Shaughnessy n.d.
Heather O'Shaughnessy. "A Brief History of Miniature Portraiture in Wax." https://www.salondecire.com/post/a-brief-history-of-miniature-portraiture-in-wax.

Ost 1992
Hans Ost. *Tizian-Studien*. Cologne: Böhlau, 1992.

Otto 1964
Gertrud Otto. *Bernhard Strigel*. Kunstwissenschlaftliche Studien 33. Munich: Deutscher Kunstverlag, 1964.

Pächt 1948
Otto Pächt. *The Master of Mary of Burgundy*. London: Faber and Faber, 1948.

Padoa Rizzo 1988
Anna Padoa Rizzo. "Agnolo di Donnino: Nuovi documenti, le fonti e la possibile indentificazione con il Maestro di Santo Spirito." *Rivista d'Arte: Studi Documentari per la Storia delle Arti in Toscana*, ser. 4., 40, no. 4 (1988), pp. 125–63.

Padoa Rizzo 1991
Anna Padoa Rizzo. "Indagini sulle botteghe di pittura del '400 in Toscana: Il Maestro di Santo Spirito e i Del Mazziere: Una conferma." *Erba d'Arno* 46 (1991), pp. 54–63.

Pagnotta 1987
Laura Pagnotta. *Giuliano Bugiardini*. Turin: Umberto Allemandi, 1987.

Pallini 2002
Germano Pallini. "Dieci canzoni d'amore di Antonio di Matteo di Meglio." *Interpres: Rivista di Studi Quattrocenteschi* 21 (2002), pp. 7–122.

Panofsky 1930
Erwin Panofsky. *Hercules am Scheideweg und andere antike Bildstoffe in der neueren Kunst*. Studien der Bibliothek Warburg 18. Leipzig: B. G. Teubner, 1930.

Panofsky 1953
Erwin Panofsky. *Early Netherlandish Painting: Its Origins and Character*. 2 vols. Cambridge, Mass.: Harvard University Press, 1953.

Parani 2018
Maria G. Parani. "Mediating Presence: Curtains in Middle and Late Byzantine Imperial Ceremonial and Portraiture." *Byzantine and Modern Greek Studies* 42, no. 1 (April 2018), pp. 1–25.

Parronchi 1965
Alessandro Parronchi. "Un 'memento mori' di Giambellino." *Arte Veneta* 19 (1965), pp. 148–50.

Pastoureau 1987
Michel Pastoureau. "L'effervescence emblématique et les origines héraldiques du portrait au XIVe siècle." *Bulletin de la Société Nationale des Antiquaires de France*, 1985 (1987), pp. 108–15.

Penny 2004–8
Nicholas Penny. *The Sixteenth Century Italian Paintings*. Vol. 1, *Paintings from Bergamo, Brescia and Cremona*. Vol. 2, *Venice 1540–1600*. National Gallery Catalogues. London: National Gallery Company, 2004–8.

Pentcheva 2007
Bissera V. Pentcheva. "Epigrams on Icons." In *Art and Text in Byzantine Culture*, edited by Liz James, pp. 120–38. Cambridge: University of Cambridge Press, 2007.

Periti 2016
Giancarla Periti. *In the Courts of Religious Ladies: Art, Vision, and Pleasure in Italian Renaissance Convents*. New Haven: Yale University Press, 2016.

Perkinson 2007
Stephen Perkinson. "Rethinking the Origins of Portraiture." *Gesta* 46, no. 2 (2007), pp. 135–57.

Perkinson 2009
Stephen Perkinson. *The Likeness of the King: A Prehistory of Portraiture in Late Medieval France*. Chicago: University of Chicago Press, 2009.

Pignatti 1971
Terisio Pignatti. *Giorgione*. Complete ed. New York: Phaidon, 1971.

Pincus 2008
Debra Pincus. "Giovanni Bellini's Humanist Signature: Pietro Bembo, Aldus Manutius and Humanism in Early Sixteenth-Century Venice." *Artibus et Historiae* 29, no. 58 (2008), pp. 89–119.

Pollard 2007
J. Graham Pollard, with the assistance of Eleonora Luciano and Maria Pollard. *Renaissance Medals*. Vol. 1, *Italy*. Vol. 2, *France, Germany, The Netherlands, and England*. Washington, D.C.: National Gallery of Art, 2007.

Pollini 1990
John Pollini. Introduction to *Roman Portraiture: Images of Character and Virtue; Selections from the J. Paul Getty Museum*, edited by John Pollini, pp. 8–13. Exh. cat. Los Angeles: Fisher Gallery, University of Southern California, 1990.

Pope-Hennessy 1987
John Pope-Hennessy, assisted by Laurence B. Kanter. *Italian Paintings*. Robert Lehman Collection 1. New York: The Metropolitan Museum of Art, in association with Princeton University Press, Princeton, N.J., 1987.

Poussin 1989
Nicolas Poussin. *Lettres et propos sur l'art*. Edited by Anthony Blunt. Collection Savoir. Paris: Hermann, 1989.

Preimesberger et al. 1999
Rudolf Preimesberger, Hannah Baader, and Nicola Suthor, eds. *Porträt*. Geschichte der klassischen Bildgattungen in Quellentexten and Kommentaren 2. Berlin: Reimer, 1999.

Pressler 2000
Ernst Pressler. *Schraubtaler und Steckmedaillen: Verborgene Kostbarkeiten*. Süddeutsche Münzkataloge 10. Stuttgart: Verlag der Münzen- und Medaillenhandlung, 2000.

Prinz 1957
Wolfram Prinz, ed. *Gemälde des Historischen Museums Frankfurt am Main: Herausgegeben zum Jahrestag des hundertjährigen Bestehens der Städtischen Gemäldesammlung im Historischen Museum*. Frankfurt am Main: Verlag Waldemar Kramer, 1957.

***Raffaello a Firenze* 1984**
Raffaello a Firenze: Dipinti e disegni delle collezioni fiorentine. Exh. cat., Palazzo Pitti, Florence. Florence: Electa, 1984.

Randolph 2014
Adrian W. B. Randolph. *Touching Objects: Intimate Experiences of Italian Fifteenth-Century Art*. New Haven: Yale University Press, 2014.

Ravà 1920
Aldo Ravà. "Il 'Camerino delle antigaglie' di Gabriele Vendramin." *Nuovo Archivio Veneto*, n.s. 22, 39 (January–June 1920), pp. 155–81.

Reiss 2022
Sheryl E. Reiss. "A Note on Raphael and Gendered Viewing." In *Maraviglia: Rezeptionsgeschichte(n) von der Antike bis in die Moderne; Festschrift für Ingo Herklotz*, edited by Peter Bell, Antje Fehrmann, Rebecca Müller, and Dominic Olariu, pp. 265–76. Studien der Kunst 45. Cologne: Böhlau, 2022.

Ricci 1913
Seymour de Ricci. *Description raisonée des peintures du Louvre*. Vol. 1, *Écoles étrangères: Italie et Espagne*. Paris: Imprimerie de l'Art, 1913.

Richter 1915
Gisela M. A. Richter. *Greek, Etruscan and Roman Bronzes*. New York: Gilliss Press, 1915.

Richter 1930
Gisela M. A. Richter. *Handbook of the Classical Collection*. Rev. ed. New York: The Metropolitan Museum of Art, 1930.

Richter 1948
Gisela M. A. Richter. *Roman Portraits*. Rev. ed. New York: The Metropolitan Museum of Art, 1948.

Richter 1953
Gisela M. A. Richter. *Handbook of the Greek Collection*. Cambridge, Mass.: Harvard University Press, 1953.

Riewerts and Pieper 1955
Theodor Riewerts and Paul Pieper. *Die Maler tom Ring, Ludger der Ältere, Hermann, Ludger der Jüngere*. Munich: Deutscher Kunstverlag, 1955.

Ring 1949
Grete Ring. *A Century of French Painting, 1400–1500*. London: Phaidon, 1949.

Ritschel 2006
Iris Ritschel. "Friedrich der Weise und seine Gefährtin: Überlegungen und Erkenntnisse zu fünf verdächtig(t)en Kunstwerken." In *"... wir wollen der Liebe Raum geben": Konkubinate geistlicher und weltlicher Fürsten um 1500*, edited by Andreas Tacke, pp. 296–341. Göttingen: Wallstein Verlag, 2006.

Rizzo 2014
Luana Rizzo. "Giovan Battista Abioso e il *Dialogus in Astrologiae Defensionem*." *Bruniana & Campanelliana* 20, no. 2 (2014), pp. 655–61.

Robin 1985
Françoise Robin. *La cour d'Anjou-Provence: La vie artistique sous le règne de René*. Paris: Picard, 1985.

Robinson 1908
Edward Robinson. "New Accessions in the Classical Department: IV. Five Greek Mirrors." *The Metropolitan Museum of Art Bulletin* 3, no. 4 (April 1908), pp. 66–70.

Robinson 2019
Matthew Robinson. "Looking Edgeways: Pursuing Acrostics in Ovid and Virgil." *Classical Quarterly* 69, no. 1 (May 2019), pp. 290–308.

Rodriguez 2018
James A. Rodriguez. "Images for Personal Devotion in an Age of Liturgical Synthesis: Bilateral Icons in Byzantium, ca. 1100–1453." PhD diss., Yale University, 2018.

***Roman Imperial Coinage* 1**
The Roman Imperial Coinage. Vol. 1, *From 31 BC to AD 69*, by C. H. V. Sutherland. Rev. ed. London: Spink and Son, 1984.
***Roman Imperial Coinage* 5.2**
The Roman Imperial Coinage. Vol. 5, pt. 2. Edited by Percy H. Webb. London: Spink and Son, 1933.
Rosenbaum 1979
Allen Rosenbaum. *Old Master Paintings from the Collection of Baron Thyssen-Bornemisza*. Exh. cat. Washington, D.C.: International Exhibitions Foundation, 1979.
Roth-Bojadzhiev 1985
Gertrud Roth-Bojadzhiev. *Studien zur Bedeutung der Vögel in der mittelalterlichen Tafelmalerei*. Cologne: Böhlau, 1985.
Rothwell Hughes 2023
Frances Rothwell Hughes. "Thinking with Heraldry on the Eve of the Reformation: A Drawing by Niklaus Manuel Deutsch." *Art History* 46, no. 3 (June 2023), pp. 484–511.
Rowlands 1985
John Rowlands. *Holbein: The Paintings of Hans Holbein the Younger; Complete Edition*. Boston: David R. Godine, 1985.
Rowley and Völlnagel 2020
Neville Rowley and Jörg Völlnagel, eds. *Zwischen Kosmos und Pathos: Berliner Werke aus Aby Warburgs Bilderatlas Mnemosyne / Between Cosmos and Pathos: Berlin Works from Aby Warburg's Mnemosyne Atlas.* Exh. cat. Berlin: Staatliche Museen zu Berlin–Preussischer Kulturbesitz, Deutscher Kunstverlag, 2020.
Rudy and Baert 2007
Kathryn M. Rudy and Barbara Baert, eds. *Weaving, Veiling, and Dressing: Textiles and Their Metaphors in the Late Middle Ages*. Medieval Church Studies 12. Turnhout, Belgium: Brepols, 2007.
Ruiz Gómez 2019
Leticia Ruiz Gómez, ed. *A Tale of Two Women Painters: Sofonisba Anguissola and Lavinia Fontana.* Translated by Jenny Dodman. Exh. cat. Madrid: Museo Nacional del Prado, 2019.
Rutherglen 2012
Sussanah Rutherglen. "Ornamental Paintings of the Venetian Renaissance." Ph.D. diss., Princeton University, 2012.
Rutherglen 2016
Susannah Rutherglen. "Painting at the Threshold: Pictures for Doors in Renaissance Venice." *Art Bulletin* 98, no. 4 (December 2016), pp. 438–65.
Safley 1996
Thomas Max Safley. "Marriage." *The Oxford Encyclopedia of the Reformation*, edited by Hans J. Hillerbrand, vol. 3, pp. 18–23. New York: Oxford University Press, 1996.
Sallay et al. 2009
Dóra Sallay, Vilmos Tátrai, and Axel Vécsey, eds. *Botticelli to Titian: Two Centuries of Italian Masterpieces*. Exh. cat. Budapest: Szépművészeti Múzeum, 2009.
Scarisbrick 2011
Diana Scarisbrick. *Portrait Jewels: Opulence and Intimacy from the Medici to the Romanovs*. London: Thames & Hudson, 2011.
Schabacker 1972
Peter H. Schabacker. "Book Reviews: Martin Davies, *Rogier van der Weyden*." *Art Quarterly* 35, no. 4 (Winter 1972), pp. 422–25.
Schade 1980
Werner Schade. *Cranach: A Family of Master Painters*. Translated from the 1974 German edition by Helen Sebba. New York: G. P. Putnam's Sons, 1980.
Scharf 1950
Alfred Scharf. *A Catalogue of Pictures and Drawings from the Collection of Sir Thomas Merton, F.R.S., at Stubbings House, Maidenhead.* London: Privately printed at Chiswick Press, 1950.
Schedl 2016
Michaela Schedl. *Tafelmalerei der Spätgotik am südlichen Mittelrhein*. Quellen und Abhandlungen zur mittelrheinischen Kirchengeschichte 135. Mainz: Selbstverlag der Gesellschaft für mittelrheinische Kirchengeschichte, 2016.
Schedl 2017
Michaela Schedl. "Caldenbach gen. Hess, Martin." *Frankfurter Personenlexikon*, August 10, 2017. https://frankfurter-personenlexikon.de/node/2578.
Scher 1994
Stephen K. Scher, ed. *The Currency of Fame: Portrait Medals of the Renaissance*. Exh. cat., Frick Collection, New York; National Gallery of Art, Washington, D.C. New York: Harry N. Abrams, in association with the Frick Collection, 1994.
Scher 2000
Stephen K. Scher, ed. *Perspectives on the Renaissance Medal*. New York: Garland Publishing; American Numismatic Society, 2000.
S. Schmidt 2018
Suzanne Karr Schmidt. *Interactive and Sculptural Printmaking in the Renaissance.* Brill's Studies in Intellectual History 270; Brill's Studies on Art, Art History, and Intellectual History 21. Leiden: Brill, 2018.
V. Schmidt 2002
Victor M. Schmidt, ed. *Italian Panel Painting of the Duecento and Trecento*. Studies in the History of Art 61; Center for Advanced Study in the Visual Arts, Symposium Papers 38. Washington, D.C.: National Gallery of Art, 2002.
V. Schmidt 2005
Victor M. Schmidt. *Painted Piety: Panel Paintings for Personal Devotion in Tuscany, 1250–1400*. Florence: Centro Di, 2005.
Schmitter 2004
Monika Schmitter. "'Virtuous Riches': The Bricolage of *Cittadini* Identities in Early Sixteenth-Century Venice." *Renaissance Quarterly* 57, no. 3 (Autumn 2004), pp. 908–69.
Schmitter 2022
Monika Schmitter. "Describing Giorgione's *Tempest*: Iconography, Genre, Interpretation." *Studies in Iconography* 43 (2022), pp. 185–222.
Schoch et al. 2001
Rainer Schoch, Matthias Mende, and Anna Scherbaum. *Albrecht Dürer, das druckgraphische Werk*. Vol. 1, *Kupferstiche, Eisenradierunger und Kaltnadelblätter.* Munich: Prestel, 2001.
Scholten 2011
Frits Scholten. *European Sculpture and Metalwork*. Robert Lehman Collection 12. New York: The Metropolitan Museum of Art, in association with Princeton University Press, Princeton, N.J., 2011.
Schönberger 1933
Guido Schönberger. "Das Porträt Heinrichs zum Jungen." In *Frankfurter Beiträge Arthur Richel gewidmet*, edited by Theodor Schwisow, pp. 13–16. Frankfurt am Main: Hauserpresse [R. Th. Hauser & Co.], 1933.
Schuarte 2022
Thomas Schaurte. "'Der recht schyltt / ist eyn dotten beyn': Vorformen der Subversion in Dürers Kupferstich *Das Wappen des Todes* von 1803." In *Das subersive Bild: Festschrift für Jürgen Müller*, edited by Betram Kaschek, Teresa Ende, Jan-David Mantzel, and Frank Schmidt, pp. 83–98. Berlin: Deutscher Kunstverlag, 2022.
Schubert et al. 2022
Anselm Schubert, Daniel Hess, Gunnar Heydenreich, Oliver Mack, and Andreas Maier, eds. *Kritischer Katalog der Luther-Bildnisse (1519–1530)*. Catalogue by Daniel Görres, Amalie Hänsch, Thomas Klinke, Wibke Ottweiler, and Aline Sindel, with Vincent Christlein. Nuremberg, 2022. https://lucascranach.org/index.php/luther/einleitung.
Schuchardt 2015
Günter Schuchardt, ed. *Cranach, Luther und die Bildnisse: Thüringer Themenjahr "Bild und Botschaft."* Exh. cat., Wartburg, Eisenach, Germany. Regensburg, Switzerland: Schnell & Steiner, 2015.
Schuttwolf et al. 1994
Allmuth Schuttwolf et al. *Gotteswort und Menschenbild: Werke von Cranach und seinen Zeitgenossen*. Exh. cat., Schloss Friedenstein zu Gotha. Gotha, Germany: Schlossmuseum Gotha; Forschungs- und Landesbibliothek Gotha, 1994.
Schütz 1972
Karl Schütz. *Lucas Cranach der Ältere und seine Werkstatt: Jubiläumsausstellung museumseigener Werke, 1472–1972*. Exh. cat. Vienna: Kunsthistorisches Museum, 1972.
Schwarz-Hermanns 2007
Sabine Schwarz-Hermanns. "Die Rundbildnisse Lucas Cranachs des Älteren: Mediale Innovation im Spannungsfeld unternehmerischer Strategie." In *Lucas Cranach 1553/2003: Wittenberger Tagungsbeiträge anlässlich des 450. Todesjahres Lucas Cranachs des Älteren*, edited by Andreas Tacke, pp. 121–33. Schriften der Stiftung Luthergedenkstätten in Sachsen-Anhalt 7. Leipzig: Evangelische Verlagsanstalt, 2007.
Segal 1973
Charles Segal. "*Felices ter et amplius*: Horace, *Odes*, I. 13." *Latomus* 32, no. 1 (January–March 1973), pp. 39–46.
Settis 2008
Salvatore Settis. "Esercizi di stile: Una Vecchia e un Bambino." In *Giorgione entmythisiert*, edited by Sylvia Ferino-Pagden, pp. 39–54. Turnhout, Belgium: Brepols, 2008.
Shapley 1979
Fern Rusk Shapley. *Catalogue of the Italian Paintings*. 2 vols. Washington, D.C.: National Gallery of Art, 1979.
Shearman 1992
John Shearman. *Only Connect: Art and the Spectator in the Italian Renaissance*. A. W. Mellon Lectures in the Fine Arts 1988; Bollingen Series 35, 37. Princeton, N.J.: Princeton University Press, 1992.
Shearman 2003
John Shearman. *Raphael in Early Modern Sources (1483–1602)*. 2 vols. New Haven: Yale University Press, 2003.
Shepherd et al. 2020
Tim Shephard, Sanna Raninenm, Serenella Sessini, and Laura Ştefănescu. *Music in the Art of Renaissance Italy 1420–1540*. London: Harvey Miller Publishers, 2020.
Sherman 2013
Allison Sherman. "Murder and Martyrdom: Titian's Gesuiti *Saint Lawrence* as a Family Peace Offering." *Artibus et Historiae* 34, no. 68 (2013), pp. 39–54.
Shestack 1967
Alan Shestack. *Master E.S.: Five Hundredth Anniversary Exhibition.* Exh. cat. Philadelphia: Philadelphia Museum of Art, 1967.
Silver 1983
Larry Silver. "Forest Primeval: Albrecht Altdorfer and the German Wilderness Landscape." *Simiolus: Netherlands Quarterly for the History of Art* 13, no. 1 (1983), pp. 4–43.

Silver 2022
Nathaniel Silver, ed. *Simone Martini in Orvieto*. Exh. cat. Boston: Isabella Stewart Gardner Museum, 2022.
Simon 1996
Jacob Simon. *The Art of the Picture Frame: Artists, Patrons and the Framing of Portraits in Britain*. Exh. cat. London: National Portrait Gallery, 1996.
Simons 1988
Patricia Simons. "Women in Frames: The Gaze, the Eye, the Profile in Renaissance Portraiture." *History Workshop*, no. 25 (Spring 1988), pp. 4–30.
Simons 2013
Patricia Simons. "The Visual Dynamics of (Un)veiling in Early Modern Culture." In *Visual Cultures of Secrecy in Early Modern Europe*, edited by Timothy McCall, Sean Roberts, and Giancarlo Fiorenza, pp. 24–54. Early Modern Studies 11. Kirksville, Mo.: Truman State University Press, 2013.
Smeyers 1999
Maurits Smeyers. *Flemish Miniatures from the 8th to the Mid-16th Century: The Medieval World on Parchment*. Turnhout, Belgium: Brepols, 1999.
Smith 1998
Jeffrey Chipps Smith. "The Practical Logistics of Art: Thoughts on the Commissioning, Displaying, and Storing of Art at the Burgundian Court." In *In Detail: New Studies of Northern Renaissance Art in Honor of Walter S. Gibson*, edited by Laurinda S. Dixon, pp. 27–48. Turnhout, Belgium: Brepols, 1998.
Soranzo 2020
Matteo Soranzo. *Giovanni Aurelio Augurello (1441–1524) and Renaissance Alchemy: A Critical Edition of* Chrysopoeia *and Other Alchemical Poems, with an Introduction, English Translation and Commentary*. Leiden: Brill, 2020.
Spallanzani and Gaeta Bertelà 1992
Marco Spallanzani and Giovanna Gaeta Bertelà, eds. *Libro d'inventario dei beni di Lorenzo il Magnifico*. Florence: Associazione Amici del Bargello, 1992.
Spinelli 2018
Riccardo Spinelli. "*La Monaca* degli Uffizi, una vedova di Casa Rinieri e il suo autore: Giuliano Bugiardini o Ridolfo del Ghirlandaio?" In *Tra archivi e storia: Scritti dedicati ad Alessandra Contini Bonacossi*, edited by Elisabetta Insabato, Rosalia Manno, Ernestina Pellegrini, and Anna Scattigno, vol. 1, pp. 91–100. Florence: Firenze University Press, 2018.
Spinosa 2006
Nicola Spinosa, ed. *Tiziano e il ritratto di corte: Da Raffaello ai Carracci*. Exh. cat., Museo di Capodimonte, Naples. Naples: Electa Napoli, 2006.
Spira 2016
Freyda Spira, with Peter Parshall. *The Power of Prints: The Legacy of William M. Ivins and A. Hyatt Mayor*. Exh. cat. New York: The Metropolitan Museum of Art, 2016.
Stadler 1936
Franz Stadler. *Hans von Kulmbach*. Vienna: Anton Schroll & Co., 1936.
Stahl 2013
Alan M. Stahl. "Roman Imperial Coins as an Inspiration for Renaissance Numismatic Imagery." In *Translatio Nummorum: Römische Kaiser in der Renaissance; Akten des internationalen Symposiums Berlin 16.–18. November 2011*, edited by Ulrike Peter and Bernhard Weisser, pp. 201–6. Mainz: Franz Philipp Rutzen, 2013.
Stahl and Waldman 1993–94
Alan M. Stahl and Louis Waldman. "The Earliest Known Medalists: The Sesto Brothers of Venice." *American Journal of Numismatics* 5/6 (1993–94), pp. 167–88, pls. 19–21.
Stange 1955
Alfred Stange. *Deutsche Malerei der Gotik*. Vol. 7, *Oberrhein, Bodensee, Schweiz und Mittelrhein in der Zeit vo 1450 bis 1500*. Munich: Deutscher Kunstverlag, 1955.
Stange 1970
Alfred Stange. *Kritisches Verzeichnis der deutschen Tafelbilder vor Dürer*. Vol. 2, *Oberrhein, Bodensee, Schweiz, Mittelrhein, Ulm, Augsburg, Allgäu, Nördlingen, von der Donau zum Neckar*. Edited by Norbert Lieb. Munich: F. Bruckmann, 1970.
Sterling et al. 1998
Charles Sterling, Maryan W. Ainsworth, Charles Talbot, Martha Wolff, Egbert Haverkamp-Begemann, Jonathan Brown, and John Hayes. *Fifteenth- to Eighteenth-Century European Paintings: France, Central Europe, The Netherlands, Spain, and Great Britain*. Robert Lehman Collection 2. New York: The Metropolitan Museum of Art, in association with Princeton University Press, Princeton, N.J., 1998.
Stoichita 2015
Victor I. Stoichita. *The Self-Aware Image. An Insight into Early Modern Meta-Painting.* Translated by Anne-Marie Glasheen; revised by Lorenzo Pericolo. Rev. ed. London: Harvey Miller Publishers, 2015.
Strauss 1977
Walter L. Strauss, ed. *The Intaglio Prints of Albrecht Dürer: Engravings, Etchings & Drypoints.* Expanded ed. New York: Kennedy Galleries and Abaris Books, 1977.
Straussman-Pflanzer and Tostmann 2021
Eve Straussman-Pflanzer and Oliver Tostmann, eds. *By Her Hand: Artemisia Gentileschi and Women Artists in Italy, 1500–1800*. Exh. cat. Hartford: Wadsworth Atheneum; Detroit: Detroit Institute of Arts, 2021.
Strieder 1993
Peter Strieder. *Tafelmalerei in Nürnberg, 1350–1550*. Königstein im Taunus, Germany: Karl Robert, 1993.
Strong 1983
Roy Strong, with contributions from V. J. Murrell. *Artists of the Tudor Court: The Portrait Miniature Rediscovered, 1520–1620*. Exh. cat. London: Victoria and Albert Museum, 1983.
Sutherland 1987
C. H. V. Sutherland. *Roman History and Coinage 44 BC–AD 69: Fifty Points of Relation from Julius Caesar to Vespasian*. Oxford: Clarendon Press, 1987.
Sutherland 2005
Elizabeth H. Sutherland. "Writing (On) Bodies: Lyric Discourse and the Production of Gender in Horace *Odes* 1.13." *Classical Philology* 100, no. 1 (January 2005), pp. 52–82.
Sweeny 1966
Barbara Sweeny. *Catalogue of Italian Paintings*. Philadelphia: John G. Johnson Collection, 1966.
Syson and Gordon 2001
Luke Syson and Dillian Gordon. *Pisanello: Painter to the Renaissance Court*. Exh. cat., National Gallery, London. London: National Gallery Company, 2001.
Syson and Thornton 2001
Luke Syson and Dora Thornton. *Objects of Virtue: Art in Renaissance Italy*. London: British Museum, 2001.
Teget-Welz and Dickel 2022
Manuel Teget-Welz and Hans Dickel, eds. *Renaissance in Franken: Hans von Kulmbach und die Kunst um Dürer*. Exh. cat., Fränkischen Galerie Kronach, Zweigmuseum des Bayerischen Nationalmuseums. Petersberg, Germany: Michael Imhof Verlag, 2022.
Temple 2018
Camilla Temple. "The Greek Anthology in the Renaissance: Epigrammatic Scenes of Reading in Spenser's *Faerie Queene*." *Studies in Philology* 115, no. 1 (Winter 2018), pp. 48–72.
Thompson 1982
David L. Thompson. *Mummy Portraits in the J. Paul Getty Museum*. 2nd ed., rev. Malibu, Calif.: J. Paul Getty Museum, 1982.
D. Thornton 1997
Dora Thornton. *The Scholar in His Study: Ownership and Experience in Renaissance Italy*. New Haven: Yale University Press, 1997.
P. Thornton 1991
Peter Thornton. *The Italian Renaissance Interior 1400–1600*. New York: Harry N. Abrams, 1991.
Trexler 1991
Richard C. Trexler. *Public Life in Renaissance Florence*. Ithaca, N.Y.: Cornell University Press, 1991.
Uzielli 1884
Gustavo Uzielli. "Sopra un sonetto attribuito a Leonardo da Vinci." In *Ricerche intorno a Leonardo da Vinci (serie seconda)*, pp. 28–114. Rome: Salviucci, 1884.
Vasari 1906
Giorgio Vasari. *Le vite de' più eccellenti pittori, scultori ed architettori*. Edited by Gaetano Milanesi. 9 vols. Florence: Sansoni, 1906.
Vasari 1960
Giorgio Vasari. *Vasari on Technique; being the Introduction to the Three Arts of Design, Architecture, Sculpture and Painting, Prefixed to the Lives of the Most Excellent Painters, Sculptors and Architects.* Translated by Louisa S. Maclehose; edited by G. Baldwin Brown. New York: Dover Publications, 1960.
Vasari 1966–87
Giorgio Vasari. *Le vite de' più eccellenti pittori, scultori e architettori: Nelle redazioni del 1550 e 1568*. Edited by Rosanna Bettarini. 6 vols. Florence: Sansoni Editore, 1966–87.
Vasari 1996
Giorgio Vasari. *Lives of the Painters, Sculptors and Architects*. Translated by Gaston du C. de Vere. 2 vols. New York: Alfred A. Knopf, 1996.
Vasari 1997
Giorgio Vasari. *Le vite de' piu eccellenti pittori, scultori e architettori nelle redazioni del 1550 e 1568.* Vol. 3, *Testo: Indice A–I.* Edited by Giovanna Gaeta Bertelà. Florence: Studio per Edizione Scelte, 1997.
Veca 1981
Alberto Veca. *Vanitas: Il simbolismo del tempo*. Exh. cat. Bergamo: Galleria Lorenzelli, 1981.
Verougstraete 2015
Hélène Verougstraete. *Frames and Supports in 15th- and 16th-Century Southern Netherlandish Painting*. Brussels: Brussels Royal Institute of Cultural Heritage, 2015. https://balat.kikirpa.be/tools/frames/IV/.
Verougstraete and Van Schoute 1998
Hélène Verougstraete and Roger Van Schoute. "The Origin and Significance of Marbling and Monochrome Paint Layers on Frames and Supports in Netherlandish Painting of the Fifteenth and Sixteenth Centuries." In *Painting Techniques, History, Materials and Studio Practice: Contributions to the Dublin Congress, 7–11 September 1998*, edited by Ashok Roy and Perry Smith, pp. 98–100. London: Published by the International Institute for Conservation of Historic and Artistic Works, 1998.
Verougstraete and Van Schoute 2000
Hélène Verougstraete and Roger Van Schoute. "Frames and Supports of Some Eyckian Paintings." In *Investigating Jan van Eyck*, edited by Susan Foister, Sue Jones, and Delphine Cool, pp. 107–17. Turnhout, Belgium: Brepols, 2000.

Verougstraete et al. 1997
Hélène Verougstraete, Roger Van Schoute, and Maurits Smeyers, eds. *Memling Studies: Proceedings of the International Colloquium (Bruges, 10–12 November 1994).* Leuven: Uitgeverij Peeters, 1997.

***Vespasiano Memoirs* 1926**
Vespasiano da Bisticci. *The Vespasiano Memoirs: Lives of Illustrious Men of the XVth Century*. Translated by William George Waters and Emily Waters. London: George Routledge and Sons, 1926.

Villa 2011
Giovanni Carlo Federico Villa, ed. *Lorenzo Lotto*. Exh. cat., Scuderie del Quirinale, Rome. Cinisello Balsamo, Milan: Silvana, 2011.

Villa 2013
Giovanni Carlo Federico Villa, ed. *Titian*. Exh. cat., Scuderie del Quirinale, Rome. Cinisello Balsamo, Milan: Silvana, 2013.

Vincent 2002
Clare Vincent. "Some Seventeenth-Century French Painted Enamel Watchcases." *Metropolitan Museum Journal* 37 (2002), pp. 89–106.

Vincent and Leopold 2015
Clare Vincent and Jan Hendrik Leopold, with Elizabeth Sullivan. *European Clocks and Watches in The Metropolitan Museum of Art*. New York: The Metropolitan Museum of Art, 2015.

Vryzidis and Papastavrou 2021
Nikolaos Vryzidis and Elena Papastavrou. "Notes on the Sanctuary Curtain: Symbolisms and Iconographies in the Greek Church." *Cahiers Balkaniques* 48 (2021). https://doi.org/10.4000/ceb.18457.

Wallace-Hadrill 1981
Andrew Wallace-Hadrill. "The Emperor and His Virtues." *Historia: Zeitschrift für Alte Geschichte* 30, no. 3 (1981), pp. 298–323.

Wallace-Hadrill 1986
Andrew Wallace-Hadrill. "Image and Authority in the Coinage of Augustus." *Journal of Roman Studies* 76 (1986), pp. 66–87.

Walsh 2005
R. J. Walsh. *Charles the Bold and Italy (1467–1477): Politics and Personnel*. Liverpool: Liverpool University Press, 2005.

Walter and Zapperi 2006
Ingeborg Walter and Roberto Zapperi. *Il ritratto dell'amata: Storie d'amore da Petrarca a Tiziano*. Rome: Donzelli, 2006.

Weber 1975
Ingrid Weber. *Deutsche, Niederländische und Französische Renaissanceplaketten 1500–1650: Modelle für Reliefs an Kult-, Prunk- und Gebrauchsgegenständed*. 2 vols. Munich: Bruckmann, 1975.

Wehle and Salinger 1947
Harry B. Wehle and Margaretta Salinger. *A Catalogue of Early Flemish, Dutch and German Paintings*. Vol. 2 of *A Catalogue of Paintings*. New York: The Metropolitan Museum of Art, 1947.

Weiss 1988
Roberto Weiss. *The Renaissance Discovery of Classical Antiquity*. 2nd ed. Oxford: Basil Blackwell, 1988.

Weitzman 1976
Kurt Weitzmann. *The Monastery of Saint Catherine at Mount Sinai: The Icons*. Vol. 1, *From the Sixth to the Tenth Century*. Princeton, N.J.: Princeton University Press, 1976.

Welch 1990
Evelyn Samuels Welch. "The Image of a Fifteenth-Century Court: Secular Frescoes for the Castello di Porta Giovia, Milan." *Journal of the Warburg and Courtauld Institutes* 53 (1990), pp. 163–84.

Welch 2019
Kathryn Welch. "Shields of Virtue(s)." In *The Alternative Augustan Age*, edited by Kit Morrell, Josiah Osgood, and Kathryn Welch, pp. 282–304. New York: Oxford University Press, 2019.

***Welt in Umbruch* 1980–81**
Welt im Umbruch: Augsburg zwischen Renaissance und Barock. Ausstellung der Stadt Augsburg in Zusammenarbeit mit der Evangelisch-Lutherischen Landeskirche in Bayern anlässlich des 450. Jubiläums der Confessio Augustana unter dem Patronat des International Council of Museums (ICOM). 3 vols. Exh. cat. Augsburg: Gesamtherstellung Augsburger Druck- und Verlagshaus, 1980–81.

Wethey 1971
Harold E. Wethey. *The Paintings of Titian*. Vol. 2, *The Portraits*. London: Phaidon, 1971.

Wethey 1987
Harold E. Wethey. *Titian and His Drawings: With Reference to Giorgione and Some Close Contemporaries*. Princeton, N.J.: Princeton University Press, 1987.

Whistler 2009
Catherine Whistler. "Titian's 'Triumph of Love,'" with a technical appendix by Jill Dunkerton. *Burlington Magazine* 151, no. 1277 (August 2009), pp. 536–42.

Whistler 2012
Catherine Whistler. "Uncovering Beauty: Titian's *Triumph of Love* in the Vendramin Collection." *Renaissance Studies* 26, no. 2 (April 2012), pp. 218–42.

Wijnands 2019
Clim Wijnands. "Reflections of the Hidden Duchess and the Moon King: The Tabula Scalata and the Engaged Beholder in Sixteenth-Century Italy." *Ikonotheka* 29 (2019), pp. 80–101.

Wildenstein 1957
Georges Wildenstein. "L'inventaire de Louis Hesselin, 1662." *Gazette des Beaux-Arts*, ser. 6, 49 (January 1957), pp. 57–63.

Williams 2017
Gareth D. Williams. *Pietro Bembo on Etna: The Ascent of a Venetian Humanist*. New York: Oxford University Press, 2017.

Williamson 1910
G. C. Williamson. *Catalogue of the Collection of Jewels and Precious Works of Art: The Property of J. Pierpont Morgan*. London: Chiswick Press, 1910.

Wilson 2004
Jean C. Wilson. "'Richement et pompeusement parée': The *collier* of Margaret of York and the Politics of Love in Late Medieval Burgundy." In *Excavating the Medieval Image: Manuscripts, Artists, Audiences; Essays in Honor of Sandra Hindman*, edited by David S. Areford and Nina A. Rowe, pp. 109–33. Aldershot, U.K.: Ashgate, 2004.

Wilson 2015
Carolyn C. Wilson, ed. *Examining Giovanni Bellini: An Art "More Human and More Divine."* Turnhout, Belgium: Brepols, 2015.

Windows 2012
Peter Windows. "New Identifications in the Drawings Collections of Gabriele Vendramin." *Master Drawings* 50, no. 1 (Autumn 2012), pp. 33–48.

Winkler 1928
Friedrich Winkler. "An Unknown Portrait of a Woman by Memling." *Apollo* 7 (1928), pp. 9–12.

Winkler 1950
Friedrich Winkler. "Rogier van der Weyden's Early Portraits." *Art Quarterly* 13 (1950), pp. 211–20.

Wixom 2007
William D. Wixom. "Late Medieval Sculpture in the Metropolitan: 1400 to 1530." *The Metropolitan Museum of Art Bulletin* 64, no. 4 (Spring 2007), pp. 1–48.

Wood 2017
Kelli Wood. "Performing Pictures: Parlor Games and Visual Engagement in Ascanio de' Mori's *Giuoco piacevole*." In *Playthings in Early Modernity: Party Games, Word Games, Mind Games*, edited by Allison Levy, pp. 9–28. Kalamazoo: Medieval Institute Publications, Western Michigan University, 2017.

Woods-Marsden 1998
Joanna Woods-Marsden. *Renaissance Self-Portraiture: The Visual Construction of Identity and the Social Status of the Artist.* New Haven: Yale University Press, 1998.

Woollett 2021
Anne T. Woollett, ed. *Holbein: Capturing Character*. Exh. cat., J. Paul Getty Museum, Los Angeles; Morgan Library and Museum, New York. Los Angeles: J. Paul Getty Museum, 2021.

Zafran 1985
Eric M. Zafran. *Master Drawings from Titian to Picasso: The Curtis O. Baer Collection*. Exh. cat., National Gallery of Art, Washington, D.C.; five other venues. Atlanta: High Museum of Art, 1985.

Zanchi 2001
Mauro Zanchi. *Andrea Previtali: Il coloritore prospettico di maniera belliniana*. Clusone, Italy: Ferrari Editrice, 2001.

Zanchi 2016
Mauro Zanchi. *In principio sarà il sole: Il coro simbolico di Lorenzo Lotto.* Florence: Giunti, 2016.

Zanker 1990
Paul Zanker. *The Power of Images in the Age of Augustus*. Translated by Alan Shapiro. Pbk. ed. Ann Arbor: University of Michigan Press, 1990.

Zehnder 1990
Frank Günter Zehnder. *Katalog der Altkölner Malerei*. Kataloge des Wallraf-Richartz-Museums 11. Cologne: Museen der Stadt Köln, 1990.

Zeri 1962
Federico Zeri. "Eccentrici fiorentini." *Bollettino d'Arte*, ser. 4, 47, no. 2/3 (April–September 1962), pp. 216–36.

Zimmermann 1995
T. C. Price Zimmermann. *Paolo Giovio: The Historian and the Crisis of Sixteenth-Century Italy*. Princeton, N.J.: Princeton University Press, 1995.

Zimmermann 2001
T. C. Price Zimmermann. "Giovio, Paolo." *Dizionario biografico degli italiani*, vol. 56, pp. 430–40. Rome: Istituto della Enciclopedia Italiana, 2001.

Zöllner 2005
Frank Zöllner. "The 'Motions of the Mind' in Renaissance Portraits: The Spiritual Dimension of Portraiture." *Zeitschrift* für *Kunstgeschichte* 68, no. 1 (2005), pp. 23–40.

Zöllner 2015
Frank Zöllner. *Sandro Botticelli*. Translated by Ishbel Flett. Munich: Prestel, 2015.

INDEX

Page numbers in *italics* refer to illustrations.

This catalogue is published in conjunction with *Hidden Faces: Covered Portraits of the Renaissance*, on view at The Metropolitan Museum of Art, New York, from April 1 through July 7, 2024.

The exhibition is made possible by the William Randolph Hearst Foundation, the Robert Lehman Foundation, and the Mellon Foundation.

This publication is made possible by the Drue E. Heinz Fund.

Published by The Metropolitan Museum of Art, New York
Mark Polizzotti, Publisher and Editor in Chief
Peter Antony, Associate Publisher for Production
Michael Sittenfeld, Associate Publisher for Editorial

Edited by Margaret Donovan
Designed by Wilcox Design
Production by Paul Booth
Bibliographic editing by Margaret Aspinwall
Image acquisitions and permissions by Josephine Rodriguez
Translations from the German by Elisabeth Lauffer

Photographs of works in The Met collection are by the Imaging Department, The Metropolitan Museum of Art, except when credited differently.

Additional photography credits: Art Heritage / Alamy Stock Photo: fig. 33; Art Institute of Chicago: fig. 8; Art Institute of Chicago / Art Resource, N.Y.: figs. 33, 34; © Ashmolean Museum: cat. 33; © Henry Barber Trust, Barber Institute of Fine Arts, University of Birmingham / Bridgeman Images: fig. 26; © Besançon, Musée des Beaux-Arts et d'Archéologie, photo by Nicolas Waltefaugle: fig. 40; Bibliothèque Nationale de France, Paris: figs. 6, 29; bpk Bildagentur / Staatliche Museen / Jörg P. Anders / Art Resource, N.Y.: figs. 14, 16, 36, cats. 26, 28; © Francesco Turio Bohm. All rights reserved 2023 / Bridgeman Images: fig. 39; Bridgeman Images: cat. 30A; © The Trustees of the British Museum: figs. 17, 46; Bundesarchiv, Koblenz: fig. 52; Reproduced by permission of Chatsworth Settlement Trustees / Bridgeman Images: fig. 20; Cleveland Museum of Art: figs. 11, 42; © Compton Verney / Bridgeman Images: fig. 47; Photo © The Courtauld / Bridgeman Images: cat. 11; © The Frick Collection: fig. 56; Gabinetto Fotografico delle Gallerie degli Uffizi: cat. 27A,B, figs. 19, 36, 53; © Germanisches Nationalmuseum: cat. 51C, photo by G. Janssen: cats. 16, 54, photo by M. Runge: cat. 51A,B; Digital image courtesy of Getty's Open Content Program: figs. 4, 7; Historisches Museum Frankfurt, photo by Horst Ziegenfusz: cats. 14, 15A,B, 35B; Institut de France—Musée Jacquemart-André, Paris, France: cat. 18; KHM-Museumsverband: fig. 22, cats. 42, 47A,B; Collection KMSKA—Flemish Community: fig. 25; © Collection Kröller-Müller Museum, Otterlo, The Netherlands, photo by Rik Klein Gotink: figs. 48, 49; © Stephan Kube / SQB: cat. 41; Kunsthaus Zürich: fig. 51; Landesmuseum Hannover, Artothek: cats. 46A,B, 48; Erich Lessing / Art Resource, N.Y.: fig. 5, cat. 29A; Lindenau-Museum Altenburg / photo by PUNCTUM@Bertram Kober: fig. 12; Image © The Metropolitan Museum of Art: cats. 1, 4, 5, 6, 7, 8, 10, 20A,B, 31, 37, 38, 39, 45, figs. 43, 55, photo by Paul Lachenauer: cats. 2, 7, photo by Mark Morosse: cats. 21, 34, photo by Juan Trujillo: cats. 3, 22, 30C, 36, 43, 50A,B, 52, 53; Ministry of Culture, Regional Directorate of Museums of Tuscany, Florence: fig. 54; Morgan Library & Museum, New York: cat. 44A,B, fig. 44; Courtesy Musea Brugge and Art in Flanders, photo by Hugo Maertens: fig. 13; Musée de l'Oeuvre Notre Dame de Strasbourg, photo Musées de Strasbourg, M. Bertola: fig. 11; © Museo Nacional Thyssen-Bornemisza, Madrid: cats. 13, 17; Museo Poldi Pezzoli: fig. 21; © National Gallery, London: cats. 9, 19, 23, fig. 30; © National Gallery, London / Art Resource, N.Y.: figs. 15, 32; Courtesy National Gallery of Art, Washington: cats. 29B, 30B, 32, 40A,B, figs. 24, 35, 41; Philadelphia Museum of Art: cat. 24, fig. 9; Courtesy of the Rhode Island School of Design Museum, Providence, R.I.: fig. 31; © RMN–Grand Palais / Art Resource, N.Y., photo by Daniel Arnaudet: cat. 25, photo by Thierry Le Mage: cat. 12A,B, photo by Franck Raux: cat. 12C; Scala / Ministero per i Beni e le Attività Culturali / Art Resource, N.Y.: figs. 3, 23, 37; Smith College Museum of Art, Northampton, Massachusetts: cat. 49A,B; Photograph courtesy of Sotheby's, Inc. © 2023: figs. 1, 50; Städel Museum, Frankfurt am Main: cat. 35A; Szépmüvészeti Múzeum / Museum of Fine Arts, Budapest, 2023: fig. 27; Teylers Museum, Haarlem, The Netherlands: fig. 2; Victoria and Albert Museum, London: fig. 28

Typeset in Vendetta and Priori by Matt Mayerchak
Printed on Condat Matte Perigord 150gsm
Separations by Professional Graphics, Inc., Rockford, Illinois
Printing and binding coordinated by Ediciones El Viso, Madrid

Cover illustrations: front: Attributed to Ridolfo Ghirlandaio, *Cover with a Mask* and *Portrait of a Woman (La Monica)*, ca. 1510 (cat. 27A,B); back: Meister der Dosenköpfe, *Elector Friedrich the Wise of Saxony* and *Cover with a Centaur*, 1525 (cat. 47A)

Page 2: Attributed to Ridolfo Ghirlandaio, *Cover with a Mask*, ca. 1510 (cat. 27A), detail; page 5: Lorenzo Lotto, *Bishop Bernardo de' Rossi*, 1505 (cat. 30A), detail; page 6: Jan van der Straet, *Vanitas*, 1594 (fig. 2), detail; p. 13: Albrecht Dürer, *Hieronymus Holzschuher, with Sliding Portrait Cover with Coat of Arms*, 1526 (fig. 16), detail; p. 40: Pisanello (Antonio Pisano), *Portrait Medal of Cecilia Gonzaga* (obverse), *Innocence and a Unicorn in a Landscape* (reverse), 1447 (cat. 4), details; p. 62: Hans Memling, *Portrait of a Man* (recto), *Flowers in a Jug* (verso), late 1480s (cat. 17), details; p. 94: Lorenzo Lotto, *Bishop Bernardo de' Rossi*, 1505 (cat. 30A), detail; p. 148: Hans Süss von Kalmbach, *Portrait of a Young Man* (recto), *Girl Making a Garland* (verso), ca. 1508 (cat. 38), details; p. 174: Lucas Cranach the Elder, *Martin Luther and Katharina von Bora*, 1525 (cat. 44A,B), details

Every effort has been made to track object provenances as thoroughly and accurately as possible based on available scholarship and traceable transactions. Despite best efforts, there is often an absence of provenance information. Provenances of objects in The Met collection are updated as additional research comes to light. Readers are encouraged to visit metmuseum.org and to search by an object's accession number for its most up-to-date information.

First printing

The Metropolitan Museum of Art
1000 Fifth Avenue
New York, New York 10028
metmuseum.org

Distributed by
Yale University Press, New Haven and London
yalebooks.com/art
yalebooks.co.uk

Cataloguing-in-Publication Data is available from the Library of Congress.
ISBN 978-1-58839-775-1